The Collected Writings Of James Henley Thornwell

THE

COLLECTED WRITINGS

OF

JAMES HENLEY THORNWELL, D.D., LL.D.,

LATE PROFESSOR OF THEOLOGY IN THE THEOLOGICAL SEMINARY
AT COLUMBIA, SOUTH CAROLINA.

EDITED BY

JOHN B. ADGER, D.D.,

AND

JOHN L. GIRARDEAU, D.D.

VOL. III.—THEOLOGICAL AND CONTROVERSIAL.

RICHMOND:
PRESBYTERIAN COMMITTEE OF PUBLICATION.
NEW YORK: ROBERT CARTER & BROS. PHILADELPHIA: ALFRED MARTIEN.
1873.

Rev. Nov. 6, 1876.

CONTENTS.

3

4   CONTENTS.

PART I.

RATIONALIST CONTROVERSY.

PREFATORY NOTE.

THESE contributions to the Controversy with the Rationalists consist of—
1. An examination of Mr. MORELL's celebrated work, entitled *The Philosophy of Religion;* 2. A discussion of the Office of Reason in regard to Revelation; and 3. A Treatise on Miracles. They were all published in the Southern Presbyterian Review, and the last one appeared likewise in the Southern Quarterly during the short period for which Dr. Thornwell was the conductor of that work.

Our authority for the titles we have given to the Examination of Morell, and to its different portions, will be found in the first pages of the second section of it. DR. THORNWELL *first* considers *the Philosophy of Religion* in the light of an argument against an external Revelation as the authoritative Standard of Religion; and *secondly*, he examines the Psychology of Morell in relation to the question, What is the nature of the Subject in which Religion inheres? There remains, for the full execution of his plan as announced, the consideration, *thirdly*, of the Essence of Religion itself, and *fourthly*, of the Mode in which Religion is produced—in other words, the question, How is the given Subject put in possession of the given Essence? These two last points he subsequently threw together, and discussed them in the form of a sermon preached in Charleston before the Young Men's Christian Association. This sermon constitutes Section *third* of the Examination of Morell's work.

Section First appeared first in October, 1849, Section Second in January, 1850, but Section Third not until April, 1856.

The discussion of the Office of Reason in regard to Revelation was published in June, 1847, as the first article of Volume First of that Review whose pages during some fifteen years were illuminated with so many of the productions of his pen. The question which he considers here is not the office of Reason in relation to doctrines *known* to be a Revelation from God—where, of course, the understanding is simply to believe—but

7

the office of Reason where the reality of the Revelation remains to be proved and the interpretation of the doctrine to be settled. The general principle is maintained that the competency of Reason to judge in any case is the measure of its right. And—a distinction being made in the contents of the Scriptures betwixt the Supernatural or what is strictly Revealed, and the Natural or what is confirmed but not made known by the Divine testimony—it is argued that the office of Reason in the Supernatural department of Revelation may be positive, but never can be negative, while in the Natural it is negative, but to a very limited extent, if at all, positive. In other words, in the Supernatural, Reason may prove, but cannot refute—in the Natural, she may refute, but cannot establish.

The Treatise on Miracles was published July, 1857, in the form of a Review of the works of TRENCH, WARDLAW and HINDS. It opens with a brief history of the Controversy with the Rationalists, and then discusses the Nature, the Apologetic Worth and the Credibility of the Miracle. It is supernatural—a temporary suspension of the laws of nature; it is, in itself, a sufficient credential of a Divine commission; it is as credible as any other fact, and may be proved by competent testimony. The possibility of the event is the sole limit to the credibility of testimony, and the question of the possibility of the Miracle is simply the question of the Existence of a personal God.

THE

STANDARD AND NATURE OF RELIGION.

A REVIEW, IN THREE SECTIONS,

OF

MORELL'S PHILOSOPHY OF RELIGION.

SECTION I.

AN EXTERNAL STANDARD VINDICATED.

"THE design of this book,"[1] we are told in the preface, "grew out of some of the reviews which appeared upon a former work of the author's, entitled An Historical and Critical View of the Speculative Philosophy of Europe in the Nineteenth Century." These reviews evinced, at least to the mind of Mr. Morell, "such a vast fluctuation of opinion," and such deplorable obscurity and confusion of ideas upon the whole subject of the connection betwixt philosophy and religion, that, in mercy to the general ignorance, and particularly in deference to a suggestion of Tholuck, he was induced "to commence a discussion" which, he evidently hoped, might have the effect of imparting intensity to the religious life, vigour to the religious literature and consistency to the religious sentiments of his country. He is at pains to inform us,[2] and we thank him for the information—the book itself furnishing abundant internal evidence, which, in the absence of such a declaration, would

[1] Page iii.   [2] Preface, p. xxxii.

9

have been decisive to the contrary—that he has not rushed "hastily and unpreparedly into the region of *theological* inquiry." "While philosophy has been the highest recreation, theology," he declares, "has ever been the serious business of my whole life. To the study of this science I gave my earliest thoughts, under the guidance of one[1] who is recognized by all parties as standing amongst the leading theologians of our age; I pursued it through many succeeding years; and if I have found any intense pleasure, or felt any deep interest in philosophy at large, it has been derived, *mainly*, from the consciousness of its high importance, as bearing upon the vastest moral and religious interests of mankind." Trained by this fitting discipline for the task, it is perhaps no presumption in Mr. Morell to have published a book which professes to be not "a popular and attractive exposition" of the questions which come within its scope, but a thorough philosophical discussion, developing "from the beginning, as far as possible in a connected and logical form," a subject which involves the fundamental principles of human knowledge, and that anything like justice may be done to it, demands, at every step, the subtlest analysis, the profoundest reasoning and the intensest power of reflection. These qualities Mr. Morell may possess in an eminent degree—he may even feel that the possession of them implies a vocation of God to give a new and nobler impulse to the religion of his country, and that, like all apostles, he is entitled to use great boldness of speech—still we cannot but suggest that, as modesty becomes the great, a little less pretension would have detracted nothing from the charms of his performance. The perpetual recurrence of phrases which seem to indicate the conviction of the author that his book is distinguished by extraordinary depth, and that he is gifted with a superior degree of mental illumination, is, to say the least of it, extremely offensive to the taste of his readers; and he will

---

[1] We learn from the North British Review that Dr. Wardlaw is the divine referred to.

probably find few who are prepared to share in the super-
cilious contempt which he lavishes upon the prospective
opponents of his system. The philosophy with which Mr.
Morell is impregnated is essentially arrogant; and it is more
to it than to him that we ascribe the pretending tone of
his work. The pervading consciousness of the weakness
and ignorance of man, the diffidence of themselves, the
profound impression of the boundlessness of nature and
of the limitless range of inquiry which lies beyond the
present grasp of our faculties, the humility, modesty and
caution which characterize the writings of the great English masters, will in vain be sought among the leading
philosophers of modern Germany and France. Aspiring
to penetrate to the very essence of things, to know them
in themselves as well as in the laws which regulate their
changes and vicissitudes, they advance to the discussion of
the sublimest problems of God, the soul and the universe
with an audacity of enterprise in which it is hard to say
whether presumption or folly is most conspicuous. They
seem to think that the human faculties are competent to all
things, that whatever reaches beyond their compass is mere
vacuity and emptiness, that omniscience, by the due use
of their favourite organon, may become the attainment
of man, as it is the prerogative of God, and that, in the
very structure of the mind, the seeds are deposited from
which may be developed the true system of the universe.

Within the limits of legitimate inquiry we would lay no
restrictions upon freedom of thought. All truly great men
are conscious of their powers; and the confidence which
they have in themselves inspires the strength, intensity and
enthusiasm which enable them to conceive and to execute
purposes worthy of their gifts. To the timid and distrustful
their excursions may often seem bold and presumptuous;
but in the most daring adventures of their genius they are
restrained, as if by an instinct, from the visionary projects
and chimerical speculations which transcend the sphere of
their capacities, as the eagle, in his loftiest flights, never

soars beyond the strength of his pinion. Confidence adjusted to the measure of power never degenerates into arrogance. It is the soul of courage, perseverance and heroic achievement; it supports its possessor amid discouragements and obstacles; it represses the melancholy, languor and fits of despondency to which the choicest spirits are subject; it gives steadiness to effort, patience to industry and sublimity to hope. But when men forget that their capacities are finite, that there are boundaries to human investigation and research, that there are questions which, from the very nature of the mind and the necessary conditions of human knowledge, never can be solved in this sublunary state—when they are determined to make their understandings the sole and adequate standard of all truth, and presumptuously assume that the end of their line is the bottom of the ocean,—this is intolerable arrogance, the very spirit of Moloch,

> "Whose trust was with the Eternal to be deemed
> Equal in strength; and rather than be less
> Cared not to be at all."

We can have no sympathy with the pretensions of any method, whether inductive or reflective, which aims at a science of being in itself, and professes to unfold the nature of the Deity, the constitution of the universe and the mysteries of creation and providence. To say, as Mr. Morell does,[1] that "our knowledge of *mind*, in the act of reflective consciousness, is perfectly adequate, that it reaches to the whole extent of its essence, that it comprehends the intuition of its existence as a *power* or *activity*, and likewise the observation of all its determinations," is sheer extravagance and rant, which can be matched by nothing but the astounding declaration of the same author, that "to talk of knowing mind beyond the direct consciousness of its spontaneous being, and all the affections it can undergo, is absurd; *there is nothing more to know.*" We are not to be

[1] History of Modern Philosophy, p. 53, vol. ii., second London edition.

surprised that such a philosophy should find nothing to
rebuke it in the awful and impenetrable depths of the Di- .
vine nature, that it should aspire to gaze directly upon the
throne of God, and profess to give a "direct apperception"
of Him[1] whom no man hath seen or can see, and whose
glory would be intolerable to mortal eyes. Titanic audacity
is the native spirit of the system; and it is in the imper-
ceptible influence of this spirit upon a mind otherwise
generous and manly that we find the explanation of the
fact that Mr. Morell, in the tone and temper of his performance, has departed so widely from the modesty of true
science.

There is one feature of the book before us which is particularly painful, and we confess our embarrassment in finding terms to express it. Hypocrisy would precisely indicate
the thing, but as that word cannot be employed without
casting a serious and, we believe, an undeserved imputation
upon the personal integrity of the author, we shall forbear
to use it. We have no doubt that he is cordial and sincere
in the zeal which he manifests for an earnest and vital religion; but what we object to is, that he should so often
employ a phraseology, and employ it in such connections,
as to convey the idea to undiscriminating readers—which
the whole tenor of his argument proves to be false—that
the earnest and vital religion which enlists his zeal embraces the distinctive features of the system of grace.
When he speaks of Christianity, in its essence, as a deep
inward life in the soul, and pours contempt upon the barren
forms and frigid deductions of logic as a substitute for
piety—when he contends for divine intuitions, heavenly impulses and a 'lofty sympathy and communion with God—
there is something in all this so much like the language
of converted men that untutored minds are apt to be
caught with the guile, and under the impression that they

[1] Ibid., p. 52. It is refreshing to contrast with such pretensions the
statements of Locke in the introduction of his celebrated Essay on the
Human Understanding.

are still clinging to the doctrines of a living, in opposition
to a formal and dead, Christianity, may imbibe, without
suspicion, a system which saps the foundations of the whole
economy of the Gospel. Mr. Morell is no friend to what
is commonly denominated Evangelical Religion. His
divine-life is not that which results from mysterious union
with the Son of God, as the Head of a glorious covenant
and the Father of a heaven-born progeny. His divine
intuitions are not the illuminations of that Spirit which
irradiates the written Word, and reveals to our hearts the
light of the knowledge of the glory of God in the face of
Jesus Christ; his communion with the Father is not the
fellowship of a child, who rejoices in the assurance of his
gracious adoption, and renders unceasing thanks for his
marvellous deliverance, through the blood of a great Mediator, from sin, condemnation and ruin. His religion
embraces no such elements; and he ought not, in candour,
to have disguised sentiments, utterly at war with the common conceptions of piety, in the very dress in which these
conceptions are uniformly presented. If he has introduced a new religion, he should not have decked it in the
habits of the old. It is the same species of dishonesty,
the same paltering in a double sense, as that to which we
object in Cousin, who, in seeming to defend the inspiration
of Prophets and Apostles, and to rebut the assaults of a
rationalistic infidelity, really denies the possibility of any
distinctive and peculiar inspiration at all, and places Divine
revelation upon the same platform with human discoveries.
We acquit Mr. Morell of any intention to deceive. We
rather suspect that he has partially imposed upon himself.
We can understand his declaration,[1] that he "does not
know that he has asserted a single result the germs and
principles of which are not patent in the writings of various
of the most eminent theologians of the Church of England, or of other orthodox communities," in no other way
than by supposing that he has been so long accustomed to

[1] Preface, p. xxxiii.

associate his own philosophical opinions with the characteristic phraseology of spiritual religion that the terms have
ceased to suggest any other ideas to his mind; so that he is
unconscious of the change of meaning which they have
imperceptibly undergone from his habits of thought.   His
honesty, however, does not diminish the danger which
results from the ambiguity of his language.   A corrupt
system, disguised in the costume of the true, is like Satan
transformed into an angel of light.   We should have
rejoiced if Mr. Morell's religion could have been more
nakedly presented.   It is not the ingenuity of his arguments,
nor the subtlety of his analysis, it is not the logical statement or the logical development of any of his principles,
from which the most serious mischief is to be apprehended :
it is from his fervour, his earnestness and zeal, which, in
seeming to aim at a higher standard of Christian life, will
enlist the sympathies of many, who feel that there is something more in the Gospel than a meagre skeleton of doctrines.   They will be apt to think that the words which he
speaks to them, resembling so often the tone of Christ and
His Apostles, are, like theirs, spirit and life.   They will
take the draught as a healthful and vivifying potion, and
find, too late, that it is a deadly mixture of hemlock and
nightshade.   Here is the danger ; in this covert insinuation
of false principles, this gilding of a nauseous pill.   If there
were less in the book which counterfeits the emotions that
spring from religion, the operation of its poison would be
comparatively circumscribed.

The danger, in the present instance, is incalculably increased by the surpassing enchantment of the style, which,
though not distinguished by the precision of Stewart, the
energy of Burke or the exquisite elegance of Hall, has a
charm about it which holds the reader spell-bound from
the beginning to the end of the volume.   We will venture
to assert that no man ever took up the book who was willing to lay it down until he had finished it; and very few,
we apprehend, have finished it who were willing to dismiss

it without another, and perhaps still another, perusal. Mr. Morell is never dull; in his abstrusest speculations, in his most refined and subtle efforts of analysis, there is an unction which fascinates the reader; he has the art, the rare and happy art, of extracting from the dry bones of metaphysics a delightful entertainment. The sorcery of his genius and the magic of his eloquence conceal the naked deformity of his principles; and attention is beguiled from the hideousness of the object by the finished beauty of the painting.

The transparency of his diction, the felicity of his illustrations, the admirable concatenation of his thoughts, his freedom from the extremes of prolixity and brevity, and his skill in evolving and presenting in beautiful coherence and consistency the most complicated processes of thought, justly entitle him to rank among the finest philosophical writers of his country. Imbued as he is with the spirit of German philosophy, and thoroughly conversant with the productions of its best masters, it is no small praise that in his own compositions he has avoided all affectation of foreign idioms, and that at a time when our language seems likely to be flooded with the influx of a "pedantic and un-English phraseology." He has found his mother-tongue amply adequate to the expression of his thoughts, and even the misty ideas of Germany, which its own authors have seldom been able to render intelligible in a dialect of amazing flexibility and compass, are seized with so firm and masculine a grasp, are so clearly defined and so luminously conveyed, that we hardly recognize their identity, and cannot but think that if Kant could rise from the dead and read his speculations in the pages of Mr. Morell, he would understand them better than in his own uncouth and barbarous jargon. We could wish that all importers of German metaphysics and German theology would imitate the example of Mr. Morell in his use of the vernacular tongue. We want no kitchen-Latin, and we strongly suspect that any ideas which refuse to be marshalled in English sentences, or to be obedient to English words, are unsuited to our soil, and had better be left to vegetate or perish on the banks of the Rhine.

As Mr. Morell nowhere tells us precisely what he means by the *philosophy of religion*, we are left to collect its import from his occasional statements of the scope and design of philosophy in general, his definition of religion, and the nature of the whole discussion. *Religion* he carefully distinguishes from *theology ;* they are, as he insists in his former work,[1] " two widely different things. Theology implies a body of truth founded upon indisputable principles, and having a connection capable of carrying our reason with it running through all its parts. Religion, on the other hand, is the spontaneous homage of our nature, poured forth with all the fragrance of holy feeling into the bosom of the Infinite. Religion may exist without a theology at all, properly so called." Or, as the same sentiments are expressed in the work before us,

"Let it be distinctly understood in the outset that we are speaking of religion now as a fact or phenomenon in human nature. There is a very common but a very loose employment of the term religion, in which it is made to designate the outward and formal principles of a community quite independently of the region of human experience, as when we speak of the Protestant religion, the religion of Mohammed, the religions of India, and the like. The mixing up of these two significations in a philosophical treatise cannot fail to give rise to unnumbered misunderstandings, and we emphatically repeat, therefore, that in our present use of the term we are not intending to express any system of truth or form of doctrine whatever, but simply an inward fact of the human consciousness—a fact, too, the essential nature of which it is of the utmost importance for us to discover."[2]

By religion, then, we are to understand not a system of doctrine or a creed, but those states of the mind and those inward experiences of the heart which spring from a sense of the Infinite and Eternal. But religion, in general, occupies a very subordinate place in the book; it is only introduced at all in order to prepare the way for what Mr.

---

[1] Vol. ii., Appendix, 2d Edition, p. 650.   [2] Pages 62, 63.

Morell denominates "the Christian consciousness." It is Christian experience, particularly, which he proposes to investigate. But what is the *philosophy* of religion? We have a clue to what the author means by it in the following passage of the preface:

"All great systems of philosophy are simply methods; they do not give us the material of truth: they only teach us how to realize it, to make it reflective, to construct it into a system."[1]

The inquiries which, in conformity with this definition—a definition, we would add, rather of logic than philosophy—we should expect to find him conducting as obviously falling under the import of his title, are such as have reference to the department of the soul in which religion is pre-eminently seated, the nature and origin of our religious affections, the laws of their development and growth, the process by which a theology may be formed, and the grounds of certainty in regard to religious truth. In this expectation we are not disappointed; these are the high themes that he discusses—the pith and staple of his argument. But we must take the liberty to say that in our humble judgment the analysis of these points, whatever appearances of candour and impartiality may be impressed upon it, was instituted and shaped with special reference to a foregone conclusion. The author was in quest of what Archimedes wanted in order to move the world—a $\pi o\nu$ $\sigma\tau\omega$—by means of which he could overturn the foundations of the Christian faith. There was a darling hypothesis in relation to the authority of the Bible which he was determined to establish; and with an eye to this result his philosophy, though digested into the form of a regular and orderly development of principles, was invented and framed. It is a species of special pleading, ingeniously disguised in the mask of philosophical research against the great distinctive feature of Protestant Christianity. When we contemplate the havoc and desolation of his theory—the Bible as an authoritative standard of faith, and creeds and confes-

[1] Page xxiv.

sions as bonds of Christian communion and fellowship, involved in a common ruin, with nothing to supply their place but the dim intimations of sentiment and feeling, chastened and regulated by the natural sympathy of earnest and awakened minds—we might be appalled at the prospect, if it were not for the consolatory reflection which the author himself has suggested, that his "philosophy does not give us the material of truth."

But to be a little more minute, the book is divided into twelve chapters, the *first* of which presents us with a general survey of the human mind. And as two of its powers are found to be of fundamental importance to the subsequent discussion, the *second* is devoted to a somewhat extended elucidation of the distinction betwixt them. In these two chapters the "philosophical groundwork" is laid of the author's whole system. If he is at fault in any essential point of his analysis, or has misapprehended the nature and relations of the "two great forms of our intellectual being" which play so conspicuous a part in his theory, his speculations labour at the threshold, the foundations are destroyed and the superstructure must fall to the ground. Since a human religion must be adjusted to the faculties of the human mind, an important step is taken toward the determination of its real nature when these faculties are explored and understood. Mr. Morell is, accordingly, conducted by his mental analysis to an inquiry into "the peculiar essence of religion in general," which he prosecutes in the *third*, and to a similar inquiry into the essence of Christianity in particular, which he prosecutes in the *fourth*, chapter of the book. He is now prepared to enter into the core of the subject; and as it is in the application of his psychology to the affiliated questions of Revelation and Inspiration, and to the construction of a valid system of Theology, that the poison of his principles most freely works, we must invite particular attention to his opinions upon these points, the development of which occupies the *fifth*, *sixth* and *seventh* chapters of the work.

Revelation he regards as a "mode of intelligence"—a process by which a new field of ideas or a new range of experience is opened to the mind. It is precisely analogous to external perception, or that more refined sensibility to beauty and goodness upon which we are dependent for the emotions of taste and the operations of conscience. It consists in the direction of an original faculty to a class of objects which it is capable of apprehending. It is wholly a subjective state, and should never be confounded with the things revealed; a spiritual clairvoyance which brings the soul into contact with spiritual realities, and enables it to gaze upon invisible glories. Hence an external revelation, or a revelation which does not exist in the mind, is a contradiction in terms. We might just as reasonably suppose that the Bible or any other book could supply the place of the senses in giving us a knowledge of the material world, as to suppose that it can supply the place of revelation in giving us a knowledge of religion. It can no more see for us in the one case than in the other; this is a personal operation, a thing which every man must do for himself. And as each individual must have his own power of perception, that he may know the existence of the objects around him, so each individual must have a personal and distinct revelation in himself, that he may come into the possession of the "Christian consciousness;" he must be brought immediately into contact with the object, and contemplate it "face to face." Inspiration is not essentially different from revelation; they are rather different aspects of the same process. As in all immediate knowledge there is an intelligent subject and an intelligible object brought into union, *revelation*, for the convenience of distinction, may be regarded as having primary reference to the act of God in presenting spiritual realities to the mind; and *inspiration* to whatever influence may be exerted upon the soul in order that it may be able to grasp and comprehend the realities presented. Revelation, in other words, gives the object; inspiration, the eye to behold it. The concurrence of both is essential to the production of knowledge. As inspiration, therefore, indicates, exclusively, a state of the mind, and that a state in which we are conscious of immediate knowledge, it cannot be affirmed of any class of writings nor of any processes of reasoning. An inspired book or an inspired argument is as senseless a form of expression as an intelligent book or an intelligent argument. Hence the whole question of an authoritative standard of religious truth, commended to our faith by the testimony of God, is summarily dismissed as involving an absurdity—a discovery which relieves us from all those perplexing speculations in relation to the proofs of a Divine commission, and the criteria which distinguish the Word of God from the delusions of man or the impostures of the Devil, upon which theologians, from the earliest age, have been accustomed, in their ignorance and folly, to waste their ingenuity. The doctrine is avowed, openly and broadly avowed, that God *cannot*, without destroying the very nature of the human understanding, put us in possession of an infallible system of truth. A book or an argument can be inspired in no other sense than as it proceeds from a man under the influence of holy and devout sensibilities, and contains the results of his reflection—in the development of which the Almighty cannot protect him from error —upon the facts of his own experience. The Pilgrim's Progress is, accordingly, Divine, or the Word of God, in precisely the same sense in which the Scriptures are Divine ; and the productions of Prophets and Apostles are entitled to no different kind of respect, however different in degree, from that which attaches to the writings of Owen and Baxter and Howe. Theology, in every case, results from the application of logic and philosophy to Christian experience; it is necessarily a deduction from subjective processes, and not the offspring of the comparison and arrangement of doctrines derived from an external source. Being the creature of the human understanding, and the understanding being above or below the immediate guidance and control

of God—we do not know exactly where the author places
it—every theology must be fallible and human, whether it
be that of Paul, or Peter, or James, or John, or—for such
is the fearful sweep of the argument—that of Jesus Christ
himself.

Having settled the principles upon which theology must
be constructed, he proceeds to apply them in the *eighth*
chapter, with remorseless havoc, to the popular faith of
his age and country. His next step is to investigate the
grounds of religious fellowship—an investigation which
turns out to be a spirited and earnest assault upon creeds
and confessions. When the Bible is gone, these beggarly
children of the understanding can, of course, show no
cause why sentence of death should not be pronounced
upon them. The *tenth* chapter, which is a sort of summary
of all his previous speculations, discusses the grounds of
certainty in reference to spiritual truth, which are resolved
partly into our own consciousness, or immediate knowledge
of its reality, and partly into the consciousness of other
similarly inspired people. The *eleventh* chapter, on the
significancy of the past, seems to us to be a logical appendage of the *seventh* or *eighth*, mercifully intended to relieve
our minds from the despondency and gloom which were
likely to overwhelm them on account of the loss of the
Bible, and the feebleness and imperfection of the instrument
which we must use in its place in "realizing" a system of
faith. After all, he tells us, among earnest and awakened
minds there is no danger of miscarriage. Error is the
fiction of bigotry rather than a stern and sober reality. All
contradictions and discordancies of opinion are only the
divergencies or polar extremities of some higher unity of
truth, in which they are blended and reconciled, as the
numberless antagonisms of nature contribute to the order
and harmony of the universe. The progress of Theology
depends upon the success of the effort to discover those
higher realities in which heresy and orthodoxy sweetly
unite, and hence all opposition to error and zeal for the

truth, overlooking the important fact that they are different phases of the same thing—that error, in other words, is only a modification of truth—are very wicked and indecent.

The relation between Philosophy and Theology is the subject of the *last* chapter, in which he undertakes to vindicate himself from the anticipated charge of Rationalism. How successful he has been we shall see hereafter; but one thing is certain, his Rationalism has but little tendency to exalt the understanding. In the pictures which he occasionally draws of a perfect Christian state, this perverse and unruly faculty, it seems, is to be held in abeyance; the soul is to be all eye, all vision, everlastingly employed in the business of looking, so completely absorbed in the rapture of its scenes that it cannot descend to the cold and barren formalities of thought.   But while the understanding is degraded, another element of our being is unduly promoted. Throughout the volume we find attributed to sympathy the effect, in producing and developing the Divine life, which the Scriptures uniformly ascribe to the Holy Spirit. Society and fellowship are, indeed, the Holy Ghost of Mr. Morell's gospel.   They beget us again to a lively hope, they refine and correct our experiences, they protect us from dangerous error, they establish our minds in the truth, and through them we are enabled to attain the stature of perfect men in Christ Jesus.

From this general survey of the scope and contents of the book, it must be obvious to the reader that we are called to contend with a new and most subtle form of infidelity.   The whole ground of controversy is shifted.   The end aimed at is the same—the destruction of the Bible as a Divine revelation, in the sense in which the Christian world has heretofore been accustomed to use the term—but the mode of attack is entirely changed.   The infidels of former times impugned Christianity either in its doctrines or evidences, but never dreamed of asserting that an external standard of faith was inconceivable and impossible.   Some denied that it was necessary, as the light of nature is suf-

ficient for all the purposes of religion; the ground generally
taken being that the Scriptures were wanting in the proofs
by which a Divine revelation ought to be authenticated, or
that they were self-condemned in consequence of the absurdity and contradiction of their contents, or that no proofs
could ascertain to others the reality of a revelation to ourselves; but whatever was the point of assault, whether
miracles, prophecy or doctrines, the genuineness and authenticity of the records, the origin and propagation of Christianity in the world and its moral influence on society, it
was always assumed that *there was sense* in the proposition
which affirmed the Bible to be a Divine and authoritative
standard of faith.   Elaborate apologies for it, under this
extraordinary character, were deemed worthy of the powers
and learning of the most gifted members of the race.   But
Mr. Morell takes a widely different position.   He undertakes to demonstrate, by a strictly *a priori* argument, drawn
from the nature of the mind and of religion, that a revealed
theology is a psychological absurdity.   His design is, from
the philosophy of Christian experience, to demolish the
foundations of Christianity itself.   His method requires
him to attack neither miracles, prophecy nor doctrines; you
may believe them all, provided you do not regard them as
proving the Bible to be a rule of faith, nor receive them on
the ground that they are attested by the seal of Heaven.
In the application of his boasted reflective method he has
plunged into the depths of consciousness and fetched from
its secret recesses the materials for proving that, in the very
nature of the case, every system of doctrine not only *is*, but
must be, human in its form and texture.   It is on this
ground that we charge him with infidelity.   He takes away
the Bible, and we deliberately assert that, when that is
gone, all is lost.   He talks, indeed, of his intuitions and
fellowship and sympathy and his all-powerful organon of
reflection, but when he proposes these as a substitute for the
lively oracles of God, our minds labour for a greater ability
of despising than they have ever had occasion to exert

before. Let the authority of the Bible be destroyed, and
Christianity must soon perish from the earth. Put its doctrines upon any other ground than a "thus saith the Lord,"
and every one of them will soon be denied, and from the
dim territory of feeling in which Mr. Morell has placed religion we shall soon cease to hear any definite reports of God.
What has been the effect upon himself since he has declined
to receive his theology from the Bible? How many of the
doctrines which he was, no doubt, taught in his infancy and
childhood has he been able to "realize" by his own method
of construction? The plan of his work has not required
him to treat of particular articles of faith, but from occasional glimpses which we catch, it is easy to collect that his
creed is anything but evangelical. The doctrine of the
incarnation, for example, is reduced to nothing but "the
realization of divine perfection in humanity." "We need,"
says the author,[1] "to have the highest conceptions of divine
justice and mercy, and the highest type of human resigna-
tion and duty realized in an historical fact, such as we can
ever gaze upon with wonder and delight; not till *then* do
they become mighty to touch the deepest springs of our
moral being." Jesus is, accordingly, represented as a finished model of ideal excellence, combining in his own person all that is pure and lovely and sublime, a living em-
bodiment of the moral abstractions which, it seems, are
powerless to affect the heart until they are reduced to "an
historical and concrete reality," and which *then*, as if by an
electric shock or a wizard's spell, can stir the depths of our
nature, rouse our dormant energies and inspire us with
zeal to imitate what we are obliged to admire. Hence the
whole mystery of godliness—of the Word made flesh—is a
very simple affair; it is just God's giving us a pattern to
copy. This is what reflection makes of it from the intuitions of religion without the Bible. Justification by faith,
the *articulus stantis aut cadentis ecclesiæ*—"the very life-
spring," as Mr. Morell admits,[2] "of the Reformation"—

---

[1] Page 241.   [2] Page 253.

fares no better in his hands as it passes, through his constructive method, from the region of experience to that of
doctrine.   It is not a little remarkable, too, and sets this
method in a very unfavourable light, that while our author
professes to have the same "*moral idea*" with Luther and
the Reformers, his statement of it as a *doctrine* is precisely
opposite to theirs.   Total depravity, and the consequent necessity of regeneration, he must, to be consistent, deny, as
his theory requires that religious sensibility, even in our
fallen state, should be viewed as an original faculty of the
soul; and from the beginning to the end of the volume
there is not a single passage which even remotely squints
at the doctrine of atonement in the sense of a satisfaction
to the justice of God for the guilt of men.   What, then, of
real Christianity does he believe?   Echo answers, What?

These specimens are sufficient to show what success
crowns the efforts of our author in constructing a theology
without the Bible.   We want no better illustration of what
is likely to become of our religion when we give up an
external standard for the dim intuitions of inspired philosophers.   We are not, however, without other lessons of
experience, which Mr. Morell must admit to be applicable.
Upon his principles, the construction of the universe is a
process exactly analogous to the construction of a creed.
The ontological systems of the German masters may, accordingly, be taken as a fair sample of what reflection is able
to achieve in the science of world-making; and, judging
from them, we can form something more than a conjecture
of the extravagance and folly which will be palmed upon
us for the pure and wholesome doctrines of the Cross, should
the same method be admitted into the department of
Christian theology.   It would be sheer insanity to suppose
that it will make less havoc of our creeds than it has made
of nature, of the soul and God.   Upon one thing we might
count with certainty—the being speedily overwhelmed with
a species of Pantheism, in which all sense of duty and religion would perish.   The fatalism of Mohammed has the merit

of being consistent, but the transcendental philosophy, as
if impelled by an irresistible instinct to contradictions and
absurdity, makes its boast, in one breath, of the demonstration of the essential and indestructible freedom of man as
its greatest triumph, and in the next does not scruple to
deduce the contingent, finite and variable from their *necessary relations* to the absolute, infinite and eternal.   No man
can turn from these speculations and laugh at the Geeta or
the Ramayuna of Valmeeki.   They teach us—what it
would be madness to disregard—that, in relation to theology, the real issue is between the Bible and a wild imagination " in endless mazes lost;" between the Bible, in other
words, and Atheism.   We do not hesitate, therefore, to rank
Mr. Morell's book in the class of infidel publications.   He
has assailed the very foundations of the faith ; and in resist-
ing his philosophy we are defending the citadel of Christianity from the artful machinations of a traitor, who, with
honeyed words of friendship and allegiance upon his tongue,
is in actual treaty to deliver it into the hands of the enemy
of God and man.

Entertaining these opinions of the character and tendency
of the work, we shall make no apology for entering with
great freedom into a critical estimate of its merits.   It is,
perhaps, only the first-fruits of what we may yet expect
from larger importations of the same philosophy into
Britain and America, and, as is generally the case with first-
fruits, it is probably the best of its kind.   We apprehend
that no man who shall undertake a similar work will be
able to bring to it a larger variety of resources, a more profound acquaintance with ancient and modern speculations,
a nicer critical sagacity or an intenser power of reflection,
than have fallen to the lot of Mr. Morell; and we are
glad that it is a man thus eminently gifted, the great hiero-
phant of German mysteries, and not the humble and contemptible retailer of oracles hawked about as divine only
because they defy all effort to understand them, who has
brought on the first serious collision in the field of English

literature betwixt evangelical religion and the new discoveries in metaphysics. The vigour of *his* assault may be taken as a fair specimen of the power and resources of the enemy ; and we rejoice in being able to say that whatever vague and undefined fears may have floated through our minds for the security of our faith while the conflict was yet at a distance, and the proportions of the foe unduly magnified by the fogs and mists through which he was contemplated, they have turned out to be, upon the first demonstration of his real dimensions and his skill in battle, like the shudder and dismay conjured up by a moonlight ghost.

The book may be considered in the double light of a philosophy and an argument, the philosophy supplying the premises of the argument. We intend to examine it in both aspects; and as in every instance of ratiocination the first and most obvious inquiry is in regard to the validity of the reasoning, Does it hold, do the premises contain the conclusion ? we shall pursue in the present case the natural order of thought, and inquire into the merits of the argument before we investigate the claims of the philosophy. We hope to show that there is a double escape from the infidelity and mysticism into which the author would conduct us—one through the inconclusiveness of his reasoning, the other through the falsehood or unsoundness of his premises. He is signally at fault in both his logic and his philosophy.

The fundamental proposition of the treatise in which its preliminary speculations were designed to terminate, and upon which its subsequent deductions are dependent for all the value they possess, is, that a valid theology is *never* the gift of Heaven, but is *always* the creature of the human understanding. This is assumed as a settled point in the last *six* chapters of the book. The *seventh*, which develops the process by which, in conformity with the laws of mind, we are able to construct a theology for ourselves, evidently takes it for granted that this is a thing which we have to do for ourselves, unless the author intended these discussions as a mere exhibition of his skill, an amusing play of

ingenuity and fancy, like Ferguson's Natural History of
Society, or Smith's Theory of the Origin of Language. If
God has given us a body of divinity, it is of very little
consequence to speculate on what might have taken place
had we been left to ourselves. Theology, in this aspect of
the case, being reduced to the condition of any other science,
perhaps the method described by our author is, as he asserts
it to be, the *only* method by which we could successfully
proceed. But the very stress of the controversy turns upon
the question, Whether we have been left to ourselves whether theology is in fact, like all other sciences, the production of man, or whether God has framed it for us ready to
our hands? The same assumption in regard to the human
origin of theology pervades all the speculations of the *eighth*
chapter, professedly on Fellowship, but really on Creeds and
Confessions. If there be a faith once delivered to the saints,
it may be our duty to contend for it, and to withdraw from
those who consent not to wholesome words, even the words
of our Lord Jesus Christ, and to the doctrine which is
according to godliness, and to reject those after the first and
second admonition who bring in damnable heresies. If
there be such a thing as a form of sound words, there may
be an obligation to teach it, and hence an analogy betwixt
the Church and the School, in consequence of which believers
may be termed *disciples*, ministers *teachers*, and Christ
the great *Prophet* of all. These things cannot be gainsaid
until we have something more than assertion that there is
no authoritative type of doctrine into which we ought to be
cast. As to the chapter on Certitude, that never could have
been written by a man in whose philosophy it was even
dreamed of that there might be a ground of assurance in
a Divine testimony fully equal to dim and misty intuitions,
which require to be corrected by the generic consciousness
of the race. Let it be admitted that God has given us a
theology, and evinced it to be His by signs and wonders or
any species of infallible proofs, and we certainly need no
firmer basis for our faith than that the mouth of the Lord

has spoken. All such speculations as those of our author are darkening counsel by words without knowledge. The relation, too, in which philosophy stands to theology—the subject of the *last* chapter of the book—is materially changed when it is denied that philosophy is the organon to form it, or when the whole question concerning the truth or falsehood of any doctrinal system is made a question of *authority,* and not a question of abstract speculation.

It is hence obvious that the human origin of theology is the soul of this system; it pervades all the author's speculations. Without it one-half of his book falls to the ground, and the conclusions which palpably contravene the popular faith are stripped of all plausibility and consistency. As a logical production his entire treatise is a failure unless this principle can be established.

Now, has it been proved? Has the author anywhere demonstrated that theology, as contradistinguished from religion, must necessarily be human, and can possess no other authority but that which attaches to it from the laws of thought? Or, has he even succeeded in showing that as a historical fact it *is* human, though it *might* have been otherwise, and therefore subject to the same criticisms to which every human production is amenable? Let it be remembered that the real issue betwixt himself and the popular faith is, Whether or not God *has* communicated in the language of man a perfect logical exposition of all the truths which in every stage of its religious development the human mind is capable of experiencing. Mr. Morell denies; the popular faith affirms. If he can make good his negative, then we must create theology for ourselves; his speculations upon that point become natural and proper, and all the conclusions which are subsequently drawn from them in relation to fellowship, certitude, and the precise office of philosophy with respect to systems of Christian doctrine, become consistent and legitimate. If, on the contrary, he fails to do so, then all these speculations are premature, they have no solid foundation in truth; and though they may still be interesting as a new and curious department of fiction, they should drop the name of philosophy or couple it with that of romance, and assume a title which would indicate the fact that their logic is purely hypothetical. Has he succeeded, or has he failed? This question we shall be able to answer by considering what the exigencies of his argument demanded, and the manner in which he has addressed himself to the task of meeting them—by comparing, in other words, what he had to do with what he has done. What, then, is necessary in order to prove that no such Divine communication as the popular faith maintains has ever been made to men? There are, obviously, only two lines of reasoning that can be pursued in an argument upon this subject. It must either be shown *a priori* that such a Divine communication is impossible, involving a contradiction to the very nature of theology, or *a posteriori* that such a Divine communication as a matter of fact never has been made, or, what upon the maxim, *de non apparentibus, etc.*, is equivalent to that, never has been proved. This last proposition may be established, in turn, either by showing that no testimony and no evidence can authenticate such a communication; or that the evidence, in the given case, falls short of what ought to be afforded; or that it is set aside by countervailing evidence; or that there is positive proof that some other method has been adopted. This seems to us to be a true statement of the logical condition of the question. Mr. Morell was bound to prove either that a Divine revelation, in the ordinary sense of the term, is impossible, a psychological absurdity, or that no book professing to be a revelation is worthy of credit; there *can* be, or there *has* been, none. This being the state of the controversy, let us proceed to examine how he has acquitted himself in disposing of these points, the last of which alone has given rise to a larger body of literature than perhaps any other subject in the world.

The premises of the argument, in both aspects, whether *a priori* or *a posteriori*, are contained in the chapters on

Revelation and Inspiration. It was evidently the design of these chapters to develop a theory which should explode the vulgar notions in relation to the Bible as at once absurd in a philosophical point of view and destitute of evidence as a matter of fact. His whole view of inspiration he represents as "a protest and an argument"[1] against "the formal use of the letter of Scripture," which is made by "those who ground their theology, professedly at least, upon an induction of individual passages, as though each passage, independently of the spirit of the whole, were of Divine authority." "To suppose that we should gain the slightest advantage" by accuracy of definitions and consistency of reasoning on the part of the sacred writers, "implies," he informs us,[2] "an entire misapprehension of what a revelation really is, and of what is the sole method by which it is possible to construct a valid theology. An actual revelation can only be made to the intuitional faculty, and a valid theology can only be constructed by giving a formal expression to the intuitions thus granted." We understand these passages, especially when taken in connection with the spirit of the whole discussion, as distinctly asserting the proposition that theology, as a formal statement of doctrine, can never be divinely communicated, and that upon the ground that it involves elements which are incompatible with the very nature of revelation—a *revealed theology* being a contradiction in terms. Clearly, if "the giving of a formal expression to the intuitions" of religion be the *sole* method by which it is *possible* to construct it, there is no place for an authoritative standard of faith.

Now does the author's theory of revelation, admitting it to be true, preclude the possibility of a Divine theology? We shall not deny—for we have no disposition to dispute about a word—that it is inconsistent with a revealed theology, in the *author's sense* of the term. We may here take occasion to say that much of the impression which his reasoning makes upon the mind of his readers is due to the ambi-

[1] Page 205.   [2] Page 175.

guity of language. They, from old associations and familiar
usage, mean one thing by revelation, and he another; and
it is hard to keep distinctly in view that conclusions which
may be legitimate in *his* sense may not be legitimate in
theirs. If Mr. Morell chooses to restrict the application
of the term to the subjective processes by which the mind
is brought into contact with spiritual realities, and then
infer that an external standard of faith' cannot be a revelation, the inference may be just; but it no more concludes
against the reality or possibility of such a standard than to
restrict the term *animal* exclusively to quadrupeds, and
then infer that neither men nor birds were animals, concludes against the truth of their existence or their possession
of life. What Mr. Morell undertakes to settle is not a
question of words and names, not whether the Bible shall
receive this title or that (no one dreams that it is a spiritual vision, or any special mode of intelligence), but
whether God *can* communicate, in writing or in any other
form, a perfect logical exposition of those very intuitions
which he makes it the office of revelation to impart. That
such a Divine communication is, in the nature of the case,
impossible—not that it cannot be *called* by a given name—
is what he represents his theory of revelation as necessarily
involving; and that, if it does not involve, it is not pertinent to the argument.

This theory is designed to give an answer to the question,
In what manner does a man become a Christian? The
essential elements included in that form of man's religious
life which he denominates the *Christian consciousness*
having been previously enumerated, he proceeds, in his
account of revelation, to describe the "process by which
such phenomena of man's interior being are produced—the
secret link which unites them with an outward causality,
and the laws by which they are brought into existence,
regulated, and finally developed to their full maturity." It
is only "in relation to the *method* by which it is communicated to the human mind" that Christianity can be prop-

erly designated "as a revelation from God."[1] That is, if we understand the author, it is the office of revelation to excite the emotions which are characteristic and distinctive of the religion of Jesus. It has reference, therefore, exclusively to what, in common language, would be styled experimental religion, and includes nothing but the means by which the state of heart is engendered, which entitles a man to be considered as a real, in contradistinction from a formal, believer. But as religion consists, essentially, in emotions, and emotions are dependent upon that form of intelligence which supplies the objects adapted to awaken them—a direct correspondency always subsisting between the intellectual and emotional activity—the question arises, To which faculty are we indebted for the objects that awaken religious emotions? We must *know* them, they must be present to the mind, or no affections can be excited; through what form of intelligence, then, do we become cognizant of spiritual realities? The answer is, Intuition.

"In considering, then, under which of the two great generic modes of intelligence we have to class the particular case involved in the idea of revelation, we can have but little hesitation in referring it, at once, to the category of *intuition*. The idea of a revelation is universally considered to imply a case of intelligence in which something is presented *directly* to the mind of the subject; in which it is conveyed by the immediate agency of God himself; in which our own efforts would have been unavailing to attain the same conceptions; in which the truth communicated could not have been drawn by inference from any data previously known; and, finally, in which the whole result is one lying beyond the reach of the logical understanding."[2]

The author then proceeds to run the parallel betwixt this account of revelation and intuition in its lowest form— that of external perception; and finding a perfect correspondence, he does not hesitate to rank them as kindred species of the same mode of intellectual activity. But, to make assurance doubly sure, he undertakes to show that revelation *cannot* be addressed to the understanding—"that the whole of the logical processes of the human mind are

[1] Page 122.   [2] Page 126.

such that the idea of a revelation is altogether incompatible
with them; that they are in no sense open to its influence,
and that they can neither be improved nor assisted by it."[1]
His meaning is that no new original elements of knowledge,
or, as Locke would call them, no new *simple ideas*, can be
imparted to the mind by definition, analysis or reasoning.
He regards revelation as a source of original and peculiar
ideas, like the eye or the ear, or what Hutcheson felicitously
styles the *internal senses* of the mind. "The object of a
revelation is to bring us altogether into another and higher
region of actual experience, to increase our mental vision,
to give us new data from which we may draw new inferences; and all this lies quite apart from the activity of the
logical faculty."[2]

The author still further, though not more plainly, develops his views in the answer he returns to the question,
"Could not a revelation from God consist in an exposition
of truth, made to us by the lips or from the pen of an
inspired messenger, that exposition coming distinctly under
the idea of a logical explication of doctrines, which it is
for mankind to receive as sent to us on Divine authority?"
Let us hear him upon this point:

"Now this is a case of considerable complexity, and one which we
must essay as clearly as possible to unravel. First of all, then, we
have no doubt whatever but that there have been agents commissioned by God to bring mankind to a proper conception of Divine
truth and comprehension of the Divine will. But now let us look a
little more closely into their real mission, and consider the means by
which alone it was possible for them to fulfil it.

"These Divine messengers, we will suppose, address their fellow-
men in the words and phrases they are accustomed to hear, and seek
in this way to expound to them the truth of God. If we imagine
ourselves, then, to be the listeners, it is needless to say that so long
as they treat of ideas which lie *within* the range of our present experience, we should be well able at once to comprehend them, and to
judge of the grounds on which they urge them upon our attention.
But it is manifest that such a discourse as I describe could in no proper
sense be termed *a revelation*. So long as the Divine teacher keeps

[1] Page 131.   [2] Page 133.

within the range of our present intellectual experience, he might indeed throw things into a new light, he might point out more accurately their connection, he might show us at once their importance and their logical consistency, but all this would not amount to *a revelation*, it would give us no *immediate* manifestation of truth from God, it would offer no conceptions lying beyond the range of our present data, it would quite fail in bringing us into contact with new realities, nor would it at all extend the sweep of our mental vision. Mere exposition always *presupposes* some familiarity with the subject in hand; one idea has always, in such a case, to be explained by another; but supposing there to be an entire blindness of mind upon the whole question, then it is manifest that all mere logical definition and explication is for the time entirely thrown away.

"Illustrations of this are as numerous as are the sciences or the subjects of human research. Let a man, for example, totally unacquainted with the matter, hear another converse with the greatest clearness about differential quantities in physics or mathematics, how much of the explanation would he be able to comprehend? He has not yet the experiences of space, number or motion on which the intelligibleness of the whole depends, and in want of these the whole of the explanations offered are involved in the darkest obscurity. Take up any other subject, such as biology, ethics or metaphysics in their higher and more recondite branches. Explication here is of no avail, unless the mind first realize for itself, and reproduce in its own thinking, the fundamental conceptions of the teacher. What is true of perceptive teaching in the case of the infant is true in a modified sense of all human education, to the most advanced stage of intelligence. You must in every instance alike take proper means to awaken the power of vision within, to furnish direct experiences to the mind; in brief, to give clear intuitions of the *elements* of truth, before you can produce any effect by the most complete process of defining or explanation.

"Let us return, then, to the supposed case of the inspired teacher, and proceed with our analysis of the conditions that are necessary to his becoming the medium of a revelation, properly so called. We have seen that if he always kept within the region of our present experience, there would be no fresh revelation made to us at all; but now let us imagine him to *transcend* the present sphere of our mental vision, it is evident from what I have first said that in such a case we should be by no means in a condition to comprehend his meaning, on the supposition, of course, that he was to confine himself to *mere exposition*. The only way in which he could give us a revelation of truth hitherto unrealized would be by becoming the agent of elevating our inward religious consciousness up to the same or a similar standard as his own, which is the same thing as if we had said that all revelation, properly so called, can be made to us primarily only in the form of religious *intuition.*" [1]

We have now said enough to put our readers completely in possession of the author's views of revelation. It implies a direct perception of spiritual realities, a gazing upon eternal verities, which, upon the principle that the eye affects the heart, produces those peculiar emotions in which the essence of religion consists. It communicates to us the elemental ideas of all religious knowledge, the primary data, without which the science of theology would be as unmeaning as the science of optics to a man born blind. As perception gives us all our original and simple ideas of matter, the moral sense our notions of the good, taste our notions of the beautiful and sublime, so revelation imparts to us the ideas of God, of Christ, of redemption and of sin. The subjective processes in all these cases are the same. Nature, the beautiful, the good, are just as truly and properly *revelations* as the verities embraced in Christian experience. There was, however, in the case of Christianity, a series of "Divine arrangements through the medium of which the loftiest and purest conceptions of truth were brought before the immediate consciousness of the Apostles, and through them of the whole age, at a time, too, when in other respects the most universal demoralization abounded on every side." [2] These arrangements the author admits to be supernatural, the result of a "Divine plan altogether distinct from the general scheme of Providence as regards human development;" but the revelation consequent upon them is purely natural. Man was elevated to a mountain which commanded prospects beyond the ordinary range of his eyes, but the vision which ensued was in strict obedience to the laws of sight.

Now we ask our readers to ponder carefully this account of revelation, and to lay their fingers on the principle which either directly or indirectly proves that a perfect standard

[1] Pages 134–137.   [2] Page 145.

of theology cannot be imparted to us by God, or that any and every theology must be the offspring of the human understanding. This account, we are told, is at once a protest and an argument against the popular notions on the subject. The protest we can find, it is patent on every page, but the *argument* we are utterly unable to discover. Does it follow that because religion as a matter of experience is Divine, therefore theology as a matter of science must be human? Does it follow that because God gives us all the direct and immediate cognitions out of which the science can be framed, therefore He is unable to construct the science Himself? Does it follow that because He makes us feel and see, therefore He is incompetent to describe either our visions or emotions? We confess that our sincerest efforts cannot render palpable to our thinking faculty the least incongruity betwixt the notions of a Divine theology and a revealed religion in the sense of Mr. Morell. For aught that we can see to the contrary, his whole psychology might be granted; all that he says of the understanding and intuition, their differences and relations, with his whole scheme of revelation, all might be granted, and yet nothing be conceded at all destructive of the doctrine that we have a faith ready developed to our hands which we are bound to receive upon the authority of God. We might no longer call it a *revealed* faith, but it would be none the less infallible and Divine on that account.

Mr. Morell admits that man can construct a theology for himself, that "he is able to give a definite form and scientific basis to his religious life, and to the spiritual truth involved in it." The intuitions of religion, like all other intuitions, can be submitted to the operations of the understanding; they can be compared, classified and arranged; they are as really the materials of a science as the facts of perception or the phenomena of conscience. Now, what is there in the process of constructing a science from religion which limits it exclusively to man? Is there any absurdity in supposing that God can communicate in writing or in some other form a perfect logical exposition of all the intuitions which in every stage of its religious history the human mind is capable of experiencing? any absurdity in supposing that God can do perfectly and infallibly for His weak and ignorant creatures what it is conceded they can do imperfectly and fallibly for themselves? What is there inconceivable in God's giving a logical and formal expression to the religious mind of man? We do not deny that a Divine theology, though it might be strictly scientific in its form, and capable of the same proofs to which all human sciences appeal, must yet challenge our assent upon a higher ground. It is to be received, not because it accords with our experience, but because it is the testimony of God. It comes to us, and must come to us, with authority. It is truth, because it proceeds from the fountain of truth. If Mr. Morell contends that this peculiarity removes it from the category of science, we shall not dispute about a word; all that we contend for is, that it is and must be a more full and complete representation of all the phenomena of religion than reflection itself could give with the aid of the best conceivable organon applied to intuitions as strong, distinct and clear as the most definite perceptions of sense.

It is clear that Mr. Morell, in representing his scheme of revelation as an *a priori* argument against the possibility of a Divine theology, has quietly assumed that the agency there described is the sole agency of the Deity in relation to the religion of His creatures. He seems to think that the Almighty exhausted Himself in the production of spiritual perceptions, and therefore *could* not reduce them to the forms of the understanding—that in the process of engendering religion he lost the ability to describe it. But where is the proof that revelation, in our author's sense, includes the whole agency of God? Not a particle is adduced, and hence, as a Divine theology is not inconsistent with a revealed religion, as there is no shadow of contradiction betwixt them, and not the slightest proof that the revelation of religion is the only form in which God condescends to His ignorant and sinful creatures, Mr. Morell has signally failed to establish, on philosophical grounds, the human origin of theology. His premises do not contain his conclusion. For aught that he has alleged to the contrary, we may be as truly indebted to the Divine benignity for a perfect and infallible standard of faith as for those other operations in consequence of which we feel the pulsations of the Christian life.

The only thing, indeed, in the whole chapter on Revelation which seems remotely to bear upon the subject is the passage already quoted, in which he states the question only to evade it. He shows, indeed, that a logical explication of doctrines could not awaken ideas in a mind destitute of the capacity to apprehend them. We may cheerfully concede that no painting can make a blind man see, that no music can ravish a deaf man with the rapture of its sounds; but still the painting and the music may both exist and be perfect in their kind. No one claims for a Divine theology the power of making men Christians; it is universally conceded that the letter killeth, but the controversy betwixt Mr. Morell and the popular faith is, whether that letter can exist. It is a poor evasion to say, because it cannot perform an office which no one has ever thought of ascribing to it, that, therefore, it is essentially and necessarily inconceivable as a real and substantive entity. All that our author proves is, that it cannot enlighten; that it can impart no new simple idea; that it presupposes all the elemental germs of thought which enter into theology, as natural philosophy presupposes the informations of sense, and psychology those of consciousness. It supposes, in other words, that men are capable of religion, but it by no means follows that because a Divine theology can neither create the religious faculty nor immediately produce its appropriate intuitions, therefore it cannot express them with logical exactness, nor describe the objects on which they are dependent. Moral philosophy cannot originate a conscience, but it may still be a scientific exhibition of all the operations of the moral nature. What Mr. Morell's argument requires him to prove is, that a Divine theology is impossible—that a science of religion being admitted, that science *cannot* be imparted to us by God, it must, from the nature of the case, be human in its origin; and this proposition is not affected by the inadequacy of such a science to accomplish a certain subjective effect, unless it can be shown that its ability to do this is the condition of its existence.

But perhaps the proof we are seeking may be found in the chapter on Inspiration. It is the object of that chapter to show that

"Inspiration does not imply anything generically new in the actual processes of the human mind; it does not involve any form of intelligence essentially different from what we already possess; it indicates rather the elevation of the religious consciousness, and with it, of course, the power of spiritual vision, to a degree of intensity peculiar to the individuals thus highly favoured. We must regard the whole process of inspiration, accordingly, as being in no sense *mechanical*, but purely dynamical; involving, not a novel and supernatural faculty, but a faculty already enjoyed, elevated *supernaturally* to an extraordinary power and susceptibility; indicating, in fact, an inward nature so perfectly harmonized to the Divine, so freed from the distorting influences of prejudice, passion and sin, so simply recipient of the Divine ideas circumambient around it, so responsive in all its strings to the breath of heaven, that truth leaves an impress upon it which answers perfectly to the objective reality."[1]

All which, being interpreted, is that *inspiration* and *holiness*, or *sanctification*, are synonymous terms. The author apprehends, in its literal sense, the benediction of our Saviour on the pure in heart, and makes them seers not only of God, but of those things of God which, the Apostle assures us, none can understand but the Spirit of God Himself. It will certainly strike our readers as a novelty that there should be any inconsistency betwixt the grace of holiness and the gift of knowledge. They will be slow to comprehend how sanctification and instruction can be contradictory processes—so much so that He who sanctifies cannot teach. "Sanctify them through thy truth: thy word is truth." "God hath from

[1] Page 151.

the beginning chosen you to salvation through sanctification of the Spirit and belief of the truth." For aught
that we can see, it may be granted to the author that the
measure of piety is the exact measure of ability to appreciate, to understand, to know Divine truth, that holiness
is essential to a living faith ; and yet it will not follow that
God cannot communicate the truth with which, as holy
beings, we are brought into harmony. If our holiness
were perfect, it would enable us, according to the author,
to apprehend the objects of religion in their concrete reality,
but not in their scientific form ; and there is nothing absurd
in the idea that the things which have aroused our moral
sensibilities should be presented, in their full and perfect
proportions, to the contemplation of the understanding.

It may be objected, however, that although Mr. Morell's
philosophy does not prove a Divine theology to be impossible
or absurd, in the strict acceptation of the terms, yet it
demonstrates what, in reference to any dispensation of God,
amounts to the same thing, that it is unnecessary or useless.
This is no doubt the real scope of his argument, though he
has been bold enough to assert that the *only* way, the *sole*
method, by which a valid theology can be constructed is by
human reflection on the phenomena of religion. But widely
different as the issues of possibility and expediency evidently
are, we shall concede, in the present instance, that the proof
of uselessness is tantamount to the proof of absurdity, and
proceed to inquire how Mr. Morell has succeeded in even
this aspect of the case. "To a man utterly ignorant," says
he,[1] "of all spiritual conceptions, and altogether insensible
to Divine things, the mere exposition of the truths and
doctrines of Christianity is *useless*. He does not grasp them
at all in their proper meaning and intensity ; ranging as
they do beyond the sphere of his present experience, the
very terms of the propositions employed awaken no corresponding idea within his mind." That is, theology,
under a certain contingency, is powerless to produce a given

[1] Page 137.

effect. But a specific incompetency and a general uselessness are very different things. Because, in a "man utterly
ignorant of all spiritual conceptions and altogether insensible to Divine things," the mere exposition of the truths
and doctrines of Christianity cannot supply the place of
faculties to apprehend them, it by no means follows that,
to the man who has spiritual conceptions and *is* "sensible
to Divine things," theology may not be of incalculable service.   To a man destitute of senses, natural philosophy
would, no doubt, be a very unintelligible jargon ; but does
it follow that it must be correspondingly useless to one who
has all the simple ideas of which it is composed?   But Mr.
Morell has himself settled the question. He represents
theology, in our present condition, as a necessity[1] of our
nature, and ascribes to it offices of immense importance in
the development of the religious life.   It is true that he
has his eye only on human theology, but the uses which
he admits are not at all dependent upon its origin, but
upon its truth.   It answers these valuable ends, not because
it has been reached by reflection, but because it has a real
existence and is capable of a real application.   It is the
thing itself which is useful, and not the mode of its discovery.   It would seem, too, that the more perfect it was,
the better ; and that the circumstance of its being Divine,
so far from detracting from its value, would immensely
enhance it.   Let us now attend to the author's admissions :

"Theology, having once been created, can be presented didactically
to the understanding before there is any awakening of the religious
nature, and can even lead the mind to whom it is presented to such
an interest in the subject as may issue in his spiritual enlightenment."[2]

Here it is obvious that the use of the Theology is not at
all dependent upon its origin; it is useful to a mind which
has not been in a situation to construct a system reflectively
for itself.   This is just what we attribute to a Divine theology ; it is the means under God of awakening the religious

1 Page 196.   2 Page 207.

nature, the incorruptible seed by which we are begotten to newness of life, and the standard to which all our experiences must be brought, and by which their soundness must be tried. This single consideration, that the science of religion may be the means of awakening the religious nature, that theology may be the parent of piety, is enough to set aside all that the author has said against the value of a logical exposition of the truths and doctrines of Christianity.

The following remarks, professedly intended to elucidate the subject, are applicable with tenfold power to such a system as the Bible claims to be. We ask nothing more than what the author has himself suggested, to remove all cavils against the letter because it killeth, while the spirit only is competent to quicken into life :

"The uses of Christian theology are—

"1. To show the internal consistency of religious truth. Little as we need to see this consistency whilst our inmost souls are burning with a deep and holy enthusiasm, yet in the ordinary state of human life, beset as we are with a thousand repressive influences, it is highly important to strengthen ourselves with every kind of armour against skepticism and indifference. In proportion as our zeal and excitement become cooler, do we need so much the more the concurring testimony of reason to support us in the pursuit of the Christian life. It is upon this we fall back when the fire of life burns dim, until we can kindle it again from the altar of God. Hence, the importance of having Christian truth presented to us in such a form that we may see its harmony with all the laws of our intellectual being, and have *their* witness to seal its truth on our hearts.

"2. Another use of Christian theology is to repel philosophical objections. The unbeliever has not the witness within himself, and, what is more, he would fain destroy the validity of the truths of Christianity to others by affirming their inconsistency with reason or with one another. The moral influences of the religious life do not *answer* these objections, although they may disarm them greatly of their force. To answer them the truth conveyed in the religious life must be made reflective and scientific; then, indeed, and not till then, can itself be maintained, and its consistency be defended upon the grounds of the philosophical objector himself.

"3. A third use of Christian theology is to preserve mankind from vague enthusiasm. A strong religious excitement is not inconsistent with a weak judgment, a feeble conscience, and active tendencies to folly, and even sin.   Under such circumstances the power of the emotions will sometimes overbalance the better dictates of Christian faith, love and obedience, so as to impel the subject of them into something bordering upon fanaticism.   Against this evil religion alone is often unable to struggle; it needs the stronger element of calm reason to curb these wandering impulses, and bring them into due subjection to duty and to truth.   Here, then, the influence of *theology* bears upon the whole case, and to its power is it mainly owing that the intense incentives offered by Christianity to the emotive nature of man have been so ordered and directed as to keep him from vague enthusiasm in his belief and an unsober fanaticism in his actions.

" 4. The last use we mention to which theology may be applied is to embody our religious ideas in a complete and connected system.   In this form they appeal to every element in the nature of man.   The moral influence they exert upon the whole spirit is coupled with the power of their appeal to the reason, and the intellect of mankind becomes *satisfied* as the heart becomes softened and renewed.

" Such, in brief, are some of the principal uses of theology, formally considered." [1]

Having shown that our author has signally failed in his *a priori* argument against the existence of a Divine standard of theology—that is, that his philosophy, even upon the supposition of its truth, is not inconsistent with the popular faith in regard to the authority of the Bible—we shall next notice the several considerations by which he attempts to prove that, as a matter of fact, no such Divine standard has ever been vouchsafed to our race.   His first argument is drawn from the proofs by which Christianity has been revealed to man.

"The aim of revelation," he informs us, "has not been formally to expound a system of doctrine to the understanding, but to educate the mind of man gradually to an inward appreciation of the truth concerning his own relation to God.   Judaism was a propædeutic to Christianity, but there was no formal definition of any one spiritual truth in the whole of that economy.   The purpose of it was to school the mind to spiritual contemplation, to awaken the religious consciousness by types and symbols and other perceptive means to the realization of certain great spiritual ideas, and to furnish words and analogies in which the truths of Christianity could be embodied and proclaimed to

[1] Pages 225–227.

the world.   If we pass on to the Christian revelation itself, the mode
of procedure we find was generically the same.   There was no *formal*
exposition of Christian doctrine in the whole of the discourses of the
Saviour.   His life and teaching, His character and suffering, His
death and resurrection, all appealed to the deeper religious nature of
man; they were adapted to awaken it to a newer and higher activity;
instead of offering a mere explication to the understanding, they were
intended to furnish altogether new experiences, to widen the sphere
of our spiritual insight, to embody a *revelation from God.*   The Apostles followed in the same course.   They did not start from Jerusalem
with a system of doctrine to propound intellectually to the world.
It would have been no revelation to the world if they had, for with
his moral and spiritual nature sunk down into insensibility and sin,
man would have had no real spiritual perception associated with the
very terms in which their arguments and propositions must have been
couched.   The Apostles went forth to awaken man's power of spiritual intuition—to impress upon the world the great conceptions of sin,
of righteousness, of judgment to come, of salvation, of purity and of
heavenly love.   This they did by their lives, their teaching, their spiritual *intensity* in action and suffering, their whole testimony to the word,
the person, the death and the resurrection of the Saviour." [1]

We do not remember ever to have seen a more signal
exemplification of a theory breaking down under its own
weight than that which is presented in the preceding extract.
The end of all revelation is to furnish, we are told, intuitional perceptions of religious truth ; it cannot, therefore, be
addressed to the understanding, neither can it contain logical and definite statements of doctrine.   But still this revelation is to be imparted through the instrumentality of
commissioned agents, and these agents fulfil their vocation
by *teaching.*   Now, if the reader will turn to the second
chapter of our author's book, in which the distinctions are
drawn out at length betwixt the intuitional and logical consciousness, he will find that the very first point insisted on
is that the " knowledge we obtain by the logical consciousness
is *representative and indirect,* while that which we obtain by
the intuitional consciousness is *presentative and immediate.*"
To produce an intuition, consequently, the mind and the
object must be brought together in actual contact.   It must

[1] Pages 139, 140.

not be some description or representation, but the reality of
truth itself, which must stand face to face with the knowing
subject.   Where essential existence or original elements of
knowledge are concerned, the power of language is utterly
inadequate to convey any ideas to the mind; the intuitions
themselves must exist, or all efforts to awaken the conceptions are utterly hopeless.   If, in conformity with these
principles, Christ and His Apostles were commissioned to
make a revelation to men whose moral and spiritual nature
was sunk down into insensibility and sin, all that they could
have done was to present the spiritual realities which they
themselves apprehended, and then impart a corresponding
power to perceive them.   They went, according to the
theory, among the blind to make known glorious objects of
sight.   Their first business must have been to place the
objects within the reach of the eye, and then purge the
eyes to behold them.   This is the only way in which we
can conceive that they could have succeeded in effecting
vision.   But what has *teaching* to do with this process?
All the knowledge acquired from another through the
medium of signs is indirect and representative, and therefore addressed not to intuition, but to the understanding.
How will our author explain this inconsistency?   He,
in the first place, represents Christ and His Apostles as
spiritual mesmerizers, whose whole business it is to bring
their fellow-men face to face with a class of transcendental
realities, and then at the very time that he is disproving the
possibility of an appeal to the understanding, he converts
them into teachers, dealing not with the realities themselves,
but with their signs and logical exponents.   They awaken
intuitions by *teaching!*   Hence, upon his own admission,
the process by which Christianity has been revealed to man
is *not* in accordance with the fundamental principles of his
system.   The inconsistency of his statements is still more
glaring in reference to the Mosaic institute.   That, it seems,
was a propædeutic to Christianity, but it had nothing logical, nothing in the way of representative instruction, and

"yet awakened the religious consciousness by types and
symbols." Now, we would humbly ask, What are types
and symbols but a *language* through which, in the one case,
instruction is communicated by means of analogy, and in
the other by means of visible and expressive signs? In
what way could these figured representations of truth suggest the spiritual realities to the mind, but through the
operations of the understanding, comparing the type with
the antitype, the sign with the thing signified? From the
author's own account, then, it is evident that both Judaism
and Christianity were propagated by appeals to the understanding, that the agents of the revelation in both cases
were, in the strict and proper sense of the term, *teachers,*
and that it was a part of their commission to embody in
language of some sort the high conceptions to which they
were anxious to elevate their race. These conceptions
when embodied in language became doctrines, so that there
must have been, to the same extent to which Christ and His
Apostles were teachers, "a formal exposition of Christian
doctrine."

But we would ask our author, How, apart from didactic
appeals—which, we have already seen, he confesses may be
the means of spiritual awakening—spiritual intuitions could
be engendered by any merely human agency? In what
way is it possible for one man to present a spiritual reality
to another, except through its verbal sign, or by a description of the occasions on which the intuitions are experienced? His whole office must be logical. He can neither
give eyes to see, nor can he bring the objects themselves
in their essential and substantive existence into contact with
the mind. He can, in other words, do nothing, according
to Mr. Morell's own psychology, but make a logical statement of his own experiences. How could the Apostles,
for example, impress upon the world the great conceptions
of sin, of righteousness, of judgment to come, of salvation,
of purity, of heavenly love, but by some definite—that is to
say, logical—expression of these very conceptions as they

existed in their own minds, or, if they were simple and
elementary ideas, by referring to the occasions or circumstances connected with their first suggestion to themselves?
The intuitions they could no more produce than they could
create a soul. Through a strong ideal presence of the
scenes amid which their own experiences had been awakened, they might rouse the latent susceptibilities of their
hearers, but their office terminated with the descriptions
suited to produce this presence, which is purely a logical process. "Their testimony to the word, the person, the death
and the resurrection of the Saviour" must, in the same
way, have been conveyed in words; they could only hope
to reach the sensibilities through the understanding; they
could set Christ and his life in vivid distinctness before the
minds of men, but it could only be by signs which represented the realities; and therefore their appeals must have
been exclusively logical. Their intensity in action and
suffering, as a mere phenomenon, suggested no definite idea;
it might have been madness, fanaticism or any other extravagance; it could have no moral import to spectators until
it was explained; and we see no way of explaining it but
by signs which should represent the moral enthusiasm from
which it sprung. Hence, according to the author's own
showing, the labours of Apostles and Evangelists were confined exclusively to the faculty which deals with signs.
They testified to facts, and embodied in words the great
moral conceptions which these facts involved; and hence
Christianity then was diffused so far as the agency of men was
employed by addresses to the logical faculty. The Apostles
taught, testified, acted; their teaching and testimony were
obviously to the understanding, and action has no meaning
except as its principles and motives are understood. Direct
appeals to the intuitional consciousness would evidently
have been preposterous. That faculty deals immediately
with things themselves; and unless the Apostles were gifted
with power to command the presence of spiritual realities
at pleasure, to bring God and Heaven and Hell into direct

contact with the minds of men, and possessed a similar
power over the hardened hearts, the slumbering consciences
and the stupid sensibility of their age—unless they could
give eyes to the blind and ears to the deaf—to have sent
them into the world to awaken religious intuitions would
have been about as sensible an errand as to have sent them
into a cemetery to quicken corpses and make the dead
entranced admirers of the beauty of nature. If they were
to be debarred from addressing the understanding, we are
utterly at a loss to conceive in what manner they would proceed. Mr. Morell has involved himself in perplexity and
contradiction by confounding the real mission of the Apostles, which was purely logical, and from the nature of the
case could not have been otherwise, with the results which
God intended to effect, and which, if he likes the expression, were purely intuitional. The whole process, as it is
described in the New Testament, is plain, simple, intelligible. It consisted, in the first place, in that very logical
explication or statement of doctrines which Mr. Morell so
much abhors; and then in a process of supernatural illumination which it was the prerogative of God alone to communicate. The Apostles described the realities of religion,
and the Holy Ghost enabled the hearers to understand.
They made the sounds, the Spirit imparted the hearing ear;
they presented the scenes, the Spirit gave the seeing eye;
they announced the truth, the Spirit vouchsafed the understanding heart. They, in other words, upon the authority
of God, proclaimed an infallible theology; and the Spirit
of all grace produced the religion of which that theology
was the logical expression. He used their truth to renew,
to sanctify, to purify, to save. Their business was to *teach;*
it was the office of an Agent more august and glorious than
themselves to awaken the conceptions which that teaching
embodied.

It is particularly in the chapter on Inspiration that the
author points out the difficulties with which the vulgar

theory of the Divine authority of the Scriptures is encumbered. We have seen that he regards inspiration as equivalent to holiness; and most of the chapter is occupied in refuting what he has chosen to designate the *mechanical* view of the question. It is, of course, indispensable to the authority of the Scriptures as the Word of God that the men who wrote them should have written as they were moved by the Holy Ghost. Any hypothesis which sets aside a Divine testimony to every statement and doctrine of the Bible is inconsistent with the exercise of that faith which the Scriptures exact, and which is the only adequate foundation of infallible assurance. So far as responsible authorship is concerned, a Divine rule of faith must be the production of God. The design of such a rule is not simply to give us truth, but truth which we know to be truth, specifically on the ground that the Lord has declared it. Hence the theory of "verbal dictation," which our author declares[1] "has been so generally abandoned by the thoughtful in the present day," is the only theory which we have ever regarded as consistent with the exigencies of the case, the only theory which makes the Bible what it professes to be, the WORD OF GOD, and an adequate and perfect measure of our faith. If its contents, in any instances, however insignificant, rest only upon the testimony of the human agents employed in writing it, in those instances we can only believe in man; the statements may be true, but they cease to be Divine and infallible, and the assent which we yield to them becomes opinion and not faith. If, therefore, the author has succeeded in demolishing the theory of verbal dictation or of a distinct commission—which he treats separately, though they are only different expressions of the same thing—it must be confessed that, however he has failed in his philosophy, he has completely triumphed in the *a posteriori* aspect of his argument.

His first consideration is, that "there is no *positive* evidence of such a verbal dictation having been granted."

[1] Page 154.

This is summary enough. But the reason assigned is still more remarkable.

"The supposition of its existence would demand a twofold kind of inspiration; each kind entirely distinct from the other. The Apostles, it is admitted, were inspired to preach and to teach *orally*, but we have the most positive evidence that this commission did not extend to their very words. Often they were involved in minor misconceptions; and sometimes they taught specific notions inconsistent with a pure spiritual Christianity, as Peter did when he was chided by Paul. The verbal scheme, therefore, demands the admission of *one* kind of inspiration having been given to the Apostles as men, thinkers, moral agents and preachers, and another kind having been granted to them as *writers.*" [1]

In the first place, this twofold inspiration is the result of Mr. Morell's own arbitrary use of language. If he chooses to describe the influences under which men are converted and sanctified as *one* kind of inspiration, the theory of verbal dictation, of course, implies another, but another by no means inconsistent with the former. The process by which a man is transferred from sin to holiness is very different from the process by which he receives a message to be announced in the terms of its conveyance. There is nothing in personal integrity incompatible with the office of a secretary or amanuensis.

In the next place, Mr. Morell begs the question in assuming that the commission of the Apostles as teachers and preachers involved no other inspiration but that which changed their hearts. The very stress of the controversy turns upon the question, What was the apostolic commission? Whatsoever it was, it is universally conceded that it extended to their writings in exactly the same sense in which it extended to their preaching. If their preaching, in the discharge of their functions as Apostles, was not verbally dictated, no more were their letters. If they *spake* not by the Holy Ghost, neither did they *write* under His suggestions. "But," says our author, "we have the most positive evidence that this commission did not extend to

[1] Page 155.

their very words." This, if it could be proved, would settle the question. But there is something in the first commission which our Saviour gave to the Twelve when He sent
them out to the lost sheep of the house of Israel which
seems to be in such palpable contradiction to this confident
assumption that we must be permitted to question whether
the evidence can be regarded as superlatively positive.
"Behold," says the Master, "I send you forth as sheep in
the midst of wolves; be ye, therefore, wise as serpents and
harmless as doves. But beware of men, for they will deliver
you up to the councils, and they will scourge you in their
synagogues, and ye shall be brought before governors and
kings for my sake, for a testimony against them and the
Gentiles. But when they deliver you up, take no thought
how or what ye shall speak; for it shall be given you in
that same hour what ye shall speak. For it is not ye that
speak, but the Spirit of your Father which speaketh in
you." Or, as it is more pointedly in Mark, "it is not ye
that speak, but the Holy Ghost." Paul, too, for whom by
the way the author has no great partiality, professed to
speak the things which had been freely revealed to him of
God, "not in the words which man's wisdom teacheth, but
the Holy Ghost teacheth," and had the arrogance to treat
his own communications "as the commandments of the
Lord." But what is the *most positive evidence* to which Mr.
Morell refers? Why that the Apostles "were often involved
in minor misconceptions, and sometimes they taught specific notions inconsistent with a pure spiritual Christianity, as
Peter did when he was chided by Paul." Peter *taught* no
such thing. He was guilty of dissimulation *in conduct*.
He knew the truth and acted in consistency with it before
that certain came from James, but when they were come,
he was tempted to humour their prejudices. Paul reproved
him distinctly upon the ground that he was acting in contradiction to what he knew to be the truth of the Gospel.
This case, therefore, only proves that Peter, as a man, was
partially sanctified; it does not prove that, as an Apostle,

he was permitted to fall into doctrinal error. As to the other minor misconceptions, to which our author refers, it will be time to explain them when we know what they are. Meanwhile, we may be permitted to remark that in this case of Peter, the author has confounded holiness of character with the apostolic commission. The only inspiration which he seems able to conceive is that of personal purity; and if a man has any remnants of sin cleaving to his flesh or his spirit, he is, according to Mr. Morell, imperfectly inspired. This, we repeat, is a begging of the question. No one maintains that the Apostles, as men, were perfect; they were sinners under the dominion of grace; but as Apostles, in their official relations, it is the doctrine of the popular faith that they were the organs of the Holy Spirit in communicating to the Church an infallible rule of faith and practice. It is no presumption against this hypothesis that they were subject to the weaknesses of fallen humanity; the treasure was put in earthen vessels, that the excellency of the power might be confessed as springing from God. It is surely miserable sophistry, when the very question in debate is, What was the apostolic commission? quietly to assume a theory, and then, make that theory the pretext for rejecting another account. And yet this is what our author has done; he assumes that the apostolic commission consisted exclusively in the elevation of the religious sensibilities, and then, upon the ground of this assumption, rejects the hypothesis of verbal dictation, as requiring a commission for the writers distinct from that of the apostolic office! We suspect that it would be no hard matter to prove any proposition in heaven or earth, if we can only be indulged in the liberty of taking our premises for granted.

The author's second argument,[1] upon which, very prudently, he does not insist, is drawn "from the fact that we find a distinctive style maintained by each separate author." He regards it "as a highly improbable, and even extra-

[1] Page 156.

vagant, supposition, without the most positive proof of it being offered, that each writer should manifest his own modes of thought, his own temperament of mind, his own educational influence, his own peculiar phraseology, and yet, notwithstanding this, every word should have been dictated to him by the Holy Spirit." If Mr. Morell had investigated, a little more fully than he seems to have done, the grounds of the popular faith, he might have found in this very circumstance, which he considers so extremely improbable and extravagant, a fresh illustration of the wisdom of God. The external proofs of inspiration, which consist in the signs of an Apostle or Prophet, found either in the writer himself, or some one commissioned to vouch for his production, require, in most cases, a knowledge of the author. And in conducting an inquiry upon this point, the internal evidence arising from style, structure and habits of thought materially contributes to a satisfactory result. In the first stage of the investigation we consider the productions simply as human compositions, and God has wisely distributed the gift of inspiration, so that while He is responsible for all that is said, the individual peculiarities of the agent shall designate the person whose instrumentality He employed. He has facilitated our inquiry into the human organ of the Holy Spirit. Having ascertained ourselves as to the human authors or their works, the next question is, as to the claims which they themselves put forward to Divine direction. What are these claims, and how are they substantiated? If they pretend to a verbal dictation, and then adduce the credentials sufficient to authenticate it, we have all which, in the way of external evidence, could be reasonably exacted. The Epistle to the Romans, for example, is put into our hands as a part of the Word of God. The first question is, Who wrote it? If it can be traced to Paul, we know that he was an Apostle of the Saviour and enjoyed whatever inspiration was attached to the apostolic office. He possessed in an eminent degree the signs of an Apostle, and if it were one of the privileges

of the office that those who were called to it should, in
their public instructions and testimonies for Jesus, speak the
language of the Holy Ghost, as soon as we are convinced
that Paul was the writer of the document, its ultimate
emanation from God is settled. Now it obviously facilitates
this inquiry to have the mind of Paul stamped upon the
letter—to have it distinctly impressed with his image, while
it contains nothing but the true and faithful sayings of God.
It is consequently no presumption against the Divine dictation of a book that it should exhibit traces of the hand
that was employed.

The third argument[1] mistakes altogether the very end
of inspiration. The purpose was to furnish a statement of
facts and an exhibition of doctrines, which should be received with a faith infallible and Divine, upon the sole consideration that God was the Author of both. Its design
was to give us a rule of faith and not a standard of opinion.
It was to be a Divine testimony; and therefore, whatever
might be the moral and religious qualifications of the writers, however competent they might have been upon their
own authority to have told us the same things, their words
could, in no sense, be received as the real oracles of God.
The Lord Himself must speak; and this being the purpose
of inspiration, verbal dictation detracts in no way from the
character or worth of the Apostles. What they were inspired to teach others was received by themselves upon the
same ultimate ground on which it is received by us. They
were channels of communication, not because they were fit
to be nothing else, but because the end intended to be
answered necessarily precluded any other relation, on their
part, to the message conveyed.

The fourth argument, which is a repetition, almost for
the hundredth time, of the incompetency of the Bible to
change the heart and enlighten the understanding, though
the author presents it here as a "moral demonstration"
against the theory of verbal dictation, has already been

[1] Page 156.

sufficiently answered in what we have said of the uses of theology. Mr. Morell ought to know how to distinguish between an inadequacy to produce a given effect and universal worthlessness. Is the eye useless because it cannot hear, or the ear useless because it cannot see? And must a Divine standard of theology be utterly good for nothing because it cannot perform the office of the Holy Spirit? Is there nothing else that it can do? Has not he himself repeatedly admitted that a human theology subserves many valuable purposes in the economy of religion? and in the name of truth and righteousness what is there in the mere circumstance that it is human to give it such an immense advantage over one that is Divine?

The theory of a distinct commission—which the author treats separately from that of verbal dictation, though they are only different expressions of the same thing—he summarily dismisses as destitute of any satisfactory evidence, and indebted for "its growth and progress in the Church to the influence of a low and mechanical view of the whole question of inspiration itself."[1] The compositions of the Prophets and Apostles, whether in the Old or New Testament, he considers as the spontaneous effusions of their own minds, prompted by the motives which usually regulate good men in their efforts to promote the welfare of their race. The purpose to write and the things they should write were equally the suggestions of their own benevolence and wisdom. The theory of a distinct commission, on the other hand, asserts that they were commanded to write by the special authority of God, and that the things which they wrote were dictated to them by the agency of the Holy Spirit. The settlement of this controversy evidently turns upon two points: the light in which the writers themselves regarded it, or, in the absence of any specific information upon this head, the light in which it was regarded by those who were competent to judge. If they claimed a distinct commission, or if those whose testimony ought to be decisive

[1] Page 160.

awarded it to them, there is an end of the dispute. With
relation to the books of the Old Testament, we receive their
verbal inspiration upon two grounds. The first is the testimony of the Jewish Church, which in the successive generations contemporary with the successive writers in its canon
known to them, however unknown to us, possessed the
means of determining with accuracy whether the several
authors exhibited themselves the external proofs of a Divine
commission, or, in the absence of such proofs, whether their
productions were vouched by the seal of those who were
competent, from the same proofs, to give an infallible
decision. The second· is the testimony of Christ and His
Apostles. These witnesses are competent to judge. Now
the question is, What judgment did they give? In what
sense did they receive these books as coming from God?
We shall not here enter into the question concerning the
notions of the Jews, although they are patent upon almost
every page of the New Testament; but we confidently
assert that Christ and His Apostles distinctly and unequivocally awarded to the Prophets of the ancient dispensation
precisely the verbal inspiration in their writings which Mr.
Morell labours to subvert. Paul declares that " all Scripture is given by inspiration of God ;" [1] Peter, a little more
definitely, that "holy men of God *spake* as they were
moved by the Holy Ghost." [2] Our Saviour rebuts a malignant accusation of the Jews by an argument which turns
upon the Divine authority of the *words* of the Old Testament; [3] and passages are again and again quoted by His
Apostles as the *ipsissima verba* of the Holy Spirit: "Well
spake the Holy Ghost," says Paul, "by Esaias the Prophet
unto our fathers." [4] "Wherefore as the Holy Ghost saith,
To-day if ye will hear his voice, harden not your hearts." [5]
The Old Testament is compendiously described as "the
oracles of God, [6] and the Apostle informs us that it was
"God who, at sundry times and in divers manners, *spake*

[1] 2 Tim. iii. 16.   [2] 2 Pet. i. 21.   [3] John x. 33–36.
[4] Acts xxviii. 25.   [5] Heb. iii. 7.   [6] Rom. iii. 2.

in time past unto the fathers by the Prophets."[1]   Paul goes
so far as to identify the Scripture with God Himself—attributing to it what was absolutely true only of Him.   "The
Scripture saith unto Pharaoh ;" "the Scripture foreseeing that
God would justify the heathen ;" "the Scripture hath concluded all under sin."   It is absolutely certain, from these
references, that Christ and His Apostles regarded the Old
Testament as *verbally* inspired, and the Prophets as nothing
but the agents through whom the Holy Ghost communicated
His will.   It is of no consequence, therefore, whether we
know the human authors of the different books or not, or
the times at which they were written, or even the country
in which they were composed; it is enough that what constituted the canon of the Jews in the days of our Saviour
was endorsed by Him and His own chosen Apostles as the
Word of God.   He and they referred to that canon as a
whole, under the well-known titles of "The Scriptures,"
"The Law," "The Prophets and the Psalms;" "treated it
generally as authoritative;" called it specifically "the Oracles
of God;" and, quoted particular passages in a way in which
they could not have quoted them if there had been no distinct
commission to write them.   But these considerations, it appears, are nothing to Mr. Morell.   Because we are not in
possession of the evidence which justified the reception of
each particular book into the Jewish canon, he triumphantly
asks what chance we have upon the hypothesis of verbal
dictation of being successful in proving the inspiration of
the Old Testament against the aggressions of the skeptic.[2]
"The fact," he adds, "upon which many lay such remarkable stress, that Christ and His Apostles honoured the Old
Testament, is nothing to the purpose, as far as the *nature*
of their [its] inspiration is concerned."   But is it nothing
to the purpose that Christ and His Apostles distinctly declare to us that it was *God* who *spake* by the Prophets,
that the Scriptures are called by our Saviour the *Word* of
God, and that particular passages are repeatedly cited as

[1] Heb. i. 1.   [2] Page 178.

the *ipsissima verba* of the Holy Ghost? Is this *kind* of honour nothing? But he continues:

"They honoured the *Divine* and the *Eternal* in the old dispensation. They honoured the men who had been servants and prophets of the Most High. They honoured the writings from which their spirit of piety and of power breathed forth. But never did they affirm the *literal* and special divinity of all the national records of the Jewish people, as preserved and read in the synagogues of that day."[1]

No doubt Christ and His Apostles honoured the Divine and the Eternal in the old dispensation, but, if the Scriptures are to be credited, they also honoured the Divine and temporary. They honoured everything that was Divine, whether it was to remain or to be done away. The Master fulfilled all righteousness. As to the *men* who had been servants and prophets of the Most High, they said very little about them—at least very little is recorded. But it is certain that they never honoured the writings of the Prophets because they were the offspring of pious and devotional feeling. It was not because the spirit of the men was in them, but because the Spirit of God was there, that they attached the importance which they did attach to the books of the Old Testament; and the passages which we have already quoted put it beyond any reasonable doubt that they did regard God as the real and responsible Author of these books. Their testimony is, or ought to be, decisive of the question.

The author's opinion of the inspiration of the New Testament may be collected from the following passage, which, though long, cannot be conveniently abridged:

"Passing from the Old Testament to the New, the same entire absence of any distinct commission given to the writers of the several books (with the exception, perhaps, of the Apocalypse of John) presents itself. Mark and Luke were not Apostles, and the latter of them distinctly professes to write from the testimony of eye-witnesses, and to claim the confidence of Theophilus, for whom his two treatises were

[1] Page 178.

composed, *on this particular ground.* Matthew and John wrote their accounts somewhat far in the first century, when the increase of the Christian converts naturally suggested the necessity of some such statements, at once for their information and for their spiritual requirements generally. Finally, Paul, as we know, wrote his letters as the state of particular churches seemed to call for them; but in no case do we find *a special commission* attached to any of these, or of the other Epistles of the New Testament.

"Added to this, the light which history sheds upon the early period of the Christian Church shows us that the writings which now compose the New Testament Canon were not at all regarded as express messages to them from God, independently of the conviction they had of the high integrity and spiritual development of the minds of the writers. They received them just as they received the oral teachings of the Apostles and Evangelists; they read them in the churches to supply the place of *their* personal instructions; and there is abundant evidence that *many other writings* beside those which now form the New Testament were read with a similar reverence and for a similar edification.

"It was only gradually, as the pressure of heresy compelled it, that a certain number of writings were agreed upon by general consent as being *purely apostolic,* and designated by the term *homologoumena,* or agreed upon. But that much contention existed as to which should be acknowledged canonical, and which not, is seen from the fact that a number of the writings now received were long termed 'antilegomena,' or contested, and that the third century had wellnigh completed its course before the *present canon* was fixed by universal consent. All this shows us that it was not any distinct commission attached to the composition of certain books or documents which imparted a Divine authority to the Apostles' writings, but that they were selected and approved by the Church itself as being veritable productions of men 'who spake as they were moved by the Holy Ghost' — men who were not inspired *in order* to write any precise documents, but who wrote such documents, amongst other labours, by virtue of their being inspired.

"The conclusion which we necessarily draw from these considerations is, that the canonicity of the New Testament Scriptures was decided upon solely on the ground of their presenting to the whole Church clear statements of *apostolical* Christianity. The idea of their being written by any special command of God or verbal dictation of the Spirit was an idea altogether foreign to the primitive churches. They knew that Christ was in Himself a Divine revelation; they knew that the Apostles had been with Him in His ministry; they knew that their hearts had been warmed with His truth, that their whole religious nature had been elevated to intense spirituality of thinking and feeling by the possession of His Spirit, and that this same Spirit was poured out without measure upon the Church. Here it was they took their stand, and in these facts they saw the reality of the apostolic inspiration; upon these realities they reposed their faith ere ever the sacred books were penned; and when they *were* penned, they regarded them as valid representations of the living truth which had already enlightened the Church, and as such alone pronounced upon their canonical and truly apostolic character." [1]

The substance of these observations may be reduced to three points: 1. That the writers of the New Testament made no pretensions to the sort of inspiration implied in the idea of a Divine commission to write. 2. That the primitive Church did not look upon their productions as the words of the Holy Ghost; and, 3. That the collection of books which constitute the canon of the New Testament was made, not that it might be an authoritative rule of faith, but that precious mementos of the Apostles and of apostolic preaching might be embodied and preserved.

Every one of these propositions is grossly and notoriously false. There are three considerations which to any candid mind put it beyond all reasonable controversy that the Apostles and Evangelists *must* have claimed the plenary inspiration for which we contend. The first is, that the Saviour, on no less than four different occasions, promised to the Twelve the verbal dictation of the Spirit when they should be called to testify for Him. The last of these promises has no limitation as to time and place, and the language in which it is couched deserves to be seriously pondered : "Howbeit, when He, the Spirit of truth, is come, He will guide you into all truth; for He shall not speak of Himself, but whatsoever He shall hear, that shall He speak, and He will show you things to come." [2] These promises explain the nature of the apostolic commission, at least so far as oral teaching was concerned. When the Apostles spake,

[1] Pages 163–165.
[2] John xvi. 13. The other instances are: Matt. x. 19, 20; Mark xiii. 11; Luke xii. 11, 12.

it was not in the words which man's wisdom teacheth, but which the Holy Ghost teacheth. The second consideration is, that the Apostles placed their writings upon the same footing exactly with their oral instructions. *Est enim Scripturæ et prædicationis par ratio.*[1] The third is, that they attributed the same authority to their own compositions which they awarded to the Scriptures of the Old Testament. Peter refers to the Epistles of Paul with the same reverence with which he refers to the canon of the Jews,[2] and Paul quotes the Law of Moses and the Gospel of Luke as entitled to equal consideration.[3] If, now, our Saviour promised the verbal dictation of the Spirit in the oral teaching of the Apostles, and they ascribed the same authority to their writings which belonged to their preaching, if they reckoned their own compositions in the same category with the Law, the Prophets and the Psalms, and distinctly traced these to the immediate suggestions of God, what more can be required to establish the unqualified falsehood of Mr. Morell's first position upon the subject? But Luke, it seems—whom, be it remembered, Paul quotes as of equal authority with Moses—virtually disclaimed this species of inspiration, since "he professes to write from the testimony of eye-witnesses, and to claim the confidence of Theophilus, for whom his two treatises were composed, *on this particular ground.*"[4] Mr. Morell is particularly unfortunate whenever he deals with Scripture. The memorable words of our Saviour to Nicodemus, "God so loved the world," etc., he very amusingly expounds[5] as a discovery of one of the Apostles—a bright ray of intuition beaming from a mind intensely heated by the marvellous scenes connected with the history of Jesus. And here he blunders sadly in reference to the beloved physician. Luke does not say that *he* wrote from

---

[1] 2 Thess. ii. 15; 1 Cor. xv. 1; John xx. 31; 1 John i. 1–4.

[2] 2 Pet. iii. 16.

[3] 1 Tim. v. 18. *The labourer is worthy of his hire* is a passage found nowhere else as quoted by Paul but in Luke x. 7, and there it occurs exactly in the words of the Apostle.

[4] Page 163.   [5] Pages 247, 248.

the testimony of eye-witnesses, but that *others* had done so.
He simply ascribes to himself, according to our English
version, an accurate knowledge of the facts, or, according
to another version, a thorough investigation of them; and
he claims the confidence of Theophilus, because he himself
was perfectly ascertained of the truth of what he wrote.
His own mind had reached certainty—by what particular
steps is not made known to us—and he was anxious to impart the same certainty to the friend to whom his treatises
are addressed.   Nothing hinders but that this very investigation may have been prompted by an impulse which terminated in that very dictation of the Spirit without which
his book is entitled to no special authority.   Mr. Morell is
not surely to learn that the theory of verbal inspiration
contemplates something more than organic influence; that
it represents the sentiments and language as the sentiments
and language of the writers as well as of the Holy Ghost.
God employed the minds of the Apostles, with all their
faculties and powers, distinctively as *minds,* and not as
machines, to communicate His own will in His own words
to mankind.   Through their thoughts, memories, reasonings,
studies and inquiries He infused His truth into their hearts,
put His words into their lips and impressed His own declarations on the written page.   How these things can be we
profess not to determine.   Our philosophy cannot penetrate
the mysteries of God.   But we have the faculty of believing
where we cannot explain.   The incarnate Word was man
and God in one person and two distinct natures, and His
divinity stamped ineffable value upon the deeds and sufferings of his humanity.   The written Word is Divine and
human in mysterious concurrence, and the Divine invests it
with all its value and authority as a conclusive standard of
faith.   "We grant," says Dr. Owen,[1] "that the sacred writers used their own abilities of mind and understanding in
the choice of words and expressions.   So the preacher
sought to find out acceptable words.   Eccles. xii. 10.   But

[1] Works, vol. ii., p. 159—Holy Spirit, book 2d, chap. i.

the Holy Spirit, who is more intimate into the minds and
skill of men than they are themselves, did so guide and
operate in them as that the words they fixed upon were as
directly and certainly from Him as if they had been spoken
to them by an audible voice." "God," says Haldane,[1]
"did not leave them to the operation of their own mind,
but has employed the operations of their mind in His Word.
The Holy Spirit could dictate to them His own words in
such a way that they would also be their own words, uttered
with the understanding. He could express the same
thought by the mouth of a thousand persons, each in his
own style." It is upon this obvious principle that God
employed them as intelligent agents, that they were required to give attendance to all the ordinary means of improving their faculties, to reading, study, meditation and
prayer, to mutual consultation and advice, and to all the
ordinances of the Christian Church. They were, by no
means, like Balaam's ass, the passive vehicles of articulate
sounds; God spoke through their *voice*, and communicated
ideas through their *minds*.

The second proposition—that the Primitive Church did
not look upon the writings of the Apostles and Evangelists
as verbally inspired—is so ludicrously false, and betrays
such disgraceful ignorance of the history of opinions upon
the subject, that very few words will be sufficient to despatch
it. It is well known to every scholar that the theory of
verbal dictation, stated often in such forms as to make the
sacred writers merely passive instruments of Divine communications, is the *oldest* theory in the Christian Church.
Justin, Athenagoras, Macarius and Chrysostom very frequently compare them to musical instruments, which obey
the breath of the performer in the sounds they emit. Macarius tells us that the Holy Scriptures are *epistles* which
God, the King, has sent to men.[2]   Chrysostom affirms that

[1] Haldane on Inspiration, p. 117.
[2] All the quotations which follow may be found with many others in
Suicerus, Article γραφη, and Conybeare's Bampton Lectures, Lecture 1

"all the Scriptures have been written and sent to us, not by servants, but by God, the Master of all"—that "the words which they utter are the words of God Himself." He tells us, farther, that even their very syllables contain some hidden treasure; that nothing is vain or superfluous about them, everything being the appointment of the wise and omniscient God. The same opinions are found also in Origen, Cyril of Alexandria, Irenæus and Gregory Thaumaturgus. And yet the Primitive Church attributed no verbal inspiration to the authors of the Gospels and Epistles! It is notorious, too, that the same terms of respect which the Jews were accustomed to appropriate to their canon were promiscuously applied by the Christian Fathers to the whole canon of the Christian Church, and to the books particularly of the New Testament.[1] They were called by Irenæus, *Divine Scriptures, Divine Oracles, Scriptures of the Lord;* by Clement of Alexandria, *Sacred Books, Divine Scriptures, Divinely-inspired Scriptures, Scriptures of the Lord, the true Evangelical Canon;* by Origen, the whole canon was called the *Ancient and New Oracles;* by Cyprian, the books of the New Testament were distinguished as *Books of the Spirit, Divine Fountains, Fountain of the Divine Fullness.* We hope Mr. Morell will look a little into history before he ventures to assert again that "in the early period of the Christian Church the writings which now compose the New Testament Canon were not all regarded as express messages to them from God."

The third proposition is, that these books were not collected because they were the canon or authoritative rule of faith, but because they contained interesting memorials of apostolic teaching and labours. If Mr. Morell has not sufficient leisure to peruse the documents of ecclesiastical antiquity, he will find in the treatise appended to the *Corpus et Syntagma Confessionum,* or the Consent of the Ancient Fathers

at the end. The reader is also referred to Taylor's Ductor Dub., Book 2d, Chap. iii., Rule 14.

[1] Paley's Evidences, Part 1, Chap. ix., § 4.

to the Doctrines of the Reformation, a very satisfactory
account of the precise light in which the Primitive Church
looked upon the Holy Scriptures. In the mean time, we
may inform our readers that she had exactly the same notions
of their Divine authority as the arbiter of faith and the
judge of controversies which all evangelical Christians now
entertain of them. "It behoveth," says Basil of Cæsarea,
"that every word and every work should be accredited by
the testimony of the inspired Scripture." "Let the inspired Scriptures," he says again, "ever be our umpire, and
on whichever side the doctrines are found accordant to the
Divine Word, to that side the award of truth may, with
entire certainty, be given." And still again, "It is the duty
of hearers, when they have been instructed in the Scriptures, to try and examine, by them, the things spoken by
their teachers, to receive whatever is consonant to those
Scriptures, and to reject whatever is alien; for thus they
will comply with the injunction of St. Paul, to prove all
things, and hold fast that which is good." "We have
known the economy of our salvation," says Irenæus, "by
no other but by those by whom the Gospel came to us;
which truly they then preached, but afterward, by the will
of God, delivered to us in the Scriptures, which were to be
the pillar and ground of our faith."

The facts upon which Mr. Morell relies to give countenance to his notions in reference to the early estimate of
the Scriptures prove to our minds exactly the reverse.
Why, when the primitive Christians were pressed by heresy,
were they so anxious to be ascertained of the apostolic writings, if these writings were not a standard of truth? Why
so cautious in their inquiries, so watchful against impostures
and frauds, so thorough in their investigations, if when
they had agreed upon the genuine productions of the Apostles they were no nearer settling their controversies than
they were before? Can any satisfactory reason be assigned,
but that of the eloquent and fervid Chrysostom?—

"The apostolical writings are the very walls of the Church. Some

one, perhaps, may ask, What then shall I do, who cannot have a Paul
to refer to? Why, if thou wilt, thou mayest still have him more
entire than many even with whom he was personally present, for it
was not the sight of Paul that made them what they were, but his
words. If thou wilt, thou mayest have Paul and Peter and John,
yea, and the whole choir of Prophets and Apostles, to converse with
thee frequently. Only take the works of these blessed men and read
their writings assiduously. But why do I say to thee. Thou mayest
have Paul? If thou wilt, thou mayest have Paul's Master; for it is
He Himself that speaketh to thee in Paul's words."

The Apostles themselves were to the first churches which
they collected the Oracles of God. They were inspired to
teach and publish the whole counsel of God in reference to
the Church. The words which they spake were not theirs,
but those of Christ who sent them. To all future generations their writings were designed to occupy the position
which they themselves occupied towards the first converts.
In these writings we now have what God originally spake
through them. The care and anxiety of the primitive
churches to guard against delusion and deceit were owing
to the belief that all apostolic compositions—that is, all compositions written either directly by themselves or commended
as inspired by their approbation—were, in the proper acceptation of the term, *canonical;* they were a rule of faith—
they were the Word of God. This being the state of the
case, no book was received as of apostolical authority but
after full and complete investigation. The evidences of its
origin were thoroughly canvassed. The question was,
What books has God sent to us? or, in the language of
Chrysostom, What epistles has God sent to us as the standard of truth? The answer was, Those which the Apostles,
in the discharge of their apostolic commission, either wrote
themselves or sanctioned as written by others. What books
were these? The Primitive Church finally settled this
question when it agreed upon the canon of the New Testament. The whole history of the matter shows that these
documents were honoured, not as memorials of Peter, James
and John, but as the words of the Master communicated

through them. Mark and Luke were not Apostles themselves, and yet they are included in the canon, and entitled
to the same authority with Paul or any other Apostle. The
reason was, that the early Church had satisfactory evidence
that they wrote under the same guidance which was promised to the Twelve. Mr. Morell is therefore grossly at fault
in maintaining that the Apostles themselves made no pretensions to verbal or plenary inspiration, that the Primitive
Church did not accord it to them, and that their writings
were not regarded as a Divine and infallible canon of truth.
The testimony of history is clearly, strongly, decidedly against
him; and any conclusions against the theory of a Divine
commission which he has drawn from the monstrous propositions which, as we have seen, have no existence but in the
fictions of his own fancy, are nothing worth. ·

There remain two other arguments by which he attempts
to set aside the plenary inspiration of the Scriptures. The
first is the defective morality of the Old Testament, and the
second is the inconsistencies and discrepancies of the sacred
writers. As to the first, it is obvious, from the whole tenor
of the New Testament, that it professes to make no new
revelations in morality; it is only a commentary on the Law
and the Prophets. The great principle which is supposed
by many to be characteristic of the Gospel, that we should
love the Lord our God with all our hearts, and our neigh-
bours as ourselves, is distinctly inculcated by Moses; while
patience under injuries, alms to the indigent and kindness
to the poor, afflicted and oppressed, are the reigning spirit
of the ancient institute. The Israelites were indeed commissioned to wage exterminating wars against the devoted
objects of Divine wrath, but in these instances they were
the scourge of God. It was not to gratify their private
resentments or national ambition, but to execute the vengeance of Heaven, that they were commanded to destroy
the tribes of Canaan. They were as the plague, pestilence
and famine in the hands of the Almighty—God was the
real destroyer; they were but the instruments of His will,

and they departed from every principle of their institute
if they suffered themselves to be influenced by private
malice. There are other instances in which deeds of treachery and deceit are *recorded*, but there is a huge difference
betwixt recording and approving them. The drunkenness of
Noah—if indeed he were drunk, which we very much doubt
—the lies of Abraham, the cruelty of Sarah, the incest of
Lot, the frauds of Jacob and the adultery of David were
written not for our example, but our warning. There are
other instances in which the moral import of the same
material action was very different then from what it is now.
There can be no doubt that in the progress of society relations may be developed and causes unfolded which shall
make an act criminal in one age that was perfectly blame-
less in another. Incest was lawful in the family of Adam;
under a certain contingency a Jew might marry his brother's
widow; and it remains to be proved that, in the early condition of Eastern civilization, the habits and customs which
now provoke our censure were possessed of the same moral
import which attaches to them now. With these distinctions and limitations, we have no hesitation in asserting
that the morality of the Old Testament is precisely what
we might expect it to be upon the theory of verbal inspiration. The great duties of piety and religion, of truth,
justice and benevolence, the charities of life, the virtues of
the citizen, the master and the man, the husband, the father
and the son, are all impressed under the ancient economy
with the sanctions peculiar to that dispensation. There is
nothing impure, immoral, unworthy of God.

As to inconsistencies and discrepancies in the sacred
writers which cannot be fairly explained, we simply deny
them. Mr. Morell charges them with inconclusiveness of
reasoning, defects of memory and contradictions to science
and themselves in their statements of fact. When he condescends to specify the instances, and to *prove* that his alle-
gations are true, it will be time to answer yet again these
exploded cavils of infidelity, which have a thousand times

been refuted, and which he ought to know to be worthless. In regard to defects of memory, we beg him to recollect that any effort to substantiate this charge may involve an effort to cast a serious imputation upon the moral character of Jesus Christ Himself. If there was anything which He distinctly and unequivocally promised to His Apostles, it was that the Holy Ghost should teach them all things and bring all things to their remembrance which He himself had said unto them.

There is indeed one specification which he has made—the inconsistency of geological speculations with the Mosaic cosmogony. Mr. Morell, however, is not ignorant that the Mosaic narrative contradicts not a single fact of descriptive geology. All that she reports of the shape of the earth, its minerals and fossils, its marks of convulsion and violence,—all these *facts* may be fully admitted, and yet not a line of Moses be impugned. It is only when the geologist proceeds to the causes of his facts, and invents hypotheses to explain them, that any inconsistency takes place; and this inconsistency is evidently not betwixt geology and religion, but geologists and Moses. It is a war of theories, of speculation and conjecture, against the historical fidelity of a record supported by evidence in comparison with which ,they dwindle into the merest figments of the brain.

There is one other consideration which demands our notice, and which we have reserved to this place, because it is evidently not an argument against the abstract possibility of a Divine theology—being not at all inconsistent with the patristic notion of organic inspiration—but against that view of the manner in which a Divine theology has been communicated which we have felt it our duty to defend. Mr. Morell asserts,

"That the whole of the *logical processes* of the human mind are such that the idea of a revelation is altogether incompatible with them, that they are in no sense open to its influence, and that they can neither be improved nor assisted by it. All our logical processes of mind, all the operations of the understanding, take place in accordance with the most fixed and determinate laws, those which are usually termed *the laws of thought*. Whatever can be inferred by these laws, whatever can be derived in any way from them, must be strictly within the natural capacity of the human mind to attain. If, on the contrary, there be anything which these laws of thought are naturally unable to reach, no extraneous influence whatever could give them the power of reaching it. The laws of thought are immovable —to alter them would be to subvert the whole constitution of the human intellect. Whatever is once within their reach is always so. Correct reasoning could never be subverted by revelation itself; bad reasoning could never be improved by it." [1]

We are not sure that we understand this passage. If the author means that our logical processes do not originate the materials upon which they are employed, what he says may be true, but it is nothing to the purpose; but if he means that the mind being already in possession of all the simple ideas upon which it is to operate, God, in consistency with its own laws, cannot secure the understanding from error, what he says is contradictory to the revelation of a theology through the agency of men, upon any other hypothesis but that of organic inspiration. The question is not whether any Divine influence can make bad reasoning good or good reasoning bad, but whether God can exempt men from the bad, and infallibly conduct them to the good, without subverting their intellectual constitution.

Mr. Morell will hardly deny that if all the conditions and laws which ought to be observed in the processes of the understanding were faithfully regarded, there would be no danger of fallacy or mistake. Error is the result of disobedience or inattention to the laws of our own nature—the punishment of intellectual guilt. The naked question then is, whether God, by any subjective influence on the soul, can preserve it from eccentricity and disorder, and keep it in harmony with the essential conditions of its healthful operation. Surely it is no subversion of the constitution of the mind to have that constitution protected from violence

[1] Pages 141, 142.

and encroachment. The soul is more truly itself when it moves in the orbit prescribed for it than when it deserts its proper path and wanders into forbidden regions. If God cannot exert a controlling influence upon the understanding, it must be because there is something in the nature of its faculties or exercises incompatible with the direct interference of the Deity. Now the faculties which belong to it are, according to our author's own statement,[1] memory, conception, imagination, abstraction and generalization, to which may be added the association of ideas; and the processes which belong to it are definition, division, judgment and reasoning, whether inductive or deductive. Not to enter at this stage of the discussion into any metaphysical analysis, it is obvious that these faculties exist, among different men, in very different degrees of perfection, and these processes are conducted with very different degrees of correctness, and yet their essential nature is the same in all. If, then, by the act of God, there can be different degrees of memory in different persons without any infringement of the laws of memory, why may there not be different degrees in the same person? If God can make one man reason better than another, without disturbing the laws of ratiocination, why cannot He make the same man reason at one time better than he reasoned at another? Can He not impart additional clearness to conception, vigour to imagination, nicety to analysis, and accuracy to the perception of those resemblances and relations upon which generalization and reasoning proceed? The truth is, one of the most mysterious features connected with the human mind is its susceptibility of growth and improvement without receiving additions to its substance. Perfectly simple and indiscerptible in its own nature, incapable of enlargement by accretion, it yet begins, in the simplest operations of sense, to exert an activity which waxes stronger and better in every successive period of its existence, and to the development of which there seem to be no natural limits. All the ex-

[1] Page 15.

pressions by which we represent this change are borrowed
from material analogies, and are evidently liable to the
abuse which, from such applications, has made the history
of philosophy too much a history of confusion. In relation to our minds, much more than in relation to our bodies,
we are fearfully and wonderfully made. And if the natural
order of improvement is a mystery, profound and impenetrable—if we are unable to comprehend, much less to explain, how a single substance, remaining unchanged in its
essence, shall exhibit those wonderful phenomena which we
can liken to nothing but growth, expansion and enlarge-
ment in material objects—surely it is too much to say that
in this world of mystery another mystery still cannot be
found, that of *supernatural* improvement, in which every
faculty shall faithfully obey the laws of its structure. To
us the idea that any creature, in any of its operations, can
be independent of God, involves a gross contradiction.
Absolute dependence is the law of its being. As without
the *concursus* of the Deity it must cease to exist, so His
sustentation and support are essential to every form of
action, every degree of development, every step in improvement. It is only in God that it can live and move, as it
is only in God that it has its subsistence. We see no more
difficulty in supposing that God can superintend and direct
the various processes of the understanding than in admitting
that He created its powers in the first instance, and impressed
upon them the laws which they ought to observe. Providence is no more wonderful than creation.

Mr. Morell admits that the Deity can exert a subjective
influence upon the intuitional faculties, that *they* can be
elevated to a supernatural degree of intensity, and that this
is actually done in the phenomenon of inspiration. Why,
then, should the understanding not be accessible to God?
If He can touch the soul in one point, why not in another?
If He can improve its vision, what hinders but that He
may regulate and assist its reflection? That He can turn
the hearts of men as the rivers of water are turned ; that the

spirits of all flesh, in the full integrity of their faculties, are as completely in His hands as clay in the hands of the potter; that He can bring every proud thought and lofty imagination into humble obedience to his will; that the whole man is absolutely and unresistingly in His power, so that He can direct its steps without a contravention of the laws of its being,—is the only hypothesis upon which the great evangelical doctrine of regeneration is consistent or possible. The work of the Spirit is represented as extending to the whole soul; it gives eyes to the blind, ears to the deaf, knowledge to the ignorant, wisdom to the foolish. It enlightens the mind, purifies the heart, cleanses the imagination, purges the conscience, stimulates the memory, quickens the judgment, and imparts an unwonted apttude in the perception of spiritual relations. As there is not a faculty which has not suffered from the ruins of the Fall, so there is not a faculty which does not share in the restoration of grace. The testimony of Scripture may be nothing to Mr. Morell; but as his presumptuous assertion is unsupported by anything in his own mental analysis; as it is inconsistent with the analogy which the case of intuition, confessed by him to be susceptible of supernatural influence, obviously suggests; as there is nothing in the nature of the understanding, in any of its faculties or exercises, which places it beyond the reach of Divine regulation; as there is no more absurdity in God's governing than in God's creating its powers,—we may safely receive the declarations of the Bible, as well as the dictates of common sense, until we have some better reason for calling them into question than the *ipse dixit* of a transcendental philosopher. And that theory is certainly reduced to a desperate extremity which allows its author no refuge but a bold and impudent denial of the essential attributes of God. Whatever does not involve a contradiction, and so prove itself to be nothing, lies within the boundless range of possibilities which Almighty power can achieve. It is the folly and blasphemy of the wicked to reduce their Creator to their

level, to make Him altogether such an one as they themselves, and to measure His resources by their own insignificant capacities. It is His prerogative to lift His hand and
swear that as He lives for ever, so He shall accomplish all
His will, and rule alike the minds and bodies He has
framed. Our God is in the heavens. He has done whatsoever He hath pleased; and if among the things which
have pleased Him were the purpose to communicate a Divine theology through the minds and understandings of
men, there could have been no impediment which His power
could not easily surmount.

We shall here finish our examination of the book before
us with reference to the soundness of its logic. The single
point to which our remarks have been directed is, whether
the conclusions are legitimately drawn from the premises.
We have admitted, for the sake of argument, the principles
of the author's philosophy. We have not called in question his psychology, his analysis of religion, or his accounts
of revelation and inspiration. Our object has been to discover whether, granting all these, the popular faith in regard to the authority of the Scriptures is necessarily subverted. We have attempted to show that though his
philosophy pretends to be an *a priori* argument against the
possibility of this notion being true, it demonstrates nothing
to the purpose; that revelation, in *his* sense, is not *exclusive*
of revelation in its common and ordinary acceptation; and
that *his* inspiration is by no means inconsistent with the
inspiration of the vulgar faith. Divest his argument of
the ambiguity of language, and of the gratuitous assumption that the agency which he admits is the *sole* agency of
God, and it is divested of all pertinency and force. We
have gone still farther, and convicted of weakness and confusion all his efforts to render useless and unnecessary the
existence of a canon such as the Bible professes to be. Out
of his own mouth have we condemned him. As a *philosophical* argument, therefore, we are compelled to say that
his book is utterly wanting—that so far from demonstrat-

ing that a revealed theology is a psychological absurdity,
he has beaten his drums and flourished his trumpets when
the enemy had not been even in sight. We have also followed him in his arguments addressed to the question as a
matter of fact. We have seen that he is at fault in charging the popular faith with a total destitution of positive
proof, and that all his objections to the plenary inspiration
of the Scriptures, whether founded on varieties of style, the
necessity of Divine illumination, the diminution of our respect for the sacred writers, the history of the canon, the
immoralities, absurdities and contradictions of the Bible,
or the alleged impossibility of a Divine revelation through
the understandings of men, are capable of an easy and
obvious refutation. The conclusion of the whole matter
is, that as an infidel assault his book is a signal failure.
For anything that he has proved to the contrary, by either
a priori or *a posteriori* reasoning, the Bible may be what
the Christian world has always been accustomed to regard
it. But a harder task remains yet to be performed. His
philosophy must be brought to the touchstone of truth;
and we hope at no distant day to be able to convince our
readers that no better success has attended his speculations
than has rewarded his efforts to apply them.

SECTION II.

RELIGION PSYCHOLOGICALLY CONSIDERED.

HAVING, in our former article, considered the work of Mr. Morell as an argument against an authoritative theology, we proceed, according to our promise, to examine the philosophy on which the argument is founded. This task we undertake with unfeigned reluctance. The questions which it involves demand a power of analysis, a patience of reflection, an intensity of thought, a depth of investigation and an amplitude of learning to which, we are conscious, we can make no pretensions. We always return from the study of the great problems of human knowledge with a conviction of littleness, incapacity and ignorance which, though the process by which it has been produced has disclosed enough to prevent us from "despairing of the ultimate possibility of philosophy," teaches us to commiserate rather than denounce the errors of others, and makes us feel that *our* position must always be that of humble and teachable inquirers. Far from dreaming of the attempt to originate an independent system of our own, or even to combine into a consistent and harmonious whole the various elements of truth which may be elicited from existing systems, we are content, in regard to these high problems, to discharge the negative office of refuting error without presuming to establish its contrary—of saying what is *not*, without undertaking to declare what *is*, truth. The work of simple destruction, though often invidious, is sometimes necessary. In the case before us we shall feel ourselves to be the authors of an incalculable good if we can convict Mr. Morell's philosophy of inconsistency and falsehood, though we should fail, in the progress of the argument, to make a single direct contribution to a sounder system.

This philosophy may be embraced under the three heads of Psychology, Religion and Revelation, together with the connection subsisting between them. The first inquiry of the author is in regard to the *subject* in which religion inheres, What is it that is religious? Then in regard to the *essence* of religion itself, What is it to be religious? And finally in relation to the *mode* in which religion is produced, How is the given subject put in possession of the given essence? The answer to the first inquiry constitutes his Psychology; to the second, his Analysis of religion in general and of Christianity in particular; to the last, his Theories of Revelation and Inspiration. As to` the connection subsisting between them, the nature of the subject determines, to some extent, the nature of religion; and the nature of religion, in its relations to the subject, determines the mode and laws of its production. Mind being given, the essential element of Religion is given; mind and religion being both given, the characteristics of Revelation are settled. This is a general outline of the discussions of the book. We begin with the Psychology; and that our readers may fully understand the strictures which we shall make upon some of the doctrines of our author, it may be well to give a preliminary statement of the essential differences which distinguish existing schools of philosophy.

I. Sir William Hamilton has very justly observed that[1] "philosophy proper is principally and primarily the *science of knowledge;* its first and most important problem being to determine, What can we know? that is, what are the conditions of our knowing, whether these lie in the nature of the object, or in the nature of the subject, of knowledge." The origin, nature, and extent of human knowledge are, accordingly, the questions which have divided the schools, and the answers which have been returned to them have

[1] Hamilton's Reid, page 808: Note.

determined the place which their authors have taken in the history of speculation.

It is now universally conceded that all knowledge begins in experience, but there is not the same agreement as to the conditions which are essential to experience, and under which alone it becomes available. In one class of opinions, the mind, at its first existence, is represented as a *tabula rasa* or a sheet of blank paper, upon which, from without, are written the characters which, contemplated by itself, constitute the sole materials of cognition. It comes into the world unfurnished, an empty room, and the world furnishes it. There is, on the one hand, a capacity to receive, and on the other a power to communicate; and the relation of the two constitutes experience. Upon the materials thus given the mind can operate—it can combine, compare, decompose and arrange—but it can add absolutely nothing to the stock which has been imparted to it as a passive recipient. Experience is restricted exclusively to sensation; the mind is a machine, and its various faculties the tools with which it works up the materials afforded in sensible phenomena. This low and contracted hypothesis, which sprang from a corruption of Locke's principles, at best partial and incomplete, was pushed to its legitimate consequences of Atheistic Materialism and the blindest chance by the celebrated authors of the French Encyclopædia. And it is to this scheme that we would confine the distinctive title of *Sensationalism*.

We need not say that the Sensationalist stumbles at the threshold. He gives no account of *knowledge:* to receive ideas, as the canvas receives the impression of the brush, is not to *know*. Intelligence involves judgment, belief, conviction of certainty, not merely that the thing is there, but, to use a sensible analogy, *seen* to be there. No mechanical activity, however delicate and refined, is competent to explain the peculiar phenomenon involved in the feeling, *I know*. Experience, therefore, must include conditions in the subject which make it capable of intelligence. There

must be a constitution of mind adapted to that specific activity by which it believes and judges, as it is only by virtue
of such a constitution that knowledge can be extracted from
experience. This preparation of the mind to know, or its
adaptation to intelligence, consists in subjecting it to laws
of belief under which it must necessarily act. Its energies
can be exercised only under the condition that it shall know
or believe. As it is the necessity of belief which distinguishes intelligent action from every other species of operation, and as there can be no belief without the belief of
something, there must be certain primary truths involved
in the very structure of the mind, which are admitted from
the simple necessity of admitting them. As undeveloped
in experience, they exist not in the form of propositions or
general conceptions, but of irresistible tendencies to certain
manners of belief when the proper occasions shall be
afforded. They are certain "necessities of thinking." But,
developed in experience and generalized into abstract statements, they are original and elementary cognitions, the
foundation and criterion of all knowledge. They are the
standard of evidence, the light of the mind, and without
them the mind could no more be conceived to know than a
blind man to see. Being in the mind, a part of its very
structure, they are not the products of experience. Essential conditions of mental activity, they are not the results
of it. As experience furnishes the occasions on which they
are developed or become manifest in consciousness, it is
obviously from experience that we know them as mere mental phenomena, in the same way that we know every other
faculty of mind; but as primitive beliefs, as vouchers and
guarantees for the truth of facts beyond "their own phenomenal reality,"[1] they are involved in the very conception

---

[1] For a masterly dissertation on the Philosophy of Common Sense, the
reader is referred to Hamilton's Reid, Appendix, Note A. We deem it
just to ourselves (and we hope we shall not be suspected of vanity) to say
that the distinction indicated in the text, and the corresponding distinction
in regard to the possibility of doubt illustrated by Hamilton, p. 744, had
occurred to us, in our own speculations, before we had ever seen his book.

of experience. "Catholic principles of all philosophy," they have been more or less distinctly recognized, in every school and by every sect, from the dawn of speculation until the present day. According to the different aspects in which they have been contemplated, they have received different titles,[1] as *innate truths, first principles, maxims, principles of common sense, general notions, categories of the understanding* and *ideas of pure reason, fundamental laws of belief* and *constituent elements of reason;* but whatever names they have borne, their character remains unchanged of original, authoritative, incomprehensible faiths.

Though the distinct recognition and articulate enunciation of these principles have played a conspicuous part in the speculations of modern philosophers, yet the admission of them can hardly be regarded as characteristic of a school. It forms a *class*, in distinction from that of the ultra Sensationalists, in which two schools[2] are embraced, discriminated from each other by the application which they make of what both equally admit. They are divided on the question of the relation which our primary cognitions sustain to the whole fabric of human knowledge.

One party represents them as wholly barren and unproductive in themselves—the forms of knowledge and indispensable to its acquisition, but not the sources from which it is derived. It is only when, acting in obedience to them, we come in contact with objective realities that we truly know. All knowledge implies the relation of subject and object; the laws of belief qualify the subject to know, but cannot give the thing to be known. Hence, we are dependent on experience for all the *objects* of knowledge. The mind, however richly furnished with all the capacities of cognition and belief, however intelligent in its own nature, cannot create by the laws of its constitution a single material

[1] See § 5, Note A, Hamilton's Reid.

[2] "What is a school? It is a certain number of systems, more or less connected by time, but especially connected by intimate relations, and still more so by a certain similarity of principles and of views." Cousin, Introduct. to the Hist. Phil., Lect. iv., Linberg's Trans., p. 97.

of thought. The description of our intelligent constitution
is an answer to the question *how* we know, but not to the
equally important question *what* we know. There must be
something distinct from a faculty, something to which it is
applied or applies itself in conformity with its nature,
before the relation of knowledge can obtain. Or, in one
word, the laws of belief are the *conditions* of knowing, but,
in themselves considered, are not knowledge. They are not
the matter of an argument, but the criterion of the truth
of any and of every premiss. According to this class of
philosophers, experience not only furnishes the occasions on
which our primitive cognitions are developed, but furnishes
the *objects* about which our faculties are conversant. It
gives us the *what* we are to know. From the importance
which this school attaches to induction, it may be pre-eminently styled the school of *Experience.*[1]

Others represent our original beliefs not merely as the
criterion of truth and the indispensable conditions of knowledge, but as the data, the αρχαι, in which are implicitly
contained all that is worthy of the name of science. We
are dependent upon experience only to awaken them, but
when once awakened and roused into action, they can conduct us to the fountain of existence and solve all the mysteries of the universe. As reason is held to be the complement of these universal and all-comprehensive principles,
this class of philosophers is commonly denominated *Rationalists.*

Differing as widely as they do in regard to the matter of
our knowledge, it is not to be wondered at that these two
great schools of Rationalism and Experience should differ
as widely in relation to its nature and extent or the precise
province of a sound philosophy. Rationalism, in all its
forms, aims at a complete science of Ontology; it pretends
to be, in the language of Cousin, "the absolute intelli-

[1] For a very full and satisfactory account of the relations of our primary
beliefs to human knowledge, the reader is referred to Stewart's Elements,
vol. ii., chap. i.

gence, the absolute explanation of everything;"[1] or, in the language of Sir William Hamilton, "it boldly places itself at the very centre of absolute being, with which it is in fact identified, and, thence surveying existence in itself and in its relations, unveils to us the nature of the Deity, and explains from first to last the derivation of all created things."[2]

The philosophy of Experience is guilty of no such extravagances. Professing to build on observation, its first and fundamental principle is that all knowledge must be relative in its nature and phenomenal in its objects. As speculations about abstract being transcend the province of legitimate induction, it dismisses them at once as frivolous and absurd, and aspires to know only those qualities and attributes of things through which they become related to our minds. What they are in themselves, or what they are to the omniscience of God, it would regard as a no less preposterous inquiry than to undertake to determine the size, number and employments of the inhabitants of the moon. Still, phenomena in its vocabulary are not synonymous, as Rationalists constantly assume, with phantoms or delusions. They are realities, the conditions of the objects corresponding to the conditions of the subjects of human knowledge, and consequently as truly real as those necessary principles of reason for the sake of which they are despised. "What *appears* to all," says Aristotle, "that we affirm *to be*, and he who would subvert this belief will himself assuredly advance nothing more deserving of credit."[3]

Claiming, therefore, only a relative knowledge of existence, the philosophy of Experience, instead of futile and abortive attempts to construct the universe, takes its stand, in conformity with the sublime maxim of Bacon,[4] as the

[1] Introduct. Hist. Phil., Lect. i., p. 24, Linberg's Trans.

[2] Edinburgh Review, Cross's Selections, vol. iii., p. 176. A masterly article on Cousin's Philosophy.

[3] Eth. Nic., Lib. x., Cap. 2; a passage repeatedly quoted by Sir William Hamilton.

[4] Nov. Organ., Aphor. i. In this age of transcendental speculation the words deserve to be repeated: Homo naturæ minister et interpres, tantum

minister, not the master—the interpreter, not the legislator, of Nature. Professing its incompetence to pronounce before-hand what kinds of creatures the Almighty should have made, and what kinds of laws the Almighty should have established, it is content to look out upon the world, and to look in upon itself, in order to discover what God has wrought. Without presuming to determine what *must* be, it humbly and patiently inquires what *is*. From the very nature of the case it pretends to no science of the Deity. To bring Him within the circle of science would be to degrade Him, to make Him a general law or a constituent element of other existences, instead of the Eternal and Self-exist-ent God.

The two schools of Rationalism and Experience are, accordingly, at war in regard to the scope and province of philosophy. Agreeing in their general views as to the indis-pensable conditions of intelligence, they differ fundament-ally in the answers which they return to the question, *What* can man know? This single consideration is enough to show the futility, or at least the delusiveness, of a classi-fication like that adopted by Mr. Morell in his former work, which brings Stewart, Reid and Brown under the same general category with Fichte, Schelling and Hegel. The problems which the former undertook to solve were the poles apart from those discussed by the latter. The former were inductive psychologists, applying the same method to the phenomena of mind which Newton had applied with such splendid results to the phenomena of matter; the latter were bold and rampant ontologists, unfolding the grounds of universal Being from the princi-ples of pure reason. The former restricted their inquiries to the phenomenal and relative, the latter pushed into the region of the absolute and infinite; the former stopped at properties and attributes, the latter plunged into the essence of all things. From Locke to Hamilton, English and

facit et intelligit quantum de naturæ ordine re vel mente observaverit, nec amplius scit aut potest.

Scotch philosophy has been for the most part a confession
of human ignorance; from Leibnitz to Hegel, German
philosophy has been for the most part an aspiration to
omniscience.[1]

After these preliminary remarks, we can have no difficulty as to the general position to which we must assign
Mr. Morell.   He is a Rationalist, coming nearer, so far as
we can collect his opinions, to the Eclecticism of France
than to any other school.   His method, the psychological,[2]
is evidently that of Cousin, and there is the same unsuccessful attempt to combine the philosophy of Experience
with that of Rationalism.

1. The treatise before us opens with an inquiry into that
which constitutes the essence of the mind.

"Now, first," says our author,[3] "whenever we speak of the mind,
or use the expression, '*myself*,' what is it, we would ask, that we
really intend to designate?   What is it in which the mind of man
essentially consists?"

The terms in which the question is propounded would
seem to indicate that Mr. Morell regards *personality* and
mind as synonymous expressions, the Ego as embracing
the *whole subject* of all the phenomena of consciousness.
And yet in another passage he obviously divorces intelligence from "*self*," and restricts the *person* to individual
peculiarities.

"Neither, lastly," says he,[4] "can the real man be the complex of
our thoughts, ideas or conceptions.   These indicate simply the existence of logical forms, intellectual laws or perceptive faculties, which
are essentially the same in all minds; they do not express the real,
concrete, individual man; they do not involve the element which

---

[1] Kant deserves to be specially excepted from this censure.   The "ontology
of pure reason" he has remorselessly demolished in his celebrated Critique.
See also Morell's History of Modern Philosophy, vol. ii., pp. 81, 82.

[2] Fragmens Philosophiques, Pref.   A translation of this Preface may
be found in the first volume of Ripley's Specimens of Foreign Standard
Literature: Boston. 1838.. See also Morell's Hist. Mod. Phil., vol. ii.
p. 484, 2d London Edit.

[3] Page 2.   [4] Page 2.

makes each human being entirely distinct from the whole mass of humanity around him; in a word, they do not constitute our *personality.*"

To us, we frankly confess, it is amazing that the essence of mind *as* mind should consist in something that is not common to all minds. But the difficulty does not stop here. The will, in which Mr. Morell fixes the essence of the man as *a mere power* of spontaneous action, is just as universal and just as uniform as the operations of intelligence. *It*, therefore, "as the *capacity* of acting independently and for ourselves," cannot be the essential principle of mind, and we are absolutely shut up by this species of logic to the idiosyncracies and oddities of individuals. It is strange that Mr. Morell, in adopting the analysis of Maine de Biran, has not admitted the limitations of Cousin, who, it seems to us, has unanswerably proved that, upon this hypothesis, we must deny the personality of reason, at least in its spontaneous manifestations, and make "*self*" and *mind* expressions of different but related realities. If the Ego is the will, then intelligence is no more of it than the organs of sense. "Reason," says Cousin,[1] adhering rigidly to his conception of personality as involving only the individual and voluntary, to the entire exclusion of the universal and absolute—"reason is not a property of individuals; therefore it is not our own, it does not belong to us, it is not human; for, once more, that which constitutes man, his intrinsic personality, is his voluntary and free activity; all which is not voluntary and free is added to man, but is not an integrant part of man." This is consistent. But what shall we say, upon this hypothesis, of the veracity of consciousness, the fundamental postulate of all philosophy, which just as clearly testifies that the operations of reason are subjective—that they are, in other words, affections of what we call *ourselves*—as that the decisions of the will are our own? The distinction betwixt reason, in its sponta-

[1] Introduct. Hist. Phil. Lect. v., Linberg's Trans. p. 127; Lecture vi., passim.

neous and reflective manifestations, does not touch the point. The "spontaneous apperception of truth,"[1] which Cousin boasts to have discovered "within the penetralia of consciousness, at a depth to which Kant never penetrated," is either a subjective act, and then it is personal, or it is only another name for the intellectual intuition of Schelling, in which the distinction of subject and object disappears, and we have the miracle of knowledge without anything known or any one to know. If M. Cousin admits that his spontaneous apperception of truth involves a percipient, relativeness and subjectivity are not only apparent, but as real as they are in reflection; if it does not involve a percipient, then we humbly submit that it is self-contradictory, and therefore equivalent to zero. A theory which defends the impersonality of reason by an assumption which denies the very possibility of thought may be safely remanded to the depths from which its author extracted it, and into which it is not at all astonishing that such a thinker as Kant never penetrated. We cannot but add that as Cousin's ontology is founded on the authority of reason, and the authority of reason founded on its impersonality, and its impersonality founded on the annihilation of thought, his speculations upon this subject end exactly where those of Hegel begin—AT NOTHING.

Mr. Morell, however, rigidly cleaves to Maine de Biran, and saves the *personal* character of reason by the extraordinary hypothesis—the most extraordinary which, we venture to say, has ever been proposed in the history of philosophy—that will, spontaneity or personality (for they are all, in his vocabulary, synonymous expressions) is the SUBSTANCE of mind—that our various faculties of intelligence sustain the same relations to the will, which, according to popular apprehension, an attribute sustains to that of which it is a

---

[1] Fragmens Philosophiques, Pref. Morell Hist. Mod. Phil. vol. ii. p. 495. We take occasion to say that this account of Cousin's Psychology is one of the clearest statements of his system that we have ever seen, apart from his own writings.

property.   That unknown substratum which, under the
appellations of *mind, soul* or *spirit,* other philosophers had
been accustomed to represent as the subject in which all
our mental capacities and energies inhere, Mr. Morell professes to have drawn from its concealment, and to have
identified with spontaneous activity, or the power of acting
independently and for ourselves.   Reason or intelligence,
accordingly, is a property of the will, in the same sense in
which extension is a property of matter.   All the operations of the mind are only so many modifications of the
will—so many manifestations of activity, not as an element
which they include, but as the *support* upon which they
depend.   "If, therefore," says he,[1] in a passage which
shows that we have not misrepresented him—"if, therefore,
in our subsequent classification of the faculties of the mind,
little appears to be said about the will, it must be remembered that we assume the activity it denotes as the essential
basis of our whole mental being, and suppose it consequently to *underlie* [the italics are his own, and show that
he means, *it is the substance of*] all our mental operations."
And again :[2] "Remembering, then, that the power of the
will runs through the whole, we may regard these two
classes [the intellectual and emotional] as exhausting the
entire sum of our mental phenomena."   And again :

"We would also again remind them that the activity of the *will*
must be regarded as running through all these different phenomena;
and that as there is involved in the spontaneous operations of the
human mind all the elements which the consciousness at all contains,
it must not be imagined that these elements have to be reflectively
realized before they can contribute their aid to our mental development.   It is, in fact, one of the most delicate and yet important of
all psychological analyses to show how the power of the will operates
through all the region of man's spontaneous life, and to prove that
our activity is equally voluntary and equally moral in its whole aspect,
although the understanding may not have brought the principles on
which we act into the clear light of reflective truth."[3]

"To talk of knowing *mind,*" he affirms in his former
[1] Pages 3, 4.   [2] Page 4.   [3] Pages 25, 26.

work,[1] "beyond the direct consciousness of its *spontaneous being* and all the affections it can undergo, is absurd; there is nothing more to *know*." By *spontaneous being* he evidently means the existence of mind as a spontaneity. Beyond this and the various properties it exhibits there is nothing to be known; in spontaneity we have the substance, in the "affections it can undergo" the attributes; and these, in their connection, exhaust the subject.

If, now, spontaneous activity is the substance of the soul, and intelligence and reason, with all our various capacities and powers, are only properties or modifications of this spontaneous activity, it necessarily follows that all thought and belief, all knowledge and emotion, are purely voluntary. When we cognize an external object immediately present in consciousness, or assent to any universal or necessary truth, such as that the whole is greater than a part, we do it by an act of the will. The cognition is spontaneous; which means, if it mean anything, that the mind is not irresistibly determined to it; and that, consequently, it might *refuse* to know when the object is actually present before it, and refuse to believe when the terms of the proposition are distinctly and adequately apprehended; which, being interpreted, is that a man may refuse to see when he sees, and refuse to believe when he knows. This very circumstance of the independence of truth, especially of necessary and absolute truth, of the human will, is one of the principal arguments of Cousin to establish the impersonality of reason. We *cannot help* believing when the evidence of truth is clearly before us, says Cousin; we believe in every case only because we *will* to believe, says Morell. Doctors differ.

But passing over this difficulty, and admitting the doctrine, hard as it is to reconcile with the obvious testimony of consciousness, that all knowledge and belief are the creatures of the will, the products of spontaneous activity, we find ourselves unable to detect in this activity the only

[1] Vol. ii., p. 53, 2d London Edition.

criterion by which our faculties are capable of distinguishing substance from attributes. "That which is in itself and conceived by itself," is the compendious definition of substance given by Spinoza,[1] and though it expresses what every human intellect must pronounce to be impossible, and contains the elements of proof that our only notion of substance is a certain relation to attributes — in other words, a postulation of the mind which we are forced to make, by the very constitution of our nature, in order to explain the existence of what is felt to be dependent—yet, as Mr. Morell admits it,[2] we will apply its canon to the case before us. Everything, then, is an attribute which cannot be recognized as self-subsistent and independent, and everything is a substance which can be construed to the mind as self-subsistent—self-subsistent in the sense that it inheres in nothing as an attribute in it. Hence, whatever is conceived by the mind as having only a dependent and relative existence, or is not conceivable as having a separate and independent existence, must be an attribute; it cannot be a substance. Apply this principle to the case before us. Is activity dependent or independent? In other words, can we conceive of it abstracted from every agent and every form of operation? Does it not just as much require a *subject* as intelligence or thought, and some definite mode of manifestation? Can it not just as properly be asked, *What* acts? as *What* thinks or believes? We confess that we are no more capable of representing to the mind absolute activity than of representing absolute intelligence or absolute motion. We can understand the proposition that the mind is active, that it performs such and such operations, but we can attach no glimmer of meaning to that other proposition, that it is activity itself. Action without something to act and some manner of action is to us as preposterously absurd as knowledge without some one to know;

[1] Spinoza, in Howe's Living Temple, Pt. ii., chap. i.
[2] This is evident from what he says of substance, p. 37; also Hamilton's Reid, p. 895, note, 1st col.

and we are unable to enter into that peculiar mode of cogitation which can be content to settle down on activity as the substratum, the self-subsisting subject, of all intellectual phenomena. That the mind is active in thought, and that activity thinks, are propositions the poles apart; that activity is a characteristic and all-pervading quality of every species of mental affection, and accordingly the highest generalization of mental phenomena, is a very different statement from that which makes it *the mind itself*. Hence, according to the canon, activity is only an attribute. Mr. Morell, in fact, admits as much.

"We do not say, indeed," says he, "that we can comprehend the very essence of the soul itself *apart* from all its determinations; but that by deep reflection upon our inmost consciousness we can comprehend the essence of the soul in connection with its operations—that we can trace it through all its changes as a *power* or pure activity, and that in this spontaneous activity alone our real personality consists." [1]

But it is essential to any positive idea of substance that it should be conceived apart from attributes. It is that "which exists in itself and is conceived by itself, or whose conception needs the conception of nothing else whereby it ought to be formed." In saying, therefore, that activity cannot in thought be abstracted from its manifestations, Mr. Morell has conceded the impossibility of his thesis, and, instead of making it the *substance*, he has only made it the universal characteristic, of mental operations.

But be it substance or accident, we venture to suggest a doubt whether such a thing as *spontaneous* activity, in the sense of Mr. Morell, does not involve a contradiction. According to this hypothesis, man is an undetermined cause, or a cause determined by nothing but his own proper energy. How shall we account for the first act? It either produced itself or it came into being by chance, for all foreign influences are, *ex hypothesi*, excluded: to have

[1] Page 3.

produced itself it must have existed as a cause before it
existed as an effect; that is, it must have existed before it
existed, which is self-contradictory.   To say that it was
produced by chance is to say that the negation of all cause
is the affirmation of some cause, or that a thing can be
and not be a cause in the same relation and at the same
time, which is also self-contradictory.   We crave from Mr.
Morell and his admirers a solution of these difficulties.
We are utterly unable to absolve the doctrine of *spontaneous*
activity from the charge of implying the doctrine of an
absolute commencement, and an absolute commencement
we are as incapable of conceiving as a triangle of four
sides.   If Mr. Morell takes man "out of the mighty chain
of cause and effect, by which all the operations of nature
are carried on from the commencement to the end of time,"
and makes him a separate and independent cause, receiving
no causal influence from without, we should like to know
how he makes a beginning?   For to us it is as plain that
all commencement must be relative as that there is any
such thing as a commencement at all.   If an absolute commencement were possible, Atheism could not be convicted
of absurdity; and we see not how they can consistently
apply the principle of causation to the proof of theism—
how they can deny that all things might have spontaneously
sprung from nothing, when they distinctly affirm that our
mental acts generate themselves.   Upon this subject there
are obviously only three suppositions that can be made—
that of the Casualist, who asserts an absolute commencement;
that of the Fatalist, who asserts an infinite series of relative
commencements; that of the Theist, who asserts a finite
series of relative commencements, carried up in the ascending scale to a necessary Being, at once Creator and Preserver, the seat of all causation, who is without beginning
of days or end of life.   The extremes of Fatalism and
Casualism are not only inconceivable—for we readily grant
that the power of thought is not the measure of existence—
but they are palpably and grossly self-contradictory, and

therefore must be false. The hypothesis of the Theist is also inconceivable. We cannot represent in thought a necessary and eternal Being; but, then, it is not self-contradictory, and upon the doctrine of excluded middle it must be true; so man must take his place in the "mighty chain of cause and effect, by which all the operations of nature are carried on from the commencement to the end of time." In the calumniated doctrine of an universal Providence, extending to all events and to all things, the only depositary of real efficiency and power, we find the true explanation of an activity which is neither casual in its origin nor a dependent link in an endless chain.[1] In God we live and move and have our being. Nature and our own minds present us with multifarious phenomena linked together as antecedent and consequent, but all are equally effects. Neither nature nor ourselves present us with an instance of a real cause. To Him that sitteth on the throne, and to Him alone, in its just and proper sense, belongs the prerogative of POWER. He speaks and it is done. He commands and it stands fast.

The proof by which Mr. Morell establishes his proposition that spontaneous activity is the substance of the soul is as remarkable as the proposition itself. His argument is what logicians call a destructive conditional, to the validity of which it is as requisite that all the suppositions which can possibly be made in the case should be given in the major, as that all but the one contained in the conclusion should be destroyed in the minor—the very species of argument which we ourselves have employed in regard to the existence of a necessary Being. Now, says Mr. Morell, the essence of mind *must* consist either in sensation, intelligence or will. It does *not* consist in sensation or intelligence; therefore it *must* consist in the will. Very plausible, no doubt. But how, we ask, does it ap-

[1] Hence we dissent totally from the doctrine laid down by Sir. Wm. Hamilton, that there is no medium between fatalism and chance. Hamilton's Reid, p. 602: Note.

pear, that it *must* consist in one of the enumerated elements? Why may it not consist in something else, in that unknown substance denominated spirit—unknown, but yet believed by virtue of the very constitution of our nature? This supposition is, at least, one which may be made in the case, which has been made by philosophers of the highest repute, and which, we venture to predict, will continue to be made by the great mass of mankind so long as the world shall stand. Then, again, in his process of destruction he removes a great deal more than he intends. He removes whatever "is essentially the same in all minds," and of course the will considered as a mere "spontaneity or capacity of acting independently and for ourselves," for in this sense it is unquestionably common to all mankind. Its modes of manifestation are various in different individuals, and in the same individual at different times; but as a faculty or a power abstracted from its effects "it is essentially the same in all minds."

We have insisted, at what may seem a disproportionate length, upon this preliminary feature of Mr. Morell's psychology, because we believe that it contains the seeds of incalculable mischief. The serious proposal of the question concerning the substance of the soul, as one that our faculties can answer, involves a complete apostasy from the fundamental principle of the Experimental school. The great masters of that philosophy would as soon have thought of gravely discussing the relations of angels to space, how they can be here and not there, or there and not here, and yet be incorporeal and unextended beings. Des Cartes, indeed, speaks of the essence of the soul, and places it in thought, as he had placed the essence of matter in extension. But he uses essence, not as synonymous with substance—for he expressly distinguishes them—but for the characteristic and discriminating quality.

If there be any principle which we regard as settled, it is that all human knowledge must be phenomenal and relative; and that science transcends its sphere when it seeks to penetrate into the region of substances or into that of efficient causes—two things which, we shall afterward have occasion to observe, Rationalists are perpetually confounding. We will not quote in confirmation of our own, the opinions of philosophers imperfectly or not at all acquainted with the modern speculations of Continental Europe. We choose rather to refer to one who is master of them all; who in depth and acuteness is a rival to Aristotle, in immensity of learning a match for Leibnitz, and in comprehensiveness of thought an equal to Bacon. We allude to Sir William Hamilton. His work on Reid has filled us with amazement at the prodigious extent and critical accuracy of his reading. The whole circle of the ancient classics, poets, philosophers and orators; the entire compass of Christian literature, Eastern and Western, from Justin to Luther, including the angry controversies and the endless disputes of the Fathers and Schoolmen; the great works of the Reformation, and the prolific productions of England, Scotland, Germany and France from the period of the Reformers until now,—all seem to be as familiar to his mind as the alphabet to other men; and, what is more remarkable, this ponderous mass of learning is no incumbrance: he has not swallowed down only, but digested, libraries, and while he carries—it is hardly extravagant to say—all the thoughts of all other men in his head, he has an immense multitude besides, precious as any he has collected, which none have ever had before him, and for which the world will always hold him in grateful remembrance. He is an honour to Scotland and an ornament to letters. Upon this subject of the nature and extent of human knowledge and the legitimate province of philosophy, we are rejoiced to find that he treads in the footsteps of his illustrious predecessors of the same school. He fully recognizes the distinction betwixt faith and science.

"All we know," says he,[1] "either of mind or matter, is only a know-

[1] Edinburgh Review, Cross's Selections, p. 181. A splendid article on Cousin's Philosophy.

ledge in each, of the particular, of the different, of the modified, of the phenomenal. We admit that the consequence of this doctrine is, that philosophy, if viewed as more than a science of the conditioned, is impossible. Departing from the particular, we can never in our highest generalizations rise above the finite; that our knowledge, whether of mind or matter, can be nothing more than a knowledge of the relative manifestations of an existence which, in itself, it is our highest wisdom to recognize as beyond the reach of philosophy."

"We know—we can know," he observes again,[1] " only what is relative. Our knowledge of qualities or phenomena is necessarily relative; for these exist only as they exist *in relation to our faculties.* The knowledge, or even the conception of a substance, in itself and apart from any qualities in relation to, and therefore cognizable or conceivable by, our minds, involves a contradiction. Of such we can form only a negative notion; that is, we can merely *conceive it as inconceivable.*" And again,[2] "We know nothing whatever of mind and matter, considered as substances; they are only known to us as a twofold series of phenomena, and we can only justify against the law of parcimony, the postulation of two substances, on the ground that the two series of phenomena are reciprocally so contrary and incompatible that the one cannot be reduced to the other, nor both be supposed to combine in the same common substance." And finally,[3] "We are aware of a phenomenon. That it exists only as known—only as a phenomenon—only as an absolute relative—we are unable to realize in thought; and there is necessarily suggested the notion of an unimaginable something, in which the phenomenon inheres—a subject or substance."

These principles are so intuitively obvious to us that we find it difficult to sympathize with men who can persuade themselves that, with our faculties, they can ever arrive at any other conception of substance but as the unknown and unknowable support of properties. It is not a matter of *knowledge,* but of *belief;* it is not an object which, in itself, is ever-present in consciousness; it is veiled from human penetration by the multitude of attributes and qualities which intervene betwixt it and the mind. It belongs to the dominion of faith and not of science. We admit its

[1] Hamilton's Reid, p. 322.
[2] Hamilton's Reid. Appendix. Note A, § 11, p. 751.
[3] Hamilton's Reid. Appendix. Note D.**

existence, not because we know it, but because we are unable *not* to believe it. The unfounded conviction that by some means we can ascend from the phenomenal to the substantial, that we can apprehend existence in itself, that we can know it simply as Being, without qualities, without properties, without any relative manifestations of its reality, that we can comprehend it in its naked essence, and track the progress of all its developments from its abstract *esse* to its countless forms throughout the universe, has given rise to all the abortive attempts of German and French speculation to fix the *absolute* as a positive element in knowledge. These speculations are not the visions of crackbrained enthusiasts. The reader who has judged of the German philosophers from the extravagant conclusions they have reached will find, upon opening their works and mastering their uncouth and barbarous dialects, and, what is often more difficult, their abstract and rugged formulas, that he is brought in contact with men of the highest order of mind, the severest powers of logic and the utmost coolness of judgment. They do not *rave*, but *reason*. They do not *dream*, but *think;* and that, too, with a rigour of abstraction, an intensity of attention, and a nicety of discrimination, which he is obliged to respect while he laments the perverseness of their application. The difficulty with them is that they begin wrong. Refusing to recognize the limits which the constitution of our nature and our obvious relations to existence have imposed upon the excursions of our faculties, and inattentive to the great law of our being, that in this sublunary state we are doomed to walk by faith much more than by sight, they undertake to bring within the circle of science the nature and foundation of all reality. Reluctant to accept any constitutional beliefs, they seek to verify the deposition of our faculties by gazing upon the things themselves with the intuition of God and grasping them in their true and essential existence. Hence, their endless quest of the absolute as the unconditioned ground of *being*. They suppose that, if they can once com-

prehend in its inmost essence what it is TO BE, they have
the data for "the absolute intelligence and absolute explanation of all things." The consequences, too well known,
which inattention, in their hands, to the necessary limits
of human knowledge has legitimately produced, show the
supreme importance of accurately fixing in our minds—to
use the homely language of Locke[1]—"how far the understanding can extend its view, how far it has faculties to
attain certainty, and in what cases it can only judge
and guess." The salutary lesson of human ignorance is
the last to which human pride submits; but a sound philosophy concurs with the sure word of inspiration in pronouncing man to be a creature of yesterday, who knows
comparatively nothing. It is precisely because we discover,
in the preliminary speculations of our author, this tendency
to transcend the sphere of our faculties, which, in its last
manifestation—when it has grasped the absolute—identifies
man with God, that we have adverted with so much earnestness to the indispensable conditions of knowledge. In the
case before us Mr. Morell has evidently made nothing of
substance. After all that he has said of spontaneity, will,
power, capacity of acting independently and for ourselves,
the real nature of the mind is as inscrutable as it was before; and although he has confidently said that beyond
what he has disclosed there is nothing more to know, the
instinctive belief of every understanding will instantane-
ously suggest that there *is* something more to know.

2. His classification of the powers of the mind comes
next in order. He divides them into two classes or orders—
"those relating to the acquisition of knowledge on the one
side, and those subserving impulse and activity on the
other." The former he terms *intellectual*, the latter *emotional*. "Between the intellectual and emotional activity,"
he observes,[2] "there always subsists a direct correspondency." The successive stages of human consciousness, in
the order of its development and in the correspondence

---

[1] Essay on Human Understanding, Introduct., § 4.   [2] Page 4.

of the intellectual and emotional activity, he presents in the following tabular view:

MIND,

COMMENCING IN

MERE FEELING (undeveloped Unity),

EVINCES A

TWOFOLD ACTIVITY.

I.	II.
Intellectual.	*Emotional.*
1st Stage. The Sensational	
Consciousness, (to which correspond)	The Instincts.
2d Stage. The Perceptive	
Consciousness, "	Animal Passions.
3d Stage. The Logical	
Consciousness, "	Relational Emotions.
4th Stage. The Intuitional	
Consciousness, "	Æsthetic, Moral and Religious Emotions.

MEETING IN

FAITH (highest or developed Unity).[1]

If it is the design of this table, as it seems to be, to indicate all our means of knowledge, it is certainly chargeable with an unaccountable defect. There is no faculty which answers to the Reflection of Locke or to the Consciousness of Reid, Stewart and Royer-Collard. Mind can unquestionably be made an object of thought to itself, and its own powers and operations, its emotions, passions and desires, are materials of knowledge as real and important as the phenomena of sense. Mr. Morell has told us how we become acquainted with our material organism, with external objects, with beauty, goodness and God, but he has omitted to tell us how we can know ourselves. He has made no allusion to that "internal perception or self-consciousness" which, according to Sir William Hamilton,[2] whose analysis, in another respect, he has followed, "is the faculty presentative or intuitive of the phenomena of the Ego or Mind."

[1] Page 5.   [2] Hamilton's Reid. Appendix B., § 1, p. 809.

In our author's substitution of the circumlocutory phrases,
Sensational Consciousness, Perceptive Consciousness, Logical Consciousness, Intuitional Consciousness, for the more
common and familiar terms, Sensation, Perception, Understanding, and Reason, we have an intimation of what he
distinctly avows in his former work,[1] that he agrees with
Sir William Hamilton [2] that Consciousness is not to be considered as a distinct and co-ordinate faculty of the mind,
taking cognizance of its other powers and operations to the
exclusion of their objects—the opinion of Reid, Stewart
and Royer-Collard—but that it is the necessary condition
of intelligence, the generic and fundamental form of all
intellectual activity. We cannot, in other words, know
without knowing that we know. We cannot think, will,
feel or remember without knowing, in the exercise and by
the exercise of these faculties or powers, that we are the
subjects of such operations. Hence, although it is strictly
true that every form of mental activity is a form of consciousness, yet there is certainly, as Sir William Hamilton
himself admits, a logical distinction betwixt a faculty *as
known* and a faculty *as exerted;* and this logical distinction
ought to be preserved in language. It has, indeed, been
preserved in the common terminology, which assigns to the
separate faculties, considered in themselves, appropriate
appellations, while the relation of each and all to our knowledge of them is denoted by consciousness. It is a word
which precisely expresses the formula, *we know that we know,*
and, when employed without an epithet restricting it to
some specific mode of cognition, indicates the complement
of all our intellectual faculties. It is, therefore, indispensable to any adequate enumeration of the sources of human
knowledge. Those who regard it as a single and distinct
power, of course, cannot omit it, and those who regard it
as the universal condition of intelligence should include it,
because it is a compendious statement of all the faculties in

[1] Hist. Mod. Phil., vol. ii., p. 13, seq.
[2] Cross's Selections, Edin. Review, vol. iii., p. 197.

detail, and in that precise relation which the classification
contemplates. In the table before us, Mr. Morell gives us
Perception *as known*, Sensation *as known*, Understanding
as known, Reason *as known*, and various departments of
Emotion *as known*, but he does not give us OURSELVES,
the mind in its integrity, *as known*. This omission is the
more remarkable as, in his history of Modern Philosophy,
he has himself suggested[1] the convenience of the term, *self-
consciousness*, "to express the mind's cognizance of its own
operations." We need not say that the faculties which he
has enumerated he has illustrated, according to his own
views of their connection and dependence, in a very graph-
ic and interesting sketch of the natural history of the
human mind.

3. Without detaining the reader with his accounts of
Sensation and External Perception, in which he has professedly followed Sir William Hamilton—and upon this
subject he could not have followed a better or a safer guide
—we come to that part of his psychology which bears more
immediately upon the main questions of his treatise, and
in which error or mistake is likely to be productive of
serious consequences. We allude to his doctrine of the
Understanding and Reason.

Understanding, as a synonym for logical consciousness,
is, so far as we know, utterly without authority in our philosophical literature; for we do not regard Coleridge as
authority for anything but literary theft. It is a term employed in a wider or narrower sense. In its wider sense
it embraces all the powers which relate to the acquisition
of knowledge, in contradistinction from those which are
subservient to impulse and activity—it answers, in other
words, precisely to the division which Mr. Morell has
styled *intellectual*. Hence the common distribution of our
faculties into those of the understanding and those of the
will. In its narrower and, as we think, its proper sense,
it denotes those higher intellectual faculties which pre-

[1] Vol. ii., p. 15: Note.

eminently distinguish man from the brute, to the exclusion
of sense, imagination, memory and fancy.   But we cannot
recollect a single instance in which it has ever been restricted to our lower cognitive faculties or to the processes
of ratiocination.   The change which Mr. Morell has introduced, or rather followed Coleridge in introducing, is a
radical departure from established usage.   There is much
more authority for identifying *reason* with the logical consciousness than understanding.   For although that word,
in its prevailing usage, is exactly synonymous with understanding, both in its narrower and wider sense, yet it has
not unfrequently been employed by writers of the highest
repute to denote precisely the Discursive Faculty.   This is
the first meaning which Johnson assigns to it, and the
meaning in which Reid systematically employs it in his
Inquiry into the Human Mind; the meaning to which
Beattie restricts it in his Essay on Truth, and which Dr.
Campbell evidently attached to it when he denied it to be
the source of our moral convictions.   We would not be
understood as objecting, however, to Mr. Morell's employment of reason as synonymous with common sense, or, as
he prefers to style it, the Intuitional Consciousness : this
is justified by the highest authority.   Dugald Stewart long
ago suggested "whether it would not, on some occasions, be
the best substitute which our language affords for intuition,
in the enlarged acceptation in which it had been made
equivalent to the ancient νους or *locus principiorum.*"   But
what we deny is, that understanding is ever equivalent to
logical consciousness as contradistinguished from reason in
its restricted application, or is ever opposed to it in any
other sense than a genus is opposed to a species.[1]   Intelligence
is one, and all our faculties, when legitimately exercised, are
harmonious and consistent with each other.   They all con-
spire in the unity of knowledge.   It is not one reason which
knows intuitively, and another reason which knows deduct-

[1] See Stewart's Elements, vol. ii., Prelim. Cons., and Hamilton's Reid,
Appendix.   Note A, § v., p. 768, seq.   Also p. 511: Note.

ively; but it is the same reason which knows in each case,
though the relations of the object to it are different, but not
repugnant or contradictory. To suppose that the logical
consciousness, operating in conformity with the laws of
thought, shall ever be exclusive of intuitive results, is to
suppose that philosophy is impossible, and that skepticism
is the highest wisdom of man.

The unity of reason and the harmony of intelligence
being kept steadily in view, we have no objections to *any*
form of phraseology which shall exactly designate the relations in which the objects of knowledge are contemplated
by the mind. There is certainly a distinction between those
faculties which are simply receptive and those which operate
upon the materials received—those which furnish us with
our simple and elementary ideas, and those which combine
them into structures of science; and if this is the distinction which Mr. Morell designed to signalize—if he means
by *intuition* the complement of all our faculties of presentative, and by *logical consciousness* the complement of all
our faculties of representative, knowledge—he has aimed at
the expression of an obvious truth, but, we must take the
liberty to say, has been extremely unfortunate in the mode
of its development.

He has, in the first place, confounded presentative and
intuitive knowledge. These knowledges have not the same
logical extension: one is a genus of which the other is a
species. All presentative is intuitive, but all intuitive is
not presentative, knowledge. Intuition may be, and is, constantly applied not only to the immediate view which the
mind has of an object in an act of presentative cognition,
but to the irresistible conviction of the vicarious character
of the representative in an act of representative cognition,
as well as to the instantaneous perception of the agreement
of subject and predicate in self-evident propositions. To
make these distinctions more obvious: knowledge, in its
strict acceptation, as contradistinguished from faith, is conversant only about realities which have been given in ex-

perience, and is either mediate or immediate.   It is immediate, when an object is apprehended in itself without relation to others; mediate, when it is known or apprehended in and through its relations.   Immediate knowledge is, again, subdivided into presentative and representative—presentative, when the object itself, and not an image, conception or notion of it, is that which is present in consciousness; representative, when it is not the object, but an image, notion or conception of it, which is present in consciousness. Hence, although all presentative knowledge is immediate, all immediate is not presentative knowledge; and although all mediate knowledge is representative, all representative is not mediate knowledge; and both presentative and representative knowledge may be intuitive.   External perception is an instance of presentative and intuitive, memory, of representative and intuitive, knowledge.   In the one case, the external object is known in itself, being actually present in consciousness; in the other, the past, which, *ex hypothesi*, cannot be present, is apprehended through a modification of the mind representing it.   But the knowledge of memory is as strictly self-evident—as strictly independent of proofs—though it may not be as perfect in degree, as the knowledge in external perception.   If, now, the logical consciousness embraces all our faculties of presentative, and the intuitional all our faculties of representative, knowledge, intuition certainly may be common to both.   It does not follow that, because an object is intuitively known, it is therefore directly and immediately given in consciousness.

His confusion of Intuition and Presentation has led him, in the next place, into a still more remarkable error—the confusion of mediate and indirect knowledge with that which is direct and immediate.   When he comes, for example, to account for our conceptions of God, though, with singular inconsistency, he uses terms expressive of presentative cognition, yet in describing the process of development by which we ascend to the lofty stage of supersensible consciousness, he gives us nothing but evolutions of reasoning—necessary deductions from our primitive and instinctive beliefs. God is not actually present as the object of consciousness; He does not stand before us as the outward object in an act of perception: it is the finite, limited, temporary and dependent which we immediately apprehend; and, in consequence of the necessary laws of mind, these suggest the infinite, eternal, independent and absolute. God, in other words, is not known in Himself—in His separate and distinct existence, as a datum of consciousness; He is apprehended in and through His works—through relations intuitively recognized and spontaneously suggesting the reality of His being. Or, we know God, as we know substance, in and through attributes. This species of knowledge is evidently indirect and mediate. Take away the limited, finite, contingent, take away the necessary belief that these require a cause, and you take away all Mr. Morell's consciousness of God; and hence we believe in God, not because He is seen or stands face to face with any of our faculties of cognition, but because *other things* are known which are utterly inexplicable except upon the supposition of the Divine existence. "The heavens declare His glory and the firmament showeth His handiwork;" "the invisible things of Him are clearly seen, being understood by the things that are made."

We agree most fully that there is a process by which the understanding can, to a limited extent, ascend from the known to the unknown; that we are so framed as that ourselves—our bodies, our souls, and nature around us—become *witnesses* for God; but the knowledge we derive in this way we should never dream of describing as immediate, presentative or direct. Mr. Morell has been betrayed into this inconsistency by making presentation co-extensive with intuition. There is no doubt that this knowledge of God is intuitive, as it results from the indestructible categories of thought—which, developed into formal statements, are self-evident propositions—in their application to the objects furnished in experience. Constituted as we are, we can neither cognize ourselves nor the world without a belief of God: the belief is inseparably connected with the cognition: we can give no reason for it but that such is the constitution of our nature that when an effect is given a cause must be admitted, and hence, while we may be said to know intuitively, we evidently do not know the cause in itself; it is mediated by the effect. The knowledge, in other words, is intuitive, but not presentative.

It is useless to adduce passages to prove what no one, perhaps, will think of disputing, that presentation and intuition are treated as synonymous; but as it may not be so readily conceded that mediate and indirect knowledge is also treated as presentative and immediate, we appeal to the following statements in justification of our assertion:

"Let us take a third instance. The mind, after it has gazed for awhile upon the phenomena of the world around, begins to ponder within itself such thoughts as these: What is this changing scene which men call nature? What then *is* nature? Of what primary elements do all things consist? What is the power and the wisdom through which their infinite forms of beauty spring forth, live, decay, and then become instinct with a new vitality? In these questions we again discern the activity of a higher state of consciousness than the understanding alone presents. The understanding, looking at the objects presented to us through the agency of perception, abstracts their properties and classifies them; in a word, it separates things into their genera and species, and there leaves them. But the pure reason, instead of separating the objects of nature and classifying them into various species, seeks rather to *unite* them, to view them all together—to find the one fundamental essence by which they are upheld; to discover the great presiding principle by which they are maintained in unbroken harmony. The understanding has simply to do with separate objects viewed in their specific or generic character; the higher reason has to do with them as forming parts of one vast totality, of which it seeks the basis, the origin and the end. With the phenomena of the human mind it is the same. The understanding merely classifies them, the pure reason inquires into the nature of the principle from which they spring, and views the human mind as a totality, expressing the will and purpose of its great Archetype.

"These two efforts of the reason to seek the nature and origin, both of the universe and the soul, lead naturally and inevitably to the conception of some common ground from which they are both derived. The soul is not self-created, but is consciously dependent upon some higher power. There must be a type after which it was formed —a self-existent essence from which it proceeded—a supreme *mind* which planned and created my mind. So also with regard to nature. If the universe, as a whole, shows the most perfect harmony, all the parts thereof symmetrically adapted to each other, all proceeding onwards like a machine infinitely complicate, yet never clashing in its minutest wheels and movements, there must be some mind vaster than the universe—one which can take it all in at a single glance, one which has planned its harmony and keeps the whole system from perturbation. In short, if there be *dependent* existence, there must be *absolute* existence—if there be temporal and finite beings, there must be an Eternal and an Infinite *One*. Thus the power of intuition, that highest elevation of the human consciousness, leads us at length into the world of eternal realities. The period of the mind's converse with mere phenomena being past, it rises at length to grasp the mystery of existence and the problem of destiny."[1]

We beg the reader to examine carefully this passage, and to lay his hand, if he can, upon anything but a very awkward and mystical statement—certainly a very feeble and inadequate one—of the common *a posteriori* argument from effect to cause. Instead of gazing directly upon the Supreme Being and standing face to face with the absolute, we gaze outwardly upon the world and inwardly upon ourselves, and are conducted by processes of natural and spontaneous inquiry to the admission of an adequate and all-sufficient Cause of the wondrous phenomena we behold. Whether our steps be from the finite to the infinite, from the dependent to the absolute, from the fleeting to the eternal, they are the steps of intelligence mediating a knowledge of God through relations which we intuitively recognize. We see Him only in the operation of His hands. He is mirrored in His works. The knowledge in this case is precisely analogous to that of the external world which the Hypothetical Realists ascribe to us. We are not directly conscious of its existence, but are conscious of effects pro-

[1] Pages 20–22.

duced in ourselves, which the constitution of our nature determines us to refer to outward and independent realities.

If Mr. Morell seriously believes that our knowledge of God is presentative, he is bound, of course, that he may be consistent with himself, to postulate a faculty through which the Divine Being may be given as the immediate object of involuntary consciousness. We have the senses through which the various properties of matter are directly and spontaneously cognized; we have taste and conscience, which bring us into contact with the beautiful and the deformed, the right and the wrong; and, to preserve the analogy, we must have some power or sense which shall be directly conversant about God—a faculty of the Divine or the absolute, sustaining the same relations to the Deity which the senses sustain to the outward world, taste to the fair, and conscience to the right. This is the only way in which the theory of presentative knowledge can be consistently carried out in its application to God. But if this be admitted, it is as absurd to talk of hunting up the Deity through the realms of matter and of mind, to be feeling, inquiring and searching after Him in the regions of the finite, limited and dependent, as it is to represent men as *seeking* the primary qualities of matter, or the elementary distinctions betwixt beauty and deformity, a virtue and a crime. All presentative knowledge comes, in the first instance, unbidden. There is no appetite or instinct for it which leads us in quest of it. We had no conception of matter until we were made conscious of its existence; beauty was an unmeaning word, and we should never have known how to set about comprehending its meaning until the experience of it was first felt; and if there be a separate and distinct *faculty* of God, He must be absolutely incognizable and inconceivable by us until He reaches us through the medium or instrumentality of this faculty. He must come into the mind like extension, figure, solidity—like beauty, virtue and all our simple and elementary cognitions. He is not to be a craving of our nature—something longed for

and yearned after; but an immediate datum of consciousness—something which we know to be, because he is now
and here present to intelligence.   But the passage which
we have just quoted from our author is directly in the
teeth of any such doctrine.   There is no presentation there
of any objective realities in themselves, but the finite, dependent and phenomenal—these are alone present in consciousness; but being cognized as *effects*, *they* give us, as
vouchers and witnesses, other existences beyond themselves.
They *testify* of God, but do not *present* God.   They develope
a belief which is natural, spontaneous and irresistible,
whose object is unknown except in so far as it may be
collected from their qualities and attributes in their relations to it.

Mr. Morell is equally at fault in the account which he
has given of the logical consciousness.   This, we have seen,
he employs as a compendious expression for all our faculties of representative knowledge.   It embraces those processes of the mind which relate to the combination, arrangement and structure of the sciences, which conduct us from
particular phenomena to general laws, which group individual existences into classes, and perform the functions
which are commonly denominated *discursive*.   Its first
office is to turn our intuitions into notions or conceptions—
to give us representatives, through the acts of the intellect,
of the real and, independent existences which are grasped
by the faculty of inward or outward perception.   It *ideal-
izes*, in other words, the matter of our direct and presentative knowledge.   It then decomposes its conceptions, fixes
upon one or more elements contained in them, abstracts
these from the rest, and makes these abstractions the grounds
of classification.   To it belong memory, the mediate knowledge of the past; imagination, the mediate knowledge of
the conceivable and possible; and, if Mr. Morell admits
such a thing as possible, prescience or the mediate knowledge of the future.   He calls this complement of faculties
logical; and we think the epithet well chosen to designate

representative in contradistinction from presentative knowledge, because it is in them that the mind is specially
cogitative—it is in them that the laws and necessary forms
of thought which it is the office of logic to investigate are
conspicuously developed. In presentation the mind *knows;*
in representation the mind *thinks.* In presentation there
is an immediate object apart from the mind; in representation nothing is directly given but the acts of the mind
itself. In presentation the mind may be regarded as comparatively passive; in representation it is wholly and essentially active. In presentation, accordingly, the prominent
matter is the object of cognition; in representation, the
categories of thought. There are two points, however, in
Mr. Morell's doctrine of the logical consciousness against
which we must enter a solemn and decided protest. The
first is, that our conceptions cannot exactly represent our
intuitions—that the remote and ultimate object, as given
in an act of mediate and representative cognition, is not
precisely the same as the immediate object in an act of
direct and presentative cognition. The other is, that the
understanding cannot enlarge our knowledge of numerical
existences; that we can only think the precise, identical
realities which have been given in experience, and can
infer and prove the substantive existence of naught beyond
them.

In relation to the first point, we can only speak of what
strikes us as the prevailing doctrine of the book, for the
author is so vague, vacillating and inconsistent in his
account of conception that we freely admit that he appears
in two passages to teach the doctrine for which we contend.
But as a general thing he maintains that the understanding
is exclusively conversant about attributes or properties.
"It has to do," he informs us, "entirely with the *attributes*
of things—separating, scrutinizing, classifying them, and
adapting them, by the aid of judgment and reasoning, to
all the purposes of human existence." "Thus every notion" [conception], he tells us in another place, "we have

of an external object—as a house, or a tree, or a flower—is
compounded of two elements, a material and a formal.
The matter is furnished by the direct sensational intuition
of a concrete reality, and this is perception; the form is
furnished by the logical faculty, which, separating the attributes of the object, as given in perception, from the essence,
constructs a notion or idea [conception] which can be clearly
defined and employed as a fixed term in the region of our
reflective knowledge." And again:

"Of mere phenomena we can gain a very good knowledge by an in-
termediate or logical process. We can have the different attributes
presented to us as *abstract ideas ;* we can put these attributes together
one by one, and thus form a conception of the whole thing *as a phenomenon ;* but this cannot be done in regard to any elementary and
essential existence. Of *substance,* for example, we can gain no conception by a logical definition; the attempt to do so has, in fact,
always ended in the denial of substance altogether, considered as an
objective reality; it becomes in this way simply the projected shadow
of our own faculties. The only refuge against this logical skepticism,
which has been uniformly attached itself to a sensational philosophy,
is in the immediacy of our higher knowledge—in the fact that we see
and feel the existence of a substantial reality around us, without the
aid of any logical idea or definition by which it can be represented or
conveyed." [1]

Mr. Morell surely cannot mean that through any representative faculty, *original* ideas can be imparted of attributes and qualities which had never been *presentatively*
given—that a blind man can be instructed in colours by a
logical definition, or a deaf man in sounds. Every simple
idea, whether of qualities or not, must, in the first instance,
have been conveyed in an act of immediate cognition.
What we understand Mr. Morell as teaching is, that the
conceptions of the understanding do not adequately represent the cognitions of intuition; that the phenomenon
does not mirror the whole reality; that there is something
given in perception which cannot be mediated by an act of
mind. It is true that this mysterious something is described
as the essence or substance of the thing perceived; and it is

[1] Page 37.

equally true that essences or substances are only matters of
belief; we neither see them nor feel them—they lie beyond
the boundaries of knowledge, whether presentative or otherwise. But we maintain that *whatever* can be perceived or
immediately known can be also imagined or conceived. We
can frame an image or notion which shall exactly correspond
to the *whole* object of an inward or outward perception.
We can represent *all the essence* that we ever knew. There
is no difference between the remote and ultimate object in
an act of representative, and the immediate and present
object in an act of immediate and presentative, cognition.
Unless Mr. Morell admits what we understand him to
deny, that the vicarious knowledge involved in conception
answers exactly to the original knowledge given in intuition, he must maintain that the knowledge of any existence but that which is now and here present in consciousness is impossible. All else becomes purely ideal—our
conceptions cease to be *representative;* for the very notion
of representation implies a reality apart from itself which,
as represented, is known. To affirm that the representative
does not truly mirror the original is to invalidate the only
conceivable process by which we can pass from the ideal to
the actual. It is to deny the fidelity of our faculties in the
irresistible conviction which we have of the reality of the
original, though mediated, idea, and thus to lay the foundation of universal skepticism. To illustrate by an example:
memory is the mediate knowledge of the past. The house,
or man, or flower which we saw yesterday, and remember
to have seen to-day, has no longer a present existence in
consciousness; what we now contemplate, and immediately
cognize, is not the thing itself, but a conception which we
feel to be its representative. According to our author,
however, this conception is partial and inadequate—it does
not embrace *all* that we saw; the most important part, the
only part indeed which was real, has been omitted. But
consciousness assures us that we distinctly and adequately
recollect our perception of yesterday—the whole perception

precisely as it was experienced; that, to accommodate the language of Mr. Hume, the present idea is an exact transcript of the former impression. If, now, consciousness deceives us in this case, if it *lies* in pronouncing that to be an adequate representative which is partial, maimed and defective, what guarantee have we for its veracity in any case? And how, especially, shall we prove that memory and all our powers of mediate knowledge are not faculties of mere delusion? Mr. Morell, it seems to us, must deny all objective existences apart from the mind, or he must admit that the understanding can frame conceptions exactly commensurate with original intuitions. This, we conceive to be the fundamental condition of the certainty of all representative knowledge. We see no alternative between pure idealism and this theory of the understanding. When it abstracts and fixes its attention upon one or more attributes, performing what Mr. Morell regards as its characteristic functions, these attributes are not absolutely conceived, but relatively, as the attributes of real things.

The other point—that the understanding cannot enlarge the boundaries of knowledge—Mr. Morell seems uniformly to treat as wellnigh self-evident.

"And yet this logical consciousness, although it is the great instrument of practical life, is entirely subjective and formal. The material with which it has to do is wholly given in sensation and perception; all that it furnishes in addition to this are forms of thought, general notions, categories and internal processes, which have an abstract or logical value, but which, when viewed alone, are absolutely void of all 'content.'" [1]

If Mr. Morell means nothing more than that the understanding can furnish no original ideas beyond the contents of intuition, the proposition, though unquestionably true, is far from being new. It is universally conceded that no powers of conception, imagination, memory or reasoning, no processes of definition, analysis or judgment, can supply the elementary notions of the senses to one who was desti-

[1] Page 16.

tute of the material organism.   But if he means, what the
tenor of his argument demands, and what we, accordingly,
understand him to assert, that, all our simple ideas being
given, the understanding or the laws of thought cannot
conduct us to the full conviction of existences lying beyond
the range of present intuition, the proposition is just as unquestionably false.   What transcends the limits of momentary experience can either not be known at all, or it must be
known through the medium of the logical consciousness.
If it cannot be known at all, then human knowledge, in
regard to external things, is limited to what is in immediate
contact with the organs of sense; in regard to internal
things, to the fleeting consciousness of the moment.   We
can know nothing of the past, we can know nothing of the
distant, we can predict nothing of the future.   In other
words, all science is a rank delusion; even our knowledge
of the material world, as embracing a wide range of existence, is an inference of the understanding, and not the
result of a direct perception of its amplitude and variety.
Upon the theory of external perception which Mr. Morell
has adopted it is intuitively obvious that we can perceive
nothing, or have a presentative cognition of nothing, but
that which is in contact with our material organism.   The
sun, moon and stars are not objects of perception, but of
inference; they are not directly, but representatively known.
We can immediately know only what is now and here present in consciousness.

"In the third place," says Sir William Hamilton,[1] "to this head we
may refer Reid's inaccuracy in regard to the precise object of perception.   This object is not, as he seems frequently to assert, any distant
reality; for we are percipient of nothing but what is in proximate
contact, in immediate relation, with our organs of sense.   Distant
realities we reach, not by perception, but by a subsequent process of
inference, founded thereon; and so far, as he somewhere says, from all
men who look upon the sun perceiving the same object, in reality
every individual, in this instance, perceives a different object, nay, a
different object in each several eye.   The doctrine of Natural Realism
requires no such untenable assumption for its basis.   It is sufficient to

[1] Hamilton's Reid, p. 814.

establish the simple fact that we are competent, as consciousness
assures us, immediately to apprehend through sense the non-ego in
certain limited relations; and it is of no consequence whatever, either
to our certainty of the reality of a material world, or to our ultimate
knowledge of its properties, whether, by this primary apprehension,
we lay hold, in the first instance, on a larger or a lesser portion of its
contents." And in another place:[1] "A thing to be known *in itself*
must be known as *actually existing*, and it cannot be known as actually
existing unless it be known as existing in its *When* and its *Where*. But
the When and Where of an object are *immediately* cognizable by the
subject, only if the When be *now* (*i. e.*, at the same moment with
the cognitive act), and the where be *here*, (*i. e.*, within the sphere of
the cognitive faculty); therefore a presentative or intuitive knowledge
is only competent of an object *present* to the mind both in *time* and
space. E converso, whatever is known, but not as *actually* existing
now and *here*, is known not in itself, as the presentative object of
an intuitive, but only as the remote object of a representative,
cognition."

Upon the hypothesis of Mr. Morell, accordingly, which
restricts the operations of the understanding to the specific
contents which have been given in actual intuitions, the
worlds which astronomy discloses to our faith are merely
subjective forms and logical processes, and not realities at
all. All the deductions of pure mathematics are sheer
delusions, inasmuch as they are the products of the understanding operating upon the primary qualities of matter,
which alone are furnished in perception. That the results
which the chemist has obtained to-day, shall, under the
same circumstances, be verified to-morrow, that like antecedents shall be attended with like consequents in all the
departments of philosophy, cannot with confidence be predicted, since that would be a present knowledge of a future
event, and involve a fact numerically different from any
which had ever been given in experience. To say that the
understanding cannot compass other realities beside the
precise identical ones which have been or are present in
consciousness is to pull down the entire fabric of human
science, to leave us nothing of nature but the small frag
ment of its objects within the immediate sphere of our

[1] Hamilton's Reid, p. 809.

faculties, to make us, without a figure, the creatures of the passing moment. All that can be maintained is, that the understanding cannot conduct us to the knowledge of existences involving elements which have not been derived from some objects of actual intuition. But it may infer and prove the existence of realities involving these elements in different degrees and different modes of combination from any that have actually fallen within the sphere of consciousness. We can prove the existence of the sun, and yet we may have never seen him. Without a specific presentation of his substantive reality, we can frame the conception of him by a combination of attributes which have been repeatedly given in other instances of intuition. We ascribe to him nothing but what we know from experience to be properties of matter, and what we know he must possess in order to produce the effects which he does produce. We believe in the existence of animals that we never saw, of lands that we are never likely to visit, of changes and convulsions that shook our globe centuries before its present inhabitants were born; and though we have no experience of the future, we can frame images of coming events, all of which may, and some of which, as the decay and dissolution of our bodies, most assuredly will, take place. Were there not a law of our nature by which we are determined to judge of the future by the past, and a uniformity of events which exactly answers to it, the physical sciences would be impossible, and prudential rules for the regulation of conduct utterly absurd.

So far, indeed, is it from being true that the understanding does not enlarge our knowledge of real existences, that it is precisely the faculty or complement of faculties which gives us the principal part of that knowledge. Intuition supplies us with very few objects, it is limited to a very narrow sphere; but in the materials which it *does* embrace it gives us the constituents of all beings that we are capable of conceiving. The understanding, impelled to action in the first instance by the presentation of realities, goes for-

ward in obedience to the laws of thought, and infers a
multitude of beings lying beyond the range of our presentation, some like those that have been given, others possessed of the same elementary qualities in different degrees
and proportions. It is impossible to say how much our
knowledge is extended—our knowledge, we mean, of veritable, objective realities—by the processes involved in
general reasoning. We can form some conception of the
immense importance of abstraction and generalization, as
subservient to intellectual improvement, by imagining what
our condition would be if we were deprived of the benefits
of language. How much better, apart from speech, would
be our knowledge than the crude apprehension of the brute?
He has, no doubt, all the intuitions of the primary qualities
of matter which we possess, but he knows them only as in
this or that object; he has never been able to abstract,
generalize, classify and name; and therefore his knowledge must always be limited to the particular things now
and here present in consciousness. He can have no science.

To us it is almost intuitively obvious that the understanding, as the organ of science, is pre-eminently the faculty of knowledge. Intuition gives us the alphabet; the
understanding combines and arranges the letters, in conformity with the necessary forms of thought, into the words
which utter the great realities of nature, whether material,
moral or intellectual. Intuition is the germ, the bud; understanding, the tree, in full and majestic proportions,
spreading its branches and scattering its fruits on all sides.
Intuition is the insect's eye, contracted to a small portion
of space and a smaller fragment of things; understanding,
the telescope, which embraces within its scope the limitless
expanse of worlds—"of planets, suns and adamantine
spheres, wheeling unshaken through the void immense."

Mr. Morell has been betrayed into his inadequate representation of the understanding as an instrument of knowledge by adhering too closely to the Kantian theory of its
nature as subjective and formal, without a reference to the

circumstances by which the theory, though essentially just, must be limited and modified. We believe most fully that there are and must be laws or categories of thought—that there must be conditions in the subject adapting it to know, as well as conditions in the object adapting it to be known. Thinking is not an arbitrary process, our faculties of representation do not operate at random; there are forms of cogitation which cannot be separated from intelligence without destroying its nature. We care not by what names they are called; they certainly exist, and it is the special function of logic to investigate and analyze them. But one thing is set over against another. These laws of the understanding are designed to qualify it to be an instrument of knowledge. They are the conditions by which a limited and finite creature can stretch its intelligence beyond the points of space and time in which its existence is fixed. The laws of thought are so adjusted to the laws of existence that whatever is true of our conceptions will always be true of the *things* which our conceptions *represent*. The operations of the understanding, though primarily and immediately about its own acts, are remotely and mediately about other objects. Its acts are *representative*, and hence it deals with realities through their symbols. If Mr. Morell had kept steadily in view the *representative* character of our logical conceptions, he would have seen that they *must* have respect to something beyond themselves which is not subjective and formal. He would have seen that every operation of mind *must* be cognitive—must involve a judgment. Every conception implies the belief that it is the image of something real, that has been given in experience; every fancy implies a *judgment* that it is the image of something possible, that *might* be given in experience. Attention to this circumstance of the cognitive character of all the operations of mind would have saved him from the error of supposing that the acts of the understanding are exclusively formal. Kant knew nothing of the distinction betwixt presentative and representative knowledge. His conceptions, therefore, involved no judgment—they were not the images of a reality, as given in intuition; they were purely the products of the mind, and corresponded to nothing beyond the domain of consciousness.   Had he recognized the truth that every intellectual act is *cognitive*, and every act of the understanding *representative*, he would have "saved the main pillars of human belief;" and while he still might have taught, what we believe he has unanswerably demonstrated, that space and time are native notions of the mind and not generalizations from experience, he would have seen that, as native notions, they are the indispensable conditions of its apprehending the time and space properties of matter, and have accorded, consequently, an objective reality to extension, solidity and figure which his theory, in its present form, denies; he would have seen that the understanding is as truly conversant about *things* as intuition—that the only difference betwixt them in this respect is, that the one deals with them and apprehends them directly, the other, through means of representatives, and that, consequently, the conclusions of the understanding, legitimately reached, must have a counterpart in objective reality as truly as the cognitions of sense.   We are sorry to say that Mr. Morell, though professing to adopt the distinctions to which we have adverted, falls again and again into the peculiarities of the Kantian hypothesis, against which they are a protest.   Take the following passage:

"Perception, viewed alone, indicates simply the *momentary consciousness* of an external reality standing before us face to face, but it gives us no *notion* which we can define and express by a term. To do this is the office of the understanding—the logical or constructive faculty, which seizes upon the concrete material that is given immediately in perception, moulds it into an idea, expresses this idea by a word or sign, and then lays it up in the memory, as it were a hewn stone, all shaped and prepared for use whenever it may be required, either for ordinary life or for constructing a scientific system. Thus every notion we have of an external object—as a house, a tree, or a flower—is compounded of two elements, a material and a formal.

The matter is furnished by the direct sensational intuition of a concrete reality; and this is perception: the form is furnished by the logical
faculty, which, separating the attributes of the object as given in perception from the essence, constructs a notion or idea, which can be
clearly defined and employed as a fixed term in the region of our
reflective knowledge." [1]

This passage, upon any theory but that of Kant—and
even upon that theory it requires modification—is absolutely
unintelligible.   Upon the theory which Mr. Morell professes to adopt it is pure gibberish.   " *The understanding
seizes upon the concrete material that is given immediately in
perception.*"   Now this "concrete material" was the "*external reality standing before us face to face.*"   Are we then
to understand that the understanding captures the outward
object *itself?*   If so, it surely has matter as well as form.
But then it *moulds* the concrete material into an *idea*, dubs
it with a name and lays it away in the memory.   What
does he mean, what can he mean, by moulding an external
reality into an idea?   But it seems that in this moulding
process, though the understanding had originally seized the
concrete reality, yet by some means or other the *essence*
slipped between its fingers, and the notion or idea lodged
away in the memory retains nothing but the qualities.   Now
what is the real process of the mind which all this nonsense
is designed to represent?   Perception gives us the external
reality in those qualities which our faculties are capable of
apprehending.   We know it in itself, and as now and here
existing.   Conception, or rather imagination, is an act of
the understanding, producing an *image* or *representative* of
the object; it seizes upon no *material* given from without;
the *immediate* matter of its knowledge is its own act, and
that act, from its very constitution, vicarious of something
beyond itself.   "A representation," says Sir William Hamilton,[2] "considered as an *object*, is logically, not really, different from a representation considered as an *act*.   Here,
object and act are the same indivisible mode of mind

---

[1] Page 72.   [2] Hamilton's Reid, p. 809.

viewed in two different relations. Considered by reference
to a mediate object represented, it is a representative object;
considered by reference to the mind representing and contemplating the representation, it is a representative act."
Hence, in every operation of the logical consciousness what
we *immediately* know is not the external reality, but a modification of the mind itself, and through that modification
we know the external object. The form and immediate
matter, therefore, cannot be separated even in thought.

Mr. Morell indeed speaks of forms and categories of
thought in such terms as to imply that the mind *creates* the
qualities which it represents in its conceptions. This, of
course, is to deny that its acts are properly representative—
to shut us up within the prison of hopeless idealism. The
laws of thought enable the mind, not *to create*, but to image,
figure or represent; they enable it to *think* a thing which is
not before it, but they do not enable it to invest it with a
single property which it does not possess; and they are
violated whenever a thing is thought otherwise than as it
actually exists. The mind as intelligent, and things as
intelligible, are adapted to each other.

We may now condense into a short compass what we conceive to be the truth, in contradistinction from Mr. Morell's
doctrine of the understanding, on the points to which we
have adverted. We believe, then, that this faculty, or rather
complement of faculties, possesses the power of representing, and of completely and adequately representing, every
individual thing, whether a concrete whole or a single attribute, which ever has been presented in intuition. "It
stamps," in the language of Aristotle, "a kind of impression of the *total process* of perception, after the manner of
one who applies a signet to wax." This is the fundamental
condition of the certainty of its results. For, as Sir William Hamilton expresses it, "it is only deserving of the
name of knowledge in so far it is conformable to the intuitions it represents." There is no separation of the essence
from the attributes in an act of recollective imagination;

what was given in intuition, and *all* that was given, is pictured in the image. As representative, we believe, in the next place, that the understanding is ultimately conversant about *things*—realities—and not fictions or empty forms. What it proves of its conceptions legitimately framed will hold good of the objects which they represent; its ideas are, if we may so speak, the *language* of reality. In the next place, it is not confined to the numerical particulars which have been actually given in intuition. It is dependent upon presentation for all the elements it employs in its representations—it can originate no new simple idea; but testimony and the evidence of facts, induction and deduction, may lead it—may compel it—to acknowledge the existence of beings which in their concrete realities have never been matters of direct experience. It frames a conception of them from the combination of the elements given in intuition in such proportions as the evidence before it seems to warrant. Thus the geologist describes the animals which perished amid what he believes to be the ruins of a former world; thus we believe in the monsters of other climes, the facts of history and the calculations of science.

After what has already been said, it is hardly necessary to devote much space to the detailed and articulate account of the distinction betwixt the logical and intuitional consciousness, upon which Mr. Morell has evidently bestowed much labour, and to which he attaches no small degree of importance in consequence of the part which it is destined to play in his subsequent speculations. His first observation is, that "the knowledge we obtain by the logical consciousness is *representative* and *indirect*, while that which we obtain by the intuitional consciousness is *presentative* and *immediate*." This is the fundamental difference of the two complements of faculties. Intuition, or, as in consequence of the ambiguity and vagueness of that term, we should prefer to call it, *Presentation*, embraces all our powers of original knowledge. Through it we are furnished with

whatsoever simple ideas we possess; it is the *beginning* of
our intellectual strength. The logical consciousness, on
the other hand, embraces all our powers of representative
knowledge; it builds the fabric of science from the materials presentatively given; it comprehends all the processes
of thought which the mind is led to carry on in consequence
of the impulse received in presentation. If Mr. Morell
had consistently adhered to this fundamental distinction,
and admitted no differences but what might naturally be
referred to it, he would have been saved from much needless confusion, perplexity and self-contradiction.

His second observation is, that "the knowledge we obtain
by the logical consciousness is *reflective;* that which we
obtain by the intuitional consciousness is spontaneous."
This distinction, we confess, has struck us with amazement.
In the first place, upon Mr. Morell's theory of the soul,
spontaneity is the indispensable condition of all intelligence;
it is of the very essence—substance—substratum, of mind.
Reflection, therefore, is not something *distinct from*, it is
only a *form* of, spontaneity. "The power of the will," he
tells us, "operates through all the region of man's spontaneous life," "our activity is equally voluntary and equally
moral in its whole aspect." In the next place, upon any
just view of the subject, what we are authorized to affirm
is, that all reflective knowledge is representative, but not
that all representative knowledge is reflective. The two
propositions are by no means convertible. Reflection is
nothing but attention to the phenomena of mind. It is
the observation—if you please, the study—of what passes
within. "The peculiar phenomena of philosophy," says
one[1] who has insisted most largely upon the spontaneous
and reflective aspects of reason, "are those of the other
world, which every man bears within himself, and which
he perceives by the aid of the inward light which is called
consciousness, as he perceives the former by the senses.
The phenomena of the inward world appear and disappear

[1] Cousin, Frag. Phil., Pref.

so rapidly that consciousness perceives them and loses sight of them almost at the same time. It is not then sufficient to observe them transiently, and while they are passing over that changing scene; *we must retain them as long as possible by attention.* We may do even still more. We may call up a phenomenon from the bosom of the night into which it has vanished, summon it again to memory, and reproduce it in our minds for the sake of contemplating it at our ease; we may recall one part of it rather than another, leave the latter in the shade, so as to bring the former into view, vary the aspects in order to go through them all and to embrace every side of the object; *this is the office of reflection.*" Reflection is to psychology what observation and experiment are to physics. Now to say that all our representative knowledge depends upon attention to the processes of our own minds, that we know only as we take cognizance of the laws and operations of our faculties, is too ridiculous for serious refutation. Even Mr. Morell starts back from the bouncing absurdity; and—with what consistency we leave it to our readers to determine—reluctantly admits that "there is evidently a sense in which all the faculties, even the logical consciousness itself, may be regarded as having a spontaneous movement, such as we have described—a sense in which we cast our knowledge spontaneously and unreflectively into a logical mould." In order to extricate himself, however, from the contradiction in which he is involved, he invents another meaning for *reflective*, in which he makes it synonymous with *scientific.* But we do not see that this subterfuge relieves him. All representative knowledge is surely not scientific, nor attained upon scientific principles. The elements of science must exist and be known representatively before science itself can be constructed, and reflection always presupposes spontaneous processes as the objects of its attention. Without spontaneity there could be no reflectivity. There would be nothing to reflect upon. Reflection, therefore, is simply an instrument or faculty of one species of representative knowledge, the organon through which science is constructed from spontaneous data, whether those data be the spontaneous facts of presentation or the spontaneous processes of representation. All the faculties and operations of mind can be made the objects of contemplation and of study. If Mr. Morell, therefore, had said that our faculties of presentation include no power of reflection, that this belonged to the logical consciousness, he would have announced a truism, but a truism about as important in reference to the object he had in view as if he had said that memory and imagination belong to the understanding and not to intuition.

His third observation is, that "the knowledge we obtain by the intuitional consciousness is *material*, that which we gain by the logical consciousness is *formal*." Now formal, as opposed to material, amounts in our judgment to about the same thing as *nothing* in contrast to *something*. That the understanding is a complement of *formal* faculties, is a proposition which we not only are able to comprehend, but fully believe; that the *knowledge* we obtain by means of these faculties is *formal*, is a proposition which we frankly confess transcends our powers of thought: a *form* without *something* to which it is attached passes our comprehension. The matter of knowledge means, if it means anything, the *object* known. Now in intuition there is but a single object, which is apprehended in itself and as really existing; in the logical consciousness there is a double object—the act of the mind representing what is immediately and presentatively known, and the thing represented, which is mediately and remotely known. The *matter*, therefore, both in intuition and the logical consciousness, is ultimately the same; it is only differently related to the mind,—in the one case it stands before us face to face; in the other case it stands before us through the forms of the understanding. Hence it is sheer nonsense to speak of the logical consciousness as *matterless*, which is equivalent to saying that it *knows*, but knows *nothing*. Mr. Morell, though expressing great admiration of Sir William Hamilton's theory, in which we heartily unite with him, departs from it precisely in the points in which it is absolutely fatal to idealism.

His fourth observation is, that "the logical consciousness tends to *separation* (analysis), the intuitional consciousness tends to *unity* (synthesis)." Analysis and synthesis, in the proper acceptation of the terms, are both expressive of purely logical processes, the one being the reverse of the other. The idea of a *whole* is a logical conception, implying the relation of parts, and presupposing both analysis and synthesis as the condition of its being framed. The induction of Aristotle, for example, is a synthesis; the deduction, an analysis. Presentation may give us things in the *lump* or *mass*—a dead unity; but the separation and subsequent recomposition of parts are offices which belong exclusively to the understanding. Mr. Morell has admitted as much:[1] "Knowing," says he, "as we do too well, that the intuitions we obtain of truth in its concrete unity are not perfect, we seek to restore and verify that truth by *analysis*—*i. e.*, by separating it into its parts, viewing each of those parts abstractedly by itself, and finding out their relative consistency, so as to put them together, by a logical and reflective construction, into a systematic and formal *whole*. Hence the impulse to know the truth *aright* gives perpetual vitality and activity to the law by which our spontaneous and intuitional life passes over into the logical and reflective. Logical reasoning is the result of human imperfection struggling after intellectual restoration." This is well and sensibly said; and as it is a clear concession that the logical consciousness *tends to unity*—that the very end of its analysis is an adequate synthesis—we cannot but marvel that either of these functions should have been ascribed to intuition. Kant's reason, accordingly, which aimed at an all-comprehensive unity of existence, is simply the understanding moving in a higher sphere, and its regulative ideas nothing but the categories under a new name and translated

[1] Page 74.

to a different province. There is no distinction, according
to him, between the powers themselves or the *modes* of their
operation; they are conversant about different objects—
reason being to the conceptions of the understanding what
the understanding is to the intuitions of sense. Kant, too,
made his reason seek after its darling unity or totality of
being, through the same processes of generalization by
which the understanding reaches its lower unities and
separate totalities in the various departments of science.

The synthetic judgments of Kant, upon which Mr. Morell seems to have shaped his conceptions of synthesis, are
not instances of synthesis at all. They are amplifications
or extensions of our knowledge—they are new materials
added to the existing stock, and are either presentative or
mediate according to the circumstances under which they
are made. The discovery of new qualities in substances is,
of course, presentative; but what he denominates *synthetic
judgments a priori* involve only simple beliefs, the object
of the belief being unknown, as in the case of substance,
or an indirect and representative knowledge of the object
as given in its relations to the things which spontaneously
suggest it. In all cases in which the ultimate object *known*
is mediated and represented, in virtue of the essential constitution of the mind, upon occasions in which other objects
are the immediate data of consciousness, the process belongs,
according to the fundamental distinction of our author, to
the logical and not the intuitional consciousness: in these
cases there is a law of belief, necessary and indestructible,
which authenticates the premises of a syllogism, conducting
us logically, not presentatively, from what is given in experience to what experience is incapable of compassing, and
which, therefore, cannot be immediately known. We grant
that such judgments are *intuitive*—the grounds of belief
are in the very structure of the soul, they involve primary
and incomprehensible cognitions; but the objective realities
apprehended in virtue of these beliefs are not themselves
directly given in consciousness. They are conceptions of

the mind *necessitated* as vicarious of real existence. The conclusion of such a syllogism is not the simple assertory judgment of presentative intuition, Something *is*, but the imperative and necessary declaration of representative intuition, Something *must* be; it is not expressed by the formula, *Something is*, because it is actually apprehended in itself and as existing, but, Something *is*, because the mind is incapable of conceiving that it is *not*. The mind does not so much affirm the reality of existence as deny the impossibility of non-existence. This is the nature of the synthesis in that class of judgments to which Mr. Morell has referred; and how it differs from what all the world has been accustomed to regard as the logical process involved in *a posteriori* reasoning, we leave it to the Rationalists to determine.

Mr. Morell's fifth note of distinction is, that " the logical consciousness is *individual;* the intuitional consciousness is *generic.*" That is, if we understand our author, the truths about which the logical consciousness is conversant depend, in no degree, for the confirmation of their certainty, upon the common consent of mankind, while the truths about which the intuitional consciousness is conversant are to be received in consequence of the universal testimony of the race.

"We all feel conscious," says he, "that *there are* certain points of truth respecting which we can appeal to our own individual understanding with unerring certainty. No amount of contradiction, for example, no weight of opposing testimony from others, could ever shake our belief in the definitions and deductions of mathematical science or the conclusions of a purely logical syllogism. On the other hand, we are equally conscious, upon due consideration, that there are truths respecting which we *distrust* our individual judgment, and gain certainty in admitting them only from the concurring testimony of other minds. (Of this nature, for example, are the main points of moral and religious truth.) Hence it appears evident that there is within us both an individual and a generic element; and that answering to them there are truths for which we may appeal to the individual reason, and truths for which we must appeal to the testimony of mankind as a whole." [1]

[1] Page 70.

He then goes on to observe that "The ground of this twofold element in our constitution, and the reconciliation of the respective claims of the individual reason and the *common sense* of humanity, is easily explained when we take into account the distinction which we have been developing between the logical and the intuitional consciousness. It will be readily seen, upon a little consideration, that the logical consciousness is stamped with a perfect individualism—the intuitional consciousness with an equally universal or generic character. The logical consciousness, as we have shown, is *formal;* and it is in those branches of knowledge which turn upon formal definitions, distinctions and deductions (such as mathematics or logic) that we feel the most perfect trust in the certainty of our individual conclusions. The understanding, in fact, is framed so as to act on certain principles, which we may term *laws of thought*, and whatever knowledge depends upon the simple application of these laws, is as certain and infallible as human nature can possibly make it. The laws of thought (or, in other words, the logical understanding) present a *fixed element* in every individual man, so that the testimony of one sound mind, in this respect, is as good as a thousand. Were not the forms of reasoning, indeed, alike for all, there could no longer be any certain communication between man and man. The intuitional consciousness, on the other hand, is not formal, but material; and in gazing upon the actual elements of knowledge, our perception of their truth in all its fullness just depends upon the extent to which the intuitive faculty is awakened and matured. The *science* of music, for example, is absolutely the same for every *human understanding;* but the real perception of harmony, upon which the science depends as its material basis, turns entirely upon the extent to which the direct sensibility for harmony is awakened. And so it is with regard to every other subject which involves a direct element of supersensual truth. The intensity with which we realize it depends upon the state of our *intuitional consciousness*, so far, at least, as the subject in question is concerned. Here there are no fixed and uniform laws of intellection, as in the logical region, but a progressive intensity from the weakest up to the strongest power of spiritual vision or of intellectual sensibility."[1]

We shall need no apology to our readers for these long extracts, when they reflect that the distinction in question plays a very prominent part in the author's subsequent speculations, especially in relation to the origin and development of the religious life and the foundations and criterion of religious certitude. The whole force of the argument

[1] Pages 71, 72.

for that species of Realism which is involved in the
modern doctrine of progress, and which Leroux has so
eloquently expounded and the Socialists have so coarsely
practised, is here presented. The individual is nothing,
humanity is everything. The genus man is not a logical
abstraction, not a second intention, but a real, substantive
entity; and mankind is not the collection of all the individuals of the human race, but something which, though
inseparable, is yet distinct, and to which each is indebted
for his human character. Something of this sort seems to
be implied in making intuition a generic element, in contradistinction from understanding as personal and individual, and depending for its perfection, not upon the
culture of the individual, but upon the development of the
race. Something very like it is directly affirmed when
our author teaches that

"Intuition being a thing not formal, but material—not uniform, but
varying—not subject to rigid laws, but exposed to all the variations
of association and temperament, being, in fact, the *function of humanity*, and not of the individual mind—the only means of getting at the
essential elements of primary intuitional truth is to grasp that which
rests on the common sympathies of mankind in its historical development, after all individual impurities and idiosyncracies have been
entirely stripped away."[1]

But, bating the vein of Realism which pervades this and
the other passages we have quoted, the proposition of the
author, so far as it has sense, is, that the operations of the
understanding are as perfect in each individual as in the
whole race collectively, and that its deliverances cannot be
affected by an appeal to the testimony of mankind—that what
it pronounces to be true must be true to *us*, though all the
race should unite in contradicting it. We can never be
assured of the certainty of intuitional truth, however,
without comparing the deliverances of *our* consciousness
with the consciousness of other men; the touchstone of
certainty is universal consent. The understanding, in other

[1] Page 73.

words, vindicates to itself the absolute right of private judgment; the intuition appeals to the authority of catholic tradition. This is the thesis. The arguments are: 1st. That, in point of fact, the most certain truths, those about which we feel it impossible to doubt, are the truths of the understanding—he instances mathematics and logic. The example of logic is unfortunate. That science is not even yet perfect. There are sundry points upon which logicians are not agreed, and others intimately connected with the subject, to which hardly any attention has been paid. The Apodictic Syllogism has been thoroughly investigated, but will Mr. Morell venture to say the same of the Inductive? Will he pretend that any writer upon logic has kept steadily and consistently in view its distinctive character as a science of forms, and never interpolated or corrupted it with considerations of matter? As to mathematics, its conclusions are certain, and certain precisely because it deals with hypothesis and not with realities. But then it is a prodigious leap from the proposition that *some* truths are certain within the circle of the understanding, to the proposition that *all* truths peculiar to it are certain—that because it admits of demonstration at all, therefore it admits of nothing *but* demonstration. The same process of argument would establish the same result in regard to intuition. What can be more indubitable to us than our own personality, our indiscerptible identity, the existence of our thoughts, feelings and volitions? "No amount of contradiction, no weight of opposing testimony from others, could ever shake our belief" in the reality of the being which every man calls *himself*, or those processes of intellect which consciousness distinctly affirms. What human understanding can withhold its assent from the great laws of causality, substance, contradiction, and excluded middle? These are all intuitive truths—we receive them on the naked deliverance of consciousness; and we can no more deny them than we can annihilate ourselves. Certainty, therefore, is not *peculiar* to the understanding as contradistinguished from intui-

tion. But, says the author, *some* intuitional truths—those,
for example, of morals and religion—are *uncertain*, in so
far as we depend upon the single testimony of our own
minds. But are not some logical truths uncertain also?
Is everything demonstrative, reduced to apodictic certainty
in the *sciences* of morals, government, politics, chemistry,
botany and history? Is it not a characteristic of the evidence upon which the ordinary business of life is conducted
that it admits of every variety of degrees, from the lowest
presumption to the highest certainty? Is there no such
thing as a calculation of chances? and no such thing as
being deceived by logical deductions? The author somewhere tells us that the "purely logical mind, though dis-
playing great acuteness, yet is ofttimes involved in a mere
empty play upon words, forms and definitions; making
endless divisions and setting up the finest distinctions,
while the real matter of truth itself either escapes out of
these abstract moulds, or perchance was never in them." [1]
One would think, therefore, that it was not so infallible
after all. As, then, certainty is not restricted to the understanding, nor the understanding to it, the same ground of
appeal, from private judgment to the verdict of the race,
exists in reference to *its* deliverances which the author
postulates from the testimony of intuition. The argument
is valid for both or neither. 2dly. His next position is,
that the intuitional consciousness is susceptible of improvement, of education, development. The logical consciousness is fixed and unchanging. If we admit the fact, it is
not so easy to discover its pertinency as an argument, so
far as intuition is concerned. We may grant that if the
understanding is the *same* in all minds, the testimony of
one is as good as the testimony of a thousand; but it does
not appear that because the degrees of intuition are different
in different minds, therefore each mind must appeal to all
others before it can be certain of its own intuitions. One
man may see *less* than another, but it does not follow that

[1] Pages 16, 17.

he is dependent upon the testimony of that other for the
assurance that he sees the little that he *does* see. We cannot comprehend why *he* should not *know* that he sees what
he sees, however little it may be, as well as others know
that they see their more. But it is positively false that the
understanding is not susceptible of progress and improvement. The powers of reasoning and of representative
thought can be developed and educated—have their germ,
expansion and maturity—as well as the powers of intuition.
The laws of thought may be fixed, but the capacity of applying, or acting in obedience to, these laws is by no means
fixed. It is a capacity which requires *culture;* and the
multiplied instances of bad reasoning in the world—to which
our author has contributed his full proportion—are so many
proofs that man must be taught to reason and to think, as
well as to *know.* There is an immense difference betwixt
the logical consciousness of a Newton and of a Hottentot,
betwixt the logical consciousness of Newton at twelve and
Newton at fifty. These *laws* of thought are the same to
all men, and to the same men at all times, but the men
themselves are not the same. If these laws were always
faithfully observed, error might be avoided; but the amount
of truth that should be discovered would depend upon the
degree to which the faculties were developed, and not upon
the laws which preserve them from deceit. But unfortunately there is a proneness to intellectual guilt in transgress-
ing the laws of thought, which is as fruitful a source of
error as defect of capacity is of ignorance; and each is to
be remedied by a proper course of intellectual culture. But
if the argument from fixed laws proves the understanding
to be fixed and unchanging, it may be retorted with equal
force against the progressiveness of intuition. It is true
that Mr. Morell affirms that this form of intellection " has
no fixed and uniform laws ;" but this is an error arising
from the relation in which he apprehends that the laws or
forms of thought stand to representative cognitions. They
are the *conditions*, not the *matter*, of this species of intel-

ligence. They are not the *things* known, but the *means* of
knowing. They solve the problem of the possibility of
mediate knowledge. Now, corresponding to them, there
are, in all instances of representative cognition, *conditions*
in the thing known, which render it capable of being apprehended by the mind. The qualities, phenomena—properties which make it cognizable, make it capable of coming
within the sphere of consciousness—are laws of intuition as
certain and fixed as the relations of things to the mind.
In other words, the adaptations of things to our faculties
are as truly laws of intuition as the adaptations of our
faculties to *think* them are laws of the logical consciousness.
Hence, if the argument from the reality of laws cuts off
the understanding from an appeal to universal consent, it
cuts off intuition also, and we are shut up to private judgment in the one case by the same process which shuts us up
to it in the other. It is no distinction, consequently, betwixt the understanding and intuition, to say that the one
is individual and the other generic. They are both equally
individual, both equally generic; both belong to *every*
man, and therefore to all men; both may subsist in different degrees, in different men, and in the same men at
different times; and both are consequently susceptible of
education and improvement.

The truth is, Mr. Morell has entirely mistaken the purpose for which philosophers are accustomed to appeal from
private judgment to the general voice of mankind. It is
not to authenticate the deliverances of intuition—not to
certify us that we see when we see or know that we know;
our own consciousness is the only voucher which we can
have in the case. Every faculty is its own witness. In
the case of the understanding, others may point out fallacies
and guard against errors, but our *own minds* must perform
the process before there is any *logical truth* to us. In the
case of intuition, the voice of mankind cannot help us if
we are destitute of the power, or if it is unawakened, nor
add a particle to the degree of clearness with which we

apprehend existences, nor to the degree of certainty with which we repose upon the data of consciousness. Others may suggest the occasions upon which the intuitions shall arise or indicate the hindrances which prevent them; but the intuitions themselves are and must be the immediate grounds of belief. From the very nature of the case all truth must be individually apprehended, though all truth is not necessarily apprehended as individual. Private judgment is always and on all subjects the last appeal. Nothing is truth to *us*, whatever it may be in itself, until it is brought in relation to our own faculties, and the extent to which they grasp it is the sole measure of our knowledge. However, there is a question upon which an appeal to common consent is an indispensable means of guarding against error, misapprehension and mistake, and of rectifying inadequate, false or perverted judgments; but that question happens to be one which concerns directly the operations of the logical understanding. It is simply whether reflection exactly represents the spontaneous movements of the soul. The distinction betwixt reflection and spontaneity has been ably and happily illustrated by Cousin:

"To know without giving an account of our knowledge to ourselves; to know and to give an account of our knowledge to ourselves—this is the only possible difference between man and man; between the people and the philosopher. In the one, reason is altogether spontaneous; it seizes at first upon its objects, but without returning upon itself and demanding an account of its procedure; in the other, reflection is added to reason, but this reflection, in its most profound investigations, cannot add to natural reason a single element which it does not already possess; it can add to it nothing but the knowledge of itself. Again, I say reflection well directed—for if it be ill directed it does not comprehend natural reason in all its parts; it leaves out some element, and repairs its mutilations only by arbitrary inventions. First to omit, then to invent—this is the common vice of almost all systems of philosophy. The office of philosophy is to reproduce in its scientific formulas the pure faith of the human race—nothing less than this faith, nothing more than this faith—this faith alone, but this faith in all its parts."[1]

[1] Phil. Frag., Pref.

This is justly and beautifully said. It is assumed that all minds are essentially the same; and when the question is, What are the phenomena of consciousness, what are the laws, faculties and constitution of the soul? this question can only be answered by unfolding the nature of its spontaneous movements. In these the constitution of the intellect is seen. But from the fleeting, delicate and intangible nature of the phenomena, it is extremely difficult to reproduce them in reflection, and make them the objects of scientific study. It is no easy thing to reconstitute the intellectual life—"to re-enter," in the language of the distinguished philosopher just quoted—"to re-enter consciousness, and there, weaned from a systematic and exclusive spirit, to analyze thought into its elements, and all its elements, and to seek out in it the characters, and all the characters, under which it is at present manifested to the eye of consciousness." This is the office of reflection. As the phenomena which it proposes to describe are essentially the same in all minds, every man becomes a witness of the truth or falsehood of the description. Common consent is a criterion of certainty, because there is little possibility that all mankind should concur in a false statement of their own intellectual operations. It is particularly in regard to our original and primitive cognitions that this appeal to the race is accustomed to be made. One of the acknowledged peculiarities which distinguish them is the *necessity* of believing, and of this necessity universal agreement is an infallible proof. We wish to know whether any given principle is a primary and necessary datum of consciousness —whether it belongs essentially to intelligence; and this question is answered by showing that it is a characteristic of all minds. But in all cases in which reflection appeals to the testimony of the race, that testimony is not regarded as the immediate ground of faith, but as a corroborative proof that we have not fallen into error. It is the deliverance of consciousness which determines belief; and when it is found that every other consciousness gives the same

deliverance, we are satisfied that our reflection has not been
partial or defective. But if the voice of mankind is against
us, we feel that we have erred somewhere, and consequently
retrace our steps, analyze thought with greater minuteness
and attention; and thus make the verdict of the race the
occasion of reflection being led to correct itself. This is
the true nature of the appeal which a sound philosophy
makes to the testimony of mankind. The question is, What
are the phenomena of spontaneity? Reflection undertakes
to answer, and the answer is certified to be correct when all
in whom these phenomena are found concur in pronouncing
it to be true. Each man answers for himself from his own
consciousness, and the philosopher feels that there is no
further occasion to review his analysis. He has been led, for
example, to announce the existence of the external world
as an original datum of consciousness. He thinks he finds
in his belief of it that criterion of necessity which distinguishes primitive cognitions, but it is so hard to seize
upon the spontaneous phenomena of the mind with certainty and precision that he may mistake prejudice, association or an early judgment for an original belief. He
appeals to other minds; he finds the belief to be universal;
he is confirmed consequently in regarding it as necessary,
and therefore natural; and hence he is satisfied that reflection has, in this case, exactly described spontaneity. It
would appear, therefore, that instead of saying the intuitional consciousness is generic, and the logical, individual,
it would be much nearer the truth to assert that the *spontaneous* consciousness, in all its operations, whether intuitional or logical, is generic, or essentially the same in all
minds; and the *reflective*, individual, or modified by personal and accidental peculiarities. And this is precisely
the distinction which Cousin makes. Reason, which, with
him, is synonymous with intelligence, without regard to our
author's distinction of a twofold form, in its spontaneous
movements is impersonal; it is not mine nor yours; it belongs
not even to humanity itself; it is identical with God; and

upon the ground that "humanity as a mass is spontaneous and not reflective," he declares that "humanity is inspired." Reason, on the other hand, in its reflective movements, when its deliverances are made the object of attention, analysis and study, is subjective and personal, or rather appears to be so from its relations to reflection, while its general relations to the Ego, in which it has entered, renders it liable, though in itself infallible and absolute, to aberrations and mistakes. "Reflection, doubt and skepticism appertain to some men," such is his language; "pure apperception and spontaneous faith appertain to all; spontaneity is the genius of humanity, as philosophy is the genius of some men. In spontaneity there is scarcely any difference between man and man. Doubtless there are some natures, more or less happily endowed, in whom thought clears its way more easily, and inspiration manifests itself with more brightness; but, in the end, though with more or less energy, thought devlopes itself spontaneously in all thinking beings; and it is this identity of spontaneity, together with the identity of absolute faith it engenders, which constitutes the identity of human kind." The distinction here indicated is just and natural, but it is very far from the distinction signalized by our author.

His sixth and final observation, that "the logical consciousness is fixed through all ages, the intuitional consciousness *progressive*," is but a consequence of his positions which we have just been discussing. We need only detain the reader to remark that the author has evidently confounded the progress or education of the *faculties* with the progress and improvement of society. The probability is, that among any cultivated people the degree to which mind is developed is not essentially different in one age from what it is in another. The thinkers of the present generation, for example, have no greater capacity of thought than the Greek philosophers, the Schoolmen, or the philosophers and divines of the sixteenth, seventeenth and eighteenth centuries. The present age may *know* more, in consequence of the

labours of those that have preceded; but as its greater
amount of knowledge, under the circumstances of the case,
involves no greater amount of effort, and as it is healthful
exercise, and not the number or variety of objects that
elicit it, which developes the mind, society may be in advance in point of knowledge—the standard of general
intelligence may be higher—while yet the standard of intellectual vigour and maturity may be essentially the same.
The tyro now begins where Newton left off, but it does
not follow that because he begins there he has the capacities
or intellectual strength of Newton. All generations, men-
tally considered, are very much upon a level. Every man
has to pass through the same periods of infancy, childhood
and youth; but in reference to the *objects* which occupy
attention, each successive age may profit by the labours of
its predecessors, and thus make superior attainments in
knowledge without a corresponding superiority of mental
intensity or power. The progress of society, therefore, is
not due, as Mr. Morell seems to intimate, to the progress
of intuition; it is not that we have *better faculties* than our
fathers, but that we employ them under better advantages.
Their eyes were as good as ours, but we stand upon a mountain. We need not add that we have no sympathy with
the mystic Realism which dreams of a destiny of humanity
apart from the destiny of the individuals who compose the
race—a destiny to which every generation is working up,
and which is yet to be enjoyed only by the last, or by those
in the last stage of development. We can hardly comprehend how that can be a destiny of *humanity* in which immense multitudes, to whom that humanity belongs, have no
immediate share, and to which they stand in no other relation than that of precursors and contributors. Least of all
do we believe that any progressive development of human
nature *as it is* will ever conduct any individual to that condition of excellence in which the " whole sensibilities of his
nature " are brought " into harmony with the Divine—with
the life of God." This consummation requires a transfor-

mation as well as education, renovation as well as progress.
We must be new creatures in Christ Jesus before we can
be partakers of a Divine nature.

Having explained the distinctions betwixt the logical
and intuitional consciousness, Mr. Morell proceeds to expound their connection and dependence. He represents
"logical reasoning as the result of human imperfection
struggling after intellectual restoration." The case is this:
The harmony of our nature with moral, intellectual and
religious truth has been disturbed and deranged, and the
consequence is "that the power of intuition is at once
diminished and rendered uncertain. The reality of things,
instead of picturing itself, as it were, upon the calm sur-
face of the soul, casts its reflection upon a mind disturbed
by evil, by passion, by prejudice, by a thousand other influences which distort the image, and tend to efface it
altogether." To correct our defective and imperfect intuitions we resort to the double processes of analysis and
synthesis. We separate the parts, compare them with each
other, and, from the perception of their consistencies and
adaptations, reconstruct our knowledge into a logical
whole, which shall more faithfully correspond to reality
than the original intuitions themselves. Upon this remarkable statement we hope to be indulged in a few observations.

As logical or representative truth is based upon and necessarily presupposes presentative, it never can be more certain than intuition. Demonstration is strictly an intuitive
process. In the pure mathematics the conceptions involved
in the definitions which are the subject matter of the
reasoning are not regarded as *representative;* they are the
things, and the only *things,* to which reference is had; and
every step in every demonstration is a direct gazing upon
some property or content of these conceptions. As the
logical consciousness only reproduces the elementary cognitions of intuition, it can add nothing to them; it can
neither increase their intensity, remove their obscurity, nor

directly reduce them to consistency. It must faithfully represent them just as they are. Inconsistencies in our reflective exhibitions of truth may indeed send us back to our original intuitions and make us repeat the occasions on which they are produced, so that we may question them with more minuteness and attention; but it is not the *intuitions* which we suppose to be defective, but our *accounts* of them. We seek to correct the inadequacies of memory by the completeness of consciousness. If a man's powers of intuition, therefore, are deranged upon any subject, no processes of ratiocination will cure him. Logic is neither eyes to the blind nor ears to the deaf. And if a man is destitute of the moral faculty, reasoning will be utterly incompetent to put him in possession of the notions of right, duty and obligation; or if his intuitional faculties are defective and disordered, he can only reason upon the defective and distorted conceptions which faithfully represent them. He can never have clearer notions till he is furnished with sounder faculties. It is true that logical exposition may be the means of awakening, developing and maturing intuitions; but then the logical expositions must come from others who have actually had the intuitions described, or from the God that made us. They cannot come from the man to be awakened. So that *his* logical consciousness cannot stand to *his* intuitional in this relation of a help. We cannot comprehend how Mr. Morell, without departing from every principle which he has previously laid down, and upon which as occasion requires he is not backward to insist, should represent the logical understanding as a remedy for dimness of vision. Did Adam have no understanding before the fall? Are the angels without it? and shall we drop it at death? Is it an endowment vouchsafed to the race only in consequence of the moral confusion and disorder which have supervened from sin, and are we to look to it as the Holy Spirit by which we are to be renovated and saved?

The true view of the subject we apprehend to be, that

the understanding is designed not to cure the disorders and remedy the imperfections, but to *supplement* the defects, of the intuitional faculties. It is the complement of intuition. Finite and limited as we are, presentative knowledge can extend but a little way; and the office of the understanding is to stretch our knowledge beyond the circle of our vision. We are so constituted that what we see shall be made the means of revealing more than we see. Presentation and Representation, Intuition, Induction and Inference are all instruments of *knowing;* and by virtue of the constitution they describe, man is able to penetrate beyond the limits of time and space to which consciousness is evidently restricted. It is, therefore, distinctly to add to his knowledge, to complete his constitution as an intelligent creature, that God has given him understanding. It is true the necessity of an understanding implies defect—intuition is the highest form of knowledge—but it is a defect which attaches to all finite creatures. They must either supplement intuition by inference, or their knowledge must be limited in time and space to the sphere of their personality. It belongs to the omnipresent God alone, as He is uncircumscribed in His being, to embrace all things in a single glance of unerring intuition. Creatures, however glorious and exalted, from the very limitation implied in being creatures, can never dispense with the faculties of mediate and representative cognition; this is the law of their condition; and a fundamental error which pervades Mr. Morell's whole account of the understanding is, that it is *not* a faculty of knowledge. Had he, in this point, risen above the philosophy of Kant, many of the paradoxes and inconsistencies of his treatise might have been obviously avoided. He professes to be a Natural Realist, and as such contends, and very properly contends, that we have faculties by which we can immediately apprehend existences; but his theory of the understanding, instead of being constructed in harmony with this hypothesis, instead of making it that complement of powers by which the mind can represent to itself the properties and qualities of absent objects, instead of treating its categories and forms as the conditions in conformity to which its representations shall be adequate and just, has made it the organ of the rankest delusions, of the most contemptible and puerile trifling.

Our author takes occasion to caution his readers, "in the outset, against the supposition that the distinction" which he has elaborately expanded between the intuitional and logical consciousness "is anything at all novel in the history of mental philosophy. So far from it," he affirms, "that it is almost as universal as philosophy itself, lying alike patent both in ancient and modern speculation."[1] This we cannot but regard as a mistake. Our acquaintance with the history of philosophy is small, but we know of no writer previously to Kant who took precisely the same views of the nature, office and operations of the understanding; and we know of no writer but Mr. Morell who has restricted reason or intuition exclusively to the faculties of presentative cognition. It would require more space than we can at present devote to the subject to discuss his ancient authorities, but we cannot forbear a word upon his modern examples. To begin with Kant: we very frankly confess that in his Critical Philosophy we never could distinguish betwixt the operations or *modes* of action which he ascribes to reason and those which he attributes to the understanding. They seem to us to be exactly the same faculty, or complement of faculties, employed about different objects, and in this opinion we are confirmed by an authority which it is seldom safe to contradict. "In the Kantian philosophy," says Sir William Hamilton, "both faculties perform the same function, both seek the one in many, the idea (*idee*) is only the conception (*begriffe*) sublimated into the inconceivable, reason only the understanding which has overleaped itself." Intellect directed to the objects beyond the domain of experience is the Kantian reason; within the domain of experience, the Kantian under-

[1] Page 27.

standing. Intellect in search of scientific unity is understanding; in search of absolute unity, the reason. Employed about the finite, limited, contingent, it is understanding; employed about the correlatives, the absolute, infinite, necessary, it is reason. Or, in one word, as the faculty of the *conditioned* it is understanding; as the faculty of the *unconditioned* it is reason. But if the science of contraries be one, the faculty in each case as an intellectual power must be the same. There is, accordingly, a much closer correspondence between Mr. Morell's logical consciousness and Kant's speculative reason than between Kant's reason and Mr. Morell's intuition; and Mr. Morell's intuition, in turn, is much more analogous to Kant's sensibility than to his reason. Mr. Morell's intuition is the presentative knowledge of supersensible realities. Kant pronounced all such knowledge to be a sheer delusion. Mr. Morell's intuition is exclusive of analysis. Kant's reason reaches its highest unity through processes of generalization. Mr. Morell's intuition has no fixed and permanent laws. Kant's reason has its *ideas* as his understanding its categories. Between Kant's *practical* reason and Mr. Morell's intuition there are some striking points of correspondence, but they are points in which Mr. Morell is inconsistent with himself. Both attribute our firm conviction of the Divine existence and of a future life to our spiritual cravings and the authoritative nature of conscience; but, in thus representing them as a *want* on the one hand and an *implication* on the other, our author abandons his fundamental principle that in intuition the object reveals itself.

Neither is Mr. Morell's intuition precisely the same with the principles of common sense or the fundamental laws of belief of the Scottish school. These were not faculties *presentative* of their objects, but vouchers of the reality of knowledge; and as to the Eclectics, they make no such distinction between reason and understanding as that signalized by Kant, Coleridge and our author, but treat the categories and ideas promiscuously as laws of reason or intelligence. "The one catholic and perennial philosophy, notwithstanding many schismatic aberrations," is not that all objective certainty depends upon the actual presentation of its realities, and that the understanding cannot conduct us beyond the circle of sensibility, but that all knowledge is ultimately founded on faith, and "the objective certainty of science upon the subjective necessity of believing." If Mr. Morell had meant by intuition nothing more than "the complement of those cognitions or principles which we receive from nature, which all men therefore possess in common, and by which they test the truth of knowledge and the morality of actions," or, if he had defined it simply as the faculty of such principles, we should have regarded him in this matter beyond the reach of any just exceptions. But this is not his doctrine.

The importance of the points upon which we have been insisting will appear from their application to the great problems of Religion. What is God? What vouchers have we for the objective certainty of His being? What kind of intercourse can be maintained betwixt Him and His creatures? These are questions which will be variously answered according to varying views of the nature and extent of human knowledge, and the offices and operations of the human faculties. We have already seen that, in describing the developments of the higher stages of the intuitional consciousness, Mr. Morell has confounded the intuition of a principle with the presentation of an object, representing our *inference* in relation to the Divine existence, authenticated by the necessary law of causation, as a direct perception of the Deity Himself. His language in many places will bear the interpretation that our knowledge of God is intuitive only in so far as it rests upon original principles of belief; but there are other passages in which he unquestionably teaches that God reveals Himself as an immediate datum of consciousness, and that we know Him in Himself precisely as we know the phenomena of matter or the operations of mind. These two sets

of statements are really inconsistent—an unjustifiable confusion of intuition and presentation—but it is easy to see
how they have arisen in the Rationalistic school.   The law
of substance has been marvellously confounded with the law
of causality, and an *inference* from an effect to its cause has,
accordingly, been treated as a perception of the relation of
a quality to a substance.   The proof of a cause has, in
other words, been taken for the presentation of a substance,
on the ground that the effect is a phenomenon which, as it
cannot *exist*, cannot be *perceived* apart from its substratum or
"fundamental essence."   To affirm, therefore, in consistency
with these principles, that the external world and ourselves
are a series of effects, is simply to affirm that they are a
series of phenomena which must inhere ,in some common
substance, and of which they are to be regarded as the
manifestations.   "In my opinion," says Cousin, "all the
laws of thought may be reduced to two—namely, the law
of causality, and that of substance.   These are two essential and fundamental laws, of which all others are only
derivatives, developed in an order by no means arbitrary."
Having shown that these two fundamental laws of thought
are absolute, he proceeds to reduce them to identity : "An
absolute cause and an absolute substance are identical in
essence, since every absolute cause must be substance in so
far as it is absolute, and every absolute substance must be
cause in order to be able to manifest itself."   To reduce
causality to substantive being, and effects to phenomenal
manifestations, is to deny the possibility of a real creation.
Substances *as* such cannot be relative and contingent : to
make them *effects* is to make them phenomena.   There can,
therefore, be but one *substance* in the universe, and all that
we have been accustomed to regard as the *works* of God are
only developments to consciousness of the Divine Being
Himself.   The world stands to Him in the same relation in
which thought and volition stand to our own minds.   This
is the necessary result of confounding causation with substance, and yet this is what Mr. Morell has done, and what

his psychology absolutely demanded to save it from self-contradiction. At one time we find him ascending, by virtue of the law of causality, from the finite, contingent and dependent to the infinite, necessary, self-existent, from effects to their causes, in the very track of the argument which he affects to despise. He finds God, not in Himself, but in His creatures. At another time, "in loftier moments of contemplation," he seems to stand upon the verge of infinity, and to gaze upon "Being (substance) in its essence, its unity, its self-existent eternity." At one time the great problem of reason is to discover the power and wisdom which gave the world its being and impressed upon nature its laws; at another "*to find the one fundamental essence* by which" all things are upheld. At one time, in a single word, God is contemplated and known as the *cause*, at another as the *substance*, of all that exists. This confusion pervades the book, and is constantly obtruded upon us in that offensive form which makes the Deity nothing but the bond of union or the principle of co-existence to His creatures. This is the plain meaning of all that eternal cant about "totality and absolute unity," about the tendency of reason to *synthesis*, which is echoed and re-echoed in various forms without any apparent consciousness of its wickedness, blasphemy and contradiction. The whole doctrine of the absolute which has played so conspicuous a part in German speculations turns upon this blunder. To get at the *cause* of all things is only to get at the *substance* in which all inhere and coexist—to get at *Being* in its necessary and fundamental laws, which, of course, would give all its manifestations.

Those who wish to see what this philosophy has achieved in other hands will do well to consult the pages of Mr. Morell on the systems of Fichte, Schelling and Hegel; and those who would appreciate its pretensions to truth and consistency would do well to study the masterly article of Sir William Hamilton upon the Eclectic Scheme of Cousin. We shall add here only a few reflections, that the reader may distinctly see where Mr. Morell's principles would conduct him.

In the first place, Deity, as absolute substance, is necessarily *impersonal*. The idea of individuality, or of separate and distinct existence, is indispensable to our conception of a Person. But *absolute Being* has no distinct existence; to distinguish is to condition it—to make it *a* being, and a being of such and such qualities, which is to destroy its absoluteness. In the next place, it obviously follows that *everything is God and God is everything*. As absolute being He is the generative principle of being in all that exists. He is their *essence*—that upon which their *esse* depends, and without which they would be mere shadows and illusions. Just as far as anything really exists, just so far it is God. He is the formal and distinguishing ingredient of its nature as an entity or existence.

Hence, it deserves further to be remarked that there can *be no such thing as real causation*. The law of substance is made to abrogate the law of causality. The absolute is not a *productive*, but a *constitutive*, principle—a fundamental element or condition, but not an *efficient* of existence. It is no more a cause in the sense in which the constitution of our nature determines us to apprehend the relation, than body is the cause of extension, mind the cause of thought, or the sun the cause of light. Absolute beauty, for example, is not the creator, but the essential element, of all particular beauties; absolute right is not the producer, but an indispensable constituent, of all particular rectitude; and absolute Being is not the maker, but the necessary ingredient or characteristic principle, of every particular being. There is then no creation, no maker of heaven and earth, no father of the spirits, nor former of the bodies of men. There is simply *ens reale*, from which what we call creatures emanate, as its properties and adjuncts. This doctrine is unblushingly avowed by the great master of the Eclectic School; and it is deeply imbedded in everything that Mr. Morell has said of the relations of the Deity to

the world. We need not say that a philosophy which contradicts a fundamental principle of belief, which denies the
law of causality, or, what is the same, absorbs it in another
and a different law, is self-condemned.

We affirm finally that every form in which the philosophy of the Absolute ever has been, and, we venture to
say, ever can be, proposed, necessarily *leads to nihilism*—
the absolute annihilation of the possibility of knowledge.
The very notion of the absolute is inconsistent with the
conditions of knowledge. Merging all difference in identity, and all variety in unity, it is evidently incompatible
with the nature of consciousness, which evidently implies,
as Cousin has lucidly explained, plurality and difference.
The only consistent hypothesis is the intellectual intuition
of Schelling, "in which there exists no distinction of subject and object—no contrast of knowledge and existence;
all difference is lost in absolute indifference—all plurality in
absolute unity. The intuition itself, reason and the absolute
are identical." But consistency is here evidently maintained
at the sacrifice of the possibility of thought. Fichte, though
his confidence in his system was so strong that he staked
his everlasting salvation on the truth of even its subordinate
features, yet confesses that it was, after all, a mere tissue of
delusions.

"The sum-total," says he, "is this: there is absolutely nothing
permanent, either without me or within me, but only an unceasing
change. I know absolutely nothing of any existence, not even my
own. I, myself, know nothing, and am nothing. Images there are—
they constitute all that apparently exists, and what they know of themselves is after the manner of images; images that pass and vanish
without there being aught to witness their transition; that consist
in fact of the images of images—without significance and without an
aim. I, myself, am one of these images; nay I am not even thus
much, but only a confused image of images. All reality is converted
into a marvellous dream, without a life to dream of, and without a
mind to dream—into a dream made up only of a dream of itself.
Perception is a dream—thought, the source of all the existence and
all the reality which I imagine to myself of *my* existence, of my power,
of my destination, is the dream of that dream."

Melancholy confession! God grant that it may serve as an awful warning to those who, with presumptuous confidence, would plunge into the fathomless abyss of the Absolute!

The certainty of God's existence rests upon no such flimsy speculations. Through the indestructible principles which are not merely, as Kant supposed, regulative laws of thought, but guarantees for the objective realities to which they conduct us, we have an assurance for the Divine existence which cannot be gainsayed without making our nature a lie. Reason conducts us to God—its laws vouch for His existence, but it is in the way of inference from what passes around us and within us. He has so constituted the human mind that all nature shall be a witness for Himself. Everything is inexplicable until He is acknowledged. But we know Him, and can know Him, only *mediately*. We spell out the syllables which record His Name as they are found in earth, in heaven and in ourselves. What is *presentatively* given is not the Almighty, but His works; but reason, from the very nature of its laws, cannot apprehend His works without the irresistible conviction that He is. The principles are intuitive by which we ascend from nature to its Author, but the substance of the Godhead never stands before us face to face as an object of vision, though these deductions of reason are felt to have an objective validity independent of the subjective necessity of believing.

Let it be granted that our knowledge of God is mediate, and that the understanding is a faculty of cognition, and the whole groundwork of Mr. Morell's system is swept away. All that remains to prove that the logical consciousness may be an adequate medium of revelation and a competent instrument of religion is to indicate the fact that through its representative conceptions it can reproduce every emotion which the original intuitions could excite. The copy can awaken all the feelings of the original. Vivid description may produce the effects of vision. The peculiar emotions of religion, consequently, are not dependent upon the power of gazing upon its actual realities. If they can be embodied so as to produce what Lord Kames denominates ideal presence, the result may be the same as if the presence were real. To this principle painting, poetry and oratory owe their power to stir the depths of the human soul—to rule like a wizard the world of the heart, to call up its sunshine or draw down its showers.

The remaining portions of the book we must reserve for another opportunity.

SECTION III.

REVELATION AND RELIGION.

THE Apostle Paul, writing to the Romans, says, "So then faith cometh by hearing, and hearing by the Word of God." In these words he first states in what the essence of a sinner's religion consists, and then how it is produced. The essence of this religion, as plainly appears from the context, he makes to be Faith in Jesus Christ. "If thou shalt confess with thy mouth the Lord Jesus, and shalt believe in thine heart that God hath raised him from the dead, thou shalt be saved. For with the heart man believeth unto righteousness, and with the mouth confession is made unto salvation." As if anxious to avoid the imputation of novelty, and to show that he taught nothing but what was contained in the lively Oracles of God, the Apostle appeals in confirmation of his doctrine to the testimony of an ancient Prophet. "For the Scripture saith, Whosoever believeth on him shall not be ashamed." I must call your especial attention to the manner in which Paul applies this passage to the case of the Gentiles, as it furnishes a strong incidental proof of his profound conviction that the very words of Scripture were the words of the Holy Ghost. He knew nothing of an inspiration of the Spirit as contradistinguished from an inspiration of the letter, and consequently does not scruple to build an argument upon a single expression, when that expression is the language of a Prophet. Because the Scripture saith *whosoever*, without limitation or restriction, the Apostle concludes that there is no difference between the Jew and the Greek. This term equally includes them both, and he accordingly has no hesitation in drawing the infer-

153

ence that "the same Lord over all is rich unto all that call
upon him." It is to be received as an universal proposition,
true in all cases and under all circumstances, and that upon
the force of a single term, that "Whosoever shall call upon
the name of the Lord shall be saved."

The religion of a sinner being compendiously embraced
by the Apostle under the head of Faith, the question arises,
How is this faith produced? The successive steps of the
process are first expanded in a series of forcible and pungent
interrogatories, and then recapitulated in this solemn language: "How then shall they call on Him in whom they
have not believed? and how shall they believe in Him of
whom they have not heard? and how shall they hear without a preacher? and how shall they preach except they be
sent?" That is, in order to the existence of faith there must
be a Divine testimony. The Word of God is its standard
and measure. That this testimony may produce faith, it
must be known—it must be imparted from without; it is
not the offspring of our own cogitations, nor the product of
our own thoughts; it comes to us in the form of a report.
But in order that it may be proposed and communicated,
there must be persons commissioned for the purpose; there
must be Apostles—men, in other words, to whom the Word
of the Lord is entrusted. This then is the Divine arrangement. A class of men is to be put in charge of that which
is to be the object of faith; this is Inspiration. They
report to others the Word of the Lord; this is Revelation;
and this report is the medium through which a saving Faith
is engendered. "So then faith cometh by hearing, and
hearing by the Word of God." Inspiration gives rise to
revelation, revelation to faith, and faith is the sum and substance of religion. If you ask the Apostle what it is to be
inspired, he briefly answers that it is to be sent with a message from God; if you ask him what he means by revelation, he as promptly replies that it is the Divine message
delivered; and if you inquire of him in regard to man's
duty, it is, compendiously, to believe the report. This is his

philosophy of religion : God sends; Apostles report; men believe.

But, simple and consistent as it seems, this account, we are told, is in palpable contradiction to the very nature of religion and the fundamental laws of the human mind. We are accordingly furnished with a theory drawn from a deeper philosophy than Prophets or Apostles ever knew, which, under the pretence of emancipating us from the bondage of the letter and giving free scope to the liberty of the spirit, has left us nothing of Christianity but the name. A revelation which reports the testimony of God, and the faith which believes it because it is His testimony, are both discarded as psychological absurdities; and as to the idea that any men or set of men have ever been commissioned to speak to others in the name of the Lord, and to challenge submission to their message on the ground of the Divine authority which attests it, this is scouted as "of all our vanities the motliest, the merest word that ever fooled the ear from out the Schoolman's jargon." The issues involved in this controversy are momentous. It is not a question about words and names ; it is a question which involves the very foundations of Christianity. These insidious efforts to undermine the authority of the Bible and to remove an external, infallible standard of faith, however disguised in the covert of philosophy, are prompted by a deep and inveterate opposition to the doctrines of the Cross. The design is to destroy the religion, and hence the fury of the efforts against the citadel in which it is lodged. It is not the casket, but the jewel, that has raised all this clamour of rancorous opposition ; and when men cry, Down with the Bible ! the real meaning of their rage is, Away with Jesus and His Cross ! Vain is all their opposition, vain the combination of philosophers and sophists; He that sitteth in the heavens shall laugh, the Lord shall have them in derision ; He hath set His Son upon the holy hill of Zion, and there he must reign until He has put down all His enemies under His feet.

The new theory of religion—I call it new, not because

any of its fundamental principles are new, they are only old errors in a new dress, but because it is supported upon new grounds—this new theory of religion I propose briefly to consider in contrast with the testimony of Paul, so that it may be seen to be untenable, even on the principles of the metaphysical philosophy behind which it has entrenched itself.

I. I shall begin with the new theory of Revelation, as the discussion of that will lead me to say all that I deem important upon the present occasion on the nature and essence of religion.

"The idea of revelation," we are told by the writer whom I have in view, "always implies a process by which knowledge, in some form or other, is communicated to an intelligent being. For a revelation at all to exist there must be an intelligent being, on the one hand, adapted to receive it, and there must be, on the other hand, a process by which this same intelligent being becomes cognizant of certain facts or ideas. Suppress either of these conditions, and no revelation can exist. The preaching of an angel would be no revelation to an idiot—a Bible in Chinese would offer none to a European. In the former case, there is no intelligence capable of receiving the ideas conveyed; in the latter case, the process of conveyance renders the whole thing practically a nonentity by allowing no idea whatever to reach the mind. We may say then, in a few words, that a revelation always indicates *a mode of intelligence.*"[1]

From this passage we see the necessity of being on our guard against the ambiguity of words. It is perhaps unfortunate that a term which in its strict and proper acceptation applies only to a part of the contents of the Sacred Volume, should have been, as in the language of theology it confessedly has been, applied to the whole canon of faith. The Scriptures themselves denominate nothing revelations but those supernatural mysteries which lie beyond the province of reason, which eye hath not seen nor ear heard, and which

---

[1] Morell's Phil. Rel., pp. 123, 124, Eng. Ed.

could not be known independently of the supernatural teaching of the Spirit. When they speak of themselves as a whole they are designated simply by some title which indicates that they are the Word of God. This is the phrase which Paul employs in writing to the Romans, and employs in the same sense in which popular usage applies *revelation*.

It is little worthy of the dignity and candour of philosophy to construct an argument upon a verbal quibble. Revelation as synonymous with the standard of faith and as covering the whole contents of Scripture, without reference to the distinction of the natural and supernatural, is not so much a mode of intelligence as a ground of belief. Its office is not subjective, but objective. It is not *in* the mind, but *to* the mind. The simplest notion that we can form of it is that it is a message from God. Its work is done when it reports what He says. What distinguishes *revealed* truth from every other species of truth is not its nature, not its object-matter, but the immediate ground of credibility. It is the measure of faith; and the argument of faith is, Thus saith the Lord. The characteristic of revelation, in the generic sense in which it is applied to the canon, is, that it contains, or rather is, a Divine testimony, and this testimony must be the immediate ground of belief—I say the *immediate ground* of belief, because the ultimate and final basis of truth in every case is the faithfulness of God in the structure of our mental constitution. We believe the reports of our senses and the data of consciousness because the constitution of our nature is such that we cannot do otherwise; but when we are asked how we know that our faculties do not deceive us, we can only appeal to the moral character of Him who has wrought these laws of belief into the very texture of our frames. But in these cases the immediate grounds of belief are found in our faculties themselves. It is ourselves that we first trust, and not God. Such truths may be discoveries, but they are not revelations; they may be clear, distinct, unquestionable, but they are not Divine. We receive them either because they are self-evident and need

no proof, or because we are able to prove them, and not
because God appears as a witness in their behalf. Revelation and a Divine testimony are one and the same thing.
How this testimony shall be received and what effects it
shall produce, whether men shall understand it or not,
whether it shall really awaken any ideas in their. minds or
create any emotions in their hearts,—these are matters which,
however important in themselves, do not at all affect the
question whether it is really a message from God. It may
be admitted that a revelation to an idiot or in an unknown
tongue, where no adequate provision was made for removing the impediments to an apprehension of its contents,
would be very senseless and absurd. But such a message
being supposed, the question whether it *is* a revelation is one
thing, and whether it is wise and judicious is another; and
in a philosophical discussion things that are separate ought
to be kept distinct.

This adroit play upon the ambiguity of the term *revelation*, in which it is made to be a mode of intelligence rather
than the measure of a Divine faith, is the corner-stone upon
which the author's whole theory of the nature and grounds
of religious truth is erected.

It is unnecessary to give a detailed account of the process
by which revelation is distinguished; it will be enough to
seize upon his fundamental principle and expose its fallacy.
His doctrine is briefly this, that revelation is a species of
intuition in which things authenticate themselves. The
realities of religion are brought directly into contact with
the mind and vouch for their own existence, just as the
material world and the forms of beauty and of virtue are
their own witnesses. We know the things that are freely
given us of God, not by the testimony of His Spirit, but
the immediate consciousness of their presence. Revelation
is a spiritual perception in which we see the invisible, and
stand face to face with the infinite and eternal. Its objects
are presented to us by God, but in no other sense than He
presents the objects of all other knowledge. The rocks,

mountains, caves and valleys of the material world, the
heavens above us and the earth beneath, are as really and
truly a revelation from Him and in the same essential sense
as the Person, offices and work of His own eternal Son.
Faith is vision, and the actual presentation of its objects its
only standard and measure.   In conformity with these
views inspiration is represented as a subjective process in
which God adapts the mind to the objects presented in revelation.   It is a clearing of the spiritual sight, a strengthening of the spiritual eye, "an especial influence wrought upon
the faculties of the subject, by virtue of which he is able to
grasp these realities in their perfect fullness and integrity.
Revelation and Inspiration, then, indicate," we are told,
"one united process, the result of which upon the human
mind is to produce a state of spiritual intuition, whose phenomena are so extraordinary that we at once separate the
agency by which they are produced from any of the ordinary principles of human development.   And yet this
agency is applied in perfect consistency with the laws and
natural operations of our spiritual nature.   Inspiration does
not imply anything generically new in the actual processes
of the human mind.   It does not involve any form of intelligence essentially different from what we already possess.
It indicates rather the elevation of the religious consciousness, and with it, of course, the power of spiritual vision,
to a degree of intensity peculiar to the individuals thus
highly favoured by God."[1]

This might be taken as a caricature of the work of the
Spirit in the effectual calling of God's children, were it not
that the author has taken special pains to show that there
can be no other kind of inspiration, without contradiction
to the laws of mind, but that which he has described.   His
inspiration is, in many respects, analogous to the saving
operations of the Spirit.   It enables its subject to understand revelation; brings him into harmony with Divine
truth; subdues the passions; represses the influence of

[1] Morell, p. 151.

sense and sanctifies the heart. It evidently stands in the same relation to his *revelation* that the regenerating and enlightening influences of grace sustain to the Scriptures of God. But an inspiration which gives rise to a revelation, which commits a message from the Holy One to the hands of men, which ends in a Divine testimony as the standard and measure of a Divine faith, he can by no means abide. The objects of religion must authenticate themselves. The consequence is, that every man, in so far as he is religious, is inspired, and "every man has his doctrine and his psalm." The inconsistency of these views with the uniform and pervading testimony of the Scriptures must strike the dullest apprehension. Paul, as we saw, solemnly declares that faith comes by hearing; this new philosophy affirms that it comes by vision. Paul declares that the immediate ground of belief is the testimony of God; this new philosophy, that it is found in the things themselves. Paul declares that inspiration imparts to men a Divine message; this new philosophy, that it purges the mind. Paul declares that it is restricted to Apostles; the new philosophy, that it is the property of the race.

All these enormous and palpable contradictions of Scripture have sprung from the gratuitous assumption that revelation is a mode of intelligence, a process of our own minds, and not an extraordinary message of God. Taking it for granted that it is nothing more than an exercise of our natural faculties in some form of cognition, the author proceeds to conclude from the laws of the disjunctive syllogism that it must be intuitive. He acknowledges but two modes of intelligence, and to one or the other of these it must belong. It cannot be a process of ratiocination; no rules of logic, no powers of combination and analysis, no force of words nor ingenuity of inference could ever have evolved the scheme of redemption or the sublime mysteries of the Cross. There are elements embraced in religion which it never could have entered the heart of man to conceive. It introduces us, in a high and sublime sense, into a

new world, exalts us to new conceptions, and unveils to us
glories beyond the suggestion of mortal thought. It bears
upon its face impressions of originality and novelty which
remove it beyond the sphere of the logical understanding,
and carry convincing evidence that, however it came, it
never could have been excogitated. This reasoning has a
show of plausibility. It labours, however, under one fatal
defect—the disjunction can be easily retorted. It is as easy
to show, on the one hand, that Christianity, as a whole,
never could have been intuitive, as it is to prove, on the
other, that it never could have been the offspring of logic.
It involves relations and dependencies which could only
have been adjusted by powers of combination. It is not a
single concrete reality, like a man, a mountain or a tree,
but a connected scheme of events, every one of them contingent in relation to our knowledge, and concatenated into
a system which cannot be grasped without calling into play
all the powers of the logical understanding. It is a system
which pre-eminently requires reasoning—a comprehensive
view of great moral principles as they are involved and
illustrated in a wonderful series of facts. What then? It
cannot be intuitional, it cannot be logical. One would
think that this obvious *reductio ad absurdum* would have
been sufficient to open the mind of a philosopher to the
fallacy of his fundamental principle. No wonder that subjective religionists hate logic; it makes sad havoc with
their finest speculations.

The notion that revelation is a mode of intelligence,
which, in plainer terms, means that it a faculty of the
human mind, is the parent or child—it is hard to say
which is the first in order of nature—of a still more serious mistake in reference to the nature of religious truth
and the peculiarities of Christian experience. This double
misconception has concealed from the author the palpable
incongruities of his system, and induced him to believe that
the doctrines of grace might be pressed to the support of
an hypothesis which, legitimately carried out, reduces them

to nonsense. To refute his scheme is simply to expose
these errors. He has made religious truth essentially different from what it is, and therefore has had to postulate a
faculty in order to cognize it. He has made the religious
life essentially different from what it is, and therefore has
had to fit the work of the Spirit to his assumptions.

1. His first error is a fundamental misconception of the
nature of religious truth. To say nothing of his chapters
upon the peculiar essence of religion in general and Christianity in particular, it is evident, from the manner in which
he attempts to set aside the popular notion of revelation,
that he looks upon religion as embracing a province of
things, a class of realities, or, if you prefer an expression
more in accordance with the theory of Locke, a collection
of simple ideas, entirely distinct from every other department of knowledge, every other sphere of existence. It is
a world to itself. And as all primitive conceptions must
come through some original faculty to which they are
adapted, there must be a peculiar faculty of religion analogous to taste or the sensibility to beauty, and to conscience
or the sensibility to right.

"Imagine yourself," says the author, "by definitions and
explications addressed to the understanding, attempting to
make a blind man, who had never gazed upon nature, comprehend the exquisite beauties in form, hue and graceful
motion, presented to the eye by a summer's landscape. It
is needless to say that all your descriptions would fall infinitely short of the actual reality—that they would not
convey the hundredth part of what one minute's gaze upon
the scene would spontaneously present—that he could only
conceive, indeed, of any portion of it by analogies taken
from the other senses. The reason of this is that he knows
the thing only formally by logical exposition; he has never
had the proper experiences, never the direct sense-percep-
tions, which are absolutely necessary to a full realization
of it. And so it is, *mutatis mutandis*, with religious truth.
You may expound, and define, and argue upon the high

themes which Christianity presents to the contemplation ;
but unless a man have the intuitions on which all mere
verbal exposition must be grounded, there is no revelation
of the spiritual reality to his mind, and there can be no
clearer perception of the actual truth than there is to the
blind man of the vision of beauty which lies veiled in
darkness around him."

Improvement in religious knowledge, accordingly, is represented as consisting in the education and development
of the religious faculty, which, at every stage of its growth,
enlarges the sphere of our actual experience and expands
the horizon of our mental vision. Religion, like taste,
presupposes an original susceptibility to a particular class
of ideas. It may be cultivated, ennobled and refined; but
the mind can never get beyond the fundamental data
which are given in this form of consciousness. All accessions to its knowledge are only new experiences; the faculty
is the parent of all the truth we can know. Reflection
may construct a science, presenting these data in their
proper order, and showing their connections, dependencies
and consequences, but to him who is destitute of the data
the science is unmeaning and nugatory. All theology, consequently, is nothing but the product of analysis and
synthesis from the materials which are given in experience.
As the science of optics to the blind and the science of
music to the deaf can be little more than jargon, so any
representative exhibitions of Divine truth to one whose
religious faculty has not yet been awakened would be worse
than idle.

We meet this whole train of reasoning by a bold and
confident denial of its fundamental assumption. Religion,
in the sense asserted, is not a simple thing—it is not a
collection of ideas at all analogous to the sensible properties
of matter or the original faculties of the mind. Neither is
it exclusively confined to any one department of our nature,
so that we can say that this is the religious sense, as we
affirm of conscience that it is a moral sense, or of taste

that it is the sense of the beautiful and fair. I do not say
that religion involves no simple ideas or primitive elements
of thought; this would be an absurdity. But I do say that
there are no intuitions peculiar to religion, requiring a
separate and distinct faculty in order to their cognition,
and which could not and would not have been developed
in the ordinary exercise of our powers. There are no
things, no objects of thought which, as such, are simply
and exclusively religious—which exist, in other words, only
in so far as they are religious. There are no simple ideas
characteristic of revelation, and which, without it, would
never have found a lodgment in the mind. On the contrary, our faculties, in the sphere of their ordinary exercise,
furnish us with all the materials out of which the whole
fabric of revealed truth is constructed. Every stone in the
sacred and august temple is hewn from the quarry of common experience. The Bible contains not a single simple
idea which, considered merely as an element of thought,
may not be found in the consciousness of every human
being who has ever exercised his wits. It is not the elements, but the combinations of these elements, that give to
revelation its peculiarity and grandeur. It is not the
stones, but the order and arrangement of the stones, that
constitute the building. Revelation deals pre-eminently
with complex ideas, particularly with what Locke denominates mixed modes, which, as they are mainly retained in
the mind by the force of words, would seem to refer revelation to the category from which our author excludes it—of
verbal exposition.

But the fallacy of the notion of a peculiar religious faculty, with its characteristic cognitions, will yet more fully
appear from a brief investigation of the nature of religion
itself. What, then, is religion? In whatever its peculiar
essence may be said to consist, one thing is universally conceded—that it grows out of the relations betwixt moral and
intelligent creatures and their God. Take away God, and

there can be no religion, because there is no object upon
which it can fasten.   Take away moral and intelligent creatures, and there can be no religion, because there are no subjects in whom it can inhere.   Prosecute the analysis, and it
will be found that the relations out of which religion arises
are those that are involved in moral government.   "They
that come unto God must believe that He is, and that He is
the rewarder of them that diligently seek Him."   It is not
a little remarkable that this conception of moral government, without which religion is a term destitute of meaning,
has wholly escaped the notice of our profound philosopher,
and we need not be astonished that a system which dispenses with obedience and law has no manner of use for the
Bible.   The essence of religion, as a subjective phenomenon,
is made to consist in a state of feeling which a dog may have
in common with his master.   There is certainly nothing
moral in a naked sense of dependence.   Men may feel that
they are in the hands of God, and hate his power.   Devils
feel it, and blaspheme although they tremble.

Having settled the principle that religion grows out of
the relations involved in moral government, we are prepared for a detailed consideration of its objective elements.
These are obviously embraced in a history of the Divine
administration—an account of the law to which obedience
is exacted, of the rewards to which it shall be entitled, and
of the doom to which transgressors shall be assigned.   It is
a history, in other words, of God's providence as unfolded in
His dealings with the race—an account of God's purposes as
already, or yet to be, developed in events.

Subjectively considered, it indicates the attitude in which
men should stand to the Divine administration—a generic
condition of the soul prompting to exercises in unison with
the requisitions of the law.   It extends not to a single faculty or power, but to the whole man; it is the loyalty of a
subject to his prince—of a dutiful son to the father that
begat him.   God, the just and righteous Ruler; man, the
subject, whether obedient or rebellious,—these are the terms

that must be given to understand religion. It is mainly conversant with relations, and those exclusively moral.

As it treats of the progress and conduct of a government, any account of it must, in the nature of the case, be to a large degree historical. Revelation in regard to it must be analogous to an explanation of the laws, constitution and history of a kingdom in past ages or in a distant quarter of the earth.

These things being so, no other intuitions are needed in order to grasp the truths of religion but those which are evolved by our circumstances in the world. The great idea of moral government is not only a primary dictum, in its germ, of every human consciousness, but is daily and hourly exemplified in more or less completeness by the relations of the Family, the School, the State. It meets us everywhere, and men can never efface it from their souls until they have extinguished the light of conscience. Truth, justice, benevolence, mercy—all those moral attributes which adorn the character of God, and which are required to be found in us—demand nothing more than the ordinary operations of our moral nature in order to be in some measure understood. Revelation consequently deals with no new and peculiar simple ideas. It is not, consequently, a faculty or mode of intelligence. Conversant about relations and historical in its form, it must be a presentation to our faculties of facts and events involving combinations of simple ideas collected from all quarters—which can only be done by report. Philosophy confirms the Apostle that faith comes by hearing.

But we may go a step farther, and show from a brief recapitulation of the distinctive doctrines of Christianity, as they are unfolded in the Scriptures, that they turn upon events which could be known only by the testimony of God. The Gospel is a history of the conception and execution of God's purposes of grace to the fallen family of man. That there should exist such a purpose is, relatively to human knowledge, a contingent event. There were no principles from which we or any creature could demonstrate it *a priori*. How then shall we know it? By intuition? It is one of the deep things of God, and none can penetrate His counsels but His own Spirit. He must reveal it, or it must remain locked up in eternal secrecy. The mediation of Christ, the grand agency by which redemption has been achieved, as actually interposed, is a history involving a series of events deriving all their significancy and importance from relations that the understanding alone can grasp. As God and Man in one Person, as Prophet, Priest and King of the Church, He performed and still continues to perform a work in which what strikes the senses is the shell; the substance lies within. How shall we know that He was the federal head and legal substitute of men? This was a sovereign and arbitrary appointment. How shall we know that He bore our sins in His own body on the tree? that He was bruised for our iniquities and wounded for our transgressions? How shall we know that He was justified in the Spirit, and that He is now seated at God's right hand, and ever liveth to make intercession for us? Evidently these things must depend upon report. Faith must come by hearing. Either, then, such a religion as Christianity *cannot* be true—not only is not true, but *cannot* be true, or at least known by us to be true—or revelation is not a mode of intelligence. In this sense such a religion cannot be revealed. The only species of revelation which it admits is that of verbal exposition. It must be a history recited or recorded, or both. Faith must lean on report.

As a religion of moral government so obviously requires this species of revelation, if revealed at all, it is worthy of remark that those who have been most malignant in their assaults against the bondage of the letter have been left to exemplify the fact, in many painful and distressing instances, that they were also emancipated from the bondage of the law. Dealing in intuitions and rhapsodies, living in a world of impalpable shapes and airy forms, they soon learn to treat with contempt the tame and sober relations which are involved in the notions of husband, citizen, friend and subject. Mysticism is an intoxicating draught—a stimulus so powerful, not unfrequently, in particular directions, that all sense of responsibility is lost, and the darkest crimes are perpetrated with as little remorse as that with which a drunkard belches forth his oaths or insults the wife of his bosom and the children of his loins. The letter is the guardian of morals as well as of truth. It teaches men— what they are often anxious to forget—that there is a law, holy, just and good, and yet terrible to evil-doers, which supports the eternal throne. It unveils a judgment to come; a day is appointed in which the world shall be judged in righteousness, and every man shall receive at the hands of impartial justice according to his deeds. This unflinching supremacy of right, this supreme dominion of law, this terrible responsibility for sin, is no doubt a griev- ous offence. But those who will not accept the provisions of grace—all in accordance with the immutable requisitions of right—may kindle a fire and walk in the light of their own sparks, but this shall they have at God's hands, they shall lie down in sorrow. Their intuitions and impulses, their dreams and inspirations, will not save them from the awful exactions of that government which was whispered in conscience, thundered on Sinai and hallowed on Calvary. God will by no means clear the guilty.

But misapprehending, as the author has done, the essen- tial nature of religious truth, he has confounded two things that are entirely distinct,—the process of giving a revelation, and the process of making a Christian. Having made Revelation a faculty in man, which, like every other faculty, is developed by exercise on its appropriate objects, he could find no other office for Inspiration but that of stimulating and strengthening the natural organ of religious truth. Revelation itself *is* the Divine life. The possession of this faculty is what makes man a religious being, and he im- proves in religion just to the extent that this form of con- sciousness is developed, cultivated and refined. Inspiration

is what quickens it into motion. Let it be granted that
there is such a species of inspiration as that here described,
it obviously does not exclude the inspiration which gives a
message from God. If religious truth is of such a nature
that in order to be known it must be reported, the fact that
an influence may be necessary to enable a man to receive
and understand the report is not inconsistent with the other
fact, that there must be some one to make the report. You
can dispense with messengers only upon the supposition that
the knowledge to be conveyed cannot be communicated by
a message. It is this misconception which has led our
author to confound inspiration with conversion. If he had
been right as to what religion is, he would have seen the
necessity of inspiration in the sense of the Apostle, who
makes it the sending of men with a testimony from God.
What it is in its own nature, how God operated upon the
minds of Apostles, and how far their own powers were
called into play, are simply curious questions, about which
the Bible has resolved nothing. The main thing is, that
those who were so sent spake not the words which man's
wisdom teacheth, but which the Holy Ghost teacheth; and
as they spake so also they wrote, as they were moved by the
Holy Ghost. Their words and writings are equally and
alike the testimony of God. The end of inspiration is to
furnish the rule of faith. *Faith* comes by hearing, and hearing by the Word of God. But, apart from the abusive
application of the term *inspiration* to the renewing and
sanctifying operations of the Spirit, the author has misrepresented that work itself in consequence of his primary
error in reference to revelation.

The notion that revelation is a faculty of peculiar intuitions the author has marvellously confounded with the evangelical doctrine of the agency of the Spirit in regeneration.
" In making these statements," says he, " we are simply putting in a more definite form what almost all classes of Christians fully admit, and what they are perpetually asserting.
Is it not allowed that men, even of intellect and learning,

may read the Bible through and through again, and yet may have no spiritual perceptions of the realities to which it refers? Do we not constantly hear it asserted that Divine truth must be spiritually understood? Nay, does not St. Paul himself tell us that the things of the Spirit of God must be spiritually discerned? And what does all this amount to but that there must be the awakening of the religious consciousness before the truth is actually revealed to us, and that it can only be revealed to us at all, essentially speaking, in the form of religious intuition?"

I am willing to admit that if religious truth consisted of a collection of simple and primitive cognitions, the only conceivable mode of making them intelligible to men would be to produce them in their consciousness. If God designed to impart to the blind the idea of colours, to the deaf the idea of sounds, or to those totally destitute of the senses the glories of heaven and the beauties of earth, it would be necessary to impart the faculties that they wanted and bring them into contact with their appropriate objects. But if Divine truth, so far as it implies intuitional elements, lays under tribute the contributions of all our faculties in the ordinary sphere of their exercise, as it involves no elements requiring a peculiar and distinctive faculty of religion, as it appeals mainly and pre-eminently to the logical understanding, the difficulty which is obviated in regeneration and conversion must be something very different from the production of a new class of cognitions. Hence, it has never been contended by evangelical divines that grace communicates new faculties to the soul. Man, since the Fall, possesses all the original powers with which he was endowed when he came from the hands of God. Nor is it contended that the Spirit awakens any dormant susceptibilities, any latent capacities which have lacked the opportunity of development and exercise. Neither this, nor anything like this, is the scriptural theory of grace; and if our author had understood the real condition of man he would have seen the true position of the Word in the economy of salvation,

and have assigned it its office without confounding it with
the work of the Spirit.

2. I proceed to expose his misconception in relation to
the end or design of Divine Revelation. He makes it, as
we have seen, a faculty in man which God developes by the
presentation of its appropriate objects, and occasionally
stimulates by the special influence of inspiration. Revelation is, therefore, the Divine life. A man is religious just
to the extent that this form of intuitional consciousness is
developed, cultivated and refined. Now, in opposition to
this, Paul asserts that revelation is *in order to* the Divine
life, the means of producing it, and rearing and expanding
it to its full proportions. He makes faith to be the very
essence of a sinner's religion, and the Word of God to be
its measure and its rule. The testimony of God without us
supplies us with the *credenda*, the things to be believed.
That exists independently of our own minds. But will the
mere report of the Divine testimony infallibly terminate in
faith? Paul promptly replies that they have not all obeyed
the Gospel, and Esaias saith, Lord, who hath believed our
report? What, then, is the difficulty? Is it that the Gospel is naturally unintelligible?—that it contains, I mean,
verbal statements involving simple ideas or primitive elements of thought which we have no faculties to grasp? Is
it that it talks of colours to a blind man, or of sounds to a
deaf one? By no means: the terms it uses are all in themselves intelligible, and intelligible by us with none but the
faculties that we bring with us into the world. It speaks of
a ruler, a judge, sin, guilt, condemnation, pardon and atonement,—all of them things which, to some extent, we are able
to conceive and to represent in thought. It is not, therefore,
that its terms are senseless; it is not as if written in Chinese
or Sanscrit, nor like the preaching of an angel to an idiot.

The difficulty is one which intuition cannot reach. If
the things revealed were actually present to the mind, the
difficulty would still exist; it would still be true that the
natural man would refuse to receive them, and that he

could not spiritually discern them.   Mr. Morell seems to
think that all that is wanted is simply the faculty of apprehension—the power of knowing the things and perceiving
them to be real.   But this is not the case.   The difficulty
lies in the moral condition of the sinner.   The sinner
remaining as he is, no presence of spiritual realities, no contact of them with the mind, however immediate and direct,
would give him a different kind of discernment from that
which he obtains from the Word.   This moral condition is
denominated in the Scriptures a state of *death;* and the term
is happily chosen, for it exactly describes depravity in its
pervading influence upon all the powers and faculties of the
man.   Holiness is called a *life,* the life of God in the soul of
man; and by pursuing the analogies which these terms suggest we may form some definite conceptions of the real hindrances among men to the cordial reception of the Word.
What, then, is life?   It evidently belongs to that class of
things which, incomprehensible in themselves and incapable
of being represented in thought, are matters of necessary
belief.   We see its effects, we witness its operations, we can
seize upon the symptoms which distinguish its presence.
But what it is in itself no mortal mind can conceive.   We
can only speak of it as the unknown cause of numberless
phenomena which we notice.   Where is life?   Is it here and
not there?   is it there and not here?   Is it in the heart, the
head, the hands, the feet?   It evidently pervades the frame;
it is the condition, the indispensable condition to the organic
action of every part of the body.   The body may be perfect in
its structure; it may have every limb and nerve and muscle,
and foreign influences may be made to mimic the operations
of life, but if life be not there these actions, or rather motions,
will be essentially distinct from those of the living man.[1]

In like manner holiness is a generic condition of the soul.
As a state or nature it is incomprehensible in itself; we

[1] NOTE BY EDITOR.—Some of these sentiments and illustrations will
be found also in Vol. I. Thel. Lect. xiv., and in Vol. II. Discourse i.
on Truth.

can no more represent it in thought than we can form an
image of power or causation. It is a something which lies at
the foundation of all the soul's exercises and operations, and
gives them a peculiar and distinctive cast. It is not itself
a habit nor a collection of habits, but the indispensable
condition of all spiritual habits. It is not here nor there,
but it pervades the whole man—the understanding, the
will, the conscience, the affections; it underlies all the dispositions and habitudes, and is felt in all the thoughts and
desires. Natural life has its characteristic functions; so
spiritual life has its distinguishing tendencies. They all
point to God. He is holy, and where this quality exists in
the creature it is attracted to Him and produces a communion, a fellowship, a familiarity, if I may so speak,
which easily detects the impressions of God wherever they
exist. It involves an union with Him that renders His
traces patent and obvious wherever they are found. Spiritual death or depravity is the opposite of all this—a generic condition of the soul in which these particular exercises
are not possible. The same faculties may remain, the same
ideas may be suggested, the same objective realities may
be conceived, the same materials of thinking may exist,
but that influence proceeding from holiness which distinguishes all the operations of the sanctified mind is wanting.
That union and fellowship with God, that mysterious
familiarity which hears and knows His voice even in its
lowest whispers, is gone. The characteristic tendencies of
the carnal mind are *from* God; it is even enmity against
God, not subject to His law nor capable of becoming so.
Now faith, in the apostolic sense, involves the recognition
of God in the Word. It believes in consequence of the
Divine testimony. It knows God's voice. When the
Gospel is proclaimed it is perceived to be a message of
love and of mercy from the eternal throne.

This faith can only exist in a holy heart. An uncon-
verted sinner can no more exercise it than the dead can rise
and walk or the blind can see. Two men may receive a

letter from the same person, or rather the same letter may be put into the hands of both. One is an intimate friend of the writer, the other an entire stranger. The stranger reads it, and apprehends exactly the same ideas, considered as mere thoughts; but he sees not the writer in it, and cannot enter into it with that sympathy, that cordiality and delight with which the friend peruses it. The Gospel is a message from God; all holy hearts see God in it, and rejoice in it because of His Name; strangers and aliens have the Word in their hands, but have not God in the Word. They may be convinced by external arguments—and such arguments abound—that it is indeed His message; but they have not that witness within themselves upon which the heart reposes with assured confidence. Now here comes in the agency of the Spirit, who imparts that new nature, that generic condition of soul, which brings the heart into sympathy with God and all that is Divine, and enables it to believe. This throws a new light around the truth, gives a new direction to the heart and imparts its influence to the whole soul. It creates an instinct for God, which infallibly recognizes His presence wherever He condescends to manifest it. There is no new faculty and there are no new ideas; but there is a new mode of exercising all the faculties and a new discernment of the old truths.

Just apprehensions, consequently, of the work of the Spirit afford no manner of countenance to the doctrine that Divine revelation involves an intuitive perception of spiritual realities. Place a sinner in heaven, and he would be no nearer to a spiritual discernment of the glories of God and the Lamb than he is in his guilt and blindness on earth. He would there need as much as here to be born of water and the Spirit, that his heart might magnify the Lord.

The apostolic theory of the relations of faith and revelation indicates an appointment of God in regard to the Divine life in beautiful analogy with his arrangements for the preservation and growth of animal existence. One

thing, as Butler has forcibly illustrated, is set over against
another. Life implies an inward state, and an external
condition to correspond to it; and in the harmony of these
conditions consists the healthfulness of being. Now, the
Word is to the spiritual man the external condition to
which his new nature is adapted—it is the element in which
it moves, and grows and flourishes. It is milk to babes,
and strong meat to those who have their senses exercised
by reason of use. If God should regenerate a man, and
leave him in the world without His truth, in some form or
other, communicated—if, for example, He should renew a
heathen, and yet give him no revelation of His will, except
as He might gather it from the instincts and impulses of
the new heart—how deplorable would be his condition!
Conceive him pregnant with celestial fire. Upon what
objects shall his mind be employed? Where shall he go to
find the materials that are suited to his taste? He has
cravings which earth cannot satisfy, and yet knows nothing
of the bread which came down from heaven, nor of the
streams which gush from Siloah's fount. He longs for
God, but his soul cannot find Him; and as he feels for
Him on the right, and He is not there, on the left, but He
is gone, he sinks down in weariness and disappointment,
to famish and die. He is in a world of enemies, of idolaters
and will-worshippers and children of the Devil. Where
is his panoply against the powers of darkness—the shield
of faith, the helmet of salvation and the sword of the Spirit?
What hopes shall support and dignify his soul? He knows
nothing of Christ, nothing of the Spirit, nothing of the
Divine promises, nothing of the glorious inheritance of the
saints in light. There is no element about him which corresponds to his disposition. No, impossible! Such an
anomaly never takes place; it cannot be endured that God's
children should be as orphans in the world, without food
or raiment or shelter. As well might we suppose that
fish should be transferred to the air and birds to the sea
as that God should new-create a soul and leave it without

the external adaptations that its wants demand. These, in this life, are found in the Bible; faith makes them realities, makes them substantial. It opens from the Scriptures a new and glorious world, to which all the faculties of the new creature are proportioned; and when it has educated and trained them for a higher sphere, they pass from its discipline to the full fruition of the things themselves. We now learn in books; we shall hereafter study things. The appointments of God in the kingdom of grace are at one with this appointment in the kingdom of nature.

The argument does not apply to infants dying in infancy, because they may be translated instantly to a sphere in which a holy nature shall have ample opportunity of expansion. But the anomaly cannot be endured that God's children should be left as sheep without a shepherd; even worse, without food, raiment or shelter.

The scriptural doctrine, moreover, guards against the absurd supposition that the life of religion consists in the development and expansion of any single power of the soul. It is not confined to any one department of thought or feeling. The *whole* man must acknowledge its influence; it thinks in the head, feels in the heart and acts in the will. It is the great pervading law of our being, leading us to find God everywhere, and, whether we eat or drink, to do all to His glory. It is the religion of a moral creature under the dominion of a moral law; not the visions of a seer, the phantoms of a dreamer, but the inspiration of a soul pregnant with celestial fire. Body, soul and spirit, all are the organs of the Divine life. It extends to all actions, to all impulses, to all ends. It reigns as well as lives. Such is Bible religion. How stunted and dwarfish, in comparison, a single faculty gazing on a single class of things—the eye playing with colours, or the ear sporting with sounds!

II. Having shown that the theory in question mistakes the nature of religious truth and the office of revelation in the economy of salvation, it only remains that the essence

of Religion should be more distinctly considered. In its
subjective and objective aspects a little has already been
said of it, but only in reference to the argument then in
hand.   It is particularly in the subjective aspect that we
propose to consider it now.   The question is, What is it to
be religious?   Particularly, What is it to be a Christian?
The word *essence* is very unfortunately applied to the subject, as it is apt to mislead by its vagueness and ambiguity.
If it is supposed that there is some *one* formal quality, some
simple and uniform idea that enters into all the exercises
that are distinctively religious (the notion evidently of our
author), it is a very great misapprehension.   When we
arrange things according to their colour it is precisely the
same quality of whiteness which characterizes all that we
classify as white.   But there is no single quality of actions
and of thoughts that causes them to be ranked under the
head of religion.   Two emotions, entirely distinct in their
own nature, having nothing in common, considered merely
as phenomena, may yet be equally religious—hope and fear,
for example.   Upon what ground are they grouped together?
The reason of the classification must evidently be sought,
not in themselves, but in the state of mind from which they
proceed.   That state of mind which is truly religious is the
condition which we have previously described as spiritual
life or holiness; but as a state we have also seen that it
belongs to the category of things which we are compelled
to believe without being able to represent in thought.   It
is rather, in fact, the condition of religion than religion
itself.   That consists in the *exercises* which proceed from this
state of the soul, and they are all distinguished by the circumstance that they are in harmony with our relations to
God.   These relations must be known before it can be determined that any given experiences are proper manifestations
of religion.   The subjective cannot be comprehended without the objective.   An universal and pervading disposition
to comply with the will of God—a heart in sympathy with
Him, is the nearest approximation that we can make to a

description of what constitutes religion as a subjective phenomenon. This is the state in which angels are, the state in which man would have been, if man had never sinned. This is the state to which when men are exalted they are said to be *saved*. This is religion in general. Now, Christianity is a scheme through which, in conformity with the nature of moral government, man is recovered from his ruin and exalted to this condition. It is the immediate end which the mediation of Christ aims at, and the attainment of this end in the case of any sinner is salvation. But the means by which Christianity produces its fruits in us is faith. This is the great requirement of the Gospel, the only medium by which we can ever be brought into harmony and fellowship with God. Hence, faith may justly be described as embracing the whole religion of a sinner. "He that believeth hath everlasting life;" "with the heart man believeth unto righteousness, and with the mouth confession is made unto salvation." It is not only the instrument by which through Christ we are justified, but the organ through which the whole Word of God operates upon the soul and builds it up in holiness. It is the great and all-comprehensive duty which springs from our relation to God under the Gospel.

I need not prosecute this inquiry any farther. It is only necessary to put the two systems, that of the Gospel and that of the subjective philosophy, side by side, in order that we may perceive the immeasurable superiority of the former. Both admit the importance of revelation, and in developing its nature the Gospel gives us three terms—the Person from whom, the persons to whom, and the message itself. Its revelation professes to be the Word of God. The new philosophy gives us but two—a thinking mind, and the things to be thought. There is no Revealer; it is a message without an author and without a messenger. Which is most reasonable? When we go a step farther, and inquire into the characteristics of the things revealed, the Gospel unfolds a system of moral government springing

from the very nature of God and His relations to His creatures, involving a series of the sublimest events that the
mind can conceive. It unveils the great drama of Providence, and shows how the Divine purposes have been working to their accomplishment from the beginning of all
things. It spans the arch of time—explains to man his
nature, his fall, his duty and his destiny. Above all, it
unveils a scheme of grace, an eternal purpose conceived in
the bosom of infinite love for the redemption of the guilty,
and executed in the fullness of time by an agency so mysterious and amazing that angels desire to look into it.
Throughout the Bible holiness reigns. God appears there
a holy God, His law supreme; and the perfection of man is
measured by his approach to the Divine excellence. Religion is there represented as a life into which we are quickened by Almighty grace, and which brings every faculty of
the soul in sweet subjection to the authority of God. What
are the revelations of the subjective philosophy? Echo
answers, What? There are no responses from the tripod,
the oracles are yet dumb. The worshipper sits, and gazes,
and feels, but what he sees and how he feels we are quietly
told that mortal language is incompetent to describe.

One of the most offensive features in this system is the
utter deceitfulness with which it avails itself of the ambiguity of language. From its free and familiar use of the
language consecrated to evangelical religion the unwary
reader is insensibly beguiled from the contemplation of its
real character. It pretends to be a *revealed* system. This
sounds fair and well. But when we look a little deeper,
it is a revelation as nature is a revelation, and when we
express our astonishment at this abuse of words, we are
told for our comfort that God made the world and that He
made us with faculties capable of knowing its existence.
He reveals the world to us by creating us with eyes to see it.
The whole work is Divine. So He made a certain class of
spiritual concretions, and made us with faculties capable
of enjoying them. This is all surely Divine!

So again it speaks of a Divine life. But when we inquire into its meaning we do not find the new birth, we do not recognize a holy nature, we do not discover an influence upon the whole soul of man which brings him into harmony with Divine truth. There is nothing supernatural, there is nothing eminently gracious. On the contrary, we meet with nothing but what takes place in regard to every function of life—just the natural faculty developed and exercised by the presentation of its appropriate objects. The faculty of religion and the faculty of imagination are brought into activity in the same way, and there is as much of grace and as much of God in the process by which a child learns to know that a stone is hard as in the process by which a man passes from death to life. God may dispose circumstances so as to hasten the development, but all religion springs from the man himself! Such, without exaggeration or caricature, is the system for which we are called upon to surrender the Bible. We are to give up God's Word and the hopes of the Gospel for the rhapsodies and ravings of every spirit who pretends to a higher development of the religious consciousness. Man must be supreme. He must be allowed to create his God, his law, his religion! The mind of every individual is the universe to him, intuition is his oracle, and he has but to look within to know his state, his prospects and his destiny!

Behold, I show you a more excellent way. "God, who at sundry times and in divers manners spake in times past unto the fathers by the Prophets, hath in these last days spoken unto us by His Son." We have a message from the skies. We are not left, like the blind, to grope in the dark, but we have an excellent Word, to which we are exhorted to take heed as unto a light that shineth in a dark place. But let us remember that the Word alone cannot save us; it is the means but not the source of life. The Bible without the Spirit is a dead letter, as the spirit without the Bible is a lying delusion. The Spirit *and* the Bible, this is the great

principle of Protestant Christianity. " The doctrine which
we defend is not only the testimony of the Scriptures, but,
still further, the testimony of the Holy Spirit. If we maintain the Scriptures against those who wish only for the
Spirit, so do we also maintain the Spirit against those who
wish for nothing but the Scriptures." The Bible without
the Spirit can rise no higher than formalism—the spirit
without the Bible will infallibly end in fanaticism. The
Bible with the Spirit will conduct to Christ, to holiness and
God. The times are threatening. With the earlier schools
of infidelity the main objection to the Scriptures was that
they inculcated the necessity of a Divine life in the soul of
man—they wanted to get quit of the Spirit; with the subjective philosophers the great difficulty is that they are not
all spirit. Surely the men of this world are like children
sitting in the market-place; if you pipe to them they refuse
to dance, if you mourn they refuse to weep.

I confess frankly my apprehensions that, if the great doctrine of the supremacy of the Scriptures should be shaken
in the popular mind, we have no security against the perpetration of the most enormous crimes in the hallowed name
of religion. If men are to draw their faith from themselves,
it will be like themselves—it will patronize their lusts and
sanctify their most outrageous excesses. It is impossible to
estimate the power of the Bible as a bit to curb where it
does not save. Of all ungovernable mobs that is the most
dangerous which acts under the frenzy of religious fanaticism. When men enthrone the Devil as their god, we may
tremble for the interests of society. Give me storms, earth-
quakes and tornadoes, plague, pestilence and famine—any
form of evil that springs from the Providence of God—but
save me from that hell, the hearts of men where the fiends
of foul delusion have taken up their lodgment. The Bible,
the Bible is the great safeguard of nations. We must reverence its holy pages as we love our country, our homes and ourselves. We must stand by the Scriptures or perish. Well

did Luther say, " If we will not drink of the water of the
fountain, so fresh and pure, God will cast us into ponds and
sloughs, and there oblige us to swallow long draughts of a
putrid and stinking water."

NOTE. In the passage " whosoever believeth," etc., it may be well to
remark that the universality is implied in the ὁ λεγων, and that Paul introduces the πας as interpretative.

THE OFFICE OF REASON IN REGARD TO REVELATION.

L ORD BACON has very justly observed, in relation
to the subject announced at the head of this article, that
Christianity maintains the "golden mediocrity between the
law of the heathen and the law of Mohammed, which have
embraced the two extremes." The heathen system attached
no importance to *truth;* "it had no constant belief or confession, but left all to the liberty of argument." In its
richer developments it was evidently the offspring of imagination, requiring no piety, but taste. Fables were its
Scriptures, poets its divines and the fine arts its altars. In
its practical operations it was an affair of State. Princes
were its priests, magistrates its guardians, and obedience to
its precepts a branch of the duties of a citizen. Destitute
of truth, it was, of course, destitute of moral power; and
from the intimate connection which subsists between the
imagination and emotions, its appeals to the fancy must
have served to inflame the passions and to augment the
corruption which it is the office of religion to repress. Cul-
tivating to excess that "forward, delusive faculty" which
Butler pronounces to be the "author of all error," while
it left the understanding without instruction and the heart
without discipline, it must have formed a species of character in which indifference to truth was strangely blended
with sensibility to beauty, and refinement of taste unnat-
urally combined with the grossness of vice and the obscen-
ities of lust.

The law of Mohammed claimed to be a revelation from
heaven; and though, in accordance with its pretensions, it
demanded faith, yet, as it presented no rational grounds of
conviction, its policy was to intimidate or bribe the understanding, according as fear, prejudice or lust was the pre-
dominant principle of action. Where it could not extort a
blind credulity, it made the passions the vehicles of its doctrines; the timid it frightened to submission, the profligate
it allured to acquiescence, and the heretic and skeptic it
wheedled and cajoled by a partial patronage of their errors.
Exclusively a system of authority, it gave no scope to discussion. Its great argument was the word of its Prophet,
its decisive sanction the sword of its soldiers, and its strongest attraction the license which it gave to voluptuous indulgences. Paganism wore the "face of error," and Mohammedanism of "imposture."

Christianity, on the contrary, attaches pre-eminent importance to *truth*, and acknowledges no faith but that which
is founded in conviction. At the same time it professes to
be from God, and therefore, as becomes it, speaks with
authority. As a system *claiming* to be *Divine*, it invites
the fullest discussion. As a system *proved* to be *Divine*, it
demands implicit submission. It both "admits and rejects
disputation with difference."

But how far "it admits" and how far "it rejects disputation"—that is, the precise province of reason in regard to
revelation—is a point which has been keenly discussed
between Socinians and the orthodox, infidels and believers
in Christianity.

It is needless to deny that the language of divines has
not always been sufficiently guarded on the subject. Their
intemperate reprobations of the spirit of perverse speculation which confounds the departments of Revelation and
Philosophy, and applies to the former measures of truth
which are obviously incompatible with its nature, have
given some pretext to the calumny that faith is inconsistent
with reason, and that Christianity repudiates an appeal to

argument. Religion, from the necessity of the case, is addressed to reason.[1] Its duties are represented as a reasonable service, and its inspired teachers, who disdained the tricks of human eloquence and disclaimed the agency of human wisdom as an adequate foundation of faith, were accustomed to resort to argument to produce conviction. It is reason which distinguishes man from the brute. Without it we should be incompetent to apprehend truth or feel the obligation of moral law—as incapable of appreciating a message from God as "the beasts which perish." To say, therefore, that Christianity puts an absolute interdict upon the exercise of reason is equivalent to saying that she exempts us from the duty of considering her claims. To prohibit *rational* is to prohibit *moral* action. To strip us of reason is to free us from law.

The question, however, in dispute, is not in regard to reason as a *faculty* of the mind, the faculty which judges of truth and falsehood, right and wrong; but in regard to reason as a compendious expression for the principles and maxims, the opinions, conclusions or prejudices which, with or without foundation, men acknowledge to be true. Locke and Witsius have both pointed out the distinction.[2] Rea-

---

[1] Cæterum Ratio, quantumvis corrupta, Ratio tamen manet, id est, ea facultas qua homo cognoscit et judicat. Adeo quidem ut homo nihil omnino, quale illudcunque sit, cognoscere et judicare valeat, nisi per rationem suam, tanquam proximum cognitionis et judicii principium et causam. Idcirco si Divinæ res, si mysteria Religionis cognoscenda sint, non aliter id fieri potest nisi per Rationem. Ipsa Fides, quum cognitio et νόησις sit et assensus, Rationis sive mentis est operatio. Idque tam est liquidum ut pro rationali non sit habendus qui in dubium id revocat. Witsius, Opera, Tom. ii., p. 588: De Usu et Abusu Rationis, § x.

[2] Locke says: "The word *reason*, in the English language, has different significations. Sometimes it is taken for true and clear principles; sometimes for clear and fair deductions from those principles; and sometimes for the cause, and particularly the final cause. But the consideration I shall have of it here is in a signification different from all these; and that is, as it stands for a faculty in man—that faculty whereby man is supposed to be distinguished from beasts, and wherein it is evident he much surpasses them." Hum. Understand., Book iv., c. 17, § 1.

Witsius says: "Ratio significat vel *Facultatem* hominis qua percepit et

son, in the one sense, is necessarily presupposed in the very
idea of revelation; but to reason in the other, it is not only
possible, but likely, that a system which shall pre-eminently
display the wisdom and the power of God shall appear to
be foolishness. "The Jews," says the Apostle, "require a
sign, and the Greeks seek after wisdom; but we preach
Christ crucified—unto the Jews a stumbling-block, and unto
the Greeks foolishness; but unto them which are called,
both Jews and Greeks, Christ the power of God and the
wisdom of God." The distinctive principles of Christianity
contradicted the distinctive principles of every sect of the
ancient philosophers. By its humbling representations of
the depravity and impotence of man it rebuked the pride
of the Stoic; the Epicurean was disgusted with its heroic
maxims of self-denial and benevolence; the Sophist was
confounded with a standard of eternal truth which poured
contempt upon his quibbling speculations; and the Rheto-
rician seemed to be degraded by a system which looked
for success not to the enticing words of man's wisdom, but
to the demonstration and power of God's Holy Spirit. The
disciples of the Porch, Lyceum and Academy all concurred
in rejecting the Gospel, not because its external evidences
were unsatisfactory or defective—these they hardly took
the trouble to examine—but because the doctrines it inculcated were inconsistent with the instructions of their masters. Here reason, or what men regarded as reason, was
plainly at war with revelation. What God pronounced to
be wisdom, the Greek denounced as foolishness. What
the Greek pronounced to be wisdom, God denounced as
foolishness. "The Lord knoweth the thoughts of the wise,
that they are vain."

In regard to doctrines which are *known* to be a revelation
from God there can be no question as to the precise office
of reason. The understanding is simply to believe. Every

judicat verumque a falso dignoscit; vel, *placita, scita, axiomata,* quæ vel
per se evidentia sunt, vel ex evidentibus certa consecutione deducta creduntur." Opera, Tom. ii., p. 585: De Usu et Abusu Rat., § iii.

proud thought and every lofty imagination must be brought in captivity to the Father of lights. When God speaks, faith is the highest exercise of reason. In His testimony we have all the elements of truth, and His veracity is the ultimate ground of certainty in every species of evidence. The resistless laws of belief which he has impressed upon the constitution of our minds, which lie at the foundation of all human knowledge, without which the materials of sense and consciousness could never be constructed into schemes of philosophy and science, derive all their authority from His own unchanging truth. Let it, for a moment, be supposed that God is willing to deceive us, and who could rely with confidence upon the information of his faculties? Who would trust his senses if the instinct by which he is impelled to do so might, after all, be a false light to seduce him into error? That instinct is the testimony of God; and what we call *reasoning* is nothing but the successive steps by which we arrive at the same testimony in the original structure of our minds. Hence belief, even in cases of the strictest demonstration, must, in the last analysis, be traced to the veracity of God. Reasoning is only a method of ascertaining what God teaches; the true ground of belief is the fact that God *does* teach the proposition in question.[1] If the laws of belief be the testimony of God, and whatever accords with them be evidence, variously denominated, according to the clearness or directness with which the accordance is felt or perceived, then knowledge and opinion both rest alike upon this testimony; the only difference betwixt them being the difference in intensity and distinctness with which that testimony is perceived. All real evidence, whether intuitive, demonstrative or probable, is only the light with which He irradiates the mind; and we follow it with confidence, because the strength

[1] Reason, says Mr. Locke, is natural revelation, whereby the eternal Father of light and fountain of all knowledge communicates to mankind that portion of truth which He has laid within the reach of their natural faculties. Hum. Understand., B. iv., c. 19, § 4.

of Israel is not a man that He should lie, or the son of man that He should repent. The distinction between faith and the ordinary forms of assent is not in the ultimate ground of certainty—that is the same in all cases—but the methods by which it is reached. Faith reaches it immediately, having Divine revelation for its object; in other cases it is reached through the medium of those laws which God has impressed upon the mental constitution. Hence it would seem that faith, being less remote from the ultimate ground of certainty, is more excellent than knowledge or opinion. As Locke has shown that demonstration is inferior to intuition,[1] the successive steps of proof increasing the possibilities of deception and mistake, so in all cases in which the testimony of God is only *mediately* perceived the exposure to fallacy is in proportion to the number of comparisons employed. When, consequently, any doctrine is known to be a matter of Divine revelation, "if we will truly consider it, more worthy is it to believe than to know as we now know."[2] There can, strictly speaking, be no improbabilities in it. And however it may appear to contradict the sentiments and opinions we have cherished, yet "the prerogative of God extendeth as well to the reason as to the will of man; so that, as we are to obey His law, though we find a reluctation in our will, so we are to believe His word, though we find a reluctation in our reason."[3] To prefer the deductions of philosophy to a Divine revelation is to relinquish the sun for the stars, to "imitate," as Perrot expresses it, "the conduct of the Cynic,

[1] See this matter very clearly discussed in Hum. Understand., B. iv., c. 2, §§ 4–9. Much of the reasoning in these sections is applicable to the subject discussed in the text.

[2] Bacon, Advancement of Learning: Works, Montagu's Edition, vol. ii., p. 299. Bacon reaches the conclusion by a process of argument different from that in the text. "For in knowledge," says he, "man's mind suffereth from sense, but in belief it suffereth from spirit, such a one as it holdeth for more authorized than itself, and so suffereth from the worthier agent."

[3] Bacon, Advancement of Learning: Works, vol. ii., p. 299, Mont. Edition.

who, not contented with the light of the sun, took a candle at noonday to search for a good man."

But the true question is, not whether an humble submission of the understanding, when God speaks and His words are rightly apprehended, be the imperative duty of man—of this there can be no doubt—but, What is the office of reason in those cases in which the reality of the revelation remains yet to be proved, and the interpretation of the doctrine remains yet to be settled?—the office of reason, not simply as a faculty of the mind, but as furnished with the lights of experience, the inductions of science and the conclusions of philosophy? Is its own wisdom the rule by which a pretended revelation must be tried or a pretended interpretation justified or condemned? Is it competent to judge of the doctrines—the things which profess to be revealed—either for the purpose of refuting, from their supposed absurdity and falsehood, the claims of the system which contains them, or, what is the same in principle, for the purpose of invalidating, upon the same grounds, the exegesis which derives them from a record confessed to be Divine? This is the question which we propose briefly to discuss.

The origin and perplexity of this question, it deserves to be remarked, are due to the fall of man. Had he retained his integrity, the operations of his reason would have been uniformly right, his perceptions of truth clear and unclouded, and no contradiction could ever have been suspected between his deductions from the light of nature and the express communications of God. As a finite creature his knowledge would necessarily have been limited; he would have been subject to ignorance, but not to error, and whatever accessions the Deity in His goodness might have chosen to impart would have been felt to harmonize with his previous attainments. But darkness of mind is the sad inheritance of sin. The irregular influences to which the Fall has exposed us, the deceitfulness of all our measures of truth when we pass the limits of intuition and demonstration, the turbulence of passion, the force of habit and the ascendency of education,—all combine to warp the understanding, make us confound prejudices and principles, and mistake the application of right and wrong. So great is the danger, if the prerogative be accorded to reason to judge of revelation, of the rejection of its doctrines because they contradict the shallow philosophy and false notions of things which have been imbibed from the schools, insinuated by custom or adopted without examination, and which, from long familiarity, are possessed of the authority of self-evident maxims, that distinguished writers,[1] particularly in modern times, since the rise of philosophical infidelity, have insisted, with more zeal than discretion, upon the external evidences of Christianity as the only ones which, in the first instance, we are at liberty to examine. Not that they suppose there is anything *unreasonable* in the Bible; on the contrary, could it be ascertained to them that *right* reason, and not prejudice and error under the name of reason, should sit in judgment upon it, their objections to a candid investigation of the internal evidences as an important branch of the inquiry into its Divine authority would probably be removed. They are not willing, however, to run the risk of having a true doctrine condemned because it contradicts a false proposition, nor of having a true revelation rejected because it contradicts a false philosophy. Whatever, they justly conclude, *proves* any system to have emanated from God, proves at the same time that its contents are worthy of His character, and that all objections to them as foolish, inconsistent or absurd must be presumptuous and vain.

But as internal improbabilities weaken external proof, they ought to have shown that the evidence of revelation can be considered as complete before the preliminary point is settled—that there is nothing on the face of it to contradict its pretensions. We would not assert, though we

---

[1] Bishop Wilson, for example, in his Critique on Butler's Analogy, and Van Mildert in his Boyle Lectures.

have heard the proposition ingeniously maintained, that, according to the natural order of thought, the *first* inquiry is obviously into the character of that which claims to be Divine, and then into the credentials or external signs by which its claims are authenticated; but it cannot be denied that it is the course actually adopted by the great majority of Christendom, who, in rejecting the corrupt systems of religion that obtain in the world, are not governed by the insufficiency and defects of the proof, but the grossness of the doctrine and the looseness of the precepts.

Rome appeals to miracles. Every saint in her calendar, by his faith when living or his bones when dead, has wrought wonders, according to the Popish legends, analogous to those of Christ and His Apostles; and yet who that believes the Bible would not feel amply justified in discarding the authority of the Pope and the dogmas of his sect, because they contradict Christianity, without being able to prove the fabulousness of monkish marvels or to expose the fraud which has attempted to palm them on the world? The *internal* evidence condemns them. Few take the trouble, and none feel themselves bound, to examine the credentials of Rome, Mohammed or Smith. It is enough that they come to us with a lie in their mouths. They teach what we *know* to be false, and no amount of external evidence can make that Divine which is eminently characteristic of the Devil. Either, then, the rejection of the Popish and Mohammedan impostures by the mass of Protestants has been prematurely made, or the investigation of internal evidences is a legitimate subject of inquiry, where the question is yet to be decided whether a system which professes to be revealed is really from God. According to the reasoning of Bishop Wilson, in his Critique upon Butler's Analogy, no religion can, in the first instance, be self-condemned. The credentials must be shown to be spurious before the doctrines can be convicted of falsehood. "The external evidences," says he, "are those which should be first studied. Indeed they are the only ones that can be considered in the first instance as essential, because they undertake to show the credentials of the messenger who professes to come with a revelation from heaven. We have no right to go farther than this in the first place. The moment the messenger is sufficiently proved to have Divine credentials, we have but one duty left—that of receiving and obeying his message, that of reading and meditating on the revelation itself, in order to conform ourselves to it with devout and cheerful submission. We have no right at all to examine the nature of the discoveries or doctrines or precepts of Christianity [and of course of no other system professing to be a revelation] with the view of determining whether they seem to us becoming the wisdom of God and agreeable to the reason of man. It is proved that the revelation is from heaven; this is enough."[1]

According to this principle, a plain, unlettered believer may be hopelessly entangled in the decrees of Councils and the edicts of Popes, how palpably soever they contradict the Word of God and his own experience as a child of grace. They profess to be a message from heaven, and produce credentials of the Divine commission or infallibility of the church in pretended prodigies and wonders which from his circumstances and education he cannot be expected, by external proofs, to convict of forgery. As he is not at liberty "to examine the nature of the discoveries or doctrines" that are taught, he cannot deny but that these accounts *may* be true. The church, consequently, *may* be infallible, and the dogmas which disgust him *may* be Divine. The Apostles insisted upon a very different rule from that of the Bishop. "Beloved, believe not every spirit," says John,[2] " but try the spirits, whether they are of God; because many false prophets are gone out into the world." But how are these impostors to be detected and exposed? By demanding their commission, examining their credentials

---

[1] Critique on Butler's Analogy, prefixed to the Analogy—sixth Glasgow Edition, pp. 86, 87.
[2] 1 John iv. 1, 2.

and insisting solely upon the external proofs of their apostleship? Nothing of the kind. John remands us to the *doctrine* as the decisive test of spurious and true revelations. "Hereby know ye the Spirit of God: Every spirit that confesseth that Jesus Christ is come in the flesh is of God; and every spirit that confesseth not that Jesus Christ is come in the flesh is not of God." "If there come any unto you," says this same Apostle[1] in guarding against the deceivers who were entered into the world, "and bring not this doctrine"—whatever else he may bring, "after the working of Satan with all power and signs and lying wonders"—"receive him not into your house, neither bid him Godspeed." "But though we or an angel from heaven," says Paul,[2] "preach any other Gospel unto you than that ye have received, let him be accursed." It is remarkable that the New Testament nowhere insists—which it must have done upon the hypothesis of Bishop Wilson—on the insufficiency of external proofs as the decisive test of imposture. The *doctrine*, and the doctrine alone, is made the turning-point of the argument. The directions of the Apostles were founded upon the obvious principle that one truth cannot contradict another; and therefore whatever contradicted the Scriptures, which were *known* to be truth, carried upon its face the impression of falsehood. It was not because the Scriptures are a Divine revelation that they were made the touchstone for trying the spirits, but because, being a Divine revelation, they are necessarily and infallibly true. The proposition is universal that whatever is repugnant to a *known truth*, no matter what may be the method by which that truth is ascertained to us—whether by the oracles of God, intuition, demonstration or experience—cannot be Divine;[3] and the application of this principle presupposes

---

[1] 2 John v. 10. [2] Gal. i. 8.

[3] Vide Locke, Hum. Understand., B. iv., c. 18, § 5. "At supposito," says Witsius, "ista de quibus disseruimus Rationis axiomata pro veris ac certis comperta esse, et ab ipso Deo, nobis per Rationem preformata; quum verum vero non possit esse contrarium, uti nec Deus sibi ipsi, consequens est, nunquam Deum supernaturali revelatione aliquid homini patefacere,

the right, which Bishop Wilson denies, to examine the nature of the doctrines, discoveries or precepts which profess to be from heaven.   Even the Papists, who of all men are most concerned to establish the coexistence of repugnant truths, admit—with the exception of a few Schoolmen, who have taught the consistency of the same things being theologically true and philosophically false, or philosophically true and theologically false—that to effect contradictions is not an element of the power of God.[1]   But if the right to interrogate the record be denied, admissions of this sort are nothing worth.

The argument from abuse is always suspicious, and if we are to be deterred from the legitimate exercise of reason on the internal evidences of revelation by the danger of applying false measures as the standard of judgment, the same plea might be pressed with no little plausibility against the investigation of the external evidences which would leave us without the possibility of any reasonable faith at all. The Greeks looked at the *doctrine* and pronounced the Gospel to be foolishness, but it is forgotten that the Jews looked at the miracles and pronounced *them* to be inadequate. The Greeks sought wisdom, the Jews required a sign.   The Greek turned away from Christ because philosophy condemned Him ; the Jew because the sign which he demanded had not been vouchsafed.   The one *abused* his reason in the field of internal evidence ; the other in the field of external evidence.   Both were wrong in the *abuse,* but why the one had not as much right to examine the message as the other the credentials of the messenger, or why a privilege should be denied to the one because it was abused, while it is still

quod repugnet veritatibus per se notis, sive rectæ rationis dictamini. Atque hactenus illa axiomata valere quodammodo pro norma possunt, ut nihil recipiatur tanquam a Deo revelatum, quod principiis natura cognitis revera contrarium est."   De Usu et Abusu Rat., § xv.

[1] Denique est primum principium in lumine naturæ: Omne est, aut non est ; quo sublato tollitur omnis cognitio.   Itaque etiam adversarii in hoc conveniunt, id non posse fieri quod implicat contradictionem.   Bellarm., De Sac. Euch. Lib. iii., c. ii., sub. fin.

accorded to the other notwithstanding its abuse, does not appear.

Bishop Butler, who has conclusively demonstrated " that objections against Christianity as distinguished from objections against its evidence are frivolous," has expressed himself with his characteristic caution and sobriety in defining the relations of Reason to Revelation. He is far, however, from endorsing the doctrine of Bishop Wilson. " I express myself with caution," says he,[1] " lest I should be mistaken to vilify reason, which is indeed the only faculty we have wherewith to judge concerning anything, even revelation itself, or be misunderstood to assert that a supposed revelation cannot be proved false from internal characters. For it may contain clear immoralities or contradictions, and either of these would prove it false. Nor will I take upon me to affirm that nothing else can possibly render any supposed revelation incredible."

It is to be regretted that this distinguished prelate, who as a thinker deserves the title of Judicious incomparably better than Hooker, has not attempted to draw the line between the use and the abuse of reason, though his sentiments may perhaps be collected from a careful attention to the tenor and spirit of the chapter from which the above extract is taken. We can only say that that chapter, in connection with some passages, to which we shall afterwards allude, in Taylor's Ductor Dubitantium, has suggested to us the views which we are about to submit.

We lay it down, then, as a general principle, that the competency of reason to judge in any case is the measure of its right. This competency may be actual or potential—actual, when we are possession of the knowledge requisite to the formation of a sound opinion ; potential, when though not in actual possession of it, we are able to acquire it. This general principle, which is only another statement of the proposition that contradictions can never be both true, involves in its application a double distinction of rev-

[1] Analogy, Part II., c. 3.

elation and a corresponding distinction in the office of reason.

Revelation may be contemplated as imparting to us truths which eye hath not seen nor ear heard, neither have entered into the heart of man to conceive, which "descend to us immediately from heaven, and communicate with no principle, no matter, no conclusion here below," or, as proclaiming upon Divine authority what we were capable of discovering without the aid of inspiration. In other words, revelation may be regarded, according to its subjects, as either supernatural or natural. "Everything in Scripture," says Taylor,[1] "is not, in the divided sense, a matter of faith"—that is, the Scripture contains some propositions which are intuitively evident without revelation; others which reason can demonstrate from premises furnished by our natural faculties; and others still which lie beyond the province of nature, are "derivatives from heaven and communicate not at all with the principles of philosophy" or science. The supernatural is that which alone is strictly and properly *revelation;* the natural is *confirmed,* but not *made known,* by the Divine testimony.

This distinction betwixt the supernatural and the natural we conceive to be important, not merely as it serves to give clearer views in reference to the office of reason, but as it equally serves to remove some popular objections, sedulously inculcated by Papists, to the universal reading of the Scriptures. The obscurity which is alleged to render them unfit for indiscriminate perusal will be found on examination to lie for the most part within the province of the natural; it is of the earth, earthy. Allusions to the events, manners, customs and institutions of an age long since past, to places of which no trace can be found, to scenery which is not familiar to us, and to modes of thought into which we find it difficult to enter—all of which were simple and

---

[1] Ductor Dubitantium, Book I., c. ii., Rule 3, §§ 21, 22. This whole Rule, though, like all Taylor's writings, very much wanting in precision and method, contains many valuable thoughts.

natural to the countrymen and contemporaries of the sacred writers—are the sources of no little perplexity and labour to their modern readers. But these things affect the costume, not the substance, of revelation—the body, not the soul. Its life must be sought in its supernatural discoveries. These are its own field, and whatever obscurity attaches to them presses as heavily upon the learned as the unlearned, the clergy as the laity. All stand upon the same level. All are equally dependent upon God for his Divine illumination; none can claim to be a master, none should submit as a slave. The august mysteries of Christianity are revealed to the meek, however untutored in this world's wisdom, and concealed from the wise, however skilled in philosophy and science. Here God is the teacher and man the disciple, and every one in this school must become a fool in order that he may be wise. The Bible incidentally treats of history, geography and ancient manners, but these are not the things which give it its value. Christ crucified is its great subject; it is the knowledge of Him that saves the soul, and that knowledge is more accessible to the poor and ignorant than to the arrogant disputers of this world.

But to resume the immediate subject of discussion: the office of reason in the supernatural department of revelation may be positive, but can never be negative;[1] in the natural it is negative, but only to a very limited extent, if at all, positive. We use the terms *positive* and *negative* to indicate the nature of the conclusion, and not the arguments by which it is reached; that being positive by which the reality of the revelation is affirmed, and that negative by which it is denied. When we say, therefore, that reason has no negative jurisdiction in regard to the supernatural, we mean that it is incompetent to infer the spuriousness of a pretended revelation from the nature of its mysteries—that

[1] There is one exception to this rule: When a professed revelation contradicts itself, another, or one which is known to be real, then reason has a negative power. This exception, however, comes under the general principle on which the rule is founded.

it cannot construct an internal argument, from discoveries
and doctrines which transcend the limits of natural attainment, to convict of falsehood what professes to be Divine.
The positive jurisdiction which, in this department, we have
conceded to reason refers to the perception of those impressions of His character which it is to be expected God would
enstamp upon His Word, those traces of power, wisdom,
goodness and glory which proclaim a Divine original as
truly as the works of nature or the dispensations of Providence. Every true revelation must authenticate itself, and
the only faculty through which its reflection of the Divine
image can be manifested to us is Reason. Unenlightened
by grace, it is confessedly incompetent to discover God in
His Word, and consequently never can exercise any positive
jurisdiction until it becomes the habitation of the Spirit.
It is to the called, and the called alone, that Christ crucified
is the power of God and the wisdom of God. The negative
power which we have accorded to reason, in the department
of the natural, implies that it is competent to say, to a certain extent, what a revelation ought not to be, though it
is not competent to say what it ought to be. It is able here
to convict a pretended revelation of imposture by showing
that it contains contradictions, palpable falsehoods or gross
absurdities, though it cannot infer that a system is truly
Divine because it is free from objections which would be
fatal to its credit. The sum of our doctrine, then, is that in
the supernatural, reason may prove, but cannot refute, the
claims of a pretended revelation; in the natural, it may
refute, but cannot establish.

This distinction of the use of reason, corresponding to
the division of the subjects of revelation, is only an application of the principle that the right of reason to judge, in
any case, springs from its competency. To justify a negative judgment upon internal grounds there must be contradiction to previous knowledge. The very idea of the supernatural involves the supposition that its discoveries are new.
The field which it occupies is inaccessible to our natural

faculties, and having no previous informations of the subjects it discloses, we cannot condemn it, on account of inconsistency with known truth. The revelation, in this aspect,
is a source of new ideas, perfectly independent of every
other source, and it is to be expected that they should differ as widely from those derived from experience as these,
in turn, differ among themselves. When truths beyond the
reach of nature are announced upon the authority of God,
a new world is opened to reason—a world of invisible realities and of mysterious things. All may be strange and unexpected, as the scenes of the moon or some distant planet
would be to a traveller from earth. Still, as such a traveller
would be guilty of great folly in refusing to credit his
senses because the appearances before him differed from
those in the world he had left, so reason would be guilty
of equal folly in rejecting the disclosures of revelation
because they are unlike the discoveries of nature. We are
no more competent to say beforehand what shall or shall
not be revealed than we are to pronounce, independently
of experience, upon the species of information which our
senses might be expected to supply. The embryo in the
womb is as capable of predicting what sort of a world it
shall enter as natural reason of predicting the things of the
Spirit of God. Revelation, again, may be likened to a new
sense unfolding to reason a new field of ideas; and it would
be no less preposterous to discredit its testimony because it is
different from that of nature than it would be to despise
the information of the eye because it differs from that of
the ear. We have no natural measures of supernatural
mysteries, and as they, therefore, cannot contradict philosophy
and science, they cannot be judged by the wisdom of men.

The relation in which we stand to the supernatural disclosures of an authentic revelation is analogous to that
which, according to the sublime aphorism of Bacon,[1] we

---

[1] Homo naturæ minister et interpres, tantum facit et intelligit quantum
de naturæ ordine re vel mente observaverit, nec amplius scit, aut potest.
Nov. Organ., Aph. I.

sustain to nature. As the phenomena of the material
world are not to be *judged*, but *seen*, so the mysteries of
heaven are not to be *judged*, but *apprehended*. Interpretation is to theology what observation and experiment are
to philosophy. As it is the business of science not to fabricate imaginary worlds and dignify hypotheses with the title
of *laws*, but patiently to investigate the facts of nature as
they really exist, so it is the business of reason in regard to
revelation not to form fantastic theories in relation to its
discoveries, doctrines and institutions, but to interpret with
humility and digest with reverence what God has chosen to
communicate. The scope of inquiry in each case is not
what ought to be, but what is. The facts of nature, reduced
to general expressions declaring their uniformity, constitute
laws, and these laws, arranged into system, constitute science or philosophy. The facts of revelation are its doctrines
or mysteries, and these reduced to method, according to their
dependencies and connections, constitute theology. Actual
phenomena furnish the materials of the one; the Word and
Oracle of God, the materials of the other.

These seem to have been the views of Bacon, who treats
revelation as an independent source of new ideas, and concedes to reason the twofold use of explication and inference,[1]
" the former, in the conception and apprehension of the
mysteries of God to us revealed, the other, in the inferring
and deriving of doctrine and direction thereupon." The
inference of Bacon, however, does not refer to the inductive
process by which the scattered instructions of revelation
are collected, compared and digested into system, but to
the application of its principles to the practical emergencies
of life. It is the inference of a chess-player, who deduces
from the positive laws of the game the most successful
method of regulating his movements; the inference of the
statesman, who devises the wisest schemes for the conduct
of the republic in conformity with the maxims and prin-

[1] Advancement of Learning: Works, Montagu's Edition, vol. ii., pp.
301, 302.

ciples of the Constitution; the inference, of daily life, in which the general laws of society are applied to the circumstances and conditions of men. It is an office of reason, in the *use* of revelation, presupposing that its reality has been proved and its maxims understood.

The doctrine which we have endeavoured to illustrate, that reason possesses no negative jurisdiction in regard to the mysteries or supernatural facts of revelation, because it possesses no previous knowledge which they can contradict, subverts the basis of the whole system of philosophical infidelity. The corner-stone of the fabric is the competency of man to determine beforehand what a revelation should contain. That, from the very nature of the case, it deals with the unknown, and contemplates us in the attitude of learners and not of teachers, of servants and interpreters and not lords and masters, is a proposition, simple and obvious as it is, which the disciples of Herbert, Bolingbroke and Hume have entirely overlooked. The legitimate conclusion from their principles is, either that man possesses, in his natural faculties and resources, the means of omniscience, or that whatever God knows beyond the reach of reason must for ever remain an impenetrable secret with Himself. The Deity, in His omnipotence, cannot impart ideas which "eye hath not seen, nor ear heard, neither have entered into the heart of man." He cannot open the eyes of the blind nor unstop the ears of the deaf. But if God can indefinitely unfold to us new sources of ideas; if He can lift the curtain which covers the invisible from mortal eyes; open worlds, peopled with realities, of which fancy had never dreamed; if He can impart to us new senses, or illustrate the unknown by analogies borrowed from the present state, as the form of the key is adapted to the ward of the lock,—then revelation may be as real as nature, as independent in its own sphere and as certain in its results.[1] Faith may be as

[1] Id primo tenendum, Axiomata Rationis certis quibusdam circumscripta esse limitibus, ultra quos eniti non valeant; Mysteria autem Fidei eos

unsuspected a means of knowledge as sense, consciousness or reason, and no more to be condemned because it is adjusted to no natural measure than one sense is to be cashiered because it speaks not the same language with its neighbour.

Those, therefore, who deny the reality of supernatural mysteries, who confound what is *above*, with what is contrary to, reason, and reduce everything to the level of natural attainment, deny the reality of *any* proper revelation at all. To be supernatural is to be above reason. That these mysteries, however, can contain no contradictions to reason must be obvious to the slightest reflection. Descending upon us immediately from heaven, their source is the bosom of God; and as they communicate with no principles of earth, we must take them just as they descend from the fountain of truth. Reason is simply the eye to apprehend the light—the ear to distinguish the sound. And the *new* truths of faith can no more be *contrary* to reason than new truths of sense, impressions of colour and sound, in the instance of the blind and deaf restored to the enjoyment of their lost senses, can be contrary to their previous attainments. All that we can say is, that reason is furnished with new materials of thought, knows something which it did not know before, is in possession of a class of ideas different from anything to which it had been previously accustomed. There can be no contradiction, however, where the terms are not the same.

We have attributed to reason a positive jurisdiction in authenticating the claims of a real revelation from the nature of its mysteries. As we demonstrate, in natural theology, the being and perfections of God from the order and beauty of His works, and infer the relations which He

limites plurimum transcendere. Sic ut nequaquam Rationi liceat mysteria isthæc eo nomine rejicere, quod nihil unquam iis simile in suis ideis ac notionibus invenerit. 1 Cor. ii. 9. Certe et id Ratio docet, multa in Dei infinitate et consilio ejus latere, quæ ipsa per se assequi non possit; Deoque dignum esse ea de se revelare quæ captum nostrum superant. Witsius, de Usu et Abusu Rat., § xx.

must sustain to the worlds He has made, so the scheme of
Providence, disclosed in revelation, may, in its majesty and
grandeur, its harmony, beneficence and purity, contain
such memorials of Deity as to render skepticism little less
than madness. In the case of Christianity, for instance,
the glory of God is so conspicuously displayed in the provisions of the Gospel that to the called it would be as easy
to doubt the shining of the sun in the heavens as the
Divine mission of Jesus. Redemption is its own witness.
We may study its doctrines and its facts in their harmony
and connection—we may compare the end with the means,
and discover the wisdom and the power, the grace and love
which animate the whole. We call it *reasonable*, not because reason discovered its doctrines or originated its precepts, but because it is consistent with itself; it is a system
made up of parts, nicely adjusted and exquisitely arranged,
and not a mass of insulated, incoherent, independent phenomena. The fitness and propriety of its provisions, the
simplicity and scope of its laws, the beauty of its rites and
the sublime purity of its code, as information upon these
points may be gathered from itself, are topics which may
not only furnish legitimate employment to reason, but task
its highest powers.

But the execution of these functions requires the illumination of the Holy Spirit. Reason can perceive very faintly
the positive proofs which revelation carries on its face,
though, as we shall afterward see, it may construct a negative argument which, if not sufficient to satisfy faith, is sufficient to rebuke unbelief.

But what we wish particularly to inculcate here is, that
an incapacity of perceiving the impressions of Deity upon
His Word creates no presumption against the truth of their
existence. It would only follow that we are weak and
blind, and not that the things themselves are either false
or unreasonable. We cannot reason from our ignorance.
Though the invisible things of God are clearly seen, being
understood by the things that are made, yet multitudes in

every age have gone down to the grave without being conducted to the great Creator by the heavens which declare
His glory, and the firmament which showeth His handiwork. The stupidity of the learner is no proof against the
truth which he fails to apprehend. It remains certain to
reason and to faith that God made the worlds, and His finger
is conspicuously displayed in their arrangement and government, though thousands have failed to recognize His hand
and to adore the wisdom which conducts the universe.
That the blind are incapable of receiving the impressions
of light and colour is no presumption against the existence
of either; and so the glory of God may be indelibly stamped
upon the Gospel, it may reflect His image, display His wisdom, and make known the manifold riches of His grace,
and yet mortal ignorance and mortal stupidity may fail to
apprehend the fact. The light shineth in darkness, and the
darkness comprehendeth it not. Hence, it is impossible,
from the mysteries of revelation, to construct an internal
argument against it, though one may be framed in its favour.

In addition to this, as we have already intimated, there
are negative considerations suggested by the contents of
revelation which go far to establish its supernatural pretensions. This point has not passed altogether without notice
in Butler's masterly treatise.[1] The argument consists in
showing that no causes, apart from the interposition of
God, are adequate to explain the appearance or to account
for the phenomena of thought involved in the subjects of
the professed revelation. One by one, all natural solutions
may be removed, every supposition may be destroyed, but
that which ascribes to God the agency which is claimed.
If, for example, human invention is alleged as a sufficient
explanation of the case, *that* may be proved to be inadequate by showing that the materials which compose the system, either as they separately exist or are combined into a
whole, are not such as could have been suggested by any
conceivable laws of association to the human mind, and

[1] See the Analogy, Part ii., chap. 3d, last sentence.

therefore must lie beyond the province of human ingenuity.
Such transcendent elements as the Trinity, the incarnation
of the Son, the work of the Spirit, personal election, and
particular redemption are not the ingredients which man
was likely to use in devising a system of religion. These
ideas never arose spontaneously in the human breast; they
are indeed so remote from the ordinary trains of thought that
the authority of a confessed revelation finds it difficult to
subdue the remonstrances of carnal reason against them.
The scheme of redemption as a whole, its conception and
gradual development, the harmony of its doctrines as delivered in successive ages and generations by patriarchs and
prophets, the correspondence of all its dispensations, and
its grand consummation in the death of Jesus and the institutions of the Gospel,—all these exhibit a reach of thought
and an amplitude of purpose which we feel it to be mockery
to chain to earth. The temple is too grand and august for
a puny architect. If, again, such a revelation should be
referred to the Devil, the argument of our Saviour is ready
with overwhelming force: a house divided against itself
cannot stand—Satan cannot be expected to cast out Satan.
The moral tone of the Gospel is too pure and elevated, its
doctrines tend too evidently to promote the glory of God,
the peace of society and the good of man, to have sprung
from hell. Its atmosphere is too clear, its light too brilliant, its hopes too sublime, to be emanations from the pit.

If Christianity should be ascribed to policy or enthusiasm, the answer is also ready that the effect does not correspond to the cause. We are competent to judge of the natural operation of these principles, and we trace none of their
peculiarities in the glorious Gospel of the blessed God.
Christianity, however, exists; it is an effect which must, like
every other, have had *some* cause. And if it can be shown
to have sprung neither from earth nor hell, the conclusion
is irresistible that its source is the bosom of God. Such is
the nature of that negative argument founded on the principle that every effect must have an adequate cause, which

reason, we think, is capable of constructing from the acknow-ledged phenomena of revelation.

We have now, we apprehend, sufficiently explained our views in saying that the office of reason in regard to super-natural mysteries can never be negative. It cannot con-demn them, because it has no law by which to try them; it is not a fit judge, because not a competent judge. It can-not say beforehand what a revelation should be, how it should be given, what it should contain, and with what evi-dence it ought to be attended. At the same time, it may study these mysteries and find God in them, while it pos-sesses the power of proving upon other grounds that they could have originated from no other source. The conclu-sion is most important that no mysteries ever can create the slightest presumption against the Divine original of the sys-tem which contains them, while they may contain irresist-ible evidence, both negative and positive, of its truth.

The office of reason in relation to those parts of revela-tion which communicate with principles of natural know-ledge we have defined to be negative and not positive, or, if positive at all, only to a very limited degree. Every sys-tem, and particularly every written system professing to be Divine, with which we are acquainted, contains not only its mysteries or supernatural facts, but allusions direct or indi-rect to a variety of subjects which fall within the limits of the human faculties. Geography, history and philosophy, the manners, customs, institutions of a distant age, the scenery and productions of other lands, and especially the appearances of human nature in its moral, social and politi-cal condition at the period of the writers, are embraced in the Sacred Records, and the statements concerning them attested by the same inspiration which covers the mysteries of the faith. In regard to these matters, the human mind, according to the extent and accuracy of its knowledge, is capable of judging between truth and falsehood, and any real inconsistency with fact is evidently fatal to the plea of in-spiration. A record pretending to this high character, which should contain anachronisms or geographical mistakes, which should blunder in its political or social allusions, reason could not hesitate to brand with the stigma of forgery. While, however, error in these matters would be evidently fatal, the strictest fidelity and truth would create no necessary inference of Divine interposition. Human causes would be adequate to explain the phenomenon, without an appeal to the supernatural agency of God. Reason, therefore, can give a negative, but not a positive decision; it can say what is *not*, but not what is, from God. If there be any exception to this principle, it is in the department of moral inquiry, though Bacon seems to reckon the purity of the Gospel among its supernatural facts.[1] He grounds upon the Word and Oracle of God, "not only those points of faith which concern the great mysteries of the Deity, of the creation, of the redemption, but likewise those which concern the law moral truly interpreted." It is revealed in the Scriptures with a degree of perfection to which the light of nature cannot aspire, and though conscience is a "sparkle of the purity of man's first estate," yet in his present fallen condition it is no adequate guide, no perfect rule; it can "check the vice, but not inform the virtue." Hence, he concludes that the doctrine of religion, as well *moral* as mystical, is not to be attained but by inspiration and revelation from God.

That the standard of rectitude displayed in the Scriptures is beyond the capacities of fallen man to discover, may, as a general truth, be admitted, and yet the positive argument arising from this fact seems to us to rise no higher than a presumption, since it is impossible to fix the limit to which the light of nature might have conducted us without the guidance of revelation. The subject of morals is not above reason, considered in itself, apart from the consequences of the fall. If man had never sinned, his moral vision would always have been clear. His incapacity, in his present state, to frame a perfect system of duty does

[1] Advancement of Learning: Works (Montagu), vol. ii., p. 300.

not pertain to nature, as such, but to nature as fallen and corrupt. It is an accidental and not an essential defect. The incapacity, however, to discover the *mysteries* of religion is absolutely natural. The angels are as much dependent upon revelation for the sublime facts of redemption as man himself. There are deep things of God, which none can penetrate but His own eternal Spirit, and none can know them but those to whom they are graciously revealed. These unfathomable depths are evidently supernatural, in a sense which cannot attach to any code of morals, however pure and exalted.

As man, even in his fallen state, possessing a moral nature, possesses necessarily *some* knowledge of moral distinctions, and as this knowledge is unquestionably capable of being enlarged and refined, we can never be certain that any particular moral discovery *could* not have been the offspring of nature. There may be violent presumptions against its natural origin, arising from the condition of those who announce it—their want of education, their early habits, prejudices and associations, and from the superiority which it evinces to the spirit and attainments of the age and country in which it first made its appearance. These and such like considerations are entitled to no little weight; but still, as we cannot definitely say how far nature *might* go, we cannot determine where the necessity of a revelation begins. Immorality is clear proof that the system containing it is not Divine, but a high morality is not decisive evidence to the contrary. It has great force in removing objections, in showing that the doctrine is not unworthy of God, and as concurring with other proofs it may make them amount to a moral demonstration; but, in itself considered, we are inclined, with Warburton, to rank it no higher than a presumption.[1] The credibility of the sacred

[1] Divine Legation, B. ix., chap. 5. His words are: "But in reverence to Truth, I hold myself obliged to own, that in my opinion the reasonableness of a doctrine pretended to come immediately from God is of itself alone no proof, but a presumption only, of such its Divine original;

writers—the reality and honesty of their convictions—may be established by their moral tone; and these, established, establish the facts to which they bear witness, and these, in turn, the Divine original of their religion; but morality here is not a direct proof of inspiration, but the means of fortifying the direct proof. The internal evidences upon which alone we would confidently rely are those drawn from the mysteries of revelation—its supernatural facts and discoveries. Here God must be seen and confessed. There can be no suspicion of nature's agency. The grand facts of redemption—these are the glory of the Gospel, and its inward witness of a heavenly birth.

The supernatural facts of revelation may, however, react upon morals, by the addition of new and impressive sanctions to its duties, and by enlarging the sphere of moral obligation. It is a low and narrow view of Christianity which those have been accustomed to take who, anxious to exalt Natural Religion upon its ruins, have artfully depicted it as a system of ceremonial rites and positive observances. It reveals, they tell us, no new duties essentially *moral* in their character; and its chief value consists not in its own peculiarities, but in the relation which they bear to the great doctrines of Natural Religion. As containing an authoritative statement of what the light of reason

because, though the excellence of a doctrine (even allowing it surpass all other moral teaching whatever) may show it to be worthy of God, yet, from that sole excellence, we cannot certainly conclude that it came immediately from Him, since we know not to what heights of moral knowledge the human understanding, unassisted by inspiration, may arrive. Not even our full experience, that all the wisdom of Greece and Rome comes extremely short of the wisdom of the Gospel, can support us in concluding with certainty that this Gospel was sent immediately from God. We can but very doubtfully guess what excellence may be produced by a well-formed and well-cultivated mind, further blessed with a vigorous temperament and a happy organization of the body. The amazement into which Sir Isaac Newton's discoveries in nature threw the learned world, as soon as men became able to comprehend their truth and utility, sufficiently shows what little conception it had that the human faculties could ever arise so high or spread so wide."

might have been able to discover without it, and as diffus-
ing, by the judicious institutions of its ministry and ordinances, and impressing, in the regularly recurring seasons
of its worship, the solemn obligations of nature which men
are prone to overlook and forget, revelation, they confess, is
not to be despised.   Still, its highest office is to anticipate
the slow discoveries of reason, to supersede the excuses of
indolence and ignorance, and to make nature effective by an
appeal to the awful majesty of God.

The shallow sophistry of these pretenders in theology,
is at once refuted[1] by the fact that the great end of redemption is not to fortify nature, but to recover it from
the ruin and degradation of the Fall: it is a scheme of *salvation*—of life to the dead, liberty to the captives and the
opening of the prison to them that are bound.   In unfold-

---

[1] This subject is very ably treated in the first chapter of the Second
Part of Butler's Analogy.   The distinction, however, which Butler
draws between natural and supernatural religion does not strike us as
being strictly just.   "The essence of natural religion" he places in religious regards to the Father; "the essence of revealed," or, as we would
prefer to call it, supernatural, "religion, in religious regards to the Son
and the Holy Ghost."   Now we apprehend that the difference betwixt them
is not in the *objects* to which they are respectively directed, but in the *relations* under which those objects are contemplated.   Supernatural religion
is founded on the relations in which God stands to us as a Redeemer and
a Saviour; natural religion, upon the relations in which He stands to us
as Creator and Governor.   The Trinity is alike the object of both.   It
was Father, Son and Holy Ghost who created Adam, and he was bound
to worship the Trinity—for there is no other God—under the pain of
idolatry.   Natural religion is as much revealed as supernatural.   If its
object be the Trinity, nature never could discover the personality of the
Deity.   Adam was dependent upon the Author of his being for the knowledge of His name.   And though, when the object of worship was once
made known, and the relations in which man stood to the Deity discovered, the duties were a matter of obvious deduction, yet, as the same
holds in supernatural religion, revelation is equally important to both.
By natural religion we understand the religion of man in his state of
nature as he came from the hands of his Maker; by supernatural religion, the religion of sinners redeemed by grace and restored to the favour
of God.   The covenant of works is natural, the covenant of grace supernatural, religion; and both are equally revealed.

ing the mysteries of grace it unfolds at the same time relations to God, to all the Persons of the Trinity, to our fellowmen and ourselves, which, as they are founded upon nothing in nature, could not be discovered without the light of revelation, and just as truly create obligations essentially moral in their character as the natural relations discoverable by reason which are so much extolled. The distinction of moral and positive duties is not a distinction of the mode in which the grounds of duty are ascertained to us, but a distinction of the grounds of duty themselves; that being moral which grows out of a moral relation, and that positive which is simply the offspring of command. The relations of redemption, which are made known by revelation, being as truly moral as the relations of creation made known, if indeed it be so, by the light of nature, this new department of relations opens a new field of duties specifically moral, which can no more be neglected without guilt than the more obvious injunctions of natural religion. To .disregard a Redeemer and a Saviour would seem to be even more aggravated depravity than not to love a Creator and Preserver. The relations in the one case are tenderer and sweeter than those in the other, and the neglect or contempt of them consequently argues intenser hardness of heart and deeper obduracy of conscience.

That the offices of the Godhead in the economy of salvation present the Deity to us in a new light, and expand the circle of our moral obligations, may be admitted; while it is not so obvious that our duties to ourselves and others are any otherwise enlarged than as they are enjoined with greater clearness and authority than unassisted reason could reach. But Christianity unquestionably binds the race together in ties unknown to nature. She establishes a sacred brotherhood in a common origin, a common ruin, a common immortality and a common Saviour, which unites the descendants of Adam into one great family, and renders wars, discords and jealousies as odious as they are, hurtful. The benevolence of the Bible is a different principle from

the benevolence of nature and that peculiar sympathy of
the redeemed—the cultivation of which is at once a duty
and a delight—founded upon a common union with their
Lord, and a common participation of the glorious Spirit, is
as much above anything attainable by unrenewed humanity as the heavens are above the earth. "A *new* commandment give I unto you, that ye love one another."

The duties of temperance and chastity which primarily
respect ourselves are placed upon a basis entirely novel, and
invested with awful sanctions by the doctrine of the Scriptures that our bodies are the temples of the Holy Ghost.
Chambering, wantonness and dissipation become, under this
view, not merely excesses, but sacrilege. They insult God
while they degrade ourselves.

In all these cases, however, in which Christianity enlarges
the field of morality by enlarging our knowledge of the
moral relations into which our duties must ultimately be
resolved, reason is competent to recognize the duty as soon as
the relation is discovered. It cannot, indeed, discover the
relation itself—this grows out of the supernatural facts of
revelation—but when they are once admitted there is nothing in the subsequent process beyond the capacities of nature.
Hence, if any duties contradictory to these relations should
be enjoined, the pretended revelation might be as confidently pronounced to be the offspring of imposture as if it
inculcated principles inconsistent with the relations discoverable by reason. The negative jurisdiction of reason in the
department of morality is the same as that which belongs to
it in the department exclusively natural. The morality
does not vary with the light by which it is perceived. The
form of communication makes no change in the essence of
the duty. We cannot, therefore, agree with Lord Bacon in
looking upon morality, in any aspect of it, as strictly supernatural. It falls within the legitimate province of reason;
and though revelation may enlarge its dominion, remove its
defects, and enforce its claims by new and more effectual
sanctions, still, as in itself it does not bear visibly the im-

press of God, it can hardly be regarded as competent to authenticate any system professing to be from Him.

It is remarkable, too, that it is only in the negative light upon which we have insisted as that in which the Scriptures present the argument from morality that so much stress has been laid upon that argument by a certain class of writers as to make it the great internal proof of revelation. Our Saviour does not say that His system is necessarily from God because it is pure, but that it cannot be from the Devil. The sublime sanctity of His precepts was a triumphant demonstration that the finger of Beelzebub had no part in his miracles; therefore *they* were Divine, and *therefore* his doctrines were to be received. The pure morality is pleaded to remove objections, and nothing more; and the principle is obviously implied that any imperfections in this respect are a conclusive refutation of the pretensions, however supported, of a professed revelation.

The negative jurisdiction which we have assigned to reason in the natural department of revelation, we are not reluctant to confess, is capable of immense abuse. This is the arena upon which shallow philosophy and spurious science have delighted to contest the claims of Christianity. The dreams of visionaries, the maxims of education and the prejudices of ignorance will in the exercise of this jurisdiction be made, to a greater or less extent, the touchstone of Divine truth, and prove the rock on which thousands shall stumble and perish. It is not to be expected, in this world of sin and error, that rights will be always rightly used. The Jews, without controversy, not only had the right, but were solemnly bound, to try the religion of Jesus by the standard of Moses and the Prophets, and yet in the exercise of this unquestionable right, the discharge of this imperative obligation, they were led to condemn the Saviour as an impostor and blasphemer. They were surely not to be denied the privilege of reasoning from the Scriptures because they reasoned badly. The use of medicine is not to be prohibited because quacks and mountebanks turn it into

poison and murder their unfortunate patients. If God
gives reason the right to judge, He gives it subject to a
fearful responsibility; and in nothing is the obligation so solemn and awful to cultivate a love of truth, to cherish a
spirit of honesty and candour, and guard the mind against
prejudice and passion, as in this very matter of weighing
the evidence of a professed revelation. When there is a
contradiction betwixt our philosophy and it, the method of
reason and of duty is to compare their respective evidences,
and lean to the side which has the preponderance. If the
principle which is contradicted be an intuitive truth or a
demonstrative conclusion, the pretended revelation must be
evidently discarded; if it be only a probable opinion, the
arguments which sustain it must be stronger than the proofs
of revelation before the latter can be justly rejected for the
former. Whatever credentials the professed revelation presents are so many positive arguments which cannot be set
aside without stronger opposing proofs. The great danger
is in over-estimating the evidence in support of a favourite
opinion. "Nothing," says Paley, "is so soon made as a
maxim." Those, consequently, who do not make conscience
of truth are under severe temptation to contract the guilt
of rejecting the Word of God on account of its opposition
to silly prejudices and hasty inductions which are assumed
to be unquestionable. This abuse of reason is a sin to which
the apostasy has exposed us. We may misjudge where we
have the right to judge, but we do it at our risk.

The most precious doctrines of the Gospel, though in the
forms of their development and the precise mode and circumstances of their application they are pre-eminently
supernatural, yet ultimately rest upon moral principles
which do not transcend the legitimate province of reason.
Justification by faith, for example, while it involves the
supernatural facts connected with the advent and offices of
Christ, at the same time proceeds upon a law—that of federal
representation, and the consequent propriety of imputation—
which belongs to the department of morals, and upon the

essential character of which, as just or unjust, reason is to some extent competent to pronounce. A false philosophy may condemn this cardinal principle of God's dispensations with man; it may be assumed as a maxim that neither sin nor righteousness can be justly imputed. The proper reply to such cavils and objections is, not that reason has no right to pronounce a judgment in the case, but that the judgment in question is contrary to truth and evidence. Those who obstinately persist in their prejudices are in the same condition with the Jews, who felt it to be impossible that He who was accursed of God—as Christ, according to the Scriptures, was shown to be by hanging on a tree—could be the Saviour of men, or their own promised Messiah. They were not wrong in applying the test of Scripture to the pretensions of Christ, but they were wrong in adopting false interpretations, in reasoning from false premises or corrupting those that were true. There is no such moral axiom as the enemies of imputation allege. The doctrine is fully consistent with reason, and if on account of it a revelation is rejected, it is rejected in concession to a false philosophy. So, again, it may be assumed that all sin consists in voluntary action, and the Bible may be spurned for teaching a better doctrine. But the species of abuse which reason undergoes in this case is analogous to that which it received at the hands of Hume when he attempted to demonstrate that miracles were incapable of proof from human testimony. Reason, in such instances, does not pronounce upon a subject entirely beyond its province, but it may grievously and sinfully err in the character of the judgment it shall render. It may prostitute its right to the cause of falsehood and hell.

Could it be shown that the doctrine of imputation involved a principle essentially iniquitous, or that states of heart, as contradistinguished from transitory acts, could not be possessed of a moral character, we should feel that the argument against Christianity were as complete as if it had been convicted of inculcating lying or authorizing fraud. And hence we regard those who by their perverse disputations

corrupt the great truths of justification and original sin not
simply as heresiarchs, but as the patrons and abettors of
gross infidelity. The world is not to be mystified by absurd
interpretations, and the issue which will ultimately be made
is not what is the sense of the Scriptures, but whether documents containing the sense which the Bible evidently does
can be inspired. The advocates of the new divinity are laying the foundations broad and deep of a new phase of philosophical infidelity—an infidelity more dangerous, because
more subtle, than that of Bolingbroke and Hume, which pretends reverence while it really insults, which, like Judas,
betrays the Son of man with a kiss. We would remind
these men that all the trains of evidence in favour of Christianity—its prophecies fulfilled, its stupendous miracles, its
salutary effects on the world—are so many positive arguments *against* their pretended axioms which they are
solemnly bound to weigh before they are authorized to dignify their crudities with the title of intuitive truths, and on
account of them dismiss the Gospel with a sneer. The
Jews were as certain that no prophet could spring from
Galilee and no good thing from Nazareth as these men that
neither sin nor righteousness can be imputed, or that all sin
must be resolved into voluntary action. They, too, may be
confounding familiar prejudices with intuitive truths, and
they too may find that the penalty of this awful abuse of
God's best gift is that they shall die in their sins. We
would not attack this species of philosophical infidelity by
putting its moral inquiries beyond the territory of reason,
but we would assault its principles themselves; and we are
much mistaken if it cannot be shown—though this is not
the place for doing so—that they are as contrary to the facts
of experience as to the Word of God, that they are shallow,
false, sophistical, having indeed the semblance of wisdom,
but the substance of folly. We should be reluctant even to
suggest the impression, by timid distinctions and sly insinu-
ations against the office of reason, that the friends of truth
are unable to meet its enemies on the moral ground which

they have chosen to occupy. We would direct our batteries against their strongholds, turn their favourite weapons against themselves, and construct the same species of argument against their cobweb theories which they have in vain fabricated against the *grace* of the Gospel. We would appeal from reason misinformed to reason rightly informed, from the drunken to the sober judge, from philosophy, falsely so called, to the true philosophy of facts.

We wish, however, to have it distinctly recollected that the province which we assign to reason in this whole department is purely negative. It is not within the compass of nature, of moral philosophy or metaphysics, with all the lights and resources which either or both can command, to devise a system of religion adequate to the wants of a sinner—to determine of what elements it ought to consist, how it shall be communicated, in what form dispensed, or under what circumstances imparted. These are secret things which belong to God, and can be known only as He chooses to reveal them to the sons of men. But, while reason cannot say what the scheme of salvation shall be, it may condemn a system which, professing to be from heaven, contradicts the obvious principles of truth and rectitude. Its office hath this extent, no more.[1] What revelation actually is must be known from its own records. The Word and Oracle of God is our only source of information. We have no sympathy with the prevailing tendency of some modern speculations to aspire at universal truths—truths which shall contain the seeds of all possible knowledge, the principles of all philosophy, and from which universal science may be deduced, by strictly *a priori* pro-

---

[1] The negative jurisdiction for which we contend is generally assumed by Protestants in their arguments against transubstantiation. Though this professes to be a supernatural mystery, yet it touches upon points of human philosophy and contradicts the most obvious principles of science; and therefore, instead of being entitled to credit on the authority of a pretended revelation, it is sufficient to damn the claims of any system which inculcates it. We feel the argument to be complete against it, because it is an absurdity.

cesses. It was to be hoped that Bacon had completely
exploded this whole method of investigation, though he
has given countenance to the possibility of some such universal science—attained, however, by induction, and not
from necessary maxims of pure reason—in his curious
speculation upon what he denominates the first philosophy.

There is but little danger that the physical sciences will
ever be cultivated upon any other principles than those of
the Novum Organum. The time has gone by when the
dreams of Rabbins and Hutchinsonians upon the letters,
points and dots of the Bible shall be substituted for the
observation of nature and the consequent generalization of
facts. Science is felt to be no longer the creature of ingenuity, but the offspring of patient attention and rigorous
induction.

But in religious and moral subjects the age is prone to
revert to the exploded method of the Schools. Discarding
in nature the safer guidance of experience, and in revelation the safer guidance of a sound interpretation, those who
aspire to the highest forms of philosophy are intent upon
constructing systems without facts, from principles which
have been woven of the stuff that dreams are made of.
The origin of this unfortunate tendency is, no doubt, to be
ascribed to an obvious defect in Mr. Locke's theory of the
sources of our knowledge. Overlooking the fact that the
understanding is, and must be, a source of ideas to itself,
he had ascribed too much to sensation and reflection. The
detection of the error has created a tendency to the opposite
extreme, and in modern times too much is attributed to
the spontaneous development of principles in the mind.
These are made the universal forms of knowledge, and as
weary a search is instituted after these magic forms as ever
the Realists embarked in after their general entities. As
many an alchemist persuaded himself, and perhaps others,
that he had found the golden secret of his toil, so these
deluded children of the mist eagerly embrace phantoms,
which they mistake for the object of their quest, and chuckle

in the imagined possession of materials from which they are prepared to fabricate God, worlds and religion. Happy mortals! no longer doomed to the slow discipline of the senses and the slower discipline of the understanding, they carry a laboratory within from which they can extract at will the essence and quintessence of all possible and real things. They wield an enchanter's wand potent as the eye of Omniscience. They need no voice from nature, the universe or God. Nature, the universe and God are all the creatures of their skill. For ourselves, doomed to drudge in an humbler sphere, we are content to know of the external world just what our senses reveal, of the world within us what reflection can bring to light, and of the world above us what the inspiration of the Almighty may vouchsafe to impart. Beyond these soundings we are lost in unfathomable depths. Here, then, we are content to abide.

Timid believers may, perhaps, be alarmed at the negative jurisdiction which we have conceded to reason in those points in which revelation touches the subjects of natural knowledge. But they have nothing to apprehend from its legitimate exercise. Not a single contradiction to any single principle of science and philosophy can be justly imputed to the Records of Christianity. Time was when infidelity exulted in the prospect of reading the doom of the Gospel in the mysteries of the stars; but astronomy now is made subservient to its glory, and the God who rules the heavens is felt to be the God of redemption. Then the bowels of the earth were ransacked, and some secret voice was invoked from the monuments of faded races and past generations to give the lie to the narrative of Moses, but Nature, in all her caverns, answered back to the testimony of inspiration. Nothing in the *facts* of the earth's history could be found in contradiction to the Sacred Records, although they were often rendered subservient to conclusions with which they are as slightly connected as a sick man's dreams with the realities of life. None dare assert that the *facts themselves* were contravened by the Bible. And who shall affirm that the deductions which they were made to yield are entitled to the prerogative of infallibility, or possess any clearer proof than the external evidence of the credibility of Moses. We repeat it, Christianity has nothing to fear from true science. It has passed the test; and whatever is the extent of the presumption of Divine interposition, arising from the fact that it touches upon philosophy in so many points, and yet contradicts it in none, it is a presumption to which our holy religion is fully entitled. How different is the case with the records of Mohammedan and Hindoo faith! The Bible is certainly singular in this respect, and it ought to be a matter of sincere gratulation to the heart of every believer.

MIRACLES.

ALL the departures from the ancient faith concerning the authority of the Scriptures which have distinguished modern speculation may be traced directly, whatever may be said of the perverseness of the heart as the ultimate cause, to an insuperable repugnance to the admission of miracles. The supernatural has been the stone of stumbling and the rock of offence. The antipathy to it has given rise to open infidelity on the one hand, and to the various types of criticism on the other, which, in consequence of their agreement in rejecting everything that transcends the ordinary agencies of nature, have been classed under the common name of *Rationalism*. If the immediate intervention of God, either in the world of matter or of mind, is assumed to be intrinsically incredible, nothing is left but to discard the records which assert and pretend to give examples of it as impudent impostures; or to seek by tortuous interpretation to reconcile accounts confessedly false with the honesty of the historian, and, what would seem to be still more difficult, with the essential divinity of the religion. The English Deists in the seventeenth and eighteenth centuries took the former course, and denounced the Bible in unmeasured terms of vituperation and abuse. They saw no middle ground between the rejection of the supernatural and the rejection of Christianity. They could not comprehend how that could, in any sense, be treated as Divine which was made up of a tissue of fables, or how they could be regarded as honest men who had palmed the grossest extravagances upon the world as sober, historical realities. Woolston may perhaps be deemed an exception. His letters upon the miracles of our Saviour are remarkable for having anticipated the method, in some degree at least, which has been carried out with such perverseness of learning and ingenuity by Strauss and Bauer. " His whole reasoning"—we use the words of Strauss himself—" turns upon the alternative, either to retain the historical reality of the miracles narrated in the Bible, and thus to sacrifice the Divine character of the narratives, and reduce the miracles to mere artifices, miserable juggleries or commonplace deceptions; or, in order to hold fast the Divine character of these narratives, to reject them entirely as details of actual occurrences, and regard them as historical representations of certain spiritual truths." His own opinion is nowhere articulately expressed, but the presumption is, from the general tenor and spirit of his book, that he was really a Deist, who resorted to allegory as a convenient cover for his malignity, and to the spiritual sense as a protection from the unspiritual weapons with which he was likely to be assailed. He was well aware, if his dilemma could be fairly and conclusively made out, which horn of it the sturdy common sense of Englishmen would adopt. A religion shrouded in figures could be no religion for them. But, with this exception, if exception it can be called,..the issue in England was, No miracles, no Christianity; the Bible must be accepted as it is, as out-and-out Divine, or wholly and absolutely rejected; it was the ancient faith or open and avowed infidelity.

The case was different in Germany. The publication of the Wolfenbüttel Fragments—an anonymous production of Reimar which pursued precisely the same line of argument with the English Deists—gave rise to a class of theologians who have undertaken to retain Christianity at the expense of the historical accuracy of its records. They agree with the Deists in repudiating all that is supernatural, but they cannot agree with them in denouncing Prophets and Apostles as impostors, or in divesting the biblical narratives of all moral and spiritual significance. The modes in which they save the credit of the sacred writers and the Divine import of the sacred history vary with the reigning philosophy, and constitute the different schools into which the class of theologians commonly known as Rationalists may be divided. The first of these schools, that founded by Eichhorn and perfected by Paulus, accepted the authenticity of the Scriptures as a narrative of facts by reducing the miraculous to the dimensions of the natural. They were only ordinary events produced by ordinary agency, which had assumed an extraordinary character in the narrative, either from the omission of circumstances necessary to explain them, or from the style in which the opinions and prejudices of the age led the spectators to describe them. Our Saviour neither wrought, nor pretended to work, miracles, and the Evangelists, properly interpreted—that is, interpreted in the light and spirit of their own times—record nothing of the kind. All was natural. Jesus was a wise and a good man, and what we are accustomed to consider as His wonders were "works of benevolence and friendship, sometimes of medical skill, sometimes also the results of accident and good fortune." In this way the history was saved, but what became of the Divine? That also was reduced to very small proportions. Jesus introduced a pure and spiritual religion, enforced it by the example of a spotless life, and confirmed it by the glory of a martyr's death. He was called of God, in the sense that providential circumstances favoured the development of His character, and His natural gifts qualified Him to become a great moral teacher.

The thorough-going attempt to reduce the supernatural in the New Testament to the dimension of the natural, to make the miracles nothing but the language in which the age signalized ordinary phenomena, is one of the most curious chapters in the history of criticism. It contained the seeds

of failure in itself; " and now," says Trench, " even in the
land of its birth it has entirely perished."

The approximation to a deeper and more earnest faith
was indicated by the systematic effort of Schleiermacher to
reconcile religion to nature without stripping it of all Divine
power.   The supernatural, in common with the Deists
and the preceding school, he discarded.   The low sense of
the natural which Paulus contended for he equally repudiated.   He wanted more of God—a religion that should
really answer to the description of God manifest in the
flesh.   The anxiety to escape from anything like a real miracle, and the longing for a system of spiritual life and power,
the revulsion alike against a material naturalism and a palpable supernaturalism, is the key to the elaborate Christology of Schleiermacher.   The conception which he had of
Christ as the archetype of perfect humanity, in whom the
consciousness of God existed in absolute strength, led him
to attribute to the Saviour an intimacy of communion with
nature and an access to her secrets which no other man
possessed.   He was familiar with her mighty energies, and
He could lay His hand upon the springs of her power, and
produce effects which to those immersed in sense should
appear to be supernatural.   Still, all that He did was to
obey her laws.   He never rose above her.   A profounder
knowledge invested Him with a deeper power, but it was
the same in kind with the power of other men.   This, of
course, was to deny the miracles without denying the phenomena of the New Testament.

Next comes a school which discards the entire histories
of the New Testament as authentic narratives of facts, and
makes them the offspring of the love, admiration and glory
with which the followers of Jesus adorned their recollec-
tions of their Master.   They were unconscious allegories,
into which their imaginations, enriched and expanded by
the prejudices, and expectations, and habits of thought
engendered by the Old Testament, threw their remem-
brances of their Lord—" the halo of glory with which the

infant Church, gradually and without any purpose of deceit, clothed its Founder and Head. His mighty personality, of which it was livingly conscious, caused it ever to surround Him with new attributes of glory. All which men had ever craved and longed for—deliverance from physical evil, dominion over the crushing powers of nature, victory over death itself—all which had ever, in a lesser measure, been attributed to any, they lent in a larger abundance, in unrestrained fullness, to Him whom they felt greater than all. The system may be most fitly characterized"—and we cordially concur in the caustic criticism of Trench—"as the Church making its Christ, and not Christ His Church."

On this scheme the history, both natural and supernatural, is fairly abandoned. There was a basis of facts in the life of Jesus, but what those facts really were we have no means of determining. He lived and died, and this is about all we can know with any certainty. What, then, becomes of the Divine? Is not that abandoned too? By no means, says Strauss. The history is altogether unessential; the absolute contents of Christianity are quite independent of it. The stories of the New Testament are only the drapery in which a grand idea is represented, and that idea may be seized and retained without clinging to the dress in which it was first presented. We may give up the Bible without surrendering aught that is Divine in Christianity itself. Here that criticism which ventures to reject the supernatural, and yet call itself Christian, seems to have reached its culminating point. Extravagance could go no farther.

Though the term *Rationalist* as a distinctive title is, for the most part, restricted to the school of Eichhorn and Paulus, we have not hesitated to extend it to them all, in consequence of their agreement in radical and fundamental principles. They all equally reject the supernatural, they all equally admit no other standard of truth but our own reason, they all equally repudiate an objective, external Divine revelation. The Divine with them is only the true,

and the true is that which authenticates itself to our own
souls. We believe because we see or feel, and not because
the mouth of the Lord has spoken. They all equally make
man the measure of his religion. To indicate the differences among themselves, the epithets Sensual and Spiritual
might be chosen, which seem to be appropriate to the different systems of philosophy they had respectively embraced.

The pretensions to a deeper spiritualism and a profounder
life have given something of currency to the peculiar system
of Schleiermacher, have detracted from the historic form
in which the Christology of the ancient faith is embodied,
and served to increase, if not to engender, a secret prejudice,
on the part of earnest inquirers, against the miraculous
features of Christianity. Men have been willing to accept
a religion which promises to satisfy the longings of their
nature without demanding an extraordinary faith; which meets
their wants without repressing the freedom of speculation.

But the point on which the Church has always insisted,
and which she makes essential to the existence of a true
faith, is, that the scheme of Christianity involves the direct
intervention of God, and that the Scriptures, which record
that scheme, are an authoritative external testimony from
Him. She is not content with a barren compliment to the
honesty and integrity of the writers, nor with the still more
barren admission that something of truth, more or less
elevated, according to the philosophy of the critic, can be
extracted from their pages. She asserts their authority to
speak in the name of God; and she commends their doctrines, not because they commend themselves by intrinsic
probability or ideal excellence, but because they are the
Word of the Lord. The fundamental postulate of the
Rationalist of every type precludes the conception of *such*
a revelation. A religion of *authority* he as indignantly
rejects as the most unblushing scoffer. Such a revelation,
being essentially supernatural, stands or falls with the
miracle. Let those, therefore, who feel themselves tempted
to join in the cry against miracles, and to depreciate them

as carnal and earthly, who would insist upon the Divine truths of Christianity to the exclusion or neglect of its equally Divine credentials, consider well what they are doing. They are giving currency to a principle which, if legitimately carried out, would rob them of those very truths in which they are disposed to rest. There is not a distinctive doctrine of the Gospel which could be known to be true independently of just such a revelation as implies the reality of miracles. There are no lines of ratiocination, no measures of experience, no range of intuition, no ideas awakened in the soul, which could authenticate to us the ends and purposes on the part of God involved in that series of stupendous facts unfolded in the biblical histories. What elevation of consciousness or what intensity of moral and spiritual enthusiasm could ever ascertain to us the appointment of a great Mediator, on the part of Heaven's high chancery, to bring in an everlasting righteousness and to open the kingdom of heaven to all believers? The sensible phenomena connected with the life and death of Jesus may, indeed, be apprehended, but their significance in the economy of God it transcends the sphere of our faculties to discover. They are the counsels of His will, which none can penetrate but His own eternal Spirit; and unless He has revealed them, our speculations about them are little better than a sick man's dreams. They must be known by a Divine testimony, or they cannot be known at all. The question, then, of miracles runs into the question concerning those very doctrines for the sake of which we affect to slight them. It is impossible to abandon the miracle, and cling to any other Christianity but that which is enkindled in our own souls from the sparks of our own reason. The consciousness of the individual or the consciousness of the Christian community, awakened and propagated by sympathy, must be the sole criterion of truth. There is no alternative; man must make his religion if God cannot give it to him.

As the question of an external, authoritative revelation

depends upon the question of the truth or possibility of
miracles, we have thought proper to contribute our mite to
the interests of religion and (may we not add?) of a sound
philosophy by a calm and candid discussion of the whole
subject. We are aware that some would have religion as
completely divorced from letters as from politics. But
such a separation is as hopelessly impossible as it is unde-
sirable, if it were possible. Religion and philosophy touch
at every point; and we agree with Suarez that no man can
be an accomplished theologian who is not, at the same time,
an accomplished metaphysician, and that no man can be an
accomplished metaphysician without imbibing principles
which should lead him to religion. Faith and reason are
distinguished, but not opposed; and though a superficial
culture may have the effect which Strauss ascribes to it,
of alienating the mind from the Sacred Records, yet a
deeper and sounder philosophy will correct the aberration.
We shall know nothing of sects or parties; but those
broad questions which mere sectaries and partisans cannot
comprehend, yet which pertain to the statesman and scholar,
are exactly the topics which ought to find a place in a
journal like this. We shall feel that we have rendered an
essential service to society if we can succeed, in any measure, in showing that the prejudice against the supernatural,
which operates unfavourably on the minds of many in
averting their attention from Divine revelation, is without
any just foundation. We hope that religion can be reconciled with science upon a safer and easier plan than the
sacrifice of either.

The works named at the head of our article[1] cover the
whole ground which we propose to occupy. We shall
pursue the method adopted by Dr. Wardlaw, and discuss,
first, the nature of miracles; then, their apologetic worth;
and, finally, their credibility.

1. What, then, is a miracle? It is obvious that the

[1] NOTE BY EDITOR.—These were Trench and Wardlaw on Miracles,
and Hinds' Inquiry into the proof, nature and extent of Inspiration.

definition should contemplate it only as a phenomenon, and
include nothing but the difference which distinguishes it
from every other species of events. There should be no
reference to the cause that produces it; that must be an
inference from the nature of the effect. Those who make,
as Mill does in his Logic, the belief of God's existence
essential to the credibility of a miracle, virtually deny that
the miracle can be employed as a proof of His being. But
there is evidently no reason in the nature of things why the
argument here cannot proceed from the effect to the cause,
as in the ordinary changes of nature. The miracle presupposes God, and so does the world. But the miracle, as a
phenomenon, may be apprehended even by the Atheist. It
is an event, and an event of a peculiar kind, and God comes
in when the inquiry is made for the cause. Hence Cudworth and Barrow, as well as the Fathers and Schoolmen,
do not hesitate to appeal to miracles as an argument for the
Divine existence. Considered as a phenomenon, in what
does the peculiarity of the miracle consist? Trench does
not give a formal definition, and we find it difficult to
determine precisely what his notion was. He explains the
terms by which miracles are distinguished in Scripture, but
these terms express only the effects upon our own minds,
the purposes for which and the power by which they are
wrought, and the operations themselves—the effect, the end,
the cause—but they do not single out that in the phenomenon by which it becomes a wonder, a sign, a power or
a work. In his comparison of miracles and nature we
have either failed to understand him or he contradicts himself. He asserts, first, that the agency of God is as immediate in the ordinary occurrences of nature as in the production of miracles. The will of God is the only power
which he recognizes anywhere, and to say "that there is
more of the will of God in a miracle than in any other
work of His is insufficient."[1] And yet in less than a
page he asserts: "An extraordinary Divine causality be-

[1] Trench's Notes on the Miracles, p. 10.

longs, then, to the essence of the miracle; more than that
ordinary which we acknowledge in everything; powers of
God other than those which have always been working;
such, indeed, as most seldom or never have been working
until now. The unresting activity of God, which at other
times hides and conceals itself behind the veil of what we
term natural laws, does in the miracle unveil itself; it steps
out from its concealment, and the hand which works is laid
bare."[1] If God immediately produces all events, what can
be meant by extraordinary Divine causality? And if the
will of God is the sole energy in nature, what are "the
powers of God other than those which have been always
working?" Has the will of God been seldom or never
exerted? If the hand of God was directly in every event,
how has it been concealed behind natural laws? There is
certainly a confusion here. The two sets of statements
must have been written under the influence of different
feelings. His anxiety to escape from a dead, mechanical
view of nature, and from Epicurean conceptions of the indolence of God, may account for his denial of all secondary agencies; the palpable features of the miracle forced
upon him the admissions of these same agencies as a standard by which it was to be tried.

The scriptural term which gives us the nearest insight
into the real nature of the miracle is precisely the one of
which Dr. Trench speaks most slightingly—the word
wonder.[2] It is true that every wonder is not a miracle, but
every miracle is a wonder. The cause of wonder is the
unexpectedness of an event; and the specific difference of
the miracle is, that it contradicts that course of nature which
we expected to find uniform. It is an event either above,
or opposed to, secondary causes. Leave out the notion of
these secondary causes, and there can be no miracle. All
is God. Admit a nature apart and distinct from God, and

[1] Trench on Miracles, p. 12.
[2] Miraculi nomen ab admiratione sumitur. Thomas Aquinas, Summa,
1, Quest. cv., Art. vii.

there is scope for an extraordinary power. The doctrine
of nature, as consisting of a series of agencies and powers,
of substances possessed of active properties in their relations to each other, by no means introduces a dead, mechanical view of the universe. God has not left the world, as
a watchmaker leaves his clock after he has wound it up,
to pursue its own course independently of any interference
from Him. He is present in every part of His dominion;
He pervades the powers which He has imparted to created
substances by his ceaseless energy. He sustains their efficiency, and he regulates all the adjustments upon which
their activity depends. He is the life of nature's life. In
Him we live, and move, and have our being. But still, in
dependence upon His sustaining care and the concurrence
of His pervading energy, nature has powers and consists of
causes which, in the same circumstances, always produce the
same effects. To the following remarks of Dr. Wardlaw
we cordially assent:

"I have already, at the very outset, given a definition of them in
other terms—as *works involving a temporary suspension of the known
laws of nature, or a deviation from the established constitution and
fixed order of the universe;* or, perhaps more correctly, of that department of the universe which constitutes *our own system,* whose
established order and laws we are capable, to the full extent requisite
for the purpose, of accurately ascertaining—works, therefore, which
can be effected by no power short of that which gave the universe its
being and its constitution and laws. In this definition, let it be
observed, I have called a miracle a suspension of the *known* laws of
nature. It is necessary to mark this. Effects, it is abundantly obvious, might be produced, such as, to those who witnessed them, might
appear, and might be believed, miraculous, while the persons by whom
they are performed are well aware, from their superior acquaintance
with the laws, and powers, and phenomena of nature, that the appearance is fallacious and the belief unfounded. The persons before
whom they are performed may be utterly unable to account for them
by any natural laws or powers *known to them;* while, in point of
fact, in place of their being suspensions of any law or laws of nature
whatsoever, they are actually the product of their operation; so that,
in the circumstances, the real miracle would have lain not in their
production, but in their *non-*production. *That* would have been the

true deviation from the settled constitution of nature. In such a case, the miracle is a miracle *only to ignorance;* that is, it is *no* miracle. A little farther development of the secrets of nature annihilates the seemingly miraculous, and only reads to the previously uninformed mind a new lesson of nature's uniformity. It becomes, therefore, an indispensable requisite to a genuine miracle that it be wrought both *on* materials, and *by* materials, of which the properties are well and familiarly known; respecting which, that is, the common course of nature is fully understood." [1]

Dr. Wardlaw subsequently criticises, and we think with justice, the distinctions and evasions by which Trench undertakes to rescue the miracle from being a violation of nature's order; to this point we shall afterward refer. We cannot forbear to quote a portion of his remarks:

"The truth is, we must understand the term *nature* in the sense usually attached to it, as relating to the constitution and laws of the physical system of our own globe. It is true that, in consequence of sin, there have been 'jarrings and disturbances' of its 'primitive order.' But it does not follow from that that there are no natural principles and laws in fixed and constant operation. And when an event occurs for which these natural principles and laws make no provision, for which they can in no way account, which is quite aside from and at variance with their ordinary uniform operations, it does not to me seem very material whether we speak of it as beyond nature, or above nature, or beside nature, or against nature, or contrary to nature—whether as a suspension, an interruption, a contravention, or a violation of nature's laws—provided we are understanding 'nature and nature's laws' as having reference to the physical economy of our own system. When, in illustration of his position that a miracle is not at all 'the infraction of a law, but only a lower law neutralized and put out of working by a superior,' Mr. Trench says, 'Continually we behold in the world around us lower laws held in restraint by higher, mechanic by dynamic, chemical by vital, physical by moral; yet we say not, when the lower thus gives place in favour of the higher, that there was any violation of law, that anything contrary to nature came to pass; rather we acknowledge the law of a greater freedom swallowing up the law of a lesser,' he seems to forget that this 'holding in restraint of one law by the operation of another' is itself *one of the very laws* whose working 'we behold in the world around us,' and that it comes, therefore, among the laws of nature as ordinarily understood—that is, as having relation to this

[1] Wardlaw on Miracles, pp. 34, 35.

said 'world around us,' to the physical order of our system. But it is manifestly unfair, in interpreting *nature*, to quit our own system, to mount to a loftier sphere, to take in a wider amplitude, to embrace the entire range of being; and then, because a thing, though a manifest contravention of the laws of 'the world around us,' of 'the nature which we know,' may not be out of harmony with nature when considered as embracing the boundless universe, and even the attributes of its Maker, thus bringing Omnipotence itself into the range of 'natural causes,' to deny the propriety of pronouncing anything whatever to be *against nature*. For this involves the fallacy of taking the same term in two senses, and because the thing in question may not be inconsistent with it in the one, concluding that it cannot be inconsistent with it in the other!" [1]

2. Having settled that the essence of the miracle consists in the contranatural or the supernatural, we are now prepared to investigate its apologetic worth. The question to be answered is briefly this—we quote the words of Mr. Trench—"Is the miracle to command, absolutely and without further question, the obedience of those in whose sight it is done, or to whom it comes as an adequately attested fact, so that the doer and the doctrine, without any more debate, shall be accepted as from God?" In other words, is the miracle in itself, from its own intrinsic character, a sufficient credential of Divine inspiration or a Divine commission?

Trench, in company with the Jewish and Pagan enemies of Christianity, and a large body of both Catholic and Protestant theologians, answers in the negative. Dr. Wardlaw answers in the affirmative, and we think that Dr. Wardlaw is right. The assumption on which the negative proceeds is, that a real miracle may be wrought by beings inferior to God. The Jews ascribed those of our Saviour to Beelzebub, the Gentiles to magic, and the Scriptures themselves warn us against the lying wonders of the Man of sin. The miracle, consequently, establishes, in the first instance, only the certainty of a superhuman origin, without determining anything as to its character. It may be heaven

[1] Wardlaw on Miracles, pp. 40, 41.

or it may be hell. To complete the proof the nature of the
doctrine must be considered. If that is approved by the
conscience or commends itself to the reason, it settles the
question as to the real source of the miracle, and the miracle,
thus authenticated as from God, confirms in turn the Divine
origin of the doctrine. We acquit this reasoning of the
charge which has often been brought against it of arguing
in a circle. When it is said that the doctrine proves the
miracle, and the miracle the doctrine, it is obvious, as Warburton has judiciously remarked, that "the term *doctrine*,
in the first proposition, is used to signify a doctrine *agreeable to the truth of things, and demonstrated to be so by natural light.* In the second proposition, the term *doctrine* is
used to signify a doctrine *immediately and in an extraordinary manner* revealed by God. So that these different
significations in the declared use of the word *doctrine*, in
two propositions, sets the whole reasoning free from that
vicious circle within which our philosophic conjurors would
confine it. In this there is no fruitless return of an unpro-
gressive argument, but a regular procession of two distinct
and different truths, till the whole reasoning becomes complete.   In truth, they afford mutual assistance to one
another, yet not by taking back after the turn has been
served what they had given, but by continuing to hold
what each had imparted to the support of the other."[1]   The
whole argument may be stated in a single sentence: The
goodness of the doctrine proves the divinity of the miracle ;
the divinity of the miracle proves not the goodness—that
would be the circle—but the divine authority of the doctrine.

But though we admit that this reasoning is valid as to
form, we cannot make the same concession in relation to its
matter. We cannot bring ourselves to believe that any
created being, whether seraph or devil, can work a real
miracle. We hold that this is the exclusive prerogative of
God. The only power which any creature possesses over
nature is the power which results from the knowledge of,

[1] Divine Legation, Book ix., chap. 5.

and consists in obedience to, her laws. No finite being can
make or unmake a single substance, nor impart to matter or
to mind a single original property. Nature is what God
made it, her laws what God appointed; and no orders of finite
intelligence, however exalted, can ever rise above nature,
for they are all parts of it, nor accomplish a single result
independently of the properties and laws which God has
ordained. They, like man, can only conquer by obeying.
They may through superior knowledge effect combinations
and invent machinery which to the ignorant and uninstructed may produce effects that shall appear to transcend
the capabilities of a creature, but they can never rise above,
nor dispense with, the laws they have mastered. They may
reach the *mirabile*, but never the *miraculum*.[1] It was to set
in a clear light the truth that the miracle from its very
essence transcends the only species of power which we can
ascribe to creatures, that we were so earnest in fixing the
definition of it as something above or contradictory to
nature. The power which works a miracle is evidently
creative; the same which first gave to the universe its being,
to all substances their properties, and to the course of things
its laws. It is the power of Omnipotence. Hence, wherever there is a real miracle, there is and must be the finger
of God. Neither can this power be delegated to a creature.

[1] The distinction between finite power and that by which a real miracle
is wrought, and between real and relative miracles, is clearly stated by
Aquinas, Summa 1, Quest. cx., Art. iv.: "Miraculum proprie dicitur, cum
aliquid sit præter ordinem naturæ. Sed non sufficit ad rationem miraculi, si aliquid fiat præter ordinem naturæ alicujus particularis: quia sic
cum aliquis projicit lapidem sursum, miraculum faceret, cum hoc sit
præter ordinem naturæ lapidis. Ex hoc ergo aliquid dicitur esse miraculum quod sit præter ordinem totius naturæ creatæ. Hoc autem non
potest facere nisi Deus; quia quicquid facit angelus, vel quæcunque alia
creatura propria virtute, hoc sit secundum ordinem naturæ creatæ; et sic
non est miraculum.

"Quia non omnis virtus naturæ creatæ est nota nobis, ideo cum aliquid
sit præter ordinem naturæ creatæ nobis notæ per virtutem creatam nobis
ignotam, est miraculum quoad nos. Sic igitur cum dæmones aliquid
faciunt sua virtute naturali, *miracula* dicuntur non simpliciter, sed quoad
nos." Compare 2. 2., Quest. clxxviii., Art. ii.

He is, in no case, even the instrument of its exercise. If imparted to him as a *habit*, it would be like every other faculty subject to his discretion; if only as a transient virtue, it would still be a part of himself, and we cannot conceive that even for a moment infinite power could be resident in the finite.[1] The Prophet or Apostle accordingly never performs the miracle. He is only the prophet of the presence of God. He announces what the Lord of nature will do, and not what he himself is about to perform. The case is well put by Dr. Wardlaw:

"Another observation still requires to be made—made, that is, more pointedly, for it has already been alluded to—I mean that in the working of a miracle there is in every case *a direct and immediate interference of Deity.* There is no transference of power from God to the divinely-commissioned messenger. Neither is there any committing of Divine Omnipotence to his discretion. The former is, in the nature of the thing, impossible. It would be making the creature for the time almighty, and that (since omnipotence can belong to none but Divinity) would be equivalent to making him God. And the latter, were it at all imaginable, would neutralize and nullify the evidence, inasmuch as it would render necessary to its validity a previous assurance of the *impeccability* of the person to whom the trust was committed—that is, an assurance, and an absolute one, of the impossibility of its being ever perverted by the improper application of the power to purposes foreign to those of his commission. Omnipotence placed at a creature's discretion is indeed as real an impossibility in the Divine administration as the endowing of a creature with the attribute itself; for, in truth, if the power remains with God, it would amount to the very same thing as God subjecting Himself to His creature's arbitrary and capricious will. There is, strictly speaking, in any miracle no agency but that of the Divine Being Himself. Even to speak of the messenger as His *instrument* is not correct. All

---

[1] The same doctrine is enunciated by Dr. Hinds, Part ii., § 4, p. 120. It is also found, as to its leading thought, in Aquinas, Summa 2. 2., Quest. clxxviii., Art. i.: "Operatio virtutum (miracles) se extendit ad omnia quæ supernaturaliter fieri possunt; quorum quidem causa est divina omnipotentia, quæ nulli creaturæ communicari protest. Et ideo impossibile est quod principium operandi miracula sit aliqua qualitas habitualiter manens in anima. Sed tamen hoc potest contingere quod sicut mens prophetæ movetur ex inspiratione divina ad aliquid supernaturaliter cognoscendum; ita etiam mens miracula facientis moveatur ad faciendum aliquid ad quod sequitur effectus miraculi, quod Deus sua virtute facit."

that the messenger does is to declare his message, to appeal to God for its truth, and if, at his word, intimating a miracle as about to be performed in proof of it, the miracle actually takes place, there is, on his part, in regard to the performance, neither agency nor instrumentality, unless the mere utterance of words, in intimation of what is about to be done, or an appeal to Heaven and petition for its being done, may be so called. God Himself is the agent, the sole and immediate agent." [1]

The miracle, according to this view, requires no extraneous support in authenticating its heavenly origin. It is an immediate manifestation of God. It proclaims His presence from the very nature of the phenomenon. But how does it become a voucher for a doctrine or the Divine commission of a teacher? Neither conclusion is implicitly contained in it, and notable difficulties have been raised as to the possibility of establishing spiritual truths by material facts. We are far from asserting that miracles are so connected in the nature of things with a Divine commission that wherever they are proved to exist inspiration must be admitted as a necessary inference. There is no logical connection that the human mind is capable of tracing between the supernatural exercises of power and the supernatural communication of knowledge. It is certainly conceivable that one might be able to heal the sick and raise the dead who could neither predict future contingencies nor speak with the authority of God. The relation betwixt the miracle and inspiration depends upon the previous announcement of its existence. The man who professes to come from God must appeal to the extraordinary intervention of His power. That appeal makes known to us a connection by virtue of which the miracle establishes the doctrine, not in its logical consecution, but by the extrinsic testimony of God—establishes the doctrine, not as a truth internally apprehended, but a matter of fact externally authenticated. It makes the Almighty a witness in the case. The previous appeal is the great canon upon which

[1] On Miracles, pp. 52, 53.

the applicability of the miracle, as a proof, depends; and
whenever it is complied with, the performance of the miracle is as a voice from heaven; it is a present God affixing
His seal to the claims of His servant. That this is the case
can, we think, be conclusively evinced by three considerations:

(1.) The miracle is an instance of the reality of that
which alone creates any presumption against the claims of
the prophet—it is an *example* of the supernatural. There
is obviously the same antecedent presumption against the
pretension to work miracles as against the pretension to
inspiration. They are phenomena which belong to the
same class, and the man who justifies his pretensions in the
one case removes all proper ground of suspicion in the
other. He goes farther; he illustrates an intimacy of connection with the Deity which inspiration supposes, and on
account of which it is inherently improbable. This argument is clearly put by Dr. Hinds:

"In the case of a person claiming to be commissioned with a message from God, the only proof which ought to be admitted is miraculous attestation of some sort. It should be required that either
the person himself should work a miracle, or that a miracle should be
so wrought, in connection with his ministry, as to remove all doubt of
its reference to him and his message. The miracle, in these cases, is,
in fact, a *specimen* of that violation of the ordinary course of nature
which the person inspired is asserting to have taken place in his appointment and ministry, and corresponds to the exhibition of *specimens* and *experiments* which we should require of a geologist, mineralogist or chemist if he asserted his discovery of any natural phenomena, especially of any at variance with received theories. In this
latter case, it would be only reasonable to require such sensible proof,
but it would be unreasonable to admit the assertion without it—without seeing the experiment or specimen ourselves, or satisfying ourselves, on the testimony of credible witnesses, that it had been seen
by others. Equally unreasonable would it be to admit any person's
claim to inspiration or extraordinary communion with God without
the appropriate test, the *earnest* of the Spirit." [1]

(2.) The miracle, in the next place, is not only a speci-

[1] Hinds' Inquiry, p. 9.

men of the supernatural in general, but a specimen of the precise kind of the supernatural which it is adduced to confirm; it is a specimen of inspiration. Here the importance of the doctrine that God is, in every case, the immediate worker of the miracle—that the power is never delegated to a creature—becomes manifest. He who appeals to the miracle with the certainty of its performance must know that God will put forth His energy. He is a prophet of the Divine purpose, and therefore, really and truly, as to the event in question, inspired. As we are indebted to Dr. Wardlaw for this feature of the argument, we shall permit him to speak for himself: [1]

"For, having said that every prophecy is a miracle, I have now further to say that every miracle is a prophecy. *The prophecy is a miracle of knowledge; the miracle is a prophecy of power.* The power by which the miracle is wrought (as may be noticed more particularly by and by), being *Divine* power, not transferred to the human messenger, but remaining God's, and God's alone, and being by God alone directly put forth for its effectuation, it is plain that a miracle, as far as the messenger is concerned whose commission and whose testimony are to be certified, is simply an intimation of such Divine power being about to be put forth by Him who alone possesses it, to produce an effect which He alone is able to accomplish. And to make this still more manifest: if we only suppose that the production of the miraculous effect is not immediate, not to take place at the moment of its intimation, but fixed in the messenger's announcement for a precise time in the somewhat distant future; in that case, when the time came, and the power was put forth, and the miracle wrought accordingly, we should have, you will at once perceive, a *miracle* and a *fulfilled prophecy* in the same event; we should have, in that one event, the evidence of the miracle of knowledge and the miracle of power united." [2]

"And there is in connection with the miracle of power, a miracle of knowledge, consisting in such a secret supernatural communication between the mind of God and the mind of His servant as imparts to

[1] The same thought is found in Dr. Hinds, but it had escaped our notice until we had read the work of Dr. Wardlaw. It is not so clearly stated by Dr. Hinds as by Dr. Wardlaw, and Dr. Hinds does not seem to have appreciated its bearing upon the testimonial character of the miracle. See Hinds' Inquiry, p. 120.

[2] On Miracles, pp. 32, 33.

the latter the perfect assurance that God *will*, at the moment, put forth the necessary power—that he certainly *will* strike in with His miraculous attestation." [1]

The miracle, therefore, being an instance, is a proof, of inspiration.

(3.) The third consideration is drawn from the character of God. It is not to be presumed that He will prostitute His power to the purposes of deception and fraud; and yet if he works a miracle at the bidding of an impostor He becomes a party to a double lie. He endorses equally the claim to supernatural power and supernatural knowledge. The whole thing becomes a scene of complicated wickedness. First, a creature with intolerable audacity professes to be in intimate communion with his Maker; then, with a still more intolerable profaneness, takes the name of God in vain, not only by pronouncing it upon his lip, but by demanding a manifestation of the Divine presence; and the supposition is that God acquiesces in his blasphemy, succumbs to his behests and fosters his designs. We cannot conceive of anything more atrocious. The miracle, as we have seen, is, in every case, the immediate operation of Divine power. The man is not even the instrument; he is only the prophet of the Divine purpose. Now, to say that God's power shall be subject to his arbitrary dictation is to say that the Almighty becomes a tool to answer the ends of imposture and falsehood, a willing instrument to propagate deceit. If a creature, by habitual virtue, were able to effect a miracle, the case would be different. We might not be competent to say how far God's goodness should interfere to restrain its discretion. But the question is of the immediate agency of God Himself; and then it is wicked to think, much more deliberately to propose the problem, how far He can lend Himself as a party to a fraud. This consideration seems to us to conclude the controversy. We concur most heartily in the earnest representation of Dr. Wardlaw:

[1] On Miracles, p. 53.

"If a man announces himself as having been commissioned by God to propound a certain doctrine or system of doctrines, *as from Him*, and for the truth of his commission and his communication appeals to works such as no power but that of God can effect; if, upon his making this appeal, these works are instantly and openly done at his bidding; there is no evading of the conclusion that this is a *Divine interposition*, at the moment, in attestation of the authority he claims, and of the truth of what is declared. The professed Divine ambassador says: '*This is from God;*' and God, by the instant intervention of the miracle, sets His seal to it—says, as by a voice from heaven, if not even more decisively, '*It is from Me!*' The sole questions requiring to be answered, in order to the legitimacy of the conclusion, are these two: '*Is the work one which God alone can do?*' and '*Is it actually done?*' If these questions are settled in the affirmative, there is no reasonable ground on which the conclusion can be withstood." [1]

The foregoing reasoning, as to the testimonial connection between the miracle and inspiration, seems to us to be abundantly confirmed by the example of our Lord. In the case of the paralytic He claimed, in the first instance, to exercise a special prerogative of God. The scribes were shocked at the blasphemy. They looked upon it as altogether incredible that a man should be intrusted with any such authority. "And Jesus, knowing their thoughts, said, Wherefore think ye evil in your hearts? For whether is easier to say, Thy sins be forgiven thee; or to say, Arise, and walk?" That is, Which is antecedently the most improbable, that I should be commissioned to forgive sin, or to control the course of nature? Is there not the same presumption against the one as the other? Are they not both equally the supernatural, and, in that respect, equally unlikely? If, now, I can demonstrate to your senses that I have the power in one case, will not that convince you that I have it also in the other? If, by a word, I can arrest this disease and restore health and energy to this palsied frame, will you not believe that I am likewise commissioned to remit sin? Their silence indicated that the scribes acknowledged the force of the appeal. They instinctively

[1] On Miracles, p. 51.

felt that if Jesus could do the one, there was no reason for
saying that He could not do the other. The intrinsic improbability of both was precisely the same. "But that ye
may know that the Son of man hath power on earth to
forgive sins, (then saith He to the sick of the palsy,) Arise,
take up thy bed, and go unto thine house. And he arose,
and departed to his house." The effect was electric; the
multitudes felt that He had made out His case, "and they
marvelled, and glorified God, which had given such power
unto men." We venture to say that the same effect would
have been produced upon every unsophisticated mind that
witnessed the scene.

In this case all the conditions of our argument are complied with. The miracle is appealed to as the proof of the
commission; it is treated as belonging to the same category
of the supernatural, as being a specimen of the kind of
thing which is claimed, and as pledging the character of
God for the truth of what is affirmed.

This case seems to us to go still farther, and implicitly to
rebuke the opinion of those who make the doctrine vouch
for the Divine original of the miracle. The Jews were
right in insisting upon the exclusive authority of God to
pardon sin. It *was* blasphemy for a creature to claim and
exercise the power in his own name. No such doctrine
could commend itself to a Jew as good. If, therefore, the
pretensions of the Saviour, in the case before us, had been
tried only upon internal grounds, or if the miracle had been
estimated only by the nature of the truth it was invoked to
sustain, there would have been some pretext for the blasphemous insinuation that He wrought His wonders by the
finger of Beelzebub. Besides, there are other instances in
which Jesus appealed from the internal improbability of
the doctrine to the external authority of the miracle. When
He announced the truths in reference to His own person,
offices and works which were so offensive to his countrymen, on account of their alleged discrepancy with the pervading tenor of the Prophets, He in no case undertakes to

obviate their prejudices by removing the ground of their objections, and showing that the doctrine was intrinsically excellent, but appeals directly and at once to the miracle as to that which ought to be an end of controversy. "The works that I do in my Father's name, they bear witness of me. If I do not the works of my Father, believe me not. But if I do, though ye believe not me, believe the works, that ye may know and believe that the Father is in me, and I in Him." He suspends the guilt of the Jews in rejecting Him upon the sufficiency of His miracles to authenticate His mission. "If I had not done among them the works which none other man did, they had not had sin."

The theory which proves the doctrine by the miracle is so much more simple, obvious and direct, and so much more in accordance with the general tone of Scripture and the spontaneous suggestions of our own minds, that no counter-hypothesis would ever have been devised had it not been for the philosophic error that real miracles may be performed by a power inherent in the spirits of evil. That error we have exposed as arising from a wrong conception of the nature of finite power, and the argument may be regarded as complete that miracles are always the great seal of heaven, infallible credentials of a Divine commission. Whoever works them must have God with him.

But it may be objected that it avails nothing to prove that God is the only author of a real miracle, and that all such miracles impress the seal of His authority upon the doctrine, so long as it is admitted that superior intelligences can produce effects which to us in our ignorance shall seem to be miraculous. We want a criterion by which to distinguish these achievements of a higher knowledge from the supernatural works of God. Cudworth applies the term *supernatural* to both classes of effects, though he is careful to indicate that the feats of demons do not transcend the sphere of nature and her laws. "Wherefore it seems," says he, "that there are two sorts of miracles or effects supernatural. First, such as, though they could not be done by any ordinary and natural causes here amongst us, and in that respect may be called supernatural, yet might notwithstanding be done, God permitting only, by the ordinary and natural power of other invisible created spirits, angels or demons. As, for example, if a stone or other heavy body should first ascend upward, and then hang in the air without any visible either mover or supporter, this would be to us a miracle or effect supernatural, and yet, according to vulgar opinion, might this be done by the natural power of created, invisible beings, angels or demons, God only permitting, without whose special providence, it is conceived, they cannot thus intermeddle with our human affairs. . . . But, secondly, there is another sort of miracles, or effects supernatural, such as are above the power of all second causes, or any natural created being whatsoever, and so can be attributed to none but God Almighty Himself, the Author of nature, who, therefore, can control it at pleasure."

The distinction is a just one, though we do not like the application of the terms *miracle* and *supernatural* to the first class; the broad line which distinguishes them from the works of God is that they are within the sphere of nature. But still, may not these achievements of the creature be palmed upon us as real miracles, and are we not in danger of being deceived by them, unless we have some criterion apart from the nature of the phenomena by which we can distinguish the real from the apparent? Must we not, after all, fall back upon the doctrine to settle the question whether a real miracle has been wrought—whether the phenomena in question are in the sphere of the natural or not? This evidently comes to the same thing with the hypothesis we have been endeavouring to set aside, and if it could be consistently maintained, all that we have said would go for nothing. But among those who concur in our views of the testimonial character of the miracle, the difficulty is commonly solved by appealing to the goodness of God. The theory is, that God will not permit His weak and ignorant creatures to be deceived by counterfeits of His own seal, He will not suffer demons to imitate miracles in cases in which they are likely to mislead, He will restrain the exercise of their power. This, if we understand him, is the position which Dr. Wardlaw has taken. It is the position taken by Mosheim in his valuable notes to Cudworth. God will never suffer anything that can be fairly taken for a miracle, or that is calculated to have that effect upon us, to be wrought in attestation of falsehood. We must be permitted to say that the inference here is contradicted by all analogy. We have no means of ascertaining beforehand how far God is likely to limit the discretion of His creatures, or to prevent the machinations of malignity and falsehood. The argument from His goodness is shown to be lame from the uniform experience of the world. We see nothing in the distinctions of Dr. Wardlaw to render that experience inapplicable to the case.

The effect of all such prevarications and evasions is to destroy the value of the miracle as a proof. If it possesses no authority in itself except as supported by foreign considerations, and if these are neither clear nor obvious, it seems to be of comparatively little use; it is better to eject it from the scheme of evidences at once. But these distinctions are altogether unnecessary. The true doctrine is, that, as the miracle proves by an evidence inherent in itself, no miracles should be admitted as the credentials of a messenger or doctrine but those which carry their authority npon their face. Doubtful miracles are in the same category with doubtful arguments; and if a religion relies upon this class alone to substantiate its claims, it relies upon a broken reed. There are unquestionably phenomena which, surveyed from a higher point of knowledge, we should perceive at once to be perfectly natural, and yet to us they may have the wonder and the marvel of the true miracle. We can lay down no criteria by which to distinguish in every case betwixt the natural and the supernatural. The effect is, where the line cannot be drawn, that the wonders are

not to be accepted. We do not know them to be miracles,
and consequently have no right to give them the weight
of miracles. When the witness is suspected, we discard
his testimony. Let it be conceded that the doctrine is good;
that only shows it to be true, and not that God has revealed
it. The same superior knowledge which enables a demon
to transcend my experience of nature, may enable him to
transcend my science; and so, after all, the good doctrine
may come to me from a very bad source. Devils sometimes speak truth, though not from the love of it. Shall
we say that God will prohibit them from trifling with our
credulity? This may be a trial of our understandings;
the design may be to measure our love of truth, and to see
whether we shall narrowly scrutinize the evidence which is
submitted to our minds. We know not how far it may be
proper that God should restrain His creatures in the exercise of their own energies. Suppose an unprincipled
man of science should go among savages, and find that his
attainments could give to him the distinction of being the
great power of God, would God arrest his exhibitions because they were deceiving and cheating the ignorant multitude? Has he ever arrested the frauds of priests who,
under the guise of a rare acquaintance with philosophy,
have gulled the populace with their marvellous achievements? This hypothesis is destitute of all probability and
of all analogy. The only consistent course is to treat all
suspected miracles as we treat all prevaricating witnesses.
And if there were no other kinds of miracles but these, we
should say that no doctrine could be authenticated by such
evidence. But, as Cudworth has suggested, there are some
miracles which carry their credentials upon their face—so
clearly above nature and all secondary causes that no one
can hesitate an instant as to their real character. There
are some things which we pronounce intuitively to be the
sole prerogative of God. Others may be doubtful, but
these are clear as light. This is the class of miracles on
which a religion must rely. These are seals where the

impression is distinct and legible—about which there can
be no hesitation or uncertainty. These are the conclusive
arguments to which a sound understanding feels itself
justified in adhering. That the criterion of the miracle
must be sought in itself, and that, where such a criterion
cannot be definitely traced, the effect of the miracle as a
proof is destroyed, is only the application to this department of evidence of the universal rules of probability. An
argument must consist in its own light; and according as
that light is feeble or strong the argument is weak or conclusive. If a man should come to us professing to be a
messenger from God, and produce no clearer credentials
than such effects as Cudworth has enumerated—the walking
upon the water, the suspending of a stone in the air, or the
cleaving of a whetstone by a razor, effects which might unquestionably be produced by higher laws suspending or
holding in check the lower—we should feel no more difficulty in rejecting him than in rejecting a pretended syllogism with two terms, or a prevaricating witness. His
pretensions might be true, but we should quote to him the
maxim, " *De non apparentibus et non existentibus, eadem est
ratio.*"

When we turn to the miracles of the Bible, with a few
trifling exceptions, which are redeemed from suspicion by
their connection with the others, as doubtful testimony may
be confirmed by corroborating circumstances,—when we
turn to the miracles of the Bible, we feel intuitively that
they are of a character in themselves and on a scale of
magnitude which render the supposition of secondary
causes ridiculously absurd. The scenes at the Red Sea,
the cleaving of the waters, the passing over of the Israelites
on dry land between the fluid walls, the pillar of cloud by
day and of fire by night, the daily supply of manna from
the skies,—effects like these carry the evidence of their
original on their face. There is no room for doubt. And
so, in the New Testament, the conversion of water into
wine; the stilling of the tempest; the raising of the dead;

the instant cure, without means or appliances, of inveterate diseases; the feeding of thousands with a few loaves,
which involves the highest possible exercise of power, that
of creation; and, above all, the resurrection of Jesus himself,—cases like these have nothing of ambiguity in them.
They reveal, at a glance, the very finger of God. The
supernatural and the contranatural are so flagrant and
glaring that he that runs may read. We may not be able
to say what a devil or an angel can do; but there are some
things which we can confidently say that he cannot do; and
these are the things from which the miracles of our religion
have been chosen.

We have insisted upon this point at some length, because
the neglect of the distinction has been at the bottom of all
the frivolous evasions which have had no other tendency
than to weaken our faith in the Divine authority of the
miracle.

The place, consequently, which we are disposed, as the
reader may already have collected, to assign to the miracle
is the very front rank in the Christian evidences. We cannot understand how the question of a revelation or a Divine
commission can be entertained at all until the credentials
are produced. Mr. Trench laments the stress which has
been laid upon them by modern apologists, and thinks it
has contributed to obscure or to weaken the spiritual power
of the Gospel. We are not prepared to deny that many
have been strenuous advocates of the miracles who were
strangers to the life of Christianity. It is one thing to
believe in miracles, and quite another to believe in the
Saviour of mankind. Faith in the Divine authority of
our religion is not necessarily faith in Christ. We admit
all that he has said of the beauty, and glory, and self-evi-
dencing light of the doctrine, and subscribe fully to the
sentiment contained in the passage of Calvin's Institutes,
to which he has referred us. That passage asserts what all
the creeds and confessions of the reformed churches, and the
creeds and confessions of martyrs and saints in all ages of

the world have always asserted, that true faith in Jesus is
not the offspring of logic or philosophy; it is no creature
of earth, but the gift of heaven, the production of God's
Holy Spirit. We would detract nothing from the inward
light and power of the Gospel, or from the need of supernatural grace. Neither, again, do we complain that Mr.
Trench has signalized the ethical value of the Christian
miracles as being at once types and prophecies of greater
works upon the soul. He has made an important contribution to our literature by the successful manner in which
he has illustrated this principle in his rich and valuable
Notes. We agree, too, that the appearance of such a being
as Jesus would have been wanting in consistency if nature
had not been made to do homage to His name. An incarnate God could hardly walk the earth without unwonted
indications of His presence. Such a wonder must needs
draw other wonders after it, and Mr. Trench has strikingly
displayed this aspect of the importance of miracles. But
still it does not follow that because miracles are graceful
complements of the mission of Christ that their only use or
their chief use is their typical relations to grace, and their
harmony with the character and claims of the Saviour.
We maintain, on the contrary, that their principal office is
to *guaranty an external, objective revelation* by which we can
try the spirits whether they be of God. They are the criterion by which a real is distinguished from a pretended
revelation, the mark by which we know that God has
spoken, and discriminate His Word from the words of
men. An external, objective, palpable test is the only one
which can meet the exigencies of the case. If men are
thrown upon their intuitions, impulses and emotions, their
pretended revelations will be as numerous and discordant as
the dialects of Babel. Each man will have his doctrine
and his psalm. The necessity of such a test has been universally acknowledged. The Catholic feels it, and appeals
to a visible, infallible society which is to judge between the
genuine and spurious; the Protestant feels it, and appeals

to his Bible; the Bible bows to the same necessity, and
appeals to MIRACLES. These, it triumphantly exclaims, distinguish my doctrines from those of every other book, and
seal them with the impress of God. Here, then, is a standard, fixed, stable, certain, with which the experiences of men
must be compared. *To the law and to the testimony; if they
speak not according to this word, it is because there is no light
in them.* A religion of authority is the only bulwark
against fanaticism on the one hand, and a dead naturalism
on the other.

We have no doubt that if the miracle should be reduced
to an obscure or subordinate position in the scheme of Christian evidences, the result would eventually be that an authoritative, external revelation would be totally discarded. This
was the progress of criticism in Germany. Those who
prevaricated with miracles prevaricated with inspiration,
and we suspect those among ourselves who are offended at
the latter have as little relish for the spirit of the Gospel,
except when it happens to chime in with the breathings of
their own minds. We have never had apprehensions of any
other species of rationalism in this country but that which
obtains in the school of Schleiermacher. We think that there
are symptoms in various quarters that it is insinuating itself
into the minds of those of our scholars and reflecting men
who have not thoroughly studied the grounds of his philosophy. It invites by its warmth, and ardour, and life; it
gives a significancy to the history of Jesus which falls in
with the pensive longings of a meditative spirit; it speaks
of redemption, and pardon, and holiness, and sin; it
employs, except in relation to the resurrection, the very
language of piety; and seems to put on a broad and permanent foundation the holy catholic Church and the communion of the saints. But as it has no external standard
of truth, it must repudiate all precise dogmatic formulas,
and reduce the doctrine to a general harmony of feeling or
pervading uniformity of sentiment. Religion must be a
life without a creed. But as the understanding must have

something to feed on, each man will be tempted to analyze
the operations of his own consciousness of God, and reduce
to the precision of logical representation the inspirations of
his own soul. And when it is seen that the religion is supported by a philosophy essentially pantheistic, that the differences betwixt holiness and sin are stripped of all moral
import, and that a stern necessity underlies the whole constitution of things, we may well tremble at the results,
should this scheme be introduced in place of an authoritative Bible. It is because we feel that the tendency of
every disparaging remark in relation to miracles is to set
aside the Bible, in the aspect of authority, that we are so
earnest to rebuke it. We love spiritual religion, but we abhor
fanaticism. We detest bigotry, but we love the *truth;* and
we believe that there is a truth in relation to God and to
ourselves which ought to be embraced in the form of definite propositions, and not apprehended as vague sentiments.
There are truths which are powerful in proportion as they
are clear and articulate, and worthless unless they are distinctly understood.

3. We come now to the last point which remains to be
discussed—the credibility of miracles; and here we enter
into the very citadel of the controversy between the friends
and opponents of Divine revelation. Here the question is
fairly encountered, Can God stand to man in the attitude
of a witness to the truth? Can He declare to other intelligent beings, the creatures of His own power, facts which
He knows, as one man can communicate knowledge to
another? Or, if we admit the possibility of individual
inspiration, in conformity with the laws of our mental constitution, Can God authenticate that inspiration to a third
party? Can He enable others to prove a commission from
Him? To answer in the affirmative is to admit the credibility of miracles. There are certainly no natural laws by
which we can recognize any communications as authoritatively from heaven. Whether the miracles be visible or
invisible; a supernatural operation upon the mind, pro-

ducing an immediate consciousness of the Divine voice, or
supernatural phenomena addressed to the senses, producing
the conviction of the Divine presence : no matter what may
be the process, it must be evidently miraculous, as out of,
and against, the ordinary course of nature.

It would be obviously impossible to show, by any direct
processes of argument, that there is anything in the mode
of the Divine existence which precludes the Deity from
holding intercourse with His creatures analogous to that
which they hold with each other. We can perceive nothing
in the nature of things which would lead us to suppose that
God could not converse with man or make man the messenger of His will.

Analogy, on the contrary, would suggest that, as persons
can here communicate with each other, as they can be
rendered conscious of each other's existence, as they can
feel the presence of one another and interchange thoughts
and emotions, the same thing might be affirmed of God.
It is certainly incumbent upon the Rationalist to show how
God is precluded from a privilege which, so far as we know,
pertains to all other personal existences. Capacity of
society and converse seem to be involved in the very nature
of personality, and it cannot be demonstrated that there is
anything more incomprehensible in the case of a Divine
than of a human testimony. How one man knows that
another man, another intelligence, is before him, how he
reads the thoughts and enters into the emotions of another
being, are problems as profoundly inscrutable as how a man
shall know that God talks with him and imparts to him
truths which neither sense nor reason could discover. It
deserves further to be considered that as all worship involves a direct address of the creature to the Deity, as man
must *talk* to God as well as obey His laws, must love and
confide in Him as well as tremble before Him—it deserves
to be considered how all this is practicable if the communications are all to be confined to the feebler party. Religion necessarily supposes some species of communion with

the object of worship, some *sense* of God; and if this is
possible, we see not why the correspondence may not be
extended into full consistency with the analogy of human
intercourse. Certain it is that the moral nature of man,
which leads him to converse with God, has in all ages induced him to hope and expect that God would converse
with him. Every age has had its pretensions to Divine
revelations; there have always been seers and prophets.
Many have been false, have had nothing intrinsic or extrinsic to recommend them, and yet they have succeeded
in gaining a temporary credit, because they addressed themselves to the natural belief that a revelation would indeed
be given. Whence this natural expectation, whence this
easy credulity, if the very conception of a direct communication from God involves a contradiction and absurdity?

Arguments of this sort are certainly not without their
weight. They never have been and they never can be
answered in the way of direct refutation. The approved
method is to set them aside by the sweeping application of
the principle upon which the Sadducees set aside the resurrection of the dead. Revelation and its proofs are equally
supernatural, and whatever is supernatural must be false.
"No just notion of the true nature of history," says Strauss,
"is possible without a perception of the inviolability of
the chain of finite causes and of the impossibility of miracles." The first negative canon which this remarkable
author prescribes for distinguishing betwixt the historical
and fabulous, is "when the narration is irreconcilable with
the known and universal laws which govern the course of
events." He affirms that "according to these laws, agreeing with all just philosophical conceptions and all credible
experience, the absolute cause never disturbs the chain of
secondary causes by single arbitrary acts of interposition,
but rather manifests itself in the production of the aggregate of finite causalities and of their reciprocal action." In
opposition to this desolating doctrine, we shall undertake to
set in a clear light the principle that in all cases of com-

petent testimony, where the witnesses have honestly related
their own convictions, and where they were in a condition
to judge of the facts, possibility is the sole natural limit to
belief. We are bound to believe, upon competent testimony,
what is not *demonstrably impossible*. The application of this
law to all other cases of antecedent improbability but the
supernatural will hardly be questioned, and we shall therefore discuss it with special reference to miracles.

It would seem to be a self-evident proposition that
whatever is, and at the same time is adapted to our cognitive faculties, is capable of being known. No doubt but
that man is a little creature, and that there are and for ever
will remain things locked up in the bosom of Omniscience
which his slender capacities are unfitted to comprehend.
But then there are other things to which his faculties are
unquestionably adjusted—which are not only cognizable in
themselves, but cognizable by him. All that is necessary
in reference to these is, that they should stand in the proper
relation to the mind. When this condition is fulfilled
knowledge must necessarily take place. If an object be
visible, and is placed before the eye in a sound and healthful condition of the organ, it must be seen; if a sound
exist, and is in the right relation to the ear, it must be
heard. Let us now take a supernatural fact, such as the
raising of Lazarus from the dead, as recorded in the Gospel
of John. There is not a single circumstance connected
with that event which lies beyond the cognizance of our
faculties. Everything that occurred could be judged of
by our senses. That he was dead, that he was buried, that
the process of putrefaction had begun, that he actually
came from the grave at the voice of Jesus, bound hand and
foot in his graveclothes, and that he subsequently took his
part in human society as a living man, are phenomena
which no more transcend the cognitive faculties of man than
the simplest circumstances of ordinary experience. We are
not now vindicating the reality of this miracle—that is not
necessary to the argument in hand. All that we contend

for is, that if it had been a fact, or if any other real instance of the kind should ever take place, there would be
nothing in the nature of the events, considered as mere
phenomena, which would place them beyond the grasp of
our instruments of knowledge. They would be capable of
being known by those who might be present at the scene—
capable of being known according to the same laws which
regulate cognition in reference to all sensible appearances.
Our senses would become the vouchers of the fact, and the
constitution of our nature the warrant for crediting our
senses.

The skeptic himself will admit that if the first facts submitted to our experience were miraculous, there could be no
antecedent presumption against them, and that we should
be bound to receive them with the same unquestioning
credence with which a child receives the earliest report of
its senses. This admission concedes all that we now contend for—the possibility of such a relation of the facts to
our faculties as to give rise to knowledge—such a connection betwixt the subject and object as to produce, according to
the laws of mind, real cognition. This being granted, the
question next arises, Does the standard of intrinsic probability, which experience furnishes in analogy, destroy this
connection? Does the constitutional belief, developed in
experience, that like antecedents are invariably followed by
like consequents, preclude us from believing, subsequently
to experience, what we should be compelled, by the essential
structure of our nature, to believe antecedently to experience?
Does analogy force a man to say that he does not see what,
if it were removed, he would be bound to say that he *does*
see?

To maintain the affirmative is to annihilate the possibility
of knowledge. The indispensable condition of all knowledge is the veracity of consciousness. We have the same
guarantee for the sensible phenomena which are out of the
analogy of experience as for those phenomena from which
that experience has been developed. If, now, conscious-

ness cannot be credited in one case, it can be credited in none—*falsum in uno, falsum in omnibus.* If we cannot believe it after experience, it must be a liar and a cheat, and we can have no grounds for believing it prior to experience. Universal skepticism becomes the dictate of wisdom, and the impossibility of truth the only maxim of philosophy. Consciousness must be believed on its own account, or it cannot be believed at all; and if believed on its own account, it is equally a guarantee for every class of facts, whether supernatural or natural. To argue backward from a standard furnished by consciousness to the mendacity of consciousness in any given case is to make it contradict itself, and thus demonstrate itself to be utterly unworthy of credit. There is no alternative betwixt admitting that, when a supernatural phenomenon is vouched for by consciousness, it is known, and therefore exists, and admitting that no phenomenon whatever can be known. This knowledge rests upon the same ultimate authority with all other knowledge.

But it may be asked, Is not the belief of the uniformity of nature a datum of consciousness, and does not the hypothesis of miracles equally make consciousness contradict itself? By no means. There is no real contradiction in the case. The datum of consciousness, as truly given, is that under the same circumstances the same antecedent will invariably be followed by the same consequent. It is not that when the antecedent is given the consequent will invariably appear, but that it will appear if the conditions upon which the operation of its cause depends are fulfilled. Cases constantly happen in which the antecedent is prevented from putting forth its efficacy; it is held in check by a power superior to itself. "Continually we behold in the world around us lower laws held in restraint by higher, mechanic by dynamic, chemical by vital, physical by moral, yet we say not when the lower thus gives place to higher that there was any violation of the law, that anything contrary to nature came to pass; rather we acknowledge the law of a greater freedom swallowing up the law of a lesser. Thus, when I lift my arm the law of gravitation is not, as far as my arm is concerned, denied or annihilated; it exists as much as ever, but is held in suspense by the higher law of my will. The chemical laws which would bring about decay in animal substances still subsist, even when they are hemmed in and hindered by the salt which keeps these substances from corruption."[1] When the consequents, therefore, in any given case are not such as we should previously have expected, the natural inference is not that our senses are mendacious, and that the facts are not what consciousness represents them to be, but that the antecedents have been modified or counteracted by the operation of some other cause. The conditions upon which their connection with their sequences depends do not obtain. The facts, as given by the senses, must be taken, and the explanation of the variety is a legitimate problem of the reason.

Suppose, for example, that a man uninstructed in physical science should visit the temple of Mecca, and behold the coffin of Mohammed, if the story be true, unsustained by any visible support, suspended in the air, would it be his duty to believe that because all experience testifies that heavy bodies left to themselves fall to the ground, therefore the phenomenon as given by his senses in the present case must be a delusion? or would it not rather be the natural inference, as he could not possibly doubt what he saw, that the coffin was not left to itself—that though inscrutable to him there must be *some* cause which counteracted and held in check the operation of gravity? "In order," says Mill,[2]

---

[1] Trench on Miracles, p. 21.

[2] Mill's System of Logic, c. **xxv.**, § 2. This representation requires to be somewhat modified, as it seems to imply that a previous knowledge of the cause is necessary to render the miracle credible, which is by no means the case. On the contrary, every phenomenon, whether natural or supernatural, must in the first instance authenticate itself, and after it has been accepted as a fact the inquiry into the cause begins. All that the constitution of our nature positively determines is, that it must have some cause, that it cannot be an absolute commencement. We do not, therefore, believe

"that any alleged fact should be contradictory to a law of causation the allegation must be, not simply that the cause existed without being followed by the effect (for that would be no uncommon occurrence), but that this happened in the absence of any adequate counteracting cause. Now, in the case of an alleged miracle the assertion is the exact opposite of this. It is that the effect was defeated, not in the absence but in consequence of a counteracting cause— namely, a direct interposition of an act of the will of some being who has power over nature, and in particular of a being whose will, having originally endowed all the causes with the powers by which they produce their effects, may well be supposed able to counteract them. A miracle, as was justly remarked by Brown, is no contradiction to the law of cause and effect; it is a new effect supposed to be produced by the introduction of a new cause." A man is, accordingly, in no case permitted to call into question the veracity of his senses; he is to admit what he sees and what he cannot but see; and when the phenomena lie beyond the range of ordinary experience, it is the dictate of philosophy to seek for a cause which is adequate to produce the effect. This is what the laws of his nature require him to do.

It is obvious, from these considerations, that if sensible miracles can exist they can be *known;* and if they can be known by those under the cognizance of whose senses they immediately fall, they can be proved to others through the medium of human testimony. The celebrated argument of Mr. Hume against this proposition proceeds upon a false assumption as to the nature of the law by which testimony authenticates a fact. He forgets that the credibility of testimony is in itself, not in the object for which it vouches; it must be believed on its own account, and not that of the phenomena asserted. In all reasoning upon this subject the principle of cause and effect lies at the basis of the process.

the miracle because we know that there is a cause which can produce it, but we know that there is such a cause because we know the effect has been produced.

A witness, strictly speaking, only puts us in possession of the convictions of his own mind and the circumstances under which those convictions were produced. These convictions are an effect for which the constitution of our nature prompts us to seek an adequate cause, and where no other satisfactory solution can be given but the reality of the facts to which the witness himself ascribes his impressions, then we admit the existence of the facts. But if any other satisfactory cause can be assigned, the testimony should not command our assent. There is room for hesitation and doubt. If a man, for example, afflicted with the jaundice should testify that the walls of a room were yellow, we might be fully persuaded of the sincerity of his own belief, but as a cause in the diseased condition of his organs could be assigned apart from the reality of the fact, we should not feel bound to receive his statement. Two questions, consequently, must always arise in estimating the value of testimony. The first respects the sincerity of the witnesses,—Do they or do they not express the real impressions that have been made upon their own minds? This may be called the fundamental condition of testimony; without it the statements of a witness cannot properly be called testimony at all. The second respects the cause of these convictions,— Are there any known principles which under the circumstances in which the witnesses were placed can account for their belief without an admission of the fact to which they themselves ascribe it? When we are satisfied upon these two points—that the witnesses are sincere, and that no causes apart from the reality of the facts can be assigned in the case, then the testimony is entitled to be received without hesitation. The presumption is always in favour of the cause actually assigned until the contrary can be established. If this be the law of testimony, it is evident that the intrinsic probability of phenomena does not directly affect their credibility. What is inherently probable may be proved upon slighter testimony than what is antecedently unlikely; not that additional credibility is imparted to the testimony, but additional credibility is imparted to the phenomena, there being two separate and independent sources of proof. The testimony is still credible only upon its own grounds. In the case, accordingly, of sensible miracles, in which the witnesses give unimpeachable proofs of the sincerity of their own belief, it is incumbent upon the skeptic to show how this belief was produced under the circumstances in which the witnesses were placed before he is at liberty to set aside the facts. He must show how the witnesses came to believe so and so if there were no foundation in reality. The testimony must be accounted for and explained, or the miracle must be admitted through the operation of the same law which authenticates testimony in every other case. It is an idle evasion to say that men sometimes lie. No doubt there are many lies and many liars in the world; but we are not speaking of a case in which men fabricate a story, giving utterance to statements which they do not themselves believe. That is not properly a case of testimony. We are speaking of instances in which the witness *honestly* believes what he says, and surely there are criteria by which sincerity can be satisfactorily established. With respect to such instances, we affirm that there can be but two suppositions—either the witness was deceived, or the facts were real. The question of the credibility of the testimony turns upon the likelihood of delusion in the case; and where it is one in which the delusion cannot be affirmed without affirming at the same time the mendacity of the senses, the miracle is proved, or no such thing as extrinsic proof exists on the face of the earth.

But it may be contended that although testimony has its own laws, and must be judged of by them, yet in the case of miracles there is a contest of opposite probabilities—the extrinsic arising from testimony in their favour, and the intrinsic arising from analogy against them; and that our belief should be determined by the preponderating evidence, which must always be the intrinsic, in consequence of its concurrence with general experience. The fallacy here consists in supposing that these two probabilities are directed to the same point. The truth is, the internal probability amounts only to this, that the same antecedents under the conditions indispensable to their operation will produce the same effects ; the external is, that in the given case the necessary conditions were not fulfilled. There is, consequently, no collision, and the law of testimony is left in undisturbed operation. It is clear that Mr. Hume would never have thought of constructing his celebrated argument against the credibility of miracles if he had not previously believed that miracles were phenomena which could never authenticate themselves—that they were in their own nature incapable of being known. This is the conclusion which he really aimed to establish under the disguise of his deceitful ratiocinations, the conclusion which legitimately flows from his premises, and a consistent element of that general system of skepticism which he undertook to rear by setting our faculties at war with each other, and making the data of consciousness contradictory either in themselves or their logical results. If he had believed miracles to be cognizable, he would perhaps have had no hesitation in admitting that what a man would be authorized to receive upon the testimony of his own senses he would be equally authorized to receive upon the testimony of the senses of other men. What is cognizable by others—all having the same essential constitution—is cognizable by us through them. We see with their eyes and hear with their ears. The only case in which the intrinsic and extrinsic probabilities come into direct collision is that in which the alleged fact involves a contradiction, and is therefore impossible. In all other cases testimony simply gives us a new effect.

The skepticism of Mr. Hume and the disciples of the same school, it is almost needless to observe, is in fatal contradiction to the whole genius and spirit of the inductive philosophy. Observers, not masters, interpreters, not legislators, of nature, we are to employ our faculties, and implicitly receive whatever in their sound and healthful con-

dition they report to be true. We are not to make phenomena, but to study those which God has submitted to
our consciousness. If antecedent presumptions should be
allowed to prevail, the extraordinary as contradistinguished
from the facts of every-day life, the new, the strange, the
uncommon, the *mirabile*, any more than the *miraculum*, never
could be established. To make a limited and uniform
experience the measure of existence is to deny that experience itself is progressive, and to reduce all ages and gene-
tions to a heartless stagnation of science. The spirit of modern philosophy revolts against this bondage. It has long
since ceased to wonder, long since learned to recognize everything as credible which is not impossible; it explores every
region of nature, every department of existence; its excursions are for facts; it asks for nothing but a sufficient extrinsic probability, and when this is furnished it proceeds with
its great work of digesting the facts into order, tracing out
their correspondences and resemblances, referring them to
general laws, and giving them their place in the ever-widen-
ing circle of science. When they are stubborn and intractable, standing out in insulation and independence, and refusing to be marshalled into systems, they are still retained as
phenomena yet to be accounted for, and salutary mementos
of human ignorance. But no man of science in the present
day would ever think of rejecting a fact because it was
strange or unaccountable. The principle is universally recognized that there are more things in heaven and earth than
are dreamed of in our philosophy. If Hume's laws were the
laws of philosophy, where would have been the sciences of
chemistry, galvanism, electricity, geology and magnetism?
With what face could the palæontologist come out with his
startling disclosures of the memorials of extinct generations
and perished races of animals? What would be said of
aerial iron and stones? and where would have been the
sublimest of all theories, the Copernican theory of the
heavens? The philosopher is one who regards everything,
or nothing, as a wonder.

The remarks of Butler are not only philosophically just, but worthy of Bacon himself, when he asserts that miracles must not be compared to common natural events, or to events which, though uncommon, are similar to what we daily experience, but to the extraordinary phenomena of nature. It is nothing worth to say that these extraordinary phenomena may be subsequently explained in the way in which physical philosophers account for events. That was not known when they were first authenticated to consciousness. They had to be believed before they could be explained. Miracles, too, when we reach a higher pinnacle of knowledge, may connect themselves as clearly with the general scheme of God as the wonders of physics. The conclusion, then, would seem to be established that as the will of God is the sole measure of existence, so the power of God or the possibility of the event is the sole limit to the credibility of testimony.

The only question, therefore, which remains to be discussed is, whether miracles are possible. This is simply the question concerning the existence of a personal God. If there is a Being of intelligence and will who created and governs the world, there can be no doubt that the same power which at first ordained can subsequently control the laws of nature, and produce effects independently of, as easily as in concurrence with, the secondary causes which He has appointed. Accordingly, none will be found to deny the physical possibility of miracles but those who deny a great First Cause, or those who resolve the relations of the finite and the infinite into a principle of immanence or identity, totally destructive of all freedom and intelligence, and of all essential separateness of being on the part of what they profess to call God. The worshippers of the supremacy of law, on the one hand, who see nothing in nature but a blind succession of events, and the philosophers of the imagined absolute upon the other, who have ascended to the fountain of universal being, and traced the process by which the conditioned has been propagated and

derived, unite in the warfare against miracles, because, in
either case, the miracle is fatal to their pretensions. They
cannot reconcile it with the stern necessity and rigid con-
tinuity which their speculations imperatively demand.
With the avowed Atheist it is useless to contend. It is
enough that he gets quit of miracles only by getting quit
of God. And if he should be induced to admit their phenomenal reality, he could as easily resort to subterfuges and
pretexts to explain them away as he can dispense with
intelligence and wisdom in accounting for the arrangement
and order of the universe. To him to whom the glorious
wonders of creation and providence, renewed with every
morning sun, to whom what Philo calls "the truly great—
the production of the heavens, the chorus of the fixed and
erratic stars, the enkindling of the solar and lunar lights, the
foundation of the earth, the outpouring of the ocean, the
course of rivers and flowing of perennial fountains, the
change of revolving seasons, and ten thousand wonders
more," reveal nothing of design, to him the most astonishing exhibitions of supernatural power could appear as
nothing but fantastic freaks. As, according to Lord Bacon,
God never wrought a miracle to convince an Atheist, it
would be frivolous to vindicate to him the possibility of
such phenomena, or to take into serious account principles
which he holds only by the abnegation of his nature. If
there be no God, we care very little whether there are miracles or not.

But there is a class of philosophers whom unlettered
Christians are very apt to regard as closely approximating
to Atheists, but who themselves profess to be very zealous
for the Divine existence and perfections, whose poison is as
insinuating as it is dangerous, and whose speculations have
mainly contributed to undermine the credibility of the
miracle. For the purpose which we have in view they
may all be reckoned as Pantheists. It is obvious that those
who, with Spinoza, start out from the notion of substance,
and by logical deduction from the elements contained in it

reduce the finite to a modification of the infinite, come to the same ultimate conclusion with those who start out from the analysis of consciousness, and by the phenomena of human knowledge are led to confound thought and existence, and identify the subject and the object. In either case, essential being is one, and the differences of things are only varieties in the modes of manifestation. In the eclectic system of Cousin both processes are combined: the infinite is the substance; the finite, the attributes or affections; the infinite is the real, the permanent, the unchanging; the finite is the phenomenal, the fluctuating, the variable; the infinite is the cause; the finite the effect. The one is the complement of the other; neither can exist, or be known, apart.

The fundamental error of Pantheism is, that it overlooks the fact of creation. Let this be denied, and we see no way of avoiding the philosophy of Spinoza or of Hegel. We must seek a logical and a necessary connection between the finite and the infinite. It must be that of a substance with its accidents, or a mind with its thoughts, or a blind cause with its effects. Deny creation, and you can conceive of no higher existence of the world than as a thought of the Eternal Mind—an object to the knowledge of God; and contemplated in this light it has no real being—it is only God himself; it is only a subjective phenomenon of the Divine nature. Postulate creation, and these eternal thoughts, or, as Plato would call them, these eternal ideas, become realized in finite substances, which have a being, dependent to be sure, but still a being of their own. They are no longer the consciousness of God himself. But creation, as distinct from emanation or development, necessarily implies the voluntary exercise of power. It is a thing which might or might not be. It is in no sense necessary. Hence the relation of the finite to the infinite, upon this hypothesis, becomes purely contingent. It is a relation instituted by will and dependent upon will. In other words, we have no longer a necessary, but a free, cause. This aspect of the case changes the whole problem of philosophy, and gives a new direction to the current of speculation. It must now flow in the channels of induction and not of deduction. When we speak of creation as contingent, we do not mean to represent it as arbitrary. The will of God, so far from being analogous to caprice, can never be divorced from His wisdom and goodness. He must always act like Himself; and if He create a world or a universe, it must be to answer an end worthy of His exalted perfections. But while nothing can be conceived as done by Him unworthy of His Name, no knowledge of His attributes can ever conduct us, *a priori*, to the nature of the particular concrete objects to which He might determine to give being. It would enable us to speak of their general character and aim, but it would throw no light upon their specific and individual differences. No man knows what kind of inhabitants there are in the moon, or whether there are any. He cannot deduce from the attributes of God any firm solution of the problem; and yet he is persuaded that, however it may be solved, these attributes are illustrated. It is one thing to be able to say, that whatever God does must be wise and good; it is quite a different thing to be able to specify what those wise and good things may be. Speculation, therefore, must abandon the law of rigid deduction when the starting-point is a free, voluntary, intelligent cause—a Person. The question then becomes one concerning the free determinations of a will regulated by wisdom and goodness. It is a question concerning design. Necessity obtains only in relation to its general character; all else is contingent. Creation gives us at once a personal God and final causes. It gives us real existences apart from God, which are precisely what He chose to make them; and final causes give us a plan which we have no means of knowing in its special adaptations and general order, except as it is manifested in the course of experience or supernaturally revealed. It is at this fact of creation that the pantheistic philosophy has stumbled; and in stumbling here it has as thoroughly exploded design as it has miracles. The argument is as complete in the one case as the other; and we would impress it upon those who permit themselves to be entangled in these cobwebs of transcendental metaphysics that while they are revolting from the supernatural on the ground that it contradicts their philosophy, and pronouncing all miracles to be absolutely impossible, they are, at the same time, revolting from all manifestations of intelligence, and pronouncing their own most familiar consciousness to be also an impossibility.

Pantheism, in its common illustrations of the universe, has more of poetry than of truth. It represents it as an organic whole, whose unity is preserved by a regular series of separate developments, concurring in a common result. This seems to be the notion, if he had any, which Strauss intended to convey when he said: "Since our idea of God requires an immediate, and our idea of the world a mediate, Divine operation, and since the idea of combination of the two species of action is inadmissible, nothing remains for us but to regard them both as so permanently and immovably united that the operation of God on the world continues for ever and everywhere twofold, both immediate and mediate; which comes just to this, that it is neither of the two, or this distinction loses its value." The universe, in conformity with what we take to be the meaning of this passage, is not unfrequently described as a living organism, the properties of matter being strictly analogous to vital forces, the development of which is like the growth of an animal body. This view, we are sorry to say, disfigures that masterly work, the Cosmos of Humboldt. The design of his introductory remarks is "not solely to draw attention to the importance and greatness of the physical history of the universe—for in the present day these are too well understood to be contested—but likewise to prove how, without detriment to the stability of special studies, we may be enabled to generalize our ideas by concentrating them in one common focus, and thus arrive at a point of view from which all the organisms and forces of nature may be seen as one living, active whole, animated by one sole impulse."

Having sufficiently indicated the point at which Pantheism diverges from the truth, and exposed the fallacy of its *a priori* demonstration of the impossibility of miracles, we cannot let it pass without rebuking the presumption of its spirit. In nothing is it more distinguished from the humility of true science than in the magnificence of its pretensions. When we consider the immensity of the universe, and the magnitude and extent of that government, physical and moral, which God has been conducting from the beginning over all His creatures, whether material or intelligent, the conclusion forces itself upon us that the plan of the universe is a point upon which we have not the faculties to dogmatize. True science, accordingly, aspiring only to a relative knowledge of existence, instead of futile and abortive attempts to construct a universe or to fix the τὸ πᾶν as a positive element of consciousness, takes its stand, in conformity with the sublime maxim of Bacon, as the minister, not the master—the interpreter, not the legislator, of nature. Professing its incompetence to pronounce beforehand what kinds of creatures the Almighty should have made, and what kinds of laws the Almighty should have established, and what kinds of agency He Himself should continue to put forth, it is content to study the phenomena presented to it, in order to discover what God has wrought. Without presuming to determine what *must* be, it humbly and patiently inquires what *is*. The spirit of true philosophy is much more a confession of ignorance than a boast of knowledge. Newton exhibited it when, after all his splendid discoveries, he compared himself to a child who had gathered up a few pebbles upon the seashore, while the great ocean of truth lay undiscovered before him. La Place exhibited it when he spoke of the immensity of nature and human science as but a point; and Butler was a living example of it in the uniform modesty of his confessions and the caution and meekness of his researches. Shall man, the creature of yesterday, who calls corruption his father and the worm his mother and his sister, who at best can only touch, in his widest excursions, the hem of Jehovah's garment—shall man undertake to counsel the Holy One as to the plan He shall pursue? Is it not intolerable arrogance in a creature whose senses are restricted to a point, who is confessedly incompetent to declare what ends it may be the design of Deity to accomplish in creation and providence, who cannot explain to us why the world has sprung into being at all, with its rich variety of scenery, vegetation and life, who is unable to tell the meaning of this little scene in the midst of which he is placed,—is it not intolerable arrogance in him to talk of comprehending the height and depth and length and breadth of that eternal purpose which began to be unfolded when creation was evoked from emptiness, and the silence and solitude of vacancy were broken by the songs of angels bursting into light, and which shall go on unfolding, in larger and fuller proportions, through the boundless cycles of eternity? Our true position is in the dust. We are of yesterday, and know nothing. This plan of God!—it is high as heaven; what can we do?—deeper than hell; what can we know? Our ignorance in regard to it is a full and sufficient answer to the folly and presumption of those who confidently assert that its order would be broken and its unity disturbed by the direct interposition of Omnipotence. Who told these philosophers that the plan itself does not contemplate interventions of the kind? Who has assured them that He who knew the end from the beginning has not projected the scheme of His government upon a scale which included the occasional exhibition of Himself in the direct exercises of power? Who has taught them that miracles are an invasion, instead of an integral portion, of the Divine administration? It is frivolous to answer objections which proceed upon the infinitely absurd supposition that we know the *whole* of the case.

But though the idea of a universe as a living, self-developing organism cannot be sustained, though the unity of nature is nothing but the harmony of Divine operations, and creation and providence only expressions of the Divine decrees, though the whole case is one which confessedly transcends our faculties, yet something we can know, and that something creates a positive presumption in favour of miracles. We know that God has erected a moral government over men, and that this sublunary state, whatever other ends it may be designed to accomplish, is a theatre for human education and improvement. We cannot resist the impression that the earth was made for man, and not man for the earth. He is master here below. This earth is a school in which God is training him for a higher and nobler state. If the end, consequently, of the present constitution and course of nature can be helped forward by occasional interpositions of the Deity in forms and circumstances which compel us to recognize His hand, the order of the world is preserved and not broken. When the Pantheist " charges the miracle with resting on a false assumption of the position which man occupies in the universe, as flattering the notion that nature is to serve him, he not to bow to nature, it is most true that it does rest on this assumption. But this is only a charge which would tell *against* it, supposing that true which, so far from being truth, is indeed his first great falsehood of all—namely, the substitution of a God of nature in the place of a God of men."[1] Admit the supremacy of God's moral government, and there is nothing which commends itself more strongly to the natural expectations of men than that He should teach His creatures what was necessary to their happiness according to the exigencies of their case. Miraculous interventions have, accordingly, been a part of the creed of humanity from the Fall to the present hour.

The argument here briefly enunciated requires to be more distinctly considered. There is no doubt that, after all, the

[1] Trench's Notes on the Miracles, p. 60.

strongest presumption which is commonly imagined to exist
against the miracle arises from the impression that it is an
interference with the reign of order and of law. It is
regarded as an arbitrary infraction of the course of nature,
or a wilful deviation from the general plan of God. It is
treated as an aimless prodigy. If this view were correct it
would be fatal to its claims. The moral argument would
be so overwhelming that we should be very reluctant to
admit any testimony in its favour. It is to obviate this
prejudice that so many attempts have been made, like the
one already noticed in Trench and rebuked by Dr. Wardlaw, to transfer the miracle to a higher sphere of nature.
Nitzsch very distinctly states the difficulty, and resolves it
in the same way that Trench has done. "If a miracle,"
says he, "were simply an event opposed to nature's laws,
a something unnatural and incomprehensible, and if the
human understanding together with entire nature experienced through its agency merely a subversive shock, then
would the defence of Christianity—a religion established
by means of a grand system of miracles—have to contend
against insurmountable difficulties. But the miracles of
revelation, with all the objective supernaturalness essentially
belonging to them, are in truth somewhat accordant with
natural laws, partly in reference to a higher order of circumstances to which the miracles relate, and which order
also is a world, a nature of its own kind, and operates upon
the lower order of things according to its mode; partly in
regard to the analogy with common nature which miracles
in some way or other retain; and, finally, on account of
their teleological perfection." [1]

The same difficulty occurs in Thomas Aquinas,[2] and his

[1] Christian Doctrine, p. 83.
[2] "A qualibet causa derivatur aliquis ordo in suos effectus, cum quælibet
causa habeat rationem principii; et ideo secundum multiplicationem causarum multiplicantur et ordines, quorum unus continetur sub altero, sicut et
causa continetur sub causa. Unde causa superior non continetur sub
ordine causæ inferioris, sed e converso; cujus exemplum apparet in rebus
humanis: nam ex patrefamilias dependet ordo domus, qui continetur sub

answer strikes us as far more direct and conclusive than any
ingenious attempts to divest the miracle of its distinctive
and essential character as a supernatural phenomenon. The
answer amounts substantially to this : the miracle is against
the *order* of nature, but not against the *end* of nature. It
is a different way of accomplishing the same ultimate design.
There is moral harmony, notwithstanding phenomenal contradiction. As one law of nature holds another in check,
as one sphere of nature is superior to another, and the superior
rules and controls the lower, and yet as all these collisions
and conflicts conduce to the great purpose of God in establishing these laws and systems, so He who is supreme
above them all may hold them all in check when the design
of all can be more effectually promoted by such an interference. There is no more confusion or jar in this omnipotent interposition of His own will in contradiction to nature
than when one part of nature thwarts and opposes another.
In the sense, then, of *disorder* as being a turning aside from
the ultimate relation of things to the great First Cause, the
miracle is not maintained. It is the highest order, the order
of ethical harmony. It introduces no confusion in the universe. It rather lubricates the wheels of nature, and gives
it a deeper significance. It breaks the apathy into which
unbroken uniformity would otherwise lull the soul. The
introduction of miracles into the moral system of the world
is analogous in its effects to the introduction of chance upon

ordine civitatis, qui procedit a civitatis rectore, cum et hic contineatur sub
ordine regis, a quo totum regnum ordinatur. Si ergo ordo rerum consideretur, prout dependet a prima causa, sic contra rerum ordinem Deus
facere non potest ; si enim sic faceret, faceret contra suam præscientiam,
aut voluntatem, aut bonitatem. Si vero consideretur rerum ordo, prout
dependet a qualibet secundarum causarum, sic Deus potest facere præter
ordinem rerum : quia ordini secundarum causarum ipse non est subjec-
tus ; sed talis ordo ei subjicitur, quasi ab eo procedens, non per necessita-
tem naturæ, sed per arbitrium voluntatis. Potuisset enim et alium ordinem rerum instituere ; unde et potest præter hunc ordinem institutum
agere, cum voluerit ; puta, agendo effectus secundarum causarum sine ipsis,
vel producendo aliquos effectus, ad quos causæ secundæ non se exten-
dunt." Summa 1, Quest. cv. Art. vi.

so large a scale. The fortuities of nature keep us constantly reminded of God, and impress us with an habitual sense of dependence. We are compelled to recognize something more than law. The miracle, in the same way, brings God distinctly before us, and has a direct tendency to promote the great moral ends for which the sun shines, the rains descend, the grass grows, and all nature moves in her steady and majestic course. Miracles and nature join in the grand chorus to the supremacy and glory of God.

The true point of view, consequently, in which the miracle is to be considered is in its ethical relations. It is not to be tried by physical, but by moral, probabilities; and if it can contribute to the furtherance of the ends for which man was made and nature ordained, if it can make nature herself more effective, we have the same reason to admit it as to admit any other arrangement of benevolence and wisdom. We degrade ourselves and we degrade our Creator when we make the physical supreme, when we make the dead uniformity of matter more important than the life and health and vigour of the soul. This subject is very ably discussed by Dr. Wardlaw, and we close our argument upon it by a pregnant extract:

"Let me illustrate my meaning by a simple comparison—a comparison taken from what is human, but in the principle of it bearing with infinitely greater force on our conclusion when transferred to what is Divine. A mechanician, let me suppose, has devised and completed a machine. Its structure in each of its parts, and in its entire complexity, is as perfect as human ingenuity and long-practised skill are capable of making it. All its movements are beautifully uniform. Its adaptation for its intended purpose is exquisite. So far as that purpose is concerned it cannot be improved. It works to admiration. In such a case the probability certainly is that the maker will not think of introducing any change, seeing in a structure thus faultless every alteration would be for the worse. The machine, therefore, would be kept going on as at the first, to the continued satisfaction of the inventor and artificer, and the delight and wonder of all who have the opportunity of examining it. Thus far all is clear. But suppose now further that circumstances should occur in which the continuance of the regular movements of the said machine exposed a human life to danger, and that by simply stopping or changing one of those movements for but a few seconds that life could be saved, and yet more, that it is in the power of the maker and owner with perfect ease to stop or to change that movement, and to do so without in the slightest degree injuring his machine, or even at all interfering with and impeding the chief purpose of its construction,—if in these circumstances we knew the maker and owner to be a man of unusual sensibility and benevolence, or even of no more than ordinary humanity, should we not feel it by far too feeble an expression to say that it was *likely* he would stop or change the movement?—should we not think we insulted himself and maligned his character if we pronounced his doing so less than *certain?* If, merely because he was enamoured of the beauty and regularity of a mechanical motion, he were to refuse interference and allow life to perish, what should we think of the man's heart, and what too of his head? Should we not look upon him with equal detestation for his cruelty and contempt for his childish imbecility, setting him down at once as a heartless monster and as a senseless fool? And if thus you would think of the fellow-man who could act such a part, what is to be thought of the God who, when a world's salvation was in the question, involving not the safety of a human life merely, or of hundreds and thousands of such lives, but the eternal well-being of millions of immortal souls, should allow that world to perish for want of evidence of His willingness to save it, rather than allow the order of the material creation to be in a single point or for a single moment interfered with, and that too although not the slightest injury was by such interference to be done to the system? For surely by no one will it be held an injury to be made subservient to a purpose incomparably transcending in importance any or all of those which by its uninterrupted regularity it is effecting.

"Excepting in one particular, the cases I have thus been comparing are closely analogous. The particular in which they differ is this: that in the case of the mechanician the evil was not by him anticipated, nor consequently the need for his interference, whereas, in the case of the Divine Creator and Ruler, all was in full anticipation, and the occasional deviations from the order of the physical creation entered as essentially into the all-perfect plan of His moral administration as the laws by which that order was fixed entered into the constitution of the physical creation itself. But such a difference there necessarily is between everything human and everything Divine, between the purposes and plans of a creature who 'knoweth not what a day may bring forth,' and the purposes and plans of Him who 'knoweth the end from the beginning.' It evidently does not, in the least degree, affect the principle of the analogy or invalidate the force of the conclusion deduced from it." Pp. 70-73.

We cannot conclude these remarks without alluding to
the fact that the researches of modern science are rapidly
exploding the prejudices which Pantheism on the one hand,
and a blind devotion to the supremacy of laws on the other,
have created and upheld against all extraordinary interventions of God. The appearances of our globe are said to be
utterly inexplicable upon any hypothesis which does not
recognize the fact that the plan of creation was so framed
from the beginning as to include at successive periods the
direct agency of the Deity. The earth proclaims from her
hills and dales, her rocks, mountains and caverns, that she
was not originally made and placed in subjection to laws
which themselves have subsequently brought her to her
present posture. She has not developed herself into her
present form, nor peopled herself with her present inhabitants. That science which at its early dawn was hailed as
the handmaid of infidelity and skepticism, and which may
yet have a controversy with the Records of our faith not
entirely adjusted, has turned the whole strength of its
resources against the fundamental principle of Rationalism.
It has broken the charm which our limited experience had
made so powerful against miracles, and has presented the
physical government of God in a light which positively
turns analogy in favour of the supernatural. The geologist
begins with miracles, every epoch in his science repeats the
number, and the whole earth to his mind is vocal with the
name. He finds their history wherever he turns, and he
would as soon think of doubting the testimony of sense as
the inference which the phenomena bear upon their face.
Future generations will wonder that in the nineteenth century men gravely disputed whether God could interpose in
the direct exercise of His power in the world He has made.
The miracle a century hence will be made as credible as any
common fact. Let the earth be explored, let its physical
history be traced, and a mighty voice will come to us from
the tombs of its perished races testifying in a thousand
instances to the miraculous hand of God. Geology and the

Bible must kiss and embrace each other, and this youngest daughter of Science will be found, like the Eastern Magi, bringing her votive offerings to the cradle of the Prince of peace. The earth can never turn traitor to its God, and its stones have already begun to cry out against those who attempted to extract from them a lesson of infidelity or Atheism.

PART II.

PAPAL CONTROVERSY.

PREFATORY NOTE.

THE reader is presented here with two contributions to the Papal Controversy, viz.: 1. An Argument against the Validity of Romish Baptism; and, 2. A Discussion of the Arguments of Romanists for the Apocrypha.

The history of the former is as follows: The Presbyterian General Assembly (Old School) meeting at Cincinnati in May, 1845, had occasion to give its judgment respecting the validity of Roman Catholic baptism, Dr. THORNWELL being present and taking a leading part in the debate, which was decided in accordance with the views he advocated. *The Princeton Review* of the following July brought out an elaborate critique upon the Assembly's decision of the question, which it is understood was from the pen of Dr. CHARLES HODGE. To this Dr. THORNWELL replied in a series of articles, which appeared in 1846, over the name of HENLEY, in the columns of the *Watchman and Observer*, published at Richmond, Virginia. No reply appeared from the other side. In order to present them in a more accessible and permanent form, these articles were subsequently collected and republished in three separate portions in *The Southern Presbyterian Review* of July and October, 1851, and January, 1852. In reproducing them here, they have been simply brought together as one treatise.

This treatise contains a masterly discussion of Justification and Sanctification, which supplies the defect of such discussion in Vol. II.

The history of the latter is sufficiently detailed in the Dedication and Preface. The former was in these words: To the Rev. Robert J. Breckinridge, D.D., an ornament to his church and a blessing to his country, a stranger to every other fear but the fear of God, the bold defender and untiring advocate of truth, liberty and religion, this book,

which owes its existence to his instrumentality, is now affectionately inscribed by the author.

The Preface bearing date July 12, 1844, was in these words:

"The history of the present publication is soon told. Some time in
the year 1841 I wrote, at the special request of a friend in Baltimore,
the Rev. Dr. Breckinridge, a short essay on the Claims of the Apocrypha
to Divine Inspiration. This was printed anonymously in the Baltimore
Visitor, as No. V. of a series of articles furnished by Protestants in a
controversy then pending with the domestic chaplains of the Archbishop
of Baltimore. From the Visitor it was copied into the Spirit of the
Nineteenth Century, some time during 1842. From the Spirit of the
Nineteenth Century it was transferred, by the editor of the Southern
Chronicle, a valuable newspaper published in this place, to his own
columns, and, without consulting me or in any way apprising me of his
design, he took the liberty, having ascertained that I was the author, to
append my name to it. Seeing it printed under my name, and, as he
might naturally suppose, by my authority, Dr. Lynch, a Roman Catholic
Priest of Charleston, of reputed cleverness and learning, no doubt regarded it as an indirect challenge to the friends of Rome to vindicate
their Mistress from the severe charges which were brought against her.
He accordingly addressed to me a series of letters, which the members
of his own sect pronounced to be very able, and to which the following
dissertations (for, though in the form of letters, they are really essays) are
a reply. The presumption is, that the full strength of the Papal cause
was exhibited by its champion; and that the reader may be able to judge
for himself of the security of the basis on which the inspiration of the
Apocrypha is made to depend, I have given the substance of Dr. Lynch's
articles in the Appendix. This work, consequently, presents an unusually
full discussion of the whole subject connected with these books. I have
insisted largely upon the dogma of infallibility—more largely, perhaps,
than many of my readers may think to be consistent with the general
design of my performance—because I regard this as the prop and bulwark of all the abominations of the Papacy. It is the stronghold, or
rather, as Robert Hall expresses it, 'the corner-stone of the whole system
of Popery—the centre of union amidst all the animosities and disputes
which may subsist on minor subjects; and the proper definition of a
Catholic is, one who professes to maintain the absolute infallibility of a
certain community styling itself the Church.'

"It is not for me to commend my own production, neither shall I seek to soften the asperity of criticism by plaintive apologies or humble confessions. In justice, however, I may state that the following pages were composed in the midst of manifold afflictions: some of the letters were written in the chamber of the sick and by the bed of the dying, and all were thrown off under a pressure of duty which left no leisure for the task but the hours which were stolen from the demands of nature. If, under circumstances so well fitted to chasten the spirit and to modify the temper, I could really harbour the malignity and bitterness which, in certain quarters, have been violently charged upon me, I must carry in my bosom the *heart* of a *demon*, and not of a *man*. 'And here will I make an end. If I have done well, and as is fitting the story, it is that which I desired; but if slenderly and meanly, it is that which I could attain unto.' "

It may be here suggested that the reader should first examine the little article on the Apocrypha, of some half dozen pages, which will be found in the Appendix, and then the letters of A. P. F. which it occasioned, before he enters on the elaborate discussion of Dr. Thornwell. That little article contains the expressions, *vassals of Rome, captives to the car of Rome, Papists, Romanists,* which A. P. F. reprobates as shocking to ears polite. He holds up himself and also his Church as models of courtesy, patience and gentleness, yet his letters sometimes betray, in spite of his efforts, a different spirit. In his reply, Dr. Thornwell was undoubtedly led to employ not only very strong language in dealing with the corrupt and pernicious teachings of Rome, but also considerable asperity of language toward his assailant personally. Having heard him express the intention, if he should live to republish, of modifying these expressions, the Editor has considered it his duty to carry out, according to his best judgment, the known wishes of the Author in this particular. No such liberty has, however, been taken with any one of his denunciations of the Romish system, but they are left to stand in all their unsparing and just severity.

In the work of removing such blemishes from this noble production the Editor has enjoyed the great advantage of the aid of Dr. T. DWIGHT WITHERSPOON, and very especially of Dr. JOHN L. GIRARDEAU—both intimate friends of the Author.

The Editor feels bound to acknowledge here some degree of error in the general statements made by him in the Preface to these Collected Writings respecting this discussion. Bishop (then Dr.) Lynch did not, as he had been led to suppose, "quit the field," nor did Dr. Thornwell "publish both sides of the controversy," except in part. The former continued his letters in reference to the first article of Dr. Thornwell, at intervals, for many months after the latter had begun to publish his letters in reply, but he never undertook any answer to them.

The first four pages of the Seventh Letter of Dr. Thornwell being found to correspond almost *verbatim* with a passage in the second of the Discourses on Truth, it was thought proper to omit those pages. Moreover, the Seventh Letter being so intimately connected with the discussion in the Sixth as to constitute just a corollary from it, the incorporation of it with that Letter was deemed advisable. This makes the number of the Letters as here presented only eighteen instead of nineteen, as they appeared in the original volume.

Touching the spelling of the names Augustine, Bellarmine, Turrettine, the reader may notice a departure in this volume from the practice of the first two. General use is various, and Dr. Thornwell's use was so likewise. It was thought best to adopt neither spelling to the exclusion of the other, only endeavouring to have each volume conformable to itself in this particular.

THE VALIDITY OF THE BAPTISM

OF THE

CHURCH OF ROME.

THE remarks which appeared in the *Princeton Review*, the July number of the past year (1845), upon the decision of the Assembly in regard to the validity of Romish baptism, deserve a more elaborate reply than they have yet received. The distinguished reputation of the scholar to whom they are ascribed, and the evident ability with which they are written—for, whatever may be said of the soundness of the argument, the ingenuity and skill with which it is put cannot be denied—entitle them to special consideration. And as the presumption is, that they embody the strongest objections which *can* be proposed to the decision in question, a refutation of them is likely to be a complete and triumphant defence of the action of the Assembly. Under ordinary circumstances, it might be attributed to arrogance in ordinary men to enter the lists with Princeton, but truth always carries such fearful odds in its favour that the advocate of a just cause need not dread, with far inferior ability, to encounter those whom he may regard in some degree the patrons of error.

As in the General Assembly it was maintained by those who denied the validity of Popish baptism that the ordinance itself was so corrupted in its constituent elements—its matter and its form—that it could not be treated as the

institution of Christ, and that the Papal communion as an
organized body, being destitute of some of the indispensable marks of a true Church, could not be recognized in that
character, the strictures of the Reviewer have been shaped
with a reference to this twofold argument.   In opposition
to the Assembly, he asserts that the essential elements of
baptism are found in the Romish ceremony, and the essential elements of a church in the Papal communion; and
what is still more remarkable, he insists that, even upon
the supposition that the Romish sect is not a church of the
Lord Jesus Christ, it by no means follows that its baptism
is not valid.   The consent of the Protestant world for
ages and generations past to the opinion which he has
espoused, without being adduced as a separate and distinct
argument, is repeatedly introduced as an offset to whatever
weight the overwhelming vote of the Assembly might carry
with it.   Such is a general view of the Princeton remarks.

Now, I propose to show that their distinguished author
has failed to prove any one of these positions,—either that
the essential elements of baptism belong to the Popish ordinance, or that without being a church Rome can have the
sacraments of Christ, or that the testimony of Protestant
Christendom is more clearly in his favour than it is against
him.   These are the points upon which issue is joined.

To the question, What constitutes the validity of baptism? the reply obviously is, The conformity of any rite
with the definition of baptism which may be collected from
the Scriptures and justified by them.   Whatever ordinance
possesses all the elements which belong to Christian baptism is Christian baptism, and should be recognized as valid
by all who bear the Christian name.   The validity of a
sacrament does not depend upon any effects which it produces, either mysterious or common, but upon its nature:
the question is, not what it does, but what it is; and whatever coincides with the appointment of Christ, so as to be
essentially the same ordinance which He instituted, must be
received as bearing His sanction.   When the Assembly,

therefore, decided that Popish baptism is not valid, it intended to assert that what in that corrupt communion is administered under the name of baptism is really a different institution from the ordinance of Christ. Rome's ceremony does not answer to a just definition of the Christian sacrament.

In enumerating the elements of baptism the Reviewer seems to have fallen into two mistakes—one wholly unimportant, the other materially affecting the question in dispute. *Intention* is treated as something distinct from the *form* of baptism; and *matter*, form and intention are represented as constituting the *essence* of the ordinance. Now, in the language of the Schools, *form* and *essence* are equivalent expressions. The *form* of a thing is that which makes it what it is, which distinguishes it from all other beings, and limits and defines our conceptions of its properties.[1] According to Aristotle it is the *forms* impressed upon the first matter which enable us to discriminate betwixt different substances. As intention, according to the statement of the Reviewer, is a part of the *essence* of baptism, it is consequently an error of arrangement to make it different from the form. The whole idea of baptism may be embraced under two heads. The Reviewer, no doubt, had his eye upon the Peripatetic division of causes, but the *intention* of which he speaks cannot be the *final* cause of Aristotle, because that was not an ingredient of the essence. The *use* of a table, or the purpose of a mechanic in making it, is no part of the *nature* of the table. But the *intention* in bap-

---

[1] τι δ' ως το ειδος; το τι ην ειναι. Arist. Met., L. vii., c. 4. "Form is that," says Stanley, quoting this passage, "which the thing itself is said to be *per se*, the being of a thing what it is, the whole common nature and essence of a thing answerable to the definition." Philos., part 4th, chap. 3d. "Now that accident," says Hobbes, "for which we give a certain name to any body, or the accident which denominates its subject, is commonly called the ESSENCE thereof, and the same essence, inasmuch as it is generated, is called the FORM." Philosophy. "Ens a forma habet," says Wolfius, "ut sit hujus generis vel speciei atque ab aliis distinguatur. Hinc scholastici aiunt, *formam dare esse rei, dare distingui*." Ontologia, Pars ii., sec. 3, c. 2, § 945.

tism is indispensable to the existence of the ordinance; it is a necessary element of a just definition, and therefore belongs appropriately to the form. The true final cause exists in the mind of God. In the case of baptism a definition which should set forth the matter and form fully and completely would coincide exactly with the logical rule which resolves a definition into the nearest genus and the specific difference. The matter, *water*, is a generic term, and suggests every other kind of ablution besides that of baptism, while the form distinguishes this particular mode of washing from every other mode of using this element.

As this mistake in arrangement, however, is a mere question of words and names, I pass to a more important error —the omission of one of the elements which, according to the great majority of Protestant confessions, enters into the essence of baptism. The *form* does not consist alone in washing with water, with solemn invocation of the name of the Trinity, and with the professed purpose of complying with the command of Christ. There must be some one to make the invocation and to apply the water. These are acts which require an agent—services which demand a servant. Not *any* application of water in the name of the Trinity, with the ostensible design of signing and sealing the blessings of the new and everlasting covenant, constitutes baptism: the water must be applied by one who is lawfully commissioned to dispense the mysteries of Christ. There must be an *instrumental*, as well as a *material* and formal, cause. This fact the Reviewer seems neither prepared to deny nor assert; and, though he takes no notice of it in his formal definition of baptism, he is yet willing to concede it for the sake of argument. The question, then, is, Do these four things enter into the baptisms administered by the authority of the Romish Church? Do her priests wash with *water* in the *name of the Trinity*, with the *professed design of complying with the command of Christ*, and are *they themselves* to be regarded as *lawful ministers* of *the Word?* The Princeton Review has undertaken, in all these instances, to prove the affirmative; and it is my purpose to show that it has signally failed—that, according to their scriptural import, not one of these particulars is found in the Popish ordinance.

I. The Reviewer expresses great surprise[1] at the statement made on the floor of the Assembly that Romanists are accustomed to corrupt the water which they use in baptism with a mixture of oil. It is rather a matter of astonishment that he himself should not have been aware of so notorious a fact. It is true that their church formularies make natural water the only thing *essential* to the *matter* of the ordinance, but it is equally indisputable that such water is only used in cases of urgent and extreme necessity. Whenever the rite is administered with solemn ceremonies—and these can never be omitted except upon a plea which is equally valid to dispense with the services of a priest—the water, instead of being applied in its natural state, in conformity with the command of Christ, is previously consecrated, or rather profaned, by the infusion of *chrism*, a holy compound of balsam and oil. Innovations upon the simplicity of the sacraments began with the spirit of superstition in the Christian Church, and grew and strengthened until they reached their consummation in the magical liturgy of Rome. The precise period at which this specific mode of consecrating the water was first introduced I am unable to determine, but there is an evident reference to it in the Ecclesiastical Hierarchy which goes under the name of Dionysius. "Immediately after the unction," says Bingham,[2] "the minister proceeded to consecrate the water, or the bishop, if he were present, consecrated it, while the priests were finishing the unction; for so the author, under the name of Dionysius, represents it. 'While the priests,' says he, 'are finishing the unction, the bishop

---

[1] "We were, therefore, greatly surprised to see that it was stated on the floor of the Assembly that Romanists did not baptize with water, but with water mixed with oil."—Princeton Review, July, 1845, p. 449.

[2] Origines Ecclesiasticæ, Lib. xi., cap. x., § 1.

comes to the Mother of Adoption (so he calls the font), and, by invocation, sanctifies the water in it; thrice pouring in some of the holy chrism, in a manner representing the sign of the cross.'"

The Catechism of the Council of Trent not only insists upon this mixture whenever baptism is performed with solemn ceremonies, but states distinctly that it has always been observed in the Catholic Church, and traces its origin to apostolical tradition. "Illud vero animadvertendum est, quamvis aqua simplex, quæ nihil aliud admixtum habet, materia apta sit ad hoc sacramehtum conficiendum, quoties scilicet baptismi ministrandi necessitas incidat, tamen ex Apostolorum traditione semper in Catholica Ecclesia observatum esse, ut cum solemnibus ceremoniis baptismus conficitur, sacrum etiam Chrisma addatur, quo baptismi effectum magis declarari perspicuum est."[1]

This same catechism divides the ceremonies of baptism, as is usual among the Romish writers upon the subject, into three classes—the first embracing those which precede, the second, those which accompany, and the third, those which follow, the administration of the ordinance. "In primis" —it begins the explanation of the first head—"igitur aqua paranda est, qua ad baptismum uti oportet. Consecratur, enim, baptismi fons, addito mysticæ unctionis oleo, neque id omni tempore fieri permissum est; sed more majorum, festi quidam dies, qui omnium celeberrimi et sanctissimi optimo jure habendi sunt, expectantur; in quorum vigiliis sacræ ablutionis aqua conficitur," etc. "In the first place, the water to be used in baptism must be prepared. The font is consecrated by adding the oil of the mystic unction. Nor can this be done at any time; but, in conformity with ancient usage, is delayed until the vigils of the most celebrated and holy festivals."[2]

Durand enumerates four kinds of blessed water, among which he includes the water of baptism, and gives a full and particular account of the mode of sanctifying it.

[1] Pars ii., cap. ii., § 11.   [2] Pars ii., cap. ii., § 60.

"In the last place, the water is mixed with chrism—as we have previously mentioned. Whence it is said in Burcard, lib. iii., *We bless the fonts of baptism with the oil of unction.* And Augustin, using the same words, subjoins that it is done more from a mystical reason than from any authority of Scripture. By a mixture of this sort the union of Christ with the Church is signified ; the chrism representing Christ, and the water the people." [1]

To the same purport is the testimony of Alcuin, the famous preceptor of Charlemagne: " These things having been completed before the fonts, and silence instituted, the priest standing, the benediction of the font follows: *Omnipotent, Eternal God*, etc. Then succeeds the consecration of the font, to be chanted, as in the preface to the mass: *Eternal God, who by the invisible power of Thy sacraments.* At the invocation of the Holy Spirit, whom the priest proclaims with a lofty voice—that is, with deep affection of mind—the blessed candle is deposited in the water, or those which had been lighted from it, to show the presence of the Spirit, the priest now saying : May He descend in this fullness of the font. The font being blessed, the Pontiff receives from the Archdeacon the chrism with oil mixed in a vase, and sprinkles it in the midst of the font in the form of a cross." [2]

[1] "Postremo sit admixtio Chrismatis in aqua, sicut dictum est. Unde dicitur in Burcardo, lib. iii., 'benedicimus fontes baptismatis oleo unctionis;' et Augustinus eisdem verbis utens subjecit quod hoc magis tacite, sive sine Scriptura, hac mystica ratione introductum est quam per aliquam Scripturam. Per hujusmodi ergo admixtionem unio Christi et Ecclesiæ significatur. Nam Chrisma est Christus, aqua populus, et dicitur : *Sanctificetur fons iste.* Ex quibus verbis ad quid fiat admixtio satis datur intelligi." De Divinis Officiis, Lib. vi., fol. cxl., Lyons Edition, 1518.

[2] "Quibus finitis ante fontes et facto silentio, stante sacerdote, sequitur benedictio fontis: *Omnipotens, sempiterne Deus*, et reliqua. Sequitur consecratio fontis, in modum præfationis decantanda: *Æterne Deus, qui invisibili potentia sacramentorum tuorum.* Ad invocationem vero Spiritus Sancti, quem sacerdos celsa voce proclamat, id est, alto mentis affectu, deponitur cereus benedictus in aquam, sive illi qui ab eo illuminati sunt, ad demonstrandam scilicet Spiritus Sancti præsentiam, sacerdote jam

These passages, from Durand and Alcuin, are extracted from their accounts of the solemnities of the GREAT SAB-BATH—the Saturday preceding Easter. This festival and Pentecost were the solemn seasons to which, in the times of Leo, the administration of baptism was confined, except in cases of necessity; and hence it is in the description of these festivals that we are to look for a detailed exhibition of the ceremonies connected with its due celebration. In the first book of Martene De Antiquis Ecclesiæ Ritibus may be seen the forms, taken from various liturgies, of consecrating the font, and the *infusion of the chrism* is, invariably, a part of the process.[1] Hurd, in his interesting work on religious rites and ceremonies, mentions among the solemnities of Easter-eve the consecration of the waters of baptism: "The officiating priest perfumes the font thrice with frankincense, after which, he takes some of the oil used in baptism, and pours it on the holy water cross-ways, mixed with chrism, and this is reserved to baptize

---

dicente: *Descendat in hanc plenitudinem fontis.* Fonte benedicto, accipit Pontifex chrisma cum oleo mixto in vase ab Archidiacono et aspergit per medium fontis in modum crucis." De Divinis Officiis, cap. xix. De Sabbato Sanctæ Vigil. Paschæ.

[1] The following specimens may be taken:—1. Ex Missali Gothico-Galli-cano: After a prayer for blessing the fonts and the exorcism of the water, the rubric directs that the water shall be blown upon three times, and the chrism infused into it in the form of a cross. Deinde insufflas aquam per tres vices, et mittis chrisma in modum crucis, et dicis—*Infusio chrismæ salutaris Domini nostri Jesu Christi, ut fiat fons aquæ salientis cunctis descendentibus in eo, in vitam æternam.* Amen. Lib. i., Art. 18, ordo i.

2. Ex Veteri Missali Gallicano: After the prayers for blessing the fonts, the rubric directs that three crosses should be made upon the water with chrism. Postea facis tres cruces super aquam de chrisma et dicis, etc. Ibid., ordo ii.

3. From an old Paris Ritual, the form of administering baptism on the great Sabbath, the Saturday preceding Easter, is extracted. Ibid., ordo x. Among the other ceremonies enumerated, the infusion of the chrism is expressly mentioned. "Inde," is the rubric for that purpose, "inde accipiens vas aureum cum chrismate, fundit chrisma in fonte in modum crucis, et expandit aquam cum manu sua, tunc baptizantur infantes, primum masculi, deinde feminæ."

all the catechumens or children who shall be brought to the church." [1]

These authorities, I trust, are sufficient to diminish the Reviewer's surprise at the statement made on the floor of the Assembly, and to put it beyond doubt that the *matter* of Romish baptism is not simple, natural water, but water artificially corrupted. Whether this corruption vitiates the sacrament to such an extent as seriously to affect its validity is not so trivial a question as the Reviewer supposes. As baptism is a species of ablution, whatever unfits the water for the purpose of cleansing unfits it for the Christian ordinance. Such mixtures as are found in nature, in springs, pools, rivers and seas, so long as they do not affect the liquidity of the fluid, do not affect its adaptation to any of the ordinary purposes of life. Men still *wash* with it. But a water which cannot be used in *washing* is not suitable matter for baptism, and as *oil* evidently impairs its cleansing properties, it destroys that very quality in water in consequence of which it is capable of representing the purifying influence of regeneration and the renewing of the Holy Ghost. No more incongruous substances can be found than water and oil, and to wash in such a mixture is not to cleanse, but defile. The significancy of the rite is affected; it is not made to consist in simply washing with water, but in washing with a water duly consecrated with oil. In the present case attention is called to the mixture; great importance is attached to it, and it is in *consequence* of the chrism that the mixed substance is used in preference to the pure, simple, natural element. It is not because it is *water*, but because it is *sanctified by oil*, that the priests employ it in baptism. This is, certainly, not making the significancy of the rite depend upon washing with water; it makes it equally depend upon the oil of the mystic unction. The very purpose of the mixture is to increase the significancy of the rite—to declare more fully the nature and effect of the bap-

[1] Hurd's History of the Rites, Ceremonies and Customs (Religious) of the Whole World, p. 218.

tism. The oil is, consequently, made a prominent element
in the compound, and it is precisely that which in ordinary
cases *fits* the water for its use. In other cases the foreign
element is left entirely out of view, and the adulterated
substance is used *as* water, and nothing but water. But
here it is not, *notwithstanding* the mixture, but, *because* of
the mixture, that the corrupted water is employed. It is not
used *as* water and nothing but water, but as water invested
with new properties in consequence of the oil. The presence of the foreign matter is an improvement, when canon-
ically introduced, upon the original appointment of the
Saviour; and so much importance is attached to it that
Rome permits simple water to be used only on the plea
which may also dispense with the services of the priest—
the plea of stern necessity. Water without the chrism may
be employed in that class of cases in which Jews, Infidels
and Turks are authorized to baptize. Through the pressure
of necessity God *may* sanctify it without the oil, but in ordinary cases the charm lies in the mystic unction.

These two circumstances seem to me to distinguish the
mixture in question from all the combinations which are
found in nature: 1. That the oil destroys the *fitness* of
water for the purpose of ablution, and so affects the significancy of the rite; and, 2. That the mixture is not used
as water, but that peculiar stress is laid upon the foreign
element. It enters into the baptism as a very important
ingredient. He who baptizes with rain or cistern water, or
water impregnated with saline mixtures, overlooks the foreign matter and attaches value only to the water. He uses
the mixture simply *as* water. But Rome makes the *corruption* of the water a part of her solemn ceremonies; the
chrism works wonders in the font, and imparts to it an efficacy which only in rare cases it would otherwise possess.
The mixture of the chrism with the water is, according to
Durand, a sign of the union between Christ and the Church;
and as an evidence of the value attached to the chrism, he
adds that *it* represents Christ, while the water represents the

people. The Catechism of the Council of Trent teaches that additional significancy is given to the water by the holy chrism. We may concede to the Reviewer "that water with oil thrown on it is still water"—that is, it may be heated and used, notwithstanding the mixture, *as* water; that wine adulterated with water continues to be wine, or may be used as such, provided the mixture is not made a matter of prominent observation. But when the foreign elements are dignified into importance, and made to play a part in the offices performed, then the water is no longer simple water, but water and oil—the wine is no longer simple wine, but wine and water. If in the sacrament of the Lord's Supper we were professedly to adulterate the wine in order to give superior efficacy to it, and to use the compound not simply *as* wine, but as wine invested with *new* properties *in consequence* of the mixture, the matter of the sacrament would be evidently vitiated, and that not because it would be a mixture, but because it would be *used as a* mixture. If the same wine were used as wine, *notwithstanding* the mixture, there would be no impropriety, but when it is used in *consequence* of the mixture, the case is manifestly different.

It is not a little remarkable that the Romanists themselves condemn a practice which seems to be fully as justifiable as their own. "But neither are they to be approved, of whom Egbert, archbishop of York, says (Excerp., cap. 42), "There are some who mix wine with the water of baptism, not rightly, because Christ did not command to be baptized with wine, but with water." [1] And yet in the very next section this writer insists on the importance of using consecrated water, and not profane, whenever the ordinance is administered, and refers among other authorities to the passage from Dionysius, already quoted, which shows that the consecra-

[1] De Antiquis Ecclesiæ Ritibus, Lib. i., cap. i., art. 14. "Sed neque probandi sunt illi," says Martene, "de quibus Egbertus Eboracensis archiepiscopus (in Excerptis), cap. 42. 'Sunt quidam, inquit, qui miscent vinum cum aqua baptismatis, non recte; quia Christus non jussit baptizari vino, sed aqua.' "

tion embraced the infusion of chrism in the form of a cross.
It is difficult to see how a mixture with wine vitiates the
sacrament, while a mixture with oil improves it. The command of Christ, which is very properly pleaded against
wine, applies as conclusively to chrism. But whatever may
be said of this self-condemnation on the part of Rome, I
think it cannot be denied that in that idolatrous communion
the *matter* of baptism is corrupted, and that the Reviewer
has consequently failed in making out his first point, that
Papal baptism is a washing with water, and that this is the
sole matter of the sacrament. But it may be asked, What,
then? Did baptism become extinct when this innovation
was first introduced among the churches that adopted it?
My reply is, That I know of no sacredness in baptism
which should entitle it to be preserved in its integrity when
the ordinance of the Lord's Supper has been confessedly
abolished in the Latin Church. Why should baptism be
perpetuated entire, and the supper transmitted with grievous mutilations? Or will it be maintained that the essence
of the supper was still retained when the cup was denied to
the laity? Is it more incredible that an outward ordinance
should be invalidated than that the precious truths which it
was designed to represent should be lost? Is the shell more
important than the substance? And shall we admit that
the cardinal doctrines of the Gospel have been damnably
corrupted in the Church of Rome, and yet be afraid to
declare that the signs and seals of the covenant have shared
the same fate? If Rome is corrupt in doctrine, I see not
why she may not be equally corrupt in ordinances, and if
she has lost one sacrament, I see not why she may not have
lost the other; and as the foundations of her apostasy were
laid in the ages immediately succeeding the time of the
Apostles, I cannot understand why the loss of the *real*
sacrament of baptism may not have been an early symptom
of degeneracy and decay.

But our business is with truth and not with consequences.
We should not be deterred from admitting a scriptural con-

clusion because it removes, with a desolating besom, the structures of antiquity. We are not to say, *a priori*, that the Church in the fifth or sixth centuries *must* have had the true sacrament of baptism, and then infer that such and such corruptions do not invalidate the ordinance. But we are first to ascertain from the Scriptures what the true sacrament of baptism is, and then judge the practice of the Church in every age by this standard. If its customs have at any time departed from the law and the testimony, let them be condemned; if they have been something essentially different from what God had enjoined, let them be denounced as spurious. The unbroken transmission of a visible Church in any line of succession is a figment of Papists and Prelatists. Conformity with the Scriptures, and not ecclesiastical genealogy, is the true touchstone of a sound church-state; and if our fathers were without the ordinances, and fed upon ashes for bread, let us only be the more thankful for the greater privileges vouchsafed to ourselves.

II. The *form* of baptism, or that which distinguishes this species of ablution from every other washing with water, consists in the relations which, according to the appointment of Christ, it sustains to the covenant of grace. The solemn invocation of the names of the Trinity,[1] though a circumstance attending the actual application of the element, and perhaps an indispensable circumstance, does not constitute the whole essence of the ordinance. A Socinian may undoubtedly employ the same formulary as ourselves. And yet, according to repeated admissions of the Reviewer himself,[2] his want of faith in the Personal distinctions of the Godhead would be sufficient to render void the pretended sacrament. To baptize in the name of Father, Son and Spirit is not to pronounce these words as an idle form or a mystical charm, but to acknowledge that solemn compact into which these glorious Agents entered, from eternity, for

[1] "Is it then correct as to the form? Is it administered in the name of the Trinity?"—Princeton Review, July, 1845, p. 450.
[2] Pages 446-468.

the redemption of the Church. It is the *faith* of the Trinity, much more than the *names* of its separate Persons, that belongs to the essence of baptism; and where this faith existed, some of the ancient fathers contended—how justly I shall not undertake to decide—that the ordinance was validly administered, even though done without the explicit mention of all the Persons of the Godhead. "He that is blessed in Christ," says Ambrose,[1] "is blessed in the name of the Father, and Son, and Holy Ghost; because the name is one and the power one. The Ethiopian eunuch, who was baptized in Christ, had the sacrament complete. If a man names only a single Person expressly in words, either Father, Son or Holy Ghost, so long as he does not deny in his faith either Father, Son or Holy Ghost, the sacrament of faith is complete; as, on the other hand, if a man in words express all the three persons, Father, Son and Holy Ghost, but in his faith diminishes the power either of the Father, or Son, or Holy Ghost, the sacrament of faith is void." Whatever objection may lie against the first part of this statement, that the explicit mention of all the Persons of the Trinity is not indispensable to the due administration of baptism, none can decently deny that to name them without believing in them is not to celebrate but to profane the ordinance.

As, therefore, the invocation of the Trinity may take place in ablutions which it is impossible to recognize as the baptism instituted by Christ, it cannot constitute the *whole* form of the sacrament. In this there is no real difference between the Reviewer and myself. He only uses the word *form* in a different sense from that in which I have been accustomed to employ it, but by no means confines the *essence* of the sacrament to what he denominates its *form*. On the contrary, he makes the *design* or *intention*[2] an essen-

[1] Bingham, Origines Ecclesiasticæ, B. xi., c. iii., sec. 3.
[2] "There is, however, a third particular included in this definition of baptism; it must be with the design to 'signify and seal our ingrafting into Christ, and partaking of the benefits of the covenant of grace, and our engagements to be the Lord's.' . . . . No washing with water, even

tial part of the ordinance, and means by it precisely what I would be understood to convey when I resolve the form of a sacrament into the relations which its material elements, according to the appointment of Christ, sustain to the covenant of grace. To eat bread and to drink wine is not necessarily to celebrate the sacrament of the Lord's Supper; to be immersed or sprinkled—a formal invocation of the names of the Trinity accompanying the deed—is not necessarily to be baptized. There must be a reference to the economy of grace, a distinct recognition of that precious scheme of redemption in its essential features and fundamental doctrines, without which ordinances are worthless and duties are bondage. That which determines a specific ablution to be Christian baptism, which impresses upon the matter what may be styled the *sacramental form*, and which, consequently, constitutes its essence as a sacrament, is the relation which it bears to the covenant of God's unchanging mercy. To deny that relation, though all the outward appearances may be retained, is to abolish the sacrament. To tamper with the essence of an ordinance is to tamper with its life. As the constitution of this relation, whatever it may be, depends exclusively upon the authority of Christ, it is competent to Him alone to define the circumstances under which it may be justly conceived to exist, to specify the conditions upon which its actual institution depends. For aught we know, He might have rendered every circumstance of personal ablution, or of eating and drinking, on the part of believers, a sacramental act. But He has chosen to restrain the sacramental relations within certain limits; and when His own prescriptions are not observed, no power of man, no intention of ministers, can impress the sacramental form upon material elements. The purpose of a family to convert its ordinary meals into memorials of the Saviour's passion, coupled with the fact

if in the name of the Trinity, is Christian baptism, unless administered with the ostensible design of signifying, sealing and applying the benefits of the covenant of grace."—Princeton Review, July, 1845, p. 448.

that they are despatched with the usual solemnities of the eucharistic feast, is not sufficient to make them, in truth, the supper of the Lord. The emblems of His broken body and shed blood are not made thus common and profane. If, to be more specific, the authority to administer the sacraments is intrusted exclusively to the ministers of the Word, the same matter employed, in the same way, by others, would be evidently destitute of the sacramental form. The *relation* to the covenant of grace, which depends upon the institution of Christ, could not be justly apprehended as subsisting, and the promises attached to the due celebration of the ordinance could not be legitimately expected to take effect.

He, therefore, that would undertake to prove that the Romish ceremony possesses the *form* or the *essential elements* of Christian baptism must not content himself with showing that Rome baptizes in the name of the Trinity. He must prove, besides, that she inculcates just views concerning the *nature* of the relationship which the outward washing sustains to the covenant of grace; that her conceptions of the covenant itself, that to which the ablution has reference, are substantially correct; and that she employs the outward elements in conformity with the conditions prescribed by the Author of the sacrament. If she is fundamentally unsound upon any of these points, she abolishes the *essence* of the ordinance, she destroys its *form*. She may, for instance, be as orthodox as Princeton represents her to be in regard to the personal and official relations of the Trinity;[1] she may teach the truth in regard to the scheme of redemption; and yet if her baptism bears a different kind of relationship to the covenant of grace from that instituted by the Redeemer, it is evident that it must be a different thing. If, on the other hand, she is sound as

[1] "There is not a church on earth which teaches the doctrine of the Trinity more accurately, thoroughly or minutely, according to the orthodoxy of the Lutheran and Reformed churches, than the Church of Rome. The personal and official relations of the adorable Trinity are also preserved."—Princeton Review, July, 1845, p. 450.

to the *nature* of the relationship, and yet corrupt as to the *object* to which the sacrament refers,[1] her baptism is only *analogous* to Christian baptism, and therefore cannot be the same. The relations are similar, but the things related are different. If, again, she holds to the truth, both as it respects the relationship itself and the things related, and yet does not administer her ordinance according to the conditions on which the sacramental form may be expected to take place, she washes, indeed, but not sacramentally; the authority of Christ is wanting. She administers no *baptism*. If to be unsound in any *one* of these points makes void a sacrament, what shall be said when there is unsoundness in *all?* Such an ordinance is trebly void. And that this is the case with Romish baptism, I think will be made to appear when the arguments of the Reviewer—the strongest, perhaps, that can be presented to show that it possesses the form or retains the essence of the Christian institute—shall have been duly weighed.

1. First, then, does Rome teach the truth in regard to the *nature* of the relationship involved in a sacrament? The answer to this question will depend upon the answer to the previous question, what the nature of the relationship is. How much soever they have differed upon other points, Protestant divines have generally agreed that one prime office assigned to the sacraments is to represent to the eye, as preaching unfolds to the ear, Christ as the substance of the new covenant. They are *signs* which teach by analogy. As water cleanses the body, so the blood of the Redeemer purges the conscience and the Spirit of the Redeemer purifies the heart. As bread and wine constitute important articles of food, and administer strength to our feeble frame, so the atonement of Christ is the food of the spiritual man, and the source of all his activity and vigour.[2] This *anal-*

---

[1] "There can be no baptism where the essence of Christianity is not preserved."—Burnet, XXXIX. Articles, art. xix., p. 242, London edition of 1837.

[2] "The signification and substance is to show us how we are fed with the body of Christ—that is, that like as material bread feedeth our body,

ogy is what Augustine meant when he said, " If sacraments had not a certain *likeness* and *representation* of the things whereof they be sacraments, then indeed they were no sacraments."[1] The things themselves unquestionably are not similar. There is no likeness between the water and the Spirit, between bread and wine and the death of Jesus, but there is a resemblance in their *relations.* Water performs a similar office for the flesh to that which the blood of Christ performs for the soul. Bread and wine sustain a relation to our natural growth similar to that which faith in Christ bears to our spiritual health. It is obvious that, regarded simply as *signs* instituted by the authority of Christ, the sacraments are happily adapted to confirm our faith in the truth and reality of the Divine promises. They place before us in a different form and under a different aspect, in a form and aspect adapted to our animal and corporeal nature, the same grounds and object of faith which the Word presents to the understanding. They do not render the promises of the covenant, in themselves considered, more sure or credible, but they help us, by images addressed to the senses, in apprehending what might otherwise be too refined for our gross perceptions.[2] They are a double preaching of the

---

so the body of Christ nailed on the cross, embraced and eaten by faith, feedeth the soul. The like representation is also made in the sacrament of baptism, that as our body is washed clean with water, so our soul is washed clean with Christ's blood."—Jewell, Defence of the Apology, Part ii., chap. x., Divis. i.

[1] Quoted by Jewell, *ibidem.*

[2] Hence Calvin very justly observes: "And as we are corporeal, always creeping on the ground, cleaving to terrestrial and carnal objects, and incapable of understanding or conceiving of anything of a spiritual nature, our merciful Lord, in His infinite indulgence, accommodates Himself to our capacity, condescending to lead us to Himself even by these earthly elements, and in the flesh itself to present to us a mirror of spiritual blessings. 'For if we were incorporeal,' as Chrysostom says, 'He would have given us these things pure and incorporeal. Now, because we have souls enclosed in bodies, He gives us spiritual things under visible emblems; not because there are such qualities in the nature of the things presented to us in the sacraments, but because they have been designated by God to this signification.'"—Institutes, B. iv., c. xiv., sec. 3.

same Gospel, and confirm the Word just as an additional witness establishes a fact. They are, in short, *visible promises*, which we cannot contemplate in their true character without an increased conviction of the truth and faithfulness of God. But in addition to this, God may be regarded as declaring through them to worthy recipients that just as certainly as water purifies the body, or as bread and wine sustain it, just so certainly shall their consciences be purged from dead works, and their spiritual strength renewed, through the blood of the Redeemer. The certainty of the material phenomena, which is a matter of daily experience, is made the pledge of an equal certainty in the analogous spiritual things. It is in this way, I conceive, that the sacraments are seals of the covenant. They not only *represent* its blessings, are not only an authorized proclamation of its promises addressed to the eye, but contain, at the same time, a solemn assurance that to those who rightly apprehend the signs the spiritual good shall be as certain as the natural consequences by which it is illustrated—that the connection between faith and salvation is as indissoluble as between washing and external purity, eating and physical strength.

Is this the doctrine of the Church of Rome? Does she regard her sacraments as instituted *signs* of spiritual things or as visible *pledges* of the faithfulness of God in the new and everlasting covenant? If so, she has been most grievously slandered by the most distinguished Protestant divines, and the *Princeton Review* is the only work, so far as I know, of any merit, which has ventured to assert that her doctrine on this subject is precisely the same with that of the Reformed Church. It is, indeed, admitted that there is a difference between Papists and Protestants as to the *mode*[1] in which the design of baptism is accomplished. But did it not occur to the Reviewer that there could be *no*

[1] "The great difference between Protestants and Romanists relates not to the design of the ordinance, but to the mode and certainty with which that design is accomplished, and the conditions attached to it. In other words, the difference relates to the efficacy and not to the design of the ordinance."—Princeton Review, July, 1845, p. 451.

difference upon this point if there were a perfect agreement
as to the nature of that *relation* which baptism sustains to
the covenant of grace? If Rome looked upon the sacraments in the same light with ourselves, as only *signs* and
seals, and nothing more than signs and seals, though she
might have disputed whether the benefits which they represent are, in every instance in which no serious obstruc-
tion exists, actually conveyed, the question as to their
inherent efficacy never *could* have been raised. She would
have taught their recipients, as we do, to look beyond the
visible symbols to the personal agency of the Holy Ghost
to render them effectual. As well might she have expected
her children to become men in understanding by reading
books in an unknown tongue, as have directed them to seek
for grace in signs and seals, without any reference to the
things represented. As it is the ideas which words suggest
that constitute knowledge, so it is Christ's words and His
benefits that constitute the value of the sacraments; and
they cannot be used with any just conception of their *real
nature* without leading the soul directly to Him. Any
theory of their office which even proposes the temptation
to stop at themselves is utterly destructive of their true
design. The questions which have been agitated with so
much zeal among the Popish theologians, whether the consecration of a priest imparts a mystic power to the external
symbols, enabling them to produce effects which, independently of his benediction, they could not accomplish; whether
his intention to bestow this magical virtue is absolutely
essential to its actual communication; whether the appropriate results of the ordinances are secured *ex opere operantis*
or *ex opere operato*, or by both conjointly,—questions of this
sort, which have been the fruitful themes of so much discussion among the sainted doctors of Rome, are too obviously
absurd to be asked upon the Protestant hypothesis. And
yet Princeton tells us that Rome and ourselves are precisely
agreed upon the *nature* of the sacraments;[1] that she, as we

[1] "Then as to the third essential part of the ordinance, the design, in

do, makes them signs and seals of the new covenant, and
consequently fixes the hopes of her children *not upon them,*
but upon the glorious Object whom they represent. So
thought not Calvin,[1] who inveighs so eloquently against the
" pestilent and fatal nature of the opinion " which he attributes to the Sophistical schools, and declares, in his celebrated Tract concerning the necessity of reforming the
Church, to have been universal before the Reformation,[2]
"that the sacraments of the New Law, or those now used
in the Christian Church, justify and confer grace, provided
we do not obstruct their operation by any mortal sin." So
thought not Turrettin,[3] who evidently treats it as the doctrine of the Papists, that the sacraments are not signs and
seals of the everlasting covenant, but true, proper, physical
causes of the grace they are said to represent. This error

this also their [Romish] baptism agrees with that of Protestants. According to our standards, the design of the sacrament is to signify, seal
and apply to believers the benefits of the new covenant. This is the
precise doctrine of the Romanists, so far as this."—Princeton Review,
July, 1845, p. 450.

[1] Institutes, B. iv., c. xiv., sec. 14.

[2] "Besides, the consecration both of baptism and of the mass differs in
no respect whatever from magical incantation. For by breathings and
whispering and unintelligible sounds they think they work mysteries.
. . . . The first thing we complain of here is, that the people are entertained with showy ceremonies, while not a word is said of their significancy and truth. For there is no use in the sacraments unless the thing
which the sign visibly represents is explained in accordance with the Word
of God. Therefore, when the people are presented with nothing but
empty figures with which to feed the eye, while they hear no doctrine
which might direct them to the proper end, they look no farther than the
external act. Hence that most pestilential superstition under which, as if
the sacraments alone were sufficient for salvation, without feeling any
solicitude about faith, or repentance, or even Christ himself, they fasten
upon the sign instead of the thing signified by it. And indeed not only
among the rude vulgar, but in the schools also, the impious dogma everywhere obtained, that the sacraments were effectual themselves, if not ob-
structed in their operation by mortal sin; as if the sacraments had been
given for any other end or use than to lead us by the hand to Christ."—
Calvin's Tracts, vol. i., pp. 138, 139, as published by Calvin Translation
Society. See also pp. 166 and 194.

[3] Turrettin, Instit. Theo., vol. iii., p. 404, Loc. xix., Qu. viii., § 3.

concerning the inherent efficacy of the sacraments Pictet[1] also declares to be *contrary to their nature*. Owen[2] felt that there was a vital controversy betwixt us and Rome on this point when he denounced Popish baptism as a *species of idolatry*. It is impossible to read the Reformed confessions, and the apologies which the Reformers made for them, without being impressed with the fact that their authors laboured under a deep conviction that the minds of the people were seduced, by the teachings of Rome, with dangerous and fatal error on the very *essence* of the sacraments, the nature of their relation to the covenant of grace, the precise office they discharge under the dispensation of the Gospel. This was, in fact, a standing topic of controversy between the two parties. Rome represented the new doctrines concerning gratuitous justification and the work of the Spirit as derogatory to the dignity and value of the sacraments, and artfully turned the tide of prejudice, growing out of the old associations of mystery and awe with which the people had been accustomed to look upon the consecrated symbols, against the restorers of the Church. The cry everlastingly was, "You have robbed the sacraments of their glory. You have degraded them into *empty shows*.[3] You have introduced your new-fangled doctrines of faith and the Spirit in their place." These and similar accusations were continually alleged against the Reformers by the Papists, showing that there was a radical difference between them as to the design of the sacraments. Rome felt that one of her strongest holds upon the people was their attachment to these mysteries of her faith, and hence she was anxious, as much as possible, to make the sacraments the seat of the war. While the Papists charged the Reformers with prostituting these solemn and august ceremonies into worthless signs, the Protestants retorted upon

[1] Pictet, Theol. Chret., L. xv., c. 4.

[2] Owen's Works, vol. xvi., p. 95: Sermon on the Chamber of Imagery.

[3] "You make Christ's sacraments," said Harding against Jewell, "to be only shows."—Richmond's British Reformers, vol. vii., p. 693.

Rome that she had converted them into charms, and had invested creatures of dust and earth, the beggarly elements of this world, with the high prerogatives of God. The question was not so much about the *mode* of operation, as Princeton insinuates, but about the *agent* that operated; it was a question whether the sacraments themselves conferred grace, or whether God the Holy Spirit conferred it, employing them simply as *means* which had no intrinsic power to do the work. It was a question whether the sacraments were really *signs* or *efficient agents;* and if this be not a question concerning their *nature*, it would be hard to raise one that is. If the impression of the Reformers was right, that Rome exalted the sacraments into true and proper *causes* of grace, there can be no doubt that, whatever she may have professed in words, she did in fact deny them to be *signs*, and consequently changed their relations to the covenant of grace, and made them *essentially* different things from what Christ had appointed. It is a matter of no sort of consequence that the Reformers themselves failed to deduce this inference. The full application of a principle is not always perceived at once, and the soundness of a conclusion depends upon the truth of the premises and the rigour of the reasoning, and not upon human authority. If the essence of the sacraments is determined by their relation to the covenant of grace, and that relation consists in their being signs and seals of its blessings, then whoever denies the reality of the signs, or teaches doctrines inconsistent with it, evidently destroys the very being of the sacraments, and what he presents under their names, whether charms or magic or physical causes of grace, are an impious and blasphemous substitution. This is precisely what Rome does. While she retains the ancient definitions, and uses the expressions *signs* and *seals*, she vacates their meaning by giving such a view of the actual offices they discharge in the economy of redemption as to make signs no more signs, seals no more seals. They cease to be, in the ordinary sense of the phrase, *means* of grace, and become *laws* of grace. She teaches a *mechanical theory* of salvation, calculated at once to exalt her priests and to degrade God, and fritters down the personality of the ever-glorious Spirit into the mere nexus which connects a cause with its effect, a law with its results. She teaches men, accordingly, to rely upon the sacraments and not upon Christ, to stop at the external act—as if water, bread and wine were our Saviours—instead of looking to Him in whom all the truths of the Gospel centre and terminate; an error which could not be committed if she held the sacraments to be real signs. These statements I shall endeavour to make good.

The official doctrine of the Church of Rome clearly is that the sacraments confer the grace which they signify *ex opere operato*.[1] If it should be conceded, for the sake of argument, that Luther, Melancthon, Calvin and Zuingle mistook the meaning of this anomalous phrase, and that the cautious definitions of Bellarmine and Dens contain the true explanation of the subject, still the conclusion will seem to be inevitable that the sacraments produce their spiritual effects either in the way of physical causes, or of mechanical instruments. Both hypotheses are inconsistent with the theory of *signs*. It would be obviously absurd to say that fire is a symbol of heat, or that the combined forces which keep the planets in their paths are *signs* of the elliptical orbits they describe, or that the screw, the lever, and the wedge represent the effects they respectively produce. The relation of a cause to its effect, or of a machine to the phenomena of motion, is widely different from that of a sign to the thing it denotes. According to Bellarmine,[2] to confer

[1] Si quis dixerit, per ipsa novæ legis Sacramenta ex opere operato non conferri gratiam, sed solam fidem divinæ promissionis ad gratiam consequendam sufficere, anathema sit. Trident. Conc., Sessio vii., Can. viii.

[2] Igitur ut intelligamus, quid sit opus operatum, notandum est, in justificatione, quam recipit aliquis, dum percipit Sacramenta, multa concurrere; nimirum, ex parte Dei, voluntatem utendi illa re sensibili; ex parte Christi, passionem ejus; ex parte ministri, potestatem, voluntatem, probitatem; ex parte suscipientis, voluntatem, fidem et pœnitentiam; denique ex parte Sacramenti, ipsam actionem externam, quæ consurgit ex debita applicatione formæ et materiæ. Ceterum ex his omnibus id, quod

grace *ex opere operato* is to confer grace by virtue of the sacramental action itself, instituted of God for this very purpose. The effect of the ordinance does not depend either upon the merit of him who receives or of him who dispenses it, but upon the fact of its due administration. Though the authority of God which institutes the rite, the death of Christ which is the ultimate meritorious ground of grace, the intention of the minister which consecrates the elements, and the dispositions of the recipient which remove obstacles from his mind, all concur in the production of the result, yet that which immediately and actively secures the justification of the sinner is the *external action* which constitutes the sacrament. This, and this alone, however other things may be subsidiary, is, according to the appointment of God,

active, et proximè, atque instrumentaliter efficit gratiam justificationis, est sola actio illa externa, quæ Sacramentum dicitur, et hæc vocatur opus operatum, accipiendo passivè (operatum) ita ut idem sit Sacramentum conferre gratiam ex opere operato, quod conferre gratiam ex vi ipsius actionis Sacramentalis à Deo ad hoc institutæ, non ex merito agentis, vel suscipientis: quod S. Augustinus lib. 4, de Baptismo, ca. 24, expressit illis verbis: *Ipsum per seipsum Sacramentum multum valet.* Nam voluntas Dei, quæ sacramento utitur, concurrit quidem activè, sed est causa principalis. Passio Christi concurrit, sed est causa meritoria, non autem effectiva, cum non sit actu, sed præterierit, licet moneat objectivè in mente Dei. Potestas, et voluntas ministri concurrunt necessariò, sed sunt causæ remotæ; requiruntur enim ad efficiendam ipsam actionem Sacramentalem, quæ postea immediatè operatur. Probitas ministri requiritur, ut ipse minister non peccet Sacramenta ministrando, non tamen ipsa est causa gratiæ in suscipiente, nec juvat suscipientem per modum Sacramenti, sed solum per modum impetrationis et exempli. Voluntas, fides, et pœnitentia in suscipiente adulto necessariò requiruntur, ut dispositiones ex parte subjecti, non ut causæ activæ: non enim fides et pœnitentia efficiunt gratiam Sacramentalem, neque dant efficaciam Sacramentis, sed solum tollunt obstacula, quæ impedirent ne Sacramenta suam efficaciam exercere possent; unde in pueris, ubi non requiritur dispositio, sine his rebus sit justificatio. Exemplum esse potest in re naturali. Si ad ligna comburenda, primum exsiccarentur ligna, deinde excutereter ignis ex silice, tum applicaretur ignis ligno, et sic tandem fieret combustio; nemo diceret, caussam immediatam combustionis esse siccitatem, aut excussionem ignis ex silice, aut applicationem ignis ad ligna, sed solum ignem, ut caussam primariam, et solum calorem, seu calefactionem, ut caussam instrumentalem. De Sacramentis, Lib. ii., cap. 1.

the immediate instrument in effecting, when not prevented by obstacles or hindrances, the grace which is signified. *How* this is done is said to be an open question in the Church of Rome;[1] but the different opinions which have divided her divines and distracted her Schoolmen may be embraced under the general theories of moral power and physical causation.[2] The patrons of the former, slow to comprehend how material elements can achieve a spiritual result, ascribe the efficiency not to the sacraments themselves, but to the agency of God. They suppose that He has pledged His omnipotence, in every instance of their due administration, to impart the benefits which the matter represents. He has inseparably connected the effectual working of His own power with the external action. Grace always accompanies the rite; their union is fixed by Divine appointment, cemented by Divine energy, and as indissolu-

---

[1] Secundo notandum, non esse controversiam de modo quo Sacramenta sint caussæ, id est, an physicè attingendo effectum, an moraliter tantum; et rursum si physicè, an per aliquam qualitatem inhærentem, an per solam Dei motionem; ista enim ad questionem fidei non pertinent: sed solùm generatim, an Sacramenta sint veræ et propriæ caussæ instrumentales justificationis, ut vere ex eo quod quis baptizatur, sequatur, ut justificetur. Nam in hoc conveniunt omnes Catholici, ut Lutherus ipse fatetur, in lib. de captiv. Babyl. cap. de Baptismo: *Arbitrati,* inquit, *sunt quam plurimi esse aliquam virtutem occultam spiritualem in verbo, et aqua, quæ operetur in anima recipientis gratiam Dei. His alii contradicentes statuunt, nihil esse virtutis in Sacramentis, sed gratiam a solo Deo dari, quia assistit ex pacto Sacramentis a se institutis: omnes tamen in hoc concedunt, Sacramenta esse efficacia signa gratiæ.* Ibid.

Salva autem fide, inter Catholicos disputatur, an Sacramenta novæ legis conferant suos effectus physicè, an tantum moraliter. Dens, De Sacram., vol. v., No. 17, p. 90.

[2] Quidam tenent causalitatem physicam, et sese explicant, quòd Sacramenta, tanquam Divinæ Omnipotentiæ instrumenta, verè et realiter concurrant ad productionem effectuum in anima, per virtutem supernaturalem a principali agente sibi communicatam, et per modum actionis transeuntis sibi unitam. Qui verò adstruunt causalitatem moralem tantûm, dicunt quidem Sacramenta non esse nuda quædam signa, nec merè talia, quibus positis, Deus gratiam infundat, sed esse velut chirographa et authentica monumenta pacti, quo Deus se quodammodo obstrinxit, ut ad præsentiam signorum Sacramentalium gratiam conferret debitè suscipientibus. Dens, Ibidem.

ble in the experience of the faithful as they are in the purpose of the Almighty. This theory, though not so gross
and palpably absurd as the other, reduces the sacraments, in
their relations to us, to the category of machines—machines
in the kingdom of God, to which spiritual phenomena may
be ascribed, just as truly as the wheel, the pulley, and the
wedge are mechanical contrivances for bending nature to
our wills. In their relations to God they would seem to be
somewhat analogous to *laws*, since they are described as
stated modes of Divine operation, and may evidently be
regarded as compendious expressions for a class of facts
which take place with unvarying uniformity. In the
schools of philosophy no more inherent efficacy is attributed
to natural laws than the Romanists, who support the theory
of moral power, are accustomed to bestow on the operation
of the sacraments. It is God in each case who acts, and
the law simply declares the regularity and order of His conduct. But, however this may be, to resolve the connection
between outward ordinances and spiritual benefits into the
fixed uniformity of a law is to make the external action, in
reference to men, a species of machine. As motion, in the
last analysis, must be attributed to God, those mechanical
instruments which are adapted to its laws are only contrivances for availing ourselves of His power to compass ends
which our own strength is inadequate to reach. Experience,
by giving us the laws of nature, acquaints us with the
methods of the Divine administration. And mechanism
consists in a skilful disposition of materials with reference
to these laws, so as to make them subsidiary to the purpose
which we propose to achieve. If, accordingly, there be a
fixed connection between the due dispensation of the sacraments and the reception of grace, we can avail ourselves of
them to secure spiritual good with as much certainty and
as little piety as we can depend upon the wheel, the pulley,
or the lever to raise enormous weights, rely upon the wedge
to break the stoutest cohesion, or trust to the screw for an
immense compression. The external action is adapted to

the law of sacramental union, as the ordinary mechanical powers are instruments adjusted to the laws of motion. Hence, regeneration is effected, in flat contradiction to the Scriptures, by the will of man, and justification is as much our own work as the erection of a building or the construction of a monument. We can use the instrument which secures it.

The other theory of the operation of the sacraments represents them as *causes.* Its advocates seem to have believed, in opposition to the prevailing conclusions of modern philosophy, that what, in material phenomena, are dignified with this appellation are possessed of a latent power to accomplish their effects. Regarding the invisible nexus which binds events in this relationship together, as something more than the established order of sequences given by experience, they were led to ascribe mysterious efficacy to the cause by which it not only preceded the effect with unvarying uniformity, but actually gave it existence. They attributed to physical facts that potency, according to their measure, which our instinctive belief of causation leads us to recognize somewhere, and sound philosophy centres in God. The sacraments, accordingly, are represented, by the advocates of their physical efficacy, as invested with a virtue, force or power in consequence of which they produce the grace they are said to signify. This theory is not only the most common in the Church of Rome, but seems to me to be the only one strictly accordant with the views of Trent. The sixth Canon of the Seventh session of that Council pronounces its usual malediction upon those who shall deny that the sacraments of the Gospel *contain* the grace which they signify, or that they *confer* that grace upon those who place no obstacles in the way.[1] But whatever may be said

---

[1] Si quis dixerit, Sacramenta novæ legis non continere gratiam quam significant, aut gratiam ipsam non ponentibus obicem non conferre, quasi signa tantum externa sint acceptæ per fidem gratiæ vel justitiæ, et notæ quædam Christianæ professionis, quibus apud homines discernuntur fideles ab infidelibus, anathema sit. Trident. Con., Sess. vii., can. vi.

of the decrees of the Council, its Catechism seems to be
clear and unambiguous. Having spoken of signs which
are only significant and monitory, it proceeds to observe[1]
that "God has instituted others which have the power, not
only of signifying, *but of effecting*, and in this class must
evidently be reckoned the sacraments of the new law. They
are signs divinely prescribed, not invented by men, which,
we certainly believe, contain in themselves the *power of
effecting the sacred thing* [the grace] which they declare." A
sacrament is defined to be[2] a "thing subjected to the senses,
which, in consequence of the appointment of God, possesses
the power, not only of signifying, but also of *effecting*, holiness and righteousness." They are said to have been instituted as "remedies and medicines for restoring and defending
the health of the soul," and are commended as pipes which
convey the merit of the Saviour's passion to the consciences
of men.[3] What language can be stronger than that which
the authors of the Catechism have employed in treating
of the first effects of the sacraments?[4] "We know," say
they, "by the light of faith"—and all true Papists must
respond Amen—"that the power of the omnipotent God

---

[1] Alia vero Deus instituit, quæ non significandi modo sed efficiendi
etiam vim haberent, atque in hoc posteriori signorum genere sacramenta
novæ legis numeranda esse liquidò apparet: signa enim sunt divinitùs
tradita, non ab hominibus inventa, quæ rei cujuspiam sacræ, quam declarant, efficientiam in se continere certò credimus. Trident. Catechism.
Pars ii., cap. i., § viii.

[2] Quare, ut explicatiùs quid sacramentum sit declaretur, docendum erit
rem esse sensibus subjectam, quæ ex Dei institutione sanctitatis, et justitiæ
tum significandæ, tum efficiendæ, vim habet. Ibid., cap. i., § x.

[3] Tertia causa fuit, ut illa tanquam remedia, ut scribit sanctus Ambro-
sius, atque Evangelici Samaritani medicamenta ad animarum sanitatem,
vel recuperandam, vel tuendam præstò essent. Virtutem enim, quæ ex
passione Christi manat, hoc est, gratiam quam ille nobis in ara crucis
meruit, per sacramenta, quasi per alveum quemdam, in nos ipsos derivari
oportet, aliter verò nemini ulla salutis spes reliqua esse poterit. Ibid.,
cap. i., § xiii.

[4] At fidei lumine cognoscimus, omnipotentis Dei virtutem in sacramentis
in esse, qua id efficiant, quod sua vi res ipsæ naturales præstare non possunt. Ibid., cap. i., § xxvi.

exists in the sacraments, and they can, consequently, effect
that which natural things, by their own energy, cannot
achieve."

In the comparison which is instituted between the sacraments of the *new* and those of the *old* dispensation, the
pre-eminence is given to the former, in consequence of possessing what the others did not possess, the ability of effecting that which their matter represents.[1] The latter availed
to the cleansing of the flesh, the former reach the impurities
of the soul; the latter were instituted simply as signs of
blessings to be afterward conferred by the ministry of the
Gospel, but the "former, flowing from the side of Christ,
who, through the Eternal Spirit, offered himself without
spot unto God, purge our consciences from dead works to
serve the living God, and so work, through the power of
Christ's blood, that grace which they signify." The general current of this phraseology seems to be incompatible
with any hypothesis but that of physical causation; the
same sort of relationship is attributed to the outward matter
and the inward grace which subsists between impulse and
motion, fire and heat.

This view of the subject is confirmed by the prevailing
tone which the Popish theologians adopt in discussing the
doctrine of the sacraments. "Grace," says Bellarmine,[2] "is
the effect of the sacrament, and hence is contained in the

---

[1] Ex iis igitur quæ de priori sacramentorum effectu, gratiâ scilicet justi-
ficante, demonstrata sunt, illud etiam planè constat, excellentiorem, et
præstantiorem vim sacramentis novæ legis inesse, quàm olim veteris legis
sacramenta habuerunt: quæ cùm infirma essent, egenaque elementa,
inquinatos sanctificabant ad emundationem carnis, non animæ: quare, ut
signa tantùm earum rerum quæ ministeriis nostris efficiendæ essent, instituta sunt. At verò sacramenta novæ legis ex Christi latere manantia,
qui per Spiritum Sanctum semetipsum obtulit immaculatum Deo, emun-
dant conscientiam nostram ab operibus mortuis, ad serviendum Deo
viventi, atque ita eam gratiam, quam significant, Christi sanguinis virtute
operantur. Ibid., cap. i., ¿ xxviii.

[2] Gratia enim effectus est sacramenti, proinde in sacramento continetur,
ut quilibet alius effectus in sua caussa. Bellarmine, De Sacramentis, Lib.
i., cap. iv.

sacrament, as every other effect is contained in its own
cause." "That which is chiefly and essentially signified,"[1]
he observes again, "by the sacraments of the new law, is
only justifying grace. For, as we shall subsequently see,
the sacraments of the new law effect that which they signify.
They do not, however, effect the passion of Christ nor
future blessedness. They presuppose, on the contrary, His
passion, and promise future blessedness; but they do, properly, import justification." In discussing the question,
whether a sacrament can be logically defined, he announces
a truth which seems to be fatal to those who, like the Reviewer, would inculcate the identity of Popish and Protestant views in regard to the nature of the sacraments. "A
sacrament, as such," says he,[2] "not only signifies, it also
sanctifies. But to signify and to sanctify belong to different
categories, the one being embraced under that of relation,
the other under that of action." "It is more proper," he
states, in another connection,[3] "to a sacrament to *sanctify*
than it is to signify." In rebutting Calvin's account of
the nature of the sacraments, he does not scruple to assert[4]
that "they are efficacious causes of grace when no obstacles
interpose." His critique of the great Reformer's definition
so strikingly illustrates the fundamental difference between
Protestants and Romanists on this whole subject that I

[1] Est autem hoc loco notandum, id quod præcipuè et essentialiter significatur per sacramentum novæ legis, esse solam gratiam justificantem.
Nam ut infrà dicemus, sacramenta novæ legis efficiunt, quod significant,
at non efficiunt passionem Christi, nec vitam beatam sed solam justificationem: passionem enim præsupponunt, et vitam beatam promittunt,
justificationem autem propriè adferunt. Ibid., cap. ix.

[2] Secundo, sacramentum, ut sacramentum, non solùm significat, sed
etiam sanctificat, ut Catholici omnes docent de sacramentis novæ legis.
Ibid., cap. x.

[3] Prima propositio: Ad rationem sacramenti in genere non satis est, ut
significet, sed requiritur etiam, ut efficiat sanctitatem seu sanctificationem:
immo magis proprium est sacramenti sanctificare, quam significare. Ibid.,
cap. xii.

[4] Sacramenta esse causas gratiæ efficaces, nisi ponatur obex. Ibid., cap.
xvi.

hope the reader will excuse me for extracting the part which
relates to the sign.   Calvin says that a sacrament is "an
outward sign, by which the Lord seals in our consciences
the promises of his good-will toward us, to support the
weakness of our faith; and we, on our part, testify our
piety toward him; in His presence and that of angels, as
well as before men."   "This whole definition," says Bellarmine,[1] "is vicious, as will evidently appear from a close examination of it word by word.   The first expression is *an
outward sign*.   This, indeed, is absolutely true, but not in
the sense in which Calvin intends it.   He means a naked
sign, a symbol which signifies only, but effects nothing.
For throughout his whole definition he contemplates no
other effects of the sacraments than to seal the promises of
God and to testify our own piety.   It is no objection to this
statement that he asserts, in his Antidote to the Council of
Trent (Sess. 7, can. 5), that *The sacraments are instruments
of justification*, for he calls them *instruments*, because they

---

[1] His explicatis refellenda est hæc definitio: tota enim est vitiosa, ut
perspicuum erit, si percurramus singula verba.   Primum verbum est,
Symbolum externum.   Quod quidem verum est absolutè, non tamen in eo
sensu, quo accipitur à Calvino. · Ille enim intelligit esse nudum symbolum, id est, symbolum quod solùm significet, non autem operetur aliquid:
nam in tota definitione non ponit alios effectus hujus symboli, nisi obsig-
nare Dei promissiones, et testificari pietatem nostram: neque obstat, quod
Calvinus dicat in Antidoto Concilii Tridentini, Sess. vii., can. v.: *Sacramenta esse instrumenta justificationis;* nam intelligit esse instrumenta, quia
excitant, vel alunt fidem; idque non per aliquam efficientiam, sed merè
objectivè.   Id quod explicat clarissimè Theodorus Beza, in lib. De summa
rei sacramentariæ, quest. 2, cum sic ait: *Unde efficacia illa sacramentorum?
A Spiritus sancti operatione in solidum, non autem a signis, nisi quatenus
externis illis objectis interiores sensus moventur.*   Hæc ille.   Qua ratione
certe signa etiam, quæ in foribus publicorum hospitiorum pendent, instrumenta dici possunt cœnationis, quia movent hominem, ut cogitet in ea
domo paratam esse mensam, etc.   At Scripturæ passim docent, sacramenta
esse res quasdam operantes, nimirum quæ mundent, lavent, sanctificent,
justificent, regenerent.   Joan. iii.; 1 Cor. vi.; Eph. v., ad Tit. iii.; Act. xxii.
Immo nusquam Scripturæ dicunt, sacramenta esse testimonia promis-
sionum Dei et nostræ pietatis, aut certè non tam expressè hoc dicunt,
ut id quod nos asserimus, nimirum quod sint causæ justificationis.   Ibid.,
cap. 16,

excite and strengthen faith, and that not efficiently, but
only objectively. Beza has very clearly expressed the same
idea in his book De Summa Rei Sacramentariæ, Question 2,
where he says: 'Whence is the efficacy of the sacraments?
It depends entirely upon the operation of the Holy Spirit,
and not upon the signs, except so far as the outward objects
may excite inward perceptions.' Thus Beza. For the same
reason, the signs which hang on the doors of inns might be
called instruments of eating, since they suggest the idea of
a table within. The Scriptures, however, everywhere teach
that the sacraments are *operative*, inasmuch as they cleanse,
wash, sanctify, justify, regenerate. John, chap. iii.; 1 Cor.
vi.; Eph. v.; Tit. iii.; Acts xxii. Never do they assert
that the sacraments are testimonies of God's promises and
of our piety; or, at least, they do not certainly teach this
with as much directness as they inculcate the doctrine which
we have asserted, that the sacraments are causes of justification." The point most offensive to the mind of Bellarmine in the doctrine of Protestants was, evidently, that
in which they represent the effect of the sacraments as depending upon the Holy Spirit and upon the truths and promises which they address to faith. He regarded the external
action as the secret of their power. When duly administered, they just as truly, according to him, confer grace as
impulse communicates motion or fire communicates heat.
They were causes containing their effects, not figuratively,
but really and properly—instruments producing their results
by immediate and direct efficiency. Precisely to the same
purport is the doctrine of Dens. "In the fourth place," says
he,[1] "a sacrament is a sign, efficacious and practical, effecting that which it signifies." The recipient is said to be
passive under its power,[2] and the sacraments are represented
as truly and properly the causes of grace to those who do

---

[1] Quartô, est signum "efficax et practicum," scilicit efficiens id, quod
significat.—Dens, De Sacram., vol. v., No. iii., p. 68.

[2] Quia subjectum non concurrit activè, sed tantùm passivè. Ibid., No. iv.,
p. 70.

not interpose obstacles [1]—"they contain the grace causally and instrumentally, and that not simply as they are signs of it, which was the case with the sacraments of the old law, but as instrumental causes from which it may be extracted.[2] Harding, the Jesuit, in his celebrated controversy with Jewell,[3] says: "There be seven sacraments, which do not only signify a holy thing, but also do sanctify and make holy those to whom they be exhibited, being such as, by institution of Christ, contain grace in them and power to sanctify." "The sacraments of the new law," he teaches again,[4] "work the thing itself that they signify, through virtue given unto them by God's ordinance to special effects of grace." "Sacraments contain grace, after such manner of speaking as we say potions and drinks contain health."[5]

The theory of causation is kept up even in the doctrine of obstacles. There is a striking analogy betwixt the resistance which is offered by material hindrances to the action of physical causes, and that of the obstacles which, according to the Romish doctors, defeat the operation of the sacraments. What is technically called an *obstacle*—I allude not to those essential ones arising from perverseness of will or from gross hypocrisy, which render void the sacrament, but to those accidental ones which do not invalidate, but only impede the efficacy of the ordinance—what is technically called an *obstacle* of this sort is either some disposition directly repugnant to the sanctifying tendency of the sacrament, or the want of such a state of mind as is suited to its action. There must be some congruity, as in material phenomena, between the tendencies of the cause and that upon

[1] An Sacramenta novæ legis causent Gratiam?

Responsio Fidei contra sectarios est, ea verè et propriè causare Gratiam non ponentibus obicem, non tanquam causas principales (hoc enim solius Dei est), sed tanquam instrumentales. Ibid., No. xvii., p. 89.

[2] Sed quòd Gratiam contineant causaliter et instrumentaliter, vel, ut dicit Steyaert, quatenùs non sunt tantùm signa Gratiæ, ut illa veteris Legis, sed et causæ instrumentales, de quibus eam depromere liceat. Ibid., No. xviii., p. 90.

[3] Richmond's British Reformers, vol. vii., p. 685.

[4] Ibid., p. 690.   [5] Ibid., p. 686.

which they are expended.   Fire has a tendency to burn, but
then the fuel must be dry.   Motion once begun has a tendency to continue, but then friction and resistance must be
removed ; and so the sacraments are fitted to sanctify, but
then the subject must be adapted to their action.[1]

Whatever may be the mode in which the sacraments
operate, whether mechanical or efficient, the relation in
which they are conceived to stand to the covenant of grace
is essentially different from that represented in the Scriptures.   Instead of being signs and seals of the benefits
of redemption, conducting the mind beyond themselves
to Jesus, the Author and Finisher of faith, they usurp the
office of the Holy Ghost, and undertake to accomplish what
He alone is pledged to effect.   It cannot be doubted that
the only Holy Spirit whom Rome practically recognizes is
what she denominates her sacraments.   Her whole theory
of grace is grossly mechanical.   The Tridentine Catechism
runs the parallel between natural and spiritual life, and
shows that the sacraments are to the latter what birth,
growth, nutriment and medicine are to the former.[2]   The

[1] Est carentia—says Dens, defining an obstacle—dispositionis necessaria ad recipiendum sacramenti effectum ; sive est defectus alicujus non
impediens valorem sacramenti, sed ejus effectum seu collationem Gratiæ
ob indispositionem suscipientis ; ut si quis in affectu peccati mortalis, vel
cum ignorantia necessariorum necessitate medii, suscipit aliquod sacramentum, præter Pœnitentiam.

Quotupliciter continget, poni obicem accidentalem?

Dupliciter: scilicet per obicem sacramenti positivum seu contrarium, et
per obicem negativum seu privativum.

Obex positivus seu contrarius sacramenti consistit in indispositione
actuali repugnante infusioni Gratiæ sanctificantis.

Talis est quodcumque peccatum actuale mortale, sive cujus actus
vel effectus in suscipiente sacramentum adhuc moraliter dici potest per-
severare; sive quod in ipsa sacramenti cujuscumque susceptione com-
mittitur.

Obex negativus consistit in carentia dispositionis necessariæ ad effectum
sacramenti ex ignorantia vel inadvertentia nullo modo, vel saltem non
graviter culpabili ; v. g. ignorantia inculpabilis necessariorum necessitate
medii.—Dens, de Sacram., vol. v., No. xxix., p. 107.

[2] Catholicæ igitur Ecclesiæ sacramenta, quemadmodum ex Scripturis
probatur, et Patrum traditione ad nos pervenit, et conciliorum testatur

sinner is renewed by baptism, strengthened by confirmation, nurtured by the eucharist, restored to health by penance, and dismissed into eternity, prepared for its awful solemnities, by extreme unction. Baptism is the birth, confirmation the growth, the eucharist the food, penance the medicine, and extreme unction the consummation of the spiritual man. Call them *causes* or call them *machines*, no matter how they act, while it is conceded that the sacraments confer grace *ex opere operato*, their relation to the economy of salvation is substantially that which the eternal Word assigns to the Third Person of the Trinity.

Lying vanities, as they are, according to the teaching of the mother of harlots, they are yet the saviours to which the millions of her deluded children cling for acceptance before God. They are accustomed to use nothing higher in the scale of excellence than the empty pageantry of cere-

auctoritas, septenario numero definita sunt. Cur autem neque plura neque pauciora numerentur, ex iis etiam rebus, quæ per similitudinem à naturali vita ad spiritualem transferuntur, probabili quadam ratione ostendi poterit. Homini enim ad vivendum, vitamque conservandam, et ex sua reique publicæ utilitate traducendam, hæc septem necessaria videntur: ut scilicet in lucem edatur, augeatur, alatur; si in morbum incidat, sanetur; imbecillitas virium reficiatur; deinde, quod ad rempublicam attinet, ut magistratus nunquam desint, quorum auctoritate, et imperio regatur; ac postremò, legitimâ sobolis propagatione seipsum et humanum genus conservet. Quæ omnia quoniam vitæ illi, quâ anima Deo vivit, respondere satis apparet, ex iis facilè sacramentorum numerus colligetur.

Baptismus.—Primus enim est baptismus, veluti ceterorum janua, quo Christo renascimur.

Confirmatio.—Deinde confirmatio, cujus virtute fit ut divina gratiâ augeamur, et roboremur. Baptizatis enim jam apostolis, ut Divus Augustinus testatur, inquit Dominus: Sedete in civitate, donec induamini virtute ex alto.

Eucharistia.—Tum Eucharistia, quâ, tanquam cibo verè cælesti, spiritus noster alitur, et sustinetur. De eâ enim dictum est à Salvatore: "Caro mea verè est cibus, et sanguis meus verè est potus."

Pœnitentia.—Sequitur quarto loco pœnitentia, cujus ope sanitas amissa restituitur, postquam peccati vulnera accepimus.

Extrema-unctio.—Posteà verò Extrema-unctio, quâ peccatorum reliquiæ tolluntur, et animi virtutes recreantur, siquidem D. Jacobus, cùm de hoc sacramento loqueretur, ita testatus est: *Et si in peccatis sit, remittentur ei.*—*Trid. Catech.*, Pars ii., cap. i., § 18.

monial pomp, or to dream of nothing better in the way of felicity than the solemn farce of sacerdotal benediction; their hopes are falsehood and their food is dust. Strangers to the true concision of the heart which they have experienced who worship God in the Spirit, rejoice in Christ Jesus, and have no confidence in the flesh, the miserable votaries of Rome confound the emotions of mysterious awe produced by the solemnities of a sensual worship with reverence for God and the impressions of grace. Doomed to grope among the beggarly elements of earth, they regale the eye, the fancy and the ear, but the heart withers. Imagination riots on imposing festivals and magnificent processions, symbols and ceremonies, libations and sacrifices; the successive stages of worship are like scenes of enchantment, but the gorgeous splendours of the liturgy, which famish the soul while they delight the sense, are sad memorials of religion "lying in state surrounded with the silent pomp of death." The Holy Ghost has been supplanted by charms, and physical causes have usurped the province of supernatural grace.

As to the point whether the sacraments are seals, it deserves to be remarked that there is a discrepancy between some of the most distinguished Popish theologians and the Catechism of Trent. The latter teaches[1] that "as God in the Old Testament was accustomed to attest the certainty of his promises by signs, so also in the New Law our Saviour Christ, having promised us the pardon of our sins, heavenly grace, the communication of the Spirit, has instituted signs subjected to the eyes and senses which serve as pledges of His truth, so that we cannot doubt but that He will be faithful to His promises." And yet of the same

---

[1] Quemadmodum igitur in veteri Testamento Deus fecerat, ut magni alicujus promissi constantiam signis testificaretur; ita etiam in novâ lege Christus Salvator noster cùm nobis peccatorum veniam, cœlestem gratiam, Spiritûs Sancti communicationem pollicitus est, quædam signa oculis et sensibus subjecta instituit; quibus eum quasi pignoribus obligatum haberemus, atque ita fidelem in promissis futurum dubitare nunquam possemus. Ibid., ¿ xiii.

doctrine, as announced by Luther, Bellarmine remarks[1]
"that it is so absurd that nothing can be conceived more so.
Signs and prodigies," he continues, " may justly be employed
for confirming the message of a preacher, since they are
known and striking of themselves, and depend not at all
upon the message.   But the sacraments have no power of
themselves; they cannot be even apprehended as sacraments
except as confirmed by the testimony of the Word.   Those
who see the sick suddenly healed, demons expelled at a
word, the blind restored to sight, and the dead raised from
their graves by a preacher of the Divine Word, are so struck
and prostrated by the intrinsic power and splendour of the

[1] Sed hæc sententia tam est absurda—ut nihil fere cogitari possit absur-
dius. Nam signa atque prodigia ad confirmandam prædicationem meritò
adhibentur, cùm sint ex se nota et illustria neque à prædicatione ulla
ratione dependeant: contrà autem sacramenta nullam ex se vim habent,
ac ne sacramenta quidem esse intelliguntur, nisi testimonio verbi confirmentur. Itaque qui à prædicatore divini verbi, vel morbos repente curari,
vel dæmones verbo pelli, vel cæcos illuminari, vel ab inferis mortuos revo-
cari conspiciunt, ipsa miraculi vi tanquam fulgore quodam ita percellun-
tur, ac prosternuntur, ut vel inviti verbis tanti viri fidem habere cogantur.
Qui verò aquis hominem ablui, quod in baptismo facimus, vident, nihil
mirantur, neque facile credunt in ea lotione aliquid sublimius latere, nisi
verbo Dei ante crediderint. Quòd si non ante sacramenta suspicere incip-
imus, quàm verbo Dei fidem habeamus; quo pacto, quæso, fieri potest, ut
sacramentis divina eloquia confirmentur? An non ridiculus esset, qui
ethnico diceret; "ut credas vera esse quæ dico, amphoram istam aquæ
super caput tuum effundam?" Egregia sane probatio; nisi enim ex Dei
verbo disceremus lotionem illam et illam unctionem ad purgandos animos
valere, quis crederet? quis id non rideret? neque enim id habet aquæ
natura, ut morbos animi curet, et cordis maculas eluat; sed quidquid in
hoc genere potest, ex institutione divina potest, divinam autem institu-
tionem divina eloquia patefaciunt.

Porrò comparatio illa, qua verbum diplomati, sacramentum sigillo ab
adversariis, passim confertur, tam est inepta, ut nihil ineptius fingi queat;
multoque rectiùs verbum Dei sigillum sacramenti, quàm sacramentum
verbi Dei sigillum dici possit. Nam ut sigillum, etiam sine diplomate,
vim suam habet atque agnoscitur et honoratur; diploma sine sigillo non
agnoscitur esse diploma, nec vim ullam habet; sic etiam verbum Dei, sine
testimonio sacramenti, suam, eamque summam habet auctoritatem; sacramentum verò sine verbi testimonio, nullam. Non igitur sacramentum, ut
illi volunt, sigillum verbi, sed verbum, sigillum sacramenti nominari
debuisset. Bellarmine, Preface to vol. iii., De Sacrament.

miracle that even against their wills they are compelled to credit his message. Those, however, who perceive a man washed with water—which is what we do in baptism—see nothing wonderful, and are slow to believe that anything of unusual sublimity lies hid in the act, unless they shall have previously credited the Word of God. If we do not begin to honour the sacraments until we have faith in the Divine Word, how, I pray, is it possible that the sacraments should confirm that Word? Would he not be ridiculous who should say to a heathen, In order that you may believe what I say, I will pour this pitcher of water upon your head? An admirable proof, truly! Unless taught by the Word of God that that washing and that unction avail to purify the soul, who would believe it? Who would not laugh at the thought? There is nothing in the nature of water to cure diseases of the mind or to cleanse the stains of the heart. Whatever virtue of this sort it possesses is derived from Divine institution, and that institution is made known by the Word of God. Besides, the comparison, so common among our adversaries, of the Word to a charter and the sacrament to its seal, is so inapt that nothing can be conceived more so. With much more propriety can the Word be called the seal of the sacrament than the sacrament, of the Word. For as the seal even without the charter has its own power, and is acknowledged and honoured, while the charter without the seal is not recognized as such, and has no force, so also the Word of God without the testimony of the sacrament has its own, and that the highest, authority, while the sacrament without the testimony of the Word has none. The sacrament, therefore, should not be called the seal of the Word, but the Word the seal of the sacrament." Many other passages of the same nature might be extracted from this writer in which the doctrine of sacramental seals is repudiated, scouted, scorned. Can it then be regarded as an authoritative dogma of Rome? Her leading theologians despise it, make it a spurn and trample in their controversies with Protestants, pronounce it the very height of absurdity, the perfection of inaptitude. The Decrees of Trent nowhere allude to it, and the only place in which it seems to be remotely favoured is a single short paragraph in the Tridentine Catechism, occurring in the midst of a long, elaborate dissertation on the sacraments. The *emphasis* most clearly, in the Church of Rome, is laid upon the power of the sacraments to sanctify. This is their distinguishing feature, this, according to Bellarmine, their *differentia*.[1] Their *essence* lies here, and whoever denies to them their power destroys their reality.

I cannot, therefore, disguise my astonishment that Princeton should have represented that the views of Rome and of ourselves in regard to the nature of the sacraments are precisely the same. She teaches that they are *causes* of grace, and we that they are *signs*. She teaches that they dispense the blessings of salvation by their own power; we, that they are nothing without the Holy Ghost. According to her, they justify, regenerate and sanctify. According to us, they point to Him who, of God, is made unto us wisdom, and righteousness, and sanctification, and redemption. According to Rome, they work infallibly where material dispositions exist. According to us, they are lifeless and unmeaning when estranged from faith. We insist that they are seals of the everlasting covenant, and Rome, if she speaks at all upon this point, mutters the confused gabble of Babel. Rome's sacraments and ours belong essentially to different categories. They are as wide apart as action and passion. Hers is a species of deity, and ours are content to be elements of earth. When she baptizes, her water penetrates the soul, purges the conscience and purifies the heart. When we baptize, we wash only the flesh, while our faith contemplates the covenant of God and His unchanging faithfulness. Our baptism *represents* what the blood of the Redeemer, applied by the eternal Spirit, performs upon the souls of believers. Rome's does the work itself. Ours is

---

[1] Proinde signum, est veluti genus; sanctificans, veluti differentia. Bellarmine, De Sacramentis, Lib. i., cap. x.

vain without the Holy Ghost. Rome's is all the Holy Ghost she needs.

From the foregoing discussion it will be seen that Rome vitiates the *form* of the sacraments by inculcating the dogma that they produce their effects *ex opere operato*. It is this principle which changes them from *means* into laws or causes of grace, and converts them into a species of machinery, by the use of which men become the architects of their spiritual fortunes. The argument, therefore, as urged against Rome, does not apply with equal force to the strictly Lutheran and the English churches, unless it can be shown that these communions embrace the principle that the sacraments confer, *ex opere operato*, the grace which they signify. The churches of the East I have no disposition to ridicule. There is sad reason to apprehend that the Gospel has long since departed from their sanctuaries. But the great Protestant communions of England and Germany, glorious from the strife of other days, I cannot contemplate, with all their defects, without veneration and love; and it will require something more than the unsupported word of the Reviewer to convince my mind that they symbolize with Rome in one of her deadliest errors.[1] The English Reformers have expressed themselves with great clearness upon the subject of the sacraments—this having been one of the hottest points of controversy in England—and their Catechisms, Letters, Protestations and Creeds are free from any tinge of error. The Articles adopted in London in 1552, and published by the king, Edward VI., in 1553, are as explicitly Protestant as words can make them. The 26th treats of the sacraments, in which it is said that " in such only as worthily

---

[1] "Besides, if baptism is null and void when administered by those who hold the doctrine of baptismal regeneration, what shall we say to the baptism in the Church of England, in the strict Lutheran churches and in all the churches of the East? On this plan we shall have to unchurch almost the whole Christian world; and Presbyterians, instead of being the most catholic of churches, and admitting the being of a church wherever we see the fruits of the Spirit, would become one of the narrowest and most bigoted of sects." Princeton Rev., July, 1845, p. 452.

receive the same they have a wholesome effect and operation, and yet not that of the work wrought (*ex opere operato*),
as some men speak; which word, as it is strange and unknown to Holy Scripture, so it engendereth no godly, but a
very superstitious, sense."[1]   The Catechism adopted by the
same Convention, and published at the same time, is almost
as bald in its definition or description as Zuingle himself
could have desired.[2]   The Articles, as now existing, have
undergone considerable changes since the reign of the good
King Edward; the clause condemning the *opus operatum*
doctrine of Rome is no longer retained, but the opposite
truth is most clearly expressed.   What there is in the
Lutheran symbols to subject them to the just imputation of
the Romish error, I am unable to discover.   Luther himself, says Bellarmine,[3] has defined a sacrament "to be nothing else than a Divine testimony, instituted for exciting and
increasing faith, which, like a miracle, confirms, and, like a
seal, ratifies, the promise of grace."   "A ceremony in the
New Testament without faith," says the Augsburg Confession,[4] "merits nothing, either for the agent or others.   It is
a dead work, according to the saying of Christ, The true
worshippers shall worship the Father in spirit and in truth.

[1] Richmond's British Reformers, p. 334.

[2] Master.   Tell me what thou callest earliest sacraments?

Scholar.   They are certain customary reverent doings and ceremonies
ordained by Christ, that by them He might put us in remembrance of His
benefits, and we might declare our profession that we be of the number of
them which are partakers of the same benefits, and which fasten all their
affiance in Him; that we are not ashamed of the name of Christ, or to be
termed Christ's scholars.   Ibid., p. 369.

[3] Princeps Lutherus, cùm in Babylone, tùm in assertione Articulorum,
nihil aliud sacramentum esse voluit nisi divinum testimonium ad excitan-
dam, vel nutriendam fidem, institutum, quod instar miraculi confirmet, et
instar sigilli obsignet promissionem gratiæ.   Quocirca Sacramenta fere
conferre solet cum vellere Gedeonis, cum signo quod Isaias obtulit regi
Achaz, cum aliis ejusmodi miraculis, atque prodigiis, quibus ad faciendam
fidem Prophetæ et Apostoli utebantur.   Bellarmine, Præf., vol. iii., De
Sacramentis.

[4] Augsburg Confession, De Missa; compare also Article xiii., which is
very strong.

The whole eleventh chapter of Hebrews proves the same: By faith Abel offered a better sacrifice; without faith it is impossible to please God. Therefore, the Mass does not merit remission of guilt or punishment *ex opere operato*. This reason clearly refutes the merit which they term *ex opere operato*." If there be any one principle of the Gospel which Luther saw in a steady light and held with a firm grasp, that principle was justification by faith—a principle as utterly opposed to the sacramental grace of Rome as to the ceremonial righteousness of the Jews; and it is grossly improbable that Luther, who understood so fully, appreciated so highly, and laboured so severely for, the liberty wherewith Christ has made us free, should have been entangled with the galling yoke of ceremonial bondage. How could he the business of whose life it was to unfold the blessedness of faith have taught, in the same breath in which he proclaimed the glories of the Cross, that we are justified by any external work, however sacred? Tell it not in Gath, publish it not in the streets of Askelon! It is true that he did teach— what the Liturgy of England is supposed to sanction—that infants are regenerated at the time of baptism, but he was far from teaching the mortal heresy of Rome, that baptism itself renews them. He treated the sacrament as only a sign and seal; but he supposed that God works in their hearts by the power of his Holy Spirit that faith upon which the grace of the sacrament depends. The sacrament, in other words, profits them precisely as it does all other believers. It is a symbol and a seal in every case, whether of infants or adults, addressed to faith. "Perhaps," says he in the Babylonian Captivity,[1] after having explained the necessity of faith to the efficacy of baptism, "perhaps the baptism of little children may be objected to what I say as to the necessity of faith. But as the Word of God is mighty to change the heart of an ungodly person, who is not less deaf nor helpless than an infant, so the prayer of the Church, to which all things are possible, changes the little child, by

---

[1] Quoted in D'Aubigné's Hist. Ref., vol. ii., p. iii., Carter's Edition.

the operation of the faith which God pours into his soul, and thus purifies and renews it." "The Anabaptists," he says again,[1] "greatly err in preventing infants from being baptized. For though little children at another time want the judgment of reason, yet when they are baptized, God so operates upon their minds that they hear His Word, and know and love Him, as formerly the holy John, in the womb of his mother, perceived the presence of Christ, and leaped for joy." If other evidence were wanting that he was far from embracing the *opus operatum* fiction of Rome, I might refer to his Sermon on Baptism, in which he denounces this heresy of schools, and while he admits that the Master of the Sentences and his followers have treated well of the dead matter of the sacraments, he asserts that "their spirit, life and use, which consist in the verity of the Divine promise and our own faith, have been left wholly untouched."[2] And nothing more is needed to vindicate the Lutheran Church than Melancthon's defence, in his Apology, of the passage already extracted from the Augsburg Confession.[3] "Here we condemn," says he, "the whole rabble of Scholastic doctors, who teach that the sacra-

[1] Potiùs graviter errant Anabaptistæ, homines fanatici ac furiosi, dum infantes baptizari prohibent. Nam etsi parvuli alio tempore judicio rationis carent, tamen dum baptizantur, sic in eorum mentibus operatur Deus, ut et verbum Dei audiant, et Deum etiam agnoscant, ac diligant; quemadmodum olim sanctus Joannes in utero matris Christi præsentiam sensit, et præ gaudio exultavit. Luther quoted in Bellarmine, Præf., as above.

[2] Esto contemptor Magistri Sententiarum cum omnibus suis scribentibus, qui tantum de materia, et forma sacramentorum scribunt, dum optimè scribunt, id est, mortuam, et occidentem literam Sacramentorum tractant; cæterum spiritum, vitam, et usum, id est, promissionis divinæ veritatem, et nostram fidem prorsus intacta relinquunt. Luther quoted in Bellarmine, De Sacram., Lib. i., cap. ii.

[3] Hic damnamus totum populum scholasticorum Doctorum, qui docent, quòd Sacramenta non ponenti obicem conferent gratiam *ex opere operato* sine bono motu utentis. Hæc simpliciter Judaica opinio est, sentire, quòd per ceremoniam justificemur, sine bono motu cordis, hoc est, sine fide: et tamen hæc impia, et superstitiosa opinio magna auctoritate docetur in tota regno Pontificio. Luther quoted in Bellarmine, De Sacram., Lib. i., cap. iii.

ments confer grace upon him who interposes no obstacle, *ex opere operato*, without any good motion on the part of the recipient. This opinion is pure Judaism—to suppose that we can be justified by a ceremony without a good motion of the heart, that is, without faith; and yet this impious and superstitious opinion is taught with great authority in the whole kingdom of the Pope." Such proofs might be indefinitely multiplied.[1] The Reviewer, I think, must have been misled by the ambiguity of the phrase, *baptismal regeneration*. It may mean regeneration produced by the ordinance itself, *ex opere operato*, or, as Bellarmine expresses it, the external action—which is the doctrine of Rome; or it may mean regeneration effected by the Spirit of God at the time of baptism—which was unquestionably the opinion of Luther, and perhaps of the compilers of the English Ritual. The first destroys the *nature* of the sacrament as a sign and seal; the other does not impair it: and hence the argument, so fatal to Rome, leaves untouched the English and Lutheran communions.

To obviate a difficulty which may suggest itself to the minds of some, it may be well to remark that the errors of an individual minister do not invalidate the ordinances dispensed by him, so long as the Church with which he is connected teaches in her symbols, and retains as a body, just conceptions of their nature. He is guilty of aggravated sin in trifling with the mysteries of Christ. But his public and official acts must be measured not by his private opinions, since it is not man's prerogative to search the heart, but by the standards of the society to which he belongs, and by whose immediate authority he acts. Those who, in Christian simplicity, receive the sacraments at his

---

[1] This matter is discussed pretty fully in the third volume of Bellarmine's " Disputationum, de Controversiis," Ingolstadt edition, 1601, which is the edition constantly referred to in these articles. The arch-Jesuit quotes passages from Luther which seem to insinuate the Papal doctrine, but which, he proves conclusively, were not intended to teach it. Bellarmine contends that it was absolutely impossible for him to teach it as long as he held the doctrine of justification by faith.

hands will receive them with profit to their souls. He, indeed, is a heretic, but his Church is sound; and the ordinances which he dispenses are those received by the Church, and not the inventions of his own mind. Hence, baptism administered in the Church of England by an Arian or a Puseyite, though the one denies the Trinity and the other the essence of the sacrament, is unquestionably valid, because the Church itself is sound upon both. And so there may be, perhaps are, priests in the Papal communion who hold the true, Protestant, scriptural doctrine of the sacraments; and yet, as they act under covenanted articles, and are consequently presumed to do what the Church intends, the ordinances dispensed by them cannot be regarded as valid. The *creed* of the Church, not the intentions of individuals, must be our standard of judgment. Here we have what the Reviewer calls "the professed, ostensible design;" and Rome's baptism I feel solemnly bound to reject, because her design is not the design of Christ. She professes to do a different thing from what the Saviour instituted.

2. The most conclusive proof that Romish baptism is essentially different from the ordinance of Christ remains yet to be considered. It might, for the sake of argument, be conceded to the Reviewer that both consist of the same matter and are administered in the same manner—that both are regarded as instituted symbols, and nothing more, which at once represent and confirm our interest in that which is represented; still, their *identity* could not be asserted unless they were signs of the same truths and seals of the same promises. It is just as essential to the form of a sacrament that it have a relation to the *right things* as that it have the right kind of relationship itself. While it must be a sign and seal, it is equally indispensable that it be a sign and seal of the *covenant of grace*. Its specific purpose, according to the Westminster Confession, is "to represent Christ and His benefits, to confirm our interest in Him, and to put a visible difference between those that belong unto the Church and the rest of the world, and

solemnly to engage them to the service of God in Christ, according to His Word." Hence all Protestants, however they have differed in other points, have regarded the sacraments as badges of Christian profession. Proclaiming, as they do to the eye, the great distinguishing features of redemption, they cannot be consistently received nor decently administered when the scheme of salvation, in its essential elements, is denied or repudiated; and as their purpose is to confirm our interest in Christ, they evidently involve such a profession of Christianity as is consistent with a reasonable hope of personal acceptance through His blood. To assert, consequently, of Romish baptism integrity of form, is to assert that he who receives it if arrived at years, and his sponsors who present him if an infant of days, make a credible profession of vital union with Him who is the substance of the eternal covenant, and in whom all its promises are yea and amen. Baptism administered to those who do not profess to believe the Gospel is evidently null and void; it is an empty ceremony, a sign and seal of nothing. The question, therefore, at issue between the Assembly and the Reviewer is, whether a man, by submitting to the Romish ordinance, becomes a "professing Christian;" or, in other words, whether, consistently with the faith that the church requires, and the obligations she imposes upon him in imparting to him this first sacrament, he *can* cherish a scriptural hope of "his engrafting into Christ, of regeneration, of remission of sins, and of his giving up unto God, through Jesus Christ, to walk in newness of life." These are the benefits which baptism signifies and seals; and if the profession which is actually made or necessarily implied is incompatible with the reception of these blessings, it is not a profession but a denial of the Gospel; and such baptism does not *seal*, but *gives the lie* to, the covenant of grace. It is important to bear in mind that the profession which the validity of the ordinance requires is not that of a general belief in Christianity, without specific reference to what is, *par eminence*, called the Gospel, but

one which is consistent with a saving interest in Christ.
The two things are evidently distinct, though the Reviewer
has more than once confounded them.   There is a loose
and general sense in which the term *Christian* is applied to
all who trace their religion, whatever may be its doctrines
or precepts, to the authority of Christ.   It is an epithet
which distinguishes them from Jews, Pagans and Mohammedans, and all who do not believe in Jesus as a teacher
sent from God.   In this application it does not indicate any
particular type of doctrine, whether Calvinism, Arianism,
Pelagianism or Socinianism; it expresses simply the fact
that whatever be the system, it is professedly received upon
the authority of Christ.

In this sense no one denies that Papists are Christians:
no one, using his terms in the strictest sense, would rank
them "in the same category"[1] with Mohammedans and
Pagans, with Jews, infidels and Turks.   They are Christians upon the same principle which extends the epithet to
Pelagians, Arians, Universalists and Socinians.   But there
is another and a stricter sense in which *Christian* denotes a
peculiar relation to Christ, and is confined exclusively to
those who believe, or profess to believe, the fundamental
doctrines of the Gospel, or what is distinctively styled the way
of salvation.   To be entitled to this application of it, something more is required than a general belief in Jesus of
Nazareth as the author of a new dispensation of religion.
The religion itself which He taught, not any system which
men may choose to ascribe to Him and recommend to the
world under the sanction of His name, but that which He
proclaimed in His own person, or committed to the inspired
founders of His Church, which is emphatically the way of
life, and the only basis of human hope, must in its leading
principles be cordially embraced.   They only can be Christians, in this strict and proper sense, who profess to receive
under the name of Christianity nothing that subverts the
economy of grace.

[1] Princeton Review, July, 1845, p. 465.

It may be cheerfully conceded, the Assembly has not denied, and the whole Protestant world has asserted, that in the first sense the Church of Rome is Christian—Christian, as the Schoolmen would say, *secundum quid*, accidentally and not essentially; Christian, as professing to trace her scheme of doctrine, whatever it may be, to the instructions of Christ. She may be Christian in this sense, and yet all her children go down to hell. She may have the name without the Gospel of Christ. As the sacraments, however, contemplate the covenant of grace as a scheme of salvation, as it is not the *name* but the *religion* of Jesus which they signify and seal, if Rome in dispensing her baptism demands a faith and imposes obligations which are inconsistent with a saving relation to Christ, however she may make professing Christians in one sense, she makes none in the only sense in which the title is important. If she does not baptize into Christianity in its peculiar and distinguishing features as the scheme of redemption and the foundation of human hope, she might as well, so far as any valuable result is concerned, baptize into the name of Confucius or Mohammed.

If she is not Christian in the second sense which I have indicated, if her Gospel is not the Gospel of Christ, her religion not the religion of the Son of God, her baptism cannot be that which He instituted. Though Christian in name, she is Antichristian in reality. The real question, consequently, is, whether or not in what she denominates baptism Rome requires a profession and imposes obligations which are inconsistent with a saving interest in Christ, or the application of those very benefits which the Christian sacrament was appointed to represent and seal. Can a man believe what she commands him to believe, and engage to do what she obliges him to do, and be at the same time a spiritual disciple of Jesus Christ? This is the issue. Princeton says that he can: the Assembly and all the Protestant world have declared that he *cannot*. To determine the matter, the profession and engagements must be previously appre-

hended which a man makes when he is baptized in the
Church of Rome. The statements of the Reviewer upon
this point are wide of the truth. By a most extraordinary
paradox, as it seems to me, the merits of which will be afterwards discussed, he has been led to maintain that the recipients of Romish baptism are not made Romanists, and that the
heresies of Popery are not exacted in the ordinance.[1] But
what says Rome herself? She certainly is a better witness
of what she actually imposes on her children than those that
are without. "Whosoever shall affirm," says the Council
of Trent,[2] "that the baptized are free from all the precepts
of holy Church, either written or delivered by tradition, so
that they are not obliged to observe them unless they will
submit to them of their own accord, let him be accursed."
This is sufficiently explicit, and so strong is the obligation
which baptism imposes to observe these precepts which
make up what Rome calls a "Christian life," that those
who when arrived at years may be disposed to relinquish
the vicarious promises of their sponsors can yet be *compelled* to redeem them.[3] It is true that the Apostles' Creed
is the summary which is actually professed at the time of
baptism, but then this contains only the heads of doctrine,
the details of which must be embraced according to the system of Rome. "The true Catholic faith, out of which none
can be saved," and into which consequently all must be

[1] "It was hence argued that the recipients of Romish baptism are made
Romanists, and are baptized into a profession of all the heresies of Popery.
This appears to us an entirely wrong view of the subject. . . . . No man,
therefore, is made a Papist by being baptized by a Papist." Princeton
Review, July, 1845, pp. 468, 469.

[2] Si quis dixerit, baptizatos liberos esse ab omnibus Sanctæ Ecclesiæ
præceptis, quæ vel scripta vel tradita sunt, ita ut ea observare non teneantur, nisi se, sua sponte, illis submittere voluerint; anathema sit. Conc.
Trident., Sess. vii., can. viii., De Baptis.

[3] Si quis dixerit, hujusmodi parvulos baptizatos, cum adoleverint, inter-
rogandos esse, an ratum haberi velint, quod patroni eorum nomine, dum
baptizarentur, polliciti sunt; et ubi se nolle responderint suo esse arbitrio relinquendos, nec alia interim pœna ad Christianam vitam cogendos,
nisi ut ab Eucharistiæ aliorumque Sacramentorum perceptione arceantur,
donec resipiscant; anathema sit. Ibid., can. xiv., De Baptis.

baptized, is the symbol of Pius IV. This creed all proselytes to the Romish Church are required publicly to adopt, and hence it must be the creed which all her children are presumed to embrace. They are at liberty to put no other interpretation upon the sacred Scriptures, much less upon minor symbols of faith, than that which the Church has authorized. Baptism is regarded as a sort of oath to observe her statutes and ordinances, and whatever articles she proposes at the time must be taken in her own sense. The *animus imponentis* determines what the catechumen must believe, or be understood to profess, when he gives his assent to those sections of the creed which treat of the holy catholic Church, the forgiveness of sins, the communion of saints, and the state of the dead. As she makes a public declaration beforehand that all whom she baptizes are subject to her authority in faith and practice, as this is the known condition on which the ordinance is dispensed, it is undeniable that those who receive it at her hands do virtually profess "her whole complicated system of truth and error," and become *ipso facto* Romanists or Papists. Her notorious claim to exact obedience afterwards upon the ground of baptism would be grossly preposterous upon any other hypothesis. Bellarmine accordingly enumerates it among the advantages of the ceremonies which Rome has appended to her ordinances that those who are baptized with them are distinguished not merely from Jews, infidels and Turks, but also from heretics or Protestants—that is, they profess by the reception of the rite with its Papal accompaniments not simply Christianity as contradistinguished from Paganism, but Popery as contradistinguished from Protestantism.[1]

The Reformers, too, seem to have understood the matter in the same light. Regarding baptism as a species of com-

---

[1] Sexta est distinctio Catholicorum ab hæreticis. Nam Sacramenta sunt quidem symbola quædam, quibus discernimur ab infidelibus, tamen ab hæreticis vix per Sacramenta distingui possumus, sed per cæremonias optimè distinguimur. Bellarm., De Sac., Lib. ii., cap. 31.

munion with the Church, which implies the sanction of its
doctrines and a promise of subjection to its precepts, they
deemed it to be inconsistent with attachment to the true
religion to submit to the institute of Rome. It was not
merely that she had corrupted by additions and obscured
by her mummeries the simple appointment of Christ—
this, though one, was not the principal ground of objection.
But, according to the Confession and Discipline of the Reformed Church of France,[1] those who received baptism at
her hands polluted their consciences by consenting to idolatry; they virtually endorsed the synagogue of Satan and
treated it as the Church of the Lord Jesus Christ. There
is a very striking passage in the "Confession and Protestation of the Christian Faith," drawn up by John Clement
on the first day of April, 1556. This Clement was a remarkable witness for the truth in the reign of Queen Mary,
and, like many others, was doomed to the stake for his
opinions, from the horrors of which he was mercifully saved
by a natural death in prison. His Confession, it would seem
from the testimony of Strype, was transcribed and circulated
as a faithful manual of the Reformed doctrines in England.
The passage to which I have referred occurs in the seventeenth article. "Howbeit," says he, "this I do confess and
believe, that no Christian man ought to bring or send his children to the Papistical church, or to require [request] baptism
of them, they being Antichrists; for in so doing he doth
confess them to be the true Church of Christ, which is a
grievous sin in the sight of God and a great offence to his
true congregation."[2] Notwithstanding this extraordinary
protestation, Clement acknowledged the validity of such

[1] In the mean while, because of those corruptions which are mingled
with the administration of that sacrament, no man can present his children to be baptized in that Church without polluting of his conscience.
Quick's Synodicon, p. 12; Confession of French Reformed Ch., art. 28.

Such as by their proxies present children to be baptized in the Church
of Rome shall be severely censured, because they consent thereby unto
idolatry. Ibid.,.p. xlvi., Discipline Fr. Ref. Ch., can. xiii.

[2] Richmond's British Reformers, vol. iv., p. 292.

baptisms: his objection to them was, not that the *child* would fail of receiving a true baptism, but that the *parent* professed by implication a false faith. He knew nothing of the Princeton theory—the Reformed Church of France had never heard of it—that baptism was simply an introduction to the Church in general, and involved a profession of the creed of no church in particular. If this hypothesis be correct, which I had previously been accustomed to consider as only a Catabaptist riddle, it is hard to perceive in what the wickedness consists of receiving baptism from Rome. If her priests are true ministers of Jesus, as Princeton affirms, and impart a valid baptism, as she also asserts; if those who submit to it hold no communion with her errors; if they are made professing Christians and not Papists, introduced into Christ's body and not into the Papal congregation, where is the sin? What have they done that deserves the censures of the Church? Surely there can be no crime in being made professing Christians, if nothing more nor worse is done. And what more? Is it that they have acquiesced in the superstitious ceremonies which precede, accompany and follow the administration of the ordinance? Was it for ceremonies only that the churches of France and Scotland and the noble army of Reformers denounced participation in the Romish rites as polluting and idolatrous, and excluded those from their own communion who had presented their children in Papistical assemblies? The Lutheran Church retained many ceremonies; was it a sin to be baptized in it? The English Church in her palmiest days was defiled with many fragments of Popery; was the participation of her baptism idolatrous? Why, then, if ceremonies are so fatal in Rome, were they not equally fatal in Germany and Britain? The truth is, ceremonies were the smallest item in the account. It was the faith of Rome which the Reformers abhorred, and because they regarded all who sought baptism at her hands as professing that faith, they subjected them to discipline as transgressors and idolaters. They believed, as all the world but Princeton believes, that he who requests baptism from Rome declares by the act that he is a Romanist. He goes to the Pope because he loves the Pope.

But whatever Reformers thought, and whatever Princeton may think, it is plain, from the testimonies already adduced, that Rome herself looks upon all to whom she administers the ordinance as bound to be Papists. The profession which is made is the profession of her own creed; the obligation assumed, an obligation to obey all her statutes and ordinances. Now, the creed of Pius IV., which is the only distinctive creed of Rome, binds the subscriber, and every human being that hopes to be saved, to receive the canons and decrees of Trent, to render true obedience to the Pope, and to submit, by consequence, to every bull which may be issued from the Pontifical throne. The very circumstance that this creed is pronounced to be indispensable to salvation shows conclusively that those must profess it to whom in baptism is imparted the remission of sins. Now the question recurs, Is such a profession consistent with a saving interest in Christ? Can a man believe the Gospel, and at the same time believe the doctrines of Trent, and the still more detestable doctrines of the memorable Constitution *Unigenitus?* Can a man "enter into an open and professed engagement to be wholly and only the Lord's," and at the same time engage to observe all the precepts, whether written or traditive, enjoined by the Papal Church?

This is substantially the issue which the Reviewer himself accepts in discussing the question whether or not the Church of Rome is a true church of the Lord Jesus Christ. "If a man," says he, "makes no profession of faith, we cannot regard him as a believer; nor can we so regard him if he makes any profession inconsistent with the existence of saving faith. And consequently, if a body of men make no profession of faith, they cannot be a church; nor can they be so regarded if they make a profession which is incompatible with saving faith in Christ. . . . . If, therefore, we deny to any man the character of a Christian on account of the profession which he makes, we must be prepared to show that such faith is incompatible with salvation. . . . . And in like manner, if we deny to any body of men the character of a church on account of its creed, we thereby assert that no man holding that creed can be saved."[1] Hence the doctrine of the Reviewer is, that a cordial profession of the Romish creed—for what signifies profession without the corresponding motion of the heart?—Rome being a true church of the Lord Jesus Christ, is not incompatible with saving faith; that a man may, in other words, be a sincere Papist, and still be a spiritual child of God. If this proposition can be sustained, no argument can be drawn from her views of the covenant to invalidate the baptism of Rome; if not, the decision of the Assembly is according to truth and righteousness.

It is amusing to see the Reviewer, after having himself given so clear a statement of the issue in dispute, proceeding in the very next breath to discuss a different question, or, if it be the same, so disguised as to suggest a different one to the mind of the reader. There are evidently two general causes which may invalidate a profession of saving faith—ignorance and error. The grounds of suspicion in the one case are defective views of the economy of grace; in the other, those that are incompatible with its principles. In the one case, we apprehend that enough of truth is not received and understood to save the soul; in the other, that wrong notions and contradictory opinions destroy its efficacy. In the one case, the resolution of our doubts depends upon the minimum of truth essential to salvation; in the other, upon the maximum of error inconsistent with it. The question then is, not, as the Reviewer intimates, whether Rome teaches truth enough to save the soul, but whether she teaches error enough to damn the soul. It is not a question of ignorance, but heresy; not whether her system falls short of the Gospel standard by defect, but whether it is inconsistent with it by error; not whether she fails to profess something that ought to be professed

[1] Princeton Review, July, 1845, p. 461.

in order to salvation, but whether she professes something that cannot be professed in consistency with salvation. These questions are obviously distinct, and yet the Reviewer has strangely blended and confounded them, confining his discussion to the first, and deducing his conclusion in reference to the second. His whole argument is a glaring instance of *ignoratio elenchi*.

There are two forms of heresy incompatible with salvation. In the one, the foundation is directly denied, in the other, necessarily subverted; in the one, the contradictory of the Gospel is openly professed, in the other, it is secretly insinuated; the one destroys by the boldness of its attacks, the other by the subtlety of its frauds. The Socinians may be taken as examples of the one; the Pelagians as illustrations of the other. This latter form of heresy is the more dangerous, because least suspected. It steals upon the soul in insidious disguises, recommends its errors by the truth it adopts, labels its poisons as healthful medicines, and administers its deadly draughts under the promise of life. To this class of heresy it was contended in the Assembly that the doctrines of the Church of Rome must be referred. Whatsoever of the Gospel she retains is employed simply as a mask to introduce her errors without suspicion. She is a fatal graft upon the living stock of Christianity, and though the root be sound, yet she, as a branch, brings forth nothing but the fruit of death. Her creed contains some truth—this cannot be disputed; it contains enormous error —this is equally unquestionable. The truth is not her creed, the error is not her creed, but the two combined; and to ascertain whether her creed is incompatible with salvation, we must take it as a *whole*, and compare the system which *as a whole* it presents with the essential principles of the Gospel. If it is inconsistent with them, or subversive of them, it cannot be regarded as a *saving creed*. The connection and dependence of the truth and error in a complicated system will determine the sense in which each is apprehended, and often give a result entirely different from that which would be reached by the isolated and sole contemplation of either. It is possible to assent to propositions which, in themselves considered, contain vital and saving truth, but yet, *as modified* by others, they may be far from having a salutary tendency. Men, for example, may profess to believe that Jesus Christ is the Saviour of the world. In making this profession they assent *in words* to a fundamental doctrine of the Gospel; and yet they may so limit and restrain it by other propositions as to make Christ, after all, the tool of human merit, and grace the foundation of a claim of law. The formularies of Rome may contain all the important principles of Christianity which the Reviewer thinks he has found there, and yet, after all, they may be so modified by the introduction of different principles as to give a result utterly incompatible with the salvation of the soul. As she teaches them, and as she requires her children to believe them, they may be essentially another Gospel. It is not enough that she mingles the elements of Christianity in her creed: she must mingle them with nothing that shall convert them into a savour of death unto death. The most discordant properties, not unfrequently, are produced by different modes of combination when the same materials are employed. Sugar and alcohol contain the same chemical ingredients, but how different their qualities and effects! And so the articles which make up the creed of a child of God may enter into the profession of a Papist, and yet the system embraced by the one be as widely different from the system of the other as alcohol from sugar. The question in dispute is, whether the *creed* of Rome is a saving creed; and as neither her truth nor her errors, separately taken, constitute her creed, it is as incongruous to argue from either *alone* as to infer the nature of a compound from the properties of one of its ingredients. And yet this is the fallacy which the Reviewer has perpetrated. He has seized upon the fundamental doctrines of the Gospel, which he asserts that Rome holds, and *because* she holds these he infers that her creed *must* be saving, without stopping to inquire whether they are not so linked and connected with fundamental errors, so checked, modified and limited, as to convey a meaning widely remote from the teachings of the Bible.

It is nothing to the purpose to say that the doctrines of the Trinity, incarnation and atonement are saving doctrines: no one denies it when they are scripturally understood and cordially embraced; and if Rome believed nothing more or nothing inconsistent with orthodox conceptions of them, the dispute would be ended. But as these constitute only a fragment of her creed, it was incumbent upon Princeton to show that her additional articles were not incompatible with the saving application of these others.

In most instances of the mixture of error with important truth, they are brought simply in juxtaposition without any attempt to define the system which results from their combination. In such cases it is hard to determine the character of the whole, and to pronounce with confidence upon its saving or pernicious tendencies. Minds are so differently constituted that the form of words which shall be the means of conducting one to salvation shall prove fatal to another. The real creed, as it is impressed upon the heart, may be very different from that which the examination of its elements might lead us beforehand to determine. But in the case of Rome no such difficulty exists. She has stated her truths; she has announced her errors: she has gone farther and detailed the system of salvation which she deduces from the whole. Her Gospel is full and minute in the directions which it gives to the sinner who inquires, with the jailer, what he must do to be saved. If these directions are inconsistent with the instructions of the Apostles, if their obvious tendency is to subvert and set aside the way of salvation as revealed in the Scriptures, the dispute is ended. Rome repudiates the covenant of grace of which baptism is a seal, and consequently destroys the form of the Christian sacrament. Now the Reviewer has nowhere attempted to show that the creed of Rome,

which is the creed of Pius IV.,[1] including the decrees of
Trent (in conformity with which it is expressly provided
that all previous symbols must be interpreted) and the subsequent bulls of the Vatican, contains nothing incompatible
with the cordial reception of the scriptural method of salvation. This, the real point in dispute, he has wisely left
untouched, and has wasted all his strength upon another—
that Rome proclaims certain propositions from which, separately taken, the essence of the Gospel may be drawn.[2]

His second argument, founded on the concession that
there are true believers in the Papacy, is not less fallacious
than the first.[3] It proceeds upon the assumption that they
were made Christians by the creed they ostensibly profess
in the sense which that Church teaches and requires her
children to adopt; that is, it begs the very question in dispute. If these true believers reject, in their hearts, the
complicated system of the Pope, and were instrumentally
converted by a different Gospel from that of Trent, the
truth of their piety is no proof that the Romish creed is
saving. Now it is certainly possible to be *in* Rome and
not to be *of* Rome—to be in nominal connection with the
Church without believing its creed; and that this is the
precise condition of true believers in the Papacy is indi-

[1] See an able article on the creed of Rome, in Papism in the Nineteenth
Century, p. 214.

[2] "If these principles are correct, we have only to apply them to the
case in hand, and ask, Does the Church of Rome retain truth enough to
save the soul? We do not understand how it is possible for any Christian
man to answer this question in the negative. They retain the doctrine of
Incarnation, which we know, from the infallible Word of God, is a life-
giving doctrine. They retain the whole doctrine of the Trinity. They
teach the doctrine of atonement, far more fully and accurately than multitudes of professedly orthodox Protestants. They hold a much higher doctrine as to the necessity of Divine influence than prevails among many
whom we recognize as Christians."—Princeton Review, July, 1845, p. 463.

[3] "It is further evident that the Church of Rome retains truth enough
to save the soul, from the fact that true believers, who have no other
means of instruction than those therein afforded, are to be found in that
communion. Wherever the fruits of the Spirit are, there is the Spirit;
and wherever the Spirit is, there is still the Church."—Ibid., p. 465.

cated by the intense anxiety which, in proportion to their
light, they generally feel to escape from her borders. But
then they are converted "by no other means of instruction
than those afforded by Rome." The *means* she affords,
and the *use* to which the Spirit of God may turn them,
are quite distinct. That the Holy Ghost should bring
light out of darkness and truth out of error is proof of
His own power and grace, but none that darkness is light
and error is truth. The godly in Babylon are saved by
the mercy of our heavenly Father, in having their attention diverted from her monstrous corruptions, and fixed
upon those propositions which, scattered up and down in
her formularies, may be made to suggest ideas not by any
means contemplated in the real creed of the Church. It
is the force of the truth that is ostensibly retained by Rome,
applied by the Spirit in a sense which Rome expressly
repudiates, which delivers these men from the power of
Satan, and introduces them into the kingdom of God. They
are saved in spite of her creed.

But, says the Reviewer, these men evince the fruits of
the Spirit, and "wherever the Spirit is, there is still the
Church." I cheerfully concede that wherever a true church
is, there is the Spirit, but I am not prepared to convert the
proposition without a limitation. If the Spirit is only in
the Church, how are men to be converted from the world?
The Bible requires them to be believers before they can
belong to the Church; they cannot be believers without the
Spirit; and according to Princeton they cannot have the
Spirit, unless they are *in* the Church. So that those who
are without are in a truly pitiable dilemma. They cannot
have the Spirit because they are not in the Church; they
cannot belong to the Church because they have not the
Spirit. What, then, is to become of them? It is our
unspeakable comfort that the Bible knows nothing of the
Princeton doctrine upon this point. The Holy Ghost is a
Sovereign, working when, where and how He chooses. In
the lowest depths of Paganism, in the dungeons of crime,

amid Hindoo temples and Indian pagodas, in the darkest
chambers of imagery, as well as the congregation of Christian people, He may be traced accomplishing the end of
election, and preparing the vessels of mercy destined from
eternity to glory. He works as well *out* of the Church as
in the Church. He knows no limits but His sovereignty,
no rule but the counsel of His will. Wherever He is, there
are life and grace, because there is union with the Son of
God. There, too, is a membership in the invisible Church;
but it is an act of the believer, subsequent to his conversion,
and founded upon it, to seek a corresponding membership
in that visible congregation to which the ordinances are
given. True faith will engender the desire to be connected
with the true Church, and hence converted Papists are,
for the most part, eager to renounce the Mother of harlots,
as those called from the world are anxious to renounce *it*.

I have now examined the arguments by which the Reviewer would prove that the Romish creed is not inconsistent with a saving interest in Christ, and the reader, I
trust, is prepared to render the verdict, They are found wanting. For aught that appears, this creed may belong to that
species of heresy which, without directly denying, subverts
the foundation by subtlety and fraud. It may take away
our Lord, not by gross and open violence, but by stratagem
and craft; it may, like Judas, betray the Son of Man with
a kiss. This was the opinion of the General Assembly. It
was on the ground of *heresy, fatal, damnable heresy*, that
Rome was declared to be apostate and her ordinances pronounced to be invalid.

It was indeed asserted, and asserted in full consistency
with this explanation of the issue, that she does not retain
truth enough to save the soul. The meaning was, that the
system resulting from the combination of her truths and
errors, the *real* creed which is the product of these jarring
and discordant elements, as developed by herself in the
accounts of the plan of salvation, leaves so little scope for
the operation of any of the distinctive doctrines of the Gos-

pel, according to their native tendencies, that the impression made upon the heart is not that of the truth, but of a lie. In the compound whole there is too little truth practically efficacious, or capable of being practically efficacious, to resist the working of the deadly errors. The poison is too strong for the healthful medicine. The Romish creed is a mixture of incongruous materials. Among these materials some truth is found, but in the tendencies of the mixture the characteristics of the truth are so lost and blended that it fails to preserve its distinctive properties or to produce its distinctive effects. It was only in this aspect of the case that she was regarded as retaining too little truth to save the soul, and that in this sense the imputation is just I shall endeavour by God's grace to prove.

The substance of the Gospel is compendiously embraced by John,[1] under the threefold record of the Spirit, the Water and the Blood; in which phraseology of his Epistle there is obviously a reference to the circumstance he very particularly mentions in the Gospel of the miraculous effusion from the Saviour's side when pierced by the spear of the soldier. The *Water* and the *Blood* I take to be emblematical expressions of the two great divisions of the work which the Redeemer came to accomplish. They define the nature and specify the elements of that salvation which He dispenses to His disciples. A change of state and a change of character, justification and sanctification, both equally indispensable, are the immediate benefits of the covenant of grace. The change of state is fitly represented by the Blood, an emblem of that death which consummated obedience to a broken law, satisfied its awful curse, brought in an everlasting righteousness, and reconciled the pardon and acceptance of sinners with the justice of God. The change of character is with equal fitness represented by the Water, the scriptural symbol of purity and holiness, the washing of regeneration and the renewing of the Holy Ghost. When, therefore, it is said that the Redeemer came by

---

[1] 1 John v. 8; compare Gospel, xix. 34.

Water and by Blood, not by Water only, but by Water and by Blood, the meaning is that He came to justify and sanctify; not simply to restore to men the lost image of God by the infusion of grace, but, as the foundation of every other blessing, to restore them to the lost favour of God by the merit of His death. The Apostle guards us against the defective view of His work which overlooks the Blood, which confounds pardon and holiness, righteousness infused and righteousness imputed. As He came by *both*, the integrity of the Gospel requires *both*; and as they flowed simultaneously and in consequence of the same act from His side, so they are indissolubly joined together in the experience of the faithful, and are imparted without confusion, and yet without division, to all who are called by God's grace. The Spirit, on the other hand, indicates the process by which these benefits, the Water and the Blood, justification and sanctification, are applied to men. It is a compendious phrase, as I understand it, for the whole of experimental religion. The Apostle represents the Spirit as bearing witness to the fact that Jesus came by Water and by Blood, which, I suppose, is done in that inward work of grace which convinces sinners of their guilt and misery, enlightens their minds in the knowledge of Christ, unites them to Him by a living faith, and seals upon their hearts a full persuasion that they are born of God. When the Spirit, the Water and the Blood are all found in their scriptural meaning and their scriptural proportions in any creed, that creed is a saving one; and error in regard to any one of them singly, or their mutual relations to each other, is always dangerous, and may be fatal. He that gives us the Blood without the Water is an Antinomian; he that retains the Water without the Blood is a Legalist; and he who, either admitting or rejecting the Water and Blood, discards the Spirit, is a Pelagian. Our Saviour has settled the question that Antinomians[1] as such cannot enter into the kingdom of heaven. Paul has taught us that Pharisees and

[1] Matt. v. 19.

Legalists are fallen from grace,[1] and Pelagians from the very nature of the case exclude themselves from Christ. These heresies are deadly, in irreconcilable opposition to the characteristic principles of the Gospel, and any creed which derives its shape and form from them, or is a consistent development of any of them, must be regarded as fatal. No man can be saved by such a creed. It is true that men professing to believe it may be saved, for they may really embrace principles in their hearts widely removed from the verbal declaration of the lips. But Antinomianism, Legalism, Pelagianism never *did*, never *can* save any one; and he who in *fact* as well as in *form* rests upon either of these systems is, if there be truth in the Bible, building his house upon the sand.

In attempting to determine the question whether a creed is a saving one, our attention must be directed to two points: What are the benefits which it proposes to communicate, and how are these benefits dispensed? A creed may be obviously sound as to *what* constitutes salvation, and yet grossly at fault as to *how* it is to be obtained. Justification and sanctification may be properly exhibited in their scriptural meaning as the great blessings of the Gospel, and yet union with Christ, through whom alone we partake of them, may be made to turn upon a principle which Christianity does not recognize, and which must infallibly defeat the hopes of all who rely on it. Who would pronounce *that* a saving creed which, while it commends Christ as the ultimate Saviour of the lost, teaches that union with Him is effected by carnal ablutions, by periodic fasts, by alms and penances; which promises eternal life to every ascetic who will starve on Fridays, flog himself on Mondays, and give tithes of all he possesses; which insists that the mere *doing* of such things is all that God requires to make men partakers of Christ, and is infallibly connected with all the benefits of the new and everlasting covenant? Who would dare to say that such a creed is a saving one? It sets forth

[1] Gal. v. 2, 3, 4.

indeed a true Saviour, but it preaches a false Gospel; it embraces many precious and glorious truths about Christ, but it can never avail to introduce the sinner into fellowship with Christ. Should it be conceded, for the sake of argument, that Rome confesses in her symbols the true nature of justification and sanctification, that she insists alike upon the reality of the atonement and the necessity of holiness, yet her creed would not be proved to be a saving one unless it were likewise shown that she inculcates the scriptural method of union with the Son. The Water and the Blood can never reach us except through the Spirit. It avails little to be taught *what* salvation is, if we are not further instructed *how* salvation may be had. In regard to both points, however, Rome is fundamentally in error. She denies alike the Blood and the Spirit, and even the Water which she professes to retain is so miserably defiled that it can hardly be received as a stream from Siloah's brook.

(1.) She denies the Blood. The Apostle, it would almost seem, had a prospective reference to her heresy when he added so emphatically that Jesus came not by Water only, but by Water and by Blood. The great cardinal doctrine of Christianity, so clearly revealed, so earnestly inculcated and so variously illustrated, that of justification by grace, is robbed in her creed of all that is distinctively evangelical and precious. The peculiarity of the Gospel is not that it teaches justification—the Law had done this before—but that it teaches justification BY GRACE. Here lie the glory of the Cross and the hopes of man. This is precisely the point at which Rome begins to pervert the truth. She does not object to justification, but justification *by grace* she cannot abide. Where the Gospel enters Rome protests. Unfortunately for those who can trace in her features the lineaments of a true church, the only justification she admits is essentially that which Paul declares impossible to man— *justification by works*. Grace, in its scriptural acceptation, at least when used in connection with this subject, she entirely repudiates as the source of all licentiousness, and sends its advocates to hell. She is not content to put forth essentially another Gospel, but she must needs belch forth her anathemas against the true Gospel of the blessed God.

There can be no question that when the Scriptures affirm that justification is by grace, they mean that it proceeds from the mercy of God in Christ Jesus, without any reference to personal obedience or inherent righteousness. To be justified freely by God's grace is to be justified without the deeds of the law. To be saved by grace is to be saved independently of works, lest any man should boast. "And if by grace, then it is no more of works; otherwise grace is no more grace. But if it be of works, then it is no more grace; otherwise work is no more work." This, then, is a settled point, that grace, in the sense in which it enters into the scriptural doctrine of justification, excludes all reference to our own performances; and any creed which attributes our acceptance, either in whole or in part, to works of righteousness which we have done, denies the grace of the Gospel. Grace and works cannot be amalgamated; the law and the Gospel are fundamentally distinct. From the very nature of the case, a compound system which proposes to justify us partly by one and partly by the other involves a contradiction in terms. "Behold, I Paul say unto you, that if ye be circumcised, Christ shall profit you nothing. For I testify again to every man that is circumcised that he is a debtor to do the whole law. Christ is become of no effect unto you, whosoever of you are justified by the law; ye are fallen from grace." To rely at all upon personal obedience is to appeal to the justice and not to the mercy of God. The argument in the Epistle to the Romans, to prove the ultimate triumph of believers over sin, proceeds on the assumption that law and grace are incapable of confusion or mixture. "Sin," says the Apostle, "shall not have dominion over you; for ye are not under the law, but under grace." This conclusion would be miserably lame if it were possible to be under both at once, or in any third state distinct from each. There are, then, but two conceivable dispensations—

one of law, the other of grace; and consequently but two possible methods of justification—one by inherent righteousness, and the other by the free mercy of God. The difference of the two systems may be placed in another light. To justify is to pronounce righteous. A holy God cannot, of course, declare that any one is righteous unless he is so. There are no fictions of law in the tribunal of Heaven—all its judgments are according to truth. A man may be righteous because he has done righteousness, and then he is justified by law; or he may be righteous because he has received righteousness as a gift, and then he is justified by grace. He may be righteous in himself, and this is the righteousness of works; or he may be righteous in another, and this is the righteousness of faith. Hence, to deny imputed righteousness is either to deny the possibility of justification at all, or to make it consist in the deeds of the law—both hypotheses involving a rejection of the grace of the Gospel. There are plainly but three possible suppositions in the case: either there is no righteousness in which a sinner is accepted, and justification is simply pardon; or it must be the righteousness of God, without the law; or the righteousness of personal obedience;—it must either be none, inherent, or imputed. The first and last suppositions are both embraced by Rome in one sweeping anathema. "Justification," she declares, is not "remission of sin merely;" and subsequently adds: "Whosoever shall affirm that men are justified solely by the imputation of the righteousness of Christ, or solely by the remission of sin, to the exclusion of grace and charity, which by the Holy Spirit is shed abroad in their hearts, and inheres in them, or that the grace by which we are justified is only the favour of God, let him be accursed."[1]

She is therefore shut up to the position which she cheerfully assumes, that men are accepted in their own personal obedience. When, according to Bellarmine,[2] we are said to

[1] Concil. Trident., Sess. vi., cap. vii., Canon de Justificat., xi.
[2] De Justificat., Lib. ii., c. iii.

be justified freely by *God's grace*, the meaning is that we are justified by the *effects* of His grace, or the personal holiness it generates within us. Such also was the view of Trent when it damned those who resolved this grace into the unmerited favour or free mercy of God. Rome, then, takes her stand upon inherent righteousness. *Justification* and *sanctification* in her vocabulary are synonymous terms, and men are justified, *not by grace*, but by their *graces*. "The sole formal cause" of justification, says Trent, "is the righteousness of God; not that by which He Himself is righteous, but that by which He makes us righteous; with which, being endued by Him, we are renewed in the spirit of our mind, and are not only accounted righteous, but are properly called righteous, and are so, receiving righteousness in ourselves, each according to his measure, which the Holy Spirit bestows upon each as He wills, and according to our respective dispositions and co-operation." "Justification," it is previously said,[1] "is not remission of sin merely, but also sanctification and the renewal of the inner man by the voluntary reception of grace and Divine gifts, so that he who was unrighteous is made righteous; and the enemy becomes a friend and an heir according to the hope of eternal life." "The state of the whole controversy," says Bellarmine,[2] "may be reduced to this simple question—whether the formal cause of absolute justification be inherent righteousness or not? To prove the affirmative is, at the same time, to refute all contrary errors. For if the formal cause of justification is inherent righteousness, it is not, of course, the indwelling righteousness of God, nor the imputed righteousness of Christ, nor solely the remission of sin, without the renovation of the inner man. And if inherent righteousness is the formal cause of absolute justification, then of course the imputation of Christ's righteousness is not required, which would dispense with an inchoate and imperfect justification. Neither is faith alone our righteousness; since faith, the Lutherans themselves being witnesses,

[1] Concil. Trident., Sess. vi., c. vii.   [2] De Justificat., Lib. ii., c. ii.

cannot absolutely justify, and therefore, according to the fourth article of the Augsburg Confession, is not reputed as righteousness by God. And so none of these errors are placed for inherent, but only for extrinsic, righteousness; or if they admit inherent, they deny that it absolutely justifies. They will all, consequently, be refuted by proving that what simply and absolutely justifies is inherent righteousness." This being the doctrine of Rome, I have no hesitation in saying that it amounts to a complete subversion of the Gospel. It substitutes *law* for *grace*, works for the sovereign mercy of God. It embraces the characteristic principle of a legal dispensation, and renders the blood of Christ of no effect. The Scriptures teach that the grace by which we are justified excludes all reference to our own works; Rome affirms that its immediate office is to produce them, and that it actually justifies only in so far as it produces them. The Scriptures teach that the obedience of Christ, freely imputed to us of God, constitutes the righteousness in which we are accepted. Rome asserts that our own obedience, achieved by the exercise of our own free wills in co-operation with the Spirit of God, is the only righteousness in which we can appear. The difference is certainly fundamental—precisely the difference between a covenant of works and a covenant of grace. Now my argument is a short one. No creed which teaches justification by the deeds of the law can be a saving one. The proof is the positive declaration of the Apostle that the thing is impossible, and that as many as are under the law are under the curse. But Rome teaches justification by the deeds of the law, and the proof is that she makes inherent righteousness or works the immediate ground of acceptance. Therefore the creed of Rome cannot be a saving one.

The second proposition in this argument is the only one, I apprehend, that can create any difficulty—that justification by inherent righteousness is justification by the deeds of the law. To my mind, however, it rests upon sure warrant of Scripture.

Paul declares, as we have seen, that there are but two methods of justification; and as they are the immediate contraries of each other, the characteristic principle of the one must be the opposite of the characteristic principle of the other. The characteristic principle of grace, however, is, that *it excludes works;* then the characteristic principle of law must be that *it admits them.* This follows necessarily from the doctrine of immediate contraries.[1] If law and grace stand in this relation to each other, as the Apostle teaches, and it is the distinctive peculiarity of grace to *reject* works, it must necessarily be the distinctive peculiarity of law to *require* them. If whatsoever is *not* of works is grace, then whatsoever *is* of works is law. Inherent righteousness most certainly does not *exclude* or *reject* works; then it must *admit* and *require* them, and consequently must be brought under the category of law.

The evasion of Rome, that the works which are excluded are only those which precede faith and justification, and are consequently destitute of merit, is nothing worth.[2] The expression of the Apostle applies indiscriminately to *all* works performed with a view to Divine acceptance; and as to merit, the word and the thing in the relations of the creature to God are both equally unknown to the Bible. According to Bellarmine,[3] the works excluded are those which are performed in the strength of nature without the assistance of grace. "Gratuitous justification," he informs us, "does not exclude merits absolutely, but only those which are proper, which proceed from ourselves and not from God." Hence, the justification which takes place in consequence of works produced by grace is as truly justification by grace as that which takes place independently of works. We may accordingly be justified freely without the deeds of the law, and yet be justified by the inherent righteous-

---

[1] Paul reasons upon this principle in the 4th chap. Hebrews. See Owen's commentary on the 3d verse.

[2] This is the evasion of Trent, Sess. vi., cap. viii.

[3] De Justificat., Lib. i., cap. xxi.; comp. cap. ix. of the same book.

ness which the Spirit effects within us. This sophistry, to which the wily Jesuit again and again recurs, is a miserable play upon the ambiguity of the word *grace*. There are two senses in which it is used: in one, which, so far as I know, is seldom or never found in the Scriptures, it implies those operations of the Spirit which are connected with holiness; in the other it denotes the sovereign mercy or unmerited favour of God. Now in this first sense it is *never* opposed to law. If it were, justification by law would be, under all circumstances and to all classes of creatures, hopelessly impossible. On the contrary, a legal dispensation, until its disadvantages are forfeited by failure, necessarily implies that degree of grace which shall fit its subjects to render the obedience exacted. It would shock all our notions of justice, it would be gross and revolting tyranny, to create beings wholly unfurnished for a work, and yet demand it from them as the condition of life. Whatever may be the law which God in the first instance prescribes to His creatures, He imparts to them strength abundantly adequate to keep it. Adam was unquestionably placed under an economy of works. If he had kept his first estate and been justified, he would have been justified as a doer of the law; and yet the ability with which he was endowed in his first creation was as truly from God as that which the saints receive at their new creation in 'Christ Jesus. Hence, it is evident that obedience does not cease to be legal because it is rendered by Divine aid. To be justified by graces is not to be justified by grace. The proud Pharisee attributed to God his superiority to other men. It was by grace that he professed to have performed his alms, penances and devotions, yet with all his pretended gratitude and love he was a legalist at heart. Legalism and Pelagianism, though generally coexistent, are not necessarily the same. That obedience is legal which is performed with a view to justification, whatever may be the strength in which it is achieved. It is the end, and not the source of it, that determines its character. And that is a legal dispensation which prescribes a law, and attaches the promise of eternal life to conformity with its precepts. To give the law is an act of grace, but to dispense the reward when the obedience has been rendered is the discharge of a debt which God's faithfulness has imposed upon His justice. The obedience itself, not the strength in which it has been performed, is all that the law contemplates. If it demanded a particular kind of obedience, then that would be a part of the precept, and consequently no *true* obedience could be rendered if the kind in question were withheld. The law looks to nothing, and can look to nothing, but the fact that the obedience it requires is given or denied, and it rewards or punishes accordingly. To resolve justification, consequently, into inherent righteousness, how sincerely soever that righteousness may be attributed to the grace of God, is to resolve it into the deeds of the law. The man who is justified, therefore, upon the principles of Rome is as truly justified by works as Adam would have been if he had kept his integrity. Adam's original nature was as much the offspring of God as the believer's new nature. Adam was free to fall, and so, according to Rome, is every true believer, good works being the result of our wills co-operating with grace. Adam was able to stand in consequence of what God had done for him, and so are the faithful of Rome. Adam's life depended upon personal obedience, and so, says Rome, does the salvation of the saints. The parallel is perfect, and the conclusion is inevitable that Rome utterly rejects the Gospel as a dispensation of grace, and turns all its glorious provisions into a covenant of works.

But what sets the legalism of Rome in a still stronger light is the estimate which she puts upon the performances of men, achieved through the co-operation of their own wills with the stimulating grace of God; for it is, after all, but a partial agency that her creed attributes to the Holy Spirit.

Tenacious of what the Schoolmen denominate the *merit of congruity*, she distinctly teaches that men in the exercise of their own free wills, concurring with the grace of God,

prepare and dispose themselves for justification.[1] God gives
them the ability to work, but it depends upon themselves
whether or not they will improve it. The diligent are
rewarded with larger accessions of strength, until finally
"they resolve to receive baptism, to begin a new life and
to keep the Divine commandments." Then the critical
point is reached, they are fully prepared to be justified, they
have done well, and deserve *ex congruo* the august benefit. If
this detestable combination of the pride of the Pelagian and
the haughtiness of the Pharisee can be termed *grace*, then it

> " Is of all our vanities the motliest,
> The merest word that ever fooled the ear
> From out the Schoolman's jargon."

My soul sickens at the blasphemy that men, independently of union with Christ, can bring themselves into a
state in which, though they have no claim upon the justice
of God, they have a claim upon His sense of decency—in
which He cannot refuse to receive them into favour without the perpetration of an ugly deed.

A system which can find a place for such a doctrine stumbles on the very threshold of Christianity, and those who
can embrace it are strangers to what be the first principles
of the Oracles of God. But the climax of iniquity and
legalism is reached in the odious dogma first broached in
the Schools, subsequently incorporated into the public symbols of the church, and audaciously defended by her most
distinguished divines, that the good works of the faithful
are truly and properly meritorious upon principles of *justice*, so that God cannot fail to reward them without the
surrender of His holiness. "We shall therefore prove,"
says Bellarmine,[2] " what all Catholics believe, that the good
works of the just are truly and properly merits, deserving
not of any reward that may be, but of eternal life itself."
" It is the will of God," he declares,[3] " that His children who have the use of reason should acquire eternal life

---

[1] Concil. Trident., Sess. vi., cap. vi., can. iv.

[2] De Justificat., Lib. v., cap. i.   [3] Ibid., cap. iii.

by their own labours and merits, so that it may be due to
them by a double title—a title of inheritance and a right of
reward—since it is more honourable to obtain by merit than
by free gift alone; God, that He might honour His sons,
has so arranged it that they can procure eternal life for
themselves by their own merits."   The merit of these works,
we are further instructed, depends partly upon the promise
of God, His own sovereign appointment which brings Him
under an obligation of debt to reward them, and partly
upon their own intrinsic excellence.[1] "Whosoever shall
affirm," says Trent, "that the good works of a justified man
are in such sense the gifts of God that they are not also his
own good merits, or that he being justified by his good
works which are wrought by him, through the grace of
God and the merits of Jesus Christ, of whom he is a living
member, does not really deserve increase of grace, eternal
life, the enjoyment of that eternal life and also increase of
glory if he dies in a state of grace, let him be accursed."[2]

With such statements before him, how can any man who
has any adequate conceptions of the distinction between
law and grace hesitate for a moment to affirm that the system of Rome is eminently legal—that, like the Jews of
old, she goes about to establish her own righteousness, and
refuses to submit to the righteousness of God?   She requires
works; these works are to be done with a view to justification and eternal life, and not only obtain but *deserve* both
in consequence of the compact of God and their own inherent excellence.   If this be not law, it would be hard to
specify an economy that is, and if it *be* law, how can the
inference be avoided that it can *save* none who rely on its
provisions?   Is there a man who can lay his hand upon his
heart and say that he honestly believes that any sinner can
consistently with the Scriptures be accepted in the righteousness in which Rome says he must be accepted before God?
If the Galatians, by submitting to circumcision, fell from

[1] Bellarm., De Justificat., Lib. v., cap. xvii.
[2] De Justificat., can. xxxii.

grace and became debtors to the whole law, what shall be said of those who boldly proclaim that heaven can be bought by works, and audaciously put eternal life to sale in the market of human merit? If such principles are saving, or a creed can be saving which admits them, in the name of truth and righteousness what creed on earth can be a damning one?

In the face of all these clear and positive proofs of the most disgusting legalism, the Reviewer asserts that Rome "holds that we are justified by the merits of Christ," and that "she teaches the doctrine of the atonement far more fully and accurately than multitudes of professedly orthodox Protestants." The proof of these bold assumptions turns upon the fact that Christ is uniformly represented as the *meritorious* cause of all the blessings we receive. Trent says, in the passages quoted by Princeton, that "our sins are freely forgiven us by the Divine mercy, for Christ's sake;" that "the meritorious cause of justification is the well-beloved and only-begotten Son of God, who, when we were enemies, for the great love wherewith He loved us, merited justification for us by His most holy passion on the cross; that Christ, by His most holy passion on the cross, merited justification for us, satisfied God the Father on our behalf; and no one can be righteous unless the merits of the passion of the Lord Jesus Christ are communicated to him." To these extracts are added two sentences from Bellarmine, one affirming that "we are justified on account of the merits of Christ," and the other, according to the Reviewer, containing a true statement of the scriptural doctrine of imputation.

As to the expression, that "Christ is the meritorious cause of pardon and acceptance," though taken by itself and apart from its connection it might be interpreted as Princeton seems to have understood it, yet Rome is far from employing it to denote our justifying righteousness, or that which immediately commends us to God. She does not mean to teach that the personal obedience of the Saviour is the ground on which a sinner is declared to be just. That which constitutes him righteous she denominates not the *meritorious*, but the *formal*, cause of justification; and as this consists in the graces of the Spirit, whatever sense should be attached to the phrase *meritorious cause*, the legal feature of her system, inherent righteousness, is by no means excluded. · But we are not left in darkness as to the meaning of the phrase itself. "The merits of the righteous," says Bellarmine,[1] "are not opposed to the merits of Christ, but spring from them; and whatsoever praise the merits of the righteous are entitled to receive redounds to the glory of the merits of Christ. He is the Vine, we are the branches; and as the branch cannot bear fruit except it abide in the vine, so we can do nothing without Christ. And as no one was ever stupid enough to assert that it detracted from the glory of the vine when its branches bore much fruit, so none but a fool would say that it detracts from the glory of Christ when His servants, by His grace, by His Spirit, by faith and charity inspired by Him, perform good works, which are so truly righteous that a crown of righteousness is due to them from a just judge. The objection is without foundation that if the merits of men are required, those of Christ are unnecessary. For the merits of men are not required on account of the insufficiency of those of Christ, but on account of their very great efficacy. For the works of Christ merited from God not only that we should obtain salvation, but that we should obtain it by our own merits; or, what is the same, they merited for us not only eternal life, but also the power of meriting it ourselves. Because God uses the sun to enlighten the world, fire to heat, and wind and showers to refresh it, it is not to be ascribed to weakness as if He were unable to accomplish these things by Himself, without sun, fire or breeze, but to His omnipotence, by which He is not only able to do these things Himself, but also to bestow upon creatures the power of doing them."

[1] De Justificat., Lib. v., cap. v.

"Neither do our merits," says Dens,[1] "diminish the virtue of those of Christ, as heretics yelp, since our merits derive all their power of meriting from those of Christ, as the branches derive their power of bearing fruit from the vine. Wherefore our merits commend the merits of Christ, inasmuch as He, by His merits, has procured for us the power of meriting." When, therefore, Trent affirms that "the meritorious cause" of justification is God's "only-begotten and well-beloved Son," she means that the passion of the Divine Redeemer has established that dispensation under which we are required to procure salvation for ourselves, and are furnished with the necessary helps for the arduous work. His atonement is the immediate ground of pardon and acceptance to no one; it simply places the race in a new relation to God, and that a relation of law, in consequence of which they can be and do what God exacts from them. Without the death of Christ they could not have been favoured with this new opportunity of life. His merits have given them another *chance*, but success or failure depends upon themselves; He merited justification by meriting that their own works should be accepted as a justifying righteousness. Hence, His *passion* is only the basis on which a *legal scheme* of salvation is erected for *fallen man*, as the goodness of God was the basis on which a similar scheme was erected for man in innocence. As God's kindness furnished Adam and gave him strength for his first trial, so the death of the Redeemer has instituted a new trial, and fitted and qualified men to comply with its provisions. Such is the honour which Rome gives to Christ.

Princeton says, however, that Rome as a community "holds that we are justified by the merits of Christ." This proposition I am constrained to deny. Some of her divines have held it, but the Church in her public symbols, in the decrees and canons of Trent, in her authorized creed, has taught no such principle. Rome teaches that we are

[1] Tract. De Merito., vol. ii., No. 35, pp. 459, 460.

justified, in the language of Bellarmine, "*on account* of the merits of Christ," but not *by* them. To say that we are justified *by* them is to affirm that they constitute the righteousness in which we are accepted; to say that we are justified *on account* of them is to teach that they are the meritorious cause of acceptance in the sense already explained. Bellarmine [1] has accurately noted the distinction. "In strict propriety of speech," says he, "it is not *on account of* (propter), but *by* (per), which is used to designate the formal cause. If one should ask *by* what man lives, *by* what fire is warm, *by* what the stars shine, it would be rightly answered *by* the soul, *by* heat, *by* light, which are formal causes. But if he should ask *on account of what* the commander triumphs, *on account of what* the soldiers fight, it will be answered not by assigning the *formal*, but the *meritorious* or *final*, cause." Hence the first sentence which Princeton has quoted from Bellarmine contains a very different view of justification from that which she asserts that the Papal community maintains. His own exposition of his terms is conclusive proof that in saying we are justified *on account* of the merits of Christ he intended to deny that we are justified *by* them, or that they constitute the righteousness which immediately commends us to God. Of precisely the same import is the next passage. Occurring in the midst of a chapter expressly devoted to the disproof of the doctrine of imputation, and taken from a book which contains an elaborate and crafty defence of inherent righteousness, it cannot, without violence to the author and violence to its connection, be interpreted as Princeton understands it. There is, indeed, no necessity for this violence. All the expressions are in perfect harmony with the dogma that Christ is the *meritorious*, in contradistinction from the *formal*, cause of justification. His merits are given to us by being made available to generate merits within us; they are given, not by imputation, but by infusion, and whatsoever efficacy our righteousness possesses, is derived from

[1] De Justificat., Lib. ii., c. 2.

the passion of Christ. If He had not died, we should neither have been able to perform works of righteousness, nor would works of righteousness have saved us. It is in consequence of what He has done that our own doings are effectual. His merits are given in the same way that His wisdom is given—the one to make us meritorious, as the other removes our ignorance; and we can present them to the Father for our sins because, in consequence of them, remission may be expected according to the tenor of the new law under which they have placed us. Our prayers, penances, satisfactions and obedience could not purge our consciences from guilt unless the blood of the Redeemer had imparted this efficacy to them, as the sun could dispense no light without the sovereign appointment of God. Such I take to be the meaning of Bellarmine.

Of what has been spoken upon the first point, the denial of the Blood, this then is the sum. It has been proved, in the first place, from the testimony of Paul, that no creed which teaches salvation by works can be a saving one; in the second place, that the creed of Rome does teach it, because she resolves our justifying righteousness into personal holiness, damns the doctrine of imputation, audaciously proclaims the figment of human merit, both of congruity and condignity, and makes Christ only the remote and ultimate cause of pardon and acceptance. These premises being established, the conclusion necessarily follows that the creed of Rome cannot be a saving one. It robs God of His glory and the Saviour of His honour; gives us ashes for bread, a scorpion for an egg, and death for life.

(2.) Rome corrupts the Water. To make acceptance with God dependent upon personal holiness is to repudiate the distinction between depravity and guilt, and to endorse the detestable doctrine of the Socinians, that repentance is an adequate ground of pardon, since it effaces those moral qualities the possession of which is what renders men liable to punishment. Rome and the Fratres Poloni differ, not in the principle on which justification immediately proceeds

—both ascribe it to inherent righteousness—but in the source whence the principle in reference to the fallen derives its efficacy. The change of character which is supposed to be inseparably connected with the favour of God and a title to happiness is, according to the Socinian hypothesis, attainable by the strength of nature without the assistance of grace. Rome, on the other hand, contends that, although free-will has not been extinguished in men by the Fall, they have become so completely the slaves of sin and the subjects of the Devil that neither Jews nor Gentiles, independently of the passion of Christ and the aid of the Spirit, could be restored to liberty and peace. The inherent righteousness by which we are justified is, in the theology of Rome, the infusion of grace; in the theology of Socinus and his followers it is the product and offspring of nature. When the question is asked *how* we obtain it, these doctors differ; but when it is inquired *what it accomplishes* or *what is its office*, Herod and Pontius Pilate are agreed; the Papist and Socinian strike hands in harmonious accord, impelled by equal fury against the most glorious truth of the glorious Gospel of the blessed God—justification by grace. That which, according to both, effaces guilt and exempts from punishment is the possession of personal righteousness. The inward purity which expunges the stain obliterates the crime. Men cease to be punishable as soon as they cease to be wicked. Though their personal identity remains unchanged, yet, as guilt attaches only to *character*, it must be expunged as soon as the character undergoes a change. God deals with men according to the present condition of their moral qualities, and he, consequently, who would escape from punishment, must escape from that moral pollution which the law condemns, and acquire those traits which the law approves. Men can cease to be guilty only by becoming just; their righteousness covers their iniquities —their purity cancels their guilt. Abandoning the grounds of displeasure against them, they procure the favour of God.

Whatever objections to this reasoning may be drawn from the ordinary conduct of Providence, and however fallacious it may be in itself, yet the conclusion at which it aims must be confessed to be plausible—it falls in with our instinctive conviction of propriety; and as the government of God is moral, dispensing rewards and punishments according to the principles of distributive justice, there is felt to be a manifest incongruity in treating the righteous, no matter how or when they become so, as if they were wicked. The fact of being righteous would seem to be sufficient to exempt from punishment, though it might entitle to no positive rewards. Accustomed to regard purity as the parent of happiness, and misery as the offspring of vice, we spontaneously pronounce it to be absurd, no less than a contradiction in terms, to suppose that the holy can ultimately perish or the good be abandoned of God. Still, the claims of violated law are sacred and immutable. God has inseparably linked together punishment and crime, and it is the dictate alike of reason and revelation—the soul that sinneth it shall die. Whatever changes may have been experienced in the moral qualities of the agent, his personal identity is untouched— he is the man who sinned; and as the wrath of God is revealed from heaven against all ungodliness and unrighteousness of men, and as the sin cannot be visited except in the person of the transgressor himself, he is the man that must suffer. It would appear, then, that if a sinner could repent of his iniquities, and undergo a complete and thorough transformation in his moral nature, so as to be possessed of all the qualities which God requires, the change in his character would create an emergency in the Divine administration, the issue of which it would be impossible for us, upon any principles of natural religion, to predict with certainty. Penal justice, constituting an indispensable ingredient of the holiness of God, would be evidently forfeited if the past offences of the guilty were permitted to escape with impunity; and yet the idea that hell should be peopled with the righteous—with those who bear the image of their

Maker, and are intent, even amid their agonies, upon the glory of His name—cannot for a moment be endured.

How, then, shall this problem be resolved? Most evidently by denying the possibility of the case. Piety instinctively suggests what reason and Scripture concur to authenticate—that the government of God is too wisely ordered in all its arrangements to permit emergencies to arise, as they often occur in human administrations, which cannot be adjusted without inconsistency, compromise or concession. It can never consequently happen, in the course of the Divine economy, that moral fitness shall be violated by dooming the upright to punishment; neither can penal justice be foregone by allowing the guilty to escape. These two principles, equally sacred and immutable, must be preserved in inviolable harmony—their demands can never be permitted to clash. Hence, the guilty must necessarily be incapable of rectitude. They can never acquire the character which moral fitness shall approve while they continue in the state which penal justice must condemn. Pardon is accordingly indispensable to repentance; the liability to punishment, or what Protestants denominate *guilt*, must be cancelled, before reformation is possible or holiness attainable. Sanctification, independently of a previous justification—previous in the order of nature, though not necessarily in the order of time—involves a gross contradiction in terms. Personal holiness, according to the uniform teachings of the Scriptures, results from union with God; and union with God necessarily implies the possession of His favour. Good works, proceeding as they do from the love of God as their source, governed by His law as their rule, and directed to His glory as their end, cannot be conceived to exist among outcasts and aliens. Men without God are without hope in the world. As the light of the sun is the prolific parent of life, beauty, vegetation and growth to the earth, so the light of the Divine countenance diffuses health, cheerfulness and vigour in the hearts of the children of men. His favour is to the moral what the sun is to the material world, and the soul that is darkened by His frown can no more "move in charity and turn upon the poles of truth" than a soil covered with perpetual night can be enriched with verdure or adorned with animals and plants. In the beautiful language of the Psalmist, His favour is life, and His loving-kindness is better than life. Union with Him is the only source of strength, purity and peace. This is what the Scripture denominates *life*.

Now, what is the condition of an unpardoned sinner? His first transgression, upon the necessary principles of retributive justice, has doomed him to the curse. But to be under the curse, and at the same time enjoy the favour of God, are contradictory states. The curse implies something inconceivably stronger than a bare negation of favour —it fixes an illimitable chasm between the sinner and his Judge. It effects that awful separation from God, that banishment from His presence, that aggregate of all that is terrible, which the Bible compendiously expresses by *death*: in this condition of wretchedness and of exile the dominion of sin must be unbroken and complete. Corruption riots on its victim. The curse which banishes from God banishes from holiness. The unpardoned sinner, consequently, from the very nature of his state, is as incapable of aspiring to holiness as a corpse is incapable of the functions of life. It is his doom, like the serpent, to crawl upon his belly and to lick the dust. The condemnation which sends him out, like Cain, from the presence of the Almighty for ever precludes the possibility of repentance, places him beyond the pale of communion with his Maker, beyond the reach of spiritual impulses, and leaves him to wither in the atmosphere of death. Such is the strength of the law to crush the victims of its penalty. All that are under the curse are dead—cut off from the fountain of life; the only works they are competent to perform are *dead* works.

The effect of a single sin upon the relations of a creature to God is by most men inadequately apprehended, in consequence of confounding spiritual death with the extinction of the moral nature. As long as habits of incurable wickedness are not formed, while conscience in any measure continues to discharge its office, and the understanding recognizes the distinctions of right and wrong, there is supposed to be a form of spiritual life, which, by vigilance and culture, may be restored to strength and nurtured to maturity. Death in trespasses and sins is represented as the result of a *course* of transgression, a permanent condition of depravity produced by the natural operation of habit. This is to confound the cause with its effects, the tree with its fruits—death as a *state* with its ultimate and complete exhibitions. According to the Scriptures, the slightest sin, like a puncture of the heart, is instantly attended with this awful catastrophe. It dissolves the union betwixt the sinner and God; it superinduces the condemnation of the law, and whatever operations the moral nature may subsequently perform are destitute of the only principle which can render them acceptable. As natural death consists in the separation of the body and soul, so spiritual death consists in the separation of the soul and God. As the body, though destitute of life, may long resist the process of putrefaction, preserving the integrity of its members and all the features and lineaments of the man; so the soul, though banished from God, may long resist what may not unaptly be styled the process of *moral putrefaction*, continuing to possess sensibility of conscience, delicacy of perception, and revolting at the thoughts of abandoned wickedness. As the body may be beautiful in death, so the soul, deserted of God and bereft of the light of holiness, may yet retain something of original brightness in its form, and reveal in the grandeur of its ruins the glory of the state from which it fell. It is a great mistake to suppose that spiritual death is the destruction of all moral susceptibilities and impressions. There may be total depravity without desperate atrocity, a complete alienation from God without degradation to the fiendishness of devils, an utter destitu-

tion of holiness without the possession of all conceivable
wickedness. The condition which the moralist and Pharisee might acknowledge to be death is that to which spiritual
death necessarily tends. As soon as the soul is cut loose
from God it begins a career which, sooner or later, effects
the prostration of the whole moral nature. It is in a state to
form the habits which bind it in fetters of massive depravity, as the body ultimately moulders in decay from which
the soul has taken its flight.

Spiritual death, consisting, as we have seen, in the separation of the soul from God, must continue to reign until a
reunion shall have been effected. There can be no holiness
until the sinner has been restored to the favour of his
Maker, and he cannot be restored to this state until the
curse of the law has been removed. He must therefore
continue to be incapable of holiness as long as the law continues to condemn. Its penalty is an awful barrier betwixt
his soul and life, and until that barrier is in some way or
other destroyed he must remain the victim of everlasting
death. Hence, the removal of the curse is the first step in
his progress to holiness; the removal of the curse implies
pardon; so that he must be pardoned before he can repent,
he must cease to be condemned before he can breathe the
atmosphere of life. Repentance and reformation, proceeding from communications of Divine love, involve the possession of Divine favour, and can never consequently obtain
among those whom God pronounces to be vessels of His
wrath. To suppose that a sinner can be sanctified is to
suppose that he can enjoy fellowship with God, and perform
those works which flow from the participations of Divine
love. To suppose that he can be sanctified without being
justified is to suppose that he can be in a condition in
which God denounces him as the object of vengeance, and
at the same time in a state of reconciliation and favour—
that he can be and not be at one and the same moment
under the curse. Repentance, therefore, implying restoration to favour and communion with God, is incompatible

with a state of condemnation which debars from both; and consequently an unpardoned sinner cannot repent.

If, now, pardon is essential to repentance, acceptance indispensable to holiness, it necessarily follows from the hypothesis of Rome, which confounds the Water and the Blood, that repentance and holiness are hopelessly impossible. The design of justification is to put the sinner in a state in which the light of the Divine countenance can be lifted up upon him, in which he can receive communications of grace and enjoy communion with God. If these manifestations of favour are indispensable to holiness, and can only be imparted when the sinner is justified, justification must be the only basis on which righteousness of life can be reared. Rome, however, has reversed this order, and made holiness essential to acceptance; the necessary consequence is, that justification is denied to be of grace, and sanctification is impossible. With all her pretended zeal for the interests of righteousness, her extravagant adulation of works, and her presumptuous confidence in merit, she has proclaimed a creed which whoever cordially embraces and consistently endeavours to embody in his life must everlastingly remain an alien from God, under sentence of condemnation, in bondage to spiritual death. Philosophy and Scripture concur in declaring that whoever would be holy must be in union with his Maker, that union with God is inseparably connected with the possession of His favour, and the possession of His favour a fruit of justification; so that whoever would be holy must necessarily be justified. Rome, on the other hand, proclaims in foolish confidence of boasting, that the sinner must begin in holiness and end in the favour of his Judge, begin at the point which he can never reach, and of course end precisely where he was—under the wrath and curse of the Almighty. Here, then, is the insuperable difficulty of Rome—she denies the Blood, and, in denying the blood, inevitably corrupts the Water; she takes away the cause, and of course must renounce the effect. Upon her hypothesis sanctification is subverted. How, then, can hers be a saving creed?

The impossibility of constructing a system of sanctification independently of a gracious justification does not strike men at once, because they are apt to confound two widely different conditions, those of a fallen and an unfallen creature. In an unfallen state, justification is possible by the deeds of the law, because personal obedience is within the power of the agent. Created in the image of God, possessed of a holy nature and governed by holy impulses, they present no obstructions in their persons and character to the free communications of Divine favour. They are united with God, and are, consequently, able to do all that His law demands. But so long as they are not justified this union is precarious; they may fall from their integrity and lose their rectitude of nature. Justification confirms this union, and renders their apostasy for ever impossible, giving them at the same time a right to whatever rewards had been promised to obedience, so that perpetual security is one of its leading and characteristic benefits. But the justification of a sinner, of a fallen being, though essentially the same, yet, in consequence of the different condition of the subject, includes the imparting of an element which in the other case was previously possessed. As an unfallen creature already enjoys the favour of God, he is simply confirmed in its possession, while a fallen creature, who, from the nature of the case, is alienated from his Maker, must first acquire this privilege before he can be confirmed in it; his union with God must be instituted as well as established. As, then, in the justification of a sinner, communion with God is to be procured as well as confirmed, he cannot be justified by deeds of law, which presuppose its existence. His acceptance must be of grace, or it cannot be effected at all. It must precede personal obedience, or personal obedience can never take place.

It is vain to allege, in extenuation of the beggarly theology of Rome, that, in consequence of the work of the Redeemer, communications of grace may be imparted to the guilty which enable them to repent, to bring forth the fruits of righteousness, and so to be justified by works. These communications either imply the possession of the Divine favour and deliverance from the condemnation of the law, or they do not. If they do, the sinner is already justified without works, and pardoned independently of repentance, which is contrary to the hypothesis. If they do not, then they leave him under the curse, in the power of spiritual death, and of course do not impart spiritual life; so that the works which they enable him to perform are only dead works. The conclusion is therefore unaffected, that without a gracious justification no sinner can be sanctified. Pardon and acceptance must precede repentance and holiness.

The *practical effects* of the Romish system are so modified by the temper and constitution of those by whom it is received as to present no uniform appearance. In some it produces an awful bondage. Anxiously solicitous about the salvation of their souls, and taught to seek for the Divine favour in works of righteousness which their hands have wrought, they exhaust the resources of their nature in vain and servile efforts to compass obedience to the law. Tortured by conscience, which always in the guilty forecasteth grievous things, groaning in spirit under the intolerable burden of aggravated guilt, they multiply devices of superstition and will-worship, in the delusive hope of bringing peace to their troubled and agitated breasts. They know nothing of the liberty of the sons of God. Strangers to that glorious spirit of adoption which the sense of acceptance generates, they feel existence to be a curse, and dread the presence of God as a terrible calamity. Their obedience is the effort of a slave to propitiate a tyrant, and after a life dragged out in galling servitude, death comes to them clothed with tenfold terror. Eternity is shrouded in insupportable gloom, and the dismal tragedy of life closes with an awful catastrophe. To such sensitive and conscientious minds Rome presents her system in the aspect of unbending severity. She imposes penances and privations, pilgrimages and fasts, vows of poverty and self-denial, haircloth and rags, the torment of the body for the good of the soul. Eternity alone can disclose the groans, the sufferings, the agony which the cells of her monks and the chambers of her nuns have witnessed among those who are anxiously inquiring wherewith they should appear before the Lord and bow themselves before the Most High God. And all this anguish has been occasioned by her devilish cruelty in suppressing the grace of God. She has refused to point the wounded spirit to the Fountain opened in the house of David for sin and for uncleanness; she has refused to proclaim a free and glorious justification through the obedience unto death of the Son of God, to open the doors of the captive and strike the fetters from the hands of the prisoner. Instead of acting as the herald of mercy, she has betrayed the cruelty of a tyrant brooding in vindictive malice over the woes and anguish which, with the scorpion whip of the law, she has wrung from hearts to which the oil of grace should have been imparted, and has rejoiced in thickening the horrors of superstition where she was bound to diffuse the light of the Gospel. Like the ancient Pharisees, she binds heavy burdens upon men and grievous to be borne, and lays them on their shoulders, and will not move them with one of her fingers. She shuts the kingdom of heaven against them, neither entering herself nor permitting others to do so. Like ancient Egypt to the Hebrews, she is literally the house of bondage. Some, like Luther, have escaped from her cruelty. The key which opened their prison doors and enabled the soul to laugh at her terrors was justification by grace. This precious truth, for which their hearts had panted in Babylon, was the talisman of joy, of peace, of holiness. Delivered from the curse of the law, the dominion of the Devil and the horrors of conscience, they could serve God acceptably with reverence and godly fear, in holiness and righteousness before Him, all the days of their lives. There are others whose apprehensions of sin are less feeble and impressive. Disposed to make a mock of its consequences, they indulge in presumptuous hopes, and treat the salvation of the soul as an easy and comparatively light matter. These Rome flatters with the deceits of a frivolous and deadly casuistry. Corrupting the first principles of morals, she makes sin to be no more sin, law to be no more law; with elaborate ingenuity she has undertaken to solve the problem, what is the minimum of decency and the maximum of sin with which men can enter into heaven; she has confounded the distinctions of truth and falsehood, of right and wrong, and left nothing certain but her own pretended authority; and all to accommodate easy consciences, to reconcile hopes of heaven with a careless and wicked life.

Such is the working of the system. Theoretically, it makes sanctification impossible; practically, it verifies the truth of the theory.

Extremes meet. An old writer has pithily observed that the least touch of a pencil will translate a laughing into a crying face. In illustration of the proverb, it would not be difficult to prove that the vaunting legalism of Rome really terminates in a filthy and disgusting antinomianism. She degrades the majesty of the Divine law, substitutes for it a fictitious standard of excellence, and represses those emotions which must characterize the heart of every true penitent. Her doctrine of venial sins, which are confessed to be transgressions of the Divine commandments, is utterly incompatible with those awful impressions of the malignity of the least departure from rectitude which the holiness of God and the atonement of the Redeemer alike impart. She teaches that men may disregard the authority of their Maker and yet not be deserving of death—that there are some precepts so insignificant, and some offences so trivial and harmless, that a few signs of the cross and muttered incantations, a little holy water, an Ave Maria or a Pater Noster, are abundantly sufficient to expiate them. Is not blasphemy written on the portals of a church which can

preach such a doctrine as this? Does she not make the
commandments of God of none effect by her traditions?

But the odious tendencies of her doctrine are not only
manifested in her slight estimate of some of the commandments—one she has absolutely expunged. The pure and
sublime idea which the Scriptures inculcate of a spiritual
God, neither possessed of a corporeal figure nor capable of
being represented by visible symbols, is as much a stranger
to the theology of Rome as to the "elegant mythology of
Greece." Hence, we are told that "to represent the persons
of the Holy Trinity by certain forms under which, as we
read in the Old and the New Testaments, they deigned to
appear, is not to be deemed contrary to religion or the law
of God." Accordingly, the second commandment is annulled
by the hierarchy (in books of popular devotion it is wholly
suppressed), the windows of Papal churches are frequently
adorned with images of the Trinity, the breviaries and mass-
books are embellished with engravings which represent God
the Father as a venerable old man, the Eternal Son in
human form, and the blessed Spirit in the shape of a dove.
Sometimes grotesque images, hardly surpassed in the fabulous creations of heathen poets, where centaurs, gorgons,
mermaids, with all manner of impossible things, hold undisputed sway, are employed to give an adequate impression
of Him who dwells in majesty unapproachable, whom no
man hath seen or can see. To picture the Holy Trinity with
three noses and four eyes and three faces—and in this form
these Divine persons are sometimes submitted to the devout
contemplation of Papal idolaters—is to give an idea of God
from which an ancient Roman or a modern Hindoo might
turn away in disgust. Such gross and extravagant symbols,
however carefully explained or allegorically interpreted,
involve a degradation of the Supreme Being which it is impossible to reconcile with the sublime announcement of our
Saviour that God is a Spirit, and they that worship Him
must worship Him in spirit and in truth. The adoration
which is paid to the Deity under any corporeal figure or

visible representation cannot be vindicated from the charge
of idolatry upon any principles which do not exempt from
the same imputation every form, whether ancient or modern,
of Pagan superstition. It is quite certain, from the accounts
of heathen philosophers and poets, that the images of their
gods were regarded simply as visible memorials of invisible
deities, as signs by which their affections were excited and
through which their worship was directed. The veneration
with which they were treated was purely of that relative
kind which the Romish doctors impute to the devotees of
their own communion.[1]   Pagan statues and Romish pictures

[1] "Nor is it of any importance whether they worship simply the idol
or God in the idol; it is always idolatry when Divine honours are paid to
an idol under any pretence whatsoever.   And as God will not be worshipped in a superstitious or idolatrous manner, whatever is conferred on
idols is taken from Him.   Let this be considered by those who seek such
miserable pretexts for the defence of that execrable idolatry with which
for many ages true religion has been overwhelmed and subverted.   The
images, they say, are not considered as gods.   Neither were the Jews so
thoughtless as not to remember that it was God by whose hand they had
been conducted out of Egypt before they made the calf.   But when Aaron
said that those were the gods by whom they had been liberated from
Egypt, they boldly assented: signifying, doubtless, that they would keep in
remembrance that God Himself was their Deliverer, while they could see
Him going before them in the calf.   Nor can we believe the heathen to
have been so stupid as to conceive that God was no other than wood and
stone.   For they changed the images at pleasure, but always retained in
their minds the same gods, and there were many images for one god; nor
did they imagine to themselves gods in proportion to the multitude of
images; besides, they daily consecrated new images, but without supposing
that they made new gods.   Read the excuses which Augustine (in Psalm
cxiii.) says were alleged by the idolaters of the age in which he lived.
When they were charged with idolatry, the vulgar replied that they worshipped not the visible figure, but the Divinity that invisibly dwelt in it.
But they whose religion was, as he expresses himself, more refined, said
that they worshipped neither the image nor the Spirit represented by it,
but that in the corporeal figure they beheld a sign of that which they
ought to worship." Calvin's Inst., Lib. i., cap. xi., § 10.   Upon this whole
subject of the idolatry of the Church of Rome the reader is referred to
Archbishop Tenison's Discourse of Idolatry, particularly to chapters x.,
xi., xii.   That the heathens did not regard their images as gods, and that
they worshipped them on the same principle vindicated by the Papists,
may be seen from Arnobius, Lactantius, Austin and divers of the Fathers.

are due to the operation of the same principle—an attempt to accommodate the receding majesty of a spiritual being to human sympathies, and to divest the adoration of an infinite object of some of its awful and mysterious veneration by reducing its grandeur to the feeble apprehension of human capacities. Fallen humanity, having originally apostatized from God, and lost the right as well as the power of intimate communion with the Father of spirits, seeks to gratify its religious aspirations by tangible objects around which its sympathies can readily cling. Unable to soar to the unapproachable light in which Deity dwells in mysterious sanctity, it spends its devotion upon humbler things, to which it imparts such Divine associations as may seem at least to reconcile the worship with the acknowledged supremacy of God. When we cannot rise to God, the religious necessities of our nature will drag Him down to us. In the Papal community the degradation of the Supreme Being seems to have reached its lowest point of disgusting fetichism in the adoration of the bread and wine of the sacramental feast. I know of nothing in the annals of heathenism that can justly be compared with this stupendous climax of absurdity, impiety, blasphemy and idolatry. The work of the cook and the product of the vintage, bread and wine, the materials of food which pass through the stages of digestion and decay, are placed before us, after having been submitted to the magical process of sacerdotal enchantment, as the eternal God in the person of the incarnate Redeemer.[1] The eucha-

A very interesting discussion of the nature and unlawfulness of image-worship may be found in Taylor's Ductor Dubitantium, book ii., chap. ii., rule 6, § 21, ad fin.; Works, vol. xii., p. 382, seq. The vain pretexts of the Papists are there so ably discussed that the reader is earnestly requested to peruse it.

[1] We submit to the reader the following description of the scene when the bread and wine are about to be destroyed and the person of the Saviour produced. It is taken from Bishop England's preface to his translation of the Roman missal, p. 78:

"We are now arrived at that part which is the most solemn, important and interesting of the entire; everything hitherto had reference remotely or proximately to the awful moment which approaches. For now the

ristic elements are not memorials of Christ nor visible symbols of his love: they are, after the pretended consecration of the priest, the Son of God himself. They are worshipped and adored, eaten and drunk, received into the stomach and passed into the bowels, as the Creator, Preserver and Saviour of mankind!

The ancient Egyptians, in paying religious veneration to inferior animals and to a certain class of vegetables, regarded them as sacred, as we learn from Herodotus and Cicero, on account of their subservience to purposes of utility. They were considered not as gods themselves, but as instruments of Divine Providence by which the interests of husbandry were promoted and noxious vermin were destroyed. But where in the whole history of mankind, among the darkest tribes of Africa or the benighted inhabitants of the isles of the sea, is another instance to be found of a superstition so degraded or a form of idolatry so horribly revolting as that which is presented in the doctrine of the Mass? The infernal incantation of the witches in Macbeth, chanting their awful dirges over the boiling caldron in which are mingled the elements of death, are to my mind less insupportably disgusting, less terrifically wicked, than those of the priests of Rome pretending to subject the Saviour of the world,

true victim is about to be produced. In a well-regulated cathedral this indeed is a moment of splendid, improving and edifying exhibition to the well-instructed Christian. The joyful hosannas of the organ have died away in deep and solemn notes which seem to be gradually lost as they ascend to the throne of God, and solemn silence pervades the church; the celebrant stands bareheaded, about to perform the most awful duty in which a man could possibly be engaged. His assistants in profound expectation await the performance of that duty; taper-bearers line the sides of the sanctuary, and with their lighted lamps await the arrival of their Lord; incense-bearers kneel, ready to envelope the altar in a cloud of perfumes which represents the prayers of the Saints, and at the moment of the consecration, when the celebrant elevates the host and the tinkling of a small bell gives notice of the arrival of the Lamb, every knee is bent, every head is bowed, gratulating music bursts upon the ear, and the lights which surround the throne of Him who comes to save a world are seen dimly blazing through the clouds of perfumed smoke which envelope this mystic place."

in cold-blood cruelty and for purposes of hire, and that in increasing millions of instances, to the unutterable agonies of Gethsemane and Calvary.

While she thus depresses the Divine standard of holiness, mutilates the first table of the law, and makes idolatry a part of devotion, she fabricates a standard of her own. She assumes to be a lawgiver, and proclaims her impious precepts upon the pains of the second death. Men may violate the law of God with impunity, but the authority of Rome must be guarded with the awful sanctions of eternity. She has instituted days, and months, and years; she has appointed confessions, penances and ceremonies; she has constructed a vast system of will-worship, and has conceded the palm of distinguished holiness to the sanctimonious hypocrites who most scrupulously comply with her minute and painful observances, although they may be living in flagrant contempt of some of the most palpable injunctions of God.

And what shall be said of the fiction of supererogatory merits, of the competency of one man to satisfy for the sins of another, and of the power of the Church to dispense indulgences for gold? What shall be said of purgatory, private masses, auricular confession and priestly absolution? What are all these but so many proofs of the desperate blindness of Rome in regard to the nature of holiness, the beauty and simplicity of spiritual truth, and the compass, purity and extent of the Divine law—so many monuments of presumptuous confidence in the resources and ability of man, and contempt for the provisions and efficacy of God's grace?

Her whole system in regard to the Water is fundamentally corrupt. She renders the sanctification of the Gospel hopelessly impossible, substituting for a spiritual devotion the grievous bondage of superstition, and for holiness of life the sanctimonious hypocrisy of will-worship.

(3.) Having shown that Rome is essentially unsound in regard to the Water and the Blood, I proceed to consider her doctrine of the Spirit, or the account which she gives of the application of redemption to the hearts and consciences of men. Upon this point, although the Reviewer has asserted that she holds "a much higher doctrine as to the necessity of Divine influence than prevails among many whom we •recognize as Christians," yet, according to the standard of the Reformation, the theology of the Vatican is in fatal and fundamental error. If we take the creed of Rome, not from the speculations of private doctors nor the peculiar opinions of chosen schools—Dominicans, Thomists and Jansenists—but from the public and authorized symbols of the Church, it seems to me impossible to deny that her theory of grace is exactly in accordance with the conditions of a legal system, and presents as wide a departure from the simplicity of the Gospel in regard to the operations of the Spirit as her views of justification in regard to the righteousness of Christ. Representing the economy of salvation as a new dispensation of law, she makes its blessings contingent and precarious, dependent upon the decision of its subjects and not upon the agency of God. As freedom and mutability of will are evidently essential to a state of proper probation—freedom, as implying the power to fulfil whatever conditions are exacted; mutability, as denoting that the power may be abused and the required obedience withheld—Rome can consistently admit no other operations of the Spirit than those which shall impart ability to stand without affecting the liability to fall.

Able to stand and liable to fall,—this is a compendious description of man in his condition of innocence, and must appertain to him under every economy which suspends acceptance upon personal performances. Hence, Rome places the destiny of the sinner in his own hands. *Suœ quisque fortunœ faber est.* Whatever may be her pretensions on the subject—and they are vain enough—the supernatural gifts which she attributes to the Spirit, since they are intended to qualify men for a legal dispensation, are no more entitled to be denominated grace than the natural endowments of the Pelagian.   They stand in the same relation to salvation, spring from the same source and are dispensed for the same end.   If, as Rome contends, we are the subjects of an original probation, whatever is necessary to fit us for the trial must be imparted on principles of justice; and it is a mere question of priority of time whether the necessary qualifications which must be possessed shall be traced to creation or to some act subsequent to birth: it is equally a question of words and names whether they shall be called nature or grace.   To be born with them is as truly to receive them from God as to acquire them by an extraordinary communication; and in either case they are intended to adapt us to the exigencies of a legal condition.   Gifts springing from the same source, directed to the same end, accomplishing the same results, are unquestionably of the same nature, whatever may be the order of time in which they are bestowed.   The only point in which the hypothesis of Rome has the advantage of the most unblushing Pelagianism is in relation, not to the doctrine of grace, but to the natural condition of man. In the Papal creed, the Fall, as a federal transgression, is admitted, and guilt and depravity confessed to be the inheritance of Adam's descendants.   In the Pelagian creed, it is denied to be any thing more than a private sin, and its penal consequences are accordingly restricted to the author of the act.   But both parties represent the *present* as a legal state—the Pelagian, as a continuance of our first trial, and, therefore, he supposes that we are born with all that is requisite to meet it; the Papist, as a new trial superinduced upon the ruins of the first, and therefore, as he must admit that we first reap the consequences of the original failure, he confesses that we are *born* in sin, yet because of the *new* dispensation he makes provisions to fit us for the race which is now set before us.   The creed of one has more truth, but not more *grace*, than the other, for both are equally a covenant of works, and equally destructive of the principles of the Gospel.

In conformity with this reasoning, no operations of the

Spirit can be justly denominated *grace* which leave the
decision of his destiny in the hands of the sinner. The
agency of God may be carried so far as to make men *able*
to stand, yet, if it depends upon themselves to stand or fall,
to use or reject the assistance which is given, there is nothing in such a state to distinguish it from the grossest legalism. The Spirit is evidently the *servant* not the *master* of
the man ; grace *obeys* but *does not reign*. All such schemes,
whatever honour they may pretend to ascribe to the Holy
Ghost, are insulting to God, since they lay a foundation for
boasting in the creature. That alone is grace, in the strict
and proper application of the term, which, independently
of works on our part, determines the will, and not only
makes it able to stand, but guards it against the possibility
of failure. As in justification it is the righteousness of
God that reigns to the exclusion of human obedience, so in
regeneration it is the will of God that reigns to the exclusion of that of man. This is the doctrine of the Scriptures. "Of His own will begat He us ;" "it is not
of him that willeth, nor of him that runneth, but of God
that showeth mercy." This is the only view of the subject which is consistent with the doctrine of gratuitous
justification, and hence those who have attributed a sovereignty to the human will which God cannot control without destroying its nature have invariably denied the imputation of the Saviour's righteousness. From the very
necessity of the case they must be legalists ; the reason why
one is justified and another not, they must seek in the
sinner himself, and, hence, justification cannot be wholly
irrespective of works. What is commonly called free-will
is as directly contradictory to the grace of the Spirit in
effectual calling as works of righteousness to the grace of
the Redeemer in justification. Grace must reign, or it
ceases to be grace, and the office of the human will is not
so much to concur with it as to obey it ; its efficacy consists
in removing the spirit of resistance and implanting the
spirit of obedience. "The grace of God," says Quesnel, in

his Moral Reflections on the New Testament, "is nothing else but His omnipotent will." "God," says a higher authority, "worketh in us both to will and to do of His good pleasure." All the analogies by which it is illustrated in Scripture show that in regeneration man is the subject of an almighty operation, extending to all the faculties of the soul, the will itself included. It is not a change *in* man—it is a change *of* man. In his natural condition he is as completely *nothing* in regard to the proper ends of his existence as if he possessed no being at all, and the power which recalls him from this state is as independent of his concurrence as that which originally created him from nothing. The human will, therefore, must be excluded from any participation in the work of regeneration, or grace ceases to be grace, man reigns, God is dethroned, and a legal system is established. Grace is the antithesis of the sovereignty of man. Hence, the Reformers, who reviewed the doctrines of grace, were deeply impressed with the indispensable necessity of laying deeply the foundation of the Spirit's work in the bondage of the human will. They perceived at a glance that gratuitous justification could not be maintained a moment if it depended upon man himself whether he should be justified or not. Luther, accordingly, while he denominated justification by grace the "*articulus stantis aut cadentis ecclesiæ*," attached no less importance to the resistless power of the Spirit in the new birth as that by which alone the grace of the former could be preserved. What appeared to his age his most extravagant paradoxes were put forth on the natural impotence of man. His sense of the necessity of maintaining the servitude of the will as the only adequate foundation of grace may be judged from the fact that he paid to Erasmus, who had written an elaborate defence of its freedom, the distinguished compliment of being the only champion of the Papacy who understood the controversy betwixt the Reformers and Rome. "I must acknowledge," says Luther, "that in this great controversy you alone have taken the bull by the horns."

It is evident that if the doctrine of justification were the hinge upon which the Reformation turned, the servitude of the will was the hinge upon which the controversy about justification turned. The supremacy of the Divine will and of Christ's righteousness stand or fall together. Effectual grace and free justification are inseparable elements of the same system. These precious truths carry in their bosom the kindred doctrines of personal election, final perseverance and particular redemption, which are so indissolubly united together that to deny one is logically, though not always in fact, to deny them all, and to admit one is logically, though not always in fact, to admit them all. These are the truths which combined into a system constitute pre-eminently the doctrines of grace, which, after having been buried and obscured for ages, with the exception of a cloister here and there, or a few hearts doomed to solitude and suffering, in which their light still dimly burned, burst upon the world in their original lustre at the time of the Reformation. These are the truths which bring glory to God in the highest, and distribute peace among men. They are the hope of our race, the stars which adorn the firmament of revelation. In their light we behold the sovereignty of God and the nothingness of man; here the Creator is supreme, while the creature is prostrate in the dust. They force from us the doxology of earth, "Not unto us, not unto us," and the pealing anthem of heaven, "The Lord God Omnipotent reigneth."

That Rome denies the efficacy of grace, which is equivalent to denying its reality, as contradistinguished from the qualification of a legal state, may be inferred not only from the logical necessity of her system, but from the canons of Trent and the subsequent bulls of her popes. The Tridentine Fathers affirm, in the first place, that liberty of will is not extinguished by the Fall; it is only enfeebled and bent. This cautious phraseology implies that notwithstanding the ruins and desolation of sin there yet lingers in man some germ of spiritual life, some latent susceptibility of holy emotions, which proper nourishment and care may develope into healthful exercise. Man is not dead in trespasses and sins, he is only crippled and exhausted; he does not require to be created anew, it is amply sufficient to nurse his attenuated power, to stop the progress of disease, and leave to nature the action of its *vis medicatrix*. "Free-will," says Andradius,[1] in explaining this very statement of the Council, "without the inspiration and assistance of the Spirit, cannot perform spiritual actions. This, however, does not result from the fact that the mind and will which man possesses from his birth are previously to conversion utterly destitute of any of the power, abilities or faculties which are necessary for beginning or consummating spiritual actions. It is rather because these natural abilities and faculties, though neither effaced nor extinguished, are so involved in the snares of sin that man cannot by his own strength extricate himself from the net; as he who is fettered with iron shoes may have the natural ability to walk, yet although he possesses he cannot use it and actually walk until the fetters are broken which hinder and retard his motion." Here is the famous distinction, which should always have been confined to the forges of Rome, between natural and moral ability. The sinner possesses the power to act, but his energies are restrained by superior strength. Conversion simply throws off the superincumbent pressure, and permits the wearied and exhausted faculties of man to develope and expand. Grace imparts no new susceptibilities, communicates no supernatural faculties; it only takes from the garden of nature the weeds which infest it.

An illustration similar in import to that of Andradius is employed by Bellarmine.[2] In answer to the question how the will can possess the power of contrary choice when it is unable to do good, he observes: "That the will is indeed free, but its liberty is bound and restrained; it becomes

---

[1] As quoted in Chemnitzii Exam. Conc. Trident., de Libero Arbitrio, p. 134.

[2] De Gratia et Lib. Arbit., Lib. vi., c. xv.

released and disentangled when the proximate power of
working is imparted to it by the preventing grace of God.
Something similar we experience in regard to the power of
vision where the sensible species is absent; man still possesses the power and liberty of seeing, for that species is not
the cause of either. The power, however, is remote, and
the liberty bound, until the species being present the power
is perfected and may be actually exercised."

The doctrine of Trent, then, plainly is, that man is possessed of natural though not of moral ability to comply
with the commandments of God; and if this doctrine has
recently been regarded as fatal in the Presbyterian Church,
it is hard to understand how it can be saving in the Church
of Rome. Anywhere and everywhere it breathes the spirit
of a legal covenant.

In the next place, the phrases by which Trent distinguishes the operations of the Spirit are studiously accommodated to this absurd theory of the freedom of the will.
Grace "excites" and "helps,"—expressions which obviously
imply that there are dormant energies to be stimulated and
fainting strength to be assisted.

But the most detestable feature in her theory is, that the
influences of the Spirit derive their efficacy not from the
will and power of God, but from the consent and concurrence of man. Such is the sovereignty of the human will
that all the efforts of the Almighty to regenerate the heart
may be rendered abortive by an obstinate resistance. The
will is above the reach of Deity Himself. God may persuade, but He cannot subdue. To ascribe such dominion to
man is utterly destructive of the reality of grace; and yet
Trent expressly teaches[1] that it is by the free consent and
co-operation of the sinner that the agency of God accomplishes his conversion—that he is fully competent to reject
the inspiration of the Spirit, and so is, what every subject
of a legal dispensation must be, able to stand and liable to
fall. The fourth canon on justification, though awkwardly

[1] De Justificatione, Sessio vi., cap. v.

and even absurdly expressed, was obviously aimed against the Lutheran, which is the scriptural, hypothèsis, that mán is passive in regeneration—a doctrine absolutely essential to preserve the completeness of the analogy betwixt Christ and Adam. There must be a double union with both in order that the effects of their respective covenants may be communicated to their respective seeds—a federal union, which renders their public conduct imputable, a personal union, through which it becomes actually imputed. Now the personal union with Adam, which consists in descent from his loins, is unquestionably instituted without any concurrence on our part. The very act which makes us men makes us his children, and by necessary consequence the heirs of his guilt and ruin. Why, then, should not our union with Christ, which is constituted in effectual calling, be also independent of our own co-operation? If our connection with the Head of the first covenant is confessedly involuntary, why should not the analogy be sustained and our connection with the Head of the second be equally involuntary? If the act which makes us the seed of Adam is prior to our possession of natural being, why should not the act which makes us the seed of Christ be also prior to our possession of spiritual existence? The truth is, we are new-created in Christ as we were originally created in Adam—we are the subjects of both operations, and active in neither. We can no more be our own spiritual than our natural fathers.

The attempt of the Dominicans to reconcile the Tridentine theory of grace with the doctrines of their great master, Augustine, deserves to be briefly noticed, as it has led to the impression which the Reviewer himself has sanctioned, that the decrees of the Fathers are ambiguous.[1] The Council said expressly that "man can dissent from God, exciting and calling him, if he should will to do so." This seems to be a plain denial of efficacious grace, and yet, by a quibble grossly contradictory and absurd, the Dominicans endeavoured to prove that it was not inconsistent with

[1] Princeton Review, April, 1846, p. 342.

their favourite doctrine. They admitted that man might
dissent if he should *will* to do so, but they denied that it is
possible to have such a will when the grace of God is imparted. It is the essence of grace to take from him the
power of willing to the contrary. In the midst of this
trivial sophistry, the Dominicans had forgotten what Bellarmine commends to their attention, that the Council had previously determined that man could *reject* the grace itself.
How could he reject it without a previous will? " The impossibility of willing to dissent," continues Bellarmine,[1] "is
utterly inconsistent with free-will, if it be maintained, as the
adversaries maintain, that this impossibility of willing to
dissent results from the fact that grace actively and intrinsically determines the will to the contrary. We have
already declared that man can believe or love God if he will;
that he cannot will, however, without assisting grace. There
is no inconsistency here, because free-will is feeble for good,
and therefore requires assistance. But when the assistance
is imparted, we affirm that man can will and not will, and
that in this way he is truly and properly free. But if, grace
being present, man cannot will to dissent, and grace being
absent he cannot will to consent, there is no liberty of will,
no departure from the opinion of heretics."

The Dominican interpretation is further contradicted by
notorious facts. For the space of a century and a half after
the dissolution of the Council of Trent a bitter and ferocious
controversy was waged in the Church of Rome upon the
doctrines of grace; and all the authoritative documents which
were published during that period were decidedly Semi-
pelagian, and sometimes worse. They are, to be sure, for
the most part negative, but they are negations of the fundamental truths of Christianity.

On the first of October, 1567, Pius V. issued a bull condemning the seventy-six propositions which were said to have
been extracted from the works of Baius. It is nothing to
my purpose whether or not this distinguished professor really

[1] De Gratia et Lib. Arbit., Lib. vi., cap. xv.

entertained all the sentiments which his enemies ascribe to him; it is enough to know what the oracle of the faithful pronounced to be heresy. Among the repudiated propositions are the following:

xx. No sin is of its own nature venial, but every sin deserves eternal punishment.

xxxv. All the works of unbelievers are sins, and the virtues of the philosophers are vices.

xxxvii. Free-will, without the assistance of God's grace, can do nothing but sin.

xxxviii. It is a Pelagian error to say that by free-will man can avoid any sin.

xxxix. What is done voluntarily, though it be done necessarily, is done freely.

xli. The only liberty which the Scriptures recognize is not from necessity, but sin.

lxv. To admit any good use of free-will, or any which is not evil, is Pelagian error, and he does injury to the grace of Christ who so thinks and teaches.

lxvi. Violence alone is repugnant to the natural liberty of man.

When the authenticity of the bull denouncing these propositions had been seriously called into question, it was solemnly confirmed by a constitution of Gregory XIII., bearing date the 28th of January, 1579.

Upon the infallible authority of two popes, Urban VIII., in 1642, and Innocent X., in 1653, five propositions, purporting to be taken from the Augustine of Jansen, were subjected to the odious imputation of heresy. These propositions asserted the impotency of man, the invincibility of grace, the certainty of predestination, and the definite nature of the atonement. I give them in order:

i. There are some commands of God which righteous and good men are absolutely unable to obey, though disposed to do it; and God does not give them so much grace that they are able to observe them.

II. Inward grace in the state of fallen nature cannot be resisted.

III. To constitute merit or demerit in the state of fallen nature, man does not require liberty from necessity; liberty from coercion being sufficient.

IV. The Semi-pelagians admitted the necessity of inward preventing grace to every act, even the beginning of faith, but their heresy consisted in this—that they maintained this grace to be such that the human will could resist or restrain it.

V. It is Semi-pelagian to say that Christ died for all men.

The first of these propositions is condemned as "rash, impious, blasphemous, heretical;" the second and third are declared to be "heretical;" the fourth is pronounced to be "false and heretical;" and all the vials of pontifical abuse seem to be emptied on the fifth; it is denominated "impious, blasphemous, contumelious, derogatory to piety, and heretical."[1]

The last document to which I shall refer is the memorable constitution *Unigenitus*, signed by Clement XI. at Rome on Friday, the 8th of September, 1713, the birthday, as Romanists assert, of the Immaculate Virgin. This Bull,[2] the professed design of which was to condemn one hundred and one propositions extracted from the work of Quesnel, entitled Moral Reflections upon each verse of the New Testament, contains a formal reprobation of the distinguishing doctrines of grace. How far in each case the censure extends it is difficult to determine. The propositions are "respectively" denounced as "false, captious, shocking, offensive to pious ears, scandalous, pernicious, rash, injurious to the Church and her practice, contumelious not only against the Church, but likewise against the secular powers, seditious, impious, blasphemous, suspected of heresy and plainly savouring thereof, and likewise favouring here-

---

[1] Leydekker's Historici Jansenismi, pp. 126, 278.   Mosheim, vol. iii., p. 332.

[2] I have made my extracts from the copy given in Lafitau's History of it.

tics, heresies and schism, erroneous, bordering very near upon heresy, often condemned, and in fine even heretical and manifestly reviving several heresies, and chiefly those which are contained in the infamous propositions of Jansenius, even in the very sense in which those propositions were condemned." The term "respectively" indicates that this medley of epithets is to be distributed—that all are not to be applied to each proposition, but only that each epithet should find a counterpart in some proposition, and each proposition be embraced under some epithet. But the allusion to Jansenius shows that, whatever may be said of the rest, the propositions containing his doctrines are to be regarded as heretical.

Among the one hundred and one condemned articles are the following truths of the Word of God, numbered as they are numbered in the Bull:

I. What else remains to the soul that has lost God and His grace but sin and the consequences of sin, haughty poverty and lazy indigence—that is, a general impotence to labour, to prayer, and to every good work?

II. The grace of Jesus Christ, the efficacious principle of every sort of good, is necessary to every good work; without it nothing either is done or can be done.

V. When God does not soften the heart by the inward unction of His grace, exhortations and external advantages serve only to harden it the more.

IX. The grace of Jesus Christ is sovereign; without it we can never confess Christ, and with it we shall never deny him.

X. Grace is the operation of God's almighty hand, which nothing can let or hinder.

XII. When God wills to save a soul at any time or place, the effect indubitably follows the determination of His will.

XIII. Whenever God wills to save a soul, and touches it with the inward hand of His grace, no human will resists Him.

XIV. However remote an obstinate sinner may be from

salvation, whenever Jesus is revealed to him in the saving light of His grace, he yields, embraces Him, humbles himself and adores the Saviour.

xix. The grace of God is nothing else than His omnipotent will. This is the idea which God Himself gives us in all the Scriptures.

xxi. The grace of Jesus Christ is strong, mighty, sovereign, invincible, being the operation of God's almighty will, the consequence and imitation of the working of God in making the Son incarnate and raising Him from the dead.

xxiii. God has given us the idea of the almighty working of His grace in representing it as a creation out of nothing, and a resurrection from the dead.

xxx. All whom God wills to save by Christ are infallibly saved.

xxxviii. The sinner is free only to evil without the grace of the Saviour.

xxxix. The will, without preventing grace, has light only to wander, heat only for rashness, strength only to its wounding. It is capable of all evil and incapable of any good.

xli. Even the natural knowledge of God, such as obtained among the Gentile philosophers, must be ascribed to God, and without grace produces only presumption, vanity and opposition to God, instead of adoration, gratitude and love.

lxix. Faith, its use, increase and reward, are wholly the gift of God's pure liberality.

lxxiii. What is the Church but the congregation of the sons of God, dwelling in His bosom, adopted in Christ, subsisting in His person, redeemed by His blood, living by His Spirit, acting by His grace, and waiting for the grace of the future life?

These documents establish by the most conclusive negative testimony that Rome repudiates the only theory of grace which can bring salvation to the lost. She utterly denies its power. The terms *efficacious grace* are indeed found in the writings of her cherished theologians, but in a sense widely different from that which the Reformers taught. It is an efficacy consisting in the skilful adaptation of motives on the part of God to the mind of man, by which the will is determined in conformity with the Divine desire. God does not determine it, but only presents considerations which from His knowledge of the man He perceives beforehand will induce it to determine itself. It is the efficacy not of power, but of persuasion; God acts the part not of a sovereign, but of an able orator. "It cannot be understood," says Bellarmine,[1] "how efficacious grace consists in an inward persuasion which may be spurned by the will, and yet infallibly accomplishes its end, unless we add that with all those whom God has infallibly decreed to draw He employs a persuasion which He sees to be adapted to their disposition, and which He certainly knows will not be despised."

It is not a little strange that Princeton should attribute to Rome a "much higher doctrine as to the necessity of Divine influence than prevails among many whom we recognize as Christians," when the orthodox portion of the Protestant world has . already condemned her opinions. The creed of Rome differs only for the worse from the creed of the Remonstrants; it is not so full and clear upon the subject of depravity, and much bolder on the freedom of the will. Still their respective theories of grace are substantially the same, and if the orthodox world in the seventeenth century conspired to suppress the errors of the Remonstrants as dangerous and fatal, what magic has extracted their malignity in the lapse of two hundred years and upward, so that they are harmless in the hands of the Pope? So striking is the similarity between the principles of the Remonstrants and the decrees of Trent that I am constrained to place them in a note in juxtaposition, that the reader may see at a glance what Princeton denominates a "much higher doctrine as to the necessity of Divine influ-

[1] De Gratia et Lib. Arbit., Lib. I., cap. xii., last sentence.

ence than prevails among many whom we recognize as Christians."[1] Both seem willing to ascribe everything to God but the conquest of the will. He may teach, enlighten, remonstrate and persuade, but He cannot subdue. The will sits as a sovereign upon her throne, and can laugh at all His thunder.

[1] I. "Man," say the Remonstrants,* "has not saving faith himself, nor by virtue of his own free-will, forasmuch as, being in a state of sin, he can neither think, will nor do by or of himself any good, especially such as proceeds from a saving faith. But it is necessary he should be regenerated and renewed by God in Christ through His Holy Spirit in his understanding, will and all his faculties, to the end that he may rightly understand, reflect upon, will and fulfil the things which are good and which accompany salvation.

II. "But we maintain that the grace of God is not only the beginning, but likewise the progress and completion, of all good; insomuch that even the regenerate themselves are not able without this previous or preventing, exciting, concomitant, and consequent grace to think, will or effect any good thing, or resist any temptation to evil; so that all good works and actions ought to be ascribed to God.

III. "Nevertheless, we do not believe that all the zeal, care and pains employed by men in order to the working out their salvation are before Faith and the spirit of Renovation vain and unprofitable, and even more prejudicial than advantageous; but on the contrary we maintain, that to hear the Word of God, to be sorry for and repent of our sins, earnestly to desire saving grace and the spirit of Renovation (which, however, cannot be done without grace), are not only not hurtful, but rather very useful and absolutely necessary to the attaining Faith and the spirit of Renovation.

IV. "The will has no power, in the state of sin and before the call, of doing any good to salvation. And, therefore, we deny that the will has, in every state of man, the liberty or freedom of willing the saving good as well as evil.

V. "Efficacious grace whereby men are converted is not irresistible, and though God works in such a manner by His Word and the internal operation of His Spirit as to communicate the power of believing and supernatural strength, and even to cause men actually to believe, yet, nevertheless, men may of themselves reject this grace, and refuse to believe, and consequently be lost through their own fault."

"In the first place," says Trent,† "the holy council maintains that it is necessary, in order to understand the doctrine of justification truly and well, that every one should acknowledge and confess that since all men

* See Brandt, History of the Reformation, vol. iii., book xxxv., pp. 87, 88.
† Concil. Trident., Sess. vi., cap. i., cap. v., can. vii.

If the creed of Rome is fatally unsound in regard to the nature of Effectual Calling, there is nothing to redeem its errors, but much to heighten its dangers, in what it teaches of the reason, office and operations of Faith, in the production of which the mystical union is completed, and upon which the whole application of redemption depends. The calling, indeed, is never effectual, and the condition of the sinner is never safe, until faith is actually wrought. To it all the promises of salvation are addressed; it is pre-eminently the work of God, that which He requires at our hands, without which it is impossible to please Him, with which it is impossible to be condemned. It is the characteristic principle of Christian life, comprising in its nature and results the whole mystery of Christian experience. " I am crucified with Christ: nevertheless I live; yet, not I, but Christ liveth in me : and the life which I now live in the flesh, I live by the faith of the Son of God, who loved me and gave Himself for me." The blessedness and joy, the light, fortitude and

had lost innocence by Adam's prevarication, and had become unclean, and, as the Apostle says, 'by nature children of wrath,' as is expressed in the decree on original sin, they are so completely the slaves of sin, and under the power of the Devil and of death, that neither could the Gentiles be liberated or rise again by the power of nature, nor even the Jews by the letter of the law of Moses. Nevertheless, free-will was not wholly extinct in them, though weakened and bowed down.

"The Council further declares that in adult persons the beginning of justification springs from the preventing grace of God through Christ Jesus—that is, from His calling wherewith they are called, having in themselves no merits—so that those who in consequence of sin were alienated from God are disposed to betake themselves to His method of justifying them by His grace, which excites and helps them, and with which grace they freely agree and co-operate. Thus, while God touches the heart of man by the illumination of His Holy Spirit, man is not altogether passive, since he receives that influence which he had power to reject, while on the other hand he could not of his free will, without the grace of God, take any step toward righteousness before Him.

"Whoever shall affirm that all works done before justification, in whatever way performed, are actually sins and deserve God's hatred, or that the more earnestly a man labours to dispose himself for grace he does but sin the more, let him be accursed."

peace, the hopes which stimulate the zeal and the beauties which adorn the character of those who love God, their change of state and the gradual transformation of their minds, are all in the Scriptures ascribed to faith. Without it the Water and the Blood are nothing worth; the invitations of the Gospel, the monitions of Providence, the persuasions of the ministry, and even the signs in the holy sacraments, are vain and nugatory, lifeless appeals, which play around the head or amuse the fancy, but are incapable of reaching the heart. The spirit of faith is the spirit of life. Faith justifies the guilty and cleanses the impure; faith is the shield in the panoply of God which quenches all the fiery darts of the wicked, the victory which overcomes the world and extracts lessons of experience from trials of patience. Faith conquers death and opens the kingdom of heaven to the triumphant saint; it is the substance of things hoped for, the evidence of things not seen.

The contrast is amazing betwixt the importance which the Scriptures everywhere attach to this grace, and that which is assigned to it in the theology of Rome. While, according to the unvarying tenor of the Gospel, which is, Believe and be saved, faith is the first, second, third thing, comprehending everything else in the department of personal religion, according to the creed of the Papacy it is at best a very slender accomplishment, having no necessary connection with salvation, capable of existing among those who are without Christ, without God, and without hope in the world. It may distinguish as well the victim of perdition as the heirs of heaven. The single fact that Rome declares that believers may be lost, while the Bible asserts that every believer shall be saved, is conclusive proof that her theology and that of the Bible are fundamentally at variance.

There are two principal points, in connection with this subject, in regard to which she is grossly and fatally unsound—the relation of faith to the Christian life, and the immediate reason of faith itself.

First. The distinguished efficacy which the Scriptures uniformly attribute to this grace does not depend upon its own intrinsic excellence, nor the natural operation of the truths, important as they are, which it receives and assimilates. These, however exalted, however cordially embraced, however admirably adapted to generate the active principles of love, hope and fear, could never achieve the splendid results which proceed from the influence of faith. As an accomplishment of the spiritual man, an integral element of inherent righteousness, charity is certainly entitled to precedence, yet charity is never said to justify; it applies neither the Water nor the Blood, but presupposes the application of them both. It is not, then, as a grace, or an act of formal obedience to the authority of God, that faith perform its wonders. The source of its power is not in itself—in moral dignity and worth it is the least of graces —nor in the propositions, abstractly considered, which it brings in contact with the understanding and the heart; the result of these could only be the production of diligence, zeal, gratitude, love, hope and fear, which, singly or combined, avail nothing in the justification of the guilty. The secret of its efficacy lies in its relation to Christ. It is a bond of union with Him. As an exercise of holiness it has its appropriate place among the elements of personal obedience. It receives the whole revelation of God, and becomes the medium through which the different emotions are excited which the various aspects of the Word are suited to inspire. Through it Divine truth penetrates the heart, presenting the terrible majesty of God, to the consternation of the guilty, and disclosing the ineffable tenderness of His love, to the consolation of the humble; but faith saves us, not because it believes the truth, but because it unites us as living members with a living Head. It is not the believer that lives or works; it is Christ who lives in him. He is our life, and faith is the channel through which His grace is efficaciously imparted. He dwells in us by His Spirit, and we dwell in Him by faith. And as He possesses

all the elements of salvation in Himself—wisdom, righteousness, sanctification and redemption—faith, which cements
a union with His person, must involve communion in His
graces. As He is emphatically the LIFE, those who are
possessed of the Son must be possessed of life. We are
justified by faith, because, in connecting us with Christ it
makes us partakers of His righteousness and death. We
are sanctified by faith, because the Spirit is communicated
from the Head to the members, revealing the true standard
of holiness in the person of the Son, presenting the true
motives of holiness in the grace and promises of the Gospel,
implanting operative principles of holiness in gratitude,
love, hope and fear, and giving efficacy to all subordinate
means by the omnipotent energy of His will. Faith saves
us, because it joins us to Him who is salvation, and who is
able to save to the uttermost all that come unto God through
Him. Such is its potency. Nothing in itself, it makes us
one with Christ; by it we suffer with Him, we die with
Him, we are buried with Him, we rise with Him, and with
Him we are destined to reign in glory.

Rome, however, knows nothing of this mystical union
with Christ, and consequently the only efficacy which she
attributes to faith in the application of redemption is that
of a spiritual grace, constituting one of the elements of the
formal cause of justification. It is a part of the righteousness in which the sinner is accepted before God. "The
principal reason," says Bellarmine,[1] "why our adversaries
attribute justification to faith alone is because they suppose
that faith does not justify after the manner of a cause, or
on account of its dignity and worth, but only relatively, as
it receives in believing what God offers in the promise.
For if they could be convinced that faith justifies by procuring, meriting, and, in its own way, beginning justification, they would undoubtedly acknowledge that the same
might be predicated of love, patience and other good acts.
We shall prove, therefore, that true and justifying faith is

---

[1] Bellarmine, De Justificatione, Lib. i., cap. xvii.; cf. Lib. i., cap. iii.

not, as the adversaries affirm, a naked and sole apprehension of righteousness, but is an efficacious cause of justification. All the arguments to this point may be reduced to three heads. The first shall be taken from those testimonies which teach that faith is a cause of justification in general, the second those which prove that in faith justification is begun, the third from those which demonstrate that by faith we please God, and procure and in some way merit justification." In developing these arguments Bellarmine repeatedly ridicules the idea that faith is an instrument which apprehends the righteousness of Christ. According to him, it contributes to our justification only in so far as it is an act of righteousness itself—its value depending not upon its relation to Christ, but upon its own intrinsic excellence. Its inherent dignity and worth are an element of personal holiness. To the same purport the Council of Trent declares that[1] "we are said to be justified by faith, because faith is the *beginning* of human salvation —the foundation and root of all justification, without which it is impossible to please God and come into the fellowship of His children." In other words, faith is the *first* grace which among adults enters into the disposition or the state of heart which is preparatory to the reception of this great blessing. It is the *first* element of righteousness which is infused into the soul, and, as being first and intimately connected with all the rest, it is the root and foundation of a holy life. But its only influence is that which it possesses as an inward grace, meritorious in itself, and capable, through the truth which it embraces, of generating other motions of good. But as the righteousness in which we are accepted must correspond to all the requisitions of the law, and as faith alone is only a partial obedience, Rome teaches that it must be combined with other graces, particularly with charity, in order to secure our justification. Charity indeed she pronounces to be the end, perfection and form of all other virtues. Without it, faith is unfinished

[1] Trident. Concil., Sess. vi., cap. viii.

and dead, incapable of meriting life or of commending to the favour of God.

If there be any one doctrine of the Bible against which Rome is particularly bitter, it is that we are justified by faith alone, without the deeds of the law. This principle strikes at the root of the whole system of infused and inherent righteousness. It removes all occasion of glorying in the flesh. It prostrates the sinner in the dust, and makes Christ the Alpha and Omega, the beginning and the end, the all-in-all of human hope. Hence, Trent enumerates no less than *seven acts*[1] as constituting the disposition preparatory to the reception of justification, among which faith is found, and *it* entitled to no other pre-eminence than that it is the first in the series, having, from the nature of its operations, a tendency and fitness to excite the rest. Hence, also, it pronounces[2] its anathema upon all who, in conformity with the Scriptures, shall affirm " that the ungodly is justified by faith only, so that it is to be understood that nothing else is to be required to co-operate therewith in order to obtain justification, and that it is on no account necessary that he should prepare and dispose himself to the effort of his own will." Hence, too, the doctrine of imputation is condemned, being consistent with no other hypothesis but that which makes faith a bond of union with Christ as a federal Head, appropriating His obedience and pleading the merits of His death. " Whosoever shall affirm that men are justified only by the imputation of the righteousness of Christ or the remission of sin, to the exclusion

---

[1] Trident. Concil., Sess. vi., cap. vi. Bellarmine remarks—De Justificatione, Lib. i., cap. xii.—" The adversaries, therefore, as we have before said, teach that justification is acquired or apprehended by faith alone. Catholics, on the other hand, and especially the Tridentine Synod, which all Catholics acknowledge as a mistress (Sess. vi., cap. 6), enumerates seven acts by which the ungodly are disposed to righteousness: faith, fear, hope, love, repentance, the purpose of receiving the sacrament, and the purpose of leading a new life and keeping the commandments of God." This opinion he endeavours in several successive chapters to establish.

[2] Conc. Trident., Sess. vi., can. ix.

of grace and charity, which is shed abroad in their hearts and inheres in them, or that the grace by which we are justified is only the favour of God, let him be accursed." [1]

It cannot fail to be observed that the Romish theory of faith is peculiarly unfavourable to the cultivation of humility. Abstracting the attention from the fullness and sufficiency of Christ, and dignifying personal obedience into a meritorious cause of salvation, it must bloat the heart with spiritual pride, and generate a temper of invidious comparison with others, equally fatal to the charity which thinketh no evil and the self-abasement which should characterize debtors to grace. When the efficacy of faith is attributed to the relation which it institutes with Christ, it is felt to be nothing in itself; every blessing is ascribed to the sovereign mercy of God; it is no more the sinner that lives, but Christ lives in him; it is no more the sinner that works, but Christ works in him. The Divine Redeemer becomes the all-in-all of his salvation—his wisdom, righteousness, sanctification and redemption. It is only when faith is apprehended as a bond of union with Christ that it produces the effect which Paul attributes to it, of excluding boasting; in every other view it furnishes a pretext for glorying in the flesh. As an instrument it exalts the Redeemer; as a meritorious grace, entering into the formal cause of justification, it exalts the sinner: as an instrument it leads us to exclaim that by the grace of God we are what we are; as a meritorious grace, to thank God that we are not as other men.

Secondly. The Papal creed is hardly less unsound in reference to the nature, than it is in reference to the office, of faith.

If there be anything in the Scriptures clearly revealed and earnestly inculcated, it is that the faith by which we apprehend the Redeemer as the foundation of our hope depends upon the *immediate testimony* of God. It is supernatural in its *evidence*, as well as supernatural in its origin.

[1] Conc. Trident., Sess. vi., can. xi.

The record which God has given of His Son bears upon its face impressions of Divinity which are alike suited to command the assent of the understanding and to captivate the affections of the heart.

The argument by which we ascend from redemption to its Author is analogous to that (though infinitely stronger in degree) which conducts us from nature to nature's God. The Almighty never works without leaving traces of Himself; a godlike peculiarity distinguishes all His operations. He cannot ride upon the heavens but His name *Jah* is proclaimed; the invisible things of Him, from the creation of the world, are clearly seen, being understood by the things that are made, even His eternal power and Godhead. But if the material workmanship of God contains such clear and decisive traces of its Divine Author—if the heavens declare His glory and the firmament showeth his handiwork—if sun, moon and stars, in their appointed orbits, demonstrate an eternal Creator, and leave the Atheist, skeptic and idolater without excuse—much more shall that stupendous economy of grace which bears pre-eminently the burden of His name reveal the perfections of His character and authenticate the Divinity of its source. The evidence that it sprang from the bosom of God, and that its voice is the harmony of the world, must be sought in itself. It stands a temple not built with hands, bearing upon its portals the sublime inscription of God's eternal purpose, of His wisdom, power, justice, goodness and grace. It is the palace of the great King, where His brightest glories are disclosed, His choicest gifts bestowed. Jesus is seen, is felt to be the image of the invisible God, the first-born of every creature. The believer has only to look upon His face, and he beholds His glory as of the only-begotten of the Father, full of grace and truth. God, who commanded the light to shine out of darkness, has shined into our hearts, and revealed the light of the knowledge of the glory of God in the face of Jesus Christ.

But while redemption contains the evidence of its heav-

enly origin, such is the deplorable darkness of the human
understanding in regard to things that pertain to God, and
such the fearful alienation of men from the perfection of
His character, that though the light shines conspicuously
among them, they are yet unable to comprehend its rays.
Christ crucified proves to all, in their natural condition,
whether Jews or Gentiles, a stumbling-block or foolishness.
Hence, to the production of faith there must be a heavenly
calling. In order that the infallible evidence which actually
exists in the truth itself may accomplish its appropriate
effects, the eternal Spirit, who sends forth His cherubim
and seraphim to touch the lips of whom He pleases, must
be graciously vouchsafed to illuminate the darkened mind,
and manifest in the provision of the Gospel the power of
God and the wisdom of God unto salvation. It is the
Spirit that quickeneth; the flesh profiteth nothing. Redemption is a spiritual mystery, and faith is the spiritual
eye, supernaturally imparted, which beholds it. He that
believeth hath the witness in himself: the divine illumination of the Spirit is the immediate and only reason of a
true and living faith. Other arguments may *convince,* but
they cannot *convert;* they may produce *opinion,* but not the
faith of the Gospel; and those who, in their blindness, rely
upon miracles and prophecy—upon the collateral and incidental proofs with which Christianity is triumphantly
vindicated from the assaults of skeptics and infidels—they
who rely upon the fallible deductions of reason to generate
an infallible assurance of faith have yet to learn in what
the testimony of God consists which establishes the hearts
of His children. *Their* witness is not within themselves;
it lies without them—in historical records, musty traditions
and the voice of antiquity. ·

The Romish doctors are not reluctant to admit that faith
is supernatural in its origin. "Whoever shall affirm," says
Trent,[1] "that man is able to believe, hope, love or repent,
as he ought, so as to attain to the grace of justification,

[1] Conc. Trident., Sess. vi., can. iii.

without the preventing influence and aid of the Holy
Spirit, let him be accursed." "It is impossible," says
Stapleton, as quoted by Owen,[1] "to produce any act of
faith, or to believe with faith, rightly so called, without
special grace and the Divine infusion of the gift of faith."
"This is firmly to be held," says Melchior Canus [2]—I again
quote from Owen—"that human authority, and all the motives before mentioned, or any other which may be used
by him who proposeth the object of faith to be believed,
are not sufficient causes of believing as we are obliged to
believe; but there is moreover necessary an internal, efficient
cause, moving us to believe, which is the especial help or
aid of God. Wherefore all external human persuasions or
arguments are not sufficient causes of faith, however the
things of faith may be sufficiently proposed by men; there
is moreover necessary an internal cause—that is, a certain
Divine light, inciting to believe, or certain internal eyes
to see, given us by the grace of God." But there is a
still more remarkable passage in Gregory of Valentia.[3]
"Whereas," saith he, "we have hitherto pleaded arguments
for the authority of Christian doctrine, which, even by
themselves, ought to suffice prudent persons to induce their
minds to belief; yet I know not whether there be not an
argument greater than they all—namely, that those who are
truly Christians do find or feel by experience their minds
so affected in this matter of faith that they are moved (and
obliged) firmly to believe, neither for any argument that we
have used, nor for any of the like sort that can be found
out by reason, but for somewhat else, which persuades our
minds in another manner, and far more effectually than any
arguments whatever." "It is God Himself, who, by the
voice of His revelation, and by a certain internal instinct
and impulse, witnesseth unto the minds of men the truth
of Christian doctrine or of the Holy Scripture." And the

[1] Owen on the Reason of Faith: Works, vol. iii., p. 364.
[2] Ibid., pp. 364, 365.
[3] Ibid., p. 365.

same doctrine is maintained by Bellarmine in the second chapter of his sixth book on grace and free-will.

All this seems wonderfully orthodox. But it is a deceitful homage rendered to the work of the Spirit. Rome grants that He enables us to believe, but departs widely from the truth, and assigns to the Spirit a mean and subsidiary office, when she undertakes to specify the evidence through which He produces a living faith. The immediate end of His illumination, according to her theology, is not to reveal the evidence which lies concealed in the Gospel itself, but to ascertain the inquirer of the Divinity of her own testimony. The office of the Spirit is to prove that she is the prophet of God, His lively oracle, which must be devoutly heard and implicitly obeyed. The testimony of the Church, and not of God's Spirit, she makes to be the immediate and adequate ground of faith. Whatever light the Spirit imparts is reflected from her face, and not from the face of Jesus Christ; and whatever witness the believer possesses, he possesses in her, and not in himself. Hence Stapleton,[1] while he admits the necessity of Divine illumination, gives it a principal reference to the judgment and testimony of the Church. "The secret testimony of the Spirit is altogether necessary, that a man may believe the testimony and judgment of the Church about the Scriptures." Bellarmine says,[2] "in order that faith may be certain in relation to its object, two infallible causes are required—the cause revealing the articles, and the cause proposing or declaring the articles revealed. For if he who reveals, and upon whose authority we rely, can be deceived, faith is obviously rendered uncertain. Therefore, the cause revealing should be none other than God. And, by parity of reason, if he who proposes or declares the articles revealed is liable to error, and can propose anything as a Divine revelation which in fact is not so, faith will be rendered wholly uncertain. Mohammedans and heretics therefore, although they suppose that they be-

[1] Owen on the Reason of Faith: Works, vol. iii., p. 365.
[2] Bellarmine, De Grat. et Lib. Arbit., Lib. vi., cap. iii.

lieve on the ground of a Divine revelation, yet in fact they
do not, but simply believe because they rashly choose to
believe, inasmuch as they acknowledge not a cause infallibly
proposing and declaring the revelation of God. For if one
should inquire of the heretics how they know that God has
revealed this or that article, they will answer, From the
Scriptures. If it should be further inquired how they
know that their interpretation of Scripture is correct, seeing
that it is differently expounded by different persons, or how
they ever know that the Scriptures are the Word of God,
they can answer nothing but that this is their opinion. They
reject the judgment of the Church, which alone God has
declared to be infallible by numberless signs and prodigies
and many other testimonies, and every one claims for himself the right of interpreting Divine Revelation. Who,
without great rashness, can believe his own private judgment of Divine things to be infallible, since such infallibility
can be proved neither by Divine promise nor human reason ?
Catholics, on the other hand, have a faith altogether certain
and infallible, since it rests on the authority of revelation.
That God has given the revelation they are equally assured,
since they hear the Church declaring the fact, which they are
certain cannot err, since its testimony is confirmed by signs and
wonders and manifold arguments." Whatever the Church
authoritatively enjoins is a material object of faith. "The
authority of the Church," says Dens, "affords the first and
sufficient argument of credibility."[1] The Rules of Faith
are divided by Dens[2] into two classes, animate and inanimate,
the latter comprehending the Holy Scriptures and tradition,
and the former embracing the Church, General Councils and
the Pope. "The animate rule of faith is that which declares
to us the truths which God has revealed, so that it may propose them with sufficient authority to be believed as it were

[1] Dens, De Virtutibus, vol. ii., No. 18, p. 27.
[2] Dens, De Regulis Fidei, vol. ii., No. 59, p. 93. See particularly De
Resolutione Fidei, vol. ii., No. 20, p. 30.

by a Divine faith." Even Erasmus,[1] half-reformer as he
was, could utter such detestable language as the following:
"With me the authority of the Church has so much weight
that I could be of the same opinion with Arians and Pelagians, had the Church signified its approbation of their doctrines. It is not that the words of Christ are not to me
sufficient, but it should not seem strange if I follow the
interpretation of the Church, through whose authority it
is that I believe the canonical Scriptures. Others may have
more genius and courage than I, but there is nothing in
which I acquiesce more confidently than the decisive judgment of the Church."

It is a point on which all Romanists are heartily agreed,
that somewhere in the Papacy, either in the Pope, a General
Council, or the Pope and a General Council combined, an
infallible tribunal exists, whose prerogative it is to settle
controversies and to determine questions of faith. From its
decisions there is no appeal; its voice is the voice of God—
it is the Urim and Thummim of the Christian Church.
The possession of such a living oracle is made the distinguishing glory of their sect. The doctors of Rome are
accustomed to boast that in consequence of this boon they
have the advantage of an infallible faith, while Protestants
are doomed to the uncertainty of opinion or the delusions
of a private spirit. Their Divine faith consequently depends upon the testimony of an infallible church, and not
upon the witness of the Spirit of truth. They believe because the Church declares, and of course must believe what
the Church declares. The practical working of the system
is to make every parish priest and every father confessor a
lord alike of the conscience and understanding. Every
man, upon the Papal hypothesis, no matter what may be his
condition and attainments, has infallible evidence that the
material objects of his faith are Divine revelations. But to
the great mass of private individuals the testimony of their

[1] Erasmus, as quoted in Waddington's History of the Reformation, vol.
ii., chap. xxiii., p. 165.

priests or confessors is all the evidence that they can have, and hence these priests and confessors must themselves be infallible. " Though there have been infinite disputes," says a writer in the Edinburgh Review, "as to where the infallibility resides, what are the doctrines it has definitively pronounced true, and who to the individual is the infallible expounder of what is thus infallibly pronounced infallible, yet he who receives this doctrine in its integrity has nothing more to do than to eject his reason, sublime his faith into credulity, and reduce his creed to these two comprehensive articles: ' I believe whatsoever the Church believes ;' ' I believe that the Church believes whatsoever my father confessor believes that she believes.' For thus he reasons: Nothing is more certain than whatsoever God says is infallibly true ; it is infallibly true that the Church says just what God says ; it is infallibly true that what the Church says is known ; and it is infallibly true that my father confessor or the parson of the next parish is an infallible expositor of what is thus infallibly known to be the Church's infallible belief, or what God has declared to be infallibly true. If any one of the links, even the last, in this strange *sorites* be supposed unsound, if it be not true that the priest is an infallible expounder to the individual of the Church's infallibility, if his judgment be only ' private judgment,' we come back at once to the perplexities of the common theory of private judgment."

Now, as the whole doctrine of Papal infallibility is a fiction, all pretences to a Divine illumination which reveals it must be a delusion of the Devil, and that faith which rests upon nothing but the testimony of men, whether collectively or individually, whether called a church, pope or council, is human, earthly, fallible—it is not the faith of God's elect. The degree of assent should rise no higher than the evidence which produces it ; and as the Romanist can never be assured that his Church is inspired, he can never have assurance, according to his principles, that Jesus Christ is the Saviour of men, much less can he be assured of his own interest in the Redeemer. Doubt, perplexity, apprehension and uncertainty must characterize his whole Christian experience.[1] As faith is measured by the testimony of the Church, and it is not the office of the Church to disclose the state of individuals, none can be certain of their own conversion or order their cause with confidence before God. They may hope for the best, but still, after all, it may be their fate to endure the worst. Unquestionably, the direct witness of the Spirit to the fact of our conversion is one of the most comfortable elements of Christian experience. It is the only evidence which is productive of full and triumphant assurance; and yet upon the hypothesis of Rome, which interposes the Church betwixt the sinner and Christ, it is difficult to conceive how the Spirit can impart this testimony to the hearts of God's children. It is, therefore, in consistency with the analogy of her faith that she denounces her anathema[2] upon those who pretend to assert that they know that they have passed from death unto life by the Spirit which God hath given them. "It is on no account to be maintained that those who are really justified ought to feel fully assured of the fact without any doubt whatever, or that none are absolved and justified but those who believe themselves to be so; or that, by this faith only, absolution and justification are procured, as if he who does not believe this doubts the promise of God and the efficacy of the death and the resurrection of Christ. For while no godly person ought to doubt the mercy of God, the merit of Christ or the virtue and efficacy of the sacraments, so, on the other hand, whosoever considers his own infirmity and corruption may doubt and fear whether he is in a state of grace, since no one can certainly and infallibly know that he has obtained the grace of God."

So important an element of personal religion is the direct witness of the Spirit that where it is cordially embraced it

---

[1] See this subject discussed in Dens, De Justificatione, vol. ii., No. 31, p. 452, seq.

[2] Conc. Trident., Sess. vi., cap. ix.

will infuse vitality into a dead system, counteract the principles of a professed Remonstrant, and mould his experience into a type of doctrine which he ostensibly rejects. It is the redeeming feature of modern Arminianism; to it the school of Wesley is indebted for its power; it is a green spot in the desert, a refreshing brook in the wilderness. Wherever it penetrates the heart it engenders a spirit of dependence upon God, a practical conviction of human imbecility, and an earnest desire for supernatural expressions of Divine favour. It maintains a constant communion with the Father of lights, an habitual anxiety to walk with God, which, whatever may be the theory of grace, keeps the soul in a posture of prayer, and cherishes a temper congenial with devotion and holiness. He that seeks for the witness of the Spirit must wait upon God; and he that obtains it has learned from the fruitlessness of his own efforts, his hours of darkness and desertion, his long agony and conflicts, that it is a boon bestowed in sovereignty, the gift of unmerited grace. It is through this doctrine that the personality of the Spirit as an element of Christian experience is most distinctly presented. It compels us to adore Him as a living Agent working according to the counsel of His will, and not to underrate Him as a mere influence connecting moral results with their causes. Rome, consequently, in discarding this doctrine from her creed, has discarded the only principle which could impregnate the putrid mass of her corruptions with the seeds of health and vigour.

Thirdly. Not satisfied with displacing faith from its proper position, and corrupting the evidence by which it is produced, Rome proceeds to still greater abominations in ascribing to the sacraments the same results in the application of redemption which the Scriptures are accustomed to ascribe to faith. The mode of operation, however, is vastly different. The sacraments, according to the Papal hypothesis, are possessed of an inherent efficacy to generate the graces which render us acceptable to God, while faith, accord-

ing to the scriptural hypothesis, makes us one with Christ.
The sacraments, according to Rome, enable us to live.
Faith, according to the Scriptures, makes us die, and Christ
lives in us. The sacraments, according to Rome, are
efficient causes of salvation. Faith, according to the Scriptures, is but an instrument which appropriates and applies
it. In the operation of the sacraments, therefore, Rome
combines the work of the Spirit and the functions of faith.
By baptism we are alike regenerated and justified; whatever takes place before the administration of the ordinance
is only in the way of preparation: that which crowns the
whole, and actually introduces us into a state of favour, is
the reception of the sacrament.[1] Those, too, who subsequently to baptism have fallen into mortal sin are recovered from their error, not by the renewed exercise of faith
in the Son of God, but by the fictitious sacrament of penance. The weak are established, not by looking unto
Jesus, the Author and Finisher of faith, and praying for
the unction from the Holy One which shall enable them to
know all things, but by submitting to episcopal manipula-
tion and trusting to episcopal anointing. If the soul feeds
upon the body and blood of the Redeemer, it is not as the
food of faith to the spiritual man, but the food of sense to
the natural man, which, instead of uniting us to Christ,
assimilates Him to our mortal flesh. Her ministers are
called to her altars by a sacrament; a sacrament blesses the
marriage of her children; her first office to the living is a
sacrament, her last office to the dying is a sacrament, and
she follows the dead into the invisible world with sacramental sorcery. Her power to bless, to justify and save
depends upon her sacraments; these constitute her spiritual
strength, these are her charms, her wands of spiritual
enchantment.

If Rome were sound upon every other point, her errors
in regard to the application of redemption are enough to
condemn her. What though she speak the truth as to the

---

[1] Conc. Trident., Sess. vi., cap. vii.

essential elements of salvation, yet if she directs to an improper method of obtaining them, she still leaves us in the gall of bitterness and in the bonds of iniquity.

The application of redemption,—this is to us the question of life and death, and a wrong answer here permanently persisted in must be irretrievably fatal. Christ will profit none who are not united to Him by faith. Baptism will not save us; confirmation will not impart to us the Spirit; the eucharist is an empty pageant, penance a delusion, and extreme unction a snare, without the faith of God's elect. Christ is the power of God and the wisdom of God unto salvation to believers—to believers only, and not to the baptized—and whatsoever creed sets aside the office of faith practically introduces another Gospel. In Christ Jesus neither circumcision avails anything, nor uncircumcision, but faith which works by love. Here, then, is the immeasurable distance between the way of life proposed in the Scriptures and that which is proposed in the Papacy. The Bible says, " Believe and be saved;" Rome says, Be baptized and be justified. It is the difference between the Spirit and the flesh, the form of godliness and its power.

I have now finished what I intended to say upon the Romish creed. Having been compared with the standard of an inspired Apostle, I think that it has been sufficiently convicted of fundamental departures from the doctrines of the Gospel. It corrupts the Blood, the Water and the Spirit. It denies the doctrine of gratuitous justification, makes the Redeemer the minister of human righteousness, converts His death into the basis of human merit, destroys the possibility of scriptural holiness, degrades the perfection of the Divine law, exalts the church into the throne of God, and erects a vast system of hypocrisy and will-worship upon the ruins of a pure and spiritual religion. Divine grace is divested of its efficacy, and the Almighty is reduced to the pitiful condition of an ancient German prince, whose sole influence consisted in the authority to persuade, but not in the power to enforce. Faith is dislodged from its legitimate position, perverted in its nature and corrupted in its evidence, while the sacraments, clothed with preternatural power, are foisted in its place. Such is the creed which, to the astonishment of the land, Princeton has pronounced to be not incompatible with a scriptural hope of life. I have never said, neither do I now assert, that all who are nominally in Rome must necessarily be of Rome—that every man, woman or child who ostensibly professes the Papal creed must be hopelessly doomed to perdition. It is the prerogative of God alone to search the heart, and He may detect germs of grace in many a breast which have never ripened into the fruit of the lips. But I do confidently assert that no man who truly believes and cordially embraces the Papal theory of salvation can, consistently with the Scriptures, be a child of God. If his heart is impregnated with the system, it is impregnated with the seeds of death. To make his own obedience, and not the righteousness of Christ, the immediate ground of his reliance; to look to the power of the human will, and not to the potency of Divine grace, as the immediate agent in conversion; to depend upon the sacraments and not upon faith for a living interest in the benefits of redemption; to defer implicitly to human authority and reject the Spirit except as He speaks through a human tribunal,—this is to be a Papist: and if these characteristics can comport with sincere discipleship in the school of Jesus, the measures of truth are confounded, humility and pride are consistent, and grace and works are synonymous expressions. Even Hooker, the semi-apologist for Papists, is compelled to admit that though in the work of redemption itself they do not join other things with Christ, yet "in the application of this inestimable treasure, that it may be effectual to their salvation, how demurely soever they confess that they seek remission of sins not otherwise than by the blood of Christ, using humbly the means appointed by Him to apply the benefits of His holy blood, they teach indeed so many things pernicious to the Christian faith, in setting down the means whereof they speak, that the very foundation of faith which they hold is thereby plainly overthrown on the force of the blood of Jesus Christ extinguished." This witness is true, and if true the baptism of Rome is nothing worth. It wants the form of the Christian ordinance, which derives its sacramental character from its relation to the covenant of grace; it is essential to it that it signifies and seals the benefits of redemption. Apart from the Gospel it cannot exist. The institute of Rome is neither a sign nor a seal, however she may apply these epithets to it; and even if it were, as she has introduced another Gospel and another scheme of salvation, she must necessarily have introduced another baptism. The one baptism of Paul is inseparably connected with the one Lord and the one faith. When the truths of the covenant are discarded, its signs lose their efficacy and its seals their power.

NOTE.—For some admirable remarks on the immoral tendencies of the Romish doctrines, see Taylor's Dissuasive from Popery. See also the preface to his Ductor Dubitantium for a brief account of Papal Casuistry. If I can do so without offence, I would also refer to a recent work on the Apocrypha for some arguments, not altogether common, upon the tendencies of Rome to skepticism, immorality and superstition. Some use has been made of this work in the present article.

ROMANIST ARGUMENTS FOR THE APOC-RYPHA DISCUSSED.

LETTER I.

PRELIMINARY STATEMENTS—COUNCIL OF TRENT AND THE CANON.

SIR: If you had been content with simply writing a review of my article on the Apocrypha, without alluding to me in any other way than as its author, I should not, perhaps, have troubled you with any notice of your strictures. But you have chosen the form of a personal address; and though the rules of courtesy do not require that anonymous letters should be answered, yet I find that your epistles are generally regarded as a challenge to discuss, through the public press, the peculiar and distinctive principles of the sect to which you belong. Such a challenge I cannot decline. Taught in the school of that illustrious philosopher who drew the first constitution of this State, I profess to be a lover of truth, and especially of the truth of God; and as I am satisfied that it has nothing to apprehend from the assaults of error so long as a country is permitted to enjoy that "capital advantage of an enlightened people, the liberty of discussing every subject which can fall within the compass of the human mind " (a liberty, as you well know, possessed by the citizens of no Papal state), I cannot bring myself to dread the results of a controversy conducted even in the spirit which you ascribe to me.

If, sir, my sensibilities were as easily wounded as your

own, I too might take offence at the asperity of temper
which you have, indeed, attempted to conceal by a veil of
affected politeness, but which, in spite of your caution, has
more than once been discovered through the flimsy disguise.
But, sir, the spirit of your letter is a matter of very little
consequence to me.

If the moderation and courtesy of the Papal priesthood
were not so exclusively confined to Protestant countries,
where they are a lean and beggarly minority,.there would
be less reason for ascribing their politeness to the dictates
of craft instead of the impulses of a generous mind. It is
certainly singular that Papists among us should make such
violent pretensions to fastidiousness of taste, when the style
of their royal masters—if the example of the popes is of
value—stands pre-eminent in letters for coarseness, vulgarity, ribaldry and abuse. *Dogs, wolves, foxes* and *adders,*
imprecations of wrath and the most horrible anathemas,
dance through their bulls, "in all the mazes of metaphorical confusion." If these models of Papal refinement are
not observed in a Protestant state, men will be apt to reflect
that an Order exists among you whose secret instructions
have reduced fraud to a system and lying to an art. How
you, sir, without "compunctious visitings of conscience,"
could magnify breaches of "the rules of courtesy" on the
part of Protestants toward the adherents of the Papal communion into serious evils which often required you "to
draw on your patience," is to me a matter of profound
astonishment. Standing as you do among the children of
the Huguenots, whose fathers tested the liberality of Rome,
and signalized their own heroic fortitude at the stake, the
gibbet and the wheel, were you not ashamed to complain
of "trifles light as air," mere "paper bullets of the brain,"
while the blood of a thousand martyrs was crying to heaven
against you? Two centuries have not yet elapsed since the
exiles of Languedoc found an asylum in this State. Who
could have dreamed that in so short a time the members
of a community which had pursued them with unrelenting

fury at home should have been found among their descendants, whining piteously about charity and politeness?
They who, in every country where their pretended spiritual
dominion has been supported by the props of secular authority, have robbed, murdered and plundered all who have
been guilty of the only crimes which Rome cannot tolerate
—freedom of thought and obedience to God—are horribly
persecuted if they are not treated with the smooth hypocrisy
of courtly address! Did you feel constrained, sir, in the
city of Charleston, where the recollection of the past cannot have perished, where the touching story of Judith
Manigault must always be remembered, to make the formal
declaration that "Catholics [meaning Papists] are not devoid of feeling?" Were you afraid that the delight which
you formerly took in sundering the tenderest ties of nature,
tearing children from their parents and husbands from
their wives, and above all your keen relish for Protestant
blood, coupled with the notorious fact that you have renounced your reason and surrendered the exercise of private
judgment, might otherwise have created a shrewd suspicion
that you possessed the nobler elements of humanity in no
marked proportions? But I am glad to learn that you are
neither "outcasts from society nor devoid of feeling;" and
I shall endeavour to treat you in the course of this controversy as men that have "discourse of reason," though I
plainly foresee that your punctilious regard to "the rules
of courtesy" will lead you to condemn my severity of spirit.
It is a precious truth that my judgment is not with man.
To employ soft and honeyed phrases in discussing questions
of everlasting importance; to deal with errors that strike
at the foundation of all human hope as if they were harmless and venial mistakes; to bless where God curses and to
make apologies where God requires us to hate,—though it may
be the aptest method of securing popular applause in a sophistical age, is cruelty to man and treachery to Heaven.
Those who, on such subjects, attach more importance to the
"rules of courtesy" than the measures of truth, do not

defend the citadel, but betray it into the hands of its enemies. Judas kissed his Master, but it was only to mark him out for destruction; the Roman soldiers saluted Jesus, Hail, King of the Jews! but it was in grim and insulting mockery. Charity for the *persons* of men, however corrupt or desperately wicked, is a Christian virtue. I have yet to learn that opinions and doctrines fall within its province. On the contrary, I apprehend that our love to the souls of men will be the exact measure of our zeal in exposing the dangers in which they are ensnared.[1] It is only among those who hardly admit the existence of such a thing as truth, who look upon all doctrines as equally involved in uncertainty and doubt—among skeptics, sophists and calculators—that a generous zeal is likely to be denounced as bigotry, a holy fervency of style mistaken for the inspiration of malice, and the dreary indifference of Pyrrhonism confounded with true liberality. Such men would have condemned Paul for his withering rebuke to Elymas the sorcerer, and Jesus Christ for his stern denunciations of the Scribes and Pharisees. Surely if there be any subject which requires pungency of language and severity of rebuke, it is the "uncasing of a grand imposture;" if there be any proper object of indignation and scorn, "it is a false prophet taken in the greatest, dearest and most dangerous cheat—the cheat of souls."

[1] "We all know," says Milton, in a passage which I shall partially quote, "that in private or personal injuries, yea, in public sufferings for the cause of Christ, His rule and example teaches us to be so far from a readiness to speak evil as not to answer the reviler in his language, though never so much provoked; yet in the detecting and convincing of any notorious enemy to truth and his country's peace, I suppose, and more than suppose, it will be nothing disagreeing from Christian meekness to handle such an one in a rougher accent, and to send home his haughtiness well bespurted with his own holy water. Nor to do this are we unauthorized either from the moral precept of Solomon, to answer him thereafter that prides himself in his folly; nor from the example of Christ and all His followers in all ages, who, in the refuting of those that resisted sound doctrine and by subtle dissimulations corrupted the minds of men, have wrought up their zealous souls into such vehemencies as nothing could be more killingly spoken."—*Animadversions upon the Remonst. Def. Pref.*

If I know my own heart, I am so far from entertaining vindictive feelings to the *persons* of Papists that I sincerely deplore their blindness, and would as cheerfully accord to them as any other citizens who have no special claims upon me the hospitalities of life. It is only in the solemn matters of religion that an impassable gulf is betwixt us. You apply, it is true, to the Papal community throughout your letters (I have three of them now before me) the title of the Catholic Church; and perhaps one ground of the offence that I have given is to be found in the fact that I have not acknowledged even indirectly your arrogant pretensions. Sir, I cannot do it until I am prepared with you to make the Word of God of none effect by vain and impious traditions, and to belie the records of authentic history. I say it in deep solemnity and with profound conviction, that so far are you from being the Holy Catholic Church that your right to be regarded as a Church of God *at all*, in any just scriptural sense, is exceedingly questionable. A community which buries the truth of God under a colossal pile of lying legends, and makes the preaching of Christ's pure Gospel a damnable sin; which annuls the signs in the holy sacraments, and by a mystic power of sacerdotal enchantment pretends to bestow the invisible grace; which, instead of the ministry of reconciliation, whose business it is to preach the Word, cheats the nations with a Pagan priesthood, whose function it is to offer up sacrifice for the living and the dead; which, instead of the pure, simple and spiritual worship that constitutes the glory of the Christian Church, dazzles the eyes with the gorgeous solemnities of Pagan superstition; a community like this—and such is the Church of Rome—can be regarded in no other light than as "a detestable system of impiety, cruelty and imposture, fabricated by the father of lies." Like the "huge and monstrous Wen," of which ancient story[1] tells us, that claimed a seat in the council of the body next to the head itself, the constitution of the Papacy is an enormous excrescence which

---

[1] See the story told in Milton, Reformation in Eng., Book ii.

has grown from the Church of Christ, and which, when opened and dissected by the implements of Divine truth, is found to be but a "heap of hard and loathsome uncleanness, a foul disfigurement and burden." The Christian world was justly indignant with the fraternal address which English Socinians submitted "to the ambassador of the mighty emperor of Fez and Morocco" at the court of Charles the Second.[1] But their own spurious charity to Papists is a no less treacherous betrayal of the cause of truth. What claims have Roman Catholics to be regarded as Christians which may not be pleaded with equal propriety in behalf of the Mohammedans? Is it that Rome professes to receive the Word of God as contained in the Scriptures of the Old and New Testaments? The false Prophet of Arabia makes the same pretension. Assisted in the composition of the Koran by an apostate Jew and a renegade Christian, he has given a lodgment to almost every heresy which had infected the Church of Christ in this rude and chaotic mass of fraud and imposture. Professing to receive the Bible, he makes it of none effect by his additions to its teaching. The *real* creed of Mohammedans has no countenance from Scripture. It is on the ground that Mohammed makes void the Word of God by his pretended revelations that he is treated by the Christian world as a blasphemer and impostor. Has not Rome equally silenced the Oracles of God in the din and clatter of a thousand wicked traditions? Her *real* creed, that which gives form and body to the system, that which is proposed alike as the rule of the living and the hope of the dying, is not only not to be found in the Bible, but contradicts every distinctive principle of the glorious Gospel of God's grace. If Mohammedans justify the heterogeneous additions of their Prophet to the acknowledged revelation of Heaven by pretending that the Bible is imperfect, and consequently inadequate as a rule of faith and practice, how much better is the conduct of Rome in reference to the same

---

[1] See Leslie's Socinian Controversy. For the authenticity of this address, see Horsley's Tracts in controversy with Dr. Priestley.

matter? She may not assume with Mohammed that the Scriptures have been corrupted, but she does assume that the Scriptures are not what God declares that they are—able not only to make us wise unto salvation, but to make "the man of God *perfect*, thoroughly furnished unto every good work."[1] Again, Rome's bulwark is tradition. Mohammed, however, far outstrips her in this matter, and appeals to a tradition preserved by the descendants of Ishmael that reaches back to the time of Abraham.

So, also, in the article of infallibility and authoritative teaching, the Arabian impostor and the Roman harlot stand on similar ground. The doctrines of the Koran are announced with no other evidence than the $\delta\upsilon\tau\grave{o}\varsigma$ $\grave{\epsilon}\varphi\eta$ of the master, and the Edicts of Trent claim to bind the world because they are the Edicts of Trent. In one respect the religion of Mohammed is purer than that of Rome; it is free from idolatry. There is in it no approximation to what Gibbon calls the "elegant mythology of Greece."

Mohammedanism and Popery are in truth successive evolutions in a great and comprehensive plan of darkness, conceived by a master mind for the purpose of destroying the kingdom of light and perpetuating the reign of death. For centuries of ignorance and guilt the god of this world possessed a consolidated empire in the unbroken dominion, among all the nations but one, of Pagan idolatry. This was the grand enemy of Christ in the apostolic age. When this fabric, however, in the provinces of ancient Rome, tottered to its fall, with his characteristic subtlety and fraud the Great Deceiver, according to the predictions of Prophets and Apostles, began another structure in the corruption of the Gospel itself, which should be equally imposing and more fatal, because it pretended a reverence for truth. Under the plausible and sanctimonious pretexts of superior piety and extraordinary zeal the simple institutions of the Gospel were gradually undermined; errors, one by one, were imperceptibly introduced; the circle of darkness con-

---

[1] 2 Tim. iii. 17.

tinued daily to extend, until in an age of profound slumber, through the deep machinations of the wicked One, the foundations of the Papacy were securely laid. The temple of the Western Antichrist, erected on the ruins of Christianity in the bounds of the Roman See, and requiring as it did the corruptions of ages to prepare, cement and consolidate its parts, owes its compactness of form and harmonious proportions to the profound policy and consummate skill of the Enemy of souls. As left by the Council of Trent, the Papal Church stands completely accoutred in the panoply of darkness—the grand instrument of Satan in the West as Mohammedanism in the East—to oppose the kingdom of God.[1] The lights are now extinguished on the altar; those in her, but not of her, who have any lingering reverence for God, are required to abandon her; her gorgeous forms and imposing ceremonies are only the funeral rites of religion; the life, spirit and glory have departed. Entertaining as I do these convictions in regard to the Papal community, I shall not pretend to sentiments which as a man I *ought* not to cherish, and as a Christian I *dare* not tolerate. Peace with Rome is rebellion against God. My love to Him, to His Church, His truth and the eternal interests of men will for ever prevent me—even indirectly by a mawkish liberality which can exist only in words—from bidding God-speed to this Babylonish merchant of souls. But I wish it to be distinctly understood that my most unsparing denunciations of doctrines and practices which seem to me to lead directly to the gates of death are not to be construed into a *personal abuse* of the Papists themselves. Little as they believe it, I would gladly save them from the awful doom of an apostate church.

With these general explanations of the spirit by which I am and shall continue to be actuated, I shall pass on to make a few remarks in vindication of the expressions at which you have taken offence as indicating ill feelings on

[1] The doctrine of the immaculate conception of the Virgin is supposed to be derived from the Koran. See Gibbon, vol. ix., chap. l., pp. 265, 266.

my part, and "with which even in quotation you are unwilling to sully your pen." These expressions, you will excuse me for saying, are perfectly proper.

Protestants designate their own churches by terms descriptive of their peculiar forms of government or the distinctive doctrines they profess. Some are called Presbyterians and some Prelatists, some Calvinists and others Arminians. You acknowledge the supremacy of the Pope; this is a distinctive feature of your system. Where, then, is the ground of offence in applying to you a term, or, as you choose to call it, a "vulgar epithet," which exactly describes a characteristic principle of your sect?

Then again, as to the phrases "vassals of Rome" and "captives to the car of Rome," they are really the least offensive terms in which your relations to the Papal See, as set forth in standard writers of your own Church, can be expressed. You must be aware, sir, or you would hardly venture to assume with so much confidence the air of a scholar, that the word *vassal* was employed by our earlier writers as equivalent to a man of valour, and was far from conveying a reproachful meaning. "The word," says Richardson, "is indeed evidently as much a term of honour as knighthood was." It is certainly a softer term than *slave*, which, according to Cicero's definition of servitude—*obedientia fracti animi et abjecti et arbitrio carentis suo*[1]—seems to be more exactly adapted to describe your state. Captivity to Christ is the glory of a Christian; and as the voice of Rome is to you the word of the Lord, I do not see why you should object to being called "captives to the car of Rome." I am afraid, sir, that the real harm of these words is not to be found in their vulgarity and coarseness, but in the unpalatable truth which they contain. If there were no sore there would be no shrinking beneath the probe. As to my "mocking language concerning the awful mystery of transubstantiation," I am not yet persuaded that there is any other mystery in this huge absurdity but "the mystery of

[1] Cicero, Paradoxon, V. i.

iniquity." To you, sir, it may be *awful;* so no doubt were calves and apes to their Egyptian worshippers.

I. Your letters contain, or profess to contain, an explanation of what the Council of Trent actually did in regard to the Canon of Scripture, a vindication of its conduct, and a laboured reply to my short arguments against the inspiration of the Apocrypha. In other words, they naturally divide themselves into three parts: a statement, the proof, and refutation. Of each, now, in its order.

In your statement of what the Council did, you have given us a definition of the word *Canon* which, since the term is not—as you seem to imply—univocal, adequately represents neither ancient nor modern usage. As I shall have occasion in another part of this discussion to revert to this subject again, it will be sufficient for my present purpose to observe that, in the modern acceptation of the term, the Scriptures are not called *canonical* because they are found in any given catalogue, but because they are authoritative as a rule of faith. The common metaphorical meaning of the Greek word *κανών* is a *rule* or *measure.* In this sense it is used by the classical writers of antiquity,[1] as well as by the great Apostle of the Gentiles.[2] Whether found in a catalogue or not, if the inspiration of a book can be adequately determined, it possesses at once canonical authority. It becomes, as far as it goes, a standard of faith. And with all due deference, sir, to your superior facilities for understanding aright the decisions of your Church, you will permit me to declare that the Council of Trent, which you so much venerate, in pronouncing the Apocrypha *canonical,* either employed the term in the sense which I have indicated, and made these books an authoritative rule of faith, or was guilty of a degree of folly which, with all my contempt for the character of its members, I am unwilling to impute to them. You inform us, sir, that a book is to be regarded as *sacred* because it is inspired, but that no book,

[1] Aristotle, Polit., lib. ii., cap. 8; Eurip., Hec., 602.
[2] Gal. vi. 16; Phil. iii. 16.

whatever its origin, is to be received as *canonical* until it is inserted in some existing *catalogue*. With this key to the interpretation of its language, the Council of Trent[1] has pronounced its anathema not only on the man who refuses to receive these books as inspired, but also on him who does not believe that they are found in a catalogue. He is as much bound, on pain of what you interpret to be excommunication, to believe in the existence of a *list* of inspired books as he is to believe in the Divine authority of the books themselves. It is not enough for him to know that the various documents which compose the Bible were written by men whose minds were guided by the Holy Ghost; he must also know that a body of men in some quarter of the world has actually inserted the names of these books in a catalogue or list. " *Risum teneatis, amici !*"

Now—to borrow an illustration from your favourite quarter—suppose one of our slaves should be converted to Popery, that is, should receive as true all the dogmas that the priests inculcate, and yet be ignorant that such a learned body as the Council of Trent had ever been convened, or, what is no uncommon thing among you, be profoundly ignorant that such a book as the Bible exists at all, would he be damned? To say nothing of his not receiving the Scriptures under such circumstances as *sacred*, he most assuredly does not receive them as *canonical* in your sense. He knows nothing of a list or catalogue in which these books are enumerated. It is an idle equivocation to say that the curse has reference only to those who know the existence of the catalogue. In that case the sin which is condemned is evidently a sheer impossibility except to a man who is stark mad. *To know* that a catalogue is composed of certain books, and this is the only way of knowing it is a catalogue,

[1] " Now if any one does not receive as sacred and *canonical* those books entire, with all their parts, as they have been usually read in the Catholic Church, and are found in the old Latin Vulgate edition, and shall knowingly and industriously contemn the aforesaid traditions, let him be anathema."—*Letter I.*

and yet *not to believe* that the books are in it, is a mental contradiction which can only be received by those whose understandings can digest the mystery of transubstantiation.

According to your statement, the venerable Fathers assembled at Trent did three things: 1. They decided what books were inspired; 2. They arranged them in a list; and, 3. They excommunicated all those heretics who would not receive both books and list. In my humble opinion, however, the holy Fathers declared what books they received as sacred and authoritative in matters of faith, and pronounced their curse upon those who did not acknowledge the same rule with themselves. I shall quote from the decree itself, *in your own translation,* a sentence which shows that your sense of the term *canonical* was foreign from their thoughts: "It has, moreover, thought proper to annex to this decree a *catalogue* of the sacred books, lest any doubt might arise which are the books *received* by this Council." You will find, on recurring to the original, that the word which you have rendered *catalogue* is not *canona,* but *indicem.* Again, sir, as the Fathers are said to *receive* these books before their own list is made, how did they do it? Evidently in the same way—unless there be one sort of faith for the people and another for divines—in which they required others to receive them, that is, as *sacred* and *canonical.* But the preceding part of the decree contains not a word about the existence of former *catalogues,* though it is particular to insert the *inspiration* of these books as well as of tradition as the ground of their reception, maintaining, at the same time, that they were, if not *the rule,* at least what is equivalent to it, the *source* (*fontem*), of every saving truth and of moral discipline. Hence, in the sense of Trent, to be sacred and canonical "is to be inspired as a rule of faith."

After this specimen of definition we are not to be astonished at still more marvellous achievements in the way of translation. The words, clear and explicit in themselves, "*pari pietatis affectu ac reverentia suscipit et veneratur,*" I find are rendered by you into English, hardly less equivocal than the language of an ancient oracle.[1] Sir, to say nothing of the obvious meaning of the words, you might have learned from your own Jesuit historian *Pallavicino*[2] that it was the intention of the Fathers in this famous decree to place the Apocrypha and unwritten traditions upon a footing of equal authority with the book which the Lutherans acknowledged as inspired. Their object was to give their Canon or rule of faith.   Determined as the Pope and his legates were to suppress the Reformation, which had then been successfully begun, and to perpetuate the atrocious abuses of the Roman court, they commenced the work of death by poisoning the waters of life at the fountain.   In the sentence immediately succeeding the anathema, we are given to understand that the preliminary measures in reference to faith were designed to indicate the manner in which the subsequent proceedings of the Council touching questions of doctrine and order should be conducted.

[1] " Receives with *due* piety and reverence, and venerates." The same blunder is found in the translation of this decree prefixed to the Douay version of the Scriptures.

[2] " Deinde quo res per futuram Sessionem statuendæ discuterentur, idem Legatus exposuit: Optimum sibi factu videri, ut primo loco recenserentur ac reciperentur libri Canonici sacrarum Literarum, quo certo constaret, *quibus armis esset in hæreticos dimicandum, et in qua basi fundanda esset Fides Catholicorum;* quorum aliqui super ea re misere angebantur, cum cernerent in eodem libro a plurimis Spiritus digitum adorari, alios contra digitum impostoris execrari. Hoc statuto tria in peculiaribus cœtibus proposita sunt. Primum, an omnia utriusque testamenti volumina essent comprobanda. Alterum, an ea comprobatio per novum examen peragenda: tertium a Bertano ac Seripando propositum, an expediret sacros libros in duas classes partiri: alteram eorum quæ ad promovendam populi pietatem pertinent, et illius ergo solum ab Ecclesia recepti tamquam boni, cujusmodi videbantur esse Proverbiorum et Sapientiæ libri, nondum ab Ecclesia probati tamquam Canonici, tametsi frequens eorum mentio haberetur apud sanctum Hieronymum et Augustinum, aliosque veteres auctores: alteram eorum, quibus etiam fidei dogmata innituntur. Sed ea divisio, tametsi ab aliquo auctore prius facta, et tunc a Seripando promota per libellum eruditissimum ea gratia conscriptum, quo cuncti libri Canonici rite expenderentur, uti revera firmam rationem non præferebat, ita nec sua specie Patres allexit, vix nacta laudatorem: quare nihil ultra de illa disputabimus."—*Pallavicino, Hist. Conc. Trident.,* lib. vi., cap. xi.

They settled the proofs and authorities to which in all their future deliberations they intended to appeal. As Luther was to be crushed, and as the armory of God's Word furnished no weapons with which this incorrigible heretic could be convicted of error, a stronger bulwark must needs be raised to protect the abuses and cover the corruptions of the Church of Rome. You cannot be ignorant, sir, that much difficulty was felt by the Council in settling the list of canonical books.[1] It was not prepared at once to outrage truth and history by making that Divine which the Church of God had never received as the work of the Holy Ghost. But, sir, without the Apocrypha and unwritten tradition, the holy Fathers were unable to construct an embankment sufficient to roll back the cleansing tide of life which Luther was endeavouring to pour into the Augean stable of Papal impurity and filth. The awful plunge was consequently taken, and these spurious books and lying legends were made standards of faith of equal authority with God's holy Word. Inspired Scripture, apocryphal productions and unwritten traditions were not only received with *due* piety and reverence, as you would have us to believe, but were received with *equal* piety and veneration, as the decree itself asserts. This, sir, is what Trent did, and, until it can be shown that all these elements of

[1] "Some thought fit to establish three ranks. The first, of those which have been always held as Divine; the second, of those whereof sometimes doubt hath been made, but by use have obtained canonical authority, in which number are the six Epistles, and the Apocalypse of the New Testament, and some small parts of the Evangelists; the third, of those whereof there *hath never been any assurance;* as are the seven of the Old Testament and some chapters of Daniel and Esther. Some thought it better to make no distinction at all, but to imitate the Council of Carthage and others, making the catalogue, and saying no more. Another opinion was that all of them should be declared to be in all parts, as they are in the Latin Bible, of Divine and equal authority. The book of Baruc troubled them most, which is not put in the number, neither by the Laodiceans, nor by those of Carthage, nor by the Pope, and therefore should be left out, as well for this reason, as because the beginning of it cannot be found. But because it was read in the Church, the Congregation, esteeming this a potent reason, resolved that it was, by the ancients, accounted a part of Jeremy and comprised with him."—*Father Paul*, p. 144.

Papal faith are really entitled to the same degree of authority and esteem—that they are all, in other words, equally
inspired—my charge of intolerable arrogance remains un-
answered against the Church of Rome.   I said, and repeat
the accusation, that she made that Divine which is notoriously human, and that inspired which, in the sense of
the Apostle, is notoriously of "private interpretation."   I
did not impeach the Council for having presumed to draw
up a catalogue of sacred and canonical books; but I did
impeach it, and do still impeach it, of one of the most awful
crimes which a mortal can commit, in having solemnly declared "Thus saith the Lord," when the Lord had neither
spoken nor sent them.   The insulted nations, heartsick
with abuses, were looking, with the anxiety of a dying man,
for the sovereign remedy which it was confidently hoped
would be prepared and administered by this long-looked-
for assembly of spiritual physicians; but when the day of
their redemption, as they fondly dreamed, had at length
arrived, and the cup of blessing was put to their lips, behold, instead of the promised cure, a deadly mixture of
hemlock and nightshade!   Five crafty cardinals and a few
dozen prelates from Spain and Italy, called together by the
authority of the Pope, and acting in slavish subjection to
his sovereign will (as if the measure of their iniquity was
now full, and the hour of their final and complete infatua-
tion had at length arrived), proceeded, with the daring
desperation of men bereft of shame and abandoned of God,
to collect the accumulated errors of ages into one enormous
pile, and to send forth, as if from the "boiling alembic of
hell," the blackening vapours of death to obscure the dawn-
ing light, to cover the earth with darkness and involve the
people in despair.   Where were truth and decency, sir,
when this miserable cabal[1] of scrambling politicians claimed

[1] When we call to mind the arts and subterfuges by which the Court
of Rome endeavoured to evade the necessity of calling a Council; its
long delays, while groaning Europe was clamouring for reform; its wily
manœuvres, when the necessity at last became inevitable, to have the
Council under its own control; the crafty policy by which it succeeded,—

to represent the *universal Church?* Is it not notorious that when the Canon of your faith was settled, even Papal Europe was so poorly represented that not a *single deputy* was found in the Council from whole nations that it assumed to govern? Its pretensions, too, to be guided by the Holy Ghost, when its whole history attests that the spirit of the Pope was the presiding spirit of the body, afford "damning proof" that it was given up to "hardness of heart and reprobacy of mind." You have favoured us, sir, with an extract from Hallam, which I shall not crave pardon for asserting is entitled to about as much respect as his *discriminating* censures of Pindar's Greek. I am surprised, sir, that you should have ventured to commend the learning of the Fathers of Trent.[1] The matter can easily be settled by an

when we look at these things—and whoever has read the history of Europe during that period cannot be ignorant of them—the language of the text cannot be deemed too severe. The Council was evidently a mere tool of the Pope.

[1] The following extracts, one from Robertson, the other from Father Paul (a Papist himself), may be taken as an offset to the testimony of Hallam, and a flat contradiction to "A. P. F.'s" account of the *learning* of the body:

"But whichever of these authors," says Robertson. referring to the histories of Father Paul, Pallavicino and Vargas "whichever of these authors an intelligent person takes for his guide in forming a judgment concerning the spirit of the Council, he must discover so much ambition as well as artifice among some of the members, so much ignorance and corruption among others ; he must observe such a large infusion of human policy and passions, mingled with such a scanty portion of that simplicity of heart, sanctity of manners and love of truth which alone qualify men to determine what doctrines are worthy of God, and what worship is acceptable to Him,—that he will find it no easy matter to believe that any extraordinary influence of the Holy Ghost hovered over this assembly and dictated its decrees."—*Charles V.*, vol. iii., b. x., p. 400.

"Neither was there among those prelates any one remarkable for learning: some of them were lawyers, perhaps learned in that profession, but of little understanding in religion ; few divines, but of less than ordinary sufficiency ; the greater number gentlemen or courtiers ; and for their dignities, some were only titular, and the major part bishops of so small cities that, supposing every one to represent his people, it could not be said that one of a thousand in Christendom was represented. But particularly of Germany there was not so much as one bishop or divine."—*Father Paul*, p. 153.

appeal to facts. Cajetan was reputed to be the most eminent man among them, "unto whom," says Father Paul,
"there was no prelate or person in the Council who would
not yield in learning, or thought himself too good to learn
of him;"[1] yet, with all his learning, he knew not a word
of Hebrew. What divine of the present day would be
deemed a scholar at all who could not read the Scriptures
in the original tongues? When the question of the authenticity of the Vulgate was under discussion in the Council,
what a holy horror was displayed of grammarians! What
shocking alarm lest the dignities of the Church should be
given to pedants, instead of divines and canonists![2] Sir,
why this dread of the Hebrew and Greek originals if your
pastors and teachers could read them? Is it not a shrewd
presumption that you made the Bible authentic in a tongue
which you *could* read, because God had made it authentic
in tongues which you *could not* read? So much for the *learning* of these venerable men.

II. Having sufficiently shown that your statement is a
series of blunders, and your eulogy on the Council wholly
unfounded, I proceed to your proof. The point which you
propose to establish is, that the Apocrypha were given by
inspiration of God. You undertake to furnish that positive
proof which I had demanded, and without which I had
asserted that no moral obligation could exist to receive
them. Before, however, you proceed to exhibit your argument, you step aside for a moment to show us the extent
of your learning in regard to the disputes which at various
times have been agitated touching the books that should be
received as inspired. Sir, the object of such statements is
obvious—you wish to create the impression that the whole
subject of the Canon is involved in inextricable confusion,
and that the only asylum for the doubting and distressed,
the only place in which the truth can be found and perplexities resolved, is the bosom of your own communion. In
your zeal to represent Protestants as without any solid

[1] Page 145.   [2] Father Paul, page 146.

foundations for their faith, it would be well to confine yourself to statements better supported than some that you have
made. That the Sadducees, as a sect, rejected all the books
of the Old Testament with the exception of the Pentateuch,
is certainly not to be received upon the conjectures of the
Fathers against the violent improbabilities which press the
assertion—improbabilities so violent that, with all his regard for the Fathers, Basnage[1] has been compelled to
soften down the proposition into the milder statement that
this skeptical sect only attributed *greater* authority to the
writings of Moses than to the rest of the Canon. If by
the Albigenses you mean the Paulicians, you can know but
little about them except what you have gathered from their
bitter and implacable enemies. The documents of their
faith have all perished. You cannot be ignorant, however, that Protestant divines have constructed a strong
argument from the very nature of their origin to rebut the
assertion which you have ventured to assume as true.

LETTER II.

THE ARGUMENT FOR INSPIRATION EXAMINED.

I COME now, sir, to the examination of your argument
for the inspiration of the Apocrypha, as well as of all
the other books which you profess to receive as sacred and
canonical. In appreciating the force and importance of this
argument it will be necessary to bear distinctly in mind
that the conclusion which you aim to establish is not to be
probably true, but *infallibly certain.* You require of those
who undertake to determine for themselves what books

[1] Basnage, History of the Jews, B. ii., ch. vi., p. 96.—Brucker, Crit.
Hist. Phil., tom. ii., pp. 721, 722. See particularly Eichhorn, who has
clearly shown that the charge is unfounded: Einleit., 4th Edit., vol. i.,
p. 136.

have been given by inspiration of God to decide the matter
with absolute certainty, or to renounce the exercise of their
private judgments. In proposing, therefore, a "more excellent way," you could not think of substituting one which
did not fulfil this high and important condition. Your
conclusion, then, is not to be a matter of opinion, but infallible truth; and if your arguments do not establish
beyond the possibility of a reasonable doubt the inspiration
of the Apocrypha, they fall short of the purpose which you
have brought them forward to sustain. Your proposition
consequently is that there is infallible evidence that the
Apocrypha were given by inspiration of God; or, to state
it in another form, that the Apocrypha were inspired is
infallibly and absolutely certain. Your general argument
may be compendiously expressed in the following syllogism:

Whatever the pastors of the Church of Rome declare to
be true must be infallibly certain;

That the Apocrypha were inspired the pastors of the
Church of Rome declare to be true;

Therefore it must be infallibly certain.

In other words, the Council of Trent *did not* err in this
particular case because it *could not* err in any case. It is
the *argumentum a non posse ad non esse*, which is then only
logically sound when the *non posse* is sufficiently established.
Since the whole weight of your reasoning rests upon the
truth of your major proposition, you have very judiciously
employed all your resources in fortifying it. Still, sir, after
all your care, it is signally exposed to heretical assaults.
In the first place, you must be aware that your argument is
vitiated by that species of paralogism which logicians denominate *ambiguity of the middle*. What is the precise extension of the words "pastors of the Church of Rome"?
They may be understood either universally, particularly, or
distributively; and you will excuse me for saying that in
the course of your first letter you have either employed
them in each of these different applications, or I have been

wholly unable to apprehend your meaning. At one time it
would seem that you mean the whole body of your priesthood collected together in a grand assembly. You speak
of " a *body* of individuals, to whom, in *their collective capacity*, God has given authority to make an unerring decision."
Then, again, you inform us that the " pastors of the Catholic Church" (meaning, of course, the Church of Rome)
" claim to compose it." In addition to this, you speak of a
single priest "presenting himself to instruct a Christian or
an infidel" as a *member of the body;* whence, the inference
is natural and necessary that *every* priest is a member of the
body. From a comparison of these various passages in your
first letter it would evidently appear that you employed the
words " pastors of the Church of Rome" in your major
proposition in their fullest extension. If, then, you meant
an assembly composed of *all* the pastors of the Church of
Rome, the Council of Trent, which comprised only a *small
portion* of your teachers, has manifestly not the shadow of
a claim to the precious virtue of infallibility. In this case
your major might be true, and yet your minor would be so
evidently false as to destroy completely the validity of your
conclusion. A body consisting of *all* the pastors of the
Church of Rome never *has* met, never *will* meet, and, from
the nature of the case, never *can* meet; and an infallibility
lodged in such an assembly for the guidance of human
faith or the regulation of human practice is just as intangible and worthless as if it were lodged with the man in the
moon. Still, whether this infallible tribunal were accessible
or not, your argument would be a sophism. It would stand
precisely thus : Whatsoever *all* the pastors of the Church of
Rome in their collective capacity declare must be infallibly
certain. That the Apocrypha were inspired *some* of the
pastors of the Church of Rome collected at Trent declared.
Therefore, it must be infallibly certain. An infallible conclusion, undoubtedly !

But, sir, the words may be taken particularly. If, however, they are to be taken in a restricted sense, you should

have told us precisely what limitation you intended to prefix, otherwise your reasoning may be still vitiated by an *ambiguous middle.* Without such an explanation we have no means of ascertaining whether the words as employed in the minor coincide as they should do with the same words as employed in the major. You should have told us under what circumstances infallibility attaches to *some* pastors of the Church of Rome, if you indeed intended to limit the phrase. That you have occasionally used it in a limited sense is evident from the fact that you attribute infallibility to the Council of Trent, which was certainly a small body compared with *all* the pastors of your entire Church. Are you prepared to say that *any* number of Popish pastors met under *any* circumstances shall be infallibly guided by the Holy Ghost in all their decisions concerning doctrine and practice—that even the *same* number which met at Trent, collected together by *accident,* or merely by *mutual consent,* would be possessed of the *same* exemption from all possibility of error which you ascribe to Trent? If you are not prepared to make this assertion, your *major* proposition is not absolutely true, but only under special limitations. These limitations are not even *stated,* much less *defined;* and while your leading proposition is left in this unsettled condition, what logician can determine whether your argument be anything more than a specious fallacy? Certain it is that it can never be regarded as conclusive until you show that all *those conditions* were fulfilled in the Council of Trent which are necessary to secure infallibility to "*some* of the pastors" of the Church of Rome. Where in all your letters have you touched this point? What was there that distinguished the Fathers of Trent from an equal number of bishops and divines met together upon their own responsibility, in such a way as to make the former infallible and the latter not? Was it the authority of the Pope? Then your argument was not complete until you had proved with absolute certainty that a Papal bull secures the guidance of the Holy Ghost. Was it the concurrence of the Emperor?

This matter is nowhere established. Was it both combined? What was it, sir? Let me remind you that as you aim at an infallible conclusion, every step of your argument must be supported by infallible proof. There must be no hidden ambiguities, no rash assumptions, no precipitate deductions. In so solemn a business you should construct a solid fabric, able to support the enormous weight which you would have us to rest upon it.

There is still another meaning which your major proposition may bear. You may have employed the words "pastors of the Church of Rome" in a distributive sense, and then you would distinctly inform us that every priest belonging to your sect shall infallibly teach the truth. The application of your argument to the condition of the ignorant and unlearned absolutely requires this sense. According to you every man, no matter what may be his condition or attainments, may have infallible evidence on the subject of the Canon. Where is he to find it? In the instructions of the priest who informs him what books were inspired and what books arose from "private interpretation"? The testimony of the single, individual priest is all the evidence that he does or can have. If, then, he has *infallible* evidence, the testimony of the priest, which is his *only* evidence, must be infallible, and consequently the priest himself must be infallible too, or incapable of teaching error. It is not enough that the water should be pure at the fountain, it must also be pure in the channels through which it is conveyed. The Council of Trent may have been infallible, but if it has only fallible expounders, the *people* can have nothing but *fallible* evidence. According to you, however, the people *do* have *infallible* evidence; therefore, the Council must have infallible expounders; therefore, every pastor must be individually infallible.[1] While your argument,

[1] "Though there have been infinite disputes as to where the infallibility resides, what are the doctrines it has definitively pronounced true, and who to the *individual* is the infallible expounder of what is thus infallibly pronounced infallible, yet he who receives this doctrine in its integrity has nothing more to do than to eject his reason, sublime his faith into credu-

however, indispensably requires this sense, you seem to disclaim it in those passages of your letters which speak of a
body of individuals in their collective capacity as the chosen
depository of the truth of God. How, I beseech you, is a
poor Protestant heretic, with no other helps but his gram-
mar and lexicon, and no other guide but his own reason, to
detect your *real* meaning in this mass of ambiguity and confusion? I would not misrepresent you, and yet I confess
that I do not understand you. I can put no intelligible
sense upon your words which shall make all the parts of
your letter consistent with themselves. You seem to have
shifted your position as often as you added to your para-
graphs. We have no less than four distinct propositions
covertly concealed under the deceitful terms of your major
premiss:

1. Whatsoever *all* the pastors of the Church of Rome
declare must be infallibly true.

2. Whatsoever *some* of the pastors of the Church of
Rome, *under certain special limitations*, declare, must be
infallibly true.

3. Whatsoever *some* of the pastors of the Church of
Rome, under *any* circumstances, declare, must be infallibly true.

4. Whatsoever *any* priest or pastor of the Church of
Rome declares must be infallibly true.

lity, and reduce his creed to these two comprehensive articles: 'I believe
whatsoever the Church believes; 'I believe that the Church believes
whatsoever my father confessor believes that she believes.' For thus he
reasons: Nothing is more certain than whatsoever God says is infallibly true; it is infallibly true that the Church says just what God says;
it is infallibly true that what the Church says is known; and it is also
infallibly true that my father confessor, or the parson of the next parish,
is an infallible expositor of what is thus infallibly known to be the Church's
infallible belief of what God has declared to be infallibly true. If any
one of the links, even the last, in this strange *sorites*, be supposed unsound,
if it be not true that the priest is an infallible expounder to the individual
of the Church's infallibility, if his judgment be only 'private judgment,'
we come back at once to the perplexities of the common theory of private
judgment."—*Edinburgh Review*, No. 139, Amer. reprint, p. 206.

Until, sir, you shall condescend to throw more light upon the intricacies of your style, your leading proposition must stand like an unknown quantity in Algebra, and for aught that appears to the contrary the letter x might have been just as safely and just as definitely substituted. Those who look for an infallible conclusion in this reasoning must not be surprised if they meet with the success which rewards the easy credulity of a child in seeking for golden treasures at the foot of the rainbow. Thousands have fully believed that they were there, but none have been able to reach the spot.

The infallibility of testimony which you attribute to the pastors of the Church of Rome you endeavour to collect from two general propositions, which it is necessary to your argument to link together as antecedent and consequent. First, you inform us that God must have "given authority to a body of individuals in their collective capacity to make an unerring decision upon the subject" of the Canon; and then you infer that if such a body exists at all it must be composed of the pastors and teachers of the Church of Rome. Until you can show that the antecedent in the proposition is necessarily true, and the consequent just as necessarily connected with it, you must acknowledge, sir, that you have failed in presenting to your readers what your extravagant pretensions require—an *infallible* conclusion. You must show, according to the process of argument which you have prescribed for yourself, not only that an infallible body exists, but that it is and can be composed of no other elements but those which you embrace under the dark and unknown phrase, "pastors of the Catholic Church." Deficiency of proof on either of these points is fatal to your cause.

It is not a little remarkable, in the history of human paradox, contradiction and absurdity, that absolute infallibility should be claimed for the testimony of those who, if tried by the ordinary laws which regulate human belief, would be found destitute of any decent pretensions to the common degree of credibility. You have presented the pastors of the Church of Rome before us distinctly in the attitude of witnesses. Their power in regard to articles of faith is simply declarative; they can only transmit to others pure and uncorrupted that which they received at the hands of the Apostles. They can add nothing to it, they can take nothing from it, and whatever they may declare to be the truth of God, according to the original preaching of the Apostles, we are bound to receive upon their testimony. Whatsoever they declare or testify to be true, according to your statement, must be infallibly certain. Now the credibility of a witness depends as much upon his moral integrity as upon his means and opportunities of knowledge. He must not only know the truth, but be disposed to speak it. As, too, our assent to testimony is ultimately founded upon our instinctive belief that every effect must have its adequate cause, when existing causes can be assigned which are sufficient to account for the deposition of a witness apart from the truth of his declarations, we are slow to rely on his veracity. In other words, when he is known to be under strong temptations to pervert, conceal or misstate facts, we proportionably subtract from the weight of his evidence, and if it should so happen that he had ever been previously detected in a lie, few would be inclined to receive his testimony. If these remarks be just, whoever would undertake to establish the credibility of your pastors must prove that they are possessed of such a degree of moral honesty as to constitute a complete exemption from all adequate temptations to bear false witness. To prove their knowledge of the subject is not enough, their integrity must also be fully made out. Any abstract arguments, however refined and ingenious, would be liable to a palpable *reductio ad absurdum* if after all their extravagant pretensions it should be ascertained from undeniable facts that your priesthood has ever been found destitute of those sterling moral qualities which lie at the foundation of all our confidence in testimony. Has it ever been shown, sir, that the

bishops of your Church have never been exposed, from their
lordly ambition and indomitable lust, to adequate motives
for bearing record to a lie? Has it ever been proved that
the purity of their manners and the sanctity of their lives
have always been such as to render them the most unexcep-
tionable witnesses on the holy subject of religion? How
will you dispose of the remarkable testimony of Pope
Adrian VI., who confessed through his nuncio to the Diet
of Nuremberg that the deplorable condition of the Church
was "caused by the sins of men, especially of the *priests*
and *prelates*"? What say you, sir, to that admirable commentary on the honesty and integrity of your pastors, the
"Centum Gravamina" of the same memorable Diet, which
was carefully and deliberately drawn up with a full know-
lege of the facts and despatched with all possible rapidity
to Rome? Do the records of the past furnish no authenticated instances in which your infallible pastors have either
testified to falsehood themselves or applauded it in others?
Sir, if all history be not a fable, the priesthood of Rome,
taken as a body, can yield in corruption, ambition, tyranny
and licentiousness to no class of men that ever cursed the
earth. If infallible honesty can be proved of them, if the
Holy Spirit has indeed been a perpetual resident in this
cage of unclean birds, if the ordinary credibility which
attaches to a *common* witness can be ascribed to them where
their pride, ambition or interest is involved, then all moral
reasoning falls to the ground, the measures of truth are
deceitful, and we may quietly renounce the exercise of judgment and yield to the caprices of fancy. No, sir; instead
of being the temple of the Lord, the habitation of the Holy
One of Israel, your dilapidated Church is a dreary spectacle
of moral desolation, peopled only by wild beasts of the
desert, full of doleful creatures, owls, satyrs and dragons.[1]

[1] "Without entering into the mazes of a frivolous and unintelligible
dispute about words, it is sufficient to remark that the supernatural and
infallible guidance of a Church which leaves it to stumble on the threshold of morality, to confound the essential distinctions of right and
wrong, to recommend the violation of the most solemn compacts, and the

Tried in the scale in which other witnesses are tried, your witnesses will be found deplorably wanting. Hence, you very wisely evade all moral considerations, and resolve your boasted infallibility, not into your own attachment to the truth, but into the stern necessity of uttering whatever God by the irresistible operation of His Spirit shall put into your mouth, as Balaam's ass, through His power, overcame the impediments of nature and spoke in the language of men. Whether you have succeeded in demonstrating by *infallible* evidence that you are the subjects—the passive and mechanical subjects—of such an uncontrollable *afflatus* from above as may entitle you to a credit which your honesty and integrity would never warrant, remains now to be inquired.

LETTER III.

THE ARGUMENT FOR AN INFALLIBLE BODY.

In resuming now the analysis of your argument, it may be well to repeat that the ultimate conclusion which you propose to reach is the infallibility of Rome as a witness for the truth. This point you endeavour to establish by showing, in the first place, that there must be some "body of individuals to whom, in their collective capacity," God has gra-

murder of men against whom not a shadow of criminality is alleged except a dissent from its dogmas, is nothing worth, but must ever ensure the ridicule and abhorrence of those who judge the tree by its fruits, and who will not be easily persuaded that the eternal fountain of love and purity inhabits the breast which 'breathes out cruelty and slaughter.' If persecution for conscience' sake is contrary to the principles of justice and the genius of Christianity, then, I say, this holy and infallible Church was so abandoned of God as to be permitted to legitimate the foulest crimes, to substitute murders for sacrifice, and to betray a total ignorance of the precepts and spirit of the religion which she professed to support; and whether the Holy Ghost condescended, at the same moment, to illuminate one hemisphere of minds so hardened and hearts so darkened, may be safely left to the judgment of common sense."—*Hall's Works*, vol. iv., p. 249.

ciously vouchsafed the precious prerogative which you claim
for your pastors. According to you, the whole question of the
truth of Christianity turns upon the existence of an infallible
tribunal on earth, from which men may receive unerring decisions in matters of faith, and without which the overwhelming majority of the race must be abandoned to hopeless and complete infidelity. If there were, indeed, no escape from the dilemma to which you have attempted to
reduce us, the means of salvation would be hardly less fatal
than the dangers from which they are appointed to rescue
us. But it may yet be found, sir, that a merciful God has
dealt more gently with His children than to commit their
fate to the teachings of a body " whose garments are dyed in
blood," whose whole career on earth, like the progress of
Joel's locusts, has been marked by ruin, and which, if its
future blessings are to be collected from its past achievements, can give us nothing but wormwood and gall, a stone
for bread and a serpent for a fish. The friends of liberty
and man, if reduced to the deplorable alternative of reaching the sacred Scriptures only on condition of submitting to
a bondage more grievous than that from which the groaning
Israelites were delivered by a strong hand and an out-
stretched arm, would, in all probability, prefer the frozen air
of infidelity to the deadly miasma of Rome. But I am
persuaded that no such dilemma, so fatal in either horn,
exists in reality; and that there is a plan by which we may
be rescued at once from the gloomy horrors of skepticism
and the despotic cruelty of Rome. To you, sir, it is utterly
inconceivable that the infinite God, whose judgments are un-
searchable and His ways past finding out, should have been
able to devise, in the exhaustless resources of His wisdom,
any plan of authenticating the record of His own will but
that which you have prescribed. You undertake to prove
that there must be a body of individuals authorized to make
an unerring decision upon the doctrines of religion as well
as the truth and inspiration of the Scriptures, from the
absolute impossibility that any other scheme could be efficient

or successful. What is this but to *limit* the Holy One of Israel? You would do well to remember that the purposes of God are not adjusted by the measures of human prudence or of human sagacity. As the heavens are high above the earth, so His thoughts are high above our thoughts, and His ways above our ways. In His hands broken pitchers and empty lamps are capable of achieving as signal execution as armed legions or chariots of fire. To judge, therefore, of the schemes of the Eternal by our own conceptions of expediency or fitness—to bring the plans of Him who is wonderful in counsel, and whose government is vast beyond the possibility of mortal conception, to the fluctuating standard of the wisdom of this world is to be guilty of presumption, equalled by nothing but the transcendent folly of the effort. A sound philosophy as well as a proper reverence for God would surely dictate that His appointments must always be efficacious and successful, simply because they *are* His appointments. We are not at liberty upon matters of this sort to indulge in vain speculations *a priori*, and pronounce of any measures that they cannot be adopted because they seem ill-suited to their ends. It is true wisdom to believe that He who originally established the connection of means and ends can accomplish His purposes by the feeblest agents, the most unpromising arrangements, or by no subsidiary instruments at all. Plausible objections avail nothing against Divine institutions. Whatever does not contradict the essential perfections of the Deity, nor involve a departure from that eternal law of right which finds its standard in the nature of God, is embraced in that boundless range of possibilities which infinite power can accomplish by a single act of the will. Any argument, therefore, which bases its conclusion upon the gratuitous assumption that the wisdom of God and the conceptions of man shall be found to harmonize is built upon the sand. To you, sir, the theory of private judgment may be encumbered with difficulties so insurmountably great as to transcend your ideas of the power of God: you can perceive no wisdom in a plan on which priests are not tyrants and the people are not slaves. But your objections are hardly less formidable than those of Jews and Greeks to the early preaching of the cross. Still, sir, Christ crucified was the power of God and the wisdom of God. In your attempt to fathom the counsels of Jehovah by arbitrary speculation, and to settle with certainty the appointments of His grace, may we not detect the degrading effects of a superstition which tolerates those who acknowledge a god in a feeble mortal and find objects of worship in departed men? Certain it is that your reasoning involves the tremendous conclusion that the great, the everlasting Jehovah, the Creator of the ends of the earth, is altogether such an one as we ourselves. Do you not tell us, in effect, that God could not have given satisfactory evidence of the truth and inspiration of His own Word without establishing a visible tribunal protected from error by His special grace? And that He is thus limited in His resources, thus necessarily tied up to the one only plan which the pastors of Rome have found so prodigiously profitable to them, according to your reasoning, must be received as an infallible truth, just as absolutely certain as an axiom in geometry. The argument by which you reach this stupendous conclusion has been wonderfully laboured, but when weighed in the balances of logical propriety, it is found as wonderfully wanting. I shall now proceed in all candour and fidelity to expose the "nakedness of the land."

With a self-sufficiency of understanding which never betrayed itself in such illustrious men as Bacon, Newton, Locke or Boyle, you undertake to enumerate all the possible expedients by which God could ascertain His creatures of the inspiration of His Word. These you reduce to *four*, and as the first three, according to you, are neither "practicable nor efficient," the fourth remains as a necessary truth. In the species of argument[1] which you have thought

[1] The argument of "A. P. F." is a destructive disjunctive conditional. It may most conveniently be expressed in two consecutive syllogisms:

A man must either judge for himself concerning the inspiration of the

proper to adopt, the validity of the reasoning depends on two circumstances : 1st. All the possible suppositions which can be conceived to be true must be actually made ; and, 2dly, Every one must be legitimately shown to be false but the one which is embraced in the conclusion. If all the others have been refuted, that must be true, provided, from the nature of the subject, some one must necessarily be admitted. In the present case it is freely conceded that there is some way of settling the Canon of Scripture, and hence your argument proceeds upon a legitimate assumption.[1]

1. Now, sir, the first question which arises upon a critical review of your argument is, Do your four schemes completely exhaust the subject ? Are these the only conceivable plans by which the inspiration of the Scriptures could be satisfactorily established ? If not, if there indeed be other methods which you have not noticed, other schemes which you have suppressed or overlooked, some one of these may be the truth, and your infallible conclusion consequently false. In Paley's celebrated argument for the benevolence of God, if he had simply stated that the Deity must either intend our happiness or misery, and had omitted entirely all notice of the third supposition, that He might be indifferent to both, the conclusion, however true in itself,

Scriptures, or rely on the authority of others. He cannot judge for himself, therefore he must rely on the authority of others. This is the first step.

If he must rely on authority, it must either be the authority of uninspired individuals, of a single inspired individual, or of an inspired body of individuals. It cannot be the first two, therefore it must be the last. Now, according to the books, this species of syllogism must contain in the *major* all the suppositions which can be conceived to be true ; then, the *minor* must remove or destroy *all but one.* That one, from the necessity of the case, becomes established in the conclusion. The argument in question violates *both* rules, and therefore, upon every view of the subject, must be a *fallacy.*

[1] " We cannot be called on to believe any proposition not sustained by adequate proof. When Almighty God deigned to inspire the words contained in the Holy Scriptures, He intended they should be held and believed to be inspired. Therefore there *does* exist some adequate proof of their inspiration."—*Letter I.*

would not have been logically just. Without pretending that I am capable of specifying all the methods by which God might authenticate His own revelation, I can at least conceive of *one*, in addition to those enumerated by you, which *might* have been adopted, which may therefore possibly be true, and which, until you have shown it to be false, must hold your triumphant conclusion in abeyance. It is possible that God Himself, by his eternal Spirit, may condescend to be the teacher of men, and enlighten their understandings to perceive in the Scriptures themselves infallible marks of their Divine original. That you should so entirely have overlooked this hypothesis—which *must* be overthrown before your argument can stand—is a little singular, since it is distinctly stated in the very chapter of the Westminster Confession to which you have alluded.[1]

"The heavens," we are told, "declare the glory of God, and the firmament showeth His handiwork." "For the invisible things of Him from the creation of the world are clearly seen, being understood by the things that are made, even His eternal power and Godhead." If the material workmanship of God bears such clear and decisive traces of its Divine and eternal Author as to leave the Atheist and idolater without excuse, who shall say that the *Word*, which He has exalted above every other manifestation of His Name, may not proclaim with greater power and a deeper emphasis that it is indeed the law of His mouth? Who shall say that the composition of the Holy Spirit in the Scriptures may not be distinguished by a majesty, grandeur and supernatural elevation which are suited to impress the reader with an irresistible conviction that these venerable documents are the true and faithful sayings of God? Is there any absurdity in asserting with a distinguished writer that "the words of God, now legible in the Scriptures, are as

---

[1] "Our full persuasion and assurance of the infallible truth and Divine authority thereof (Holy Scriptures) is from the inward work of the Holy Spirit, bearing witness by and with the Word in our hearts."— *Westminster Confession*, chap. i. v.

much beyond the words of men as the mighty works which Christ did were above their works, and His prophecies beyond their knowledge"? Jehovah has left the outward universe to speak for itself. Sun, moon and stars in their appointed orbits proclaim an eternal Creator, and require no body of men, "of individuals in their collective capacity," to interpret their voice, or to teach the world that "the hand which made them is Divine." Why may not the Scriptures, brighter and more glorious than the sun, be left in the same way, as they run their appointed course, to testify to all that their source "was the bosom of God, and their voice the harmony of the world"? Is not the character of God as clearly portrayed in them as in the mute memorials of His power which exist around us and above us? Why should an infallible body be required to make known the Divine original of the Bible when it is not necessary to establish the creation of the heavens and the earth? It is then a possible supposition that the Word of God may be its own witness, that the sacred pages may themselves contain infallible evidence of their heavenly origin which shall leave those without excuse who reject or disregard them. They may contain the decisive proofs of their own inspiration, and by their own light make good their pretensions to canonical authority.

The fact that multitudes who hold the Bible in their hand do not perceive these infallible tokens of its supernatural origin is no objection, upon your own principles, to the existence of such irrefragable evidence. The reality of the evidence is one thing, the power of perceiving it quite another. It is no objection to the brilliancy of the sun that it fails to illuminate the blind. Such is the deplorable darkness of the human understanding in regard to the things that pertain to God, and such the fearful alienation of men from the perfection of His character, that though the light shines conspicuously among them they are yet unable to comprehend its rays. Hence, to the production of faith, in order that the evidence, the infallible evidence which actually exists, may accomplish its appropriate effects, the "Eternal Spirit who sends forth His cherubim and seraphim to touch the lips of whom He pleases" must be graciously vouchsafed to illuminate the darkened mind, and remove the impediments of spiritual vision. The infallible evidence is in the Scriptures; the power of perceiving it is the gift of God. Your own writers, sir, acknowledge, and you among the number, that the infallible evidence which your Church professes to present cannot produce faith without God's grace, so that evidence may be infallible and yet not effectual, through the folly and perverseness of men. Bellarmine declares that "the arguments which render the articles of our faith credible are not such as to produce an undoubted faith, unless the mind be Divinely assisted."[1] And you have told us that the teaching of your pastors meets with a firmer and readier assent among minds that have been touched by the Spirit of God.[2] Now, sir, if your infallible evidence can yet be ineffectual through the blindness and wickedness of men, you cannot say that the Scriptures are not infallible witnesses of their own authority because all who possess them do not receive their testimony. In either case the illumination of God's Spirit is the means by which faith is really produced. According to you, it inclines the understanding to receive the teaching of the pastors of your Church; according to the doctrine of the Westminster divines, it enlightens the mind to perceive the impressions of Jehovah's character and Jehovah's hand in the sacred oracles themselves.

There is, then, evidently, a fifth supposition by which an humble inquirer after truth may be assured of the Divine

[1] "Argumenta enim quæ articulos fidei nostræ credibiles faciunt non talia sunt ut fidem omnino indubitatam reddant, nisi mens divinitus adjuvetur." De Grat. et Lib. Arb., Lib. vi., cap. iii.

[2] "We should ever bear in mind, too, that if this be the method adopted by Almighty God, if in reality, as the hypothesis requires, He speaks to that individual through this teacher, *His Divine grace* will influence the mind of the novice to yield a more ready and firm assent than the tendency of our nature and the unaided motives of human authority would produce." *Letter* I.

inspiration and canonical authority of the Holy Scriptures. God Himself may be his teacher, and the illumination of His Spirit may be the means by which, from infallible evidence contained in the books themselves, their Divine inspiration may be certainly collected. Whether true or false, right or wrong, this has been the doctrine of the Church of God from the beginning.[1] And before you can hope to

---

[1] As a specimen of what have been the sentiments of distinguished writers, I give a few extracts, selected from the midst of many others equally striking, which may be found arranged in Owen's admirable Discourse on the Reason of Faith. Works, vol. iii., p. 359, seq. The following passage from Clemens Alexandrinus is remarkable as asserting at once the sufficiency of Scripture and the right of private judgment in opposition to all human authority:

Οὐ γὰρ ἁπλῶς ἀποφαινομένοις ἀνθρώποις προσέχοιμεν δις καὶ ἀνταποφάινεσθαι ἐπ' ἴσης ἔξεστιν. Εἰ δ' οὐκ ἀρχεῖ μόνον ἁπλῶς εἰπεῖν τὸ δόξαν, ἀλλὰ πιστώσασθαι δεῖ το λεχθὲν οὐ τὴν ἐξ ἀνθρώπων ἀναμένομεν μαρτυρίαν, ἀλλὰ τῇ τοῦ Κυρίου φωνῇ πιστούμεθα τὸ ζητούμενον. Ἡ πάσων ἀποδείξεων ἐχέγγυοτέρα μᾶλλον δὲ ἡ μόνη ἀπόδειξις ὑυσα τυγχάνει. Οὕτως οὖν καὶ ἡμεῖς ἀπ' αὐτῶν περὶ ἀυτῶν τῶν γραφῶν τελέιως ἀποδεικνύντες ἐκ πίστεως πειθόμεθα ἀποδεικτικῶς. Strom., Lib. vii., cap. xvi. "For we would not attend or give credit simply to the definitions of men, seeing we have a right also to define in contradiction unto them. And as it is not sufficient merely to say or assert what appears to be the truth, but also to beget a belief of what is spoken, we expect not the testimony of men, but confirm that which is inquired about with the voice of the Lord, which is more full and firm than any demonstration; yea, which rather is the only demonstration. Thus we, taking our demonstration of the Scripture out of the Scripture, are assured by *faith* as by demonstration."

Basil on Psalm cxv. says: Πίστις, οὐχ' ἡ γεομετρικαῖς ἀνάγκαις, ἀλλ' ἡ ταῖς τοῦ πνεύματος ἐνεργέιαις ἐκγινομένη. "Faith is not the effect of geometrical demonstrations, but of the efficacy of the Spirit."

Nemes. de Hom., cap. ii.: Ἡ τῶν θειων λογιῶν διδασκαλία τὸ πιστὸν ἀφ' ἑαυτῆς ἔχουσα διὰ τὸ θεόπνευστον εἶναι. "The teaching of Divine oracles has its credibility from *itself*, because of their Divine inspiration."

The words of Austin (Conf. Lib. ii., cap. iii.) are too well known to require to be cited.

The second Council of Orange, in the beginning of the sixth century, in its fifth and seventh canons, is explicit to my purpose. Fleury, b. xxxii. 12: Si quis sicut augmentum ita etiam initium fidei, ipsumque credulitatis affectum, ... non per gratiæ donum, id est, per inspirationem Spiritus Sancti, corrigentem voluntatem nostram ab infidelitate ad fidem, ab impietate ad pietatem, sed naturaliter nobis inesse dicit, apostolicis dogmatibus adversarius approbatur. Si quis per naturæ vigorem bonum aliquid

overthrow it you must be prepared to prove—what, I think, you will find an irksome undertaking—that the Scriptures do not bear any signs or marks characteristic of their Author,

quod ad salutem pertinet vitæ æternæ cogitare ut expedit, aut eligere, sive salutari, id est, evangelicæ prædicationi consentire posse confirmat absque illuminatione et inspiratione Spiritus Sancti, qui dat omnibus suavitatem in consentiendo et credendo veritati, hæretico fallitur spiritu: "If any one say that the beginning or increase of faith and the very affection of belief is in us, not by the gift of grace—that is, by the inspiration of the Holy Spirit correcting our will from infidelity to faith, from impiety to piety—but by nature, he is an enemy to the doctrine of the Apostles. If any man affirm that he can by the vigour of nature think anything good which pertains to salvation as he ought, or choose to consent to saving—that is, to evangelical—preaching without the illumination and inspiration of the Holy Spirit, who gives to all the sweet relish in consenting to and believing the truth, he is deceived by an heretical spirit."

Arnobius advers. Gentes, Lib. iii., c. i., says: "Neque enim stare sine assertoribus non potest religio Christiana? Aut eo esse comprobatur vera, si adstipulatores habuerit plurimos, et auctoritatem ab hominibus sumpserit? Suis illa contenta est viribus et veritatis propriæ fundaminibus nititur nec spolietur sua vi, etiam si nullum habeat vindicem, immo si linguæ omnes contra faciant contraque nitantur et ad fidem illius abrogandam consensionis unitæ animositate conspirent." "Shall it be said that the Christian religion cannot maintain itself without the aid of men to vindicate its truth? Or shall its truth be said to depend on the warranty and authority of man? No, Christianity is sufficient for itself, in its own inherent strength, and stands firm upon the basis of its own inherent truth; it could lose none of its power, though it had not a single advocate. Nay, it would maintain its ground, though all the tongues of men were to contradict and resist it, and to combine with rage and fury to effect its destruction."

The great Athanasius (Orat. Cont. Gent., c. i.) says:

Ἀ'υπάρκεις μὲν γάρ ἐιστιν ἀι ἄγιαι κἀι θεόπνευςται γραφὰι πρὸς τὴν τῆς ἀληθέιας' ἀπαγγελίαν. "The Christian faith carries within itself the discovery of its own authority, and the Holy Scriptures which God has inspired are all-sufficient in themselves for the evidence of their own truth." There is a beautiful passage to the same purport in Baptista Mantuanus de Patient. Lib. iii., cap. ii. It concludes as follows: "Cur ergo non omnes credunt evangelio? Quod non omnes trahuntur a Deo. Sed longa opus est disputatione? Firmiter sacris Scripturis ideo credimus quod divinam inspirationem intus accepimus." "Why, then, do not all believe the Gospel? Because all are not drawn of God. But what need of any long disputation? We, therefore, firmly believe the Scriptures because we have received a Divine inspiration." Those who wish to find a large collection of Patristic passages bearing on this point will meet with ample satisfaction in chap. ix. of Good's Rule of Faith. The whole subject is ably

and that God's grace will not be vouchsafed to the humble
inquirer to enable him to perceive, according to the prayer
of the Psalmist, " wondrous things out of His law." Unless
you can disprove this fifth hypothesis, and show it to be—
what you have asserted of three that you have named—
neither " practicable nor efficient," your triumphant argument vanishes into air; it violates the very first law of that
species of complex syllogism to which it may be easily
reduced. You have beaten your drum, and flourished your
trumpets, and shouted victory when you had not been even
in reach of the enemy's camp. If a man, sir, reasoning
upon the seasons of the year, should undertake to prove
that it *must be winter* because it was neither spring nor
autumn, his argument would be precisely like yours for an
infallible tribunal of faith. His hearers might well ask
why it might not be *summer;* and your readers may well ask
why this *fifth* supposition, which you have so strangely suppressed when it must have been under your eyes, may not
be, after all your elaborate discussion, the true method of
God. In this ancient doctrine of the Church of God there
may be an escape from your fatal dilemma, and men may
find a sure and infallible passage to heaven without making a journey to Rome to be guided in the way. Upon
your principles of reasoning dilemmas are easily made, but
very fortunately they are just as easily avoided. Their
horns, weak and powerless as a Papal bull's, cannot gore the
stubborn and refractory. He who should infer that a sick
man must be scorching with fever because he is not aching
in all his bones with a shivering ague, would, in this pitiful
foolery, present a forcible example of the sort of sophism in
which you have boasted as triumphant argument.

discussed in Calvin's Institutes, Owen on the Reason of Faith and his kindred treatise, and Halyburton's inimitable essay on the Nature of Faith.
Some valuable hints may also be found in Lancaster's Bampton Lectures,
Jackson on the Creed, and Chalmers' Evidences. I cannot forbear, however, to advert to the two beautiful illustrations of the power of the Scriptures to authenticate themselves, which Justin Martyr and Francis Junius
have given us in their accounts of their own conversion.

2. Your reasoning is not only radically defective in consequence of an imperfect enumeration of particulars, but fatally unsuccessful in establishing the *impossibility* of those which you have actually undertaken to refute. The minor premiss is as lame as the major, and your argument at best can yield us nothing but a "lame and impotent conclusion." Your *fourth* method derives its claims to our confidence and regard from the pretended fact that all other schemes are neither "practicable nor efficient." Unless, therefore, this can be made clearly to appear, your reasoning must fall to the ground. Have you *proved* it? So far from it, the objections which you have adduced against your first three methods apply just as powerfully to the fourth, and prove, if they prove anything, that neither one of the methods specified by you can possibly be the truth. The arguments, for instance, which you have employed to overthrow the Protestant theory of private judgment, as implying the responsibility of men for their opinions, and a consequent exemption from all human authority, may be employed with equal success to demolish the pretensions of an infallible tribunal, or to show that such a body can neither be "practicable nor efficient."

Why then is private judgment inadmissible? Why is it that each man is not at liberty to examine for himself, and form his own opinions upon those solemn subjects in which his own individual happiness is so deeply concerned? Because, according to you, unless a man could speak with the tongues of men and angels, unless he comprehended all mysteries and all knowledge, unless, in other words, his mind was a living encyclopædia of science, he must be incapable of estimating properly the historical and internal evidences of the Divine original of the Scriptures. Like the Jewish Cabalists, you have rendered the judgments of the people utterly worthless to them in that matter which, of all others, is most important to their happiness. Maimonides[1] goes a little beyond you. He not only makes Logic,

[1] More Nebochim, pars i., c. 34.

Mathematics and Natural Philosophy indispensable to our progress in Divine knowledge, but absolutely necessary in order to settle the foundation of religion in the being and attributes of God; and according to him, those who are unfurnished with these scientific accomplishments must either settle down into dreary Atheism, or make up their deficiencies by submitting implicitly to cabalistical instruction! You, I presume, would grant that a man could be assured of the existence of the Deity without an intimate acquaintance with Latin, Greek, Hebrew, Syriac, Chaldee, and divers modern tongues, or without being master of Mathematics, Chemistry, Geology, Natural History and Physics. These things, on your scheme, are only necessary to settle the *inspiration* of the Scriptures.

Let us grant, for a moment, that all this immense apparatus of learning is necessary to settle a plain, simple, historical fact; what becomes of the skill and competency of your infallible body? If it is to decide according to the evidence, and all these boundless attainments are absolutely requisite in order to a just appreciation of the evidence, every individual member of your unerring corps must be deeply versed in all human lore, as well as blessed with an "almost supernatural accuracy of judgment," before the body can be qualified, according to your statements, to make an infallible decision. Suppose, sir, Europe and America were ransacked, how many individuals could be found, each of whom should possess the varied and extensive attainments which you make indispensable in settling a plain question of fact connected with the events of an earlier age? How many of the pastors of the Church of Rome would be entitled to a seat in a General Council composed only of those who could abide your test of competency to decide on matters of faith? Certain it is that there was not a single individual in the whole Council of Trent who possessed even a *tithe* of the learning without which, in your view, an accurate decision is hopeless. As we have already seen, those holy Fathers seemed to be fully persuaded that

"Hebrew roots were only found
To flourish best in barren ground."

Their skill in Samaritan, Coptic, Arabic and Syric *versions* may be readily conjectured from their profound acquaintance with the original text. If they were deeply versed in the mysteries of Chemistry and Geology, they must have been endowed with an extraordinary prolepsis which has no parallel in the recorded history of man. How, then, could these venerable men decide with "absolute certainty" when all the evidence in the case was high above, out of their reach? You tell us, sir, that they made their decision "after patient examination and a thorough investigation of all the evidence they could find on the subject." But yet, upon your own showing, the historical and internal proofs of inspiration were inaccessible not only to the prelates themselves, but to the whole rabble of divines who assisted them in their deliberations. How does it happen, then, that their decision is entitled to be received with absolute certainty? But perhaps you will say that the Fathers possessed some other evidence—that they themselves were supernaturally inspired, or irresistibly guided by God's grace to make an unerring decision? To say nothing of the fact that your argument, in order to be conclusive, requires you to show that the same supernatural assistance cannot be vouchsafed to individuals as well as to a body, I would simply ask, *How* could the Fathers *know* that they were inspired? You have made all human *knowledge* a necessary means of judging of *inspiration*. A man must be able "to refute all the objections brought from these different sources against the intrinsic truth, and, consequently, internal evidence of the Divine inspiration, of the Scriptures." If, then, a man cannot be satisfied of the inspiration of the Scriptures until he is able to perceive the intrinsic truth of their teachings—that is, until he can show that scientific objections are really groundless—how can he be satisfied of his own inspiration until he can, in like manner, determine that the propositions suggested to him are not contradictory to any truth received or taught in the wide circle of human science? And how, I beseech you, can the *people* be assured that any body of men has been supernaturally guided, until *they* are able to refute all the objections from all the departments of human knowledge to the decrees of the body? Will you say that inspiration, *once settled*, answers all objections? Very true. But how is the inspiration to be settled? You say that *an individual* cannot judge of inspiration until he is able to refute all objections and to defend the truths that profess to be inspired. No more, I apprehend, can a *body* of individuals. But a body of individuals may be *inspired* to judge of the inspiration of others. But how are they to determine their own inspiration? They must still be able to refute all possible objections, and perceive the intrinsic truth of what they are taught, themselves, or their own inspiration is uncertain; and the people need it just as much to judge of the inspiration of a council as of the inspiration of the Scriptures. So that your circle of science becomes necessary sooner or later for a body of men, if it be necessary for a private individual.

You perceive, then, that your argument against the rights of the people may be turned with a desolating edge against yourself. Like an unnatural mother, it devours its own conclusion. If, sir, the infallibility of a body depends upon the illumination of God's Spirit, it will be hard to show why God can supernaturally enlighten every man in a special assembly, and yet be unable to enlighten private individuals in their separate capacity. How the mere fact of human congregation, under any circumstances, can confer additional power upon God's Holy Spirit you have nowhere explained, and I think that you will hardly undertake the task.

Upon your own showing, then, your triumphant argument is a beggarly sophism. Your objections to private judgment prove too much, and therefore prove nothing. Whatever is simply necessary to establish *inspiration* applies as much to the inspiration of Trent as to the inspiration of David, Isaiah and Paul. As I am now exclusively engaged in the examination of your argument, I shall not turn aside from my purpose to indicate the manner in which a plain, unlettered man can become morally certain, from the historical and collateral evidences of inspiration, that the authors of the Bible wrote as they were moved by the Holy Ghost. Your long, involved and intricate account of the learning and attainments required for this end could easily be shown, and has been triumphantly shown, to be a mere phantom of the brain. You are fond, sir, of raising imaginary difficulties in the way of the humble inquirer after the truth, in order that you may find a ready market for the wares of Rome. But in this instance your own feet have been caught in the pit which your hands have dug. When you condescend to inform me how the Fathers of Trent could decide with infallible certainty upon the inspiration of the Scriptures, without the learning which is necessary, in your view, to understand the evidence, if they themselves were uninspired; or how, if inspired, they could, without this learning, either be certain themselves of the fact or establish it with infallible certainty to the mass of the people, who, without your learning, must judge of the inspiration of the holy Council,—when consistently with your principles you resolve these difficulties, one of the objections to your argument will cease. Until then it must continue to be a striking example of that sort of paralogism by which the same premises *prove* and *disprove* at the same time.

3. But, sir, the chapter of your misfortunes is not yet closed. Your favourite, triumphant, oft-repeated argument not only labours under the two serious and fatal defects which have already been illustrated, but, what is just as bad, even upon the supposition that it is logically sound, it fails to answer your purpose. It does not yield you what your cause requires—an *infallible* conclusion. At its best estate it is a broken reed, which can only pierce the bosom

of him that leans on it. You infer that a certain plan must be the true one because all others are false. It is evident that it must be absolutely certain that the others are false, before it can be absolutely certain that the one insisted on is true. The degree of certainty which attaches to any hypothesis drawn from the destruction of all other suppositions is just the degree of certainty with which the others have been removed. The measure of their falsehood is the measure of its truth. If there be any probability in them, that probability amounts to a positive argument against the conclusion erected on their ruins.

Now, sir, upon the gratuitous assumption that your argument is legitimate and regular, your conclusion cannot be infallible unless it is absolutely certain that the three methods of determining the inspiration of the Scriptures which you have pronounced to be neither "practicable nor efficient" are grossly and palpably absurd. They must be *unquestionably false* or your conclusion cannot be *unquestionably true*. If there be the least degree of probability in favour of any one of these schemes, that probability, however slight, is fatal to the *infallible certainty* required by your cause. Your conclusion, in such a case, can only result from a comparison of opposing probabilities; it can only have a *preponderance* of evidence, and therefore can only be *probable* at best.

I venture to assert, upon the approved principles of Papal casuistry, that two, most certainly, of your condemned suppositions are just as likely to be true, or can at least be as harmlessly adopted, as that which you have taken into favour. We are told by your doctors that a *probable* opinion may be safely followed, and their standard of probability is the approbation of a doctor or the example of the good—"*Sufficit opinio alicujus gravis doctoris, aut bonorum exemplum.*"

Try your third supposition by this standard, and does it not become exceedingly probable? Why have you passed it over with so vague, superficial and unsatisfactory a notice?

Were you afraid that there was death in the pot? You surely, sir, cannot be ignorant that scores of your leading divines have boldly maintained the infallibility of the Pope —*a single individual* whom they have regarded as divinely commissioned to instruct the faithful. The Council of Florence decided that the Pope was primate of the Universal Church; that he is the true Lieutenant of Christ—the father and *teacher* of all Christians; and that unto him *full* power is committed to feed, direct and govern the Catholic Church under Christ. He, then, it would seem, is the very individual to whom that Council would refer us for satisfactory information concerning the Canon of Scripture and every other point of faith. The prelates of the Lateran Council under Leo X. offered the most fulsome and disgusting flatteries to that skeptical Pontiff, calling him *King* of *kings* and *Monarch of the earth*, and ascribing to him all power, above all powers of heaven and earth. The Legates of Trent would not permit the question of the Pope's authority to be discussed, because the Pontiff himself, while he was yet ignorant of the temper of the Fathers, was secretly afraid that they might follow the examples of Constance and Basil. Pighius, Gretser, Bellarmine and Gregory of Valentia have ascribed infallibility to the head of your Church in the most explicit and unmeasured terms.[1]

[1] Gregory of Valentia carried the doctrine of the infallibility of the Pope so far as to maintain that his decisions were unerring, whether made with care and attention or not. His words are:

"Sive Pontifex, in definiendo studium adhibeat, sive non adhibeat; modo tamen controversiam definiat, infallibiliter certe definiet, atque adeo re ipsa utitur authoritate sibi a Christo concessa."—*Analys. Fid., Qu.* 6.

Augustinus Triumphus observes: "Novum symbolum condere solum ad Papam spectat, quia est caput fidei Christianæ, cujus auctoritate omnia quæ ad fidem spectant firmantur et roborantur."—*Qu.* 59, *Art.* 1.

This same writer, treating of ecclesiastical power, observes again: " Error est non credere Pontificem Romanum universalis Ecclesiæ pastorem, Petri successorem, et Christi Vicarium, supra temporalia et spiritualia universalem non habere primatum, in quem, quandoque multi labuntur, dictæ potestatis ignorantiæ, quæ cum sit infinita eo quod magnus est dominus et magna virtus ejus et magnitudinis ejus non est finis, omnis creatus intellectus in ejus perscrutatione invenitur deficere."—*Præf. P.,* John

It is generally understood, too, that this doctrine is maintained by the whole body of the Jesuits. To my mind, wicked and blasphemous as it is, this is a less exceptionable doctrine than that which you have defended. A single individual can be more easily reached, more prompt in his decisions, and is always ready to answer the calls of the faithful. To collect a Council is a slow and tedious process, and the infallibility slumbers while the Council is dissolved.

The infallibility of a *single* individual, which is your third hypothesis, is *probable* upon the well-known principles of your most distinguished casuists. You ought to have shown, therefore, that this opinion is *palpably absurd*. Write a book upon this subject and send it to Rome, and it may possibly lead to your promotion in the Church. However, let Gregory XVI. be first gathered to his fathers, as he might not brook so flat a contradiction to his own published opinions.[1] I am inclined to think that, to the major-

xxii. But the climax of absurdity and blasphemy is fairly reached in the following passage from Bellarmine, De Rom. Pont., Lib. iv., cap. v.: "Si autem Papa erraret præcipiendo vitia, vel prohibendo virtutes, teneretur Ecclesia credere vitia esse bona et virtutes malas, nisi vellet contra conscientiam peccare."

Scores of passages to the like effect may be collected from the writings of the Popes themselves.

[1] I have before me the French translation of a book written by the present Pontiff when he was Cardinal Maur Cappellari, entitled the Triumph of the Holy See and of the Church, in which the dogma of the Pope's infallibility is fully and curiously discussed. His Holiness repudiates with horror the Gallican doctrine of the superiority of Councils, and stoutly maintains that the Government of the Church is an absolute monarchy, of which the Pontiff is the infallible head. It is a little singular that A. P. F. should dismiss with contempt, as unworthy of discussion, the precise opinions which his master at Rome holds to be essential to the stability of the faith; and whether the *real* doctrine of the Papacy is more likely to be gathered from an obscure priest or from the supreme Father of the faithful, I leave it to the reader to determine. As a specimen of the Pope's book I give two extracts at random, as they may be found in the French version of Abbé Jammes:

"Le Pape, ainsi qu'il a été prouvé, est un vrai monarque; donc il doit être pourvu des moyens necessaires à l'exercice de son autorité monarchique. Mais le moyen le plus necessaire à cette fin sera celui qui ôtera tout prétexte à ses sujets de refuser de se soumettre à ses décisions et à ses

ity of Papal minds, there is so much probability in this
third opinion that if your letter had been written by a
Jesuit at Rome it would in fact have been made the *infallible
conclusion.*   Certain it is that you have not offered a single

lois, et son *infaillibilité* seule peut avoir cette efficacité.   Donc le Pape est
infaillible."—*Prelim. Dis.*, vol. i., p. 174, § 82.
   "Quoique, après tout ce qui été dit jusqu' à présent, il ne dût pas être
nécessaire de rien ajouter d'avantage, je chercherai encore à les tirer de
leurs erreurs par des argumens plus pressans.   Parmi toutes les sociétés,
celle-là seule est infaillible, qui constitue la vèritable Eglise; c'est de
foi: mais il n'y a pas de vèritable Eglise sans Pierre; nous l'avons dé-
montré: donc l'infaillibilité appartient exclusivement à la société qui est
unie a Pierre et à ses successeurs.   Or cette union avec Pierre ou avec le
Pape ne serait pas une note suffisante pour distinguer entre plusieurs
sociétés celle qui serait infaillible, si cette union ne contribuait en quelque
maniere par son concours à faire jouir cette société du privilége de l'infaillibilité; donc elle doit réellement y contribuer et y concourir.   Mais
l'Eglise doit avoir, dans ses définitions, une infaillibilité perpetuelle et
durable jusqu' a la fin des siècles; donc le même perpetuité, la même
durée jusqu' à la fin des siècles doit être assurée au concours de cette union
de l'Eglise avec le Pape, laquelle est attachée a l'infaillibilité de l'Eglise
elle-même.   D'ou il s'ensuit que, dans le cas d'un point quelconque a
définir, il sera aussi vrai de dire, avant même qu'il ait lieu, que ce concours positif et explicite ne manquera pas, qu'il est vrai de dire que
l'Eglise est infaillible dans la décision qu'elle portera, et qu'elle ne tom-
bera pas dans l'erreur.   Mais, s'il est certain que, toutes les fois qu'il
s'agira de definir un point de foi, on pourra compter sur le concours de
l'union de l'Eglise avec le Pape, il doit être également certain que Dieu
ne permettra jamais que le Pape ne donne pas son assentiment à des véri-
tés de foi, puisque, sans cet assentiment, il ne saurait, y avoir de vèritable
définition de l'Eglise.   Donc, si ce concours doit être continuel et per-
pétuel, Dieu devra continuellement et perpétuellement incliner le Pape à
donner son assentiment aux verités de fois; et il ne permettra jamais que
le Pape, comme tel, s'eloigne de la vraie croyance.   En effet, s'il n'en
etait pas ainsi, et que Dieu pût permettre que le Pape, en cette qualité,
abandonnât la verité, il pourrait arriver que, par sa primauté dans l'Eglise,
et par le droit qu'il a, pour le maintien de l'unité, comme dit saint
Thomas, de proposer le point de foi, il entrainât l'Eglise avec lui dans
l'erreur.   Donc Dieu a dû accorder au Pape, comme tel, le privilége
d'une infaillibilité indépendante de l'Eglise, indépendante de cette so-
cieté, a l'infaillibilité de laquelle il contribue et concourt par le moyen de
l'union de celle-ci avec lui.   Les novateurs ne peuvent rejeter cette con-
séquence sans nier la nécessité du concours du Pape; et s'ils la nient, ils
se rangent parmi les schismatiques et les protestans, qui se font une Eglise
separée du Pape."—Vol. i., c. ii., pp. 206–208.

argument against it. You play off upon Esdras and the
Jewish Sanhedrim, and sundry questions which "more
veteran scholars than you" have found it hard to decide,
and then conclude with inimitable self-complacency that
the "third method cannot be admitted." [1] Sir, when you
write again let me beseech you to write in syllogisms. If
you have *disproved* the infallibility of the Pope, I cannot
find your premises; and yet, unless you have done it, your
triumphant conclusion is a mere *petitio principii.* Your
own doctors will rise up against you if you undertake this
task; you are self-condemned if you do not.

Then again, your first hypothesis—the theory of private
judgment—must have some little probability in its favour,
or such mighty minds as those of Newton, Bacon, Locke
and Chillingworth would not have adopted it with so much
cordiality, nor would such multitudes of the race have
sealed their regard for it at the stake, the gibbet and the
wheel. A principle confessedly the keystone that supports
the arch of religious liberty, which emancipates the human
mind from ghostly tyranny and calls upon the nations
to behold their God, which lies at the foundation of the
glorious fabric of American freedom and distinguishes the
Constitutions of all our States, is not to be dismissed without examination as grossly false or palpably absurd. The
conditions which you have prescribed for its exercise are
not only arbitrary and capable of being turned to capital
advantage against you, but, as I shall show when I come to
the examination of your second argument, they have been
virtually withdrawn by yourself. You have actually admitted, sir, all that the friends of private judgment deem
to be important in the case. According to your own statement, the ignorant and unlearned may be assured, upon
sufficient grounds, of the genuineness and authenticity of
the books of the New Testament. This foundation being
laid, inspiration will naturally follow. So that, notwith-

---

[1] NOTE BY EDITOR.—It is understood that Bishop Lynch, since the late
Council of the Vatican, is no longer unable to admit "the third method."

standing all your objections, private judgment remains unaffected in the strength and glory of its intrinsic probability.

How, then, upon a just estimate of its merits, stands your boasted argument? Why, there are *only four* suppositions that can be made in the case. The first and third of these are so extremely *probable* that millions of the human race have believed them to be true. Therefore the *fourth* must be *infallibly certain!* Weighed in the balances of logical propriety, the infallible certainty of your conclusion turns out to be like Berkeley's "vanishing ghosts of departed quantities."

LETTER IV.

HISTORICAL ARGUMENT.

WE owe it to the goodness of God that the most corrupt and dangerous principles are not unfrequently combined in the same person with a confusion of understanding which effectually destroys their capacity of mischief and renders the triumph of truth more illustrious and complete. Error, in fact, is so multiform and various, so heterogeneous in its parts and mutually repulsive in its elements, that it requires a mind of extraordinary power to construct a fabric of such discordant materials having even the appearance of regularity and order. Truth, on the other hand, is simple and uniform. Her body, like that of the beautiful Osiris, is composed of homogeneous and well-adjusted parts; and as, in the progress of discovery or the light of patient investigation, limb is added to limb, and member to member, the mind perceives in the harmony of the proportions and the exquisite symmetry of the form a mysterious charm which, like the magic of musical enchantment, chains its sympathies and captivates its powers. The fascinations of falsehood are essentially distinguished from the "divine, enchanting ravishment" of truth by their peculiar effects upon the health and vigour of the soul. Whatever pleasure they administer is like the profound slumber produced by powerful drugs or stupefying potions, in which the joys that are experienced are the unnatural results of a temporary delirium, or, as Milton expresses it, of that "sweet madness" in which the soul is robbed of its energies and rendered impotent for future exertion; but "the sober certainty of waking bliss, a sacred and homefelt delight," a manly and solid satisfaction which at once refreshes and invigorates the mind, belongs exclusively to the province of truth. Hence philosophy, which is only another name for the love of truth, was warmly commended among the ancient sages as the health and medicine of the soul, the choicest gift of heaven and the richest jewel of earth. Falsehood, however it may exhilarate, always *confounds*, and the stimulus, however powerful, which it may impart to the faculties of the mind, can produce nothing more substantial or real than the vain phantoms of a sick man's dream. Hence, defences of error are almost always inconsistent with themselves, and the advocate of truth has often no harder task than to place the different statements of the sophist or deceiver in immediate juxtaposition, and leave them, in their war of contradictions, to demolish the system which their master had laboriously toiled to erect. The most finished productions of superstition, infidelity and Atheism, when resolved into their constituent parts, are found to be wanting in that beautiful consistency which springs from the bosom of God, and which is written, as if by the finger of Heaven, upon every system of truth.

Without intending to degrade your understanding, you must permit me to call attention to the fact that the different portions of your own compositions are "like two prevaricating witnesses, who flatly contradict each other, though neither of them speaks the truth." This confusion of ideas is perhaps to be attributed to the nature of the cause which, with more

zeal than prudence, you undertook to defend. Consistency
cannot be expected from the advocates of a black and bloody
superstition which sprang from the father of lies, whose
appropriate element is darkness, and whose legitimate effect
upon the life is to form a character homogeneous in nothing
but implacable enmity to God. We are not to be astonished,
therefore, to find that your elaborate defence of the infallibility of a body which solemnly sanctioned one of the
most deliberate and atrocious frauds[1] that ever disgraced
the annals of mankind should be so awkwardly adjusted in
its parts as to resemble nothing more distinctly than the
monstrous picture with which Horace opens his epistle to
the Pisos. They who receive not the truth in the love of
it are smitten with such madness, blindness and astonishment of heart as to grope at noonday, even as the blind

[1] "When John Huss, the Bohemian Reformer, was arrested, cast into
prison and publicly burnt alive at Constance, in spite of a "safe-conduct"
given him by the Emperor Sigismund, merely because he refused to belie
his conscience by abjuring his pretended heresy, all was executed under
the eyes and by the express authority of the Council, who solemnly decreed that the safe-conduct of the Emperor ought to be considered as no
impediment to the exercise of ecclesiastical jurisdiction, but that, notwithstanding, it was perfectly competent for the ecclesiastical judge to
take cognizance of his errors and to *punish* them agreeably to the dictates
of justice, although he presented himself before them in dependence upon
that protection but for which he would have declined appearing. Nor
were they satisfied with this impious decision alone. Because murmurs
were heard on account of the violation of a legal protection, they had the
audacity to add, that since the said John Huss had, by impugning the
orthodox faith, forfeited every privilege, and since no promise or faith
was binding, either by human or divine right, in prejudice of the Catholic
faith, the said emperor had done as became his royal majesty in violating
his safe-conduct, and that whoever, of any rank or sect, dares to impugn
the justice of the holy Council or of his majesty, in relation to their proceedings with John Huss, shall be punished without hope of pardon as a
favourer of heretical pravity, and guilty of the crime of high treason."—
Hall, vol. iv., p. 245. See *L'Enfant's Council of Constance*, vol. ii., p. 491.
   The third Council of Lateran, Canon XVI., decreed that *all oaths* contrary to the utility of the Church and to the institutions of the Fathers
are to be regarded as perjuries, and therefore not to be kept. "Non enim
dicenda sunt juramenta, sed potius perjuria, quæ contra utilitatem eccle-
siasticam et sanctorum patrum renitent instituta."

gropeth in darkness, and to feel for the wall in the full blaze
of the meridian sun.   The blandishments of error, like the
subtle allurements of Samson's wife, may rob the noblest
genius of its strength, and leave it in the midst of its
enemies dark, dark, irrecoverably dark.   I am far from
contemplating such instances of mental eclipse with feelings
of exultation or delight.   There cannot be a more appalling
spectacle in nature than a mind in ruins; and in the righteous severity of God, which visits the advocates of error by
sealing up the intellectual eyeball in impenetrable night,
we may learn the awful majesty of truth and the tremendous danger of trifling with the light.   This disastrous
judgment is the portentous herald of a deeper woe.   It is
therefore with feelings of the profoundest pity, and with
the most heartfelt reciprocation of your prayer on my behalf, that I am now compelled to expose that tissue of inconsistencies, contradictions and unwarrantable assumptions
which constitutes your second argument; and if, sir, you
shall be made to feel, as I sincerely trust you may, that you
have been only weaving a tangled web of sophistry and
deceit, you should take a salutary warning, and before you
finally stumble on the dark mountains contemplate the
severity of God in them that fall.

   Your object is to exhibit the historical grounds for believing that God has in fact established, through Jesus Christ,
a commissioned delegate from Heaven, "a body of individuals to whom in their collective capacity He has given
authority to make an unerring decision" on the subject of
the Canon.   These historical proofs, you inform us, contain
nothing that transcends the means or surpasses the understanding even of an Indian or a negro.   Now, what are
these historical proofs, and whence are they derived?   The
recorded *facts of the New Testament received on the authority
of the Apostles and Evangelists!*   You appeal to "certain
histories written by persons who lived at the same time with
the Saviour, and were for years in daily and intimate intercourse with Him, and the *accuracy* of whose reports is uni-

versally acknowledged and can be *easily* substantiated." In other words, the *genuineness* and *authenticity* of the books of the New Testament are matters so simple and plain that there is nothing in the evidence "above or contrary to the means and understanding of an Indian or a negro." These books contain satisfactory proof of the miracles of Christ; these miracles establish His Divine commission, and consequently impart Divine authority to whatever He enjoined; and as a body of infallible teachers to be perpetuated to the end of time was His provision for preserving His truth pure in the world, that arrangement unquestionably possessed the sanction of God. Such is your argument. Now, sir, if the books of the New Testament are to be received as credible testimony to the miracles of Christ, why not on the subject of their own inspiration? Are you not aware that the great historical "argument on which Protestants rely in proving the inspiration of the Scriptures presupposes only the *genuineness* of the books and the *credibility*" of their authors? You have yourself admitted that the teaching of the Apostles was supernaturally protected from error, and if their oral instructions were dictated by the Holy Ghost, why should that august and glorious visitant desert them when they took the *pen* to accomplish the same object, when absent, which, when present, they accomplished by the *tongue?*[1] They themselves declare that their writ-

[1] "We have seen how fully gifted the Apostles were for the business of their mission. They worked miracles, they spake with tongues, they explained mysteries, they interpreted prophecies, they discerned the true from the false pretences to the Spirit, and all this for the temporary and occasional discharge of their ministry. Is it possible, then, to suppose them to be deserted by their Divine Enlightener when they sat down to the other part of their work to frame a rule for the lasting service of the Church? Can we believe that that Spirit which so bountifully assisted them in their assemblies had withdrawn Himself when they retired to their private oratories, or that when their *speech* was with all power their *writings* should convey no more than the weak and fallible dictates of human knowledge? To suppose the endowments of the Spirit to be so capriciously bestowed would make it look more like a mockery than a gift." *Warburton, Doct. of Grace*, book i., chap. v.

ings possessed the same authority with their oral instructions. Peter[1] ranks the Epistles of Paul with the Scriptures of the Old Testament, which were confessed to be inspired, and Paul exhorts the Thessalonians to hold fast the traditions which they had received from him, either by word or epistle.[2] If, then, the *credibility* of these books is a matter so plain and palpable, and can be so "easily substantiated"—and such is your concession—what need of Hebrew, Greek, Latin, Syriac, Chaldee and divers modern tongues, together with Geology, Chemistry, Natural History, and almost every science, to make out their *inspiration?* They assert it, and they are to be believed; therefore one would think they might be believed by a simple, unlettered man, without being master of a library of which Charleston and perhaps Columbia is too poor to boast! I had always thought that the only difficulty in making out the external proof of inspiration was in establishing the *credibility* of the books which profess to be inspired. It had struck me that if it were once settled that their own testimony was to be received, the matter was at an end. But it seems now that the *credibility* of a witness is no proof that he speaks the *truth*, and though "the *accuracy* of his statements can be easily substantiated, even to the mind of an Indian or a negro," there is one fact about which he cannot be believed, except by a man who carries all the learning of Europe and America in his head. Nay, with all the advantages of a "larger library than Charleston can boast of," with the tongues alike of the dead and living, with universal Science pouring her treasures in boundless profusion at his feet, with an almost "supernatural accuracy of judgment," added to other marvellous accomplishments, it is still doubtful whether, in the way of private judgment, a man could ever be assured that *credible* books are to be *believed* on the subject of their origin![3] But just let one of

[1] 2 Pet. iii. 15, 16.   [2] 2 Thess. ii. 15.
[3] "Whether any investigation in either or both classes" (that is, of external and internal evidence), "carried on even under the most favour-

an infallible body present himself before a Christian or an
infidel, an Indian or a negro, and how changed the scene!
As if at the waving of a wizard's wand the mists are dis-
pelled, the shadows disappear, a flood of light removes all
lingering doubt, and an infant mind can surmount those
giant difficulties which "veteran scholars" and "sage philosophers" were unable to subdue. This teacher can achieve
these mighty wonders before it is *proved* that he belongs to
an unerring band; there is magic in his *voice.* Just let him
ope his ponderous lips and give the word, and the sun of
the Scriptures no longer "looks through the horizontal misty
air shorn of his beams, no longer stands in awful eclipse
scattering disastrous twilight over half the nations," but
shines out in the full effulgence of meridian day!

It is strange to me that you did not perceive the egregious absurdity of attempting to establish the infallible
authority of a body of individuals upon historical grounds,
when you denied the possibility of proving the infallible
authority of the Scriptures by the same process.

The evidence in both cases is precisely of the same nature.
The inspiration of Rome turns upon a promise which is
said to have been made nearly two thousand years ago; the
inspiration of the New Testament turns upon facts which
are said to have occurred at the time. Both the promises
and the facts are to be found, if found at all, in this very
New Testament. Now, how does it happen that when the
point to be proved is the pretended promise made to the
pastors of Rome, the New Testament becomes amazingly
accurate, and the proofs of its credibility are neither above
nor contrary "to the means or understanding of an Indian
or a negro," but when the point to be proved is the facts
which establish the inspiration of the writers, then the New
Testament becomes involved in a cloud of uncertainty which
no human learning is able to remove? Your argument, sir,

able circumstances, will unerringly prove the inspiration of any books of
the Scripture, I leave to be mooted by those who choose to undertake the
task." *Letter* I.

has certainly placed you in a sad dilemma. You cannot make out the historical proofs of Papal infallibility without making out at the same time the historical proofs of scriptural inspiration. Both must be traced through the same channels to the age of the Apostles.

Now, one of two things must be true—either the credibility of the Scriptures can be substantiated to a plain unlettered man, or it cannot. If it can be, then there is no need of your infallible body to authenticate their inspiration, since that matter can be easily gathered from their own pages. If it cannot, then your argument from the Scriptures to an Indian or a negro in favour of an infallible body is inadmissible, since he is incapable of apprehending the premises from which your conclusion is drawn. You have taken both horns of this dilemma, pushing Protestants with one and upholding Popery with the other, and both are fatal to you. Now, as it is rather difficult to be on both sides of the same question at the same time, you must adhere to one or the other. If you adhere to your first position, that all human learning is necessary to settle the credibility of the Scriptures, then you must seek other proofs of an infallible body than those which you think you have gathered from the Apostles. You must first establish the infallibility of the body that claims to teach us, and then receive the Sacred Oracles at their hand. A circulating syllogism proves nothing ; and if he who establishes the credibility of the Scriptures by an infallible body, and then establishes the infallibility of the body from the credibility of the Scriptures, does not reason in a circle, I am at a loss to apprehend the nature of that sophism. If you adhere to your other position, that the accuracy of the Evangelists can be easily substantiated, then your objections to private judgment are fairly given up, and you surrender the point that a man can decide for himself with absolute certainty concerning the inspiration of the Bible. Take which horn you please, your cause is ruined, but you have chosen both !

The process by which you endeavour to elicit an infallible

body of teachers from the Scriptures is in perfect keeping
with the rest of your argument. You do not pretend that
they contain any express testimony to the fact; neither
do you deduce from them any marks by which your unerring
guides of faith can be discriminated from those who introduce errors and attempt to change the religion of Christ.
How then does it appear that such infallible instructors were
appointed? Why, there is no other way in which God could
accomplish His purpose of transmitting Christianity pure
and uncorrupted to the remotest generations of men! This
is the sum and substance of the argument for the sake of
which you have made yourself so consummately inconsistent,
by contradicting your previous statements in regard to the
credibility of the Scriptures! "Some adequate provision
must be made against the error and change-seeking tendency
of man," and as Christianity is appointed to be learned from
persons delegated to teach in the name and by the authority
of Christ, "that provision must evidently and necessarily be
directed to preserve that body of teachers by the power of
God from error, and to make them in fact teach all things
whatsoever He had taught them."

That an infallible body of teachers presents the only effectual means of perpetuating the religion of Christ, unadulterated with error, is so exceedingly unlikely that it
would require nothing less than a constant miracle to preserve a system transmitted in this way from corruptions,
additions and radical changes. Unless each individual
pastor were himself infallible, fatal errors might be widely
disseminated before the body could be collected together to
separate the chaff from the wheat and to distinguish the
precious from the vile. Three centuries have hardly
passed away since the last General Council of the Roman
Church was first convened. In that lapse of time how
many unauthorized opinions may have gained currency
among the pastors of your Church, and have perverted your
flocks from the true doctrines of Rome! The truth is,
without a perpetual superintendence over the mind and

heart of every solitary teacher, amounting to a miraculous
protection from error, the plan of transmitting a system of
religion by oral tradition is the most unsafe, uncertain and
liable to abuse of any that could be adopted. The com-
monest story cannot pass through a single community without gathering additions as it goes. How then shall a complicated system of religion be handed down from generation
to generation, passed on from lip to lip, and from age to
age, and lose nothing of its original integrity, and gain
nothing from the invention of man? Sir, *your* " common sense," and " the common sense of an Indian or negro,"
might lead you "to expect that this is the course which
the Saviour would adopt," but nothing but His own Word
could render it credible to me. No, sir, God has taken a
different method to guard against the " error and change-
seeking tendencies of men." He has committed His holy
religion to *written documents,* which are to abide as an infallible standard of faith till the heavens and the earth are
no more. There, and there alone, we are to seek the truth.
By them, and them alone, all the spirits are to be tried, all
the teachers are to be judged; and if Roman pastors, with
their wicked pretensions to infallible authority, speak not
according to these Records, they are to be cast out as lying
prophets whom the Lord hath not sent.

You have totally misconceived the appropriate functions
of the Christian ministry. Sir, the preachers of the Gospel
were never designed to be the lords of the people's faith,
but helpers of their joy. They are to propose, but it
belongs to the Scriptures alone to confirm or prove, the doctrines of religion. The infallible standard is in the Bible,
and they who are noble will, like the Bereans, test the instructions of their pastors by the true and faithful sayings
of God.

You must remember, sir, that the Scriptures, which you
have admitted to be credible, which were written by men
under a special promise of Christ to be protected from error

and instructed in the truth, profess to be a perfect rule of faith and practice. "Their accuracy can be easily substantiated," even to the most illiterate understanding. Why, then, should there be an infallible stream of tradition kept up by a constant miracle running parallel with the infallible stream of Scripture, which can be and has been preserved pure by the ordinary providence of God? Is a large variety of means for the accomplishment of any effect, when a few are abundantly adequate, characteristic of the works of God? Is it His ordinary course to multiply agents when a single cause is sufficient for His purpose? Your assumption, then, that a body of infallible teachers is necessary to preserve the doctrines of Christianity in their original purity is wholly groundless, and your argument, consequently, may be given to the winds. The Bible shows us a more excellent way.

You have indirectly insisted upon the promises of Christ that He would send the Spirit to guide His disciples into all truth, and be with them to assist and bless them in preaching His Gospel to the ends of the earth. But, sir, these promises do not serve your purpose. The first was fulfilled in each of the Apostles, and if it is to be applied in a similar form to all their successors, it would prove the full inspiration of every lawful minister of God. This is more than you are willing to admit. You have already told us that no single individual is to be received as an infallible teacher, but that the authority to make an unerring decision belongs exclusively " to a body of individuals in their collective capacity." Our Saviour said nothing of such a body; His promise in reference to the Apostles was evidently *personal*, and applied to them in the official relations which each sustained as a steward of the mysteries of God. How, then, was the promise accomplished to succeeding ages? By leading the Apostles, under the inspiration of the Holy Ghost, to record the infallible instructions of Christ, which should be a perpetual rule of faith, containing all things im-

portant for man to know or for man to do.[1] These venerable
men *live* in their books: "for books are not absolutely dead
things, but do contain a progeny of life in them, to be as
active as that soul whose progeny they are; nay, they do

[1] See this subject ably and satisfactorily discussed in Warburton's Doctrine of Grace, pt. i., and Bishop Heber's Bampton Lectures. The reader
will excuse the following extract from the 7th of Heber's Lectures:

"It appears, then, that the advent of the Paraclete, and his abode
among men, would be, during any period of Christian history, sufficiently
evinced by the existence of one or more inspired individuals, whose authority should govern, whose lights should guide, whose promises should
console their less distinguished brethren, and by whom, and in whom, as
the agents and organs of His will, the Holy Ghost should be recognized
as Sovereign of the Church Universal. But if this be conceded, it will
signify but very little, or (to speak more boldly, perhaps, but not less accurately) it will be a circumstance altogether insignificant, whether the instruction afforded be oral or epistolary; whether the government be carried
on by the authority of a present lawgiver, or through the medium of re-
scripts bearing his seal, and, no less than his personal mandates, compulsory
on the obedience of the faithful. In every government, whether human or
Divine, the amanuensis of a sovereign is an agent of his will, no less ordinary and effectual than his herald; and St. Paul both might and did lay
claim to an equal deference when, in the name and on behalf of that
Spirit by whom he was actuated, he censured by his letters the incestuous
Corinthian, as if he had, when present and by word of mouth, pronounced
the ecclesiastical sentence. It follows that the Holy Ghost as accurately
fulfilled the engagement of Christ, as the Patron and Governor of Christians, by the writings of the inspired person when absent as by his actual
presence and preaching. And if St. Paul, having once by Divine authority set in order the Asiatic and Grecian churches, had departed for
Spain, or Britain, or some other country at so great a distance as to render
all subsequent communication impossible, yet still, so long as the instructions left behind sufficed for the wants and interests of the community,
that community would not have ceased to be guided and governed by the
Holy Ghost through the writings of His chosen servant. But that authority which we allow to the writings of an absent Apostle we cannot,
without offending against every analogy of reason and custom, deny to
those which a deceased Apostle has left behind him. For the authority of
such writings, I need hardly observe, is of an official, not of a personal
nature. It does not consist in their having emanated from Peter or James
or John, abstractly considered (in which case, the authority of any one of
them might, undoubtedly, terminate with his life), but their authority is
founded in that faith which receives these persons as accredited agents of the
Almighty. We reverence their communications as the latest edicts of the
Paraclete; and we believe all further communications to have ceased for

preserve, as in a vial, the purest efficacy and extraction of that living intellect that bred them. A good book is the precious life-blood of a master-spirit, embalmed and treasured up on purpose to a life beyond life." It is in the Records which they left that we now find the Spirit of inspiration; there is His abode, there the place of His supreme illumination, and in these books, consequently, Christianity must be sought in its purity and vigour.

The other promise pledges the assistance of Christ to those who preach the truth. It is a standing encouragement to all ministers that in faithfully dispensing the Word of God according to the law and the testimony their labour should not be in vain in the Lord. Our Saviour had previously given a command to go into all the world and preach the Gospel to every creature. The prospect of success in the fulfilment of this solemn injunction, from the condition of society, the prejudices of the Jews, the philosophy of the Greeks and the superstition of the Romans, was far from encouraging. To support their faith and quicken their hopes their ascending Saviour pledged His almighty power to make His truth effectual in bringing down lofty imaginations and subduing the hearts of men in captivity to His cross. The promise in that passage is

a time; not because these eminent servants of God have long since gone to their reward, for it were as easy for the Holy Spirit to raise up other prophets in their room as it was originally to qualify them for that high office—not because we apprehend that the good Spirit is become indifferent to the welfare of the Church, for this would be in utter contradiction to the gracious assurance of our Saviour; but because sufficient light has been already afforded for the government of our hopes and tempers; and because no subsequent question has occurred for which the Scriptures already given had not already and sufficiently provided. . . . .

"We conclude, then, as Warburton has long since concluded (though he arrived at the same truth by a process somewhat different, and encumbered its definition by circumstances which I have shown to be irrelevant), —we conclude that it is by the revelation of the Christian covenant, and by the preservation of the knowledge thus communicated to the ancient Church in the Scriptures of the New Testament, that the Holy Ghost has manifested and continues, as the Vicar and Successor of Christ, to manifest his protecting care of Christianity."

not that they should speak the truth, and nothing but the truth, but that in speaking the truth, in preaching whatever He had commanded, He would be with them always, even to the end of the world; and this promise has never failed.

Your letter contains a few incidental statements, introduced in the way of cumulative testimony, to confirm the pretensions of your infallible body. You tell us first that it can trace its predecessors in an unbroken line up to the age of the Apostles themselves. So far is this from being the truth, that not a single priest in your Church can have any absolute certainty that he is a priest at all unless he be invested with the prerogative of God to search the hearts and try the reins of the children of men. Intention, on your principles, is an essential element of a valid ordination! How can a priest be assured that his bishop intended to ordain him, or how can the bishop be assured that he himself was lawfully consecrated? The whole matter is involved in confusion, and you cannot know whether you are pastors at all or not.

Again, you inform us of the prodigious numbers that have been converted by the labours of your infallible teachers. Sir, the world loveth its own, and it is characteristic of the broad road which leads to death that thousands are journeying its downward course. Mohammed laid the foundations of an empire which in the course of eighty years extended farther than the Roman arms for eight hundred years had been able to spread the jurisdiction of the Cæsars. In this comparatively short space of time there were brought under the sway of the Crescent the Grecian, Persian and Mogul States, with many others of inferior importance, and yet Mohammedanism, notwithstanding its unparalleled success, was a gross system of imposture and fraud. The purity of a system is not to be determined by the multitudes that embrace it. How significant is the question of our Saviour, "When the Son of man cometh, shall He find faith on the earth?" "Fear not, *little* flock, it is your Father's good pleasure to give you the kingdom."

Why have you omitted all mention of the meekness and patience that have always been characteristic of the Church of God? Were you conscious, sir, that you had no claims to that discriminating badge of the faithful? Did the past rise up before you in horrible distinctness and warn you to forbear? Rome, Papal Rome, which professes to be the humble, meek, patient, suffering Church of God, is literally steeped in human gore. Your pastors have inflicted more sufferings upon men, have shed more human blood, have invented a greater variety of tortures, have more deeply revelled in human misery and feasted on human groans, than all the tyrants, bigots and despots of all the other systems of superstition and oppression that have ever appeared in the world from the fall of man to the present day. To Papal Rome the foul pre-eminence of cruelty must unquestionably be awarded. The holy ministers of the Inquisition, under the sacred name of religion, have tested to its utmost limits the capacity of human endurance; every bone, muscle, sinew and nerve has been effectually sounded, and the precise point ascertained at which agony is no longer tolerable, and the convulsed and quivering spirit must quit its tenement of clay. The degree of refinement and perfection to which the art of torment has been carried in these infernal prisons is enough to make humanity shudder and religion sicken, and nothing but the most invincible blindness could ever confound these habitations of cruelty, these dark corners of the earth, with the means of grace and the elements of salvation. How preposterous, while breathing out slaughter and cruelty, exhibiting more the spirit of cannibals than the temper of Christians, to claim to be the Holy Catholic Church, the chosen depository of truth, the special temple of the Holy Ghost!

Having, as you suppose, sufficiently proved that an infallible body exists, you next proceed to show us that it must be composed of the pastors and teachers of your own communion. This part of your argument need not detain me long, as I have clearly refuted your proofs of the existence of such a body. Still, if it did exist, the mere *claim* of Rome would not establish her pretensions to be received as an unerring tribunal of faith. Theudas and Judas each *claimed* to be the promised Messiah of the Jews. Moham- med claimed to be a true prophet of God, and the Devil himself sometimes claims to be an angel of light. If an arrogant claim is sufficient to establish a right, and such a right is founded in absolute certainty, how long would the distinctions of truth and falsehood, of virtue and vice, be preserved among men?

LETTER V.

INFALLIBILITY—HISTORICAL DIFFICULTIES.

THE infallibility of the Papal Church is a doctrine so momentous in its consequences as to deserve a more ex- tended view than a simple refutation of the arguments by which you have endeavoured to support it. This, sir, is the πρωτον ψευδος of your system, the foundation of those enormous corruptions in doctrine and abuses in discipline by which you have enslaved the consciences of men, and transmuted the pure and glorious Gospel of Christ into a dark and malignant superstition, which through fear of your malediction keeps its deluded victims in bondage in this world, and from the certain malediction of God dooms them to perdition in the world to come. Your pretensions to the unerring guidance of the Holy Ghost render change impossible and reformation hopeless. Whatever you have been in the past ages of your history you are to-day; and the errors which in other times ignorance engendered from a warm imagination, or which avarice and ambition have found it convenient to present to the world as the offspring of truth, must still be defended and still carried out into all their legitimate results. The impositions which you practised in an age of darkness must now be justified in an age of light. The absurdities of the past, which sprang from the blind superstition of monks and priests or from the lordly pretensions of popes and prelates, must now be fathered upon the Spirit of God, and that aid which neither reason nor the Scriptures impart to your dogmas must be supported by an arrogant claim to the control and supervision of the Holy Ghost. This is your last resort; and when this corner-stone is removed your whole system totters to its fall. It is the impression of Divine authority that conceals from your parasites the hideous proportions of the Papal fabric; it is this which throws a charm of solemnity around it, and renders that awful and venerable which seen in its true light would at once be pronounced the temple of Antichrist. The question, therefore, of infallibility is to you a question of life and death. The very being of the Papacy depends upon maintaining the spell by which you have so long deluded the nations of the earth. Let this wand of your enchantment be broken and the chambers of your imagery disclosed, and darker abominations will be revealed than those which the prophet beheld in the temple of the Lord at Jerusalem.

In pretending to the distinguished prerogative of infallibility, there is a prodigious and astonishing contrast between the weakness of your proofs and the extravagance of your claims. It seems that you act upon the principle by which Tertullian once supported a palpable absurdity, and resolve to believe it, because, under the circumstances of the case, it is absolutely *impossible* that it *can be true.*

The ordinary arguments which your writers are accustomed to adduce proceed upon a principle radically false. They reason from expediency to fact, and because an infallible tribunal is supposed to be a proper appointment for suppressing heresy and terminating controversy in matters of faith, it is rashly inferred that such a tribunal has been actually established. The inconsistency of such an arrangement with that peculiar probation which the moral government of God involves, in which our characters are tested,

our principles developed and the real inclinations of the
heart made manifest—a probation which necessarily supposes temptations, dangers and trials, both in apprehending
the truth and in discharging the duties of life—seems to
form no part of their estimate. With such a condition of
moral discipline the plan which the providence of God has
appointed for arriving at certainty upon the truths of the
Gospel is perfectly consistent. The truth is committed to
written documents; the reception of those documents depends in a great degree upon the state of the heart, which,
as the medium through which it must pass, imparts its own
tinge to the evidence submitted. They that are willing to
comply with the commandments are in that mental condition which disposes them to receive and justly to appreciate
the truth of God; and to all such the Spirit of grace, which
the Saviour bequeathed as a legacy to the Church, will impart an infallible assurance to establish their minds. A
plan like this is in harmonious accordance with every other
feature of the moral government of God. The understanding is as really tested as the heart, or rather the dispositions
of the heart—the *moral* character of the man is really exhibited by his dealings with the truth. There is in the first
instance no overwhelming evidence which quells opposition,
silences prejudice and conceals the native enmity of man
against spiritual light. There is no resistless demonstration
which compels assent, and which, by rendering us timid in
indulging inclination, may make us less visibly vicious, but
not less really depraved nor more truly virtuous. There
is no portentous sign from heaven which startles the skeptic
in his parleys with error, and forces him to receive what
his nature leads him to detest. The true evidence of the
Gospel is a growing evidence, sufficient always to create
obligation and to produce assurance, but effectual only as
the heart expands in fellowship with God and becomes
assimilated to the spirits of the just. It is precisely the
evidence which is suited to our moral condition. And any
views of expediency which would prompt us to expect a

different kind of evidence—an evidence which should stifle or repress those peculiar traits of character by which error is engendered—would be inconsistent with the state in which we are placed. Hence, we are told that it must *needs be* that heresies should come, that they which are approved may be made manifest. Our real condition requires the possibility of error; and God consequently has made no arrangements for absolutely terminating controversies and settling questions of faith without regard to the moral sympathies of men. Upon the supposition, however, that a kind of evidence was intended to be provided by which the truth might be infallibly apprehended while the heart continued in rebellion against God; by which the possibility of cavil might be removed and no plausible pretext be afforded to the sophist; by which, in fact, the light actually vouchsafed should not only be sufficient, but wholly irresistible,—if the object had been to extirpate error and to prevent controversy, it would have been a less circuitous method to have made *each* man personally infallible, and thus have secured the reception of the truth. The argument from expediency is certainly as strong in favour of individual infallibility as in favour of the infallibility of a special body: it is even stronger, for the end desired to be gained could be much more speedily and effectually accomplished. Errors would not only be checked but *prevented*, controversy would be torn up by the roots, and the whole world would be made to harmonize in symbols of faith.[1]

[1] "But it is more useful and fit, you say, for deciding of controversies, to have, besides an infallible rule to go by, a living, infallible judge to determine them; and from hence you conclude that certainly there is such a judge. But why, then, may not another say that it is yet more useful, for many excellent purposes, that all the patriarchs should be infallible, than that the Pope only should? Another, that it would be yet more useful that all the archbishops of every province should be so, than that the patriarchs only should be so. Another, that it would be yet more useful if all the bishops of every diocese were so. Another, that it would be yet more available that all the parsons of every parish should be so. Another, that it would yet be more excellent if all the fathers of families were so. And, lastly, another, that it were much more to be desired that

The method of reasoning, consequently, from expediency to fact is fallacious and unsafe; and if the magnificent pretensions of your sect rest upon no firmer basis than deceitful notions of utility and convenience, they are indeed built upon the sand. Instead of a solid and a noble fabric of imposing strength and commanding grandeur, you present us with a structure as weak and contemptible as the toy-houses of children constructed of cards.

There are no less than three different opinions entertained in your Church as to the organ through which its infallibility is exercised or manifested. This single circumstance is enough to involve the whole claim 'in contempt. If it be not infallibly certain where the infallible tribunal is, in case of emergency, to be found, the old logical maxim applies with undiminished force, *de non apparentibus et non existentibus eadem est ratio.* To settle controversies it is not enough that a judge exists; his existence must be known and his court accessible. Uncertainty as to the seat of an infallible authority is just as fatal to the legitimate exercise of its functions as uncertainty in regard to the being of the authority in the abstract. To resolve our doubts and remove our difficulties some of your doctors refer us to the Pope as the vicar of Christ, the head of the Church, the teacher of the faithful, and plead the decisions of councils in behalf of his pretensions. As the centre of unity to the Church and the fountain or source of ecclesiastical power, they represent him as possessed of an authority as absolute as that with which the head controls the members of the

every man and every woman were so: just as much as the prevention of controversies is better than the decision of them, and the prevention of heresies better than the condemnation of them; and upon this ground, conclude by your own very consequence that not only a general council, nor only the Pope, but all the patriarchs, archbishops, bishops, pastors, fathers, nay, all men in the world, are infallible. If you say now, as I am sure you will, that this conclusion is most gross and absurd, against sense and experience, then must also the ground be false from which it evidently and undeniably follows—viz.: that that course of dealing with men seems always more fit to Divine Providence which seems most fit to human reason."—*Chillingworth*, vol. i., p. 249; Oxford edition of 1838.

body. Hence, your bishops are nothing but his vicars; and in token of their bondage they are not content with the usual oaths of allegiance by which subjects are held in obedience to their sovereign, but they enter into a solemn obligation to appear personally before him every three years to give an account of their stewardship, or else to excuse themselves by an adequate deputy. "As in a disciplined army," says Dr. Milner, a modern writer of your sect, in a charge which, though intrinsically worthless, excited too much controversy to be speedily forgotten—"as in a disciplined army the soldiers obey their officers, and these, other officers of superior rank, who themselves are subject to a commander-in-chief, so in the Catholic Church, extending, as it does, from the rising to the setting sun, the faithful of all nations are guided by their pastors, who in their turns are submissive to the prelates, *whilst the whole body is subordinate to one supreme pastor*, whose seat is the rallying-point and centre of them all." In this exquisite system of slavery the Pope is evidently the sovereign authority—the whole body is subordinate to him, and whatever infallibility the Church possesses, it must be found in the person of her supreme pastor as the centre and rallying-point of the whole. Under any other theory of infallibility this, it may be well to remark, is and must be the practical working of your system. Your leading maxim is obedience; there must be no investigation of the right to command, no regard to the propriety of the precepts; the whole duty of the people is summed up in a single word, *obey*. This system of absolute submission runs up unchecked until it terminates in the Sovereign Pontiff at Rome, whose edicts and decrees, by necessary consequence, none can question, and who is therefore the absolute lord of Papal faith. This seems to be the inevitable result of that slavish doctrine of passive obedience which your pastors inculcate, and without which your Church would expire in a day. Hence, whether you lodge infallibility with councils, with the body of the pastors at large, or give the Pope an ultimate veto upon the decisions of œcumenical synods, to this complexion, under the theory of implicit obedience, it must unavoidably come at last; and the practical impression upon the people will be precisely that which, we are told by intelligent travellers, prevails in Italy—"the Pope is greater than God." [1]

It is evident that the infallibility of the Pope cannot be separated from his claim to supremacy. To prove that he is not *supreme* is, in other words, to prove that he is not infallible. Now, to those who maintain that the infallible authority of the Church is to be sought in the person of his Holiness, this serious historical difficulty arises: Where was that infallibility before a Supreme Pastor existed? It is a fact sustained by the very amplest testimony that as late, at least, as the seventh century, the bishops of the Church, not excepting the bishops of Rome, whatever accidental differences prevailed among them, were regarded at least as officially *equal*. According to Jerome, every bishop, whether of Rome, Eugubium, Constantinople, Rhegium, Alexandria or Tanis, possessed the same merit and the same priesthood. [2] "There is but one bishopric in the Church," says Cyprian, "and every bishop has an undivided portion in it;" [3] that is, it is *one* office, and the power of all who are invested with it is precisely the same. In his letter to Pope Stephen this doctrine is still more distinctly announced, but it is fully brought out in the speech which he delivered at the opening of the great Council of Carthage. "For no one of us," says he, "makes himself bishop of bishops, and compels his colleagues, by tyrannical power, to a necessity of complying; forasmuch as every bishop, according to the liberty and power that is granted him, is free to act as he sees fit; and

---

[1] "Il papa e più che Dio per noi altri."—For a remarkable account of the extravagant adulation which has been heaped upon the Popes, see Erasmus on 1 Tim. i. 6.

[2] Epist. ci., ad Evang.—Ubicunque fuerit Episcopus, sive Romæ, sive Eugubii, sive Constantinopoli, sive Rhegii, sive Alexandriæ, sive Tania, ejusdem meriti, ejusdem est et Sacerdotii.

[3] De Unitat. Eccles. Episcopatus unus est, cujus a singulis in solidum pars tenetur. § v.

can no more be judged by others than he can judge them. But let us all expect the judgment of our Lord Jesus Christ, who only hath power both to invest us with the government of His Church and to pass sentence upon our actions."

But an authority which ought to be decisive on this question is to be found in the testimony of Gregory the Great, who was filled with horror at the arrogant pretensions of the patriarch of Constantinople to be treated as a universal bishop, and in the strongest terms reprobated the idea that any such title could be lawfully applied to any person whatever.[1]

During these six centuries in which the Church was without a visible head, when there was neither centre of unity nor rallying-point to the whole, when, in the modern sense, there was no such thing as a pope, where was the infallibility of the body? Most evidently it could not have been in the bishop of Rome; he was not then what he is now; and those who contend that he constitutes now the infallible tribunal of the Church are reduced to the awkward necessity of maintaining either that there was *then* no infallible tribunal at all, or that it has since been transferred from its ancient seat to the person of the Pope. If the latter alternative should be assumed, upon what grounds and by what authority was the transfer made? When, where and how? These are questions which require to be answered with absolute certainty before we can have any absolute certainty that the bishop of Rome is not as liable to error now as he was in the days of Firmilian.[2]

The theory which lodges infallibility with general councils is pressed with historical difficulties just as strong as those which lie against the infallibility of the Pope. If you

[1] Epist., lib. vi., epist. 30.—Ego fidenter dico, quod quisquis se Universalem Sacerdotem vocat vel vocari desiderat, in elatione sua, Antichristum præcurrit. "I affirm with confidence that whoever calls himself, or wishes to be called *universal Bishop*, in this lifting up of himself is the forerunner of Antichrist."

[2] See his Epistle to Pope Stephen, charging him both with error and schism.—*Cypriani Epistolæ*, ep. lxxv.

except the Synod at Jerusalem in the age of the Apostles, which can hardly be called œcumenical or general, there was no such thing as a general council of the Church until the first quarter of the fourth century. For two hundred years, consequently, after the last of the Apostles had fallen asleep, the Church had neglected to speak, though numerous and dangerous heresies had been industriously circulated, through the only organ by which she could pronounce an infallible decision. During all that time she was shorn of her strength. Is it probable, is it credible, that while the most fatal errors were disseminated in regard to the person of Christ, and the wildest vagaries were indulged by the Montanists and Gnostics, there existed an authority to which the whole Church deferred as supreme, and which by a single word was competent to crush these growing delusions? Why did the Fathers ply so strenuously the strong arguments of scriptural truth, the words and teachings of Prophets and Apostles, if there was indeed a stronger argument to which they might resort, and from whose decision there was no appeal? A judge that neglects to act in critical emergencies just at the time when his authority is needed is little to be preferred to no judge at all.

There is still another historical fact which it is difficult to reconcile with synodical supremacy. The early councils attributed the authority of the canons which they settled to the sanction of the emperor. They pretended to no infallible jurisdiction; their decrees were not set forth as the Word of God; the veto of the emperor destroyed them; his favour made them obligatory as far as his power extended.[1] Were the Apostles thus helpless without the imperial sanction? Did their instructions acquire the force of Divine laws from the favour of Nero or the patronage of the Cæsars? If the councils were as infallible as the Apostles, why did they not proclaim their edicts in the name of God, and, whether the emperors approved or condemned, maintain their absolute power to bind the conscience by the au-

[1] See Barrow, Suprem. Pope, and passages referred to, Suppos. 6.

thority of Christ? These councils were evidently expedients of peace, adopted by the government as well as by the Church for the purpose of securing uniformity of faith and preventing religious disturbances in the empire. They were not regarded as the unerring representatives of Christ; the deference paid to the writings of the Apostles was never paid to them; they were not acknowledged as the organ of the Spirit. Others, again, maintain that no council is infallible whose convocation and decisions have not alike received the sanction of the Pope. These persons are truly in a sad dilemma; for all the early councils were confessedly convened by the mandate of the emperor, and many were acknowledged as authoritative in their own day whose canons were opposed by the bishop of Rome. According to this principle, there was no such thing as infallibility in the Church until the Pope acquired the dominion of an earthly prince, and could assemble the subjects of the realm from different quarters of the globe by his own sovereign authority.[1]

If, as a last desperate resort against all these historical objections, it should be asserted that the unanimous consent of all the pastors of the Church was a sufficient proof of the infallible truth of any system of doctrines, the question might still be asked, whether such unanimity has ever prevailed, and how in reference to any given point it can be ascertained. The idea of reaching the truth by a system of eclecticism, collecting only the doctrines which have never been disputed, is utterly unworthy of a rational understanding. It proceeds upon the wholly gratuitous assumption that nothing important has ever been denied, or nothing evidently true has ever been questioned. The history of religion, however, affords the most abundant proof that the vanity of man, even apart from considerations of interest, may be an adequate motive for attacking the most sacred opinions and the most venerable institutions, while others less important are protected from insult by their acknow-

[1] See Barrow, Suprem. Pope, and passages referred to, Suppos. 6.

ledged insignificance. Such is the weakness of humanity
that fame is often more precious than truth, and he who
cannot hope to rise to distinction by contributing to the
general fund of human knowledge is sometimes tempted to
seek notoriety from the profane attempt to demolish the
temple erected by the labour of years. The very grandeur
of the edifice provokes the efforts of infatuated vanity. To
suppose, consequently, that those doctrines of religion are
alone infallibly true which have met with universal approbation is to overlook the weakness and folly of man, and to
attribute to his conduct in regard to religion a wisdom and
propriety which the history of the past by no·means sustains. It is much more natural to suppose that the most
important truths should be the subjects of the fiercest con-
tentions, that ambitious churchmen who had been defeated
in their views of personal aggrandizement should endeavour
to wreak their vengeance and gratify their vanity by aiming their blows at the very vitals of Christianity. Hence,
we find, in fact, that a large share of the distractions of
Christendom, the most pestiferous and deadly errors, have
owed their origin to the spleen and mortification of their
authors. How much, too, ambition, the master-sin by
which angels fell, has corrupted the Church and perverted
the right ways of the Lord, the whole history of the Papacy
abundantly attests. Arius failed in obtaining a bishopric,
and vented his malignity in attacking the very foundation
of the faith. The extent to which prejudice, mere prejudice,
prevailed in the controversies of the Iconoclasts and Mono-
thelites is an amusing commentary on the harmony of
priests in fundamental doctrines; and there is an instance
on record of a famous interpreter who confessedly distorted
a passage of Scripture from its just and obvious meaning
because the leader of another sect had endorsed it in his
commentaries. A man, consequently, who should act upon
the famous maxim, *quod semper, quod ubique, quod ab omnibus*, in the formation of his creed, and resolve to admit
nothing as infallible truth which had not the mark of uni-

versal consent, might condense his articles in a very narrow
compass.   Not a single distinctive feature of revelation upon
this absurd hypothesis would be regarded as an essential
element of faith.   The plenary inspiration of the Scriptures
has been confessedly denied by distinguished divines, whole
books of the Bible have been ruthlessly discarded from the
Canon, and even popes themselves are said to have treated
the history of Jesus as a gainful fable.   It is important,
therefore, to believe nothing about the inspiration of the
Scriptures!   The doctrine of the Trinity has been bitterly
assailed, the incarnation of the Redeemer openly derided,
and the work of the Spirit denounced as enthusiasm.   While
one council has determined that Christ was the eternal Son
of the Father, another with equal pretensions to infallibility
has decided against His Divinity.   Nothing, therefore, is
infallibly certain about the person of Christ, and a man
may be a very good Catholic, according to the maxim in
question, without any opinion of the Saviour at all!   Nay,
the very being of God may be lawfully discarded from a
creed collected in this way, since the successors of the Fisherman, unless they are greatly belied, have not occasionally
scrupled to indulge in skeptical doubts upon this prime
article of religion!   This unanimous consent of the pastors
of the Church, therefore, is a mere phantom of the brain,
always mocking our efforts to compass it, and retreating
before us like the verge of the horizon.   It is "*vox et præ-
terea nihil.*"

But suppose such an unanimous consent existed in fact
in reference to all the doctrines of Christianity, suppose
that no pastors of the Church had ever been heretical, how
is an Indian or negro to become acquainted with the testimony that embraces all the priests that have ever said or
sung the services of the Church, from the age of the Apostles to the period of his own existence?   To achieve such
a task would require a critical apparatus hardly less formidable than that which you pronounce to be essential to the
settlement of the Canon.

I have now reviewed the leading theories in regard to the seat of the infallibility of your Church which have been maintained among you, and have shown them to be encompassed with historical difficulties fatal to their truth. There is one general objection of the same kind which covers them all, and which, upon the approved principle of logic, that two contradictories cannot possibly both be true, would seem to settle the matter. It is indubitably certain that popes have contradicted popes, councils have contradicted councils, and pastors have contradicted pastors, and all have contradicted the Scriptures. Notwithstanding your vain boasts of the unchanging uniformity of your system, and the perfect consistency and harmony of the doctrines of faith which your Church in every age has inculcated, it is still historically true that you have exhibited at different periods such variety of tenets as to render you wonderfully like the administration of Lord Chatham as inimitably described by Burke. Your *syntagma confessionum* would present a scene "so checkered and speckled; a piece of joinery so crossly indented and whimsically dovetailed; a cabinet so variously inlaid; such a piece of diversified mosaic, such a tesselated pavement without cement—here a bit of black stone, and there a bit of white—that it might be indeed a very curious show, but utterly unsafe to touch and unsure to stand on."

In the short compass of twenty-three years, to give a specimen of your wonderful consistency, we have idolatry both abolished and established by the councils of a Church which, according to Bossuet, never varies—the Council of Constantinople unanimously decreeing the removal of images and the abolition of image-worship, and the second Council of Nice re-establishing both, and pronouncing an anathema on all who had concurred in the previous decision. The second Council of Ephesus approved and sanctioned the impiety of Eutyches, and the Council of Chalcedon condemned it. The fourth Council of Lateran asserted the doctrine of a physical change in the eucharistic elements, in express contradiction to the teachings of the Primitive Church, and the evident declarations of the Apostles of the Lord. The second Council of Orange gave its sanction to some of the leading doctrines of the school of Augustine, and the Council of Trent threw the Church into the arms of Pelagius. Thus, at different periods every type of doctrine has prevailed in the bosom of an unchangeable Church. She has been distracted with every variety of sect, tormented with every kind of controversy, convulsed with every species of heresy, and at last has settled down upon a platform which annihilates the Word of God, denounces the doctrines of Christ and His Apostles, and bars the gates of salvation against men.

That the *Scriptures*, and not the priesthood or any infallible body of men, were the only channels through which an infallible knowledge of Divine truth was to be acquired, is so clearly the doctrine of the Primitive Church, which was founded by the hands of the Apostles themselves, as to be absolutely fatal to any of the forms in which the pretensions of Rome are asserted. Among the host of testimonies that might be adduced to establish and corroborate this vital point the following may be deemed a sufficient exposition of the views of the Fathers: "Look not," says Chrysostom, "for any other teacher; you have the oracles of God; no one can teach like them. Any other instructor may from some erroneous principle conceal from you many things of the greatest importance, and therefore I exhort you to procure for yourselves Bibles. Have them for your constant instructors, and in all your trials have recourse to them for the remedies you need."[1]

"It behooveth," says Basil, "that every word and every work should be accredited by the testimony of the inspired Scripture."[2] "It is the duty of hearers," he observes again, "when they have been instructed in the Scriptures, to try

---

[1] See also Chrysostom's 3d Hom. de Laz. The truth is, a volume might be collected from this Father in support of my position.

[2] Moralia, Regula xxvi.

and examine by them the things spoken by their teachers, to receive whatever is consonant to those Scriptures, and to reject whatever is alien."[1]   "Without the Word," says Clemens Alexandrinus, "all religious investigation is vain ; the holy prophetic Scriptures are the foundation of religious truth, the rule of life, the high road to salvation."[2]

"Whence," says Cyprian, "is this tradition [alluding to a pretended tradition of Stephen, bishop of Rome]? Is it delivered down to us on the authority of the Lord and of the Gospel, or from the precepts and writings of the Apostles? For God Himself testifies that those things which are *written* are to be observed. Josh. i. 8. And the Lord, sending his Apostles, commands the nations to be baptized and to be taught to observe whatsoever He has commanded. If, therefore, it be *prescribed in the Gospel or contained in the Epistles or Acts of the Apostles,* by all means let this Divine and holy tradition be observed. What obstinacy, what presumption, to prefer the tradition of men to the Divine ordinance, without considering that God is angry and provoked whenever human tradition breaks and overlooks the Divine commands!"[3]

In the Scriptures, then, according to these venerable men, and in the Scriptures alone, we possess the charter of our faith, pure and uncorrupted as it came from the inspired breasts of the Apostles; and the Holy Spirit, in moving these chosen ambassadors of Christ to commit His infallible teachings to imperishable records, secured that certainty in the transmission of Christian doctrine which completely obviates the necessity of an infallible body of men. Here *is,* according to the Fathers, what all history shows the priesthood of Rome *is not*—a safe, wise, adequate, successful provision against the error and change-making tendency of man.

I need not add that this appears to be the uniform doctrine of the Scriptures themselves ; not only do they assert

---

[1] Moralia, Reg. lxxii.   [2] Admon. to the Gentiles.
[3] Epist. lxxiv. Pompeio, §§ ii. iii.

their own sufficiency and completeness as a rule of faith,
but that they were written with the design of handing
down, in their integrity and purity, the doctrines which the
Apostles taught and the early Christians received. The
Evangelist Luke, in recording the motives which induced
him to commit his Gospel to writing, states distinctly that
his object was that the "certainty" of those things which
had been previously communicated by oral teaching might
be fully apprehended. He proceeds upon the just and
natural principle that written documents presented a safer
channel ᵥfor the transmission of truth than verbal tradition. Peter, when about to put off his mortal tabernacle,
makes provision for perpetuating the faith after his decease
by *writing* his second Epistle. Here was the time and here
was the place for the pretended founder of the Papacy to
assert the prerogatives of his see. But not a word does he
utter of living teachers—of any infallible tribunal composed
of men. To his mind *written memorials* were the true security for preserving entire apostolical instructions.[1] But

[1] "The claim of infallibility, or even authority, to prescribe magisterially
to the opinions and consciences of men, whether in an individual or in
assemblies and collections of men, is never to be admitted. Admitted,
said I? It is not to be heard with patience, unless it be supported by a
miracle; and this very text of Scripture (2 Pet. i. 20, 21) is manifestly, of
all others, the most adverse to the arrogant pretensions of the Roman
Pontiff. Had it been the intention of God that Christians, after the death
of the Apostles, should take the sense of Scripture, in all obscure and
doubtful passages, from the mouth of an infallible interpreter, whose decisions in all points of doctrine, faith and practice should be oracular and
final, *this* was the occasion for the Apostle to have mentioned it, to have
told us plainly whither we should resort for the unerring explication of
those prophecies which, it seems, so well deserve to be studied and understood. And from St. Peter, in particular, of all the Apostles, this information was in all reason to be expected, if, as the vain tradition goes, the
oracular gift was to be lodged with his successors. This, too, was the
time when the mention of the thing was most likely to occur to the Apostle's thoughts, when he was about to be removed from the superintendence
of the Church, and was composing an Epistle for the direction of the
flock which he so faithfully had fed, after his departure. Yet St. Peter,
at this critical season, when his mind was filled with an interested care
for the welfare of the Church after his decease, upon an occasion which

the grand and fatal objection to the doctrine of infallibility, in whatever form it is asserted, is, that it is totally destitute of the only kind of proof by which it can be possibly supported. To exempt a single individual or any body of men from the possibility of error is the exclusive prerogative of God. It depends upon Him, therefore, and upon Him alone, to declare whether He has granted this distinction to the Popes of Rome, the councils of the Church, or the whole body of its pastors. This is a fact which can only be substantiated by a *Divine revelation*. This is the sort of evidence which the case requires, and without such evidence all such pretensions are vain, delusive, arrogant and blasphemous. Abstract reasoning can avail nothing; there must be a plain declaration from the Lord. Where, I ask, and ask triumphantly, is such a declaration to be found? Where has God confirmed by miracles the extravagant claims of the Papal community? To look for it in the Scriptures would involve the supposition that the Scriptures are already known to be inspired—the proof would become destructive of the end for which it was sought. Papists tell us that we cannot be assured that the Scriptures are divinely inspired until we are assured that the decisions of the Church are infallible. It would be, then, most preposterous in them to remand us to the Scriptures to prove their claims, when the only authenticity they ascribe to the Scriptures is derived from these claims. Still, we may safely challenge them to produce from the Bible a single passage which directly asserts or by necessary implication involves the proposition—either that the Pope, in his official rela-

might naturally lead him to mention all means of instruction that were likely to be provided,—in these circumstances St. Peter gives not the most distant intimation of a living oracle to be perpetually maintained in the succession of the Roman bishops. On the contrary, he overthrows their aspiring claims by doing that which supersedes the supposed necessity of any such institution; he lays down a plain rule, which, judiciously applied, may enable every private Christian to interpret the written oracles of prophecy in all points of general importance for himself."— *Horsley's Sermons*, vol. i., Serm. 15.

tions, is an infallible expounder of the faith, or that general councils are unerring in their decisions, or that the whole body of pastors shall be preserved inviolably from error. On the contrary, it is worthy to be noticed how the Ephesian elders are solemnly assured that from even among themselves, among the very teachers of the Church, grievous wolves should arise, not sparing the flock. And the voice of all history—though the Bible says nothing specifically about them, as never contemplating such a phenomenon—the voice of all history abundantly attests that councils *have* erred, and so dissipates the idle fiction of their infallibility. Is there, then, any other revelation beside the Sacred Oracles from which the infallibility of the Church may be gathered? What messenger has ever been commissioned to proclaim this truth, and to seal his commission by miraculous achievements? Where has the voice of God ever commanded us to submit to Rome as His representative and vicar? Where are the Divine credentials of Papal infallibility? Until these questions are satisfactorily answered, Rome must be viewed in the light of an impostor, assuming to herself that supreme deference which is due exclusively to the Spirit of God. Her pretensions must be regarded as the offspring of fraud, engendered by ambition and nurtured by interest, which none can acknowledge without treason against God and perdition to themselves. Like the harlot in the Proverbs of Solomon, she stands arrayed in gaudy attire to beguile the simple, but her feet take hold on death and her steps lead down to hell.

LETTER VI.

INFALLIBILITY AND SKEPTICISM.

To abandon the exercise of private judgment, and intrust the understanding to the guidance of teachers arrogant enough to claim infallibility without producing the credentials of a Divine commission, is to encourage a despotism which none ean sanction without the express authority of God. Private judgment, indeed, can never be wholly set aside; the pretensions of an infallible instructor must be submitted to the understandings of men, and finally determined by each man's convictions of truth and justice. The ultimate appeal must be to that very reason which, in its independent exercise, is dreaded as the parent of so much mischief, the prolific source of so much schism. It is a circumstance, however, not sufficiently regarded that the pretensions of Rome to that degree of inspiration which she arrogantly claims cannot be admitted without striking at the basis of all human knowledge, confounding the distinctions of truth and falsehood, and laying the foundations of a skepticism more malignant and desolating than the worst calamities which can possibly result from the free and unhampered indulgence of private opinion. As extremes are so intimately connected that the least touch of the pencil can translate expressions of joy into symptoms of sorrow, so those who seek to remove the occasions of difference, to terminate schism, extinguish controversy and establish religion upon the strongest grounds of absolute certainty, by resorting to a guide that claims infallibility without those signs and wonders which indubitably declare that God's Spirit is in him and God's hand upon him, pursue a course having, in reality, a striking and inevitable tendency to conduct the mind to a dreary and hopeless Pyrrhonism. There can be no assurance of truth without a corresponding confidence in our faculties; the light which we enjoy, the convictions of our minds, the appearances of things to the human understanding,—these are to us the measures of truth and falsehood. Whoever is not content to receive the information of his senses, the reports of his consciousness and the evident conclusions of his own mind, deduced in conformity with those fundamental laws of belief which are presupposed in all its operations; whoever, in other words, looks upon his faculties as instruments of falsehood, and distrusts the clearest exercise of his powers; whoever refuses to take upon trust what the very constitution of his nature inclines him to believe,—must rest content with the cheerless prospect of perpetual ignorance.

There can be no knowledge without previous belief, determined by the law of our nature, and liable to no suspicions of deception, because ultimately resolvable into the veracity of God. There are certain primary convictions—certain original principles, as Aristotle calls them—through which we know and believe everything else, and which must, therefore, themselves be received with paramount certainty. These instinctive elements of natural faith constitute the standard of evidence, the foundation of truth, the groundwork of knowledge. Truth is the natural and necessary aliment of the soul; and the faculties of the mind, in their original constitution, were evidently adjusted with a special reference to its pursuit, investigation and enjoyment. As the stability of external nature responds harmoniously to our instinctive belief of the uniformity of its laws, so all the elements of faith which enter into the essential constitution of the mind are as admirably and unerringly adapted to their appropriate objects. Whatever, consequently, has a tendency to unsettle a man's confidence in the legitimate and natural exercise of his faculties, or to call into question what a distinguished philosopher has denominated the "fundamental laws of human belief," has an equal tendency to introduce a general skepticism, in which the distinctions of truth and falsehood are confounded, and the elements of life and death promiscuously

mingled. To bring the different powers of the soul into a
state of unnatural collision; to set our faculties at war; to
involve their functions in suspicion; to make the deductions
of the understanding contradict the original convictions of
our nature,—is effectually to sap the foundations of knowledge, to annihilate all certainty, to reduce truth and falsehood to a common insignificance, and expose the mind to
endless perplexity, confusion and despair. Now this is precisely the result which the Church of Rome accomplishes
in the minds of those who are foolish enough to receive her
as an infallible teacher and her instructions as infallible
truth. She subverts the original constitution of the mind,
contradicts the primary and instinctive convictions of every
human understanding, and pronounces that to be *absolutely
certain* which God, through the essential principles of human
belief, declares to be *absolutely false*. She destroys the only
foundation of evidence, extinguishes its light, surrounds
her followers with an artificial darkness, and invites them
to a repose from which no voice of truth can awaken them,
no force of argument arouse them. He that yields his
understanding to the guidance of Rome must frequently
meet with cases in which the information of his faculties is
clear and unambiguous, and the constitution of his nature
prompts him to one view, while the infallible authority to
which he has submitted requires a contrary faith. Hence,
if he be consistent, he must follow his guide, because,
according to the terms of the hypothesis, the guide is infallible, and consequently distrust the strongest convictions
of his own understanding. If, in such clear cases, the reason of men deceives them, as deceive them it must if the
teacher be indeed incapable of error, how shall it ever be
known when to trust their faculties at all? If they must
regard that light which contradicts the sentiments of their
pretended instructor as a temptation of the Devil, designed
in the providence of God to test their fidelity, how shall
they ever be able to distinguish these false appearances from
the real illuminations of truth? Is it not evident that they

must always be children in understanding, shrivelled up in intellectual dwarfishness by a comfortless Pyrrhonism— ever learning and never able to come to the knowledge of the truth?

It is a singular fact that, by pretending to infallibility, Rome occupies the same position in regard to religion which Hume maintained in relation to philosophy.[1] She is a skeptical dogmatist, and by making the same principles conduce to contradictory results, she virtually pronounces truth to be impossible and "reduces knowledge to zero." The doctrine of transubstantiation, for instance, cannot be admitted without involving in uncertainty the information of our senses, and rendering doubtful the only evidence upon which all our conceptions of the phenomena of matter must ultimately depend. Upon the authority of Rome we are required to believe that what our senses pronounce to be bread, what the minutest analysis which chemistry can institute is able to resolve into nothing but the constituent elements of bread, what every sense pronounces to be ma- terial, is yet the incarnate Son of God—soul, body and Divinity, full and entire, perfect and complete. Here Rome and the senses are evidently at war; and here that infallible Church is made to despise one of the original principles of belief which God has impressed on the constitution of the mind. If, in reference to the magical wafer, which the juggling incantations of a priest have transformed into the person of the Saviour of the world, our senses cannot be regarded as worthy of our confidence, how are we to know when to trust them at all? Why may not all our impres- sions of colour, of touch and of taste be just as delusive as those which deceive us in reference to this bread? There can be no other evidence of any sensible phenomenon than is possessed of the fact that the wafer is bread; and if this evidence is fallacious and uncertain, the existence of matter

---

[1] For a discussion of the relation of the fundamental data of conscious- ness to the reality of knowledge, see Sir W. Hamilton's Article on the Philosophy of Perception, *Discussions on Philosophy*, p. 84.

may be a chimera, or the speculation of Spinoza may not be unsound, that only one substance obtains in the universe, and that substance is God. If Rome is to be believed in opposition to the senses, the ·paramount authority of our primary convictions is at once overthrown; the constitution of our nature is rendered subject to suspicion; the measures of truth are involved in perplexity, and man is set afloat upon the boundless sea of speculation without chart, compass or rudder. The standard by which opinions must be ultimately tried is called into question, and the only thing which can be regarded as absolutely certain is the utter uncertainty of everything on earth. It is intuitively clear that if our faculties cannot be trusted in one case which falls within the sphere of their legitimate jurisdiction, they cannot be trusted in another. If they cannot be credited when, with every mark of truth, they inform us of physical phenomena, they can no more be credited when they inform us of the infallibility of the Church; if our *primary* convictions are doubtful, all other impressions must be delusive and deceitful. So far as we are able to ascertain, one thing, under such circumstances, is just as true as another; the sophist is the only philosopher, skepticism the only form of wisdom.

In conformity with what reason would lead us to expect, we find from actual experience that in Papal countries, where the infallibility of the Church is maintained without limitation or reserve, the intelligent members of the community have no real belief in any of the distinctive doctrines of religion. Hence, too, "the chair of St. Peter" has been so frequently filled by those who despised every principle embraced in the noble confession of that distinguished Apostle. Leo X., John XXIII. and Clement VII., Cardinal Bembo, Politian, Pomponatius, and a host of others, distinguished alike by their offices and attainments in the very heart of the Papal dominions, are renowned, many in the annals of infidelity, all in the history of religious hypocrisy.

The Schoolmen, indeed, did not hesitate to maintain the
assertion that opinions might be philosophically true and
yet theologically false, or theologically true and at the same
time philosophically false. . In other words, they maintained that truth might consist with open contradictions,
which is equivalent to saying that its existence was impossible, or at least inconceivable.   There can be no doubt that
the speculations of the Schoolmen prepared the way for the
extensive desolations of what has been called *philosophical
infidelity*[1] in modern times, and just as little doubt that the
violence which is offered by the creed of Rome to the original principles of human belief introduced the Schoolmen
into those curious refinements of perverse dialectics which
effectually destroyed the unity of truth, but without which
they were compelled to abandon the infallible dicta of an
arrogant community.   Modern infidelity, in all its forms, is

[1] Many valuable hints concerning the connection betwixt the scholastic
philosophy and the skepticism by which it was rapidly succeeded may be
found in Ogilvie's Inquiry into the causes of infidelity and skepticism.
The seed was evidently planted by the Schoolmen of the Middle Ages
which subsequently bore such bitter fruit; they encouraged the spirit of
captious dialectics, that absurd inattention to the fundamental laws of
belief as the basis of philosophy, which in other hands was to subvert the
foundations of all that was fair, venerable or sacred.   The reader may be
pleased with the following extract from a learned and valuable work:
"Imo, unde scholastici suas quodlibeticas et frivolas questiones, nisi ex
hac scepticismi lacuna, hauserunt.   Hoc bene notavit Jansenius (August,
tom. ii., Lib. Proœm., cap. xxviii.).   Scholastici, inquit, nimio philosophiæ
amore quasi ebrii, arcana illa mysteria gratiæ sepulta deletaque, secundùm humanæ rationis regulas, eruere, penetrare, formare, judicare, voluerunt.   Hinc ille ardor de quolibet disputandi, quidlibet eorum in dubium
revocandi.   Hinc eorum theologia innumerabilium opinionum farragine
referta est, per quas fere omnia, quantumcunque contraria, facta sunt pro-
babilia; quæ secundùm eorum pronunciata, cuilibet tueri licet.   Ita vix
quicquam certi, præter fidem, formandarum opinionum novarum promp-
titudo reliquum fecit.   Præcipitii enim pœna suspendium, εποχη hoc est;
temeritatis, omnis hesitantia et incertitudo.   Nihil enim naturalius et
vicinius quàm ut homines ex Peripateticis fiant Academici, quorum illi,
sublucente ratiuncula, sententiam extemplò precipitant; hi, temeritatis
ducti pœnitentia, semper hesitant; et nunc hoc, nunc illud, animo fluctu-
ante, displicit, placet; unde fit ut quod eis hodie probabile est, cras falsum judicetur." *Galæi Philos. General.*, Par. ii., Lib. i., c. iv.

much more intimately connected with the influence of the
Papacy than seems to be generally apprehended.   From the
very nature of the case, Popery must be the parent of skepticism, and the dogmas of Rome cannot be admitted without making a double standard of truth and destroying all
its consistency and harmony.   Those, however, who are not
prepared for the dreary shades of unmitigated skepticism
will much prefer the legitimate conclusions of their own
understanding to the wretched tattle of the Papal priesthood.   Fully assured that a standard of truth in reality
exists, uniform and stable, they can never believe that God
has subjected their minds to the control of men who can
deliberately trifle with the constitution of their nature, and
make its inherent propensities and instinctive faith a matter
of mockery.   The very fact that these miserable guides contradict the universal bias of mankind is sufficient to show that
they are blind leaders of the blind, and that, instead of having a commission from Heaven, they derive their claims from
the father of lies.   God Himself in His acknowledged revelations appeals to the authority of our primary convictions.
The miracles of Jesus Christ were addressed to the senses,
to human eyes and human ears, and in all His expostula-
tions with the Jews our Saviour evidently assumes the absolute certainty of sense and consciousness—the ultimate sources
of all human knowledge—as well as the irresistible authority
of those original principles which constitute the tests of
truth.   We cannot conceive, indeed, that a Divine revelation could be possibly authenticated without assuming the
credibility of our faculties.   To shake our confidence in
them is to render belief impossible, no matter what may be
the subject proposed or the evidence submitted.   It is idle,
in fact, to talk of evidence—which is only the light in which
the mind perceives the reality of truth—if all our perceptions are to be called into question or involved in uncertainty.
Any pretended teacher, therefore, who does not authenticate
his claims to Divine authority by performing miracles which

none could achieve unless God were with him, any teacher who belies his pretensions by opening his mouth in what every law of our nature requires us to denounce as falsehood, must be regarded as a child of darkness, the enemy of light and the foe of man. No Divine revelation can be more certain than the testimony of sense or the evidence of consciousness. Through one of these sources every idea must be conveyed to the mind; and whatever teacher undertakes to set them aside is the father of skepticism, and requires of man a homage which, though he may profess to render, it is utterly impossible to pay. If the evidence that such a teacher were really sent from God were equal to the evidence of sense or consciousness, the mind would then be involved in the state of contradiction in which it is impossible to form an opinion; the teacher and our nature, like two negatives in English, would destroy each other, and our real faith would be expressed by a cipher. The mind, in other words, would be a perfect blank, a stagnant pool of ignorance and doubt, a mere chaos of discordant elements, the sport of endless confusion and caprice. It is vain to pretend that we honour God in cordially receiving what the constitution of our nature prompts us to reject, that the merit of the faith is enhanced by the difficulties which we struggle to subdue. When these difficulties arise from perverse dispositions, from stubborn prejudices, impetuous passions or pride of understanding, there may be some foundation for the plea; but when they lie in the very nature of the evidence, he that commends his faith on such ground glories in the fact that his assent is strong just in proportion as the evidence is weak, and amounts to absolute certainty when, upon the most favourable hypothesis that can be made in the case, there is, in truth, no evidence at all. The Papist, for instance, may regard it as a wonderful triumph of devout respect for the authority of God that he really believes that bread and wine are transformed into the person of his glorious Redeemer, the accidents of bread and

wine remaining still unchanged.[1]   But then it is impossible
that the evidence in favour of this supposition can ever be
stronger than the evidence against it.   Let us grant that it
may be equal.   What, then, is the real state of the case?
God in the constitution of our nature requires us to believe
the reality of the bread; through an infallible Church He
requires us to believe the nature of the change.   We are
just as certain that He speaks through the essential constitution of the human mind as through a general Council of
the Roman Church.   To say, therefore, that we honour Him
by despising our nature, and being absolutely certain that
the Church is right, is just to say that when the evidence is
precisely on a poise it is insulting to God not to disregard
His first revelation through the reason of man.   Transubstantiation is not a mystery, but an absurdity, not a difficulty, but a contradiction, not something which transcends
the legitimate province of reason, but a fact which is repugnant to every principle of human belief—a fact which no
man can receive without denying the paramount authority
of those elementary truths which are implanted in our
nature as the germ of all subsequent knowledge and philosophy, and without which even the infallibility of a teacher
cannot possibly be proved.   Rome, then, in proposing this
dogma as an article of faith, is the patron of skepticism,
and undermines the very foundation on which alone she can
rest her authority to dictate at all.   In requiring us to
believe this monstrous absurdity she is guilty of the equally
stupendous folly of requiring us to believe, and at the same
time deny, the certainty of sense as a means of information;

[1] Trent teaches that by the consecration of the bread and wine the
whole substance of the bread is converted into the substance of the body
of Christ our Lord, and the whole substance of the wine into the substance of His blood (Sess. xiii., chap. iv.); that Christ, whole and entire,
exists under the species of bread, and in every particle thereof, and under
the species of wine and in all its parts (Ibid., c. iii.).   Our Lord Jesus Christ,
true God and man, says the Council in chap. i., is truly, really and substantially contained in the pure sacrament of the holy eucharist, after the
consecration of the bread and wine, and under the species of those sensible objects.

to believe the certainty of sense in order to substantiate the infallibility of the Church, which ultimately rests on the Divine commission of Christ as established by miracles addressed to the senses, and acknowledged by them to be indisputable facts; to deny the certainty of sense in order to sustain the enormous figment that all the sensible properties of the bread can remain unchanged after its substance has been physically transmuted into the complex person of the Divine Redeemer. How such egregious trifling with the intellectual nature of mankind differs from the false philosophy of Hume in its legitimate effects and inevitable tendencies, I leave to be determined by those who are fond of a riddle or tickled with a paradox. It is enough for me to know that no one can consistently be a Papist without ceasing to be a man, nor subscribe to the infallible dogmas of that apostate community without virtually inculcating that truth is a fiction, and that evidence is "of all our vanities the motliest, the merest word that ever fooled the ear from out the Schoolman's jargon."

The history of Greek philosophy and the controversies on the subject of transubstantiation reveal a remarkable coincidence between the ancient Skeptics of Greece and the modern doctors of Rome: they are alike in the principles with which they set out, and remarkably alike in the positive but inconsistent dogmatism upon the most solemn and important subjects with which they professed to terminate their inquiries. The distinctive features of the school of Pyrrho may be accurately ascertained from his division of philosophy and the answers which he gives to those great questions which naturally arise from his distribution of the subject. "Whoever," says the founder of this ill-omened sect—"whoever would live happily ought to look to three things: first, how things are in themselves; secondly, in what relation man stands to them; and, lastly, what will be the inevitable consequence of such relations." The followers of this blind and infatuated guide called into question the veracity of the senses, and endeavoured to show that there

was no unalterable standard of truth in conformity with
which our judgments should be formed. They regarded
mankind as walking literally in a vain show, and pronounced
it to be impossible to ascribe with certainty any real existence to the objects which surround us. Hence they recommended a suspension of judgment—an entire absence from
all positive assertion, as the dictate of wisdom. Their propositions were to be thrown into the form of *questions*, not
that the answers could ever be determined, but that the
uncertainty of knowledge might be clearly indicated and
the vacancy of the mind distinctly acknowledged. This fluctuating state of opinion, or rather this abstinence from anything sufficiently positive to be called opinion, was regarded
by the Skeptics as the true method of securing felicity. To
embrace skepticism was to embrace a life of tranquillity, in
which the indifference of the mind to truth and falsehood
happily responded to the uncertainty of things; and as
nothing was allowed to be real, the anxieties of hope, the
perturbations of fear and all the inquietude of passion were
suppressed by the removal of the causes which produce
them. This was the theory, but the rules of life which
these philosophers prescribed (and in this matter with a
strange inconsistency they were dogmatical and positive)
were completely at war with their speculative doctrines.
They recommended a moderation of desire which evidently
implied that there were real causes in existence to disturb
the equanimity of the soul; and, like the Romanists, while
in one breath they rejected the authority of the senses, in
the very next they assumed their information as the basis of
practical wisdom.

It will be remembered that, in the progress of opinion,
the Skeptics introduced the Epicureans. The true tendency
of Pyrrhonism is to destroy all interest in human affairs,
to bring about a state of complete indifference, to shroud
the mind in a listless apathy, to produce an intellectual
swoon in which, though the powers exist, their exercise is
entirely suspended. To confound the distinctions of truth

and falsehood, to render knowledge impossible or certainty absurd, is to divest the mind of all motive to exertion and remove from character the stability of principle. The investigation of truth is the proper employment of the human understanding; the possession of truth constitutes its wealth; the love of truth its glory; and sympathy with truth its health and vigour. A greater curse cannot, consequently, be inflicted on the race than to repress the mind in its noble aspirations by pronouncing its pursuits to be vain and nugatory. Society could not exist, every faculty of the soul would wither, and pine, and die, unless something were believed, something cherished and loved. To deny that there are any principles in any department of human inquiry on which we may repose with confidence and safety is to reduce man to a condition of torpor which nature cannot and will not tolerate. The activity of the soul must be exerted; and if debarred from the generous pursuit of truth, it will vent its inclinations in lawless pleasure and gratify its lusts with unrestrained licentiousness. The Sophists are natural precursors of Atheists and Libertines. It was so in Greece; it was so in the Middle Ages; it is still so where the Roman hierarchy is unchecked in its influence by the warning and example of Protestant teachers. The reality of the passions, of pride, ambition, avarice and revenge, is a matter of feeling which the refinements of skepticism are unable to dissipate. These will exert unlimited sway where the sacred majesty of truth has been disrobed of its power; these will remain as certainties when all other things are involved in doubt; and skepticism can do no more, from the very nature of man, than to remove the checks from appetite and lust, and give the reins to the indulgence of desire. In charging, therefore, the Church of Rome with embracing the fundamental principles of skepticism, I bring an awful accusation against her. She disturbs the foundations of society; she sanctions principles which, if legitimately carried out, would obliterate all science, all morality, all regulated freedom and all religion.

Instead of being the representative of Christ, who came to bear witness to the truth, she stands on the same platform with Pyrrhonists, Sophists, Atheists and Epicureans.   Hence we should not be surprised that Rome is now, and ever has been, in every period of her history, the mortal enemy of free discussion.   Those who acknowledge no invariable standard of truth must regard investigation as idle and argument as vain.   And Rome, too, is just skeptic enough to discard all sense of moral obligation and to gratify her characteristic lusts—ambition and avarice—without the annoyances of compunction and remorse.   These passions, like beasts of prey, seek the cover of darkness for their crimes; and the history of the past affords the fullest authority for saying that Rome has found it convenient to envelop truth in obscurity, in order that she might promote her own aggrandizement without molestation or disturbance. Nothing, indeed, can more strikingly illustrate her indifference to truth, and the steady zeal with which she pursues her purposes of pride, than her shameful policy in reference to books.   Her expurgatory and prohibitory indexes embrace the choicest monuments of learning; her sons are debarred from holding communion with the master-spirits of the race to whom science, philosophy and liberty are under the deepest obligations.   Among the works which to this day are proscribed by the proper authorities at Rome are the writings of Bacon, Milton and Locke.   Even the more liberal of her own children who have had the audacity to prefer candour to the interests of the hierarchy have been rudely enrolled on the list of proscription.   Du Pin, De Thou and Fenelon stand side by side with Cave, Robertson and Bingham.   Rome dreads nothing so much as liberty of thought.   Light is death to her cause; and consequently truth, philosophy and reason, the Book of God and the books of men, must be suppressed, silenced and condemned, lest the slumbers of the people should be broken, the sun of righteousness arise, and the frauds and impostures of an arrogant community exposed to the gaze of day.   She can

only flourish among a nation of sophists, among a people
who have lost the love of truth and seek from authority
what ought to be sustained by evidence.

To the Papal sect we are also indebted for the first re-
straints upon the freedom of the press.[1] Till the unhal-

[1] "The first instances of books printed with *Imprimaturs*, or official per-
missions, are two printed at Cologne, and sanctioned by the University in
1479 (one of them a Bible), and another at Heidelberg, in 1480, authorized by the Patriarch of Venice. The oldest mandate that is known for
appointing a *Book-Censor* is one issued by Berthold, Archbishop of Mentz,
in the year 1486, forbidding persons to translate any books out of the
Latin, Greek or other languages into the vulgar tongue, or, when translated, to sell or dispose of them, unless admitted to be sold by certain
doctors and masters of the University of Erfurt. In 1501, Pope Alexander VI. published a Bull prohibiting any books to be printed without the
approbation of the Archbishops of Cologne, Mentz, Treves and Magde-
burg, or their Vicars-General, or officials in spirituals, in those respective
provinces. The year following, Ferdinand and Isabella, sovereigns of
Spain, published a royal ordinance charging the Presidents of the Chan-
cellaries of Valladolid and Ciudad Real, and the Archbishops of Toledo,
Seville and Grenada, and the Bishops of Burgos, Salamanca and Zamora,
with everything relative to the examination, censure, impression, impor-
tation and sale of books. In the Council of Lateran, held under Leo X.,
in 1515, it was decreed that no book should be printed at Rome, nor in
other cities and dioceses, unless, if at Rome, it had been examined by the
Vicar of his Holiness and the Master of the Palace; or, if elsewhere, by
the Bishop of the diocese, or a doctor appointed by him, and had received
the signature, under pain of excommunication and burning of the book."—
Townley's Essays on various subjects, etc.

The above extract has been taken from Mendham's Literary Policy of
the Church of Rome—a work which condenses much rare and valuable
information, illustrating the savage ferocity of Popes and Councils in reference to the independent productions of the human mind. The infamous
decree of the Council of Lateran was confirmed by Trent, and Rome is
to-day as bigoted and bitter, as much the enemy of light and knowledge,
as she was three hundred years ago. The Encyclical Letter of the present
Pope, dated August 15, 1832, among other precious maledictions of the rights
of man, denounces the "fatal and detestable liberty of publishing whatever one chooses" (*deterrima illa ac nunquam satis execranda et detestabilis libertas artis librariæ ad scripta quælibet edenda in vulgus*); and the
Letter of Cardinal Barthelemi Pacca, dated August 16, 1832, addressed to
the Abbe de Mennais, which may be regarded as an authoritative exposition of the Encyclical Letter itself, condemns the doctrines of the
Avinci—a periodical publication which exerted great influence at the time

lowed usurpations of Rome had devised the expedient of suppressing thought by preventing its propagation, "books," says Milton, "were ever as freely admitted into the world as any other birth; the issue of the brain was no more stifled than the issue of the womb; no envious Juno sat cross-legged over the nativity of any man's intellectual off-spring; but if it proved a monster, who denies but that it was justly burnt or sunk into the sea? But that a book in a worse condition than a peccant soul should be to stand before a jury ere it be born to the world, and undergo, yet in darkness, the judgment of Rhadamanth and his col-leagues ere it can pass the ferry backwards into light, was never heard before, till that mysterious iniquity, provoked and troubled at the first entrance of reformation, sought out new limbos and new hells wherein they might include our books also within the number of the damned."

How the literary policy of Rome can be reconciled with any decent regard for the authority of truth or the enlarge-ment of the mind it is impossible to discover. If Truth indeed be "strong next to the Almighty, she needs no policies, nor stratagems, nor licensings to make her victo-rious ; these are the shifts and defences that Error uses against her power." It is the owls and bats of the world that love to expatiate in darkness : the eagle gazes on the sun, and his flight is as lofty as his vision is clear. Truth rises from the conflicts of discussion noble and puissant; untarnished by the smoke and dust of the collision, she shakes her invincible locks, and, like a strong man re-freshed by reason of wine, rejoices to run her race. That

in reference to freedom of religion and the freedom of the press. Liberal sentiments on these subjects the Cardinal declares to be highly reprehen-sible, inconsistent alike with the doctrines, the maxims and the practice of the Church. In July, 1834, the Pope issued another infernal bulletin against light, knowledge and liberty, occasioned by a new work of Men-nais, entitled the Words of a Believer. This document far surpasses in the violence of its tyrannical principles the Encyclical Letter of August 15. These facts show what *Rome now is*. I allude to them now incident-ally, as I shall have occasion hereafter to notice them more fully.

cause which is propped by prohibitions and anathemas, which appoints spiritual midwives to slay the man-children born into the world, which, like kings, is stronger in legions than in arguments, bears a shrewd presumption on its face that it is not the cause of the Father of lights.

It is a beautiful arrangement of infinite wisdom that they who assert so stupendous a claim as that of infallibility, without the least proof of Divine authority, should yet so completely stumble on the very threshold of philosophy as to make their stupidity much more remarkable than their pretensions to knowledge. It would be amusing, if it were not so humiliating, to see these arrogant empirics swelling with pompous promises to dispel all doubt, obscurity and confusion from the doctrines of religion, and to establish Christianity upon the firm basis of infallible truth, while the words have scarcely escaped from their lips before they contradict every principle of human belief, and teach us to regard all certainty and evidence as mere chimeras. They promise to give us infallible assurance, and end by instructing us that such a thing as assurance is utterly impossible. Surely they are the men, and wisdom will die with them! How true it is that the wicked are ensnared in the work of their own hands! How true the exclamation of the poet,—

"Oh what a tangled web we weave
When first we practise to deceive!"

It deserves to be added that, in inculcating a spirit of skepticism and denying a permanent standard of truth, the Church of Rome impeaches the immutability of moral distinctions, and declares herself to be a child of the devil and an enemy of all righteousness. She unsettles the foundations of right and wrong. She is as loose in her principles as she is corrupt in her practices. Consistently with her statements on the subject of transubstantiation, it is impossible to establish an unchanging standard of moral obligation; and as she evidently begins in Pyrrhonism, she must necessarily end in Epicureanism. The enormous corrup-

tions of the clergy which provoked the indignation of
Europe at the time of the Reformation, their rapacity,
licentiousness and lust, were not the occasional abuses of
wicked men, foreign to the system and abhorrent to the
principles of the mass of the Church.   They were the
legitimate, natural, necessary results of that spirit of skepticism which Romanism must engender among all who
reflect upon the foundations of knowledge or the nature of
evidence.   They were the bitter fruit of her graceless pretensions to infallibility.[1]

As the priesthood of Rome, in their mortal opposition to
the natural measures of truth and certainty, have virtually
claimed to be the arbiters of truth, it was not unreasonable
to expect that they should likewise claim to be lords of the
conscience and arbiters of duty.   Hence we find, in fact,
that by the name and pretended authority of God they
have instituted a standard of morality which completely
sets aside the eternal principles of rectitude, and makes the
interests of the Papacy, which means nothing more than the
wealth and power of the hierarchy, the supreme object of
pursuit.   That is right, according to the philosophy of Rome,
which enlarges the dominion of the priests or increases the
revenues of the Pope.   Actions take their moral complexion,
not from their influence on the relations which men sustain
to society or the relations in which they stand to their God,
but from the bearing which they have upon the temporal
grandeur of the Roman See.   The Papists, like the Scriptures, divide mankind into two great classes; but the righteous, according to Rome, are not those who are distinguished
by works of faith, benevolence and charity: these she has
felt it her special vocation to pursue, in every corner of the
earth, with fire and sword, with stripes and torture, im-
prisonment and death.   Moral accomplishments are nothing,
in her eye, as she acknowledges no standard of duty which

---

[1] NOTE BY EDITOR.—For a discussion of the relation between error in
speculation and lubricity of moral principle, between skepticism and
immorality, see Discourse of the Author on Truth, vol. ii., p. 486.

does not award to her the sublime position which reason and the Scriptures accord to the Almighty as centre of the moral system, to whom are all things, for whom are all things, and by whom are all things. Her just ones may be polluted by every crime which humanity can perpetrate— by incest, adultery, murder and treason; they may, like Hildebrand, be firebrands of hell, like John XII., the beastly impersonations of lust; yet all is right: they are the salt of the earth, the excellent ones in whom Rome takes delight, if they prefer her interests above their chief joy. The supremacy of homage and affection which she claims for herself places her on the throne of the Eternal, regulates the standard of morality according to the measures which are best adapted to promote her authority, completely sets aside the glory of God, which is and ought to be the chief end of man, and reverses all those arrangements of Infinite Wisdom by which the harmony of the universe has been nicely adjusted in accordance with the moral laws, which spring necessarily from the Divine perfections. He that makes the glory of God the end of his being, and the perfections of God his standard of rectitude, is certainly in unison with all that we know of that vast system of government, embracing the universe and compassing eternity, under which we live. But such grand and magnificent conceptions of duty, the views of the Bible, of truth and of nature, find no encouragement from the niggard politicians of Rome. They see in man but a slave for their lusts; and their whole system of morality is a sordid calculation of interest, their duties are feudal services, and the solemn sanctions of religion are only introduced to give currency and success to their nefarious frauds. Wealth and power are the watchwords of the hierarchy. The visible and invisible worlds are alike the sources of their merchandise, souls are their spoils and the patronage of sin the ultimate issue of their policy. The doctrine of indulgences, the practice of auricular confession, the system of penances, the invention of purgatory and the detestable principle of

private masses are only links in a chain of despotism by
which Rome binds the consciences of men, in order to seize
the possession of their treasures. The whole scheme of
Papal abominations is directed with unerring sagacity to
the secular aggrandizement of the clergy.[1] Every doctrine

[1] "What can we think of redeeming souls out of purgatory, or preserving them from it by tricks, or some mean pageantry, but that it is a foul
piece of merchandise? What is to be said of implicit obedience, the
priestly dominion over consciences, the keeping the Scriptures out of the
people's hands and the worship of God in a strange tongue, but that these
are so many arts to hoodwink the world, and to deliver it up into the
hands of the ambitious clergy? What can we think of superstition and
idolatry of images, and all the other pomp of the Roman worship, but
that by these things the people were to be kept up in a gross notion of
religion as a splendid business, and that priests have a trick of saving
them if they will but take care to humour them, and leave that matter
wholly in their hands? And to sum up all, what can we think of that
constellation of prodigies in the Sacrament of the Altar but that it is an
art to bring the world by wholesale to renounce their reason and sense,
and to have a most wonderful veneration for a sort of men who can, with
a word, perform the most astonishing thing that ever was?"—*Burnet,
Hist. Ref.*

"Of all the contrivances to enthral mankind and to usurp the entire
command of them, that of auricular confession appears the most impudent
and the most effectual. That one set of men could persuade all other
men that it was their duty to come and reveal to them everything which
they had done, and everything which they meant to do, would not be
credible if it were not proved by the fact. This circumstance rendered
the clergy masters of the secrets of every family; it rendered them, too,
the universal advisers; when any person's intentions were laid before a
clergyman, it was his business to explain what was lawful and what was
not, and under this pretext to give what counsel he pleased. In this
manner the clergy became masters of the whole system of human life;
*the two objects they chiefly pursued were to increase the riches of the order
and to gratify their senses and pride.* By using all their arts to cajole the
great and wealthy, and attacking them in moments of weakness, sickness
and at the hour of death, they obtained great and numerous bequests to
the Church; by abusing the opportunities they enjoyed with women, they
indulged their lusts; and by the direction they obtained in the manage-
ment of every family and every event, they exercised their love of
power when they could not draw an accession of wealth."—*Villers on
Reform.*

The doctrine of private masses is one of the worst corruptions of the
Romish Church. What Rome teaches to be Jesus Christ is actually sold
in the market, and the solemn oblation of the Son of God is professed to

has its place in the scale of profit; power and money are the grand and decisive tests of truth and righteousness; and every principle is estimated by Rome according to its weight in the balances of ambition and avarice. Expediency, in its most enlarged acceptation, is a dangerous test of moral obligation; but when restricted to the contemptible ends which the Papacy contemplates, when all the duties of mankind are measured by the interests, the secular interests, of a wicked corporation, we may rest assured that the most detestable vices will pass unrebuked, monsters of iniquity be canonized as saints, and the laws which hold the universe in order be revoked in subservience to the paltry purposes of sacerdotal intolerance. Rome claims the power of binding the conscience. She professes to wield the authority of God, and her injunctions, audacious as they are, she has the moral effrontery to proclaim in the name of the Most High. She consequently is at once a lawgiver and a judge. Truth is what she declares and righteousness is what she approves. Such stupendous claims on the part of ignorant, erring and sinful mortals like ourselves must exert a disastrous influence on the purity of morals, and sanctify the filthy dreams of men as the inspired revelations of the Father of truth. It is impossible, under such circumstances, but that interest should be made the ultimate standard of propriety, and the whole moral order of the universe involved in corresponding confusion, by making that which

be made for dollars and cents. We have masses for penitents, masses for the dead, masses at privileged altars, all which command a price in the shambles and increase the revenues of the grasping priesthood. To the disgrace of the hierarchy it deserves to be mentioned that they frequently received large sums of money for masses which they never had the honesty to say. Llorente tells us of a Spanish priest who had been paid for eleven thousand eight hundred masses which he never said. We are informed of a church in Venice, in 1743, that was in arrears for sixteen thousand four hundred masses. What a traffic in human souls! Cheated of their money, cheated of their liberty, cheated of their hopes, cheated of salvation,—how mournful the condition of the blinded, infatuated Papists! What a stupendous system for accumulating power and wealth in the hands of the clergy!

ought never to be an end the supreme object of human pursuit.

The moral system of the Jesuits, as developed in their secret instructions and the writings of their celebrated casuists, breathes the true spirit of the Papacy. These men are the sworn subjects of the Roman Pontiff; to promote the interests of their sect is the single purpose of their lives, and their code of morality is based upon the principles which support the foundation of the Papal throne. In the Jesuits, consequently, we behold the legitimate effects of the Papal system; in them it is unrestrained by the voice of nature, the authority of conscience or veneration for God. They are *Papists*—pure, genuine, undulterated *Papists;* they have endeavoured to divest themselves of every quality which is not in unison with the authority of Rome; they have made the Pope their god for whom they live, in whom they trust and to whom they have surrendered their health and strength and all things. It is only in them, or those who breathe a kindred spirit with themselves, that the true tendencies of Romanism have ever been fully developed. Thousands in Rome have not been able to be fully of Rome, and the influence of Popery has been secretly modified by numberless restraining circumstances in their position, relations and condition of society.

To take the doctrines of the Jesuits as the true standard of Papal authority cannot be censured as injustice by those who consider the intimate connection which subsists between licentiousness and skepticism. There is not a single distinctive feature of Jesuitism which may not be justified by the necessary tendencies of the acknowledged principles of Rome.[1] These men have embodied the spirit of the Church; they have digested its doctrines into order; they have reduced its enormities to logical consistency, and held up

---

[1] "One cannot condemn the Jesuits without condemning at the same time the whole ancient school of the Roman Church." Claude's Defence of the Reformation, Part I., chap. iii., § 9. The proofs are furnished in connection with the passage.

before us a faithful mirror in which we may contemplate
the hideous deformities of a body which claims to be the
Church of God, but has inscribed in indelible characters on
its front *the synagogue of Satan.* Hence, the Papal guardians of the press, in their zeal to stem the torrent of falsehood and repress the spread of dangerous speculations, while
they have eviscerated the Fathers, prohibited the writings
of the early Reformers and condemned the most precious
monuments of philosophy and learning, have suffered the
productions of Jesuitical casuists to stalk abroad into the
light of day with the *imprimatur* of the Church upon them.
These works are studied in Papal schools and colleges; systems formed in accordance with the doctrines of Molina
have free circulation where Locke, Cudworth and Bacon
are not permitted to enter. If the moral system of the
Jesuits was unpalatable to Rome, why has the order been
revived? Why has power been granted to its members to
apply themselves *to the education of youth, to direct colleges
and seminaries, to hear confessions, to preach and administer
the sacraments?* Pius VII., in allusion to the Jesuits, and
in vindication of his odious conduct in turning them loose
to desolate society, states, " he would deem it a great crime
toward God if amidst the dangers of the Christian republic
he should neglect to employ the aids which the special providence of God had put in his power, and if placed in the
bark of St. Peter and tossed by continual storms, he should
refuse to employ the vigorous and experienced rowers who
volunteer their services." The peculiar services which the
Jesuits have rendered to the interests of the Papacy have
been owing to the lubricity of their moral principles. It is
not their superior zeal, but the superior pliancy of their
consciences, which has made them such " vigorous and experienced rowers," and in condescending to accept their labours
Rome has endorsed the enormities of their system and
actually sanctioned their atrocious immoralities.

The most detestable principles of this graceless order
have not only received in this way the indirect sanction of

the head of the Papacy, but may be found embodied in the
recorded canons of general Councils. That the end justifies
the means, that the interests of the priesthood are superior
to the claims of truth, justice and humanity, is necessarily
implied in the decree of the Council of Lateran, that no
oaths are binding which conflict with the advantage of the
Catholic Church, that to keep them is perjury rather than
fidelity. What fraud have the Jesuits ever recommended
or committed that can exceed in iniquity the bloody proceedings of the Council of Constance in reference to Huss?
What spirit have they ever breathed more deeply imbued
with cruelty and slaughter than the edict of Lateran to
kings and magistrates to extirpate heretics from the face of
the earth? The principle on which the sixteenth canon of
the third Council of Lateran proceeds covers the doctrine
of mental reservations. If the end justify the means, if we
can be perjured with impunity to protect the authority of
the priesthood, a good intention will certainly sanctify any
other lie, and a man may be always sure that he is free from
sin if he can only be sure of his allegiance to Rome and his
antipathy to heretics.

The doctrine of probability is in full accordance with the
spirit of Papacy in substituting authority for evidence and
making the opinions of men the arbiters of faith.[1] And
yet these three cardinal principles of intention, mental reservation, and probability, which are so thoroughly and completely Papal, cover the whole ground of Jesuitical atrocity.[2]
How absurd, then, to pretend that the tendencies of the
Church should not be gathered from the system of the
Jesuits! On the contrary, it is plain that they are the

[1] On the effects of the doctrine of probability there are some admirable
remarks in Taylor, vol. xi., pp. 348–351.

[2] The Jesuit, Casnedi, maintained in a published work that at the day
of judgment God will say to many, "Come, my well-beloved, you who
have committed murder, blasphemed, etc., because you believed that in so
doing you were right." For a popular exposition of the morality of the
Jesuists the reader is referred to Pascal's Provincial Letters with Nicole's
Notes.

only consistent exponents of Romish doctrine; and should that Church ever rise to its former ascendency among the nations of the earth, should it ever reclaim its ancient authority, the type which it would assume will be impressed upon it by the hands of the Jesuits. There is no standard, however, by which Rome can be judged that can vindicate her character from flagrant immorality. Her priests in all ages have been the pests of the earth, and that inhuman law which, for the purpose of wedding them more completely to the interests of the Church, has debarred them from one of the prime institutions of God, has made them the dread of innocence and the horror of chastity. I take no pleasure in drawing the sickening picture of their depravity. The moral condition of Europe at the time of the Reformation, superinduced by the principles and policy of the popes, the profligacy of the clergy, the corruption of the people, the gross superstition which covered the nations,—these are the fruits of *Papal infallibility.* That apostate community commenced its career by unsettling the standards of truth and knowledge. Skepticism prepared the way for licentiousness. When the standard of truth was gone the standard of morals could not abide; and as fixed principles were removed nothing remained but the authority of Rome, who usurped the place of God, became the arbiter of truth to the understanding and of morals to the heart by making her own interests, her avarice and ambition, the standard of both.

LETTER VII.

INFALLIBILITY AND SUPERSTITION.

WHEN our Saviour declared to the woman of Samaria, God is a Spirit and they that worship Him must worship Him in spirit and in truth, He announced in this sublime proposition the just distinction between pure and undefiled

religion and the various forms of superstition, idolatry and
will-worship. That the highest felicity of man is to be
found alone in sympathetic alliance with the Author of his
being is the dictate alike of experience, philosophy and
Scripture. To restore the communion which sin has inter-
rupted, to transform man again into the image of his Maker,
and to fit his nature to receive communications of Divine
love, is the scope and purpose of the Christian Revelation.
Harmonious fellowship with God necessarily presupposes
a knowledge of His character, since it is an interchange
of friendship which cannot be conceived when the parties
are strangers to each other. Hence, the foundation of
religion must be laid in a just (though from the nature of
the case it must be inadequate) conception of the attributes
of Deity, a proper apprehension of His moral economy, and
a firm belief of that amazing condescension by which He
becomes conversable with men. He that cometh to God
must believe that He is, and that He is a rewarder of them
that diligently seek Him. The opposite extremes of true
religion, both equally founded in ignorance of God, though
under different forms of application, are superstition and
Atheism. From Atheism—which, as it dispenses with the
sanctions of decency and morality, is a prolific fountain of
bitterness and death—proceed the waters of infidelity, blasphemy, profaneness and impiety; from superstition—which
distinguished philosophers[1] in ancient and modern times, ·
have pronounced to be more disastrous to the interest of
man than Atheism itself—flow the streams of idolatry,
fanaticism and spiritual bondage. By a fatality of error,
which seems to be characteristic of this grand apostasy, the
Church of Rome is at once the patron of Atheism and the
parent of superstition.[2] Intent upon nothing but her own

---

[1] Plutarch and Bacon. Both have drawn the contrast between Atheism
and superstition, and both have expressed the opinion that Atheism is the
more harmless of the two. Warburton, in his Divine Legation, has
reviewed the sentiments of both with his usual ability and force.

[2] That I am not singular in ascribing to the same cause in different

aggrandizement, she asks of men only the decencies of external homage; and so they are content to swell her train and increase her power, it is a matter of comparative indifference whether they acknowledge the existence of God, reverence His truth, love His character or yield obedience to His laws. Her arbitrary pretensions to infallible authority disgust the intelligent, and while, like the heathen philosophers and the Pagan priests, who occupied a higher form of knowledge than pertained to the vulgar, they silently acquiesce in existing institutions, they maintain in their hearts a profound contempt for the whole system of popular delusion.

That the Church of Rome encourages a mean and slavish superstition will sufficiently appear from considering the nature of superstition itself. According to the etymology of Vossius,[1] it denotes religious excess. Any corruption of

aspects such opposite effects, will be seen from the following passages in works which have very few points of coincidence:

"For *infidelity* and *superstition* are, for the most part, near allied, as proceeding from the same weakness of judgment or same corruption of heart. Those guilty fears and apprehensions of an avenging Deity which drive some persons into *superstition* do as naturally drive others of a more hard and stubborn temper into *infidelity* or *Atheism*. The same causes, working differently in different persons or in the same person at different times, produce both, and it has been a common observation, justifiable by some noted instances, that no men whatever have been more apt to exceed in *superstition* at the sight of danger than those who at other times have been most highly *profane*."—Waterland's Works, vol. viii., pp. 57, 58.

"*Atheism* and *superstition* are of the same origin; they both have their rise from the same cause, the same defect in the mind of man—our want of capacity in discerning the truth, and natural ignorance of the Divine essence. Men that from their most early youth have not been imbued with the principles of the true religion, or have not afterward continued to be strictly educated in the same, are all in great danger of falling either into the *one* or the *other*, according to the difference there is in the temperament and complexion they are of, the circumstances they are in, and the company they converse with."—Second part of the Fable of the Bees, p. 374, quoted by Waterland, *ibidem*.

[1] "Quando in cultu ultra modum legitimum aliquid *superest*, sive quando cultus modum rectum superstat atque excedit."—*Vossii, Etymologicum in* Superstitio.

"But the word" [superstition], says Waterland, "properly imports any

the true religion, every modification of its doctrines or
addition to its precepts, comes, according to this view, under
the head of superstition.   In the estimation of others, its
derivation imports a species of idolatry founded on the impression that the souls of the departed preserve their interest in sublunary things.[1]   This sense is evidently embraced
in the wider meaning of religious excess, and we may consequently adopt with safety the more general acceptation
which the first etymology naturally suggests.

The causes of superstition, as developed by illustrious
writers of antiquity as well as by modern philosophers and
divines, in unison with the voice of universal experience,
may be traced to the influence of zeal or fear in minds
unenlightened by the knowledge of God.[2]   Plutarch and
Bacon concur in making the reproach or contumely of the
Divine Being, in ascribing to Him a character which He
does not deserve, of imperfection, weakness, cruelty and
revenge, an essential element of this religious excess.   Taylor[3] has copiously declaimed on fear as the fruitful source
of superstitious inventions.   Hooker[4] has shown that an
ignorant zeal is as prolific in corruptions as servile dread;
and Bentley[5] has proved that a multitude of observances,
which first commenced in simple superstition, were turned

religious excesses, either as to matter, manner or degree. There may be a
superstitious awe when it is wrong placed, or is of a wrong kind, or exceeds
in measure; and whenever we speak of a superstitious *belief*, or *worship*, or
practice, we always intend some kind of religious *excess*. Any *false* religion, or false part of a true one, is a species of superstition, because it is
more than it should be, and betokens excess."—Waterland, *ibidem*.

[1] Warburton gives a different explanation: "The Latin word *superstitio*
hath a reference to the love we bear to our children in the desire that they
should survive us, being formed upon the observation of certain religious
practices deemed efficacious for procuring that happy event."—Div. Leg.,
b. iii., § 6. For the view in the text, see Taylor, vol. v., p. 127, Heber's
edition.

[2] Timor inanis deorum. Cic. de Nat. Deo. i. 42.

[3] Vol. v., Sermon ix., pp. 126–139.

[4] Ecclesiast. Polity, b. v., sect. 3. The reader will find it an exquisite
passage, but it is too long to introduce here.

[5] Sermon upon Popery, vol. iii., Works, pp. 253, 254.

by the artful policy of Rome into sources of profit, so that
the dreams of enthusiasts and the extravagance of ascetics
received the sanction of infallible authority, and were proclaimed as expressions of the will of God. From the follies of mystics, the excesses of fanatics, the legends of martyrs and the frauds of the priesthood, whatever could be
converted into materials of power or made available to
purposes of gain has been craftily selected; and Romanism
as it now stands is so widely removed from the simplicity
of the Gospel that only enough of similitude is preserved to
make its deformity more clear and disgusting. It sustains,
in fact, the same relations to primitive Christianity which
ancient Paganism sustained to the primeval revelations
imparted to our race. It bears—to accommodate a simile
of Bacon's—the same resemblance to the true religion which
an ape bears to a man. To develop the corruptions of the
Papal hierarchy, which stamp that Church with the impress
of superstition, would be to transcribe its distinctive doctrines and peculiar practices. The range of discussion
would be too vast for a limited essay. I shall therefore
content myself with briefly showing how completely the
Church of Rome is imbued with the spirit of ancient
Paganism.[1]

The Pagan tendencies of Rome appear, in the first place,
from the appeal which she makes to the assistance of the senses
in aiding the conception and directing the worship of the
Supreme Being.[2] But in tracing the origin of transubstantiation, and the consequent absurdity of the Mass, we are struck
with another coincidence between the practices and doctrines

---

[1] See this subject fully and elaborately discussed in Gale's Court of the
Gentiles, part iii., book ii., chap. ii.

Bishop Horsley says: "The Church of Rome is at this day a corrupt
Church, a Church corrupted with idolatry—with idolatry very much the
same in kind and in degree with the worst that ever prevailed among the
Egyptians or the Canaanites, till within one or two centuries, at the most,
of the time of Moses."—Dissert. on Prophecies of the Messiah Dispersed
among the Heathen, Works, vol. ii., p. 289.

[2] For a discussion of this point see pp. 373–377 of this work.

of Rome and the rites and customs of Pagan antiquity. That
the terms and phrases and peculiar ceremonies which were
applied to the mysteries of the heathen superstition have
been transferred to the institutions of the Christian system,
and have vitiated and corrupted the sacraments of the
Gospel, is now generally admitted.[1] It is in the teachings

[1] The following extract from Casaubon's sixteenth Exercitation on the
Annals of Baronius will sustain the assertion of the text:

"Pii patres, quum intelligerent, quo facilius ad veritatis amorem cor-
ruptas superstitione mentes traducerent; et verba sacrorum illorum quam-
plurima, in suos usus transtulerunt; et cum doctrinæ veræ capita aliquot
sic tractarunt, tum ritus etiam nonnullos ejusmodi instituerunt; ut vide-
antur cum Paulo dicere gentibus voluisse, α αγνοουντες ευσεβειτε, ταυτα
καταγγελλομεν υμιν. Hinc igitur est, quod sacramenta patres appellarunt
mysteria, μνησεις, τελετας, τελειωσεις, εποπτειας, sive εποψειας, τελεστηρια;
interdum etiam, οργια, sed rarius; peculiariter vero eucharistiam τελετων
τελετην. Dicitur etiam autonomastice το μνστηριον aut numero multitudinis
τα μνστηρια. Apud patres passim de sacra communione leges φρικτα
μνστηρια vel το ευπορρητον μνστηριον: Gregorio Magno, 'magnum et pa-
vendum mysterium.' Μνεισθαι in veterum monumentis sæpe leges pro
cœnæ dominicæ fieri particeps: μνησιν pro ipsa actione; μνστης est sacerdos, qui etiam dicitur ο μνσταγωγων et ο ιεροτελεστης. In liturgiis Græcis et
alibi etiam η ιερα τελετη et η κρυφια και ετιφοβος τελετη est eucharistia.
Quemadmodum autem gradus quidem in mysteriis paganicis servati
sunt, sic Dionysius universam των τελετων την ιερουγιαν traditionem sacramentorum distinguit in tres actiones, quæ et ritibus et temporibus erant
divisæ; prima est *purgatio;* altera *initiatio;* tertia *consummatio.* Spem
meliorem morientibus attulisse mysteria Attica dicebat paulo ante M. Tul-
lius. Patres, contra, certam salutem et vitam æternam Christi mysteria
digne percipientibus affere, confirmabant; qui illa contemnerent, servari
non posse; finem vero et fructum ultimum sacramentorum, *deificationem*,
dicere non dubitarunt, quum scirent vanarum superstitionum auctores,
suis *epoptis* eum honorem audere spondere. Passim igitur legas apud
patres, της ιερας μνσταγωγιας τελος ειναι θειωσιν, finem sacramentorum esse,
ut qui vera fide illa perciperent, in futura vita dii evadant. Athanasius
verbo θεοποιεισθαι in eam rem est usus; quod mox ab eodem explicatur,
participatione spiritus conjungimur deitati. De symbolis sacramentorum
per quæ divinæ illæ ceremoniæ celebrantur, nihil attinet hoc loco dicere;
illud vero quod est et appellatum fidei symbolum, diversi est generis et
fidelibus tesseræ usum præstat per quam se mutuo agnoscunt, qui pietati
sacramento dixerunt; cujus modi tesseras fuisse etiam in paganorum
mysteriis ostendimus. Formulæ illi in mysteriis peragendis usurpatæ,
procul este profani, respondet in liturgia hæc per diaconos pronuntiari
solita; *omnes catechumeni, foras discedete, omnes possessi, omnes non
initiati.* Noctu ritus multi in mysteriis peregebantur; noctu etiam ini-

of heathen priests, in secret orgies of gross impiety and
flagrant indecency, and not in the instructions of Christ
and His Apostles, that we are to look for the mysteries
which in the Papal sect envelop the seals of the Christian
covenant. As the progress of corruption is always downward, what was begun in mystery ended in absurdity; the
extravagant terms in which the Fathers described the sacrament of the supper in evident rivalry of the Eleusinian
mysteries, the unnatural awe with which they invested a
simple institution, led in after times to this form of idolatry,
which transcended the follies of their Pagan guides.

But in no part of the Papal system is the spirit of
heathenism more completely carried out than in the respect and veneration which are paid to the persons and
relics of the saints. The deification of distinguished bene-
factors was perhaps the last form in which ancient idolatry
corrupted the objects of worship. The canonizations of
Rome differ but little in their spirit and tendency from the
apotheoses of antiquity. The records of martyrdom have
been explored, fabulous legends promoted into history, for

tiatio Christianorum inchoabatur; Gaudentio nominatur *splendidissima
nox vigiliarum.* Quod autem dicebamus dé silentio in sacris opertaneis
servari a paginis solito, id institutum veteres Christiani sic probarunt, ut
religiosa ejus observatione mystas omnes longe superarint. Quemadmodum igitur dicit Seneca, sanctiora sacrorum solis initiatis fuisse nota,
et Jamblichus de philosophia Pythagoreorum in τα απορρητα, quæ efferi
non poterant, et τα εκφορα, quæ foras effere jus erat; ita universam doc-
trinam Christianam veteres, distinguebant in τα εκφορα, id est, ea quæ
enuntiari apud omnes poterant, et τα απορρητα arcana temere non vul-
ganda: inquit Basilius, *dogmata silentio premuntur, præconia publicantur.*
Chrysostomus de iis qui baptizantur pro mortuis: *cupio quidem perspicue
rem dicere; sed propter non initiatos non audeo; hi interpretationem reddunt
difficiliorem; dum nos cogunt, aut perspicue non dicere, aut arcana, quæ
taceri debent, apud ipsos efferre.* Atque ut εξορχεισθαι τα μυστηρια dixerunt
pagani, de iis qui arcana mysteriorum evulgabant, ita dixit Dionysius,
vide ne enunties aut parum reverenter habeas sancta sanctorum. Passim apud
Augustinum leges, *sacramentum quod norunt fideles.* In Johannem tract.
xi. autem sic: *Omnes catechumeni jam credunt in nomine Christi.* SED
JESUS NON SE CREDIT IIS. Mox, *Interrogemus catechumenum, Manducas
carnem filii hominis? nescit quid dicimus.* Iterum, *Nesciunt catechumeni quid
accipiant Christiani; erubescant ergo quia nesciunt.*"

the purpose of exalting to the rank and dignity of intercessors with the Father a host of obscure and worthless
individuals, some of whom were the creatures of fiction,
others rank and disgusting impostors, and a multitude still
a disgrace to humanity. The eloquent declamation of the
Fathers on the glory which attached to a crown of martyrdom, the distinguished rewards in a future state which they
confidently promised to those who should shed their blood
for religion, combined with the assurance of corresponding
honours and a lasting reputation upon earth, were suited to
encourage imposture and frauds—leading some to seek in
the fires of persecution a full expiation for past iniquities,
and hundreds more, when the storm had abated, to magnify
sufferings which had only stopped short of death. It was
perfectly natural that the Primitive Church should concede
unwonted tokens of gratitude to the memories of martyred
champions and the persons of living confessors. Nor are
we to be astonished that their names should be commem-
orated with the pomp and solemnity of public festivals
among those who had witnessed the signal effects of such
imposing institutions upon the zeal and energy of their
Pagan countrymen. What at first was extravagant admiration, finally settled into feelings of devotion; these sacred
heroes became invested with supernatural perfections; from
mortal men they imperceptibly grew, in the sentiments of
the multitude, to the awful dignity of demigods and saviours, and finally received that religious homage which
was due exclusively to the King Eternal. The system of
Rome as it stands to-day, having confirmed the growing
superstition of ages, is as completely a system of polytheism
as that of ancient Egypt or Greece. The Virgin Mary is
as truly regarded as Divine as her famous prototype Cy-
bele or Ceres; and the whole rabble of saints are as truly
adored in the churches of Rome as the elegant gods of
Olympus were worshipped in the temples of Greece. To
say that the homage accorded to these subordinate divinities
is inferior in kind and different in principle is a feeble and

worthless evasion. Magnificent temples are erected to their
memories, in which their worship is "adorned with the
accustomed pomp of libations and festivals, altars and
sacrifices." In the solemn oblation of the Mass, which,
according to the Papal creed, is the most awful mystery of
religion and the highest act of supreme adoration, the
honour of the saints is as conspicuous a part of the service
as the glory of the Lord Jesus Christ.[1] Their relics are
conceived to be invested with supernatural power; their
bones or nails, the remnants of their dress or the accidental appendages of their person, are beheld with awful veneration
or sought with incredible avidity, being regarded as possessed of a charm like "the eye of newt and the toe of frog,"
which no machinations can resist, no evil successfully assail.
As the name of God sanctifies the altars consecrated to His
worship, so the names of these saints sanctify the altars
devoted to their memories; and vast distinctions are made
in the price and value of the sacrifice according to the spot
on which the same priest offers precisely the very same
victim. In the case of these privileged altars it is evidently
the name of the saint which gives peculiar value to the
gift, though that gift is declared to be none other than the
Son of God himself. To these circumstances, which unquestionably indicate more than mortal respect, may be
added the vast importance which the worship and creed of
Rome attach to their pretended intercession. They execute

[1] The following prayer occurs in the Ordinary of the Mass: "Receive,
O Holy Trinity, this oblation which we make to Thee in memory of the
Passion, Resurrection and Ascension of our Lord Jesus Christ, and in
honour of the blessed Mary, ever a Virgin, of blessed John Baptist, the
holy Apostles Peter and Paul, and of all the Saints; that it may be available to their honour and our salvation; and may they vouchsafe to in-
tercede for us in heaven whose memory we celebrate on earth. Through
the same Christ our Lord."—*England's Translation of the Rom. Miss.*,
p. 281. Here Christ, the eternal Son of God, is distinctly said to be
offered up in honour of all the saints. What can that man withhold from
them who gives them his Saviour? His *heart* surely is a small boon compared with this august oblation. And yet Trent has the audacity to declare that they are not worshipped with homage truly Divine!

a priestly function at the right hand of God which it is
hard to distinguish from the office of the Redeemer; in
fact, their performances in heaven seem to be designed to
stimulate the lazy diligence of Christ, and to remind Him
of the wants of His brethren, which the absorbing contemplation of His own glory might otherwise exclude from His
thoughts. It is the saints who keep us fresh in the memory
of God, and sustain our cause against the careless indifference of an advocate whom Rome has discovered not to be
sufficiently touched with the feeling of our infirmities,
though Paul declares that he sympathizes in all points with
His brethren, and ever liveth to make intercession for
them.

To these multiplied saints, in accordance with the true
spirit of ancient Paganism, different departments of nature
are intrusted, different portions of the universe assigned.
Some protect their votaries from fire, and others from the
power of the storm. Some guard from the pestilence that
walketh in darkness, and others from the arrow that flieth
at noonday. Some are gods of the hills, and others of
the plains. Their worshippers, too, like the patrons of ju-
dicial astrology, have distributed among them and allotted
to their special providence and care the different limbs and
members of the human frame. It is the province of one to
heal disorders of the throat; another cures diseases of
the eye. One is the shield from the violence of fever, and
another preserves from the horrors of the plague. In addition to this, each faithful Papist is constantly attended by
a guardian angel and a guardian saint, to whom he may flee
in all his troubles, whose care of his person never slumbers,
whose zeal for his good is never fatigued. If this be not
the Pagan system of tutelar divinities and household gods,
it is hopeless to seek for resemblances among objects precisely alike; for a difference of name, where no other discrepancies are discernible, is sufficient to establish a difference of things! The fatherly interest, the unceasing vigilance, the deep devotion with which these heavenly spirits

superintend the affairs of the faithful, cannot be explained upon any principles which deny to them the essential attributes of God. The prayers which are offered at their shrines, the incense which is burnt before their images, the awful sanctity which invests their relics, the stupendous miracles which the very enunciation of their names is believed to have achieved, are signal proofs that they are regarded as really and truly Divine.[1]   The nice distinctions of

[1] The following may be taken as a specimen of the honour which is ascribed to the saints. Let the reader judge whether more importance be attached to the intercession of Christ than to the prayers of His departed servants:

"O God, who wast pleased to send blessed Patrick, thy bishop and confessor, to preach thy glory to the Gentiles, grant that by his *merits* and *intercession* we may through Thy mercy be enabled to perform what Thou commandest."   Take again the Collect for St. George's Day: "O God, who, by the merits and prayers of blessed George, thy martyr, fillest the hearts of thy people with joy, mercifully grant that the blessing we ask in his name (per eum) we may happily obtain by Thy grace." Festival of St. Peter's Chair, at Rome, Collect: "O God, who, by delivering to Thy blessed Apostle Peter the keys of the kingdom of heaven, didst give him the power of binding and loosing, grant that, by his intercession, we may be freed from the bonds of our sins."   In what is called the Secret it is said: "May the intercession, we beseech Thee, O Lord, of blessed Peter, the Apostle, render the prayers and offerings of Thy Church acceptable to Thee, that the mysteries we celebrate in his honour may obtain for us the pardon of our sins."

The Apostles are addressed in the following hymn, as the dispensers alike of temporal and spiritual blessings to their earthly suppliants:

> "Vos Sæculorum Judices,
> Et vera mundi lumina,
> Votis precamur cordium ;
> Audite voces supplicum.
> Qui templa cœli clauditis
> Serasque verbo solvitis,
> Nos a reatu noxios
> Solvi jubete, quæsumus.
> Præcepta quorum protinus
> Languor salusque sentiunt
> Sanate mente languidas ;
> Augete nos virtutibus."

> O you, true lights of human kind,
> And judges of the world designed,

worship which the Church of Rome artfully endeavours to draw for the purpose of evading the dreadful imputation of idolatry are purely fictitious and imaginary. That the language in which alone the Fathers of Trent recognized the Scriptures as authentic is too poor to express the subtlety of these refinements, is a violent presumption against them, and that the Greek from which they are extracted does not justify these niceties of devotion, must be admitted by all who are capable of appreciating the force of words. Certain it is that no sanction is found in the Scriptures for the arbitrary gradations of worship which the Papacy is anxious to inculcate under the terms δουλεια (dulia), υπερ-δουλεια (hyper-dulia), and λατρεια (latria).[1]   Whatever forced inter-

> To you our hearty vows we show:
> Hear your petitioners below.
> The gates of heaven by your command
> Are fastened close or open stand;
> Grant, we beseech you, then, that we
> From sinful slavery may be free.
> Sickness and health your power obey;
> This comes, and that you drive away.
> Then from our souls all sickness chase,
> Let healing virtues take its place.

These extracts may be found in the Vespers or Evening Office of the English Papists. The Secret is from the Pocket Missal. See Bamp. Lect. for 1807, from which I have taken them, not having the original works at hand.

[1] " They pretend that the reverence which they pay to images is ειδωλοδουλεια (service of images), but deny that it is ειδωλολατρεια (worship of images). For in this manner they express themselves when they maintain that the reverence which they call *dulia* may be given to statues or pictures without injury to God. They consider themselves, therefore, liable to no blame, while they are only the servants of their idols and not worshippers of them, as though worship were not rather inferior to service. And yet, while they seek to shelter themselves under a Greek term, they contradict themselves in the most childish manner. For since the Greek word λατρευειν signifies nothing else but to worship, what they say is equivalent to a confession that they adore their images, but without adoration. Nor can they justly object that I am trying to ensnare them with words : they betray their own ignorance in their endeavours to raise a mist before the eyes of the simple. But, however eloquent they may be, they will never be able, by their rhetoric, to prove one and the same thing to

pretations may be put upon the language of the Romish
Breviaries in the prayers which are addressed to the other
saints, the worship of the Virgin is evidently in the highest
form of supreme adoration. She is not only invoked as
being likely to prove a successful intercessor with the Saviour, but solemnly entreated to *command* her Son to answer
the petitions of her servants.[1] She is exalted above all that

be two different things. Let them point out, I say, a difference, in fact,
that they may be accounted different from ancient idolaters. For as an
adulterer or homicide will not escape the imputation of guilt by giving
his crime a new and arbitrary name, so it is absurd that these persons
should be exculpated by the subtle invention of a name, if they really
differ in no respect from those idolaters whom they themselves are constrained to condemn. But their case is so far from being different from
that of former idolaters that the source of all the evil is a preposterous
emulation, with which they have rivalled them by their minds in con-
triving, and their hands in forming, visible symbols of the Deity."—*Calvin's Inst.*, lib. i., cap. xi., § 11.

[1] This blasphemous language, which is justified by the services of the
Church, was stoutly defended by Harding in his controversy with Bishop
Jewell. "If now," says he, "any spiritual man, such as St. Bernard was,
deeply considering the great honour and dignity of Christ's mother, do,
in excess of mind, spiritually sport with her, bidding her to remember
that she is a mother, and that thereby she has a certain right to command
her Son, and require in a most sweet manner that she use her right, is
this either impiously or impudently spoken? Is not he, rather, most
impious and impudent that findeth fault therewith?"

The following note, which occurs in the Bampton Lecture for 1807,
p. 238, presents an awful view of the devotions which, in their authorized books, the English Papists render to the Virgin:

"In the common office for her we have the hymn Ave Maria Stella,
which contains the following petitions (*Vespers*, p. 131):

> "Solve vincla reis,
> Profer lumen cæcis,
> Mala nostra pelle,
> Bona cuncta posce.
> Monstra te esse matrem,
> Sumat per te preces
> Qui pro nobis natus
> Tulit esse tuus."

> The sinner's bonds unbind,
> Our evils drive away,
> Bring light unto the blind,
> For grace and blessings pray.

is called God; "she approaches," according to Damiani, a celebrated divine of the eleventh century—"she approaches the golden tribunal of Divine Majesty, not *asking*, but *commanding*, not a *handmaid*, but a *mistress*." We are taught by Albertus Magnus that "Mary prays as a daughter, requests as a sister and *commands* as a mother." Another writer informs us that "the blessed Virgin, for the salvation

> Thyself a mother show;
> May He receive thy prayer,
> Who for the debts we owe
> From thee would breathe our air.

"In the office of Matins in Advent is the blessing, 'Nos, cum prole pia, benedicat Virgo Maria,' which junction of the two names in this way must shock every true Christian: 'May the Virgin Mary, with her pious Son, bless us.'—*Primer*, p. 75. At p. 99 we have the hymn where she is called upon to 'protect us at the hour of death,' and she is called '*Mother of Grace*,' '*Mother of Mercy*.' 'Mater gratiæ, mater misericordiæ, tu nos ab noste protege et hora mortis suscipe.' At p. 290 I find this recommendation to her: 'O holy Mary, I commend myself, my soul and body, to thy blessed trust and singular custody, and into the bosom of thy mercy, this day and daily, and at the hour of my death; and I commend to thee all my hope and comfort, all my distresses and miseries, my life and the end thereof, that by thy most holy intercession and merits all my works may be directed and disposed, according to thine and thy Son's will. Amen.' My readers will by this time be both wearied and disgusted, but I must add the prayer which immediately follows: 'O Mary, Mother of God and gracious Virgin, the true comforter of all afflicted persons crying to thee, by that great joy wherewith thou wert comforted when thou didst know our Lord Jesus was gloriously risen from the dead, be a comfort to my soul, and vouchsafe to help me with thine and God's only-begotten Son in that last day when I shall rise again with body and soul, and shall give account of all my actions; to the end that I may be able by thee, O pious Mother and Virgin, to avoid the sentence of perpetual damnation, and happily come to eternal joys with all the elect of God. Amen.' It must be remembered, that it is not to what might be disclaimed as obsolete canons or mere opinions of the Schools (not to any fooleries of a St. Buonaventure or Cardinal Bona) that I am referring the reader, but to what is the actual and daily practice of the Romanists in these kingdoms. I can add even the express recommendation of one of their bishops."

How just is the satire implied in the pithy remark of Bishop Bull, that "such is the worship given to the blessed Virgin by many in the Church of Rome that they deserve to be called Mariani rather than Christiani!"—*Serm. on Luke* i., 48, 49: Works, vol. i., p. 107.

of her supplicants, can not only supplicate her son as other saints do, but also by her maternal authority *command* her son. Therefore the Church prays, ' *Monstra te esse matrem ;*' as if saying to the Virgin, Supplicate for us after the manner of a command and with a mother's authority." To her the characteristic titles of God, the peculiar offices of Christ and the distinctive work of the Holy Spirit are clearly and unblushingly ascribed in approved formularies of Papal devotion.[1] If this be not idolatry, if this be not the worship of the creature more than the Creator, it is impossible to understand the meaning of terms. If there be in this case any real distinction between δουλεια (dulia) and λατρεια (latria), the δουλεια (dulia) is rendered to God, and the λατρεια (latria) to the Virgin. She is the fountain of grace, and He is the obedient servant of her will.

There is a species of superstition extravagantly fostered by veneration for the images and relics of saints, which was severely condemned by the Pagan philosophers of antiquity,· though extremely common among their countrymen, and is as warmly encouraged by the bigoted priesthood of Rome. It consists in the practical impression that there is no grand and uniform plan in the government of the world, founded in goodness, adjusted in wisdom and accomplished by a minute and controlling Providence; but that all the events of this sublunary state are single, insulated acts, arising from the humour of different beings, suggested, for the most part, by particular emergencies, and directed generally to

[1] In addition to the proofs of this awful accusation furnished in the preceding note, I appeal to the Encyclical Letter of the Pope, dated August 15, 1832:

"We send you a letter on this most joyful day, on which we celebrate a solemn festival commemorative of the triumph of the most holy Virgin, who was taken up to heaven; that she, whom we have found our patroness and preserver in all our greatest calamities, may also be propitious to us whilst writing to you, and *guide our mind by her heavenly inspiration to such counsels as shall be most wholesome for the flock of Christ.*" In the same document the same Pope ascribes to this same creature the glorious offices of Christ. He declares that she is his " *chief confidence,*" " *his only ground of hope.*"

mercenary ends.   That it secured "deliverance from unnecessary terrors and exemption from false alarms," was one
of the chief commendations of the lax philosophy of Epicurus, in which religion and superstition were, contrary to
the opinions of the most distinguished sages of antiquity,
strangely and absurdly confounded.   The legitimate fear
of God was involved in the same condemnation and exposed
to the same severity of ridicule with the fear of omens,
prodigies and portents.[1]   To the minds of the people, who
admitted a plurality of gods possessed of different attributes
and intent upon opposite designs, it was certainly impossible
to communicate those enlarged conceptions of a harmonious
scheme of Providence carried on by the power of a super-
intending mind, which are only consistent with such views
of the supremacy of one Being as the philosophers themselves faintly apprehended.   Polytheism must always be
the parent of imaginary terrors.   The stability and peace
of a well-ordered mind, that unshaken tranquillity which
is neither alarmed at the flight of birds, the coruscations of
meteors nor eclipses of the moon, proceeds from a firm persuasion that there is *one* God, who sitteth in the heavens
and whose counsel none can resist.

[1] Hence Virgil says:

> " Felix qui potuit rerum cognoscere causas,
> Atque metus omnes, et inexorabile fatum
> Subjecit pedibus, strepitumque Acherontis avari."—*Georg.* ii. 490.

> Happy the man who, studying nature's laws,
> Through known effects can trace the secret cause—
> His mind possessing in a quiet state,
> Fearless of fortune and resigned to Fate!

Speaking of religion, Lucretius says:

> " Quæ caput a cœli regionibus ostendebat,
> Horribili super aspectu mortalibus instans."—i., 65.

> Mankind ——— long the tyrant power
> Of superstition swayed, uplifting proud
> Her head to heaven, and with horrific limbs
> Brooding o'er earth.—*Goode's Lucretius.*

To suppose that different portions of the universe are assigned to the care of different divinities, possessed themselves of contradictory qualities and ruling their departments by contradictory laws, is to maintain—if the happiness of men consists in their favour or is at all dependent upon obedience to their will—that we must ever be the victims of dread, unable to escape the "barking waves of Scylla," without being exposed to equal dangers from Charybdis. Such are the rivalries and jealousies among these conflicting deities, such the variety of their views and the discordance of their plans, that the patronage of one is always likely to secure the malediction of the rest; and if one department of nature be rendered subservient to our comfort, all other elements are turned in fury against us. Under these circumstances men's lives must be passed in continual apprehension. They view nature not as a connected whole, conducted by general laws, in which all the parts have a mutual relation to each other, but as broken into fragments by opposing powers, made up of the territories of hostile princes, in which every event is a declaration of war, every appearance, whether common or accidental, a Divine prognostic. To appease the anger and to secure the approbation of such formidable enemies will lead to a thousand devices of servility and ignorance. Every phenomenon will be watched with the intensest solicitude; the meteors of heaven, the thunders in the air, the prodigies of earth will all be pressed into the service of religion, and anxiously questioned on the purposes of the gods. Charms, sorcery and witchcraft, the multiplied forms of divination and augury, servile flattery and debasing adulation, must be the abundant harvest of evils which is reaped from that ignorance of Divine Providence and the stability of nature which is involved in the acknowledgment of a multitude of gods. Epicurus distinctly perceived the folly of imaginary terrors, but in suggesting a remedy overlooked the fact that the cause was not to be found, as he evidently thought, in the admission of Providence,[1] but in its virtual denial by ascribing the course of the world to the distracting counsels of innumerable agents.   Just conceptions of Providence presuppose the absolute unity of the Supreme Being, and Polytheism is no less fatal to the interests of piety than Atheism itself.

That the Church of Rome encourages that form of superstition which heathen philosophers had the perspicacity to condemn, which heathen poets, such as Horace, Virgil and Lucretius, endeavoured to escape by fleeing to the opposite extreme of irreligion, and which the very constitution of our mind rebukes in its instinctive belief of the uniformity of nature, is too apparent to need much illustration.   The account which Plutarch has given of the religious excesses of his countrymen may be applied with equal justice, but with intenser severity, to the countless devices of Rome. The same absurd and uncouth adorations, rollings in the mire, dippings in the sea, the same contortions of the face, and indecent postures on the earth, the same charms, sulphurations and ablutions, which he indignantly charges upon the "Greeks, inventors of barbarian ills," are carried to a still more extravagant extent among the Papal inventors of worse than barbarian enormities.   The people sit in darkness and the valley of the shadow of death.   The heavens to them are redundant with omens, the earth is fraught with prodigies, the church is a magazine of charms, and the priests are potent and irresistible wizards, who rule

---

[1] " Cætera, quæ fieri in terris cœloque tuentur
    Mortales, pavidis cum pendent mentibus sæpe,
    Efficiunt animos humiles formidine divum,
    Depressosque premunt ad terram ; propterea quod,
    Ignorantia causarum conferre deorum
    Cogit ad imperium res, et concedere regnum."—*Lucr.* i., 49.

    ———— Whate'er in heaven,
    In earth man sees mysterious, shakes his mind,
    With sacred awe o'erwhelms him, and his soul
    Bows to the dust ; the cause of things concealed
    Once from his vision, instant to the gods
    All empire he transfers, all rule supreme ;
    And doubtful whence they spring, with headlong haste
    Calls them the workmanship of powers divine.—*Goode's Lucretius.*

the course of nature and govern the destinies of men by the bones, images and fragments, real or fictitious, of the slumbering dead.   In the Treasure of Exorcisms, the Roman Ritual and the Flagellum Dæmonum we have minute and specific directions for casting devils out of the possessed, and for extracting from these lying spirits a veracious testimony to the distinctive doctrines of the Papacy.[1]   The holy water, the paschal wax, the consecrated oil, medals, swords, bells and roses, hallowed upon the Sunday called Lætare Jerusalem, are charged with the power of conferring temporal benedictions and averting spiritual calamities. The Agnus Dei is a celebrated charm in the annals of Romish sorcery.[2]   It possesses the power of expelling demons, securing the remission of venial sins, of healing diseases of the body and promoting the health of the soul. Holy water has also achieved stupendous wonders : broken limbs have been restored by its efficacy, and insanity itself has yielded to its power.[3]   Whole flocks and herds are not

[1] The story of the exorcising of Martha Brosser, A.D. 1599, may be found in the history of Thuanus, lib. cxiii. The reader will find it an admirable specimen of the *black art*.

[2] Urban V. sent three Agnos Dei to the Greek Emperor, with these verses :

"Balsam, pure wax and chrism-liquor clear
Make up this precious lamb I send thee here.
All lightning it dispels and each ill sprite :
Remedies sin and makes the heart contrite ;
Even as the blood that Christ for us did shed,
It helps the childbed's pains, and gives good speed
Unto the birth.   Great gifts it still doth win
To all that wear it and that worthy bin.
It quells the rage of fire, and cleanly bore,
It brings from shipwreck safely to the shore."

The forms for blessing holy water and the other implements of Papal magic and blasphemy may found in the Book of Holy Ceremonies. I had marked out some of the prayers to be copied, but I have already furnished sufficient materials to establish the position of the text.

[3] See the dialogues of St. Gregory and Bede. St. Fortunatus restored a broken thigh with holy water ; St. Malachias brought a madman to his senses by the same prescription ; and St. Hilarion healed divers of the sick with holy bread and oil. These are only specimens, and very moderate ones, of the legends of the saints. The magic of Rome turns the course of nature into a theatre of wonders.

unfrequently brought to the priest to receive his blessing, and we have approved formularies for charming the cattle and putting a spell upon the possessions of the faithful. Rome is indeed a powerful enchantress. Even the sacraments become Circean mixtures in her hands, dispensing mysterious effects to all who receive them from her priestly magicians; being indeed a substitute for virtue, a complete exemption from the necessity of grace.[1]

The type of character and religious opinion, the pervading tone of sentiment and feeling, which any system produces on the mass of its votaries, is a just criterion of its real tendencies. The influence of a sect is not to be exclusively determined from abstract statements or controversial expositions, but from the fruits which it naturally brings forth in the hearts and lives of those who belong to it. The application of this test is particularly just in the case of Romanism, since the priests possess unlimited control over the minds and consciences of their subjects. They are consequently responsible for the moral condition, the religious observances, the customs and opinions of Papal communities. Hence, the system of Rome in its practical operations can be better ascertained from the spiritual state of the mass of the people than from the briefs of Popes, the canons of Councils and the decisions of doctors. It is seen among the people embodied in the life; its legitimate tendencies are reduced to the test of actual experience; we know what it is by beholding what it does. Tried by this standard, it seems to me that Romanism cannot be regarded in any other light than as a debasing system of idolatrous superstition, in which the hopes of mankind are made to depend upon the charms of magic and the effects of sorcery,

---

[1] "Upon the Sacraments themselves," says Bishop Taylor, "they are taught to rely with so little of moral and virtuous dispositions that the efficacy of one is made to lessen the necessity of the other; and the sacraments are taught to be so effectual by an inherent virtue that they are not so much made the instruments of virtue as the suppletory; not so much to increase as to make amends for the want of grace."— *Works,* vol. x., p. 241.

instead of the glorious principles of the doctrine of Christ.
It is indeed a kingdom of darkness, in which the Prince of
the power of the air sits enthroned in terror, envelops the
people in the blackness of spiritual night, and shrouds their
minds in the grim repose of death. Where the raven wings
of superstition and idolatry overshadow a land the spirit of
enterprise is uniformly broken, the energies of the soul are
stifled and suppressed, and the noblest affections of the heart
are chilled, blighted and perverted by the malignant influence of error. The picture which Taylor draws of the
Papal population of Ireland,[1] which Townsend gives of the

[1] I give a single specimen of the abject superstition of the Papists, upon
the authority of Jeremy Taylor: "But we have observed amongst the
generality of the Irish such a declension of Christianity, so great credulity to believe every superstitious story, such confidence in vanity, such
groundless pertinacity, such vicious lives, so little sense of true religion
and the fear of God, so much care to obey the priests and so little to obey
God, such intolerable ignorance, such fond oaths and manners of swearing, thinking themselves more obliged by swearing on the Mass-book than
the four Gospels, and St. Patrick's Mass-book more than any new one;
swearing by their father's soul, by their gossip's hand, by other things
which are the product of those many tales that are told them; their not
knowing upon what account they refuse to come to church, but now they
are old, and never did or their countrymen do not, or their fathers or
grandfathers never did, or that their ancestors were priests and they will
not alter from their religion; and after all they can give no account of their
religion, what it is, only they believe as their priests bid them, and go to
mass, which they understand not, and reckon their beads to tell the number and the tale of their prayers, and abstain from eggs and flesh in Lent,
and visit St. Patrick's Well, and leave pins and ribbons, yarn or thread in
their holy wells, and pray to God, St. Mary, St. Patrick, St. Columbanus
and St. Bridget, and desire to be buried with St. Francis' cord about them,
and to fast on Saturdays in honour of Our Lady. . . . I shall give one particular instance of their miserable superstition and blindness. I was lately,
within a few months, very much troubled with petitions and earnest
requests for the restoring a bell which a person of quality had in his
hands at the time of and ever since the late rebellion. I could not guess
at the reasons of their so great and violent importunity, but told the peti-
tioners if they could prove that bell to be theirs, the gentleman was willing to pay the full value of it, though he had no obligation to do so, that
I know of, but charity. But this was so far from satisfying them that still
the importunity increased, which made me diligently to inquire into the
secret of it. The first cause I found was that a dying person in the par-

bigoted peasantry of Spain, the condition of the Church in
Silesia, Italy, Portugal and South America, disclose the
features of the Papacy in their true light, and demonstrate
beyond the possibility of doubt that it is a system of the
same sort, founded on the same principles, and aiming at the
same results, with the monstrous mythology of the Hindoos.
They are ennobled by none of those sublime and elevated
views of the moral government of God, and the magnificent
economy of His grace through the Lord Jesus Christ, which
alone can impart tranquillity to the conscience, stability to
the character and consistency to the life. They recognize
God in none of the operations of His hands: priests, saints,
images and relics, beads, bells, oil and water so completely
engross their attention and contract their conceptions that
they can rise to nothing higher in the scale of excellence
than the empty pageantry of ceremonial pomp, or dream
of nothing better in the way of felicity than the solemn
farce of sacerdotal benediction. Their hopes are vanity
and their food is dust. To the true Christian they present
a scene as melancholy and moving as that which stirred the
spirit of the Apostle when he beheld the citizens of Athens
wholly given to idolatry; in the possession of the strong
man armed, it requires something mightier than argument,

ish desired to have it rung before him to church, and pretended he could
not die in peace if it were denied him, and that the keeping of that bell
did anciently belong to that family from father to son; but because this
seemed nothing but a fond and unreasonable superstition, I inquired farther,
and found at last that they believed this bell came from heaven, and that it
used to be carried from place to place, and to end controversies by oath,
which the worst men durst not violate if they swore upon that bell, and
the best men amongst them durst not but believe them; that if this bell
was rung before the corpse to the grave, it would help him out of purgatory, and that, therefore, when any one died, the friends of the deceased
did, whilst the bell was in their possession, hire it for the behoof of their
dead, and that by this means that family was in part maintained. I was
troubled to see under what spirit of delusion these poor souls do lie, how
infinitely their credulity is abused, how certainly they believe in trifles
and perfectly rely on vanity, and how little they regard the truths of God,
and how not at all they drink of the waters of salvation."—Works, vol. x.:
Pref. to Dissuasive from Popery, p. cxxi., seq.

stronger than the light of truth, to break the spell of spiritual enchantment which leads them on to death, to dissipate
the deep delusions of priestly imposture which are sealing
their souls for hell. The mind recoils at the thought of the
terrible account which their blind guides, who have acted
the part of mad diviners, must render in the day of final
retribution, when the blood of countless souls shall be
required at their hands. The priests of other supersti-
tions may plead to some extent irremediable ignorance for
their errors, idolatries and crimes—the way of righteousness had never been revealed to them—but the priests of
Rome have no cloak for their wickedness; they have deliberately extinguished the light of revelation, have sinned
wilfully after they had received the knowledge of the
truth, have insulted the Saviour and despised the Spirit—
betrayed the one, like Judas, with a kiss, and reduced the
other to a mere magician, and must consequently expect
the severity of judgment at the hands of the Almighty
Disposer of events.

The Pagan tendencies of Rome appear, in the last place,
from her substitution of a vain and imposing ritual, copied
from the models of her heathen ancestors, for the pure and
spiritual worship of the Gospel. The Saviour has told us
that God requires the homage of the heart, and that all our
services, in order to be accepted by Him with whom we
have to do, must be rendered in the name of the Son, by
the grace of the Spirit, and according to the requirements
of the written Word. To worship God in spirit and truth
is to bring to the employment that knowledge of His name,
that profound veneration for His character, that cordial
sympathy with the moral perfections of His nature, which
presuppose an intimate acquaintance with the economy of
His grace through Jesus Christ, the renovation of the heart
by the effectual operation of the Holy Ghost, and a constant spirit of compliance with all His statutes and ordinances. It is indeed the spirit of love and of obedience;
and both necessarily suppose that knowledge which is iden-

tified with faith and proceeds from the disclosures of the written Word. Whatever is not required is not obedience, and therefore cannot be worship, which must always be measured by the will of God. Upon comparing the worship which Rome prescribes with that which the Gospel requires, they will be found to differ in every essential element of acceptable homage. The Gospel confines our worship exclusively to God; Rome scatters it upon a thousand objects whom she has exalted to the rank of divinities. The Gospel directs that all our services should be offered exclusively in the name of Christ; Rome has as many intercessors as gods, and as many mediators as priests. The Gospel requires the affections of the heart, purified and prompted by the Holy Ghost; Rome prescribes beads and genuflexions, scourgings and pilgrimages, fasts and penances, and particularly the magic of what she calls *sacraments*, which are an excellent substitute for grace. The end which the Gospel proposes is to restore the sinner to communion with God—to make him, indeed, a spiritual man, and hence the appeals which it makes to the assistance of the senses are few and simple; the end contemplated by Rome is to awaken emotions of mysterious awe, which shall ultimately redound to the advantage of the priesthood, and hence her services are exclusively directed to the eye, the ear and the fancy. If she succeeds in reaching the imagination, and produces a due veneration for the gorgeous solemnities which pass before us, she has compassed her design, and excited the only species of religious emotion with which she is acquainted. The difference between spiritual affections and sentimental impressions, which is indeed the difference between faith and sense, is utterly unknown to the blinded priesthood of the Papal apostasy. Imposing festivals and magnificent processions, symbols and ceremonies, libations and sacrifices, —these proclaim the poverty of her spirit, the vanity of her mind: they are sad memorials of "religion lying in state, surrounded with the silent pomp of death."

LETTER VIII.

INFALLIBILITY AND CIVIL GOVERNMENT.

THE extravagant pretensions of the Romish sect to the Divine prerogative of infallibility are not only fatal to the interests of truth, morality and religion but equally destructive of the rights of magistrates and the ends for which governments were instituted. To define the connection which ought to subsist between Church and State, to prescribe their mutual relations and subserviencies, and mark their points of separation and contact, are problems of polity which have tasked the resources of the mightiest minds, and which their highest powers have been inadequate to solve. The difficulties, however, have not arisen from the inherent nature of the subject, but from the force of ancient institutions and early prejudices to blind and enslave the understanding. The masterly abilities of Warburton were certainly competent to the discussion of this or any other subject; the zeal of eloquence and power of argument with which he has presented the importance of religion as conducing to the success and stability of the State are, perhaps, irresistible; yet the attentive reader will perceive that none of his reasonings, however unanswerably they prove the value of the Church and the need of its aid, establish the necessity of a federal alliance. The gratuitous assumption which vitiates the logic of this celebrated book is the ancient opinion, that Christianity could not contribute its influence to the peace and order of society without being supported by the State. "The props and buttresses of secular authority" were conceived to be essential not only to the prosperity, but also to the *being* of the Church; as if, in the language of Milton, "the Church were a vine in this respect, that she cannot subsist without clasping about the elm of worldly strength and felicity." It is found from experience, however, and might be deduced from the nature of its principles, that Christianity is then most powerful, and sustains the government by its strongest sanctions, when it stands alone, commending itself to every man's conscience by truth and purity. Alliance with the State corrupts and weakens spiritual authority. It debases the Church into a secular institution; makes emolument and splendour more important objects than righteousness and truth; defeats the ends for which it has been instituted; and, instead of adding weight to the laws of man, detracts from the authority of the laws of God. Church and State, distinct as they are in their offices and ends, clothed with powers of a different species and supported by sanctions essentially unlike, fulfil their respective courses with less confusion and disturbance when each is restrained within its own appropriate jurisdiction. The harmony of the spheres is preserved by the regularity and order with which they revolve in their appointed orbits. The protection of life, property and person is the leading end for which governments were instituted; the restoration of man to the image of God, through faith in the scheme of supernatural revelation, is the grand purpose for which the Church was established. The State views man as a member of society, and deals exclusively with external acts; the Church regards him as the creature of God, and demands integrity in the inward parts. The State secures the interests of time; the Church provides for a blessed immortality. The State is concerned about the bodies of men; the Church is solicitous for the deathless soul. Racks, gibbets, dungeons and tortures are the props and muniments of secular authority; truth and love, "the sword of the Spirit" and "the cords of a man," are the mighty weapons of the spiritual host. To maintain with a recent writer, whose work is far inferior in compactness and precision to the treatise of Warburton, that one of the distinctive ends of government is to propagate the truths of religion, is to destroy the Church as a separate institution and make it an appendage to the State. The administration of religion, under this view, becomes as completely a *part* of the government as courts of justice or halls of legislation.

The doctrine of Rome, on the mutual relations of the temporal and spiritual power, leads to consequences as fatal to the liberty of States as those of Warburton or Gladstone to the independence, purity and efficiency of the Church. Three different views have been taken of this subject by distinguished writers in the Papal communion. The Canonists[1] and Jesuits,[2] for the most part, carrying out the idea

[1] For an amusing effort to evade the claims of the Canon law, vide Gibert, vol. ii., pp. 511, 512.

[2] The doctrine seems to be embodied in the Jesuit's oath, which the learned Archbishop Usher drew from undoubted records in Paris and published to the world. In that oath it is asserted that the Pope, by virtue of the keys given to his holiness by Jesus Christ, hath power to depose heretical kings, princes, states, commonwealths and governments, all *being illegal* without his sacred confirmation; and consequently all allegiance is renounced to any such *rulers*. The entire document is as follows:

" I, A. B., now in the presence of Almighty God, the blessed Virgin Mary, the blessed Michael the Archangel, the blessed St. John Baptist, the holy Apostles St. Peter and St. Paul, and the saints and sacred host of heaven, and to you, my ghostly father, do declare from my heart, without mental reservation, that his holiness Pope Urban is Christ's vicar-general, and is the true and only head of the Catholic or universal Church throughout the earth; and that, by the virtue of the keys of binding and loosing given to his Holiness by my Saviour Jesus Christ, he hath power to depose heretical kings, princes, states, commonwealths and governments, all being illegal without his sacred confirmation, and that they may be safely destroyed; therefore, to the utmost of my power, I shall and will defend this doctrine and his Holiness's rights and customs against all usurpers of the heretical authority whatsoever, especially against the now pretended authority and Church of England, and all adherents, in regard that they and she be usurpal and heretical, opposing the sacred Mother Church of Rome. I do renounce and disown any allegiance as due to any heretical king, prince or state named *Protestant*, or obedience to any of their inferior magistrates or officers. I do further declare, that the doctrines of the Church of England, of the Calvinists, Huguenots, and of others of the name of *Protestants*, are damnable, and they themselves are damned, and to be damned, that will not forsake the same. I do further declare, that I will help, assist and advise all or any of his holiness's agents, in any place wherever I shall be, in England, Scotland and in Ireland, or in any other territory or kingdom I shall come to, and do my utmost to extirpate the heretical Protestants' doctrine, and to destroy all their pretended powers, legal or otherwise. I do further promise and declare, that, not-

that the Pope is the vicar of God upon earth, clothe him
with all the plenitude of power, in relation to sublunary
things, which belongs to Deity Himself. It is his prerogative to fix the boundaries of nations, to appoint the habitations of the people, and to set over them the basest of
men. From him kings derive their authority to reign
and princes to decree justice; upon him the rulers and
judges of the earth are dependent alike for the sceptre and
the sword; it is his, like Jupiter in Homer, to "shake his
ambrosial curls and give the nod—the stamp of fate, the
sanction of a god." In the sentence against Frederick II.,
passed in the Council of Lyons, which, according to Bellarmine, represented without doubt the universal Church, this
extravagant pretension to *absolute power* is assumed.[1] At

withstanding, I am dispensed to assume any religion heretical for the pro-
pagating of the Mother Church's interest, to keep secret and private all
her agents' counsels from time to time, as they intrust me, and not to
divulge, directly or indirectly, by word, writing or circumstance whatsoever; but to execute all that shall be proposed, given in charge or discovered unto me by you, my ghostly father, or by any of this sacred convent. All which, I, A. B., do swear, by the blessed Trinity, and blessed
sacrament which I now am to receive, to perform and on my part to keep
inviolably; and do call all the heavenly and glorious host of heaven to
witness these my real intentions to keep this my oath. In testimony
hereof, I take this most holy and blessed sacrament of the eucharist; and
witness the same further with my hand and seal in the face of this holy
convent, this ———— day of ————, An. Dom.," &c.

[1] " Nos itaque super præmissis et compluribus aliis ejus nefandis exces-
sibus, cum fratribus nostris, et sacro concilio deliberatione præhabita dili-
genti, cum Jesu Christi vices licet immeriti teneamus in terris, nobisque
in beati Petri Apostoli persona sit dictum: ' *Quodcumque ligaveris super
terram, &c.*' Memoratum principem, qui se imperio et regnis omnique
honore ac dignitate reddidit tam indignum, quique propter suas iniquitates
a Deo ne regnet vel imperet est abjectus, suis ligatum peccatis, et abjec-
tum, omnique honore et dignitate privatum a Domino ostendimus, denun-
ciamus, ac nihilo minus sententiando privamus; omnes, qui ei juramento
fidelitatis tenentur adstricti, a juramento hujusmodi perpetuo absolventes;
autoritate apostolica firmiter inhibendo, ne quisquam de cætero sibi tamquam imperatori vel regi pareat vel intendat, et decernendo quoslibet, qui
deinceps ei velut imperatori aut regi consilium vel auxilium præstiterint
seu favorem, ipso facto excommunicationis vinculo subjacere. Illi autem
ad quos in eodem imperio imperatoris spectat electio, eligant libere suc-

the close of the second session of the fifth Council of Lateran, an oration was delivered by Cajetan, which abounds in
fulsome adulation of the Pope, representing him as the *vicar
of the Omnipotent God*, invested alike with temporal power
and ecclesiastical authority, and exhorting him, in blasphemous application of the language of the Psalmist, to "gird
his sword upon his thigh and proceed to reign over all the
powers of the earth." [1]

The Pontiffs, in their damnatory sentences, are particularly fond of quoting, in accommodation to themselves, the
words of Jeremiah : "I have set thee over the nations and
over the kingdoms," as well as the words of Christ to Peter,
in the largest and most absolute sense.   To be the *vicar*
of the *Omnipotent God* is to be Lord of lords and King
of kings.   In the famous controversy betwixt Boniface
VIII. and Philip the Fair, the insolent pontiff boldly asserted that "The king of France, and all other kings and
princes whatsoever, were obliged, by a Divine command, to
submit to the authority of the Popes, as well in all political
and civil matters as in those of a religious nature."   These
doctrines are fully brought out in the memorable Bull,
"*Unam Sanctam*," in which it is maintained that "Jesus
had granted a twofold power to the Church—or, in other
words, *the spiritual* and *temporal sword*—and subjected the
whole human race to the authority of the Roman Pontiff,"

cessorem. De præfato vero Siciliæ regno providere curabimus, cum eorun-
dum fratrum nostrorum consilio, sicut viderimus expedire."—*Labb., Concil.*,
Tom. xi., p. 645.
  [1] "Assequctur autem hoc, te volente, teque imperante, si tu ipse, pater
sancte, omnipotentis Dei cujus vices in terris non solum honore dignitatis,
sed etiam studio voluntatis gerere debes: si ipsius Dei potentiam, perfec-
tionem, sapientiamque imitaberis. Atqui ut in primis potentiam imiteris,
accingere, pater sancte, gladio tuo, tuo inquam accingere: binos enim
habes, unum tibi reliquis que hujus mundi principibus communem: alterum tibi proprium, atque ita tuum, ut illum alius nemo nisi a te habere
possit. Hoc itaque gladio tuo, qui ecclesiasticæ potestatis est, accingere,
potentissime, et accingere super femur tuum, id est, super universas humani
generis potestates."—*Labb., Concil.*, Tom. xiv., p. 75.

whom they were bound to obey on pain of eternal damnation.[1]

There is another view, which has been approved by the Church in every possible way, by the voice of her doctors, the bulls of Popes and the decrees of Councils, which reaches the same practical results on grounds less flagrantly wicked or detestably blasphemous. It is the opinion maintained by Baronius, Bellarmine, Binius, Carranza, Perron, Turrecrema and Pighius, and abounding *ad nauseam* in the documents of Gregory VII. The Pope, according to these writers, is not absolute lord of the infidel world. His special jurisdiction is the guardianship and care of the Church. In protecting his flock, however, from the encroachments of error and the dangers of schism, he is clothed with plenary power to disturb the government of nations and destroy the institutions of states. He has a broad commission from heaven to provide for the welfare and prosperity of the Church, and whatever powers may be found subservient to the fulfilment of this delegated trust are indirectly vested in his hands. Like a Roman dictator, his business is to see that the republic of the faithful receives no damage; and if kings and rulers should be regarded as dangerous to the interests of the Church, kings and rulers may be laid aside at his sovereign pleasure. If there be a single principle which can be called the *doctrine* of the Romish sect, to which its infallibility is solemnly pledged, and which has been exemplified in repeated *acts*, this is the principle. Thomas Aquinas distinctly teaches that the Church can absolve believing subjects from the power and dominion of infidel kings. Ægidius maintains that the power of the Church, which is fully embodied in the sovereign Pontiff, extends not only to spiritual interests but also to temporal affairs. Thomas Cajetan defines the power

---

[1] Gibert, Corpus Juris Canonici, vol. ii., p. 513, sums up the famous bull of Boniface VIII., De Majoritate et Obedientia, in these pregnant words : "Definit terrenam potestatem spirituali ita subdi, ut illa possit ab ista institui et destitui."

of the Pope almost in the very words with which I have
described this general opinion.[1] Those who wish to see a
sickening list of the Popish writers who have maintained
this notion of Pontifical power will find ample satisfaction
in the treatise of Bellarmine, De Potestate. Private writers, however, are of little value, compared with Councils
and Popes themselves. Gregory VII., in a Roman synod
consisting of one hundred and ten bishops, presumed, for
the honour and protection of the Church, to depose Henry
from the government of Germany and Italy, and transfer
his dominions to another man. This sentence, as Bellarmine triumphantly boasts, was afterward confirmed by
Victor, Urban, Pascal, Gelasius and Calixtus, in the Synods
of Beneventine, Placentia, Rome, Colonia and Rheims.[2] I
need not insist upon the cases of Boniface and Philip the

[1] "Aquinas: Potest tamen juste per sententiam, vel ordinationem Ecclesiæ,
auctoritatem Dei habentis, tale jus dominii, vel prælationis tolli; quia infi-
deles merito suæ infidelitatis merentur potestatem amittere super fideles,
qui transferuntur in filios Dei; sed hoc quidem Ecclesia quandoque facit,
quandoque non facit."—*Bellarm., Tract. De Potest. Summ. Pontif.*, p. 11.

"Ægidius: Sed, inquit, diceret aliquis, quod Reges et Principes spiritualiter non temporaliter subsint Ecclesiæ. Sed hæc dicentes vim argumenti non capiunt: nam si solum spiritualiter Reges et Principes subessent
Ecclesiæ, non esset gladius sub gladio: non essent temporalia sub spiritual-
ibus; non esset ordo in potestatibus; non reducerentur infima in suprema
per media. Hæc ille, qui toto illo tractatu hoc probat, potestatem Ecclesiæ, quæ plenissima est in Summo Pontifice, non ad sola spiritualia, sed
etiam ad temporalia se extendere."—*Ibid.*, p. 13.

"Cajetan: Ideo suæ potestati duo conveniunt: primo, quod non est
directe respectu temporalium: secundo, quod est respectu temporalium in
ordine ad spiritualia: hoc enim habet ex eo, quod ad supremum finem
omnia ordinari debent, etiam temporalia ab eo procul dubio, cujus interest
ad illum finem omnes dirigere, ut est Christi Vicarius; primum autem ex
natura suæ potestatis consequitur."—*Ibid.*, p. 15.

[2] "Quapropter confidens de judicio et misericordia Dei, ejusque piissimæ
matris semper virginis Mariæ, fultus vestra auctoritate, sæpe nominatum
Henricum, quem regem dicunt, omnesque fautores ejus excommunicationi
subjicio et anathematis vinculis alligo; et iterum regnum Teutonicorum et
Italiæ, ex parte Omnipotentis Dei et vestra, interdicens ei, omnem potestatem et dignitatem illi regiam tollo et ut nullus Christianorum ei sicut
regi obediat interdico, omnesque qui ei juraverunt vel jurabunt de regni
dominatione a juramenti promissione absolvo."—*Labbe*, vol. x., p. 384.

Fair, Paul III. and Henry VIII., Pius V. and the Virgin Queen. The memorable Bull, *in Cœna Domini*, issued by Pius V. in 1567, should not be suffered to pass without notice. This atrocious document prostrates the power of kings and magistrates at the foot of the Pope, subverts the independence of States and nations, and makes the sword of monarchs and rulers the pliant tool of Pontifical despotism.[1] Even in the nineteenth century the successors of the Fisherman are regaled with dreams of terrestrial grandeur, and Pius VII., in the plenitude of spiritual power, poured all the vials of his wrath upon the head of Napoleon.

Directly or indirectly, more or less distinctly, *eight* general councils have endorsed the doctrine of the temporal jurisdiction of the Pope—the fourth and fifth of Lateran, those of Lyons, Vienna, Pisa, Constance, Basil and Trent. The third canon of the fourth Council of Lateran is intended to provide for the extirpation of heresy. It is there decreed that if any temporal lord, after the admonition of the Church, should neglect to purge his realm from heretical pravity, he shall be excommunicated by his metropolitan and suffragans. If he should still fail to give satisfaction for a year, his contumacy shall be announced to the Sovereign Pontiff, who shall proceed to absolve his subjects from their allegiance, and transfer his dominions to any usurper willing and able to exterminate heretics and restore the faith.[2] "If this," says Bellarmine, "is not the

---

[1] For a particular account of this famous Bull the reader is particularly referred to Giannone Istor. di Napoli, lib. 33, cap. iv., who may there see its audacious interference with the right of kings, magistrates and rulers fully exposed.

[2] "Si vero Dominus Temporalis requisitus et monitus ab Ecclesia, terram suam purgare neglexerit ab hac hæretica fœditate, per metropolitanum et cœteros comprovinciales episcopos excommunicationis vinculo innodetur. Et, si satisfacere contempserit infra annum, significetur hoc summo Pontifici, ut ex tunc ipse vassalos ab ejus fidelitate denunciet absolutos, et terram exponat Catholicis occupandam, qui eam exterminatis hæreticis sine ulla contradictione possideant et in fidei puritate conservent."—*Labbe*, vol. xi., p. 148.

voice of the Catholic Church, where, I pray, shall we find it?" The Council of Trent—that I may not occupy the reader with a tedious display of the insolence, arrogance and pride of Vienna, Constance, Pisa and Basil—the Council of Trent, in its twenty-fifth session, passed a statute in relation to duelling, which seems to assume something more definite and tangible than spiritual power. The temporal sovereign who permits a duel to take place in his dominions is punished not only with excommunication, but *with the loss of the place* in which the combat occurred. The duellists and their seconds are condemned in the same statute to perpetual infamy, the *forfeiture of their goods*, and deprived, if they should fall, of Christian burial, while those who were merely spectators of the scene are sentenced to eternal malediction.[1]

The inevitable tendency of these arbitrary claims to secular authority is to merge the *State in the Church*. Kings and emperors, nations and communities, become merely the instruments, the pliant tools, of spiritual dominion. The kingdoms of the earth are inferior principalities to a magnificent hierarchy, the first places of which are reserved for ecclesiastical dignitaries. The higher commands the lower; and so the Pope can set his feet upon the neck of kings,

---

[1] "Detestabilis duellorum usus fabricante diabolo introductus, ut cruenta corporum morte animarum etiam perniciem lucretur, ex Christiano orbe penitus exterminetur. Imperator, reges, duces, principes, marchiones, comites, et quocumque alio nomine domini temporales, qui locum ad monomachiam in terris suis inter Christianos concesserint, eo ipso sint excommunicati ac jurisdictione et dominio civitatis, castri, aut loci, in quo vel apud quem duellum fieri permiserint, quod ab Ecclesia obtinent, privati intelligantur; et, si feudalia sint, directis dominis statim acquirantur. Qui vero pugnam commiserint, et qui eorum patroni vocantur, excommunicationis, ac omnium bonorum suorum proscriptionis, ac perpetuæ infamiæ pœnam incurrant; et ut homicidæ juxta sacros canones puniri debeant; et si in ipso conflictu decesserint, perpetuo careant ecclesiastica sepultura. Illi etiam, qui, consilium in causa duelli tam in jure quam facto dederint, aut alia quacumque ratione ad id quemquam suaserint, necnon spectatores, excommunicationis ac perpetuæ maledictionis vinculo teneantur; non obstante quocumque privilegio, seu prava consuetudine etiam immemorabili."—*Labbe*, vol. xiv., p. 916.

and bind their nobles in fetters of iron. The Church *in-cludes* the State, as the greater includes the less, as a bishop includes a priest, and a priest includes a deacon. The natural consequence is, that the *supreme* allegiance of the faithful is due primarily to the head of the Church. In a conflict of power between princes and popes, the first and highest duty of all the vassals of Rome is to maintain her honour and support her claims. Hence the Jesuit in his secret oath renounces allegiance to all earthly powers which have not been confirmed by the Holy See, and devotes his life and soul to the undivided service of the Pope. The Romish Church, too, sets her face like a flint against the subjection of her spiritual officers to the legal tribunals of the State, and has positively prohibited the intolerable pre-sumption in laymen, though kings and magistrates, of de-manding oaths of allegiance from the lofty members of her hierarchy.[1] They are specially and emphatically her sub-jects, and she cannot consent that their fealty should be transferred to others. Such principles are fatal to the in-dependence of nations ; and just in proportion as the doc-trines of Rome gain the ascendency among any people, just in the same proportion a secret enemy is cherished, slowly but surely plotting the destruction of all institutions, how-

---

[1] "Nimis de jure Divino quidam laici usurpare conantur, cum viros ecclesiasticos, nihil temporale detinentes ab eis, ad præstandum sibi fideli-tatis juramenta compellunt. Quia vero, secundum Apostolum, *servus suo Domino stat aut cadit*, sacri auctoritate concilii prohibemus, ne tales clerici personis sæcularibus præstare cogantur hujusmodi juramentum."—*IV. Lateran, Can.* 43 : *Labbe, vol.* xi., *p.* 191.

That ecclesiastical officers should be tried only in ecclesiastical courts is the standing doctrine of the Canon Law. I select a few extracts from Gibert's Corpus Juris Canonici, vol. iii., p. 530 :

"Ut nullus judicum neque presbyterum, neque diaconum vel clericum ullum aut juniores ecclesiæ sine scientia Pontificis per se distringat aut damnare præsumat. Clericus de omni crimine coram judice ecclesiastico debet conveniri. In sacris canonibus generaliter traditur ut de omni cri-mine clericus debeat coram ecclesiastico judico conveniri.

"A sæculari potestate nec ligari, nec solvi sacerdotem posse, manifestum est."

ever noble or sublime, that may happen to contradict the humour of a bigoted Italian prince, or be inconsistent with decrees passed in ages of darkness, superstition and despotism. The slaves of the Papacy are taught to conceal their weapons until they are ready to strike—to disguise their hemlock and nightshade until they can prepare the deadly potation with the certain prospect of success. But when once they become master of the sceptre and the sword, they are to strike for Rome, sell the liberties of the country to their spiritual lord, raise the banner of inhuman persecution, and purge the land from the damning stain of heretical pravity with the blood of its noblest sons.

La Fayette is reported to have said that if ever the liberties of this country should be destroyed, it would be by the machinations of Romish priests. They are all, in fact, the sworn subjects of a *foreign potentate;* they acknowledge an earthly king who has repeatedly denounced every distinctive principle for which our fathers bled. The priesthood of Rome is a formidable body. The moral elements which bind the human family together in the ties of truth, fidelity and honour are feeble to them as Samson's withes or pointless as Priam's darts. To the outward eye all may be fair and seemly; but the country which they truly love is that which is prepared to bow the knee to the authority of Rome and lick the Pontiff's feet. All other lands are accursed of God, and their vocation is to reclaim them from their ruin, to bring them into the holy fold, to overturn and overturn and overturn, until the Man of Sin is prepared to pronounce his magic benediction.

The immortal Milton, "the champion and martyr of English liberty," as well as the "glory of English literature," the bold defender of the freedom of the press, the rights of conscience and the rights of man, gave it as his deliberate opinion that a Christian commonwealth, in consequence of the Pope's pretensions to political power and the idolatrous nature of his religious rites, ought not to tolerate his dan-

gerous sect.[1] When destitute of power or forming only a
fraction of the community, Papists may do no serious harm,
but the serpent in the fable had lost nothing of its venom
though it had lost its muscular activity.   They whose eyes,
night and day, are turned to the Eternal City, whose prayers
are hourly ascending for its glory and whose zeal is devoted
to its highest prosperity; they who are persuaded that the
ark of God is there, and that the hopes of man are centred
in the favour of the monarch who sits upon the seven hills;
they who are bound, under an awful curse, to maintain the
princely and Divine prerogatives which superstition, fanaticism, pride and ambition have attributed to this august and
venerable mortal,—are not the men to love a land which is
darkened by his frown or blasted by his bitter execrations.
They may take the usual oath of allegiance, but Lateran
has taught them that *oaths are breath* when the interests of
the Church demand their violation.   There is but one tie
which is stronger than death—the tie which binds them to
Rome.   Living or dying, in all states and conditions, in
poverty or wealth, at home or abroad, wherever they are or
whatever they do, *Rome* must never be forgotten.   The
claims of brotherhood, friendship, patriotism and honour—
all that is dear on earth in private relations or public institutions—all must be sacrificed when the voice of Rome
commands it.   She holds in her hands the dread retributions
of eternity; heaven or hell depends upon her nod; and
when she brings to bear her terrific sanctions, her faithful
children throughout the world, to avoid the impending
storm, nestle beneath her wings.   Where is the State, community or nation on the whole face of the earth that can
thunder with a voice like Rome?   What are laws, statutes,
ordinances and oaths when a single word from the Eternal
City can turn them, in the eyes of Papists, to vanity and
wind?   When was it ever known that a faithful son of the
Church respected the laws as much as his priest, his country

[1] See the question discussed, "How far the religion of the Church of
Rome is tolerable?" in Taylor's 'Liberty of Prophesying,' § xx.

as much as Rome, the highest tribunal of the land as much as the Pope? It is idle to attempt to disguise the fact that the religion of the Pope is essentially seditious. In its grasping ambition it tramples upon thrones, principalities and powers, subverts the liberty of nations, destroys the independence of States, and makes the sword and the sceptre alike subservient to its own relentless despotism. These results so obviously follow from the claims to temporal authority, which have already been considered, that many Papists have been disposed to restrict the power of the Pope wholly within spiritual bounds. Hence a third view—that maintained by the Parliament of Paris and endorsed by the Gallican clergy—remains to be considered.

According to this view, kings and rulers are not subject to the Sovereign Pontiff in the conduct of their secular affairs. Their jurisdiction is distinct from his: he moves in the orbit of spiritual dominion, and they in the orbit of temporal authority; he deals in matters of supernatural faith, and they in matters of civil obedience. This theory is beautiful and the distinction is just, but the doctrine of infallibility renders them practically worthless. The Pope has power to define articles of faith and to instruct the faithful in the will of God. Whatever he proposes as an article of faith must, of course, be received with undoubting faith. To admit the right of the people to determine what are articles of faith, and what are not, would be to introduce the odious principle of the right of private judgment. Then if the Pope has plenary power to define the articles of Catholic faith, and if everything is to be received as an article of faith which he proposes as such, he can easily introduce his arbitrary claims to temporal jurisdiction under the convenient disguise of supernatural revelation. He will not directly assert that he possesses the power of deposing kings or subverting nations, but it is the will of God that heretical magistrates should not be encouraged, and obedience to their laws is a sanction of their crimes. He might caution the faithful not to be partakers in other men's sins, and guard them especially from encouraging the great in rebellion against God. The nice distinctions of the Gallican Church are mere dust and ashes, unless the doctrine of infallibility is denied and the right of private judgment maintained. If the people are bound to believe whatever the Pope may prescribe as an article of faith, the door is thrown wide open—as open as Hildebrand himself could wish it—for the introduction of all manner of treason. It is an idle evasion to say that although men are not judges of spiritual matters, yet they are judges of temporal matters, and therefore capable of deciding when the Sovereign Pontiff invades the territory of temporal jurisdiction. This plea would be good if the Sovereign Pontiff were *fallible*. They might then oppose their judgments to his decision. But if he be *infallible*, and pronounces a principle to be an *article of faith* which they beforehand would have viewed as belonging to the sphere of the civil magistrate, they must, of course, yield their fallible opinion to an *infallible* decision. A crust of bread is mutton, wine and beef, the sacred wafer is the Redeemer of men, soul, body and divinity, if Rome pronounces them to be so. It is not more unreasonable that we should abandon our judgments about political rights at the bidding of his Holiness than that we should renounce our confidence—instinctive though it be—in the report of our senses. Practically, therefore, the theory of the Gallican clergy is no security from the encroachments of Rome; so long as infallibility is maintained, it will poison the purest principles and corrupt the fairest schemes. It affords an abundant entrance for that indirect power over States, nations and empires for which doctors have pleaded, councils decreed and popes intrigued.

It is a pungent saying of Passavan, that "Satan tendered the earth and all its glory to Immanuel, and met with a peremptory rejection; he afterwards made the same overture to the Pope, who accepted the offer with thanks and with the annexed condition of worshipping the Prince of Darkness." The subtle arts and crafty machinations by which, from small beginnings, the popes have usurped, under various pretexts, the right of universal dominion, are a pregnant proof of an intimate alliance with the father of lies. Their first interferences in the affairs of States were slow and gradual; they were content to use their spiritual authority in instigating subjects to rebellion or embroiling nations in war. Encouraged by success, they rose higher and higher in their claims, until the summit of pontifical arrogance was reached in the person of Hildebrand. What a chasm between Gregory I. and Gregory VII., filled up with gins, snares and nets, fraud, hypocrisy and lies! While "the successors of St. Peter" have pretended to labour for the salvation of souls, it is plain that nations have been their game, kings their victims and diadems their hope. The golden vision of universal empire, which encouraged the zeal, quickened the efforts and soothed the anxieties of Gregory VII., has never ceased to float before the minds of his successors, and make them at once the enemies of man and the objects of abhorrence to God. Their eyes are fixed upon the *Earth*, and the cup of their ambition will never be full until, from east to west, from north to south, every kindred, tongue and language, all the tribes and families of man, shall acknowledge the Pope as king of kings and lord of lords. To accomplish this grand and magnificent purpose, Jesuits are found in every country, plying their labours with untiring zeal. Their voice is heard amid the roar of the cataract in the forests of the savage, or it charms the circles of the giddy and the gay in the saloons of refinement and elegance. Their shadows are seen in the dusky light of the convict's cell, and their persons are found in the halls of the great and the palaces of kings. They stoop to instruct the child in its alphabet and the young in philosophy, and delight to discuss with senators and statesmen the policy of States. Hunger, cold and all the inclemencies of the sky are cheerfully endured in their exhausting journeys; the frosts of winter consume them by night and sleep departs from their eyes, and yet their zeal is invin-

cible and their industry untiring. There is one glorious
object which animates their hopes, which lifts them above
the ordinary passions of man, and renders them insensible
to danger and fearless of death. That object is the *triumph
of Rome*. For her they have sacrificed moral character,
personal comforts, the delights of patriotism and the endear-
ments of home. To her they are devoted with a terrible
enthusiasm, which is cool and collected, because too intense
to be vented in passion or wasted in extravagance; and if
Rome should ever triumph, they are the men whose principles shall be lord of the ascendant and dictate law to all
the nations of the earth. In their diligence, industry, zeal
and enthusiasm let the people of this country learn their
danger and provide for their safety.

There are peculiar principles in the constitution of the
polity of Rome which render it an engine of tremendous
power. The doctrine of auricular confession establishes a
system of espionage which is absolutely fatal to personal independence, and from the intimate connection between priests
and bishops, and bishops and the Pope, all the important
secrets of the earth can easily be transmitted to the Vatican.
What can be more alarming than a whole army scattered
through the length and breadth of the land in close and
secret correspondence with a tyrant who detests every principle that makes life dear or a country glorious? The
ingenuity of earth and hell could not devise a more successful expedient for prostrating liberty, enslaving the conscience, and introducing the Pope to an intimate acquaintance with all the purposes and interests of man, than the
scheme of auricular confession. It opens a window into
the chambers of the heart, and permits a mortal to read
those secrets which it is the sole prerogative of God to know.

I have now, I apprehend, sufficiently shown that, according to the principles of Rome, the civil power is subservient
to the spiritual, the State is a tool of the Church. It will
be seen at a glance that such an assumption is not only fatal
to the independence of States, but equally fatal to liberty

of conscience and toleration of dissenters. The right to persecute is a legitimate deduction from the relative position in which the Church and State, on the pontifical hypothesis, stand to each other. It is the business of the magistrate to propagate religion, and as his weapons are exclusively carnal—the dungeon, pillory and rack—he has a right to employ them in exacting uniformity of faith. Bossuet was able to boast that on one point all Christians had long been unanimous—the right of the civil magistrate to propagate truth by the sword. In every form and shape, by the writings of private individuals, the bulls of popes, the canons of councils, and above all by public, flagrant, inhuman acts of murder, rapine and violence, the Holy See has asserted its claim to mould the faith of men, through the arm of the magistrate, to its own detestable model. I need not insist on the ruthless crusades against the innocent victims of Languedoc and Provence, on the infernal atrocities of the Inquisition or the awful massacre of St. Bartholomew's; the annals of the Papacy are written in blood. From almost every quarter of the globe the victims of its cruelties shall send their cries to Heaven for vengeance on their destroyers. It is enough to know that if the infallibility of Rome were not pledged through her Pope and councils to the ferocious principles of persecution, it results necessarily from the views which she takes of the State. In her eyes want of conformity with her own faith is an act of rebellion, a contumacious rejection of civil authority, and should therefore be punished by the temporal power, on the same ground as that on which punishment for incest, rape or murder is justified. It is, first, according to her, the duty of governments as such to spread her faith at the point of the bayonet and with garments rolled in blood. The truth is, the only principle which can secure an equal toleration and uphold the liberty of conscience is the absolute *separation* of Church and State. They cannot contract an alliance without engendering the monster *Intolerance*. Cæsar and God must be kept distinct; the State, when it assumes the propagation of religion as one of its distinctive ends, is travelling beyond its limits, and laying the foundation of bigotry, intolerance and despotism; and no Church on earth has a right to commend its doctrines or enforce its discipline by pains, penalties or civil disabilities. To keep the State within the bounds of its appropriate jurisdiction is the secret of civil liberty, and to restrain the Church within its own department of spiritual instruction is the secret of religious liberty. When these two grand organizations of God cross the orbits of each other they menace the earth with anarchy, confusion and blood. They can never coalesce; and all arbitrary unions, like the converse of the sons of God with the daughters of men, are productive only of giants famous for rebellion and full of cruelty.

I shall now close what I intended to suggest on the infallibility of the Romish Church. It will be remembered that you, sir, made this the medium of your triumphant proof of the inspiration of the Apocrypha. I have met and refuted all your arguments, and shown in addition that every theory of Papal infallibility, whether that of councils, popes, or the body of the Church, is compassed with historical difficulties fatal to its truth. I have proved, moreover, that such extravagant pretensions are utterly inconsistent with truth, morality, religion and liberty—the highest and noblest interests of man. The state of the argument, then, is just this: *First*, Infallibility is a *fiction*, resting upon no authority of Scripture, upon no principles of reason, and contradicted by the testimony of the best and purest ages of the Church. Therefore any argument which is based upon this "worthless coinage of the brain" may be safely given to the winds, and therefore your proof of the inspiration of the Apocrypha would have been just as conclusive if you had appealed to the testimony of the man in the moon. *Secondly*, If infallibility be admitted, then truth, morality, religion and liberty must fall to the ground; for it is absolutely inconsistent with all these distinguished blessings. Here, then, is a perfect *reductio ad absurdum;*

so that infallibility destroys itself, and leaves us in quiet possession of private judgment, with all the benefits that follow in its train.

LETTER IX.

APOCRYPHA NOT QUOTED IN THE NEW TESTAMENT.

BEFORE proceeding to the third general division of your letters, I shall pause for a moment to discuss a point which would detain me too long in its proper place, and which may be taken as a fair illustration of your mode of resolving any question involving the laws of literary criticism. When I read your effort to prove that Christ and the Apostles in their recorded instruction actually quoted or referred to passages of the Apocrypha, I was forcibly reminded of those ingenious and discriminating authors who have been able to discover what they supposed to be unquestionable traces of the doctrines of the Cabala in the Lord's Prayer and the Epistles of Paul. Those who can be convinced by the parade of texts which you have strung together in your second letter ought not to withhold their assent from the learned speculations of Knorrius, confirmed as they are by the authority of so laborious a writer as Buddæus. A man of sufficient perspicacity to find the Cabala in the memorable declaration of Paul, " It is a faithful saying, and worthy of all acceptation, that Christ Jesus came into the world to save sinners," who should also detect in the New Testament traces of Apocryphal lore, would only exercise in a different way the same faculty of critical second-sight. He that can discern disembodied spirits requires perhaps no additional organs to perceive a devil. The passages which you have followed Huetius in adducing as genuine quotations from the Apocrypha, I am sure will strike no one in the same light but those who are previously persuaded that if these books are not, they ought to have been, quoted by Christ and his

Apostles. The strongest evidence, I apprehend, upon which
your position can be made to rest will be found in an appeal
to a General Council. If you could induce some such body
as that of Trent to decree that these passages are quotations,
why then quotations they would have to be considered.

The first text which you give us as a quotation from the
Apocrypha is the golden rule of our Saviour: "Therefore
all things whatsoever ye would that men should do to you,
do ye even so to them; for this is the law and the prophets."[1] Matt. vii. 12; Luke vi. 31. This you would have
us to believe was suggested to the Saviour by Tobit iv. 15,
which in the Douay version is rendered, "See thou never
do to another what thou wouldest hate to have done to thee
by another." The reader, however, will observe that this
is not a translation but a paraphrase. The original is,
ο μισεις μηδενι ποιησης—"What thou hatest do to no one."
Now the question is, whether the four words that constitute
the substance of the Apocryphal passage suggested to our
Lord the fifteen words which in the original embody the
golden rule as found in the memorable Sermon on the Mount.
There is evidently no quotation in the case, since there is
but a single word which they have in common. Neither, on
the other hand, is there any such coincidence of thought as
to warrant the supposition that our Saviour had in his mind
the passage from Tobit when he announced the principle
recorded in Matthew. Our Saviour's precept, as Grotius
has very properly observed, is *positive*, while that in Tobit
is *negative*. In the Sermon on the Mount our Saviour tells
us what to perform, and Tobit, in his instructions to his son,
what to avoid; the one resolves us in the things that are
right, and the other in the things that are wrong. One, in
short, is a *command*, the other a *prohibition*. There is no
more coincidence of thought betwixt these two passages

---

[1] Huetius, who also gives the golden rule as a quotation from this passage of Tobit, admits, at the same time, that it might have been suggested
as a dictate of nature.—*Demonstratio Evangel., Propos.* iv., p. 361: *De
Libro Tobiæ.*

than between Ex. xx. 15, "Thou shalt not steal," and
Rom. xiii. 7, "Render, therefore, to all their dues." And
yet who would dream of maintaining that the precept of
Paul is either a literal quotation of the eighth commandment, or was necessarily suggested by the form in which it
is recorded in the book of Exodus? "What thou hatest,"
says Tobit, "do to none." "What thou lovest," says our
Saviour, substantially, "do to all." If, now, our Saviour
quoted from Tobit, upon the same principle of criticism
every positive, contrary to the usual order of thought, must
be suggested by its corresponding negative. But our Saviour
himself has put the matter beyond the possibility of doubt.
The rule which He gave us was a compendious expression
of the moral instructions of the Law and the Prophets. As
you have freely acknowledged that the Apocryphal writings
were not to be found in the Canon of the Jewish Church,
you will hardly contend that the " *Law* and the *Prophets*"
embraced any of those books which Josephus mentions as
not being possessed of equal authority with the twenty-two
which he had previously enumerated. You will also admit—
for it would certainly be useless to deny—that the canonical
books of the Old Testament were divided into three classes:
the *Law*, the *Prophets*, and the *Hagiographa*. Now, if the
Saviour Himself is to be trusted, His memorable rule must
have been suggested by something which is found not in
any Apocryphal writer, but in the *Law* and the *Prophets*,
in the acknowledged Canon of the Jewish Church. His
Sermon on the Mount is in fact a Divine exposition of the
ethical code which is contained in the Old Testament, with
special reference to the corruptions and abuses which ignorant and wicked teachers had introduced and fostered. He
explains the moral law, and maintains its strictness, purity
and extent in opposition to the destructive glosses of the
Scribes, Pharisees and Doctors.

The golden rule itself is evidently nothing but a statement, in another form, of the principle of universal love.
Our own expectations from others are made the standard of

our conduct towards them—that is, our love to ourselves is
to be the exact measure of our love to other men.   The
passage in Matt. xxii. 35–40 will throw additional light
upon this whole subject.   Our Saviour there condenses the
law into two great commandments—love to God, and love to
man; and then adds that "on these two commandments
hang all the *Law* and the *Prophets*."   It is evident, therefore, that Matt. vii. 12 teaches precisely the same thing as
Matt. xxii. 39 : "Thou shalt love thy neighbour as thyself;"
and this passage is a literal quotation, not from Tobit, but
from the book of Leviticus (xix. 18).   This was the text
upon which our Saviour's mind was unquestionably fixed
when he announced his celebrated maxim; it was, in fact,
constantly before his eyes, and so frequently explained, as
well as earnestly inculcated and enforced by so many new
and peculiar sanctions, as to be almost entitled to the name
of a new commandment.   Between the rule in Leviticus
and the precept of our Saviour there is an exact coincidence of thought.   Both are positive, and both make our
regard for ourselves the standard of our treatment to others.
One is the text and the other a faithful commentary.
"Love thy neighbour as thyself," says the Law—"What
you would love to have done to you, do to others," says the
Saviour.   How it could fail to strike your attention that
the passage in Leviticus was especially before the mind of
our Redeemer, when he refers you so distinctly to the *Law*,
surpasses my comprehension.

You are hardly more successful in your attempt to deduce
the magnificent description of the heavenly Jerusalem in
the Apocalypse of John from what you suppose to be a corresponding passage in the same book of Tobit.[1]   You have
again followed the Douay version, which, however it may
agree with the Vulgate, does not precisely render the original.   The English reader will find the passage to which
you refer in Tobit xiii. 15–18 of the authorized translation.

There can be evidently no quotation in this passage, since

---

[1] Vide Huetii, Demonstratio, Propos. iv., pp. 361, 362: De Libro Tobiæ.

John is describing a vision just as he saw it. He *saw* the jasper, gold and precious stones which adorned the foundations of the holy city, and testifies what he had seen. He does not pretend to give us a picture of the fancy, but a *real view*, and of course his language must be suggested by the things themselves. In such descriptions quotations may be introduced to embellish or adorn, but most assuredly the names of things themselves must be suggested by the objects before the mind. Again, the whole description is so strikingly analogous to several passages in Isaiah and Ezekiel that if there be any allusion to other writers at all it is to these venerable Prophets. The twelve gates in the vision of John correspond precisely to the twelve gates in the vision of Ezekiel (xlviii. 31–34). The golden reed with which the angel measured the city, and the gates thereof and the wall thereof, may be in allusion to the measuring-reed and the line of flax in Ezekiel xl. 3. The garnishing of the foundations of the wall with all manner of precious stones corresponds with the promise of Isaiah (liv. 11, 12): "I will lay thy stones with fair colours, and lay thy foundation with sapphires. And I will make thy windows of agates, and thy gates of carbuncles, and all thy borders of pleasant stones." The brilliant illumination of the city by the presence of God is in exact accordance with Isaiah xxiv. 23; lx. 19, 20. The truth is, these precious stones with which the city was adorned, as seen by John, are the common and familiar figures by which the glory of the Church is constantly depicted in the sacred writings. The splendid decorations of Solomon's temple, independently of any other cause, would naturally suggest these symbolical embellishments. That they occur, consequently, in different writers, and in the same connection, is no proof whatever of quotation or reference; it only shows a familiar and common method of illustration. If the Church, for instance, be compared to a kingdom, two or a dozen writers might describe its peculiarities in conformity with this scriptural metaphor, and yet be ignorant of each other's compositions.

The metaphor itself would suggest analogous trains of thought. So when the Church is compared to a city, to a splendid and magnificent city, the usual appendages of walls, gates and ornaments will be obviously presented to the mind, or if it be compared to a temple, the splendour and pomp of Solomon's unparalleled edifice would probably be the first association in a Jewish understanding.

It manifests, therefore, the strangest inattention to the laws of thought to suppose that the description of the holy city in the Apocalypse of John must needs be taken from the rhapsody of Tobit, because both speak of walls and foundations, jasper, amethyst and gold. It is much more probable that Tobit borrowed from Chronicles, Ezekiel and Isaiah.

Your attempt to make 1 Cor. x. 9, 10 a quotation from Judith scarcely needs refutation.[1] Paul is appealing to the recorded history of the "fathers," as furnishing salutary examples of practical instruction. He gives us, consequently, a brief summary of the leading events connected with their removal from Egypt and their ultimate settlement in Canaan. This summary, of course, is taken from the history itself. It is just an epitome of what may be

---

[1] "Thirdly, in favour of the book of Judith they bring two citations—one made by St. Paul when he said, *They were destroyed by the destroyer*, and another by St. James, who said, *The Scripture was fulfilled, and Abraham was called the friend of God;* both which passages (if there were any credit to be given to Serarius) are borrowed out of the eighth chapter of Judith, as we read them in the Latin paraphrase of that book; for in the *Greek copies* there is never a word like them to be found. But whom shall the Jesuit persuade that the Apostles quoted a *Latin paraphrase* which was not extant in their time? Or if we should grant that the Greek or Chaldean copies had as much in them of old as the Latin hath now, yet who would believe that St. Paul and St. James alluded rather to the book of Judith than to the book of Numbers,* where they *that were destroyed by the destroyer* are upon record at large, and to the book of Genesis,† where the story of Abraham is recited, together with the second book of the Chronicles,‡ where Abraham is called the *friend of God*, and the book of Esay,‖ where God himself saith of him, "*Abraham my friend*."—*Cosin, Scholast. Hist. Can.*, p. 25.

* Numb. xiv., xvi.   † Gen. xv.–xviii.   ‡ 2 Chron. xx. 7.   ‖ Isa. xli. 8.

found fully recorded in the books of Moses. The passage in Judith, therefore, is just as much a quotation from the Pentateuch as that of Paul. Strictly, however, neither passage is a quotation. Both writers have simply availed themselves of the same facts to inculcate lessons of piety and wisdom.

Your fourth passage is equally unfortunate. Matthew xiii. 43 is not a quotation from the book of Wisdom, but is a palpable allusion to Daniel xi. 3 and Proverbs iv. 18. The passage in Matthew is, "Then shall the righteous shine forth as the sun in the kingdom of their Father." The passage in Wisdom is, "In the time of their visitation they shall shine and run to and fro like sparks among the stubble."

Now, how is it possible that "running to and fro like sparks among the stubble" could ever suggest the idea of the brilliancy of the sun in the firmament of heaven? If in the book of Wisdom it had been written that the right-eous should be like glow-worms or fire-flies, there would have been just as solid foundations for saying that this gave rise to the magnificent image of the Saviour in depicting the fate of the just at the end of the world. The expres-sion in Daniel is suited to the dignity of the subject: "They that be wise shall shine as the brightness of the firmament," or as it is in Proverbs, "The path of the just is as the shining light, that shineth more and more unto the perfect day."

Equally futile is your attempt to make 1 Cor. vi. 2 a quotation from Wisdom iii. 8. It is, in fact, only another form of stating the promise that the kingdom and the great-ness of the kingdom under the whole heaven shall be given to the people of the saints of the most high God. Paul had before his mind the ultimate triumph of the kingdom of God, which is the burden of prophetic inspiration and the constant subject of believing prayer. We have precisely the same idea in Psalm xlix. 14: "Like sheep they are laid in the grave; death shall feed on them, and the upright shall have dominion over them in the morning." And in Daniel vii. 32: "Judgment was given to the saints of the Most High, and the time came that the saints possessed the kingdom."

Wisdom[1] iv. 10 and Hebrews xi. 15 are both in pointed reference to Genesis v. 22–24, and therefore neither is a quotation from the other. Paul was not in the habit of dealing with second-hand authorities. He therefore goes to the original record for the history of Enoch, and not to a doubtful and obscure writer some centuries afterwards.

[1] "In the first place, for the canonizing of the book of Wisdom they produce St. Paul, and say that Rom. xi. 34 (Who hath made known the mind of the Lord, or who hath been His counsellor?) is taken out of Wisdom ix. 13 (For what man is he that can know the counsel of God, or who can think what the will of the Lord is?). But Gretser is somewhat ashamed of this instance, and our answer to it is, that the sentence which St. Paul citeth is clearly taken out of Esay xl. 13, where both the sense and the words (in that translation which the Apostle followed) are altogether the *same*, as in the book of Wisdom they are not. Secondly, as much may we say to what they note upon Heb. i. 3, where Christ is called *the brightness of His Father's glory*, alluding to Sap. vii. 26, where Wisdom is called *the brightness of everlasting light*. For as it is not certain whether St. Paul ever saw that book of Wisdom or no, which, for aught we know, was not extant before his time, nor compiled by any other author than Philo, the Hellenist Jew of Alexandria, so there be several expressions in the *undoubted Scriptures* concerning the *representation*, the *splendour*, the *wisdom* and the *glory* of God, whereunto he might allude in this his Epistle to the Hebrews, as he had done before in his Epistle to the Colossians and in his second Epistle to the Corinthians, setting forth Christ there to be the *image of the invisible God* and the *first-born of every creature, by whom all things were created and do still consist;* the substance and ground whereof may be found in Ezekiel i. 28; Isaiah ix. 6 and lx. 1; Psalm ii. 7 and cxxxvi. 5; 2 Samuel vii. 14; Jeremiah li. 15 and x. 12; to some of which places the Apostle himself refers in this place to the Hebrews. Thirdly, that which is said of Enoch (Heb. xi. 5) needs not the book of Wisdom to confirm it, for the story is clear in Genesis, and in the translation of the Septuagint (which St. Paul followed) the words are alike. Fourthly, that *the powers which be are ordained of God* was said by the wisdom of God itself in Solomon (Prov. viii. 15, 16); and, fifthly, *that God is no accepter of persons* is taken out of the words of Moses in Deuteronomy (x. 17). And yet there are that refer both these maxims to the book of Wisdom, as if St. Paul had found them nowhere else."—*Cosin, Scholast. Hist. Can.*, pp. 23, 24.

On comparing Heb. i. 3 with Wisdom vii. 26, there is but a single word which they possess in common. The ideas are evidently not the same; Paul is treating of a person, and the author of Wisdom of an attribute. How the use of a solitary word can establish a coincidence in the passages themselves I am utterly unable to comprehend. To make out a *quotation* or a reference there must be either identity of expression or identity of thought, and where neither is found no quotation exists.

Romans xi. 34, if quoted at all, is quoted from Isaiah and not from Wisdom. The prominent idea of the passage frequently occurs both in Job and the Prophet: Job xv. 8; Isaiah lx. 13, etc. The analogy in Rom. ix. 21 occurs in Jeremiah and Proverbs as well as the book of Wisdom: Jer. xviii. 6; Prov. xvi. 4. Romans i. 20 is a plain allusion to the nineteenth Psalm. The passage in Eph. vi. 13–20 is much more analogous to Isaiah lix. 17 than to anything that occurs in the book of Wisdom. It is evidently, however, an *original* passage. The preceding train of thought naturally and obviously suggested this beautiful account of Christian armour; it grew almost unavoidably out of the metaphor employed.

Romans i. 20 is in evident allusion to Psalm xix. 1, and not, as you pretend, to Wisdom xiii. 4, 5.

The connection between love and obedience is one of the most familiar and common ideas in the whole Pentateuch. You will find it in Deut. vi. 5, 6; x. 12, etc.; and it is just this connection which our Saviour insists on in John xiv. 15–22.

Proverbs xv. 27; xx. 21 are much more analogous to 1 Tim. vi. 9 than the passage which you have extracted from Ecclesiasticus. The train of thought in the parable of the rich fool in the Gospel might have been more readily discovered in the Psalms of David than the obscure authority to which you have referred us. (See Ps. lxix. 10, seq.)

Matthew xix. 17 is plainly a reference to Lev. xviii. 5. That Hebrews xi. 35 contains a reference to 2 Maccabees

vi. 18–31, in which an account is given of the martyrdom of Eleazar, is not so certain as you seem to apprehend; even if it were certain, nothing is proved but the historical fidelity of the narrative, which is far from being identical with inspiration.[1]

I have now noticed the several instances in which you profess to have discovered traces of the Apocrypha in the writers of the New Testament; and I think that any candid reader must be fully convinced that in every case in which an allusion exists at all, it is to the Jewish Canon, and not to the corrupt additions of the Council of Trent. But still nothing would be gained by satisfactory proof that Christ and his Apostles made use of the Apocrypha. Mere quotations prove nothing but the existence of the books from which they are made. Paul introduces lines from the heathen poets in various parts of his writings, and many have supposed that a striking analogy subsists between portions of the Gospel of John and the speculations of Philo. Nothing is gained, therefore, in behalf of the inspiration of the Apocryphal books by proving that quotations were made from them by Christ and his Apostles. This may

---

[1] " Where for the *persons* the matter is not so sure. For other men are of another mind, and Paulus Burgensis (whose additions have the honour, even among the Romanists themselves, to be printed with Lyra's Notes and the ordinary gloss upon the Bible) understands not St. Paul here to have spoken of Eleazar and his brethren in the time of the Maccabees, but of the saints and martyrs of God that had been tortured in his own time, under the New Testament. And for the canonical authority of the book (if any book be here cited), whatever it was, the reference here made to it gave it no more authority of authentic Scripture than the words immediately following gave to another received story among the Hebrews, that Esay the Prophet *was sawn asunder to death*. Whereunto, though the Apostle might have reference when he said, *They were stoned, they were sawn asunder, were tempted, were slain with the sword, they wandered about in sheepskins and goatskins, being destitute, afflicted, tormented,* yet who ever made all these instances before St. Paul wrote them to be authentic and canonical Scripture? or who can with reason deny (if Monsieur Perron's reason were good) but that the story of Esay's death ought to be *canonized*, as well as the story of Eleazar and his seven brethren in the Maccabees, seeing there is as much reason for the one as there can be given for the other ?"—*Cosin, Scholast. Hist Can.,* pp. 27, 28.

have been done, and yet the books themselves be entitled to no more reverence than Tully's Offices or Seneca's Epistles.[1]

In the progress of this discussion your apparent want of acquaintance with the Word of God has struck me with painful and humiliating force. The books in *your* Bible which you seem to have studied the most are those which the Church of God, in ancient and modern times, has unanimously excluded from the sacred Canon. The Law and the Prophets, to which our Saviour so often alludes, seem to be unknown to you; and however clear his references to these venerable documents, you can seize upon nothing but Tobit, Judith and Wisdom. If you find a single phrase which can be tortured into a remote approximation to coincidence of thought, you instantly leap for joy like Archimedes from his bath, and expose yourself in the ecstasy of your delight. In a paraphrase of a passage in Tobit you scent out the golden rule of the Son of God, though that rule had been revealed in the Law of the Lord centuries before Tobit was born or blind. In that same precious compound of superstition and folly you meet with something about the city of the Jews adorned with gold, jasper and precious stones, and behold! the magnificent description of the entranced Apostle dwindles down into a puerile plagiarism; sparks and stubble give you the clue to the glorious picture which our Saviour has drawn of the final condition of the blessed; and Paul cannot allude to the ultimate triumphs of the kingdom of God without being indebted to a feeble passage in the book of Wisdom. There was an effort to destroy the fame of the author of Paradise Lost by robbing him of the praise of original invention in his noble production. The immortal bard was denounced as a *plagiary*. Permit me to say that you have succeeded no better than the wretched slanderer of the greatest, brightest, most glorious name that adorns the

---

[1] Vide, on this subject of quotations, Rainoldi Censura Librorum Apocryphorum, Prælectio vii., vol. i., p. 77.

annals of English literature. The case was much more plausibly made out that Milton borrowed from obscurer men than that Christ and His Apostles have quoted from the Apocrypha.

LETTER X.

THE APOCRYPHA AND THE JEWISH CANON.

I HAVE now reached the third partition of your letters, in which you attempt—whether successfully or not remains yet to be determined—to refute my arguments against the inspiration of the Apocrypha. You have undertaken to show that the authors of these books wrote "as they were moved by the Holy Ghost," and that their productions are, by consequence, entitled to *equal* veneration and authority with the Law, the Prophets and the Psalms.

As your refutation begins with a desultory notice of my first argument, it will be necessary to present the argument itself distinctly but briefly, and then discuss the validity of your reply. I assumed as true what is capable of being proved by abundant testimony, and what you yourself have freely admitted, that these books are not to be found in the Jewish Canon. The question naturally arises why they were excluded, or, what is substantially the same, why they were not introduced: my answer was, Because they were not inspired. That their exclusion from the Jewish Canon is satisfactory evidence to us that they were destitute of Divine authority was made to appear from a very simple and conclusive process of reasoning. If they were inspired, the Canon of the Jews was evidently defective, as it failed to present the *whole rule of faith* which God had revealed to the Church. But that no such defect existed in their sacred library was made to appear from the silence of our Saviour, who nowhere insinuates that their standard of faith was incomplete, and—what is still more conclusive—

from his recorded approbation of the Jewish Canon just as
it stood. Their Canon, then, could not possibly have been
defective, and therefore the Apocrypha could not possibly
have been inspired. The leading proposition of my argument was of that peculiar species in which the destruction
or removal of the consequent is, by logical necessity, the
destruction or removal of the antecedent. The only points,
therefore, in which, as the Schoolmen would have informed
you, this argument could have been successfully assailed
were in the connection of the two propositions which constitute the hypothesis on which it rests, or the validity of
the process by which the consequent was denied. To give
a complete and satisfactory refutation you would be required
to show either that the rejection of the Apocrypha from the
Canon of the Jews, though written by inspiration of God,
did not render it defective, or that the Canon was not sanctioned as complete by Jesus Christ and his Apostles.

As to the first, you have entirely mistaken the point of
my argument in supposing that it turned essentially upon
the proof of moral delinquency in the Jews in excluding
the Apocrypha from their sacred library. It is true, sir,
that I cannot conceive how the writers of those books could
possibly have been *Prophets*, and yet no evidence of the
fact be made to appear until centuries after they were dead.
If they had been sent of God as teachers to their own generation or to generations which were then unborn, some
credentials of their Divine commission would seem to be
essential. They would either have been charged with the
power of performing wonders which none could achieve
unless God were with him, or their heavenly vocation would
have been attested by those who were known to be possessed
of the Holy Ghost. There would surely have been some
evidence—enough to constitute an adequate foundation of
faith—that these writers were messengers of God, declaring
the things which they had received from Him. In conformity with the old logical maxim, *de non existentibus et non
apparentibus eadem est ratio*, they might just as well not be

inspired at all as not be able to authenticate the fact.   Unproved inspiration is to the reader no inspiration.   Hence, I
did not regard it as a violent assumption that if these men
were really inspired there must have existed satisfactory
evidence of their Divine illumination.   You yourself have
told us that "when Almighty God deigned to inspire the
works contained in the Holy Scriptures, He intended they
should be held and believed to be inspired."   Accordingly,
sir, the authors of the Apocrypha must have presented to
their contemporaries such attestations of their commission
from Heaven as to have rendered obedience imperative and
faith indispensable.   The Jews, therefore, in rejecting their
productions from the sacred Canon must have resisted the
authority of God, and in pronouncing them not to be inspired must have been guilty of a flagrant fraud.

The charge of fraud, however—which, of course, is hypo-
thetically made—is only incidentally introduced, and does
not constitute, as in your reply you seem to have supposed,
the essence of the argument.   It was urged chiefly for the
purpose of setting in a strong light the *moral* necessity
which to my mind seemed to rest upon the Saviour of
vindicating the authority of these books, if, as you pretend,
they were really the Word of God.

The real difficulty which the Romanist is required to
explain is, how a document could be perfect and complete
when one-fifth of its pages were actually omitted.   Every
book which God had given to the Jews, through the Divine
inspiration of His Prophets, was entitled to be a part of
their rule of faith; and a complete collection of such books
would constitute their Canon or entire rule of faith.   Now,
if the Apocrypha were inspired productions, even Trent
being witness, they were canonical, and therefore their presence was indispensably essential to the integrity of the
Canon.   They were a part of the rule which God had
given, and yet our Saviour treats the rule as *perfect* when
it is miserably cheated of its fair proportions—that is, upon
this new system of Papal mathematics, *some* of the parts

are made equal to the whole. Such is the substance of the argument which you were required to answer. Every step was so plainly stated in my original essay that I do not see how you failed to understand it. Now, sir, what is your answer? To what you conceive to be the leading proposition of my argument you have nothing to reply but that the Jews might possibly have been ignorant of the supernatural character of the books, or that no public tribunal existed possessed of legitimate authority to introduce them into the Canon. Your answer consists, in other words, of nothing more nor less than a pitiful defence of the honesty of the Jews! The ancient people of God were guilty of no fraud in rejecting a host of canonical books because they had not the means of ascertaining that the books were inspired! They were not to blame. God had furnished them with no satisfactory proofs that the Apocryphal authors were His Prophets, and therefore they were not at liberty to treat their compositions as clothed with Divine authority! Your answer, sir, is such a wonderful specimen of reasoning that you must excuse me for presenting it and my argument in the form of conditional syllogisms. My argument was: If the Apocrypha were inspired the Canon of the Jews was defective; but the Canon of the Jews was not defective; therefore the Apocrypha were not inspired. Now the reader will observe that the validity of the argument does nôt depend upon the causes which induced the Jews to exclude the Apocrypha, but simply upon the fact that they were excluded. The causes might have been ignorance or fraud; as I intimated in the original essay, the *fact* is all that is essential. Your answer is: If there is not satisfactory evidence that a book is inspired, there is no fraud in excluding it from the Canon; there was not satisfactory evidence that the Apocrypha were inspired; therefore there was no fraud in excluding them from the Canon. What now is the conclusion of this resistless logic? What end is answered or what point is gained? It follows, we are told, for we have to receive it on authority, that my "argument is valueless and crumbles under its own irresistible weight." You exhibit the tact of a practised logician in evading the point of my argument, and, like an artful pupil, when the question proposed by the master is too hard you *answer another*.

You are aware, sir, that the very existence of your cause depends upon the truth of my consequent, and accordingly whatever of reasoning there is in your essay is devoted to the proofs by which my minor proposition was established. You deny, in other words, that Jesus Christ or His Apostles ever treated the Jewish Canon as possessed of Divine authority, or even referred to it at all. In refuting this extravagant assertion I must correct a series of errors (into one of which you were led by Du Pin) which tinge your whole performance, and which, when once detected, leave in a pitiable plight nine-tenths of your second epistle. Your fundamental error consists in your restricted application of the term *Canon* to a mere *catalogue* or *list*. The common metaphorical meaning of the Greek word κανών, as I have already had occasion to remark, is a *rule* or *measure*. In this sense it is used by the classical writers of antiquity, as well as by the great Apostle of the Gentiles. The subordinate meanings which we find attached to it in Suicer and Du Fresne may be easily deduced from its original application to a rule or measure. In the early ecclesiastical writers it is sometimes employed, as Eichhorn properly observes, to designate simply a *book*, and particularly a book that served in general for the use of the Church. The collection of hymns which was to be sung on festivals, and the list of members who were connected with the Church, received alike this common appellation. Again, it was applied to the approved catalogue of books that might be read in the public assemblies of the faithful for instruction and edification; and in modern times it is used to designate those inspired writings which constitute the rule of faith.[1]

---

[1] Eichhorn's Einleitung, vol. i., cap. 1, § 15, pp. 102, 103. The text is almost a literal translation of the passage.

The Scriptures therefore are said to be *canonical*, not because their various books are numbered in a list or digested
into any particular order, but because they are authoritative
standards of Divine truth; and the whole collection of
sacred writings is called by pre-eminence the *Canon*, not
because it is a collection, but because, in embodied form, it
presents the entire rule of faith.[1] It is inspiration, therefore, and that alone, which entitles a book to be regarded as
canonical, because it is inspiration alone that invests it with
authority to command our faith.   If there were but *one* inspired book on the face of the earth, that book would be

---

[1] " The infinitely good God, having favoured mankind with a revelation
of His will, has thereby obliged all those who are blessed with the knowledge thereof to regard it as the unerring rule of their faith and practice.
Under this character, the Prophets, Apostles and other writers of the
sacred books published and delivered them to the world; and on this
account they were dignified above all others with the titles of the *Canon*
and the *canonical*. The word *Canon* is originally Greek, and did, in that
language, as well as in the Latin afterward, commonly denote *that which
was a rule or standard by which other things were to be examined and judged*.
And inasmuch as the books of inspiration contained the most remarkable
rules and the most important directions of all others, the collection of
them in time obtained the name of the *Canon*, and each book was called
canonical."—*Jones' New and Full Method for Settling the Canon*, etc.; pt. 1,
c. i., p. 17, vol. i. See also Lardner's Supple., chap. 1, § 3, vol. v., p. 257
of Works; Chalmers' Evidences of Christianity, Book iv., chap. 1 ; Owen
on Hebrews, Exercit. i., § 2. That the definition which has been given in
the text is abundantly confirmed by approved Papal authorities, the following extracts will place beyond question. Ferus says: Scriptura dicitur
canonica, id est, *regularis*, quia a Deo nobis data vitæ et veritatis regula,
qua omnia probamus et juxta quam vivamus. Jacobus Andradius says:
Minimè sibi displicere eorum sententiam, qui *canonicos* ideo appellari
dicunt [Scripturæ] libros quia pietatis et fidei et religionis Canonem, hoc
est, regulam atque normam e cœlis summo Dei beneficio ad nos delatam
continent amplissimam. Nam cum omnipotentis Dei incorruptissima et
integerrima voluntas humanarum esse debat actionum et voluntatum
norma: meritò sana à canone et regula nomen accipere ii codices debuere,
quibus Divina mysteria atque voluntas comprehensa. And Bellarmine,
whom Rainold styles the Prince of Jesuits, affirms: Kemnitium rectè
deduxisse ex Augustino, libros sacros Scripturæ ideo dictos *canonicos*,
quod sint instar regulæ. These extracts may be found in Rainol. Censura,
Prælect. iv., vol. i., p. 61.

the Canon, though it would be perfectly absurd to talk of
a catalogue or list of one book. Accordingly, the distinguished German critic to whom I have already referred
treats *canonical* and *inspired* as synonymous terms. The
Jews, it is important to state, did not apply the term *Canon*
to the collection of their sacred writings. They described
the books themselves in terms expressive of their Divine
origin, arranged them in convenient general divisions, but
did not confine themselves to any one specific enumeration.
The books were computed indiscriminately, so as to suit the
number of letters either in the Hebrew or Greek alphabets.
The Jews knew nothing of the magic of a list. Philo and
Josephus, for instance, never speak of the "Canon," but of
the "compositions of their prophets," their "sacred books,"
"the oracles of God," using such terms as denoted inspiration. This was the only canonical authority of which they
dreamed. This it was that distinguished their books from
the works of the Gentiles, and exalted their faith above the
deductions of a fallible philosophy. If, then, *canonical* and
inspired, as applied to the Scriptures, are synonymous terms,
to insert a book in the Canon is simply to be convinced of
its Divine inspiration. The very evidence which proves it
to come from God makes it canonical. In other words, the
proofs of inspiration and the proofs of canonical authority
are *one* and the *same thing*. Hence, instead of requiring
some great and imposing assembly, like the *cheneseth hagadolah* of the Jews or your own favourite Council of Trent,
to settle the Canon of Scripture, it is a work which every
one must achieve for himself. The external proofs of inspiration which consist in the signs of an Apostle or a Prophet—found either in the writer himself, or some one commissioned to vouch for his production—are as easy and obvious as the external proof that any body of men are supernaturally guarded from error.[1]

---

[1] "The inspiration of a writer," says Jahn, "can only be proved by Divine testimony. Nevertheless, nothing more can be required than that a
man who has proved his Divine miracles or prophecies should assert that

The contemporaries of Moses would know, from the miraculous credentials by which his commission was sustained, that his compositions were the supernatural dictates of God. They would consequently be a *canon* to his countrymen. As other Prophets successively arose, their instructions, supported by similar credentials, would receive a similar distinction. The Canon in this way would be gradually enlarged. Writers might be found who gave no external proofs themselves that they wrote as they were moved by the Holy Ghost, and yet their writings might be authenticated by those who were unquestionably possessed of the prophetic spirit, and on this account these compositions would also be added to the existing Canon. We read in the Scriptures that "all Israel, from Dan even to Beersheba, knew that Samuel was established to be a Prophet of the Lord." (1 Sam. iv. 20.) How did they know it? There was no great synagogue to publish the fact or authenticate its truth. There was no great council to settle the matter by an infallible canon, but there was something better and higher: "The Lord was with him," and attested by miracles the supernatural character of His servant. Now, precisely in the same way could the claims of every other Prophet be established, and the evidences of Divine inspiration be speedily and extensively diffused. The sacred books circulated among the people, as well as preserved in the Library of the Temple[1] by the priests, would have every moral protection from corruption, forgery or frauds. The innovations of the priests would be speedily detected by the people, and the changes of the people just as readily exposed by the priests. In the multitude of copies, as in the book or books in question are free from error."—*Introduct. O. T.*, cap. ii., pp. 34, 35, *Turner's Translation.*

The reader will find this subject very clearly presented in Sermon xxiii. of Van Mildert's Boyle Lectures.

[1] The existence of such a Temple Library will hardly be disputed by any sober critic. Traces of it may be found before the captivity in Deut. xxxi. 26; Joshua xxiv. 26; 1 Samuel x. 25. After the captivity the evidence is complete: Josephus, Antiq., L. iii., c. i., § 7; L. v., c. i., § 17; De Bello. Jud., L. vii., c. v., § 5. See also Eichhorn, Einleit., vol. i., § 3.

the multitude of counsellors, there would be safety.[1] To this must be added the sleepless providence of God, which would preserve His Word, which He hath exalted above every other manifestation of His name, amid all the assaults of its enemies, and transmit it to future generations unimpaired by the fires of persecution, as the burning bush was protected from the flame.[2]

It is a favourite scheme of the Papists to represent the settling of the Canon as a work of gigantic toil and formidable mystery. It evidently, however, reduces itself to a simple question of fact: What books were written by men whose claims to inspiration were either directly or remotely established by miracles? It is a question, therefore, of no more difficulty than the authenticity of the sacred books. To illustrate the matter in the case of the New Testament: the churches that received the Epistles from Paul could have had no doubts of their canonical authority, because they knew that the Apostle was supernaturally inspired as a teacher of the faith. He produced in abundance the signs of an Apostle. So also the writings of the other Apostles would be recognized by their contemporary brethren as the Word of the Lord. The books actually written by the Apostles or approved by their sanction would be known by living witnesses of the fact. The historical proofs of this fact—that is, the testimony of credible witnesses—would be sufficient in all future time to attest the inspiration of any given work. If a man, for example, in the third century is doubtful of the Epistle to the Romans, all that is necessary to settle his mind is to convince him that Paul actually wrote it. This being done, its inspiration follows as a matter of course. If a book, on the other hand, which pretended to be inspired could produce no adequate proofs of

---

[1] This subject is ably discussed by Abbadie in a short compass. See Christ. Relig., vol. i., ¿ 3, c. 6.

[2] Upon the manner in which the Canon was gradually formed, and for a full and satisfactory explanation of the doubts which existed in the primitive Church in reference to some of the books of the New Testament, see Lancaster's Bampton Lectures.

apostolic origin or apostolic sanction, its claims would have to be rejected, unless its author could exhibit in his own person the signs of a heavenly messenger. The congregations in possession of inspired records were accustomed, as we gather from the Apostles themselves, to transmit their treasures to the rest of their brethren, so that in process of time this free circulation of the sacred books would put them in the hands of all the portions of the Church; and as each Church became satisfied of their apostolic origin, it received them likewise as canonical and Divine, and in this way a common Canon was gradually settled. The idea that a council or any mere ecclesiastical body could settle the Canon is perfectly preposterous. To settle the Canon is to settle the inspiration of the sacred books; to settle the inspiration of the sacred books is to prove that they were written by Divine Prophets; and to prove this fact is to prove either that the Prophets themselves established their pretensions by miraculous achievements, or were sanctioned by those who were already in possession of supernatural credentials. Now, what can a council do in a matter of this sort but give the testimony of the men who compose it? Its authority as a council is nothing. It may be entitled to deference and respect as embodying the testimony of credible witnesses. Everything, however, will depend upon the honesty, accuracy, fidelity and opportunities of the individual members who constitute the synod.

Having now shown what a canon is, how a book is determined to be canonical, and how the Canon was gradually collected, little need be said in refutation of your extravagant account of the origin and settlement of the Canon of the Jews.

I could have predicted beforehand, from your known partiality for synods and councils, that you would have found in the *great synagogue* of Ezra an adequate tribunal for adjusting the rule of faith. You would never, at least, have rested in your inquiries until you had met with *some body of men* in whose decision your Papal proclivity to con-

fide in the authority of man might be humoured or indulged.
As to the wolf in the fable no possible combination of letters could be made to spell anything but *agnus*, so your
inherent love for a Council would lead you to embrace any
floating tradition by which you could construct a plausible
story that such a tribunal had settled the Canon of the Jews.
But, sir, where is the proof that this great synagogue ever
existed? The first notice which we have of it is contained
in the Talmud, a book which began about five hundred
years after this synagogue is said to have perished. You
are more modest, however, than some of your predecessors.
Genebrard, not content, like yourself, with a single council,
has fabricated two other synods to complete the work which
Ezra had begun.[1] By one of these imaginary bodies the
books of Tobias and Ecclesiasticus were added to the Canon,
and by the other the remaining works of the Apocrypha.
The great synagogue which you have endorsed was a regular ecclesiastical body, in which might be discerned, to use
your own words, "a general council of the Church in the
old law, claiming and exercising by the authority of God
the power of teaching the faithful what were the inspired
books." Beyond the traditions of the Rabbins, what evidence are you able to produce that a body so evidently extraordinary as this is reported to have been is anything more
than a fiction? You are probably aware, sir, that Jahn pronounces the story to be a fable, in which he is confirmed by
what in a question of literary criticism is still higher authority, the opinion of Eichhorn.[2] We are not wanting in

---

[1] Hottinger, Thesaur. Phil., Lib. i., c. i., quest. 1, p. 110.

[2] "The Jews attribute the establishment of the Canon to what they call
the Great Synagogue, which during more than two hundred years, from
Zerubbabel down to Simon the Just, was composed of the prophets and the
most eminent men of the nation. But the whole story respecting this
synagogue, which first occurs in the Talmud, is utterly unworthy of credit.
It is evidently a fictitious representation of the historic truth that the
men who are said to have constituted the synagogue were chiefly instrumental in the new regulation of the State, and in the constitution of the
Jewish Church, and consequently in the collecting and fixing the holy

Jewish writers from the period of Ezra to the advent of Christ and the compilation of the Talmud, and it is certainly astonishing, if the synagogue had been a historical entity of so much importance as the traditions of the Rabbins ascribe to it, that some authentic notice has not been taken of its history, organization and proceedings. How, sir, will you explain this wonderful phenomenon? Then, again, the one hundred and twenty men who composed this assembly are said all to have flourished at the same time, and so Daniel and Simon the Just are made contemporaries, although there could have been, according to Prideaux, little less than two hundred and fifty years between them. The whole story is so ridiculous and absurd as to carry the stamp of falsehood upon its face. It no doubt arose from the fact that Ezra was assisted in restoring the constitution of the Jewish State, and publishing a correct edition of the Scriptures of the Canon as already existing, by the "principal elders, who lived in a continual succession from the first return of the Jews after the Babylonish captivity to the death of Simon the Just."[1] That Ezra could not have settled the Canon of Scripture is clear from the fact that most of the books already existed and were known to be the compositions of Prophets. There is no evidence that he furnished additional proof of the inspiration of Moses, David or Isaiah, and yet this he must have done if he made them canonical.[2]

books upon which this constitution was established."—*Jahn's Introd., Turner's Trans.*, p. 45.

See also Eichhorn's Einleit., vol. i., § 5. An account of this great synagogue may be found in Bartolocci, Bibliotheca Rabbinica, vol. iv., p. 2, on the word "Cheneseth Hagadolah;" Buxtorf, Tiberias, c. x., xi.; Leusden, Philol. Heb., Dissert. ix., § 4, p. 73.

[1] Prideaux, Part I., book iv., p. 265. In addition to the authority of Jahn, see also Knapp's Lectures, vol. i., art. i., § 4, p. 81.

[2] "But the great work of Ezra was his collecting together and setting forth a correct edition of the Holy Scriptures, which he laboured much in, and went a great way in the perfecting of it. This both Christians and Jews gave him the honour of, and many of the ancient Fathers attribute more to him in this particular than the Jews themselves; for they hold that all the Scriptures were lost and destroyed in the Babylonish captivity, and that Ezra restored them all again by Divine inspiration. Thus saith

The truth is, he did nothing more in reference to existing books than discharge the duties of a critical editor. His labours were precisely of the same kind as those of Griesbach, Knapp and Mill. He might have been guided by inspiration in executing these functions, for he was confessedly an inspired man, but the ancient books which he published were just as canonical before he was born as they were after he was dead.

"What authority," you state with ineffable simplicity, "they [the Jews] thought necessary and sufficient to amend the Canon I have never met laid down by any of them. Nor do they treat of the evidence sufficient to establish the inspiration of a book." The authority, it is plain, is the evidence of inspiration, and that, in its external division, is the exhibition of miraculous credentials. Whoever claimed to be inspired, and sustained his pretensions by signs and wonders which none could do unless God were with him, was in fact inspired, and whatever he wrote under the influence of inspiration belonged of necessity to the Canon.[1]

Irenæus, and thus say Tertullian, Clemens Alexandrinus, Basil and others. But they had no other foundation for it than that fabulous relation which we have of it in the 14th chapter of the second Apocryphal book of Esdras—a book too absurd for the Romanists themselves to receive into their Canon."—Prideaux, Part I., book iv., p. 270.

[1] "In the case of a person claiming to be commissioned with a message from God, the only proof which ought to be admitted is miraculous attestation of some sort. It should be required that either the person himself should work a miracle, or that a miracle should be so wrought in connection with his ministry as to remove all doubt of its reference to him and his message. The miracle, in these cases, is, in fact, a specimen of that violation of the ordinary course of nature which the person inspired is asserting to have taken place in his appointment and ministry; and corresponds to the exhibition of *specimens* and *experiments* which we should require of a geologist, mineralogist or chemist if he asserted his discovery of any natural phenomena, especially of any at variance with received theories."—*Hinds on Inspiration*, pp. 9, 10. "The Bible is said to be inspired in no other sense than the government of the Israelites might be termed inspired; that is, the *persons* who wrote the Bible, and those who were appointed to govern God's people of old, were divinely commissioned and miraculously qualified, as far as was needful, for their respective employments. This being so, the inspiration of Scripture is not,

Your distinction, accordingly, between not inserting a book really inspired in a canon, and rejecting it from a canon through defect of proof or want of authority, is wholly gratuitous and absurd. As the only way in which a book can be inserted into the Canon is to acknowledge its Divine authority as a rule of faith—that is, to receive it as inspired—so the only way of rejecting it is to deny or not be convinced of its inspiration. A book cannot be rejected after its inspiration is established; we may refuse to obey its instructions, but if we know it to be inspired, it must be regarded as speaking with authority. Whether we hear or whether we forbear, it still is entitled to be considered as a rule. Those that would not submit to the government of Christ were still treated and punished as his subjects. His right of dominion was not at all impaired by their disobedience.

You are quite mistaken, therefore, in supposing that the charge of rejecting the Apocrypha from the Canon cannot be sustained against the Jews, unless they had proof that these books were inspired, and possessed a tribunal whose function it was to insert them into the Canon. They were rejected from the Canon, from the very nature of the case, if they were not believed to be inspired.[1]

by the strict rule of division, opposed to the inspiration of persons, but forms one branch of that multifarious ministry in which those persons were engaged. . . . . The proof requisite for establishing the Divine authority of any writings, when, as in the case of the Bible, the testimonial miracles of the authors can be no longer witnessed, is either—1, That some miracle be implied in the authorship; or, 2, That there be satisfactory testimony that the writers were persons who performed miracles; or, 3, That there be satisfactory testimony that the writings were recognized as works of inspiration by persons who must have been assured of this on the evidence of miracles."—*Ibid.*, p. 27, 28.

[1] I find that Rainold in his admirable work has taken the same view. In rebutting the very distinction of A. P. F., which, in the days of this great scholar, was urged by Canus and Sixtus Senensis, he thus proceeds: "Concidit ergo alterum exceptionis Sixti membrum: nunc ad alterum, quod ita habet: *Etsi non receperunt in canonem, tamen non rejecerunt; aliud enim non recipere, aliud rejicere.* At idem planè est ad id de quo agimus, non accipere et rejicere. Nam mutemus verba prioris ratiocina-

All your blunders upon this subject have arisen from the ambiguity of the word *Canon,* and from the preposterous idea that there is something peculiarly mysterious and profound in making a collection of sacred works. It seems never to have entered your head that there is nothing more wonderful or abstruse in gathering together the accredited writings of the Holy Ghost than in making a collection of the acknowledged publications of a human author. The difficulty of the subject is not in the collection, but in the proof that the separate pieces, in either case, are genuine. Inspiration is the mark of a genuine work of the Spirit, and miracles are the infallible marks of inspiration.

These preliminary suggestions in reference to the nature and authority of the Canon furnish the keys to a satisfactory solution of all your difficulties. Your refutation of the minor proposition of my argument will be found so essentially wanting in every element of strength that it may safely be pronounced as worthless as you have represented my own to be, and will assuredly "crumble under its own irresistible weight."

tionis nostræ, et dicamus : *Si quæ unquam Ecclesia verum et certum testimonium dare potuit de Libris canonicis Sacræ Scripturæ, de Libris certè Veteris Testamenti vetus Ecclesia Judaica potuit. At ea hos, qui sunt in controversia, libros in canonem non recipit.* Ergo *recipiendi non sunt.* Quid jam lucratus est Canus? Nobis satis probasse non esse recipiendos, quod enim Christus apud Matthæum dicit, *qui vos recipit, me recipit,* id apud Lucam sic effertur, *qui vos rejicit, me rejicit,* et alibi *qui non colligit mecum spargit :* hic *non recipi est rejici,* ut in virtutis via regreditur, quicunque non progreditur, et in Apocalypsi, *foris erunt canes, et venefici, et scortatores, et homicidæ, et idolatræ, et quisquis amat, et committit mendacium.* Quid his proderit *non rejici,* si non recipiantur? Verùm est ista distinctio adhuc plenius refutetur, ego non modo non receptos hos libros, sed et rejectos fuisse docebo. Quid est enim rejicere, nisi negare esse canonicos? Quid non recipere, quàm (ut levius in Cani gratiam interpreter) dubitare num sint recipiendi?"—*Cens. Lib. Apoc.,* Prælect. ix., vol. i., p. 86.

LETTER XI.

SILENCE OF CHRIST AS TO THE APOCRYPHA.

THAT the Jewish Canon was not defective was made to appear from the silence of Christ in reference to any omission impairing its integrity, from His recorded conversations in which He evidently sanctioned it as complete, and from the instructions of His Apostles who spake as they were moved by the Holy Ghost.

Your reply to these several distinct proofs of my minor proposition I shall now examine in the order which seems to me to be most convenient for fully presenting the subject.

First, then, you deny that our Saviour or His Apostles ever referred to the Canon of the Jews at all, and in order to give some semblance of truth to this gross and palpable error, you avail yourself of the ambiguity of a term, and endeavour to "imbosk in the dark, bushy and tangled forest" of verbal technicalities. It is freely conceded that our Saviour nowhere enumerates, by their specific names or titles, all the books which compose the Jewish Scriptures. He never pretended, so far as it appears from the sacred records, to give an accurate list or formal catalogue of all the inspired writings which the Jews received as the infallible standard of supernatural truth. But what is this to the point? Even if we take *canon* in your own arbitrary sense of it, you have grossly failed to sustain your monstrous hypothesis. It is certainly one thing to refer to a canon, and quite a different thing to enumerate all the books which compose it. Such general terms as *the Works of Homer, the Works of Plato* or *the Works of Cicero* evidently embrace a complete collection of their various performances; and to refer to them under these titles is to refer to the catalogue or list of their literary labours. If the question were asked, What were the works of Homer?

could it be answered in any other way than by enumerating the specific books of which he was supposed to be the author?

Now, if the Jews applied any general and comprehensive titles to the whole body of their sacred writings, and if our Saviour referred to these documents under those titles, he referred unquestionably to the catalogue or list of their Divine compositions; that is, in your own sense, he referred unquestionably to the *Canon* of his countrymen. Have you yet to learn, sir, that the phrases "Scriptures," "Holy Scriptures," "Sacred Books," and such like expressions, which are continually occurring in Philo and Josephus, were the common and familiar designations of those works which were believed to have proceeded from the Spirit of God?[1] Have you further to learn that the division of their sacred books into three parts, the Law, the Prophets and the rest of the books, was an ancient classification?[2] Certainly, sir, there is as much evidence of these facts as of the existence of an infallible "council of the Church in the old law" in the days of Ezra. If, now, our Saviour and His Apostles ever referred to the inspired documents of the Jewish faith under the general and comprehensive title of the "Scriptures," or under the threefold division of their books which ancient usage had sanctioned, they referred, beyond all question, to their *Canon*, in the sense of a catalogue or list of their Divine compositions. That they did refer, however, to the Scriptures generally, you yourself admit. How, then, can you deny the obvious conclusion, without maintaining that the general does not include the particulars, the whole is not composed of its parts? Homer

[1] Hottinger, Thesaur. Phil., lib. i., c. 2, § 3; Leusden, Phil. Heb., Dissert. i., § 1; Eichhorn, Einleit., c. i., § 6; Jahn, Introd., Prelim. Observ., § 1.

[2] That this was an ancient division may be gathered from the fact that it appears to have been of long standing in the time of Jesus the son of Sirach. We find it in his Prologue. See Leusden, Phil. Heb., Dissert. ii., § 1; Hottinger, Thesaur. Phil., lib. ii., c. i., § 1; Eichhorn, Einleit., c. i., § 6; Jahn, pt. i., § 103.

sometimes nodded; and you, too, in a moment of unlucky forgetfulness, have virtually acknowledged that there *can be* a reference to *a canon* when the name itself is not mentioned, and when there is no complete enumeration of the specific books which constitute the list. You have appealed to Flavius Josephus for the purpose of showing "what were the ideas of the Jews" on the subject of their national Canon. What evidence have you, sir, that will not as clearly apply to the case of Christ and His Apostles, that Josephus, in the celebrated passage to which you allude, refers to the Canon, since he only mentions the general division of the sacred books into three leading parts, and mentions the *number*, not the *names*, of the works that belong to each division?[1] The same divisions are mentioned by our Saviour (Luke xxiv. 44): "All things must be fulfilled which are written in the Law of Moses, and in the Prophets, and in the Psalms, concerning me," and yet you deny that in this passage of Luke, or in any other passage of the New Testament, there is *any reference* at all to the Canon of the Jews! I am at a loss to understand how a reference to a general classification when found in Josephus should be a reference to the Canon, but when found in the mouth of our Saviour should be entirely different. It is vain to allege that because Josephus mentions the *number* of books in each department this is equivalent to the men-

---

[1] This passage occurs in Josephus contra Ap., lib. i., § 8. It may be thus rendered: "For we have not innumerable books which contradict each other; but only twenty-two, which comprise the history of all times past, and are justly held to be Divine. Five of these books proceed from Moses; they contain laws and accounts of the origin of men, and extend to his death. Accordingly, they include not much less than a period of three thousand years. From the death of Moses to the death of Artaxerxes, who, after Xerxes, reigned over the Persians, the Prophets who lived after Moses have recorded, in thirteen books, what happened in their time. The other four books contain songs of praise to God and rules of life for man. Since Artaxerxes up to our time, everything has been recorded; but these writings are not held to be so worthy of credit as those written earlier, because after that time there was no regular succession of Prophets."

tion of a *canon*. The *number* of books may be gathered from the catalogue, but it is no more the catalogue itself than the general heads under which the list is arranged. If I should say that there are twenty thousand volumes in the library of the South Carolina College, would that be the same as a list of the books? If I should say that the books which it contains might be conveniently arranged under the four departments of Law, Divinity, Philosophy and Belles Lettres, and that each department contains five thousand volumes, would that be equivalent to a *catalogue* of the library? It is perfectly plain, sir, that Josephus no more gives us a list of the sacred writings of the Jews —which, with you, is the only way of referring to their Canon—than Christ and His Apostles; and there is no line of argument by which you can show that he refers to the Canon in the passage which you have extracted from his works that will not also show that Christ himself refers to it in the passage recorded by Luke. You yourself, then, being judge, your broad and unqualified assertion, that "there is not in the whole New Testament a single passage showing that Christ and His Apostles ever referred to the *canon, catalogue* or *list* of inspired books held among the Jews," is a pure fabrication of the brain. Your imagination was evidently commencing that grand process of unreal formations which finally resulted in the stupendous creation of a "general council of the Church in the old law, claiming and exercising by the authority of God the power of teaching the faithful what were the inspired books." I tremble for history in this process of travail. Labouring mountains produce a mouse, but labouring priests bring forth facts from the womb of fancy, are delivered of gods in the shape of bread, and produce redeemers in the form of saints.

If, upon your own hypothesis that a *canon* and a *list* of inspired books are synonymous terms, your position is grossly and palpably erroneous, how triumphant becomes its refutation upon the true view of the case, that the Canon of the Jews was their authoritative standard of faith! What Philo and Josephus denoted by the terms "Scriptures," "Holy Scriptures," "Sacred Books," "Oracles of God," and such like expressions, was precisely the same thing which is now denoted by the compendious appellation *canon*. This word was not at that time in use in reference to the sacred books, but in those connections in which we would naturally use it they always employed some phraseology which indicated the Divine authority of the books. *All* books which were written by Prophets or inspired men belonged to the class of Holy Scriptures, and those which were destitute of any satisfactory claims to a supernatural origin were ranked in a different category. As, then, the Jews evidently meant by the *Scriptures* precisely what we mean by *the Canon* or canonical books, our Saviour's references, as also those of His Apostles, to the Jewish rule of faith under this general designation were references to the national Canon. Wherever the word occurs in allusion to the sacred books, the corresponding term *canon* may be safely substituted, and not the slightest change will be made in the meaning. With these explanations I now proceed to show that our Saviour did quote, approve and sanction, as complete, the inspired rule of faith which the Jews in his own day professed to acknowledge.[1]

1. First, he appealed to it under its ancient division into three general departments, the Law, the Prophets and the Psalms. Luke xxiv. 44. This, according to Leusden, was the first general partition of the sacred books. What in this category is called *Psalms*—the first book of a class being put for the whole class—was subsequently denominated *Hagiographa;* the phrase employed by the Jews (*Ketubim*) being less definite and precise. The books of

---

[1] In my original essay I made no special references to show that Christ and His Apostles had quoted and approved the Jewish Canon, because I never dreamed that any human being would think of denying so plain a proposition. It appeared to me like proving that the sun shines at noonday.

this third division, as would appear from the term *Ketubim* itself, were usually described by a periphrasis, as there was no general name which exactly comprehended them all. Hence, in the former Prologue of Jesus the grandson of Sirach, they are simply mentioned under the vague title of the "rest of the books." Josephus also applies to them a similar appellation. The Psalms being the first in order under the general class of Hagiographa, our Saviour, in conformity with the Jewish method of citation, mentions them as including the rest of the Ketubim.[1] It appears, too, that Jesus was accustomed to introduce repeated allusions to the books of the Old Testament under a twofold division—which not unfrequently occurs in the remains of the Fathers—the Law and the Prophets.[2] (Matt. v. 17; vii. 12; xi. 13; xxii. 40; Luke xvi. 16.)

2. Not only did Christ and His Apostles appeal to the Canon of the Jews in a general way, but they appealed to it as possessed of Divine authority. They made a broad distinction between it and all the writings of man. Paul says expressly, in evident allusion to the sacred books of his nation, "All Scripture is given by inspiration of God." (2 Tim. iii. 16.)

Peter declares that "prophecy came not in old time by the will of man, but holy men of God spake as they were moved by the Holy Ghost." Our Saviour refers the Jews to the Scriptures, which they were in the habit of reading as containing the words of everlasting life, for a satisfactory defence of His own supernatural commission. Then, again, particular passages are repeatedly introduced as the *ipsissima verba* of the Holy Ghost.[3] These facts incontestably

---

[1] The *Psalms* of our Saviour's arrangement and the *Hagiographa* of later classifications are evidently the same. There being no single word by which all the books of this class could be denoted, led, necessarily, to a periphrastic description, or to the mention of a single book as a reference to the series.

[2] Suicer on the word γραφή, § 7.

[3] The following passages show the light in which the Jewish Canon was held by the writers of the New Testament. I have before me a list of

prove that the Jewish Canon was sanctioned by Christ, approved by His Apostles, and commended to the Church as the lively oracles of God.

The estimate which Christ and His Apostles put upon the Scriptures of the Old Testament may be gathered from the fact that they uniformly treat Christianity as only a development of Judaism. It was a *new* dispensation of an *old* religion. Hence, in their arguments with Jews and Gentiles, in their instructions to all classes and conditions of men, they refer to the Scriptures—the Law, the Prophets and the Psalms—for a Divine confirmation of all the doctrines which they taught. The New Testament is only an inspired exposition of the principles contained in the Old. Every doctrine which Christ or His Apostles announced may be found in the existing Canon of their day. Whatever changes they made or novelties they taught respected the organization and not the essence of the Church. Hence, the primitive Christians, even before a single Gospel or Epistle had been indited, had a written rule of faith. They were never for a moment, as the Papists pretend, left to oral tradition for the doctrines of their creed.

3. But the Jewish Canon was also held to be *complete*. In the original essay this point was presented as a legitimate and obvious inference from the silence of the Saviour in reference to any defects in the sacred library of his countrymen. Now, the strength of this argument must depend on the strength of the presumption that if such defects in reality existed, the Messiah would have felt Himself bound to correct and remove them. According to the hypothesis of Rome, one-fifth of the revelation of God was deprived of that equal veneration and authority to which it was justly entitled with the Law, the Prophets and the Psalms. Now

direct quotations made from the Old Testament by the writers of the New, amounting to about 272. Yet there is no *reference* to the Jewish Canon!

Matt. xi. 13, xv. 3-6, xix. 4-6, xxii. 31-43, xxvi. 54; Luke xvi. 16, 29, 31, xviii. 31, xxiv. 25-27, 44-46; Mark vii. 9, 13; John v. 39, 46, x. 34; Acts iii. 18, xxviii. 25; Rom. i. 2, iv. 3-24; Gal. iii. 8, 16; Heb. iii. 7, xii. 25; 1 Pet. i. 11; 2 Pet. i. 21.

the question is, whether that great Prophet of the Church "who was clad with zeal as a cloak," who came to "magnify the Law and make it honourable," and who expressly declared that He had "not refrained His lips" from speaking righteousness in the great congregation, nor concealed from it the *truth* and loving-kindness of the Lord—the question is, whether such a Prophet would suffer so large a part of the light of revelation to be extinguished without uttering a single word in its defence. Upwards of fourteen hundred years before He was born His Father had distinctly announced, "I will put my words in His mouth, and He shall speak unto them *all* that I shall command Him." He came, then, not only as a Priest and King, but also as a Teacher, a teacher of God's truth, and yet permitted a body of that truth almost equal in bulk to the whole New Testament to be "buried in the dust of death." If He raised no warning voice, no cry of expostulation, if He stood silent by when such violence was done to the sacred records of the faith, how could He say, "Thy law is within my heart, lo, I have not refrained my lips, O Lord, thou knowest"? The Jews had excluded the Apocrypha, either wilfully or ignorantly: if wilfully, they were guilty of a fraud, and that fraud ought to have been rebuked; if ignorantly, they were involved in a great calamity, and their illustrious Prophet would not have left them in their darkness and error. So that upon every view of the subject the silence of Christ is wholly unaccountable if these books were really inspired. It becomes simple and natural upon the supposition that they were merely human productions. He would have, in that case, no more occasion to mention them than to mention the writings of the Greek philosophers.

Now, sir, what is your answer to this plain argument from the silence of Christ? Why, you tell us in your third distinction that it is not so perfectly certain that Christ observed any such silence as I have attributed to Him. You inform us, in conformity with the testimony of John—for that is the only passage which bears upon the

point—that Jesus *did* a great many things which are not
recorded, therefore He must also have *said* a great many
things which have not been preserved. I confess that I do
not exactly perceive the consequence. But let that pass.
Let us admit that He may have *said* as well as *done* a great
many things which have never been written, is it likely
that the Apostles and Evangelists would have omitted what
their Master had taught in reference to a subject so vastly
important as the very *constitution* of His Church? No history perhaps records *all* the sayings and doings of the Continental Congress, but that certainly would not deserve the
name of a history that should neglect to make the most distant reference to the Declaration of Independence. Whatever other things the sacred writers have passed in silence
and neglect, we may feel perfectly certain that they have
not concealed or suppressed the instructions of their Master
in regard to so fundamental a matter as the rule of faith.
The very same arguments that render it improbable that
our Saviour would have failed to correct the defects of the
Jewish Canon, if any defects had existed, render it also
improbable that His biographers would have neglected to
record the substance, at least, of what He had taught upon
the subject. If we grant, however, that their silence is no
proof of their Master's silence, you have gained nothing.
You have only avoided one difficulty by plunging into
another. You would have the silence of the Apostles and
Evangelists to explain, instead of the silence of Christ.
For this and all other difficulties, however, you have a
stereotyped solution at hand. What Christ did not choose
to do in person upon earth, and what His Apostles failed to
perform however clearly within the compass of their sacred
commission, may yet be accomplished by a standing tribunal, a general council of the Church, like the fictitious synagogue of Ezra, "claiming and exercising by the authority
of God the power of teaching the faithful what were the
inspired works." But as every error accumulates additions
in its progress—*vires acquirit eundo*—so your infallible body

possesses some larger powers in your second letter than it was represented to possess in your first. You have brought it so often before the public, and exposed it to view in such tattered apparel, that it has finally lost its modesty, and begins to speak more "swelling words of vanity" than it dared to utter at its first appearance. In your first letter councils could do no more, on the head of doctrine, than merely declare and define what had always been the faith of the Church. They possessed no power to make *new* articles of faith; they could only announce with infallible certainty what had always been the *old*. In your second letter these councils rise a step higher and become prophets themselves, intrusted with new revelations, which neither Christ nor His Apostles had ever communicated to the Church. It seems that it is a matter of no sort of consequence whether Christ or His Apostles in their own persons had ever testified to the inspiration of the Apocrypha—that is, had ever taught that the Apocrypha were inspired: an infallible council could subsequently teach it for them. How? If Christ and His Apostles had never taught it, the members of the council could not receive it from tradition; they must therefore ascertain the fact by *immediate revelation*. What your councils will become next it is impossible to augur; they already claim to be the voice of the Lord; they will perhaps aspire to be God himself. I shall add nothing here to what I have already said touching your pretensions to infallibility. My previous numbers are a full refutation of this stupendous folly.

You are extremely unfortunate in your attempt to refute from *analogy* my obvious inference from the silence of the Saviour. You appeal to the case of the Sadducees and Samaritans, who, according to you, denied all the books of the Jewish Canon but the five books of Moses, and yet were not rebuked by the Saviour for their wicked infidelity.

Now, sir, that the Sadducees denied the Divine authority of the Prophets and Ketubim I think it will be difficult

for you or any other man to prove. It has been supposed
that because our Saviour refutes their skeptical opinions in
regard to the resurrection of the dead by a passage extracted
from the Pentateuch, therefore they denied the inspiration
of any other books. But it will be seen, by inspecting the
context, that they had drawn their cavils from a distinctive
provision of the Jewish law. They had virtually asserted
that the Pentateuch denied the resurrection, since in a given
case its peculiar requisitions, according to their view, would
introduce confusion and discord into the future state. The
Saviour met their difficulties by correcting their misappre-
hensions in regard to the nature of the future life, and by
distinctly showing that Moses had taught the doctrine which
they supposed he had condemned. Among the Fathers,
Origen, Tertullian, Jerome and Athanasius have endorsed
this calumny upon the faith of the Sadducees. It was first
called in question by Drusius, and subsequently refuted with
such triumphant success by Joseph Scaliger that Bishop
Bull pronounces his argument to be decisive of the question. That must be a bad cause in a matter of literary
criticism which such men as Scaliger, Spanheim, Pearson,
Bull, Jortin, Waterland and Eichhorn, to say nothing of
Brucker, Buddæus and Basnage, unite to condemn, and
yet all these men are found arrayed against the patristic
opinion that the Sadducees rejected the Prophets and the
Psalms.[1]

It is universally acknowledged that the Samaritans denied
the Divine authority of the whole Jewish Canon, with the
exception of the Pentateuch, but it is not so clear that the
Saviour failed to rebuke them. You are probably aware,
sir, that distinguished commentators, both in ancient and
modern times, have regarded John iv. 22 as a pointed
reproof of Samaritan infidelity, and it was incumbent upon
you to prove that this common interpretation was erroneous
before you could confidently assume that the whole matter

[1] Brucker, vol. ii., p. 721; Pearson, Vindicat. Ignat., part i., c. vii.,
p. 467; Bull, Harm. Apost. Diss. Post., cap. x., § 14.

was permitted to pass *sub silentio* by Christ.[1]   Again, it was hardly necessary to rebuke the Samaritans, as our Saviour's notorious concurrence in the faith of the Jews was an open, public and sufficient condemnation of the errors and defects of this remarkable people.

The inconsistency of the various solutions which you have suggested to the palpable difficulty arising from the silence of Christ affords an amusing illustration of human weakness.   First, it was not so absolutely certain that Christ was silent, since He performed many signs and wonders which have never been committed to written records.   Then, again, He could afford to be silent, as He had established an infallible tribunal abundantly competent to supply all His deficiencies and teach the faithful to the end of time.   In an analogous case, that of the Sadducees and Samaritans, He probably was silent, as there is no evidence whatever that He rebuked the former for a sin which they never committed, and very strong evidence that He reproved the latter for an omission of which they were undoubtedly guilty!   So you seem to oscillate between a denial and admission of the silence of Christ.   Like a man walking upon ice, you tread with wary steps, lest your next movement should engulf you. Finally, however, after all your vibrations, you "screw your courage to the sticking place," and settle down in grim despair upon a probable solution by which you seem determined to abide.   You stoutly deny that Christ was silent in the matter, and promise to prove "that Christ and His Apostles *did* take some steps, not indeed to insert those books in the Jewish Canon, but to give them to the Christians as divinely-inspired works."   Apart from the testimony of an *infallible* Church, the only proof which you present in your second letter of this miserable fiction is drawn from the assumption that in the New Testament quotations are made from the Apocryphal writers, and from the admitted

---

[1] Such is the interpretation put upon this passage by Ammonius, Grotius, Lampe, Tholuck and others. Tholuck's comment is specially deserving of notice.

fact that these books were early embodied in the Septuagint. The first position you have entirely failed to substantiate. There is no proof whatever that a single passage from any of the books of the Apocrypha is introduced into the documents which compose the New Testament. The passage, Rom. xi. 34, which of all others seems to be most analogous to a corresponding text in the book of Wisdom (ix. 31), is confessed by several of the Fathers, Tertullian, Basil and Ambrose, as well as by modern authors of the Papal sect, to have been borrowed from the canonical prophet Isaiah, xl. 13.[1] If, however, it could be proved that the Apocrypha were quoted by Christ and His Apostles, this would not establish their Divine inspiration, unless it could also be shown that *every* book quoted in the New Testament was on that account inspired. I can conceive of no other major proposition which would answer the ends of the argument. But surely, sir, you would not hazard a statement like this! It is more than Trent would dare to assert, that the heathen poets whose verses are found in the Epistles of Paul were holy men of Greece who spake as they were moved by the Holy Ghost. It is an old logical maxim that an argument which proves too much proves in reality nothing.

Your reasoning from the second fact is easily set aside. You proceed on the assumption, for which you quote the authority of Walton, that in the time of Christ and His Apostles the Septuagint contained the Apocrypha.[2] You

---

[1] See Number IX. of this series of letters.

[2] I have seen no reason, since writing my original essay, to change the opinion which I then expressed, that the Septuagint in the time of Christ did *not* contain the Apocrypha. If these documents were in the hands of the Apostles, why were they never quoted? How does it happen that not a single allusion is made to them nor a single passage extracted from them? But the subject is too unimportant to allow much time to be spent upon it. I shall just observe that I am sustained in my opinion by Eichhorn as well as Schmidius. The passage from Walton proves nothing as to the *time* when the union betwixt the Septuagint and Apocrypha took place. A. P. F.'s eulogy upon Walton's competency to settle a question of this sort is not a little amusing, since probably the most exceptionable part of his famous Prolegomena is in relation to the origin of the Sep-

then infer that "if those books were uninspired, the Saviour and His Apostles were certainly bound *positively to reject them*." Now, as I have already shown from the very nature of the case, to insert a book into the Canon is to receive it as inspired, and to reject a book is to be not persuaded or convinced of its Divine inspiration, or, to pronounce it uninspired. As there is no evidence that a single man, woman or child in the whole land of Judea looked upon the Apocrypha as inspired productions, what need was there that Christ should positively assert what no one thought of denying? His silence was conclusive proof that He acquiesced in the popular opinion. It was beyond all controversy the positive rejection for which you so earnestly plead.

You have admitted that the Jews had no satisfactory evidence that the Apocrypha were inspired, that they were excluded from the Jewish Canon, and of course a complete separation as to authority was made between them and the sacred books! Every end was consequently answered which could have been effected by the most pointed denunciation of these books. There was no need for Christ to speak, unless He intended to *add* these works to the sacred Canon. Then it would have been necessary to show the Jews their error in refusing to admit the Divine authority of Tobit, Judith and Wisdom. The truth is, you have been led into this fallacious argument by the ambiguity of the sentence that the *Septuagint contained the Apocrypha.* You evidently treat the phrase as conveying the idea that whatever books were inserted in that version were possessed of equal authority. The only meaning, however, which the words can consistently bear is that wherever there were copies of the Greek version of the Old Testament there were also copies of the Greek documents which we now style the *Apocrypha.* They usually went together, and that for the purpose of presenting in regular series the remarkable history of God's chosen people. In this way a complete col-

tuagint. He ought not to be read upon this point without Hody at hand to correct his partiality for the fable of Aristæus.

lection was made of Jewish literature, inspired and uninspired. The line was clearly drawn between the Divine
and human, but as they both met in the common point of
Jewish history, they were united together in one collection.
Thus much might have been gathered from the famous passage of Josephus which was evidently before your eyes.
" We have not," says he, " innumerable books which contradict each other, but only twenty-two, which comprise
the *history* of all times past. . . . Since Artaxerxes up to
our time, *everything has been recorded.*" In the eyes of
Josephus, then, both the canonical and Apocryphal books
contained the *history* of his nation, and therefore had a common quality which might serve as a bond of union, but the
difference between them lay in this: the twenty-two books
were "justly held to be Divine;" those composed since the
time of Artaxerxes " were not so worthy of credit, because
after that time there was no regular succession of Prophets"
or inspired writers. Another circumstance which undoubtedly contributed in no small degree to the popularity of
those works was their singular adaptation to the religious
spirit of the age. The Jews, like the Papists, had obscured
the revelation of God, and, trusting in the vain traditions
of man, had mistaken superstition for piety and sentiment
for grace. Hence, they would be likely to regard (particularly the Hellenists) these Apocryphal documents with the
same sort of veneration with which we now contemplate
the monuments of illustrious teachers of the truth.

It is, certainly, no commendation of these books to say
that they were written with that subordinate degree of inspiration which the Jews denominate the "*daughter of the
voice.*"[1] The stories of the Rabbins concerning this singular method of supernatural communication reveal a degree of superstition and betray a fondness for magical
delusion which sufficiently illustrate the real source of
their famous "*bath quol.*" In attributing to the writings

[1] For an account of this species of inspiration, see Witsii Opera, vol. i.,
lib. i., c. 3; Lightfoot on Matt. iii. 17.

of the Apocrypha this peculiar species of inspiration, they
naturally awakened a suspicion that much of the esteem in
which they held them may be ultimately traced to their
own patronage of something not very remote from the black
art. A strong inclination to credulity and magic was, according to Lightfoot, a characteristic of the Jews under the
second temple, and I know of nothing better suited to a
humour of this sort than the book of Tobit, unless it be the
Arabian Nights.

You seem to think that if these books were not admitted
into the Septuagint until after the time of Christ, it must
have been done with the sanction of the Apostles in such
a way as to imply that they were divinely inspired. This
would follow only upon the hypothesis that when admitted
they were admitted as inspired. If they were introduced
into connection with the Septuagint simply as historical
works covering an interesting period of the Jewish annals,
or as moral compositions pervaded by an elevated tone of
religious sentiment, there would be no more objection to in-
corporating them with the Septuagint than to placing them
on the same shelf in a bookcase. The Apostles, I presume,
would not have objected to their followers that they studied
the writings of the heathen philosophers, provided they did
not make Plato and Aristotle arbiters of their faith. It
was not the perusal of the books, or the places in which
they were found, that could make a matter of exception.
So long as they were treated simply as human compositions,
possessed of no Divine authority, and to be ultimately tried
in all their doctrines by the sacred Canon, the Apostles would
hardly object to the study of them. It was no part of their
creed to denounce freedom of inquiry; on the other hand,
they inculcated the noble and generous maxim, "Prove all
things, hold fast that which is good." Paul did not hesitate
to quote the heathen poets; and if the Hellenistic Jews and
the early Christians could not place the Apocrypha by the
side of their canonical books without sanctioning the inspiration of the former, how could Paul weave whole sentences

of heathen poetry into his own Divine compositions without, at the same time, endorsing the supernatural inspiration of Aratus, Menander and Epimenides? The argument from the Septuagint's containing the Apocrypha is so evidently preposterous that it need be pressed no farther. Let it lie in its glory, and let peace be with it.

The whole matter in dispute betwixt us is brought down at last to this plain issue: the Apocrypha must be rejected from the sacred canon and treated simply as human compositions, unless it can be shown that Christ and His Apostles did sanction their Divine inspiration and authorize their use as standards of faith. Up to the time of Christ there was no satisfactory proof that they constituted any part of the oracles of God. Whatever evidence, therefore, now exists of their supernatural character must have been developed in the age of the Apostles. Their inspiration must have been approved by men who gave unquestionable evidence that they spake as they were moved by the Holy Ghost. This is the proof which the case demands; and if you fail to produce it, you are only spending your strength for that which is not bread, and your labour for that which satisfieth not.

LETTER XII.

THE APOCRYPHA AND THE JEWISH CHURCH—THE APOCRYPHA AND THE PRIMITIVE CHURCH.

To you and all your predecessors in this field of controversy the conduct of the Jewish Church—to whom were committed the oracles of God—in regard to the Apocrypha has been so seriously embarrassing, that your efforts to explain it in consistency with your own views of their Divine original are a powerful illustration of the desperate expedients to which men may be driven by extremity of circumstances who are

resolved not to receive the truth. The rule of Augustine is
so palpably just, that the authority of a book must depend
on the testimony of contemporary witnesses, that the absence of all such testimony in the present case, or of any
testimony at all for a long series not of years alone but of
centuries, is felt to be a huge impediment to your cause.
As you cannot suborn the ancient people of God to give the
least countenance to your vain and arrogant pretensions, you
expend all your ingenuity upon fruitless and abortive efforts
to reconcile the exclusion of the Apocryphal books from the
Jewish Canon with your modern hypothesis of their Divine
inspiration. The Jesuits cannot disguise their spleen at the
stubborn and intractable conduct of the sons of Abraham.
In the true spirit of some of the venerable Fathers of
Trent,[1] Bellarmine speaks of the Jewish synagogue with
great contempt, representing it to be, from its very name, a
collection of cattle rather than men. And Campianus, his
inferior in learning, though his superior in elegance, treats
its Canon as a mere grammatical affair dependent upon the
characters of the Hebrew alphabet, and incapable of being
increased after the books had reached the charmed number
of the letters. Others again have endeavoured to show that
the Jews, as a body, always entertained a profound respect
for these disputed documents, and that some of the nation
actually received them as divinely inspired.[2] But of all

---

[1] The spirit of the Fathers of Trent may be gathered from the following
extract:
   "To these reasons, which the major part applauded, others added also
that if the providence of God hath given an authentical Scripture to the
Synagogue, and an authentical New Testament to the Grecians, it cannot
be said without derogation that the Church of Rome, more beloved than
the rest, hath wanted this great benefit, and therefore that the same Holy
Ghost who did dictate the holy books hath dictated also that translation
which ought to be accepted by the Church of Rome."—*Father Paul*, p.
147. For a full and able refutation of Campianus and Bellarmine upon
this subject, see Rainold, Cens. Lib. Apoc., Prælect. xi., tom. i., p. 96, etc.
   [2] This opinion is attributed by Melchior Canus to Cochlæus, but the *persons* among the Jews who *did* receive these books have never been brought
to light.

the theories which have ever been invented, that which you
have borrowed from Melchior Canus, and endorsed, is beyond controversy the most unfortunate. It turns upon a
distinction which I have already shown to be false, which
Bellarmine himself saw to be untenable and consequently
passed without discussion, and which, as presented by you,
is absolutely fatal to your cause. You deny that the Jews
rejected the Apocrypha because they had no satisfactory
evidence that the books were inspired, or possessed no tribunal competent to enlarge the extent of the Canon. They
did not receive them, you admit; but as no body commissioned to pronounce an authoritative judgment probably
existed, there could be no rejection in the case. You lay
great stress upon the arbitrary distinction of Canus, that
there is a vast difference between *not receiving* a book as
Divine and positively *rejecting* it as a human composition.[1]

Now, sir, you have only to turn to your second letter to
perceive what you regarded as satisfactory proof that in the
days of Ezra an infallible tribunal existed, a council of the
Church in the old law commissioned by God for the express
purpose of teaching the faithful what were the inspired
books. In your first and subsequent letters conclusive evidence is furnished of your firm conviction that many of
these Apocryphal books were written *before* the time of the
great synagogue, and consequently must have been in existence at the period of Ezra. You attribute, for instance,
the book of Wisdom to Solomon; Baruch, according to you,
was originally an integral portion of Jeremiah; and the internal evidence is strong that the book of Tobit was written
some six or seven hundred years before the advent of Christ.
Then, again, the Song of the Three Children, the History
of Susannah, together with the Story of Bel and the Dragon,
you represent as having been originally parts of Daniel.
The additions to the book of Esther, too, you make to be a

---

[1] "Aliud est enim non accipere, aliud rejicere. Certe Judæi intra suum
Canonem hos libros publica authoritate minime receperunt, tametsi nonnulli ex illis sacros et Divinos esse crediderint."—Lib. ii., cap. x.

portion of the book itself. From these statements it is
evident that when the Jewish Canon was settled some of
the Apocryphal books were in being. Here, then, is a curious question: if a body specially commissioned to teach the
faithful what were the inspired books should omit to enumerate among them any that were truly inspired, would not
such omission be exactly tantamount to positive rejection?
It would be vain to say that no sufficient evidence existed
that the omitted books were really inspired; the very object
of appointing such a body is to afford that evidence. Neither
can it be pretended that the books, though in being at the
time, might be unknown to the tribunal; since, according
to the very terms of its commission, it was authorized to
pronounce with infallible certainty what books were inspired. Hence, such a body must have known all the
inspired books that were extant at the time, and its failure
to insert any book in the Canon becomes, by consequence,
a damning proof of its human and earthly origin. Now,
if an infallible council settled the Canon of the Jewish
Church—and such, we have seen, is your hypothesis—if, at
the time when the Canon was settled, Baruch, Wisdom and
Tobit, the additions to Daniel and the additions to Esther,
were extant, if it is undeniably certain that these compositions were not inserted, is not the conclusion irresistible
that they were rejected by a body competent to determine
their character? Will you be pleased to explain upon any
other hypothesis how it happened that if Baruch was an
integral portion of Jeremiah, the great synagogue separated
it from the rest of the book? Let me ask you again, if
Wisdom were written by Solomon, and was, as you say,
truly inspired, why did it not receive at the hands of the
council the same treatment with Proverbs, Ecclesiastes and
Canticles? How comes it that the Song of the Three Children and the Story of Bel and the Dragon did not pass
into the Canon with the rest of Daniel? Why were the
additions to the book of Esther excluded? And why was

Tobias, your darling Tobias, prevented from being enrolled among the authoritative documents of faith?

One of two things is intuitively evident—either the tribunal which settled the Canon of the Jews was not competent to teach the faithful what were the inspired books, or Baruch, Wisdom and Tobit were rejected. If you accede to the first proposition, you contradict your position affirming the existence of an infallible tribunal in the time of Ezra for settling the Canon; if you admit the latter, you contradict your repeated declarations that the Jews did not reject the Apocrypha, since, according to this view, they must have rejected *some* of them. So that self-contradiction awaits you whichever horn of the dilemma you choose to adopt. If, however, you concede what upon the preceding statement of the case cannot be consistently denied, that any portion of the Apocrypha was rejected, then, according to your own hypothesis, you have the testimony of an infallible body against the inspiration of the rejected portion. This reduces you to a still more deplorable dilemma; and how you will extricate yourself it is impossible for me to determine. On the one hand, the Great Synagogue of Ezra stares you in the face, pronouncing with infallible certainty that certain books are not inspired; on the other, you are damned by the Council of Trent if you do not receive it as infallible truth that these same books are inspired. "When Greek meets Greek, then comes the tug of war."

My purpose in exposing the suicidal character of your argument is simply to show that upon every view of the case the testimony of the Jewish Church is clear and decided against the inspiration of the books whose Divine authority you have undertaken to defend. That testimony you cannot evade. Your nice distinctions are wholly ineffectual, and if you cannot rebut the decision of the Jewish Church by the authoritative instructions of Christ or His Apostles, your cause is hopeless. Let the reader, then, bear distinctly in mind that what you are required to prove is the historical fact that our blessed Saviour, or His in-

spired Apostles, committed the Apocrypha to the Christian
Church as infallible standards of faith.   Up to the time of
Christ we find them treated as human compositions; and
we must continue to regard them in the same light, unless
it can be shown that our great Prophet has otherwise instructed the Church.

In your pretended refutation of the second argument of
my original essay you undertake the hopeless task of proving that the Primitive Church received these books from the
hands of the Apostles as inspired productions.   Your reasoning, if a series of assumptions can be called reasoning,
may be reduced to the following syllogism :   Whatever books
the Primitive Church received as inspired must have been
received upon the authority of Christ and His Apostles;
the Apocrypha were received by the Primitive Church as
inspired; therefore they must have been received upon the
authority of Christ and His Apostles.   The testimony of
the Primitive Church is consequently your medium of proof—
a testimony, in this case, which, as we shall subsequently see,
is not pointed and direct, but only mediate and inferential.

This argument or syllogism is grossly at fault in two particulars.   In the first place, the major proposition is not
logically necessary, and you have not attempted to show the
connection between the subject and predicate.   For aught
that appears to the contrary, the primitive Christians might
have received books as inspired without the sanction of
Christ or His Apostles.   Certain it is that you have nowhere proved that they could not have done it.   You tell
us that "if they united in receiving those works as inspired,
then is our [the Papal] cause fully sustained; for they would
not have thus united unless they had been taught by the
Apostles that these books formed a part of the Word of
God."   How does it appear that they would not have united
except upon the specified condition?   All that I can find in
the shape of proof is, "that they were tried in the furnace
of persecution, and laid down their lives by thousands,
rather than swerve one jot or tittle from the truth handed

down to them"! That they were exposed to dangers, sufferings and death is evident, but that this proves anything
more than the sincerity of their convictions I am utterly
unable to perceive. We may grant that they would not
have added to the sacred Canon books which they did not
believe to be inspired; but then the question is, whether their
belief was always founded on apostolic teaching? Might
they not be mistaken as to what Christ and His Apostles
had actually taught? If they were fallible, liable to be
misled by designing men, the crafts of the Devil or the
deceitful workings of their own hearts, they might have
been perfectly sincere and yet have received error in the
place of truth. Even in the days of the Apostles, and
among the congregations collected by their labours, the
mystery of iniquity had begun to work; and none can read
the Epistle of Paul to the Galatians without being deeply
convinced that the faith of professing Christians was not
always adjusted to the standard of inspired instruction.
Paul admonishes the Ephesian Elders that even among
themselves should men arise speaking perverse things, to
draw disciples after them; and the exhortations to the seven
churches of Asia reveal anything but a necessary connection between the actual belief of the people and the lessons
which they had received from inspired teachers. The faith,
consequently, of the primitive Christians is an exceedingly
uncertain medium through which to arrive at the doctrines
of Christ and His Apostles; and yet, unless there be an
exact correspondence between them—unless the one answers
to the other as an image corresponds to its original, the seal
to its impression, the purpose of your argument is not
answered. You infer that such *must* have been the doctrine
of Christ because such was the faith of the Church. Now,
if there be any possibility of error or deception on the part
of the Church, the force of your conclusion is proportionably
weakened. It may be true, as a matter of fact, that the
Primitive Church did not receive any other Canon but that
of Christ and His Apostles; but then, in order to determine

this point, it must be previously known what books our
Saviour received and what books the Primitive Church
received. When the documents included in their respective
Canons are fully ascertained, and each Canon becomes consequently known, we can then compare them and pronounce
upon their mutual agreement or discrepancy. But if one
of the Canons be unknown, I see no clue by which a knowledge of the other will enable us to resolve our difficulties.
It is true that the Canon of Christ and His Apostles ought
to be the Canon of the Christian Church, but he who should
reason from right to reality, from what should be to what
is, will find himself halting on many a lame conclusion.
Now, in the present case your professed design is to ascertain
what books Christ and His Apostles delivered to the Church
as the Word of God: this is the unknown fact to be settled.
You attempt to settle it by appealing to the faith of the
primitive Christians. Your argument, of course, depends
on the assumption that the primitive Christians believed
nothing but what Christ and His Apostles actually taught;
and of this assumption the only proof which you furnish
goes no farther than to establish the sincerity of the primitive disciples—a point which can answer your purpose only
on the gratuitous hypothesis that none can be in error and
at the same time sincere, or that none can be deceived without being also necessarily hypocrites. When you shall have
succeeded in proving that *honesty* and *mistake* are incompatible terms, mutually contradictory and destructive of each
other, then, and not till then, your argument will have
something of logical coherence. To put the weakness of
your reasoning in a clearer light: if it were admitted—
which, however, cannot be done consistently with truth—
that the early Christians did, in fact, believe that the Apocryphal books were inspired, this would be a moral phenomenon demanding explanation. In all reasoning upon
testimony the principle of cause and effect lies at the basis
of the process. A witness simply puts us in possession of
the convictions of his own mind. These convictions are an

effect for which the constitution of our nature prompts us
to seek an adequate cause; and when no other satisfactory
solution can be given but the reality of the facts to which
he himself ascribes his impressions, then we admit the existence of the facts. But if any other cause can be assigned
the testimony should not command our assent. If a man
afflicted with the jaundice should testify that the walls of
a room were yellow, we might be fully persuaded of the
sincerity of his own belief; but as an adequate cause, apart
from the reality of the fact, could be assigned for his conviction, we should not feel bound to receive his statement.
Two questions, consequently, must always arise in estimating the value of testimony: the first respects the sincerity of the witnesses—do they or do they not express the
real impressions that have been made upon their own minds?
The second respects the cause of these convictions—are there
any known principles which can account for them without
an admission of the facts to which the witnesses attribute
them? When we are satisfied that the witnesses are sincere, and that no causes apart from the reality of the facts
can be assigned in the case, then the testimony is entitled to
be received without hesitation. Such being the laws which
regulate the value of testimony, you were bound, after
having shown that the primitive Christians believed the
Apocrypha to be inspired—you were bound to show, in addition, that no other assignable cause could satisfactorily
account for this belief, this moral effect, but the authority
of Christ and His Apostles.

In the mean time, it may be well to apprize you of the
fact that the actual faith of the Primitive Church, *as such*, is
not received by Protestants as an authoritative standard of
truth. There is always a previous inquiry into the grounds
of that faith, and if they should be found weak, futile or
insufficient, thinking men feel no more obligation to reason
badly because good men before them have done so, than to
disregard any of the sacred principles of justice because
distinguished saints have fallen into grievous sins. The

Church of Jesus Christ in the present day does not believe
in the Divine authority of those books which it admits to
be canonical because the ancient Church regarded them in
the same light, but because there is satisfactory evidence
that they were composed by men who wrote as they were
moved by the Holy Ghost. The esteem in which they were
held by the first Christians amounts to nothing more than a
presumption that there was sufficient proof of their supernatural origin; but that proof itself, and not the effect which
it had on the minds of others, must be the ultimate historical ground of faith. Historical testimony puts us in possession of this proof; it lays before us the facts upon which
the primitive Christians formed their judgment, and puts us
as nearly as possible in the same relative situation with
themselves, so that we can form an opinion upon the same
evidence which was first submitted to their understandings.
History bridges over the chasm of time, and makes us contemporary with the events which it sets in order before us.
Hence, it is absolutely false to say that the Church now
receives any document as inspired because the Church
anciently received it; the Church now has the same facts
in history which the Church anciently saw and heard, and
consequently founds its judgment upon the same data. The
only difference is in regard to the *medium* through which
the knowledge of the facts is reached, but the ultimate
ground of faith is the same in both cases. If, for example,
I were asked why I receive the Epistle of Paul to the
Romans as an inspired composition, I would answer not
because the Primitive Church received it—that would only
create a presumption in its favour—but because there is satisfactory proof that Paul wrote it, and equally conclusive
evidence that Paul attested by miracles his supernatural
commission as a teacher of the faithful. Now, sir, if you
could adduce any adequate historical testimony that Christ
and His Apostles gave their sanction to the Apocrypha as
inspired compositions, you would then be able to adduce
a sufficient ground of faith. I have already admitted that

wherever a document can be shown to have been written by persons empowered to achieve miracles as the proofs of their commission, or wherever a document can be shown to have received the approbation and sanction of those who were supernaturally commissioned, the historical evidence of its inspiration is complete. If you could, therefore, produce from the sacred Scriptures, or from any contemporary writers worthy of credit, direct statements of the fact, or of other facts necessarily involving it, that Christ and His Apostles delivered to the Church the documents in question as the Word of God, you would then allege something to the purpose. But, sir, not a particle of such testimony have you been able to adduce. You have simply inquired what the Primitive Church believed, and without pausing to investigate the grounds of its belief or the possibility of mistake, you have boldly assumed that it could believe nothing but what it had received upon inspired authority.

But, in the second place, your syllogism is just as faulty in the minor as it is in the major proposition. It so happens, as a matter of fact, that the primitive Christians did not receive any other Canon but that of the Jews, which was also the Canon of Christ and His Apostles. They might have received another, so that their endorsement of a book is no necessary proof of its Divine authority, but as it is historically true that they did not, your minor proposition is utterly without support, and my original assertion, that the unbroken testimony of the Church for four centuries is against the inspiration of the Apocrypha, remains unshaken, notwithstanding your multiplied quotations and elaborate trifling in attempting to refute it.

LETTER XIII.

THE APOCRYPHA AND ANCIENT VERSIONS OF SCRIPTURE—THE APOCRYPHA AND THE APOSTOLIC FATHERS.

THAT the Primitive Church ascribed to the Apocrypha the same canonical authority which they were accustomed to attribute to Moses, the Prophets and the Psalms, you endeavour to collect from the facts that these books were embodied in all the ancient versions of the Bible and quoted by the Fathers, and not only quoted, but quoted distinctly as sacred Scripture. "The manner," you inform us, " in which the Christians of the first four centuries acted in regard to these writings shows that they were left to them by the Apostles as inspired." The first peculiarity in their manner of acting which discloses the sentiments of the primitive disciples is to be found in the circumstance which you have gratuitously assumed, "that all these books, or parts of books, were contained in the Old Testament as used by the early Christians in the infancy of the Church."

I shall not here interrupt the tenor of the argument to expose the rashness of your inferences on the subject of some of these ancient versions. It is enough for my present purpose to observe that upon the supposition that the facts are precisely as you have stated them to be, the conclusion by no means follows which you were anxious to deduce. You have already expressed the opinion that antecedently to the advent of the Saviour, when there was no satisfactory proof of their Divine inspiration and no tribunal commissioned to enlarge the dimensions of the Canon, and when of course they could not have been received as any portion of the rule of faith, these very books were yet embodied in the version of the Seventy. How does it happen that the Hellenistic Jews could incorporate into their translation of the canonical books others which they were known not to receive as inspired, while the same privilege

is denied to the Christian Church? What is there in the
change of dispensation that shall make it a certain proof
after the advent of Christ that a work is believed to be
inspired if found in juxtaposition to those which are confessed to be Divine, when the same collocation under the
previous economy carried no such inference along with it?
I had always supposed that the major proposition of an
argument should be *universally* true, and that when *any*
particular case is adduced which proves an exception to its
general application, the argument ceases to be conclusive.
Reasoning is only a felicitous method of applying to the
parts that which is confessed to be true of the whole, and
when it is found from experience or any other source of
information that the process of arrangement has been wrong,
and that the separate elements do not possess the properties
which constitute the class, the leading proposition becomes
false and the argument is said to be refuted. In the present case you evidently reason on the principle that whatever books are embraced in the same volume with those
which are confessedly inspired must be believed to be also
inspired by those who sanction the combination. Now, to
assert that there are numerous instances in which such a
mixture of the human and Divine has been sanctioned as
the proposition supposes to be impossible is to accumulate
refutations on each other. In addition to the case of the
Jews, which has already been adduced, the Greeks to this
day reject the Apocrypha from the Canon, although they
give them a place in their copies of the Scriptures. Who
believes that because these books are found in the authorized English translation of the Bible, therefore the Church
of England receives them as inspired? or that the large
body of Protestant churches which adopt that translation
defers to their authority as supreme? There can be little
doubt that the incorporation of the Apocrypha with the
Septuagint was the real cause of their being subsequently
embraced in the later translations of the Scriptures. The
old Italic version was made from that of the Seventy, and

of course contained precisely the same books with the original from which it was made.   The Hebrew Scriptures were "quite inaccessible," says Bishop Marsh, "to Latin translators in Europe and Africa during the first three centuries. In those ages the Jews themselves who inhabited Greece, Italy and Africa read the Old Testament in the Greek version.   Thus the Greek Bible became to the Latin Christians a kind of *original* from which they derived their own translations of the Scriptures."[1]   If the Peschito version was, as it is said to have been, made directly from the Hebrew, it could not originally have contained the Apocrypha; these books must have been subsequently added from the Greek copies in which they were circulated.   Whatever currency, consequently, these spurious documents obtained among the early Christians is due to the Septuagint; and as upon your own hypothesis their insertion in that version took place previously to the advent of Christ, when the books were confessed not to be inspired, we must look for other motives besides an appeal to Divine authority for the amalgamation of human and Divine in the same volume.   If, however, you prefer the hypothesis that the mixture in question was made subsequently to the incarnation of the Saviour, after the Apostles and apostolic Fathers had fallen asleep, the phenomenon can be satisfactorily explained without resorting to the fiction of inspiration.

There are obvious considerations, apart from any convictions of Divine authority, that would lead the Christians, especially of the third century, as well as the Jews, to a diligent study of these books.   They do not seem to have been much in vogue in the Christian Church for the first two centuries after Christ.   We find scarcely any allusion to them in the apostolic Fathers, no quotations in Justin Martyr, and no certain proof that they were generally read.   But a mystic spirit soon corrupted the piety of the Church—a spirit of dreamy superstition, similar to that which Lightfoot attributes to the Jews of the second Temple, which these books

[1] Marsh, Comp. View, chap. vi., p. 99.

were well adapted to foster, and which, as it gained ground, would prompt its victims to regard their follies as signal illustrations of *piety*. This congeniality with a false spirit of religion, coupled with their relations to the history of God's ancient people, would give them a popularity which some of them certainly did not deserve; they would be regarded with that sort of religious veneration with which the Christians of the present day contemplate the works of distinguished divines, and would be bound up in the same volume with their Bibles, for convenience of reference, just as the Scotch combine in the same book the Scriptures of God and the metrical version of the Psalms by Rouse.

It may be well to observe, moreover, that this argument from ancient versions proves entirely too much; it proves, if it prove anything, that the books which Rome herself rejects as Apocryphal must be a part of the Canon. The third and fourth books of Esdras, together with the Prayer of Manasses, are actually embodied in that very translation of the Bible which the Council of Trent pronounces to be authentic.[1] The fourth book of Esdras, though not found in the Septuagint, is found in existing manuscripts of the Vulgate. The third book of Esdras occurs in the principal copies of the Septuagint, with the exception of the Complutensian edition and those which are derived from it. The Prayer of Manasses is inserted in manuscripts of the Vulgate at the end of Chronicles, and is certainly found in some editions of the Septuagint. The third book of Maccabees, too, is to be found in the most ancient manuscripts of the Septuagint now extant. Why, then, are not these books canonical? They are introduced into approved copies of the Bible; they occur in translations which the early Christians were accustomed to consult; and if they could be embodied in the same volume with the canonical Scriptures without being received as inspired, I see not why the same privilege might not be extended to Wisdom, Tobit and Judith.

[1] Marsh, Comp. View, chap. vi., pp. 108, 109 (note).

Dismissing, therefore, your argument from the case of the ancient versions as less than nothing and altogether lighter than vanity, I proceed to that upon which Bellarmine rests the strength of your cause—the quotations from the Christian Fathers. It is to be regretted that you have not, like this distinguished Jesuit, precisely specified the point upon which the discussion should be made to turn. I am at a loss to understand whether you regard a quotation, though unaccompanied with any expressions of respect that would seem to imply inspiration, as sufficient proof, or whether you design to confine the argument to those allusions in which the Apocrypha are said to be *Divine*. You are just as profuse in bringing forward instances in which there is nothing stronger than a mere accommodation of the words of the Apocrypha, as in adducing passages which seem to invest them with a sacred authority. Bellarmine, on the other hand, restricted the argument to those quotations in which these works are cited as *Divine*.[1] I have already shown that mere quotations can prove nothing but the existence of a book, and to accommodate a passage is only to endorse the particular sentiment which it contains, without any necessary approbation of the work itself.

To prove that the Fathers quoted the Apocrypha is a very different thing from proving that they believed these documents to be infallible standards of faith. Paul quoted the heathen poets, and the ancient infidels quoted, in scorn, the canonical Scriptures. It is therefore truly unfortunate for your cause that you have loaded your articles with numerous extracts, which, if they were faithfully given—in many cases they are not—from the original works of the Fathers, would prove nothing more than that they had *read* the books which Rome pronounces to be inspired, and adopted from them sentiments and opinions which they

---

[1] Disputat. de Cont., lib. i., c. x., vol. i., p. 34. His words are: "Apostoli enim poterant sine aliis testimoniis declarare libros illos esse canonicos, quod et fecerunt: alioqui nunquam Cyprianus et Clemens, et alii quos citabimus, tam constanter dixissent eos esse Divinos."

deemed to be applicable to their own purposes. By the
same method of reasoning, there is hardly a Protestant
writer of any note who might not be convicted of acceding
to the authority of the Romish canon. If you will turn to
the works of Bishop Butler, and consult his fourth sermon
upon the Government of the Tongue, you will find, in the
very small compass of that single discourse, more extracts
from the Apocryphal books than you have been able to
collect from all the writings of the apostolic Fathers. The
fifth sermon concludes, as the fourth had done, with a passage from the son of Sirach; and the sixth almost opens
with one. In the sermons of Donne, Barrow and Jeremy
Taylor we find all classes of books, heathen and Christian,
gay and grave, lively and severe, indiscriminately quoted
in the margin; and yet these men would have thought it a
most preposterous conclusion that because they enriched
their own compositions, *plenis manibus*, with the spoils of
others, therefore they believed in the Divine inspiration of
Aristotle and Tully, Lactantius and Origen, Euripides and
Horace. Even the humble writer of these lines could not
escape the imputation of Romanism if to quote a book and
to believe it inspired are necessarily connected. In his own
published sermon upon the Vanity and Glory of Man,
written long after his essay on the Apocrypha had been
anonymously committed to the press, an extract is made
from the book of Wisdom; and in his unpublished lectures
upon the Origin and Progress of Idolatry the splendid
Apocryphal passage on the same subject is introduced with
commendation and applause. If bare quotations are to be
regarded as satisfactory proofs of a supernatural origin, the
cause of Rome can be sustained by " reasons as plentiful as
blackberries." It is evident, however, that quotations themselves can prove nothing to the purpose; it is the manner
in which the quotations are made and the ends to which
they are applied. If the Apocrypha are not quoted as
infallible standards of faith of equal authority with Moses,
the Prophets and the Psalms, or if there are not circum-

stances attending the quotations which show indisputably
that the writers regarded them as the Word of God, from
whose decision there was no appeal, nothing can be gathered
from the fact in behalf of these works which could not
also be collected from similar quotations in behalf of the
heathen philosophers and poets. Why the ancient Fathers
should be denied the privilege, conceded to all writers, of
adorning their compositions with elegant expressions or
judicious sentiments which might chance to strike them in
the compass of their reading, it is difficult for me to comprehend. It is certainly ridiculous to say that because a
man writes upon religious subjects he shall not lay all the
resources of his knowledge under tribute to supply him
with apt similitudes or fitting illustrations. Surely he is
permitted to bring the treasures of his learning to the feet
of his Redeemer, and to honour his Master with the spoils
which he has gathered in his literary excursions.

From the apostolic Fathers you have pretended to present
us with nothing but quotations, unaccompanied with a single
expression that indicates the light in which the original
works were regarded. If, therefore, your extracts had been
accurate, you would have gained nothing but the gratifica-
tion which springs from the display of learning. But by
some strange fatality of blundering, which seems like an
evil genius to attend you, you have only exhibited your
misconceptions of the meaning of the Fathers and of the
tongue in which their works were written. That the reader
may be able to form an adequate estimate of the nature and
value of your services as a literary critic, I shall examine
your extracts from the apostolic Fathers with a degree of
attention which they do not deserve. And first from Barnabas :·

*Λέγει γὰρ ὁ προφήτης ἐπὶ τὸν Γσραήλ· Οὐὰι τῇ ψυχῇ αὐτῶν
ὅτι βεβούλευνται βουλὴν πονηρὰν καθ᾽ ἑαυτῶν εἰπόντες· δήσωμεν τὸν δικαιον, ὅτι δύσχρηστος ἡμῖν ἐστι.* But what saith
the Prophet against Israel : Woe be to their souls, because
they have taken wicked counsel against themselves, saying,

Let us, therefore, lie in wait for the just, because he is not
for your turn.—*Barnab. Epist.*, § 6.

"This passage," you tell us, "is composed of two texts,
Isaias iii. 9, ' Woe to their soul, for evils are rendered to
them,' and Wisdom ii. 12, ' Let us, therefore, lie in wait for
the just, because he is not for our turn.' Here St. Barnabas quotes in the same sentence, and as of equal inspired
authority, the book of Isaias, contained in the Canon of the
Jews, and that of Wisdom; one of those you boldly declare
to be of no more authority than Seneca's Letters or Tully's
Offices." Will the reader believe, after this confident statement, that the whole passage as quoted by Barnabas occurs
almost *verbatim* in the book of Isaiah as found in the version
of the Seventy? This, as we have already seen, at a very
early period supplanted the Hebrew originals, and became
itself the source of appeal and the fountain of authority.
This venerable translation Barnabas used, and from it has
introduced the text which you have attributed to the book
of Wisdom, but which is not there to be found. In your
fourth letter you seem to be sensible that you had gone a
little too far in relation to this passage, and if you had gen-
erously and magnanimously confessed your error, I should
have passed the matter over without any notice. If you
had not obliquely insinuated a doubt whether Barnabas
drew from the Septuagint or not, when the thing is as plain
as anything of that sort can possibly be made, I should
have given you credit for an honesty and candour to which
I am afraid your lame apology shows you not to be entitled.
"Candour," you tell us, with a ludicrous gravity, when you
were about to act with a very questionable regard to its
precepts, "requires that I should make a remark on a passage in my last letter." The passage to which you refer is
the one before us; now what is the remark? "I did not
at that moment [when writing the letter] recollect that the
passage from Isaias was one in which the translation of the
Septuagint varies from the Hebrew as we have it now. St.
Barnabas does not quote the Septuagint exactly, but he

approaches so nearly as to make it possible, nay, probable, that the difference resulted from a varying reading of the text." I shall now give the passage as found in the Septuagint:

Οὐαὶ τῇ ψυχῇ αὐτῶν, διότι βεβούλευνται βουλὴν πονηρὰν καθ' ἑαυτῶν, εἰπόντες· δήσωμεν τὸν δίκαιον, ὅτι δύσχρηστος ἡμῖν ἐστι.—*Isaiah* iii. 9, 10.

Now, the only difference in the passage as quoted by Barnabas and as found in Isaiah is in the fifth word, the causal particle διοτι, of which in Barnabas the first syllable is wanting. But the part of the sentence which you ascribe in your third letter to Wisdom is, *verbatim et literatim*, the same in the Father and the Prophet. But the beauty of the whole matter lies in this: in your third letter you were absolutely certain that a text was quoted from Wisdom, when the principal word in the text was not to be found in the passage to which you referred us. Barnabas says, δήσωμεν τὸν δίκαιον. In Wisdom it is written, ἐνεδρεύσωμεν δὲ τὸν δίκαιον. But in your fourth letter the *omission* of a single syllable is sufficient to raise a doubt—makes it only probable that a quotation is intended. You were quite confident that a sentence is taken from Wisdom when the leading word is changed, another word added, and the sense materially altered; you are not so sure that it can be from Isaiah when the sense, words and everything but one poor harmless syllable are exactly preserved. If, sir, you could find passages in the Fathers so nearly corresponding to passages in the Apocrypha as those of Barnabas and Isaiah, we should not be troubled with your doubts; it would be no longer a "possible, nay, a probable," matter that they were genuine quotations; we should hear the yell of triumph, the chuckle of delight and the insulting tones of defiance. If, however, there be the least hesitation in admitting that Barnabas quoted from Isaiah, it is irresistibly evident that he *could not* have quoted from Wisdom. Instead, then, of its being so very clear that the good Father "quotes in the same sentence, and as of equal inspired authority, the book of

Isaiah, contained in the Canon of the Jews, and that of
Wisdom, one of those you boldly declare to be of no more
authority than Seneca's Letters or Tully's Offices," it is
absolutely certain that no allusion is made whatever to the
Apocryphal production. So much for your first effort to
find the Apocrypha in the Fathers!

Your second attempt is like unto your first. In xix.[1] of
this same Epistle of Barnabas a passage occurs which you
have discovered to be a quotation from the book of Ecclesiasticus (iv. 28, 31), though you have not been at the pains
in this particular instance to account for the manifest discrepancies between the son of Sirach and the Father by a
"varying reading" of the text. It is *never* doubtful whether the *Apocrypha* were quoted, but as Papists have a cordial abhorrence of the Bible, they are slow to discern quotations from the Canon among those whom they honour.

It will be perceived, upon consulting the original, that
your translation of Barnabas and the Douay version of
Ecclesiasticus, which you have copied without change, are
neither of them consistent with the original text. According to you, there are three coincidences in these passages,
which show that the one must have been taken from the
other. The first which you have italicized is the exhortation to *strive*, but unfortunately no such exhortation is found

---

[1] The translation of Barnabas is as follows: "Thou shalt not be forward to speak, for the mouth is the snare of death; strive with thy soul
for all thy might. Reach not out thy hand to receive, and withhold it
not when thou shouldst give." The originals are as follows:

Barnabas—Οὐκ ἔση πρόγλωσσος· παγὶς γὰρ στόμα θανάτου. Ὅσον δίνασαι
ὑπὲρ τὴν ψυχήν σου ἁγνεύσεις. Μὴ γίνου πρὸς μὲν τὸ λαβεῖν ἐκτείνων τὰς
χεῖρας, πρὸς δὲ τὸ δοῦναι συσπῶν.

Ecclesiasticus—Ἕως τοῦ θανάτου ἀγώνισαι περὶ τῆς ἀληθείας, καὶ Κύριος ὁ
θεὸς πολεμήσει ὑπὲρ σοῦ. Μὴ γίνου τραχὺς ἐν γλώσσῃ σου, καὶ νωθρὸς καὶ
παρειμένος ἐν τοῖς ἔργοις σου. Μὴ ἔστω ἡ χείρ σου ἐκτεταμένη εἰς τὸ λαβεῖν,
καὶ ἐν τῷ ἀποδιδόναι συνεσταλμένη.

The version of Ecclesiasticus is in these words: "*Strive for justice for thy
soul*, and even unto death fight for justice, and God will overthrow thy
enemies for thee. *Be not hasty in thy tongue*, and slack and remiss in thy
works. *Let not thy hand be stretched out to receive, and shut when thou
shouldst give.*" I have given the italics as found in A. P. F.'s citation.

in Barnabas.   The good Father is insisting upon the duties
of benevolence, charity and temperance, and in the passage
before us exhorts his readers to *cultivate chastity*, even beyond
the resources of their natural strength.   There is nothing
in the Greek that can by any possibility be made to correspond with the sentence in your version : " Strive with thy
soul for all thy might."

The conjectural reading of Cotelerius, which you seem to
have followed, ὑπὲρ τῆς ψυχῆς σου ἀγωνεύσεις, is liable to
serious objections.   In the first place, the word ἀγωνεύσεις,
which that critic would substitute for the received reading,
ἀγνεύσεις, belongs to no language under the sun—most
certainly it is not Greek ; it is justified neither by the
usage of the classics, the authors of the Septuagint nor the
writers of the New Testament.   The legitimate word to
express the idea of striving is ἀγωνίζω.   In the second place,
the new reading gives a sense wholly unsuited to the connection in which the passage is found.   It occurs among a
series of earnest exhortations to specific duties.   It is preceded by solemn admonitions against severity to servants,
avarice and volubility, and succeeded by directions equally
definite and precise.   Now, to introduce an abstract proposition which covers a multitude of duties in the midst of
specific, definite and precise instructions is, to say the least
of it, exceedingly awkward.   The old reading, which makes
the passage an exhortation to the practice of chastity, suits
the nature of the context, and on that account is to be decidedly preferred.   In the third place, there is no need of
emendation.   The preposition seems to be used in its common acceptation when followed by the accusative of excess,
and ψυχήν may be regarded as a compendious expression
for the powers of the man.   This word is frequently used
to designate the whole man, and in such connections is
equivalent to ἄνθρωπος, and every Greek scholar knows
that ὑπὲρ ἄνθρωπον may be properly rendered " *beyond
human strength*."[1]

[1] Viger, De Idiotismis, c. ix., sect. 9, Reg. 1.

Turned into English, and substituting the imperative for the future, the passage in Barnabas upon which you found your first coincidence is simply this: "As far as you are able, beyond your strength, cultivate chastity." Employ not only your natural resources—these alone are not to be trusted—but seek a strength beyond your own, even the all-sufficient grace of God. What now in the corresponding passage says Jesus the son of Sirach?—"Strive for *truth* even unto death:" a marvellous coincidence with the exhortation to purity; an extraordinary quotation, when there is not a single word in the two clauses alike! One is exhorting to stability of opinion, and the other to innocence of life.

The next coincidence is the exhortation in relation to the *tongue*. In the clauses containing this advice the principal words, as found in Greek, are widely different in their meaning. Barnabas uses a word (πρόγλωσσος) which denotes excessive volubility, and he gives advice, therefore, precisely similar to that recorded in the first chapter and nineteenth verse of the Epistle of James: "Be slow to speak." The son of Sirach, on the other hand, is exhorting to civility of speech, and uses expressions which, when literally translated, amount to this: "Be not *rough* with your tongue." The Latin version surely should not supersede the Greek, and I know of no copies of the Septuagint that give the reading ταχύς which the Latin translators seem to have followed,[1] though some copies do give θρασύς. Either of these readings harmonizes exactly with the succeeding verse: "Be not as *a lion in thy house*, nor *frantic among* thy servants." This sentence illustrates what he means by being "rough-tongued;" it is to betray the fury and ferocity of the lion among those who are dependent upon us. The coincidence, then, in this passage between Barnabas and Ecclesiasticus is just the coincidence between an admonition not to be loquacious or excessively talkative, and an admonition to overcome acer-

---

[1] I say, *seem to have followed*, because the phrase adopted by the Vulgate, *citatus in lingua*, is evidently susceptible of a rendering consistent with the common reading: "Be not *violently excited* in thy tongue or speech."

bity of speech.   One says, in effect, " Be silent ;" the other
says, " Be gentle."   It is very obvious that the sentiment
in Barnabas was suggested by the passage in James upon
the same subject.

The last coincidence which you notice is in reference to
what is said of illiberality, or avarice ; and here I freely
admit that there is a coincidence both of expression and
sentiment, but a coincidence just of that sort which betrays
no marks of design.   It is a repetition in both cases of one
of those common maxims which are to be found in all
writers upon morals.   The sentiment is evidently the same
with that which Paul attributes to the Saviour in Acts xx.
35, and which is likewise suggested by numerous passages
in the heathen sages of antiquity.   Barnabas says, " Extend
not thy hand to receive; close it not to give."   Our Saviour
says, " It is more blessed to give than to receive."   In
almost precisely the same words, Artemidorus says, " To
give is better than to receive."[1]   Ælian says, " It is better
to enrich others than to be rich ourselves,"[2] and a similar
sentiment occurs in Aristotle.[3]   Coincidences of this sort
evidently show that such aphorisms must be regarded as the
spontaneous suggestions of the mind to those who observe,
with the eye of the moralist, the vicissitudes of men and
manners.   The same process of thought by which they become the property of one understanding renders them the
possession of others.   They belong to those common topics
which, whoever attempts to discuss, will, according to Johnson, " find unexpected coincidences of his thoughts with
those of other writers," growing out of the very nature
of the subject, and implying no design to imitate or adopt.

The next passage with which you favour us is taken from
a part of the Epistle of Polycarp to the Philippians, which
is now preserved only in a Latin translation.   We cannot

---

[1] Oneirocr., iv. 3.   [2] H. V., xix. 13.
[3] Nichom., iv. 1.   For many striking illustrations of the same sentiment
to be found in various authors, the reader is referred to Kuinoel, Wolfius
and Wetstein, on Acts xx. 35.

consequently determine with certainty what precisely were the words which the Father employed. You seem to be quite certain that he had his eye upon Tobit xii. 9: "For alms delivereth from death." The whole passage to which [1] you refer in Polycarp is in these words: "*Quum potestis benefacere nolite deferre: quia eleemosyna de morte liberat. Omnes vobis invicem subjecti estote: conversationem vestram irreprehensibilem habentes in gentibus.*" [1] In commenting upon this extract, you inform us that "St. Polycarp, like St. Barnabas, quotes in the same breath an author" whom all admit to be inspired (1 Peter ii. 12), and another whom Protestants reject (Tob. xii. 9).

If we admit, in the first place, that Polycarp quoted from Tobias, it will by no means follow that he regarded the book as inspired or canonical. He simply accommodates a sentence which suited his present purpose, just as Paul adopted from Menander the memorable aphorism, "Evil communications corrupt good manners." But, in the second place, the passage in Tobit is itself a quotation—a *literal* quotation from the tenth chapter and second verse of the book of Proverbs, where it is rendered in our English version, "Righteousness delivereth from death." The coincidence of the sentiment in the contexts creates a presumption that the one passage was suggested by the other. Solomon's context is, "Treasures of wickedness profit nothing;" and that of Tobit is, "It is better to give alms than to lay up gold." Solomon adds, "Righteousness delivereth from death;" and Tobit adds that "Alms deliver from death." Now the Hebrew word which Solomon employs for righteousness (צְדָקָה) is not unfrequently rendered by the Seventy, ἐλεημοσύνη, alms, the very word which is found in the Greek translation of this passage of Tobit. If, then, Tobit was originally written in Hebrew, as was doubtless the case, there being Hebrew copies extant in the time of Origen,

---

[1] The passage may be thus translated: "When it is in your power to do good, defer it not, for *alms delivereth from death.* Be all of you subject one to another, *having your conversation honest among the Gentiles.*"

the probability is that the same word which occurs in Proverbs was used in this place.   The Jews were accustomed
to interpret the passage in Solomon precisely as it has been
rendered by the Greek translators of Tobit.[1]   Hence, in the
original, this text of Tobit was in all probability an exact
quotation from the corresponding text in Proverbs.   It is
worthy of remark, that there are several Hebrew copies of
Tobit extant at this day, translated, it is generally supposed,
from the Greek.   Two of these have been published—one
by Sebastian Munster, and another by Paul Fagius.   Huetius possessed another in manuscript, differing somewhat
from both, but according more closely with that of Munster.
The editions of Munster and Fagius were reprinted in the
London Polyglot, and may be found in the fourth volume
of Walton, with the Latin translations of these distinguished
scholars annexed.   Both these copies, in the passage before
us, concur, *literatim et punctuatim*, with the passage in Proverbs, which is certainly a strong presumption that Solomon's Hebrew and Tobit's Greek (or rather his translator's)
are precisely equivalent.

Now the question is, Which did the Father quote—the
Septuagint translation of Solomon, or the Greek translation
of Tobit—since both were versions of the same original?
Your answer is, that he quoted Tobit.   How can that be
known?   His own Greek is lost, and we have no means of
ascertaining what word he used.   If he employed the term
διχαιοσύνη, *righteousness*, then Solomon, as found in the
LXX., was quoted; if he employed ἐλεημοσύνη, *alms*, then
the Greek version of Tobit was quoted.   How shall we
determine which word was employed?   The Latin translation affords no certain clue, since either term might be
rendered *eleemosyne*, both corresponding as they do to the
Hebrew, and the one always, and the other frequently, meaning the same thing as *eleemosyne*.

Your next passage is from the first Epistle of Clement to

[1] Rosenmuller on Prov. x. 2.

the Corinthians, which, you say, is compounded of Wisdom xi. 22 and xii. 12.

There is, however, an exact agreement in *sense*, although not a verbal correspondence, between this passage and Daniel iv. 35 (32 in LXX.), and Burton is of opinion that Clement had specially in his eye Isaiah xlv. 9, and Rom. ix. 19, 20. The idea is one continually occurring in the canonical Scriptures, and I think it doubtful whether the Father had any particular passage in his mind, for his words exactly tally with no one text or combination of texts in the Scriptures. I shall present, however, Clement, Wisdom and Daniel, that the reader may judge for himself whether the Father had not as much reference to Daniel as to Wisdom; and as in this case I do not object to your translation, I shall dispense with the original.

Clement says: "Who shall say to Him, What dost Thou? or who shall resist the power of His strength?"

Wisdom: "For who shall say to Thee, What hast Thou done? and who shall resist the strength of Thy arm?"

Daniel says: "He doeth according to His will in the army of heaven and among the inhabitants of earth, and none can stay His hand, or say unto Him, What dost Thou?"

The coincidence with Daniel is more striking from the succeeding sentence in Clement: "When He wills and as He wills, He has done all things, and none of His decrees shall pass away."

Your last reference to the apostolic Fathers is peculiarly unfortunate. You appeal to the abstract which Clement has given us of the history of Judith in the fifty-fifth section of his epistle, and would insinuate the belief that there was something in the passage to favour the idea that the book was inspired. But what is the fact? The history of Judith is commended as a laudable example in the same connection with the story of Œdipus and the heathen accounts of such devoted men as Codrus, Lycurgus and Scipio Africanus. A wonderful proof of inspiration, truly! Clement, no doubt, believed the authenticity of the book, but that is a very different matter from its Divine inspiration. The only passage in the reference of Clement upon which you fasten as a *quotation* from Judith happens very strangely *not* to be one.[1] If you will turn to the originals, you will find that the words translated "deliver" are very different in Judith and Clement, and the epithet with which Judith distinguished the Lord is omitted by the Father, and the name of Holofernes is not mentioned in Judith, though it is in Clement. There is nothing, I may add, in the account which Clement gives of Esther that can be remotely tortured into proof that he deemed the Apocryphal portions to be inspired. He appeals to her history simply as true, and intimates nothing of the origin of the book.

Such, then, are your abortive efforts to find a tradition in the apostolic Fathers that Christ and His Apostles delivered the Apocrypha to the Christian Church as the oracles of God. If the Apostles in their own writings said nothing on the subject, this is the age and these the men upon whom, according to Bellarmine himself, we must rely.   Con-

---

[1] I shall give the whole passage as it appears in Archbishop's Wake's translation :

"Nay, and even the Gentiles themselves have given us examples of this kind, for we read how many kings and princes, in times of pestilence, being warned by their oracles, have given up themselves unto death, that by their own blood they might deliver their country from destruction. Others have forsaken their cities, that so they might put an end to the seditions of them. We know how many among ourselves have given up themselves unto bonds, that thereby they might free others from them; others have sold themselves into bondage, that they might feed their brethren with the price of themselves, and even many women, being strengthened by the grace of God, have done many glorious and manly things on such occasions. The blessed Judith, when her city was besieged, desired the elders that they would suffer her to go into the camp of their enemies, and she went out exposing herself to danger for the love she bare to her country and her people that were besieged, and the Lord delivered Holofernes into the hands of a woman. Nor did Esther, being perfect in faith, expose herself to any less hazard for the delivery of the twelve tribes of Israel in danger of being destroyed, for by fasting and humbling herself she entreated the great Maker of all things, the God of spirits, so that, beholding the humility of her soul, he delivered the people for whose sake she was in peril."—c. lv.

temporary writers or the next generation, this wily Jesuit admits, are the legitimate witnesses of the authenticity of facts. Here, after the Apostles had fallen asleep, and the last of those who had seen or been taught by them is gathered to his fathers, there remains not a single intimation, not a distant hint, not even a remote insinuation, that these spurious documents which Rome has canonized are part and parcel of our faith. Who now shall tell us what Christ and His Apostles had taught? Who shall be able to penetrate the past when the only light which could guide us is withdrawn for ever? What witnesses shall we evoke when those alone who were competent to testify have kept the silence of the grave? It is perfectly plain that if up to the commencement of the second century nothing is known about any such instructions on the subject of the Apocrypha as you attribute to Christ, nothing can be satisfactorily ascertained afterward. The witnesses are too far removed from the facts. That nothing was known, however, when the last of the apostolic Fathers was called to his reward must be assumed as true until it is proved to be false. The silence of these men is death to your cause. In vain have you endeavoured to make them break that silence; your efforts have only recoiled upon your own character as a scholar and a critic.

LETTER XIV.

PATRISTIC TERMS APPLIED TO THE APOCRYPHA.

THE only plausible argument in support of your proposition that the Primitive Church received the Apocrypha as inspired is derived from the fact that the early Fathers, in introducing quotations from these disputed books, not unfrequently applied to them the same expressions with which they were accustomed to distinguish the canonical records.

Upon this point, as I have hinted already, Bellarmine principally dwelt. He refers, as you have done in your fourth and succeeding letters, to passages of the ancient writers in which they not only accommodate the language of the Apocrypha, but also denominate it *Scripture,* sometimes without any qualifying epithet, and sometimes with the titles, in addition, *sacred, holy* or *Divine.* To infer from a circumstance like this that they regarded these works as possessed of the same authority with Moses, the Prophets and the Psalms, or the acknowledged compositions of the Apostles and Evangelists, is to be guilty of a gross paralogism. Those who reason in this way manifestly take for granted that the term *Scripture* is *exclusively* applicable to inspired compositions; but where is the evidence of this fact? It is freely conceded that this is a common and familiar designation of the canonical books, but it by no means follows that it is restricted in its usage *exclusively* to them. To say that because all inspired writings are Scripture, therefore all Scripture must also be necessarily inspired, is to assume as true what will be found with a single exception to be invariably false, that the simple converse of an universal affirmative proposition is equivalent to the original statement. Your reasoning, if I understand it, is this: the Primitive Church believed the Apocrypha to be inspired because the Fathers quoted them as Scripture, and all Scripture must be inspired because all books confessedly inspired are denominated Scripture. This specimen of logic cannot be more happily illustrated than by a parallel case. He who should ascribe to the beasts of the field the distinctive excellences of men because beasts and men are alike said to be subject to decay, would reason precisely as you do in deducing the Divine authority of the books in question from the application to them of the same titles which are given to the sacred Canon. When your argument is stated in the form of syllogism, which, after all, is the real test of conclusive reasoning, it will be found to contain the miserable fallacy of an undistributed middle. The inspired books are called

Scripture; the Apocrypha are called *Scripture;* therefore the
Apocrypha are inspired. Before you were at liberty to
draw the triumphant conclusion which you seem to think
you have legitimately reached, it was evidently incumbent
upon you to prove (for this was the major proposition which
the case required) that whatever is called *Scripture* or
Divine Scripture must have been written under the supernatural influence of the Holy Spirit. This is unquestionably the basis of your argument; and in pity to the cause
which you had undertaken to sustain, you should have
placed it upon grounds less treacherous and deceitful than
its being the converse of a statement universally acknowledged to be true. Why, therefore, did you not manfully
meet the point, and prepare the way for your multiplied
quotations by showing at the outset what is certainly far
from evident, that *Scripture* and *inspiration* are coextensive
in their import? It is not a little remarkable that you
should have expended so much labour in evincing that the
Apocrypha were often characterized by this appellation, and
yet have passed in profound silence the other proposition,
which was equally important, that *all* books so denominated
must be *inspired.* Believe me, sir, it was a most unfortunate oversight; it leaves your conclusion halting upon a
single premiss—about as good a support as a solitary crutch
to a man destitute of legs. All that your extracts are capable of proving may be fully granted, that the books in question were often distinguished by the title of *Scripture;* but
it is a broad leap from an ambiguous expression of this sort
to the conclusion which you have collected.

There are several considerations which indisputably show
that such appellations as *Scripture, Divine Scripture,* etc.,
were generic terms as used among the Fathers, having a
much larger extension than your argument seems to suppose. While they included as a part of their meaning those
works which were acknowledged to be the offspring of the
Holy Ghost, they were also applied to other departments
of composition, in which no other spirit was conceived to

predominate but the spirit of devotion. *Scripture* itself is
synonymous with *writing*, and is consequently an appropriate term for designating anything recorded with the pen.
The epithets *sacred, holy* and *Divine* not unfrequently imply
what is suited to produce, to stimulate or quicken the devout
affections of the heart; and the whole phrase, *Divine Scripture*, was employed among the ancients to denote that peculiar class of composition which we denominate *religious* in
opposition to *profane*. Even in our own tongue the word
Scripture, contrary to its present acceptation, was used
among the earlier writers with a latitude of meaning analogous to that which obtained in the language from which
it was derived. It was not only applied to any written
document whatever, whether sacred or profane, but was
even extended to *inscriptions on a tomb*.[1] The Greek
word γραφή was perhaps more general than the English term *writing*, as it embraced not only the work of the
scribe but the performance of the painter. We are so
accustomed, however, to the definite and restricted application of the word *Scripture*, and particularly the plural
Scriptures, to the inspired records of our faith, that we
experience no little difficulty in divesting ourselves of this
association when the term is mentioned, and in going back
to the thoughts and feelings of an age when it suggested
nothing so peculiar, emphatic and precise. The Christian
Fathers themselves seem to have laboured under a measure
of embarrassment in selecting from the general and extensive phrases which were best adapted to the purpose appropriate titles of distinction and respect for the sacred volume.
If there had been any one phrase which the usage of the
language would have authorized them to adopt as a specific
and exclusive name for their inspired documents, they would
hardly have accumulated so many titles as are found scattered through their writings. The *definite* word would have
been uniformly, or at least generally, adopted. But no such
definite appellation existed, and they were obliged to employ

---

[1] See Richardson's Dictionary, word *Scripture*.

generic terms in a peculiar and emphatic sense when they
appealed to their rule of faith. Sometimes the sacred Canon
was denominated *the Holy Scriptures*, sometimes *the Oracles
of the Lord*, sometimes *Divine Scriptures, Divine Oracles,
Divinely Inspired Scriptures, Scriptures of the Lord, the
True Evangelical Canon, the Old and New Testament, the
Ancient and New Scriptures, the Ancient and New Oracles,
Books of the Spirit, Divine Fountains, Fountains of the
Divine Fullness*.[1] In this abundance of phrases—and only
a part is given—there is an obvious effort to convey a precise idea by terms which were felt to be general, a constant
endeavour to limit in a particular case what, according to
the laws of the language, was susceptible of a larger extension. Hence, while it is true that such phrases were *pre-
eminently* applied to the Word of God, we must know that
a given book is the Word of God before we can determine whether these titles are bestowed on it in the restricted
and emphatic sense or in their usual and wider signification. That the Fathers were accustomed to use them in
both applications it requires but little acquaintance with
their writings to be assured.

Eusebius testifies that Irenæus, whom you have represented as endorsing the Apocrypha, cited as *Scripture* one
of the weakest performances of ecclesiastical antiquity—the
Shepherd of Hermas. His words are worthy of being fully
exhibited: "Nor did he (Irenæus) only know, but he also
receives the Scripture of the Shepherd, saying: Well therefore spake the *Scripture* which says, 'First of all, believe there
is one God who created and formed all things, and what follows.'"[2] Here it is evident that Scripture means only a
written document, and has no reference whatever to any
impression of supernatural origin. The meaning of Irenæus, as Lardner very justly expounds it,[3] is exactly this:
"Well spake that writing, work or book which says." "It

[1] See a collection of these titles in Paley's Evidences of Christianity,
part i., chap. ix.
[2] H. E., lib. v., c. 8.   [3] Works, vol. ii., p. 186 (London Ed., 1834).

is certain," continues the author of the Credibility, "that
Irenæus himself had so used this word γραφή or Scripture.
Giving an account of the Epistle of Clement, written to the
Corinthians in the name of the Church of Rome, he says:
'The Church of Rome sent a most excellent *Scripture* (that
is, Epistle) to the Corinthians.'   And afterward, 'from that
Scripture one may learn the apostolical tradition of the
Church.'"   Eusebius himself uses the term ἐπιστολή as
synonymous with γραφή.   "Polycarp," says he, "in his
Scripture to the Philippians, still extant, has made use of
certain testimonies taken from the First Epistle of Peter."[1]
Among the Apocryphal books of the New Testament which
he utterly rejects from any reasonable claim to inspired
authority he mentions the *Scripture* of the Acts of Paul.[2]
Clement of Alexandria, who figures largely in your pages,
applies the term *Scriptures* to the compositions of the heathen authors with which Ptolemy adorned his library, as
well as to the sacred and canonical books.[3]

If the word were not confessedly general and indefinite,
nothing could be inferred from it as a term of reference
after the Apocrypha had become incorporated into the sacred
volume—and but few references were made to them before—
and had begun to be used as a means of instruction in the
congregations of the faithful.   They would naturally receive
the same titles which belonged to the collection as a whole.
The name of the volume would be adopted for the convenience of citation, and nothing could be deduced from a
quotation of this sort but the existence of the book in the
specified volume.

Nothing is added to the strength of the argument by
citing passages from the Fathers in which the Apocrypha
are denominated *sacred* or *Divine* Scripture.   To say nothing of the fact that such quotations occur, for the most part,
after the custom to which allusion has just been made obtained
extensive prevalence, there is abundant evidence that this

---

[1] H. E., lib. iv., c. 14.   [2] Ibid., lib. iii., c. 25.
[3] Strom., lib. i., cap. xxii.

and equivalent phraseology were often employed to convey
the idea of *religious literature.* Divine Scripture, in numerous instances, means precisely the same thing as an *edifying book* or a composition upon religious subjects. Dionysius, surnamed the Areopagite, quoting a passage from the
Epistles of Ignatius, styles him the *Divine* Ignatius.[1] Polycrates, the metropolitan bishop of Ephesus, said of Melito
that " he was governed in all things by the Holy Ghost."[2]
Cyril, appealing to a decree of the Council of Nice, calls it
a *Divine* and *most holy oracle,* and speaks of its decisions as
divinely inspired.[3] Melchior Canus admits that Innocent
III. pronounced the words of Augustine to be *holy Scripture,* just as the Pontifical laws are called *holy* to distinguish them from the statutes of princes.[4] So, too, the
decrees of councils and the decisions of the Church were
called *holy* and *Divine,* because they related to the subject
of religion.

But what places it beyond all doubt that the honourable
epithets with which the Fathers adorn the Apocrypha were
not intended to convey the idea of inspiration, is that in
some instances those very writers who reject them from the
Canon yet quote them under the same titles. Origen, who
in professedly enumerating the books which constituted the
rule of faith excluded the Apocrypha from the Canon, did
not scruple to refer to the Wisdom of Solomon and of
the son of Sirach, to the Maccabees, Tobit and Judith, as
Scriptures or the *Divine Word* (ϑεῖος λόγος).[5] Jerome,
whose testimony is as explicit as language can make it, cites
a passage from the book of Ecclesiasticus and calls it
Divine Scripture.[6] Now, when we compare his statement
concerning this book and that of Wisdom, that they should
be read for popular edification in life and manners, and not

---

[1] De Div. Nom., cap. iv., sect. 9.   [2] Euseb. H. E., lib. v., c. 24.
[3] De Trinitat., lib. i.
[4] Rainold, Censura Librorum Apocry., Prælect. vi., vol. i., p. 67.
[5] De Princip., ii. 1, opp. 1, p. 79. Cont. Cels., viii., opp. 1, p. 778, etc.
[6] Epist. 92, ad Julian.

for the establishing of any doctrine in the Church, we understand at once what meaning to attach to his laudatory
notice of Ecclesiasticus. Epiphanius, as Bellarmine admits,
acknowledged no books but those which were found in the
Hebrew Canon, and Rome herself does not pretend that
the Apostolical Constitutions are the inspired Word of God.
Yet, Epiphanius quotes them as *Divine Scripture*,[1] a clear
and triumphant proof that this phrase was by no means
equivalent to inspired writings. One of the clearest passages for illustrating the meaning of this phrase is found
in his disputation against Ætius.[2] He there enumerates
the books which constitute the Hebrew Canon, then the
writings of the New Testament, and having completed his
account of the books that were inspired, he mentions Wisdom, Ecclesiasticus and such like books as *Divine Scriptures*.
His design was to show that Ætius could defend his heresies
neither from the books which the Church admitted as
inspired, nor from those other writings upon religious subjects which were allowed to be read for the purpose of personal improvement. The very structure of the passage
shows that he made a marked distinction between the
Apocrypha and canonical books, though both were equally
denominated *Divine Scripture*. Cyprian, too, quotes the
Apocrypha as *sacred Scripture*, but at the same time he
shows unequivocally that he did not regard them as an
authoritative standard of faith. Having on one occasion
cited a sentence from the book of Tobit, he proceeds to *confirm* it by the "*testimony of truth*"—that is, by a passage
from the Acts of the Apostles, a canonical book, evidently
implying that though the Apocrypha were *Divine Scripture*,
they were not on that account the Word of God.[3] This
same Father also cites the third and fourth books of Esdras,
and the argument is just as strong that he regarded them as
inspired, though Rome rejects them, as it is in favour of the
books in question.

There is another circumstance which to my mind settles

[1] Hæres, 80.   [2] Ibid., 75, Cont. Æt.   [3] De Oper. et Eleemos, § vi.

the matter that the ancients used the expressions which they apply to the Apocrypha without intending to commend those documents as *inspired*. They make a distinction in the authority due to books which yet they expressly honoured as Divine. It is evident that all truly inspired writings, Trent itself being witness, must be received with equal veneration and piety. There may be a difference in the value of the truths which are communicated in different books, but there can be no difference in *authority* when all proceed from the Father of lights, with whom is no variableness, neither shadow of turning. Inspiration secures a complete exemption from error, and the Divine testimony is entitled to the same consideration whether it be interposed to establish a *primary* or a *secondary* principle. Whenever God speaks, no matter what may be the subject on which He chooses to address us, His voice is entitled to absolute obedience, and we are as much bound to believe what seems in itself to be of subordinate importance when He proclaims it, as we are to receive the weightier matters of the law. All inspired Scripture, therefore, stands on the same footing of authority.[1] When, therefore, a writer treats one

---

[1] This is well expressed by Bishop Marsh, Comp. View, p. 90. His words are as follows:

"But it is really absurd to talk of a *medium* between canonical and uncanonical, or of *degrees* of canonicity. Let us ask what the Church of England *understands* by a canonical book. This question is answered in the sixth article. It is a book to which we may appeal in confirmation of *doctrines*. It belongs to the *Canon*, or to the *rule* of faith. And the very same explanation is given in the corresponding decree of the Council of Trent—namely, that which passed at the fourth session; for, after an enumeration of the books called sacred and canonical (*sacri et canonici*), the decree concludes with the observation that the authorities above stated are those which the council proposes to use in confirmation of *doctrines* (*in confirmandis dogmatibus*). Every book, therefore, must either *be* or *not* be acknowledged as a work of authority for the establishment of doctrines. Between its absolute rejection and its absolute admission there is no medium. When the question relates to the establishment of *doctrines*, a book must have *full* authority for that purpose, or its authority is worth *nothing*. And hence the Council of Trent very consistently ascribed *equal* authority to them all. No writer, therefore, belonging to

book as of less authority than another, it is equivalent to
saying that the subordinate book is *not* inspired.   Now the
Fathers *did* treat books which they pronounced to be *sacred*
and *Divine* as of inferior authority, and therefore sacred and
Divine with them must have been something very different
from inspiration.   Junilius, in his Treatise de Partibus
Divinæ Legis, in speaking of the "authority of the Divine
books," expressly declares that "some are possessed of perfect authority, some middle, and some of *none at all*."   It is
impossible that any Christian man, who had the least reverence for the testimony of God, could say of what He had
revealed by His Spirit that it possessed no authority at all.
And yet Junilius, a Christian bishop in the sixth century,
asserts this of books which in his day were received as *holy*
and *Divine*.   The conclusion is unavoidable that in such
connections these words mean something very different
from inspired.

The testimony of Augustine is equally explicit in the
matter.   He was a member of that Council of Carthage
which is supposed to have canonized the Apocryphal books,
and of course received them as Divine Scripture.   Speaking
of the books of Maccabees, however, he justifies their reception by the Church, *chiefly* on account of the moral tendency
of the history.[1]   It is plain that he could not have regarded
them as *inspired*, since their inspiration would have been

the Church of *Rome* could represent their authority as *unequal* without
impugning that decree of the Council of Trent."

To the same purport is the following declaration of Lindanus in Pano-
plia Evang., as quoted by Rainold, Cens. Lib. Apoc., Prælect. xxiv., vol. i.,
p. 203:

"Eos impio se sacrilegio contaminare, qui in Scripturarum Christian-
arum corpore, quosdam quasi gradus authoritatis conantur locare quòd
unam, eandemque Spiritus Sancti vocem impio humanæ stultitiæ discern-
iculo audent in varias impares discerpere ac distribuere authoritatis classes."

[1] Augustine says: "Hanc Scripturam quæ appellatur *Macchabæorum*,
non habent Judæi sicut Legem et Prophetas et Psalmos quibus Dominus
testimonium prohibit. . . . Sed recepta est ab Ecclesia non inutiliter, si
sobriè legatur vel audiatur, maximè propter illos Macchabæos qui pro Dei
lege sicut veri martyres à persecutoribus tam indigna atque horrenda perpessi sunt."—*Cont. Gaudent. Donat.*, lib. i., c. xxxi.

the strongest of all possible reasons for receiving them. He receives them only because they might be profitably read and heard, and they were Divine in no other sense than as being subservient to the purpose of edification and improvement.

As, now, such phrases as *Divine Scripture* are confessedly ambiguous, as a meaning may be put upon them justified by the nature of the words and by ancient usage quite distinct from that of inspiration, it certainly devolves upon those who adduce the adoption of such expressions by the ancient Fathers, as sustaining the decision of the Council of Trent, to prove unanswerably that *Divine* Scripture and *inspired* Scripture are uniformly used as synonymous terms by the early writers, or their whole argument falls to the ground. It is one thing to assert that books are Divine in the sense that they may be profitably read or devoutly studied; it is quite another to affirm that their authors wrote as they were moved by the Holy Ghost.

The issue betwixt us and Rome is on the point of *inspiration*. She affirms that *God* is the Author of these books, and we deny it. The question is not whether the primitive churches read them or not, whether the early Fathers quoted them or not, or whether they regarded them as instructive or not, or whether they pronounced them *Divine* or not; the question is, Was God their Author? And while this is the issue, the Romanist only exposes himself and his cause to contempt by elaborate proofs of what no Protestant would deem it of any importance to dispute with him.

It would be well for you to bear in mind what you will find strikingly illustrated in the Offices of Tully,[1] the marked difference between the looseness of popular language and the accuracy of scientific disquisition. As the Primitive Church entertained no doubts of the exclusive claims of the Hebrew Canon, as this was a settled matter, there was no danger of being misunderstood in employing words in a *general* sense which had a peculiar and emphatic application only to a particular class of books. They were not likely to mislead,

---

[1] Lib. ii., c. 10.

any more than to cite the Apocrypha now as belonging to
the Old Testament would be construed into a recognition of
their Divine authority, or to speak of Watts, Hervey, Owen
and Newton as *holy* men, illustrious divines and spiritual
writers would be regarded as tantamount to the assertion
that they were supernaturally inspired. All the epithets
with which we distinguish the sacred Scriptures have a loose
and popular as well as a strict and scientific sense, and hence
the mere use of the words determines nothing as to the character of the writings. An argument constructed upon this
foundation would prove too much even for Rome; it would
authorize Barnabas, Clement, Ignatius, the Apocryphal book
of Isaiah, the book of Henoch, and the third and fourth books
of Esdras, the writings of Augustine, the canons of councils and the decrees of popes, to claim a place in the same
category with Moses, the Prophets, the Psalms, Evangelists
and Apostles. All these rejected documents were *quoted* by
the Fathers, quoted distinctly as Scripture, in some instances
as Divine Scripture, and, what is still more remarkable, as
divinely inspired Scripture. This is the language which
Nicholas[1] employs in regard to the Fathers, and which Cyril[2]
applies to the Council of Nice.

It may be, therefore, regarded as indisputably settled that
Divine Scripture and such like expressions were not equivalent to a *proper* name for the canonical books.

If, therefore, we wish to ascertain what were the sentiments of the Primitive Church in relation to the extent of
the Canon, we must appeal to more definite sources of information than a collection of passages which may be just
as accurately interpreted to mean that the disputed books
were *religious* in opposition to profane as that they were
inspired in opposition to human. Loose and popular expressions are not the proper materials for an argument of
this sort. Incidental statements, occasionally dropped in
the midst of discourses upon other matters, do not constitute

[1] Epist. ad Michæl. Imp. (Rainold, Prælect. xxiv., vol. i., p. 201).
[2] De Trinitate, lib. i. (Rainold, Ibid.).

the *testimony* of the Primitive Church. *That* should, manifestly, be sought in those places of the ancient writers in which they were professedly treating of the standard of faith, and avow it as their design to set forth the books which were received as supernaturally inspired. We have numerous passages in which these books are the subject of discussion; we have divers catalogues, made by different writers and at different times during the first four centuries, of all the documents which the Church received as the rule of faith, in different forms and under different circumstances; the whole matter is repeatedly brought before us; we have line upon line, precept on precept, here a little and there a little; and in such passages, and such passages alone, I insist upon it, is the testimony of the Primitive Church to be sought. In those parts of the Patristical remains where it is the express purpose of the writer to declare what books were believed to be of God, we may expect precision, accuracy and care. The witness is put upon the stand, answers, as it were, under oath, and guards his phraseology, provided he be honest, so as to convey an adequate impression of the truth. The astronomer speaks in popular language of the sun's rising and setting and pursuing his course through the heavens, and yet it would be preposterous to charge him with denying the elementary principles of his science or teaching a system that has long been exploded, because he employs expressions which, though sufficiently exact for the ordinary intercourse of life, are not philosophically precise. So, in a loose and familiar acceptation, the primitive Fathers speak of the Apocrypha as *Divine Scripture*, intending to convey no other idea but that they belonged to a class of religious literature, and might be profitably studied for personal improvement; and it is equally preposterous from such general expressions to infer that they taught the supernatural inspiration of the books. For the real opinions of the astronomer you would appeal to his language when he is professedly treating of the heavenly bodies; then you would expect him to weigh his words, to avoid the looseness of popular discourse, and to employ no terms which are not scientifically just. So for the real opinions of the Fathers upon the subject of the Canon we should appeal to their statements when they professedly give us an accurate account or formal catalogue of the inspired works. Then we should expect them to use terms in a strictly scientific sense; and if *in such connections* the Apocrypha were ever introduced as a part of the Word of God, there would be something like testimony in behalf of the pretensions of Rome. But it is worthy of remark that in every case in which the ancient writers used the terms *Scripture* and *Divine Scripture* in their restricted and emphatic application, in all instances in which they are professedly treating of the Canon of inspiration, they never extend them to the Apocrypha. In none of the catalogues which they have given us of the books which God has graciously imparted as the Rule of Faith are these spurious records to be found. The voice of Christian antiquity accords with the voice of the Jewish Church, and both combine to condemn the arrogance and blasphemy of Trent.

Nothing, sir, can reveal more clearly the desperate extremities to which you are driven in support of a sinking cause than that, instead of giving those plain, pointed and direct statements which the Fathers themselves intended to be, and which common sense suggests must be, their testimony upon the subject, you hunt up and down through all the remains of antiquity, and preserve your soul from absolute despair by seizing, here and there, upon a few popular expressions, which, by being tortured into a special and restricted sense, may be made to look with some degree of favour on your claims. You never seem to be aware of the egregious absurdity of bending the accurate to the loose, instead of the loose to the accurate. Upon the same principle, if you should meet with a passage in the private and confidential letter of a man of science in which he employed the language of the vulgar, you would at once construe it into the true exposition of his system, and make his phil-

osophical treatises succumb to his popular expressions.
There is an apparent discrepancy, and that must be reconciled by *torturing* philosophy and *dignifying* the dialect of
the vulgar.

If, sir, there existed an apparent inconsistency between
the statements of a witness, publicly given, when he stood
forth in the face of the world to make his deposition, and
incidental expressions, touching the matter in dispute, dropped from him in the course of conversation upon other
subjects, and if you regarded him as a man of veracity who
would not really contradict himself, would you feel bound
to explain his professed testimony by his loose conversation,
or to reconcile his loose conversation with his professed testimony? Which would you regard as the standard by which
the other was to be measured? Which, in other words,
would be what might be properly called his *testimony?* It
is certainly the dictate of common sense to explain the loose
by the accurate.

Cicero, in one of his philosophical treatises, in conformity
with the example of illustrious predecessors, maintained
that he who possessed one of the virtues must necessarily
possess them all. In a popular work he subsequently remarked that a man might be just without being prudent.
Here appeared to be a discrepancy, and upon your principles
of criticism the true method of explaining it was to deny
that he held prudence to be a virtue. The philosopher,
however, has solved the difficulty himself by assuring us
that there was no real inconsistency, since in the one case
the terms were employed with precision and accuracy, and
in the other with popular laxness. *Alia est illa*, says he—
and it would be well for you to remember the remark—
*cum veritas ipsa limatur in disputatione, subtilitas: alia, cum
ad opinionem communem omnis accommodatur oratio.*

If the plain and obvious principles which I have briefly
suggested be applied to the criticism of the ancient documents which have survived the ravages of time, we shall
find that there is not a single record of the first four cen-

turies which sustains the decision of Trent. The unbroken testimony of that whole period is clearly, decidedly, unanswerably, against that unparalleled deed of atrocity and guilt. And how else can it be regarded but as a downright insult to the understandings of men, when the formal catalogues of the Primitive Church are produced, when the passages are brought forward in which the best and noblest champions of the faith undertake professedly to recount the books of the Canon, when they come forward for the express purpose of bearing testimony in the matter before us,—how else can it be regarded but as a downright insult to the understandings of men to tell us that this is not the voice of antiquity, that these recorded statements are not the true statements of the case, because it so happens that other books besides those included in the lists of inspiration were not treated as absolutely heathenish and profane? For this, as we have seen, when fairly interpreted, is the real amount of the testimony in favour of the Apocrypha. The ancient Church treated them as religious and edifying books, just precisely as the modern Church regards the compositions of Howe, Owen and Scott. Therefore, we are gravely told, they must be inspired.

When I reflect upon your whole course of argument upon this subject, I can hardly persuade myself that you are able to peruse your own lucubrations without losing your gravity.

You set out with the purpose of proving that Christ and His Apostles had delivered the Apocrypha to the Christian Church as inspired documents. This was a perfectly plain and intelligible proposition; it respected a simple matter of fact, the legitimate proof of which was credible testimony, and we had a right to expect that you would produce some record of the Apostles, or some authentic evidence from those who were contemporary with them, in which it was directly stated that such was the case. But these reasonable expectations are excited only to be blasted. Nothing of the sort appears in any part of your letters; but, as if in mockery of our hopes, you put us off with a

series of quotations, which, allowing them all the weight
that can possibly be given to them, prove nothing more
than the existence of the books in the apostolic age.   Then
we are to infer, it would seem, that Christ and His Apostles
delivered the Apocrypha to the Christian Church as inspired, because the books existed in the apostolic age.   But
hold! You have, perhaps, some stronger reasons in reserve.
The Primitive Church believed them to be inspired; therefore, beyond all question, they must be inspired.   Now,
granting what I am unable to perceive, the legitimacy of
your *therefore* in the present case, how does it appear that
such was the faith of the Primitive Church?   This point,
you inform us, is as clear as noonday, for the Fathers of
the ancient Church actually quoted these very books, and
pronounced them to be useful and edifying compositions.
This is demonstration plain and irrefragable as holy writ,
and he who cannot see the proofs of inspiration in conduct
of this kind must be a stubborn and refractory spirit that
deserves the damnation which Trent has denounced.   The
substance of your letters may be embodied in the following
beautiful sorites:

The Apocrypha were quoted by the Primitive Church.

Whatever it quoted it believed to be inspired.

Whatever it believed to be inspired it had received from
the hands of Christ and His Apostles.

Therefore the Apocrypha were delivered to the Church
by Christ and His Apostles as inspired documents!

LETTER XV.

TESTIMONIES FROM THE SECOND CENTURY.

THAT the reader may distinctly apprehend how slender
is the basis upon which the Church of Rome has erected
her portentous additions to the Scriptures, I proceed to ex-

amine, in detail, the various testimonies upon which you have relied to prove the inspiration of the Apocrypha. This task, it is true, is in a great degree unnecessary, since it has already been conclusively demonstrated that your method of procedure is fallacious. But as in the weakness of your attempted refutation, you have only shown the strength of the position that within the period embraced in this discussion—the first four centuries of the Christian era—not a single writer can be found who regarded these documents as the Word of God, it may be of service to the interests of righteousness to cross-examine your witnesses one by one, and to show, as the result, that upon the subject of the books of the Canon the voice of antiquity is harmonious and clear. Still, however, it deserves to be remarked that if you had been as successful as you evidently hoped to be in establishing the fact that the primitive Fathers, to whom you have appealed, coincided upon this point with the Council of Trent, your original proposition would not have been sustained. Your purpose was to prove that Christ or His Apostles had given to the Christian Church the authority of which, according to you, the Jews were not possessed, to insert these books into the sacred Canon. It was testimony in behalf of this fact of which you were in quest, and such testimony you cannot surely pretend to have produced in the beggarly quotations with which you have amused us. Since, however, you have failed, signally failed, as a slight investigation will render indubitable, in your laborious endeavours to prove that the Canon of the Fathers was the same with the Canon of Rome, how overwhelming must be your defeat whenever you shall condescend to undertake the discussion of the other, your main and leading proposition !

1. The first writer of the second century to whom you have appealed is Justin Martyr. You produce a passage from the first Apology, which Justin himself professes to have borrowed from the books of *Moses*, but which you are certain, in defiance of his own unequivocal assertion, must

have been condensed from a corresponding passage in the
Wisdom of Jesus the son of Sirach. It is not, therefore,
a question between *you* and *me*, but a question between *you*
and the *Father himself*, whether or not he has quoted the
Apocrypha. In the midst of proof of the moral agency
of man, and a consequent refutation of the dangerous and
absurd pretensions of libertines and fatalists, Justin observes,
"The Holy Prophetic Spirit taught us these things, having
said through *Moses* that God spoke thus to the first formed
man: Behold, before you are good and evil; choose the
good." [1] "It might seem," you inform us in your curious
and amusing criticism upon this passage, "that St. Justin
thought that Moses declares God spoke thus to Adam; but
in his writings he appears too well acquainted with the
Scriptures, and to have studied the account of the creation
too accurately, to commit such a mistake. I have not the
means," you continue, "of discovering whether there be
any grounds for supposing some error of the manuscript in
recording the name, or whether we are forced to say that he
meant that Moses gives us an account of the creation and
of the facts, though he does not record the words which elsewhere the Holy and Prophetic Spirit testifies were spoken,
or that St. Justin, in fine, erred in memory, confounding one
part of Scripture with another. This much is certain, that
the words attributed by him to the Holy and Prophetic
Spirit are found in Ecclesiasticus xv., from which they are
evidently condensed."

It is not a little singular that the holy Father should have
been too accurately acquainted with the Scriptures to commit the mistake, if indeed a mistake it can be called, which
his words most obviously seem to imply, and yet at the same
time have possessed a memory so treacherous and erring as
to confound one part of Scripture with another. The ques-

---

[1] Ἐδίδαξε καὶ ἡμᾶς ταῦτα τὸ ἅγιον προφητικὸν πνεῦμα διὰ Μωσέως φῆσαι τῷ
πρώτῳ πλασθέντι ἀνθρώπῳ εἰρῆσθαι ὑπὸ τόν θεὸν ὄντως, ἰδοὺ πρὸ προσώπου σου
τὸ ἀγαθὸν καὶ τὸ κακόν· ἐκλεξαι τὸ ἀγαθόν. Apol. i., § 44, p. 69, Paris edition,
1742.

tion, too, might naturally be asked, why, if the memory only were in fault, it is not just as likely that Justin has confounded what Moses is recorded to have said in the fifteenth and nineteenth verses of the thirteenth chapter of Deuteronomy to his assembled countrymen with what God announced to the progenitor of the race, as that he has mistaken the son of Sirach for the author of the Pentateuch. As there exists not a particle of evidence that the name of Moses has been corruptly foisted into the next, we are compelled to acknowledge that the good Father, even if he had really, though unconsciously, condensed the passage in question from the corresponding passage in the Wisdom of Jesus, treats it as inspired, and ascribes it to the Holy Prophetic Spirit, not because it is found in Ecclesiasticus, but because he supposed it had been written by the Jewish legislator. The words are certainly contained in the Pentateuch, though not in the connection in which they are quoted by Justin. Moses nowhere says, *totidem verbis*, that God employed such language to the father of the race, but he distinctly teaches what is equivalent to it—that Adam was placed under a legal dispensation, in which life was promised as the reward of obedience, and death threatened as the penalty of transgression. As such a dispensation might be conveniently described in the very words which Justin has quoted, and as Moses actually employed them in the thirtieth chapter of the book of Deuteronomy,[1] it is no rash presumption to suppose that they were simply accommodated, in the passage before us, to express the condition in which man was placed, as Paul accommodates a portion of the same chapter in his beautiful description of the economy of grace.[2] The point which Justin had in view was to prove the freedom of the human will, a point necessarily involved in a state of probation, and which, therefore, would be sufficiently established by showing what Moses had unquestionably taught—that man was made the subject of law. "It appears from the Scriptures," he would say—if I may be allowed to para-

[1] Verses 15 and 19.   [2] Vide Romans x. 6, 7, 8.

phrase his meaning—" it appears from the Scriptures, that man is a responsible, voluntary agent, because, when originally formed by God, it was made to depend upon his own choice, upon the free decisions of his own will, whether he should be eternally happy or miserable; life and death were set before him; an easy probation was assigned him; and hence it follows that the power of election necessarily belonged to him. The very language which Moses employed in a different connection so exactly describes the nature of the trial to which our first father was subjected that it may fitly be considered as the terms in which God addressed him when He set before him the blessing and the curse in the garden of Eden." [1] If this view of the passage be correct, there is evidently no necessity of contradicting the statements of Justin himself, and of making him quote from one book when he professes to have borrowed from another. You have consequently not succeeded, and I may venture to assert that you will never succeed, in bringing up a single exception to the sweeping remark of Bishop Cosin, that Justin Martyr, "in all his works, citeth not so much as any one passage out of the Apocryphal books, nor maketh the least mention of them at all." This is certainly astonishing, since in his Dialogue with Trypho the Jew the subject invited him to incidental notices of the conduct and temper of the Jewish people in regard to the Scriptures. Though you are right in supposing that quotations in that conference from the Apocryphal works as authoritative decisions of the matters in dispute would have been inadmissible, yet it was manifestly not out of place to expose the hardness of heart and blindness of mind which persevered in the rejection of inspired documents after satisfactory proof had been furnished that they proceeded from God. Justin reproaches the Jews with their obduracy and malice, with their deliberate contempt of the light of truth, and their fraudulent

---

[1] The Editor of Justin has accordingly remarked, in a note upon the passage, "Si sensus consideretur, satis hæc congruunt cum iis quæ Deus Adamo dixit."

suppression of Messianic texts in the Prophets and the Psalms,[1] but not a syllable does he whisper of what would have been still more conclusive proof of their terrible fatuity, not a syllable does he whisper of their suppressing, in addition to single passages and isolated texts, whole books of the Bible. This is strange if the Jews indeed had been guilty of such an atrocity. So much for the testimony of Justin.

2. Your next witness is Irenæus of Lyons. You produce passages from him in which it is conceded that he quotes the Apocryphal books of Wisdom and of Baruch, and the corrupt additions to the prophecy of Daniel.[2]

As, however, he introduces his quotations with no expressions of peculiar respect or religious veneration, which show that the sentiment is not simply accommodated because it accords with the judgment of the writer, but is received with deference and reverential submission as an authoritative statement of Divine truth—as Irenæus drops no hint of any uncommon or extraordinary regard for the documents in question, beyond what he felt for other works, and works confessedly of human composition, of which he has also availed himself, I am wholly at a loss to determine what use you can possibly make of his testimony. Where does he say that these books are supernaturally inspired, that they constitute a part of the Rule of Faith—an integral portion of the written revelation which God has given of His will? What language does he apply to them from which it can be gathered that he looked upon them as possessed of equal authority and entitled to equal veneration with the Law, the Prophets and the Psalms? If the mere fact that Irenæus has *quoted* them is sufficient to canonize Wisdom, Baruch and the additions to Daniel, Rome must

[1] Vide Conference with Trypho, § 72, 73, for a specimen of these charges of fraudulent dealing with the Scriptures.

[2] Wisdom vi. 20 is quoted Contra Hæres, lib. iv., cap. xxxviii.; Baruch iv. 36, 37, and Baruch v. entire are quoted, lib. v., cap. xxxv. The story of Susannah is quoted, lib. iv., cap. xxvi.; Bel and the Dragon, lib. iv., cap. v.

considerably enlarge her Canon, since the same argument
would embrace in its sweeping conclusion divers other
books which have never been esteemed as supernaturally
inspired. In the sixth chapter of his fourth book against
heresies he quotes a passage from Justin Martyr, and
endorses the sentiment as fully and completely as in any of
the cases in which he appeals to the Apocrypha.[1] In the
twenty-eighth chapter of the fifth book of the same great
work a sentence is introduced from Ignatius' Epistle to
the Romans,[2] and in the fourth chapter of the fourth book
a nameless author is commended,[3] who is probably the same
that Eusebius denominates an apostolical presbyter. But
what is most striking and remarkable of all, in the twentieth chapter of the fourth book the Shepherd of Hermas
is not only quoted, but quoted distinctively as *Scripture*.[4]
Now, are we to infer that Justin, Ignatius and Hermas all
wrote as they were moved by the Holy Ghost ? Or shall we
not rather conclude that the argument from Irenæus proves
too much, and therefore, upon logical principles, is absolutely
worthless ?

If you should object that Baruch is quoted under the
name of Jeremiah, and the additions to Daniel under the
name of that Prophet, you yourself have supplied us with
the materials of solving the difficulty. "The book of Baruch
was at that time joined to the book of Jeremiah," and con-

---

[1] Καὶ καλῶς Ἰουστῖνος ἐν τῷ πρὸς Μαρκίωνα συντάγματι φησίν· ὅτι αὐτῷ τῷ
κυρίῳ οὐδ' ἂν ἐπείσθειεν, ἄλλον θεὸν καταγγέλλοντι παρὰ τὸν δημιουργόν . . . We
cannot complete the passage from Justin, since his own work has suffered
more terribly from the ravages of time than even that of Irenæus. The
Latin is as follows: Et bene Justinus in eo libro qui est ad Marcionem ait:
*Quoniam ipsi quoque Domino non credidissem, alterum Deum annuntianti,
præter fabricatorem et factorem et nutritorem nostrum.*

[2] Ὡς εἶπέ τις τῶν ἡμετέρων, διὰ τὴν πρὸς θεὸν μαρτυρίαν κατακριθεὶς πρὸς θηρία·
ὅτι σῖτός εἰμι θεοῦ, καὶ δι' ὀδόντων θηρίων ἀλήθομαι, ἵνα καθαρὸς ἄρτος εὑρεθῶ.

[3] Et bene qui dixit ipsum immensum Patrem in Filio mensuratum;
mensura enim Patris, Filius, quoniam et capit eum.

[4] Καλῶς οὖν εἶπεν ἡ γραφὴ ἡ λέγουσα· Πρῶτον πάντων πίστευσον, ὅτι εἷς ἐστὶν
ὁ θεὸς, ὁ τὰ πάντα κτίσας καὶ καταρτίσας καὶ ποιήσας ἐκ τοῦ μὴ ὄντος εἰς τὸ
εἶναι τὰ πάντα.

sequently the name of the Prophet must have been used in reference to the book. It was the *title* of the work in the Alexandrine versions which were then in use. Those, therefore, who appealed to it under that title no more expressed the belief that Jeremiah composed it than those who refer to the Preaching of Peter imply the conviction that Peter was its author. Huetius informs us that in the ancient list of the books of the Bible, which served as a guide to the copyists in their labour of transcription, the name of *Baruch* was not introduced, but that his work was embraced under the title of *Jeremiah*.[1] The stories of Susannah and of Bel and the Dragon in the same way were joined to the prophecy of Daniel, and were consequently quoted under the general name of the book. As we cannot for a moment suppose that Irenæus was so stupid as really to believe that Jeremiah was the author of a work which in its very first sentence professed to be written by another man, it is indisputably clear that the name of the Prophet is no otherwise employed than as the distinctive designation of the book, and consequently the use of it determines nothing in reference to the question whether or not Baruch was regarded as an inspired production. Jeremiah and Daniel, in the quotations of Irenæus, being used only in a titular sense, the quotations themselves afford not a particle of proof touching the point which you introduced them to establish.

3. You next entertain us with a series of passages from Clement of Alexandria—and the number might have been greatly increased—in which, because he cites Ecclesiasticus and Tobias under the title of *Scripture*, appeals to Wisdom as the work of Solomon, and distinguishes it, moreover, by the epithet *Divine*, quotes Baruch under the name of *Jeremiah*, and honours it, in addition, as *Divine Scripture*, you would have us infer that he regarded these works as an in-

---

[1] Librarii volumina sacra exscribentes, in eorum indice Baruchi nomen non reperirent qui sub Jeremiæ titulo continebatur.—*Demonstratio, Prop.* iv., *De Proph. Baruch*, p. 453.

tegral portion of the Canon of Faith. The number and
variety of the quotations occurring in Clement from the
Apocryphal documents should be no matter of surprise
when we call to mind the peculiar esteem in which they
were held by the Jews in the city of his residence and
labours. Surrounded as he was by those who revered them
as monuments of their national history—the history of a
people whom God had distinguished as His chosen inheritance, and who had prepared the way for that glorious dispensation in which Clement rejoiced—it was not to be presumed that he would be entirely exempt from the general
sentiment, especially when he found that *some* of these
books, in the midst of many defects, were largely impregnated with the spirit of devotion. He would naturally be
led to treat them with the same partiality which the Jews
entertained for them. As to them had been committed the
oracles of God, and the Canon of inspiration had been received at their hands, his feeling in regard to other books
preserved among this same extraordinary people would
obviously take its complexion from them. He would consequently be led not to regard the Apocrypha as inspired—
for the Jews never did it—but to treat them as religious
and devout compositions, to study them for the purpose of
personal improvement, to read them in the same way in
which Baxter and Owen and Howe are perused in the modern Church, and to adorn his writings with contributions
levied from their stores, as Protestant divines appeal to the
works of standard though uninspired authors. The ambiguous titles of commendation and respect which Clement
applies to them, it has already been demonstrated, do not
involve the belief of inspiration; epithets equally distinctive
and laudatory he does not scruple to bestow upon divers
other books[1] which make no pretensions to a place in the
Canon—some of which indeed were genuine, others grossly
spurious, others still absolutely heathenish—books which,
though Clement has quoted and commended, he distinctly

[1] Eusebius, H. E., lib. vi., c. 13.

intimates were possessed of no authority as an inspired rule of faith.

If now it can be shown that the principle upon which you have made this Father endorse the inspiration of Wisdom and Tobias, Ecclesiasticus and Baruch, will also canonize Barnabas and Hermas, Clement of Rome, and if not the Gospels according to the Hebrews and Egyptians, yet certainly the Preaching of Peter, the fourth book of Esdras, and even the pretended verses of the Sibyl, every candid mind must acknowledge that your argument is worthless, and that the same titles which are commonly employed in introducing quotations from the canonical books may also be applied to other works which are confessedly destitute of any claim to a supernatural origin.

(1.) Barnabas is repeatedly cited[1] in the books of the Stromata, and in three distinct instances receives the very appellation of authority which Clement usually bestows upon Paul. He is not only called the *Apostle Barnabas*, but in one remarkable passage seems to be treated, like the oath of confirmation, as an end of strife.[2] "For this," says Clement, "I need not use many words, but only to allege the testimony of the apostolic Barnabas, who was one of the seventy and fellow-labourer of Paul." Now, if there ever was an officer in the Christian Church entitled to command the faith and to bind the consciences of men, that officer was the *Apostle*. Paul usually commences his Epistles with a distinct assertion of his apostolic office, and the Church itself is erected "on the foundation of the Prophets and *Apostles*, Jesus Christ Himself being the chief corner-

---

[1] Stromat., lib. ii., cap. vi. (sub fine), Εἰκότως οὖν ὁ Ἀπόστολος Βαρνάβας φησίν: "Rightly, therefore, says the Apostle Barnabas." This is precisely the form in which Clement sometimes quotes the inspired writers. For example, a passage from the Psalms is thus introduced, Strom., lib. ii., c. xv.: Εἰκότως οὖν φησὶν ὁ Προφήτης: "Rightly, therefore, says the Prophet." For other quotations from Barnabas, see Strom., lib. ii., cap. xv., xviii.; lib. v., cap. x.

[2] Strom., ii. 20: Οὐ μοι δεῖ πλειόνων λόγων, παραθεμένω μάρτυν τὸν ἀποστολικὸν Βαρνάβαν, etc. It is remarkable that in this passage, as the context will show, Barnabas seems to be quoted *to prove a doctrine*.

stone." To the *Apostles* the promise was originally made
that the Holy Spirit should be imparted as a Divine
Teacher, who should guide them into all truth and bring
to their remembrance the instructions of the Son. To call
a man an *Apostle*, therefore, would seem to be equivalent to
pronouncing him *inspired*. It was an office furnished with
the gift of supernatural wisdom and infallible knowledge,
and yet Clement does not scruple to distinguish "the fellow-labourer of Paul" with this high title of authority.
Did Clement believe that Barnabas was actually inspired?
Let a single fact answer the question. He *contradicts*[1] the
exposition which Barnabas had given of the Mosaic prohibition, "Thou shalt not eat of the hyena nor the hare,"
which, says Cotelerius, "he would by no means have done
if he had believed that Barnabas was entitled to a place in
the Canon."

The epithet *Apostle*, the distinguishing title of the inspired
founders of the Church, must consequently have been applied
to him in an inferior and subordinate sense. To me it seems
self-evident that to call a book *Scripture* is no stronger proof
of inspiration than to affirm that it was written by an *Apostle*. In fact, it is much more likely that such a general
term as *Scripture*, in its own nature applicable to every
variety of composition, should be promiscuously employed,
than that an official designation of the highest rank should

[1] "There is no inconsiderable proof to be made out of the works of Clemens Alexandrinus himself *that he did not look upon this Epistle* [Barna-
bas'] *as having any manner of authority*, but on the contrary *took the
liberty to oppose and contradict it when he saw fit*. One instance will be sufficient. In Pædag., lib. ii., c. x., p. 188, he cites the explication of Barnabas on that law of Moses, *Thou shalt not eat of the hyena nor the hare*—
that is, not be like those animals in their lascivious qualities. He does not,
indeed, name Barnabas as in other places, but nothing can be more evident than that he refers to the Epistle of Barnabas, ch. x. After which
he adds, that though he doubted not but Moses designed a prohibition of
adultery by prohibiting these animals, οὐ μὲν τὰ τῇδε ἐξηγήσει τῶν συμβολ-
ικῶς εἰρημένων συγκατίθεμαι, yet he *could not agree with the symbolical explication some gave of the place*—viz., that the hyena changes its sex yearly,
and is sometimes male and sometimes female, as Barnabas saith. After
which he largely disputes against the fact."—*Jones on Can.*, part iii., c. 40.

be attributed to those who possessed none of the extraordinary endowments that give a right to the title. As, then, uninspired men among the ancient writers were unquestionably denominated *Apostles*, it is not incredible that uninspired books should have been in like manner denominated *Scripture*.

(2.) Clement of Rome is also quoted[1] in the Stromata, and quoted as an *Apostle*. Upon your principle of reasoning, accordingly, his Epistle to the Corinthians ought to be inserted in the sacred library of the Church.

(3.) But how will you dispose of the Shepherd of Hermas? It was evidently a favourite with Clement, and is sometimes described in language which, if you had found it in connection with Wisdom and Tobias, Ecclesiasticus and Baruch, you would perhaps have paraded as triumphant proof of their Divine authority. Let me call your attention to two remarkable passages. In the twenty-ninth chapter of the first book of the Stromata a quotation is introduced from the Shepherd in these words:[2] "Divinely, therefore, says the power which speaks to Hermas by revelation." Again, at the close of the first chapter of the second book,[3] another quotation is introduced in terms almost as strong: "The power that appeared in vision to Hermas, says." Now here is a power which speaks *divinely*, reveals things in *visions*, and performs the offices in regard to Hermas which are described in the same words with the supernatural communications of the Holy Ghost to the Prophets. Did Clement mean to assert that the Pastor of Hermas was an inspired production? Most unquestionably not,[4] and yet

---

[1] Strom., lib. i., c. 7: Αὐτίκα ὁ Κλήμενς ἐν τῇ πρὸς Κορινθίους ἐπιστολῇ, κατὰ λέξιν, φησί. Again, Strom., iv., c. 17: Ναὶ μὴν ἐν τῇ πρὸς Κορινθίους ἐπιστολῇ ὁ Ἀπόστολος Κλήμενς.

[2] Θείως τοίνυν ἡ Δύναμις ἡ τῷ Ἑρμᾷ κατὰ ἀποκάλυψιν λαλοῦσα.

[3] Φησὶ γὰρ ἐν τῷ ὁράματι τῷ Ἑρμᾷ ἡ Δύναμις, ἡ φανεῖσα.

[4] That the Shepherd of Hermas never was received as canonical may be gathered from the following testimonies: Euseb., H. E., lib. iii., c. iii., xxv.; Tertull., de Oratione, c. xii.; Origen, Hom. viii. in Numeros x., in Jos. i., in Psalm xxxvii.; Athanasius, de Decret. Nicænæ Synod. et in Epistola Pasch.

he has employed no language in reference to any of the books of the Apocrypha which is more explicit, more pointed or more decided than the commendations lavished on the Shepherd. You say that Wisdom must be inspired because Clement calls it *Divine* Wisdom, but Hermas also, according to him, speaks *divinely*. Nay, the argument for Hermas is far more powerful. He not only speaks *divinely*, he speaks by *revelation;* he declares things which have been opened in *visions*, and receives communications from the lips of an angel, like Daniel in his prophecy and John in the Apocalypse.

(4.) The Preaching of Peter, a document which Clement must have known to be apocryphal, he not only cites, but cites distinctly under the name of the Apostle. His most usual form of quotation is, "Peter says in the Preachings," or simply, "Peter says," when there had been a previous mention of the book.[1] Now, upon the same principles of criticism from which you have inferred that Clement received Wisdom as the work of Solomon, it must also be maintained that he regarded the Preaching as a genuine production of the Apostle. The argument is just as strong in the one case as it is in the other. Because a passage is introduced from Wisdom, and treated without scruple as a saying of Solomon, you boldly conclude that Solomon was declared to be the author of the book, but precisely the same is done in reference to Peter and the Apocryphal work which bears the title of his Preaching. I presume, however, that you will not think of contending that the holy Father looked upon the Preaching as a part of the Canon, which he certainly must have done if he believed it to be composed by one of the original Apostles. His meaning, you would probably inform us, is evidently nothing more than this: "Peter is represented as saying" in a book which

[1] Πέτρος ἐν τῷ κηρύγματι λέγει. *Strom.*, lib. vi., c. v. Again, in the same chapter, referring to the same book—αὐτὸς διασαφήσει Πέτρος. Two other references are in the same chapter, besides various others in the first and second books.

is known by the title of his *Preaching*. On the same ground it may be said that in similar quotations from Wisdom all that the Father intended to assert was, that Solomon is represented to have said in a book which is distinguished by his name. In other words, in both instances the documents are quoted according to their titles.

(5.) If the principle be true which you have assumed as the basis of your argument throughout this discussion—if the principle be true that whatever books are quoted by the Fathers in the same way with the canonical Scriptures must themselves be inspired, then the fourth book of Esdras, which Rome rejects, and Bellarmine declares to be disfigured with fables, the dreams of Rabbins and Talmudists, deserves to be inserted in the Sacred Library. In the sixteenth chapter of the third book of the Stromata you will find a passage from this miserable work, standing, in your view, upon consecrated ground (for you frequently insist on it as a matter of some moment when a text from the Apocrypha is introduced in connection with one from the Canon), with Jeremy on one hand and Job on the other. Nay, it would seem, if we confine ourselves simply to the language, that Esdras was regarded as a fit companion for these venerable men. His book is quoted as the work of a *prophet*—"says the Prophet Esdras."[1]

Now, sir, is the fourth book of Esdras inspired? Listen to Cardinal Bellarmine: "The third and fourth books of Esdras are apocryphal; and although they are cited by the Fathers, yet, without doubt, they are not canonical, since no council has ever referred them to the Canon. The fourth book is found neither in Hebrew nor Greek, and contains

---

[1] Ἐπικατάρατος δὲ ἡ ἡμέρα, ἐν ᾗ ἐτέχθην, καὶ μὴ ἔστω ἐπευκτέα, ὁ Ἰερεμίας φησὶν. οὐ τὴν γένεσιν ἁπλῶς ἐπικατάρατον λέγων, ἀλλ' ἀποδυσπετῶν ἐπὶ τοῖς ἁμαρτήμασι τὸν λαὸν καὶ τῇ ἀπειθείᾳ· ἐπιφέρει γοῦν διὰ τί γὰρ ἐγεννήθην, τοῦ βλέπειν κόπους καὶ πόνους καὶ διετέλεσαν ἐν αἰσχύνῃ αἱ ἡμέραι μου; αὐτίκα πάντες οἱ κηρύσσοντες τὴν ἀλήθειαν, διὰ τὴν ἀπείθειαν τῶν ἀκινόντων ἐδιώκοντό τε καὶ ἐκινδύνευον. Διὰ τί γὰρ οὐκ ἐγένετο ἡ μήτρα τῆς μητρός μου τάφος, ἵνα μὴ ἴδω τὸν μόχθον τοῦ Ἰακὼβ, καὶ τὸν κόπον τοῦ γένους Ἰσραήλ; Ἐσδρας ὁ προφήτης λέγει. Strom., iii., c. xvi.

(chap. vi.) certain fabulous things concerning the fish Henoch and Leviathan, which were too large for the seas to hold. These stories are the dreams of Rabbins and Talmudists."[1] And yet a work which is thus summarily condemned by one of the brightest ornaments of your Church is quoted by a Christian Father, in connection with Jeremiah and Job, as the production of a Prophet! What a commentary upon your principles of criticism!

(6.) Let me now call your attention to the manner in which Clement has treated the verses of the Sibyl. I shall not stop to inquire whether the collection which Justin, Theophilus and himself commended were the genuine verses of the ancient Sibyl or an impudent forgery of a later date. It is enough for my purpose to observe that the book extant in the second century under the well-known name of the Heathen Prophetess is not only quoted by Clement, but, what is much more remarkable, distinguished as *prophetic and Divine Scripture*.[2] What will you say to this astounding fact? Are you prepared to assert that he esteemed the Sibyl of equal authority with Isaiah, Jeremiah and David, or regarded her verses as entitled to equal vene-

---

[1] Apocryphi sunt liber . . . . tertius et quartus Esdræ. . . . . Quartus autem Esdræ citatur quidem ab Ambrosio . . . . tamen sine dubio non est canonicus, cum a nullo concilio referatur in canonem, et non inveniatur neque Hebraicè neque Græcè, ac demum contineat (cap. 6) quædam fabulosa de pisce Henoch et Leviatham quos maria capere non poterant, quæ Rabbinorum, Talmudistarum somnia sunt.—*Bellarm. de Verb. Dei*, lib. i., cap. xx.

[2] As a specimen of his treatment of the Sibylline verses, take the following passage, *Cohort. ad Gentes*, c. 8:

Ὥρα τοίνυν, τῶν ἄλλων ἡμῖν τῇ τάξει προδιηνυσμένων ἐπὶ τὰς προφετικὰς ἰέναι γραφάς. Καὶ γὰρ οἱ χρησμοὶ, τὰς εἰς τὴν θεοσέβειαν ἡμῖν ἀφορμὰς ἐναργέστατα προτείνοντες, θεμελιοῦσί τὴν ἀλήθειαν· γραφαὶ δὲ αἱ θεῖαι, καὶ πολιτεῖαι σώφρονες, σίντομοι σωτηρίας ὁδοί· γυμναὶ κομμωτικῆς, καὶ τῆς ἐκτὸς καλλιφωνίας καὶ στωμυλίας, καὶ κολακείας ὑπάρχουσαι, ἀνιστῶσιν ἀγχόμενον ὑπὸ κακίας τὸν ἄνθρωπον, ὑπεριδοῦσαι τὸν ὄλισθον τὸν βιωτικὸν, μῇ καὶ τῇ αὐτῇ φωνῇ πολλὰ θεραπεύουσαι, ἀποτρέπουσαι μὲν ἡμᾶς τῆς ἐπιζημίου ἀπάτης, προτρέπουσαι δὲ ἐμφανῶς εἰς πρόνπτον σωτηρίαν· αὐτίκα γοῦν ἡ προφῆτις ἡμῖν ᾄσατω πρώτη Σίβυλλα, τὸ ᾆσμα τὸ σωτήριον. Where can anything be produced so strong in favour of the Apocrypha?

ration with the Law, the Prophets and the Psalms?   And
yet, if the names *Scripture, Divine Scripture*, and such like
expressions are sufficient to prove inspiration—and upon
these you have chiefly relied in urging the testimony of
Clement in behalf of the Apocrypha—the books of the
Sibyl have the same claims to a place in the Canon as Wisdom, Tobias and Baruch.   The "two passages"[1] upon
which you insist with peculiar emphasis will be found,
when carefully examined, to afford no sort of countenance
to your cause.   The first is taken from the twenty-first
chapter of the first book of Stromata, and occurs in the
midst of an argument to prove what was notoriously a

[1] "Let me now call your attention to two passages from the first and the
fourth books of his Stromaton, from which we may learn something of the
contents of the Scripture, as it was in the hands of this writer:

"'During this (the Babylonian) captivity, lived Esther and Mordecai,
whose book is had, as also that of the Maccabees.   During the same captivity, Misael, Ananias and Agarias, unwilling to adore the statue, were
cast into the furnace of fire and were saved by an angel that appeared to
them.   Then, too, Daniel having been cast into a pit of lions, because of
Dagon, and nourished by Abacum through the providence of God, was
saved after seven days.   In this time, too, happened the sign of Jonah.
And Tobias, because of the angel Raphael, takes Sara to wife, whose first
seven husbands Satan had slain; and after his marriage his father Tobit
recovers his sight.   Then Zorobabel, having conquered his rivals in wisdom, obtained from Darius the rebuilding of Jerusalem.'

"The next passage is: 'How great is the perfection of Moses, who preferred to die with his people rather than to remain alone in life!   But
Judith, too, made perfect among women, when the city was besieged,
having besought the elders, went into the camp of the strangers, despising
every danger for sake of her country, delivering herself to her enemies
with faith in God.   And soon she received the reward of that faith when
she, a woman, acted manfully against the enemy and obtained the head
of Holophernes.   And Esther, also, was perfect in faith, freeing Israel
from tyrannical power and the cruelty of a satrap.   She, a single woman,
resisted the innumerable armed forces, annulling through faith the
tyrant's decree.   Him she rendered meek and crushed Aman; and by
her perfect prayer to God preserved Israel unhurt.   I mention not Susannah and the sister of Moses; how this one led the hosts with the Prophet, the chief of all the women among the Hebrews, renowned for wisdom; and the other being led forth even to death for her high purity,
when she was condemned by her incontinent lovers, remained an un-
haken martyr of chastity.'"

favourite dogma with the Fathers, that heathen literature was derived from the Jews. Clement shows that Moses was earlier than the Greek philosophers, theogonists and poets, and that, consequently, whatever was valuable in Gentile learning might be historically traced to the pure fountains of Hebrew theology. He, accordingly, after having given a synoptical statement of Greek chronologies, presents us with a compendious recital of Jewish history. He fixes, in the first place, the age of Moses, then exhibits in rapid review the leading events between Moses and David, and David and the Captivity, and finally mentions the most remarkable facts that occurred during the period of the Exile. In connection with this your first passage is introduced. Now, all that Clement's argument required was that the statements which he gathered from the Apocrypha should be historically true. It was not important that they should be confirmed by Divine inspiration or delivered only by writers who were guided by the Spirit of God. It was enough that he believed them to be true. *Historical credibility* and *supernatural inspiration* are not terms of the same extension. The histories of Herodotus and Livy are, without doubt, to be received as authentic. Does it follow that they must also be regarded as inspired or Divine? Why then may not the history of the Maccabees, the narrative of Tobit and the story of Susannah be received as a faithful exhibition of the facts which they record, without being clothed with supernatural authority? Clement simply informs us "that during this period lived Esther and Mordecai, whose book is had, as also that of the Maccabees." But is there a single syllable which indicates that either book was inspired? We know, in fact, that Esther was, but if we had not other information we should never be able to collect it from this passage. Again, he says, "Tobias, because of the angel Raphael, takes Sara to wife, whose first seven husbands Satan had slain; and after their marriage his father Tobit recovers his sight." In other words, Clement simply abridges a well-known narrative without the slightest expression of opinion as to the source from which it originated.   The book of Tobit was a part of the general body of Jewish literature, and as such is introduced by the Father.   But what puts it beyond all doubt that Clement did not confine himself in this passage, as you would have us to suppose, to the canonical books, the very next sentence to the last which you have quoted refers to the fourth book of Esdras (which Rome declares to be apocryphal), and mentions a fact which is recorded in the fourteenth chapter of that fabulous production.   Clement attributes to Esdras a *renovation* of the sacred oracles, in evident allusion to the story that the books of the Law had been burnt and were miraculously restored after the captivity.   " Esdras afterwards "—these are the words of the Father [1]—" returned to his country and by him were achieved the redemption of the people and the recension and *renewal* of the divinely-inspired oracles."

Your second passage, which may be found in the nineteenth chapter of the fourth book of the Stromata, is little more than a quotation from Clement of Rome's Epistle to the Corinthians ; and as you have already insisted upon it as found in the apostolic Father, I need not here repeat the answer which has already been given.   That Susannah—a fact to which you attach no small degree of importance—should be named in connection with Moses, Miriam and Esther, is no more surprising than that Socrates should have been lauded as a martyr and honoured as a prophet of the Logos of God.[2]

4. I see nothing in any of the extracts which you have given from Tertullian that can possibly be tortured into the semblance of an argument.   Without insisting on the point which, I think, is susceptible of an easy demonstration, that some of the passages in which you represent him as

---

[1] Κὰι μετὰ Εσδρα εἰς τὴν πατρωαν γῆν ἀναζείγνυσι. δι ὃν γίνεται ἡ ἀπολίτρωσις τοῦ λαου καὶ ὁ τῶν θεοπνεύστων ἀναγνωρισμὸς κὰι ἀνακαινισμὸς λογίων. —*Strom.*, lib. i., cap. xxi. Irenæus also endorsed the same story: *Contra Hæres.* lib. iii., c. xxi.; cf. *Euseb.*, H. E., lib. v., cap. viii.

[2] *Strom.*, lib. iv., cap. xix.; *Justin Martyr*, Apol., i. 5.

quoting the Apocrypha are, in fact, citations from the canonical books, it is sufficient to observe that he drops not a
single expression from which it can be necessarily inferred
that he believed these works, however freely he might have
used them, to be entitled to equal veneration and respect
with the undisputed Canon of the Jews. If he appeals to
Wisdom and Baruch under the names respectively of *Solomon* and *Jeremiah*, it is only in consequence of the title of
the books. There is, in fact, as much evidence that he deferred to the fourth book of Esdras as canonical authority
as you have been able to adduce in favour of the documents
which Rome has appended to the Word of God. In the
treatise De Habitu Muliebri there occurs, in the third
chapter, an evident allusion to the apocryphal story, which
the Fathers seem to have received without suspicion, of the
miraculous restoration of the Jewish books, after the return
from the Babylonian captivity, by the agency of Esdras.
"*Omne instrumentum*" is the language of Tertullian, "*Judaicæ
Literaturæ per Esdram constat restauratum.*"

The expression, *oculi Domini alti*, which may be found
near the beginning of the tract De Prescriptione Hæreticorum, seems to have been suggested by a corresponding
phrase in the eighth chapter of the fourth book of Esdras,
Domine cujus oculi elevati (v. 20). Very nearly an exact
quotation from this same fabulous production is introduced
again in the sixteenth section of the fourth book of the
work against Marcion, *Loquere in aures audientium.*

It is susceptible of the clearest proof that Tertullian did
not scruple to refer to a book as *Scripture* which he knew
at the time not to be inspired. So that if your argument
had been even stronger than it is, if you had produced—as
you have not—citations from his writings in which this
distinguished Father applies to the Apocrypha the usual
appellations of the canonical books, your conclusion could
not have followed from your premises. On two separate
occasions Tertullian denominates the Pastor of Hermas
Scripture, and yet in one of the instances, in the very con-

nection in which he refers to it under this honourable title, he distinctly testifies that it possessed no Divine authority, but was universally rejected as apocryphal and spurious.[1] So, again, in the seventeenth chapter of his Dissertation upon Baptism, he speaks of a composition which he declares to be spurious as the *Scripture* which an Asiatic presbyter had forged under the name of Paul.[2]

The author of the Poetical Books against Marcion, which pass under the name of Tertullian, seems to have entertained not the slightest suspicion that this "Prince of the Latin Church" called into question the integrity or completeness of the Hebrew Canon.   He informs us that the twenty-four wings of the elders in the Apocalypse were symbolical representations of the twenty-four books which compose the Old Testament ; the number twenty-four being doubtless made, as we learn from Jerome that it was sometimes done, by separating Lamentations from the prophecy of Jeremiah, and Ruth from the book of Judges.

> "Alarum numerus antiqua volumina signat,
> Esse satis certa viginti quatuor ista
> Quæ Domini cecinere vias et tempora pacis."
>
> *Carm. Advers. Marc.*, lib. iv.

It may be gathered as an important inference from the examination which has just been instituted into the leading documents of the second century, that all writings, professedly religious, whether human or supernatural in their origin, were referred by the Fathers to a common class, and

[1] The second passage from Tertullian I shall insert entire: Sed cederem tibi, si *Scriptura* Pastoris, quæ sola mœchos amat, divino instrumento meruisset incidi, si non ab omni concilio Ecclesiarum etiam vestrarum inter Apocrypha et falsa judicaretur.—*De Pudicit.*, c. x. Tertullian wrote this when he was a Montanist. That, however, is of no importance, since the critical purpose for which it is adduced is to show that he may call a book *Scripture* and yet believe it to be *apocryphal*.

[2] Quòd si quæ Pauli perperàm Scripta legunt, exemplum Theclæ ad licentiam mulierum docendi tinguendique defendunt, sciant in Asia Presbyterum, qui eam *Scripturam* construxit, quasi titulo Pauli de suo cumulans, convictum atque confessum id se amore Pauli fecisse, loco discessisse.

embraced under a common appellation. This was done in order that a broad line might be drawn between the monuments of Pagan literature and the productions of those who sought to be governed by the fear of God. The sacred and profane were not to be promiscuously blended or confounded; the acknowledged compositions of the sons of light, uninspired though they might be, were not to be included in the same category with the vain discussions and false philosophy of the children of darkness. They belonged to a different department of thought—a department possessing much in common with those Divine Books which the Spirit had given as a rule of faith. Whatever was written with a pious intention and promised to promote holiness of life was consequently ranked in the same class with the inspired Scriptures, to distinguish them effectually from the whole body of heathen literature. When the Fathers, therefore, use such terms as you have insisted to be a proof of inspiration, they meant no more than that the writings which they quote were suited to develope the graces of the Spirit and to quicken diligence and zeal. They were *religious* books—religious in opposition to profane—books which might not only be perused without detriment, but studied with positive advantage. *Divine Scripture* and such like expressions were terms, to speak in logical language, denoting a subaltern genus which embraced under it two distinct species —*inspired* and *uninspired* productions. These species were distinguished from each other by the difference of their origin; but as they agreed in the common property of being subservient to the interests of piety, and by this common property were alike removed from all other works, they received, in consequence, a common name. There must have been some phraseology by which even an uninspired literature that the faithful might commend could be discriminated from heathen letters; and as the leading difference between them was, that one was Divine in its tendencies and ends, while the other was sensual, earthly and devilish, no terms could possibly have been selected more appropriate than those which were actually applied by the early Fathers to Hermas, Barnabas and Clement, as well as to Wisdom, Tobit and Baruch.   Let the reader, then, bear in mind that, according to the usage of the Primitive Church, *Divine Scripture* was a *generic* term, including in its meaning whatever might be profitably read—whatever was fitted to foster devotion and to inspire diligence in the Christian life, and the language of the Fathers will present no difficulty.

LETTER XVI.

TESTIMONIES FROM THE THIRD CENTURY.

THE same erroneous principles of criticism which betrayed the weakness of your cause in your appeal to the writings of the second century have signally misled you in the inferences which you have drawn from what you call the testimony of the third century.

1. Cyprian, bishop of Carthage, with whom you commence your account of this period, and to whom you seem willing to defer with absolute submission, will be found, I apprehend, when so interpreted as to be consistent with himself, to afford no more countenance to the adulterated Canon of Rome than his celebrated "master," Tertullian.[1] It deserves to be remarked, though I shall not insist upon the fact in the argument, that several of the passages which you have culled from the writings of this distinguished Father are taken from a treatise upon which, in the judgment of scholars, no certain reliance can be placed.   The Testimonies against the Jews to Quirinus, even by those who allow it to be genuine, is acknowledged to be so largely corrupted that it is impossible to distinguish what is truly

---

[1] Nunquam Cyprianum absque Tertulliani lectione unam diem præterisse, ac sibi crebre dicere solitum: Da magistrum, Tertullianum significans.— *Vita per Jac. Pamilium.*

Cyprian's from what has been subsequently added by others.[1] A work of this sort should evidently " be quoted," as Lardner has justly observed, "with some particular caution ;" you, however, have used it as freely, certainly with as little appearance of suspicion, as if you had been perfectly assured that every sentence, line and word stood precisely as they came from the hands of the venerable bishop of Carthage.

(1.) Your favourite Tobias is the first book which you attempt to canonize by the assistance of this Father, and verily you could not, in the whole range of the Apocrypha, have selected a work more admirably adapted to furnish a complete refutation of your whole process of argument. It is admitted that Cyprian has repeatedly quoted this document, and in some instances quoted it as *Divine Scripture*. But that this does not amount to an admission of its canonical authority—that it implies no more than that the work was historically true in its statements, and suited to promote the purposes of piety—is plain from the fact that while he acknowledges it to be *Divine Scripture*, he virtually asserts that it was not *inspired*. He draws a broad distinction between it and the unerring testimony of revealed truth ; and although he was willing to accommodate its sentiments, breathe its devotion and commend its morality, he was too well acquainted with its nature and origin to depend upon it for a proof of doctrine. Accordingly, in the treatise De

---

[1] Stephen Baluze had paid great attention to the study of Cyprian, and possessed twenty-one manuscripts of this particular treatise. His opinion, therefore, is entitled to great weight : Si qua sunt loca in operibus sancti Cypriani, de quibus pronuntiari non possit ea certe illius esse, id vero in primis asseri potest de libris Testimoniorum ad Quirinum. Plures enim codices plus habent quam vulgatæ editionis, alii minus. Itaque, quoniam impossibile est discernere ea quæ vere Cypriani sunt ab iis quæ post illum a studiosis addita sunt, nos retinuimus ea quæ reperta nobis sunt in antiquis exemplaribus manuscriptis. Porro duo tantum priores libri extant in editione Spirensi, in veteri Venetâ, et in eâ quam Remboldus procuravit. Erasmus tertiam emisit ex codice scripto monasterii Gemblacensis. Habui autem unum et viginti exemplaria vetera horum librorum, quorum tamen quinque habent tantum libros duos priores.—*Baluz. Not. ad Cyprian.*, p. 596, as quoted in Lardner, vol. iii., pp. 17, 18 (marg.).

Opere et Eleemosynis, having cited and briefly expounded
the passage, " Prayer is good with fasting and alms " (Tob.
xii. 8), he proceeds:[1] "The angel reveals, and manifests,
and confirms the truth that our petitions are rendered effectual by alms, that our lives are redeemed from peril by alms,
and that by alms our souls are delivered from death.   Nor
do we allege these things, dearest brethren, so as not to
prove what the angel Raphael has said by the testimony of
truth.   In the Acts of the Apostles the truth of the fact is
established; and that souls are delivered by alms, not only
from the second, but also from the first, death, is confirmed
alike by fact and experience."   He then appeals to the history of Tabitha, and to divers passages in the canonical
Scriptures, as the *proof* of what he had cited from the book
of Tobit.   What is this but a virtual declaration that this
document, however valuable on other accounts, was no part
of the rule of faith, and could not be adduced to bind the
conscience with the authority of God?   Cyprian appeals to
it, but instead of relying upon it, as he does upon the Acts,
Gospels, Genesis and Proverbs, proceeds to confirm the sentiment which he had quoted by what he denominated the
testimony of truth.   This phrase, if we may judge from the
connection, evidently means the testimony of Him who cannot lie—who, embracing the past, the present, and the
future in a single glance of unerring intuition, is emphatically the Father of lights.   His law, according to the
Psalmist, is the fountain of truth, and His testimony must
be regarded as the seal of truth.   When Cyprian, therefore, applies this expression, as he unquestionably does in the
present instance, to the plain declarations of the Acts, the
Gospels, Genesis and Proverbs, he can mean nothing less

---

[1] Revelat angelus et manifestat, et firmat, eleemosynis petitiones nostras
efficaces fieri, eleemosynis vitam de periculis redemi, eleemosynis a morte
animos liberari.   Nec sic, fratres carissimi, ista proferrimus, ut non quod
Raphaël angelus dixit veritatis testimonio comprobemus.   In Actibus
Apostolorum facti fides posita est, et quod eleemosynis non tantum a secunda, sed a prima morte animæ liberentur, gestæ et impletæ rei proba-
tione compertum est.—§ vi.

than that these books are to be received as authoritative
standards of faith; and when he distinguishes the teaching
of Tobit, as we see that he has done, from the Testimony of
Truth, what other idea can be conveyed but that this work
is not entitled to a place in the category of inspired Scriptures? We have, consequently, *his own* statements against
your inference. You maintained that he deferred to Tobit
with the same submission, veneration and respect which he
awarded to the books that are not disputed; he, on the
other hand, assures us that while he believed it to be *Divine
Scripture,* a godly and edifying book, he still regarded it
merely as a human production, which, so far from being
competent to regulate our faith, needed itself to be confirmed by a higher sanction than the authority of its author
—even the Testimony of essential Truth.

(2.) You next attempt to show that Cyprian received Wisdom and Ecclesiasticus as inspired compositions, and your
proof is derived from the fact that he repeatedly quotes
them under the name of Solomon, and through Solomon
attributes them to the Holy Spirit. He seldom speaks of
them absolutely and without qualification as the testimony
of God, but whenever he alludes to them as the work of
the Spirit it is plainly on the supposition that they were
actually written by Solomon. In other words, the evidence
is precisely the same that he held them to be Solomon's as
that he held them to be supernaturally inspired. He introduces, for instance, a passage from the third chapter of
Wisdom—the first upon your list—in these words:[1] "By
Solomon the Holy Spirit hath shown and forecautioned us,
saying;" and again:[2] "The Holy Spirit teaches by Solomon." So, too, Ecclesiasticus is quoted in these words:[3]

[1] Per Salomonem Spiritus Sanctus ostendit et præcinit, dicens.—*De
Exhort. Martyrii,* § xii.
[2] Sed et per Salomonem docet Spiritus Sanctus, eos, &c.—*De Mortalitate,* §
xxiii.
[3] Sed et Salomon in Spiritu Sancto constitutus testatur et docet.—
Epist. iii.

"Solomon also, guided by the Holy Ghost, testifies and teaches."

It is evident from these passages—and they are the strongest which can be produced—that it is only a *conditional* inspiration which Cyprian attributes to Ecclesiasticus and Wisdom. If he believed that they were written by Solomon, then he unquestionably received them as inspired. Now, you have confidently asserted the consequent of this proposition, but have nowhere condescended to furnish us with any portion of the evidence by which the antecedent is established. Every Protestant is willing to concede that if these books were the productions of Solomon they deserve to be inserted in the sacred Canon. But the real question is, whether or not Solomon was their author. If there is no satisfactory evidence that Cyprian believed them to be his, then there is no satisfactory evidence that he believed them to be inspired. They came from God, in the view of this Father, only on the supposition that they came from Solomon. But where is the proof that Cyprian believed them to have been written by him? On this point, which is vital to your argument, you have left us completely in the dark. If it can be shown, however, that he did not believe that Solomon was their author, then he furnishes no testimony whatever in behalf of their inspiration, since we can never reason, in hypothetical propositions, from the removal of the antecedent to the establishment or removal of the consequent. Cyprian says that they were inspired *if* Solomon wrote them, but where does he say that Solomon wrote them? Unless he has said so, your conclusion is drawn from no premises which he has supplied. Now, I maintain that there is satisfactory evidence that neither Cyprian nor any other intelligent Father really believed that Wisdom and Ecclesiasticus were the compositions of Solomon. Augustine has distinctly informed us that though they were usually ascribed to him, it was not because they were reputed to be his, but because they were imitations of his style. In the twentieth chapter of the seven-

teenth book of the treatise De Civitate Dei, after having
mentioned the three books, Proverbs, Ecclesiastes and Canticles, which were universally acknowledged to have been
by Solomon, he adds:[1] "Two other books, one of which is
called Wisdom, the other Ecclesiasticus, have also from custom, on account of some similarity of style, received their
titles from the name of Solomon. That they are not his,
however, the more learned entertain no doubt." So also in
his Speculum de libro Ezechielis:[2] "Among these"—that
is, the books written before the advent of Christ, which the
Jews rejected from the Canon, but which the Christian
Church treated with respect—"among these are two which
by many are called by the name of Solomon, on account, as
I suppose, of a certain similarity of style, for that they are
not Solomon's admits of no question among the more
learned. It does not indeed appear who was the author of
the book of Wisdom, but that the other, which we call
Ecclesiasticus, was written by a Jesus who was surnamed
Sirach must be acknowledged by all who have read the
book through."

If now Cyprian were among the more learned doctors of
the Church—and you have given him a distinguished place
in your introductory eulogium on his character—he did not
believe, according to the testimony of Augustine, that these
disputed books were written by Solomon, and therefore

[1] Prophetasse etiam ipse reperitur in suis libris, qui tres recepti sunt in
auctoritatem canonicam, Proverba, Ecclesiastes, et Canticum Canticorum.
Alii vero duo, quorum unus *Sapientia*, alter *Ecclesiasticus* dicitur, propter
eloquii nonnullam similitudinem, ut Salomonis dicantur, obtinuit consuetudo: non autem esse ipsius, non dubitant doctiores.—*S. Augustini Epi-
copi de Civitate Dei*, lib. xvii., cap. xx.

[2] Sed non sunt omittendi et hi, quos quidem ante Salvatoris adventum
constat esse conscriptos, sed eos non receptos à Judæis, recipit tamen ejusdem Salvatoris Ecclesia. In his sunt duo qui Salomonis à pluribus
appellantur, propter quandam, sicut existimo, eloquii similitudinem.
Nam Salomonis non esse, nihil dubitant quique doctiores. Nec tamen ejus
qui *Sapientiæ* dicitur, quisnam sit auctor apparet. Illum verò alterum,
quem vocamus *Ecclesiasticum*, quòd Jesus quidam scripserit, qui cognomi-
natur Sirach, constat inter eos qui eundem librum totum legerunt.—*S.
Augustini Episcopi Speculum de libro Ezechielis.*

there is not a particle of evidence that he held them to be inspired. In fact, it is altogether incredible that any critic of ordinary intelligence could be persuaded that an inspired man was the author of a work which not only bore upon its face the name of another individual, but contained in its preface a satisfactory account of its original composition in one language and its subsequent translation into another. Here is a book which professes to have been written by one Jesus. The proof of its inspiration turns upon the fact that it was *not* written, as it professes to be, by Jesus, but by Solomon; that is, it can only be proved to be inspired by being proved to open with a lie—in other words, it is shown to be the testimony of infallible truth by being shown to contain a palpable falsehood ! The ridiculous evasion of Bellarmine, that Jesus diligently collected and reduced into a volume the maxims of Solomon, so that Ecclesiasticus might with propriety be attributed to each,[1] is refuted by the Prologue which is prefixed to the book. It is there stated that the original author, " when he had much given himself to the reading of the Law and the Prophets and other books of our (Jewish) fathers, and had gotten therein good judgment, was drawn on also himself to write something pertaining to learning and wisdom." This looks very little like collecting and digesting the maxims of Solomon. Ecclesiasticus evidently purports to be an original work, suggested not by the study of Solomon alone, but by the whole Canon of the Jews. It is true that it is an imitation, and in many instances a very successful imitation, of the pointed and sententious style of the wise monarch of Israel.

Besides the similarity of style, which was perhaps the original ground for attributing this work to Solomon, two other reasons may be assigned for quoting both it and Wisdom under his name, as we see that Cyprian has done. In

---

[1] At Epiphanius in hæresi Anomœorum, et alii nonnulli auctorem libri hujus Jesum Sirach esse volunt. Respondeo, facilè potuisse fieri, ut Jesus Sirach sententias Salomonis à se diligenter collectas in unum volumen redegerit, ita uterque auctor dici poterit.—*De Verbo Dei*, lib. i., cap. xiv.

the first place, it was a rapid and convenient mode of reference. The name of Solomon was a part of the professed
title of the book of Wisdom, but as it was notorious that
he was not the author of it, it would have been silly, hyper-
critical nicety always to have resorted in referring to it to
the awkward periphrasis, *the author of the book called the
Wisdom of Solomon.* To quote it by its title implied no belief that its title was just. Clemens Alexandrinus appealed
to the fourth book of Esdras under the name of *the Prophet
Ezra.* Baruch is frequently cited under the name of Jeremiah, and the Preaching of Peter was accommodated by
Clement under the name of *the Apostle.*

As the book of Ecclesiasticus, on account of its striking
analogy to the compositions of Solomon, was in all probability designated by his name—just as we call a great poet
a Homer, or a great conqueror *another Alexander*—the
Fathers would feel no hesitation in adopting a common and
popular title, especially when the work itself contained an
effectual antidote against all erroneous impressions. " In
the Gospel of Luke," says Rainold,[1] "Christ is called the
son of Joseph, as likewise in the Gospel of John. Luke,

[1] Apud Lucam Christus Josephi filius dicitur, similiter et apud Johannem. Quanquam Lucas alibi id explicat, dicens *Christum fuisse filium
Josephi ut putabatur,* et Philippus ad Nathanælem *Invenimus* (inquit) *Jesum filium Joseph, de quo scripsit Moses in lege et Prophetæ.* Atqui Moses
in lege adumbravit Christum per Melchisedecum sine patre ut hominem,
sine matre ut Deum. Et prophetarum princeps Esaias, *Ecce* (inquit)
virgo concipiet et pariet filium, unde patet Christum ut hominem non habu-
isse patrem, adeoque poterat Philippus prius intellexisse Josephum non
fuisse verè patrem Jesu. Si intellexerit ergo ad commoditatem significa-
tionis sic loquutus est sed ignorarit id Philippus, sciebat certè beata virgo
eum a Spiritu Sancto conceptum esse, ipsa tamen apud Lucam, *Ecce* (inquit)
pater tuus et ego cruciati quærebamus te. Cum sciret non fuisse Josephum
Christi patrem, appellat tamen Josephum patrem, primò quia, sic putabatur esse, secundò propter reverentiam, qua usus est Christus erga Josephum, tanquam patrem. Eodem modo verisimile est Patres, cùm citarint
libros Sapienti et Ecclesiastici sub nomine Salomonis, usos esse eo nomine, non quod Salomonis esse putarint sed significandi commoditatem
sequutos, appellationem vulgò usitatam retinuisse.—*De Libris Apocryphis,
Prælectio* xix., vol. i., p. 154.

however, elsewhere explains it, saying that Christ was the son of Joseph, *as it was supposed*, and Philip says to Nathanael, We have found Jesus the son of Joseph, of whom Moses in the law, and the prophets have written.   Yet Moses in the Law adumbrated Christ by Melchisedec without father as man, without mother as God; and Isaiah, the prince of Prophets, says, Behold, a virgin shall conceive and bring forth a son.   Hence, it is evident that Christ as man had no father, and so Philip might have known that Joseph was not in reality the father of Jesus.   If he did know it, he used the phrase only for convenience of reference. But if Philip were ignorant of the fact, the blessed Virgin certainly knew that Jesus had been conceived by the power of the Holy Ghost, and yet she says in the Gospel of Luke, Behold, thy father and I have sought thee sorrowing. Though she knew that Joseph was not the father of Christ, yet she calls him his *father;* in the first place, because he was reputed to be so, and in the second on account of the filial reverence with which Christ uniformly treated Joseph. In the same way it is likely that the Fathers, in citing the books of Wisdom and Ecclesiasticus under the name of Solomon, did so, not because they imputed them to him, but for convenience of reference they retained a common and popular designation."   To this may be added, as the same learned writer has intimated, that they used the name of Solomon to conciliate greater reverence and esteem for the sentiments which they had chosen to accommodate.   These books were so strikingly analogous to those of Solomon that they might be studied, in the opinion of Fathers, with safety and advantage.   Their authors, whoever they were, breathed the spirit of devotion, and hence their productions were applauded, as the modern Church warmly commends Owen, Charnock and Scott.   Wisdom, Ecclesiasticus, Tobit and Judith were regarded as good elementary works of religion, which might be placed with success in the hands of novices, to prepare them for the higher mysteries of the faith.   Such,

at least, is the testimony of Athanasius.[1] In his famous
Festal Epistle, after having given a catalogue of the inspired
books of the Old and New Testament, he adds : "There
are also other books besides these, not indeed admitted to the
Canon, but ordained by the Fathers to be read by such as
have recently come over [to Christianity], and who wish to
receive instruction in the doctrine of piety—the Wisdom of
Solomon, the Wisdom of Sirach, and Esther, and Judith,
and Tobit, the Doctrine of the Apostles, as it is called, and
the Shepherd."

But whether the explanations which have been given of
the manner in which the Fathers quote Wisdom and Ecclesiasticus be satisfactory or not, one thing is absolutely certain—that their ascribing them to Solomon in incidental references is no proof whatever that they really believed them
to be his. Bellarmine appeals to Basil as having cited
Ecclesiasticus in this way, and yet Basil unequivocally
asserts that only *three books*, Proverbs, Ecclesiastes and
Canticles, were written by Solomon. Jerome, too, has been
guilty of the same method of citation, and has just as
strongly affirmed that no other books can be properly
ascribed to Solomon but those which are found in the Jewish Canon.[2] It is unnecessary to adduce more examples.

---

[1] Εστὶ καὶ ἕτερα βιβλία τούτων ἔξωθεν, οὐ κανονιζόμενα μὲν, τετυπωμένα δὲ
παρὰ τῶν πατέρων ἀναγινώσκεσθαι τοῖς ἄρτι προσερχομένοις καὶ βουλομένοις
κατηχεῖσθαι τὸν τῆς εὐσεβείας λόγον. Σοφία Σολομῶντος, καὶ σοφια Σιρὰχ, καὶ
Εσθὴρ, καὶ Ιουδὶθ, καὶ Τοβίας, καὶ διδαχὴ καλουμένη τῶν Ἀποστόλων, καὶ ὁ
Ποιμήν.—*Athanasius, Epistola Festalis,* Opp. i., p. 961, ed. Bened.

[2] Ita videtis judicio Cani posse negari consequutionem illius argumenti :
patres hos libros à Salomone scriptos putarunt, ergo sunt ab eo scripti. Nunc
istius enthymematis antecedens examinemus. *Patres existimarunt hos
libros à Salomone scriptos,* ad quod confirmandum primum enthymema pertinet, *patres citarunt hos libros sub nomine Salomonis, ergo existimarunt ab eo
scriptos.* Hic quoque claudicat consequutio; in illis enim qui librum
Sapientiæ sub Salomonis nomine citarunt, fuit Basilius, qui tamen apertè
inficiatur eum à Salomone scriptum, ubi tres omnino sacros libros Sal-
omoni adscribit, τρεῖς πάσας ἔγνωμεν τὸν Σαλομῶντος τὰς πραγματείας.
Hieronymus etiam ex eorum numero est, qui Ecclesiasticum sub nomine
Salomonis citant. At alius est idem Hieronymus, ubi tres libros à Salomone scriptos dicit, *Fertur* (inquit) *et \alius qui à Siracide scriptus est,*

One single instance is sufficient to maim a conclusion drawn from the only circumstance which can be tortured into anything like evidence that Cyprian or any other Father imputed the documents in question to the pen of Solomon. It will now be remembered that the leading proposition of your argument was this: If Cyprian believed that Solomon was the author of Ecclesiasticus and Wisdom, he believed them to be inspired. It was incumbent on you to prove the antecedent, which you have not so much as attempted to do. I, on the other hand, have shown that it is false, or, at least, that there is not a particle of evidence in its favour. The argument then stands in this way: If Cyprian believed that Ecclesiasticus and Wisdom were written by Solomon, he believed them to be inspired. But *he did not believe* that they were written by Solomon. Here in my opinion the syllogism halts—*claudicat consecutio*—and Wisdom and Ecclesiasticus are left precisely where they were before you appealed to the testimony of Cyprian.

(3.) The claims of Baruch and the additions to Daniel to a place in the Canon you endeavour to vindicate by the same process of argument which we have seen to be worthless in the case of Ecclesiasticus and Wisdom. Because Cyprian has quoted the one under the name of Jeremiah, and the other under the name of Daniel—that is, because he has referred to the books by their notorious and ordinary titles—you would have us to believe that he really looked upon these venerable Prophets as the authors of the documents in question. The futility of such reasoning has already been sufficiently exposed, and therefore, without further ceremony, we may dismiss the testimony of Cyprian in behalf of these works as having no existence but in your own mind.

(4.) His quotations from the Maccabees are no more remarkable than a quotation which he has made from the third book of Esdras; and if his conviction of the historical

---

Salomonis; et adhuc alius ψευδεπίγραφος qui Sapientia Salomonis inscribitur.—*Rainold., De Libris Apocryphis, Prælectio* xviii., vol. i., p. 152.

credibility of the narrative in the one case is sufficient to canonize the books, his full and cordial accommodation of a sentiment in the other must be equally valid for the same purpose. The truth is, the argument is stronger in behalf of Esdras, since Cyprian not only quotes it, but quotes it in the very same form in which Christ and His Apostles were accustomed to cite the writings of the Old Testament. "Custom without truth," says he,[1] "is only antiquity of error: wherefore, having abandoned error, let us follow truth, knowing that truth, according to Esdras, conquers, as it is written, 'Truth endureth and is always strong: it liveth and conquereth for evermore.'"

2. In what you call the testimony of Hippolytus and Dionysius you have presented us with nothing which requires an answer. They quote and comment on passages contained in the disputed books, but I have yet to learn that anything can be gathered from a fact of this sort but the existence of the works in the age of the writers, and their knowledge and probable approbation of their contents. But you were truly bold to insist on what is called the Apostolical Constitutions as evidence in your favour. It is true that the Apocrypha are quoted in this collection, but it is not true that the citations which occur imply that there was any Divine authority in the writings from which they were made. On the contrary, we have in the fifty-seventh chapter of the second book a catalogue or list of the books which were directed to be read in the churches, and not a syllable is whispered concerning Wisdom, Ecclesiasticus, Tobit, Judith, or any of the works which Rome has added to the Canon—a pregnant proof that to quote a book and to believe it inspired are two very different things. The only books which are mentioned in connection with the Old Testament are the Pentateuch, Joshua, Judges,

---

[1] Nam consuetudo sine veritate, vetustas erroris est. Propter quod relicto errore sequamur veritatem, scientes quia et apud Esdram veritas vincit, sicut scriptum est: Veritas manet et invalescit in æternum, et vivit et obtinet in sæcula sæculorum.—Epistola lxxiv.

Kings, Chronicles, the Return from Babylon by Ezra—that is, Ezra, Nehemiah and Esther, David, Solomon, Job and the sixteen Prophets.[1] Here, then, is the Canon of the Apostolical Constitutions; and though it is a document which is notoriously spurious,[2] yet as you have chosen to appeal to its authority, I hope that in this matter you will abide by its decision.

LETTER XVII.

TESTIMONIES FROM THE FOURTH CENTURY.

You open the testimony of the fourth century with the Council of Nice. It is wholly immaterial to the argument whether I "despise its decisions" or reverence its decrees, since the only question before us has reference to the Canon, which, whether right or wrong, it believed to be Divine. I may observe, however, that while I embrace its admirable creed with cordial acquiescence, I cannot but regret that so distinguished and venerable a body should have sanctioned the principle of religious persecution, and indirectly, if not positively, endorsed the odious doctrine that pains, penalties and civil disabilities are appropriate instruments for promoting uniformity of faith. The age of Constantine is, no doubt, a period in the history of the Church upon which Romanists love to linger. Then were laid the foundations of that secular authority and that joyous and imposing pomp of ceremonial which subsequently enabled the Man of Sin to tread upon the necks of kings, to bind their nobles with fetters of iron, and to banish all that was pure and spiritual from the temple of God.

[1] Ἀναγινωσκέτω τὰ Μωσέως καὶ Ἰησοῦ τοῦ Ναυῆ τὰ τῶν κριτῶν καὶ τῶν βασιλειῶν· τὰ τῶν παραλειπομένων καὶ τὰ τῆς ἐπανόδου· πρὸς τούτοις τὰ τοῦ Ἰὼβ καὶ τὸν Σολομῶνος καὶ τὰ τῶν ἑκκαίδεκα προφητῶν· ἀνὰ δύο δὲ γενομένων ἀναγνωσμάτων, ἑτερός τις τοὺς του Δαβίδ ψαλλέτω ὑμνους.

[2] For a clear and satisfactory dissertation upon the value of the Apostolical Constitutions, see Lardner, vol. iv., p. 194, et seq.

> "Ah, Constantine! of how much ill was cause,
> Not thy conversion, but those rich domains
> That the first wealthy pope received of thee!"

1. But discarding all discussion of the merits of the council, and of the peculiar corruptions of the age in which it was convened, let us confine ourselves to the matter in hand, and endeavour to ascertain whether the wickedness and folly in reference to the Scriptures were perpetrated at Nice which upward of twelve hundred years afterward formed a fit introduction to the atrocities of Trent. To discover the opinions of a council the simplest method is to appeal to the acts, the authentic proceedings, of the body itself; but as in the creed, canons and synodical epistle, the only clear and unquestionable monuments of the doings of Nice that have survived the ravages of time, not a single hint is given touching the books which the Fathers received as inspired, you have been obliged to resort to collateral and indirect evidence, and that of the vaguest kind. The testimony upon which you have relied is a passage of Jerome and a few quotations found in the work of an obscure scribbler, Gelasius Cyzicenus. In replying to your arguments I shall reverse the order in which you have marshalled your witnesses, and begin with Gelasius.

(1.) This writer has given us a history of the Council of Nice written a hundred and fifty years after the body had been dissolved, collected from documents of which nothing is known with certainty, and consequently nothing can be pronounced with confidence. He pretends to have preserved the discussions and debates which occurred in the synod betwixt the orthodox and the Arians, but speeches reported under such circumstances are evidently entitled to small consideration.[1] Worthless, however, as his history is, you have appealed to it as possessing upon this subject "some value." "At the time," you inform us, "when

---

[1] The reader may form some conception of the value of this historian from the "Admonitio ad Lectorem" prefixed to his work in *Labbæus and Cossart*, vol. ii., p. 103.

Gelasius wrote there were many monuments of the Council of Nice still extant which have since perished.   The sentiments of the Fathers could be easily ascertained, and it is utterly incredible that if they were unanimously opposed to the inspiration of any books of the Old Testament save those in the Jewish Canon, he would have dared them to assert the contrary or to put in their mouths expressions directly opposed to what they would have used."   Let this be granted, and where is the proof that Gelasius attributed to the orthodox any sentiments or "put into their mouths" any speeches inconsistent with a cordial rejection of the whole Apocrypha from the list of inspired compositions? In the passages which you have adduced he simply represents the Fathers as quoting the book of Baruch under the name of Jeremiah and the book of Wisdom under the name of Solomon.   Now it is perfectly conceivable that they might have appealed to these works in their arguments against the Arians, as setting forth the sentiments of God's ancient and chosen people upon the matter in dispute, without implying, or intending to imply, that their declarations were to be received as authoritative statements of truth. Their object might have been to show that the Church, under the former dispensation, was as far removed from Arianism as under the latter.   These books were legitimate sources of proof as to the actual creed of the Jews, or at least a part of the nation, in the age of the writers, and there was consequently no impropriety in using them as a probable exposition of the national faith.   In fact, they have been used in modern times for precisely the same purpose in the able work of Allix, entitled "The Judgment of the Jewish Church against the Unitarians."   "We make use of their authority," says he, "not to prove any doctrine which is in dispute, as if they contained a Divine Revelation and a decision of an inspired writer, but to witness what was the faith of the Jewish Church in the time when the authors of those Apocryphal books did flourish."[1]

---

[1] See Allix's *Judgment of the Jewish Church*, etc., c. v., p. 66.

It is, hence, by no means certain that the Fathers of
Nice, if indeed they quoted the Apocrypha at all, intended
to sanction the inspiration of the works. That they referred
to Baruch under the name of Jeremiah, and to Wisdom
under the name of Solomon, proves no more than that these
were the ordinary and familiar titles of the books. If, however, you insist on the proposition that nothing was quoted
against the Arians which was not regarded by the council
as inspired, and admit that Gelasius is a fit witness of what
was quoted, your argument will prove a little too much. This
writer testifies that the Fathers cited two grossly spurious
documents—not only cited them, but cited them as *Scripture*, and cited them apparently to prove a doctrine. In the
eighteenth chapter of the second book of his history he
exhibits at length the reply of the bishops to the Arian
exposition of Proverbs viii. 22: "The Lord possessed me
in the beginning of His ways, before His works of old."
In the course of the reply, which was intrusted to Eusebius, these words occur:[1] "Enough has been said, as it
appears to me, and the proofs have clearly shown, O philosopher, that the Son of God was the former of the rational
wisdom spoken of by Solomon, and of all the creatures, and
was not a mere instrument. But in order to exhibit the
exposition of this matter in a clearer light, and to come
more speedily to the sense of the passage, we will declare
certain things from the Scripture. Moses, the Prophet,
when about to die, as it is written in the book of the

---

[1] Ἱκανὰ εἶναι μοι δοκεῖ τὰ λεχθέντα, καὶ ἁι ἀπολέιξεις παρέστησαν, ὦ φιλόσοφε,
ὅτι ὁ υἱὸς τοῦ Θεοῦ ἐστιν, ὁ καὶ τὴν ἐν Σολομῶντι τι λογιστικὴν σοφίαν
κτίσας, καὶ πάντα τὰ κτιστὰ, καὶ οὐκ ἐργαλεῖον, ἵνα δέ σοι σαφεστέραν τὴν ἀληθῆ
τῶν πραγμάτων ἀπόδειξιν παραστήσωμεν, καὶ τάχιον ἔλθωμεν ἐπὶ τὸν νόμον τοῦ
πράγματος, καὶ τῆς θεωρίας ἁυτὸν, τὰ ἐκ τῆς γραφῆς λέξωμεν. μέλλων ὁ προφήτης
Μωσῆς ἐξίεναι τὸν βίον, ὡς γέγραπται ἐν βίβλῳ ἀνὰ ληψεως Μωσέως, προσκαλεσ-
άμενος Ἰησοῦν υἱὸν Ναυῆ, καὶ διαλεγόμενος πρὸς ἁυτὸν, ἔφη καὶ προεθεάσατο
με ὁ Θεὸς πρὸ καταβολῆς κόσμου, εἶναί με τῆς διαθήκης ἁυτου μεσίτην. καὶ ἐν
βίβλῳ λόγων μυστικῶν Μωσέως, ἁυτὸς Μωσῆς προεῖπε πέρι τὸν Δαβὶδ καὶ
Σολομῶντος.—*Gelasii Historia*, lib. ii., c. 18. For a particular account of
the apocryphal book called Assumption of Moses, see Fabricius, *Cod.
Pseud. V. T.*, tom. i., p. 839.

Assumption of Moses, called to him Joshua, the son of Nun, and thus addressed him : 'God foresaw, before the foundation of the world, that I should be the mediator of His testament,' and in the book of the Mystic Speeches of Moses, Moses himself spake beforehand of David and Solomon."

Here are two books, both of them confessedly apocryphal, one called the Assumption of Moses, the other his Mystic Speeches, which the historian Eusebius, in the name of all the bishops, is represented by Gelasius as employing under the title of *Scripture* against the anonymous champion of Arianism. Now, you must either admit that Nice held these works to be inspired, or deny that their citation of a book as Scripture is any proof that the Fathers received it as inspired. If you take the first proposition, and maintain that Nice canonized these books, why has Rome rejected them ? Upon what authority is the decision of the first general council set at naught and despised ? Upon what grounds do you concur with Nice in receiving Judith, Baruch and Wisdom, and refuse your assent when you have precisely the same evidence that it sanctioned the inspiration of these legends of Moses? But you cannot, as a consistent Romanist, admit that the Assumption of Moses was treated as canonical at Nice. If not, then its quotation of a book is no proof that the work was held to be inspired, and you have consequently lost your labour in proving that it quoted Baruch, Judith and Wisdom. It deserves, however, to be remarked, that if you had succeeded in your design you would have sapped the foundation of the principal excuse which Bellarmine offers for the heresy of Jerome in rejecting all of the Apocrypha, with the exception of Judith, from the Canon.[1] "I admit," says he, "that Jerome was of this opinion, because as yet no general council had determined anything concerning any of these books, with the

[1] Admitto igitur Hieronymum in ea fuisse opinione, quia nondum generale concilium de his libris aliquid statuerat, excepto libro Judith, quem etiam Hieronymus postea recepit.—*Bellar.*, *De Verbo Dei*, lib. i., cap. x.

exception of Judith, which Jerome afterwards received."
And yet, according to you, a general council *had determined something*. Baruch and Wisdom were put upon
the same footing with Judith. Thus priest contradicts
priest, and Jesuit devours Jesuit.

(2.) Let us now turn to the testimony of Jerome. In
his preface to the book of Judith he observes: "But because the Council of Nice is read to have counted this book
in the number of Sacred Scriptures, I have complied with
your request, or rather demand."[1] It will be observed here
that Jerome does not state the fact upon his own authority—
he was not even born when the Council of Nice was assembled—but upon the authority of a *nameless writer*, whose
book it does not appear had ever been seen by himself. "It
is read," says he; but where and by whom? To these questions the Father furnishes no manner of reply. We have,
then, *not Jerome*, but an anonymous scribbler, of whom
nothing is known but his obscurity, testifying to the reception on the part of Nice of the book of Judith. Completely, therefore, without foundation is the bold statement
of Bellarmine, that Jerome opposed the authority of Nice
to the opinion of the Jewish Church, and was himself a
witness that the Nicene Synod had received the book of
Judith into the Canon of Scripture.[2] That *somebody*, no
one knows who, had somewhere, no one knows where, read

---

[1] Sed quia hunc librum Synodus Nicæna in numero S. Scripturarum
legitur computasse, acquievi postulationi vestræ, immo exactioni.—*S. Hier.,
Præf. in Libr. Judith.*

[2] Librum Judith egregium testimonium habere à Synodo Nicæna 1, omnium synodorum generalium prima et celeberrima, testatur S. Hieronymus
præfatione in Judith. Ac ne fortè Kemnitius dicat librum Judith sanctum
esse, sed non plenæ auctoritatis ad fidei dogmata confirmanda, notanda
sunt verba S. Hieronymi : asserit enim sanctissimus Doctor, apud Hebræos
librum Judith numerari in sanctis libris, qui tamen non sint idonei ad
dogmata fidei comprobanda : deinde huic Hebræorum sententiæ opponit
Nicænæ Synodi auctoritatem : igitur teste Hieronymo, Nicæna Synodus
librum Judith ita retulit in numerum sacrorum librorum, et eum ido-
neum esse censuerit ad fidei dogmata confirmanda.—*Bellar., De Verbo Dei*,
lib. i., cap. xii.

or heard that this was the case, is the sum and substance of what Jerome asserts—a precious testimony truly!

1st. That Jerome himself did not believe his anonymous witness, that he referred to the matter simply as a *rumour* and not as a fact,[1] may be gathered from his own account of the book of Judith. In his preface to the books of Solomon he says, "The Church indeed reads the book of Judith, but does not receive it among the canonical Scriptures."[2] Again, in the Prologus Galeatus: "the book of Judith is not in the Canon."[3] If he believed that the Council of Nice truly represented the faith of the Church, and yet believed that, according to the faith of the Church, the book of Judith was *not* canonical, he must have believed that the nameless author to whom he alludes had either ignorantly or wilfully lied. There was no alternative. If this author told the truth, Judith *was* canonical, and the Church received it as such; but Judith was *not* canonical, says Jerome, and the Church did not receive it as such; therefore this author could not have spoken the truth. This reasoning can be evaded only by saying that Nice did not represent the faith of the Church; that is, that the three hundred and eighteen bishops who were assembled there did not know the books which were generally received as inspired—a supposition too absurd to receive a moment's attention.

2dly. It is susceptible of the clearest demonstration that the prominent actors in the Synod of Nice received neither Judith nor any of the books which Protestants reject as a

---

[1] Erasmus and Stapleton so understood the matter. Erasmus says: Non affirmat Hieronymus approbatum fuisse hunc librum Judith in Synodo Nicæna, sed ait, in numero est literarum Legitur computasse.—*Erasm., in Cens. Præfat. Hieron.* Stapleton says: Hieronymus hoc de Synodo Nicæna tantum ex fama referre videtur. Synodus, inquit, *Legitur* computasse, nam alibi apertè dubitat.—*Lib. ix., Princip., c. xii.*

[2] Sicut ergo Judith et Tobi et Machabæorum libros legit quidem Ecclesia sed inter canonicas Scripturas non recipit.—*S. Hier., Præf. in Libr. Salom.*

[3] Liber Judith non est in canone.—*S. Hier. in Prol. Gal.*

part of the Canon; a fact which is wholly inexplicable if
Jerome's witness is worthy of credit. Eusebius, who, according to Gelasius, was more than once the organ of the
council, and who certainly must have known all of importance that occurred in the body, has not only left no intimations in any of his writings that Judith was so conspicuously honoured, but uniformly treats the whole Apocrypha
as disputed and uninspired compositions. In the twelfth
chapter of the sixth book of his Ecclesiastical History he
speaks of the Wisdom of Solomon and of Jesus the son
of Sirach as works which were not admitted into the Canon.[1]
In the second book of his Chronicles,[2] according to the version of Jerome, he distinguishes betwixt the Maccabees and
the inspired records of the Jews, and places the former in
the same category with the writings of Josephus and Julius
Africanus, and expressly states that they were not received
among Sacred Scriptures. "From the time of Zerubbabel,"
he states in the eighth book of the Demonstratio Evan-
gelica,[3] "to the time of the Saviour, no Divine book was
published." And Jerome informs us that he pronounced
the additions to Daniel to be totally destitute of Divine
authority.[4]

Athanasius, another prominent member of the Council
of Nice, expressly rejects the Apocrypha from any claim to

[1] Κέχρηται δ᾽ ἐν αὐτοῖς καὶ ταῖς ἀπὸ τῶν ἀντιλεγομένων γραφῶν μαρτυρίαις.
τῆς τε λεγομένης Σαλομῶντος σοφίας, καὶ τῆς Ιησοῦ τοῦ Σιρὰχ, καὶ τῆς πρὸς
'Εβραίους επιστολῆς, τῆς τε Βαρνάβα καὶ Κλήμεντος καὶ Ιούδα.—Eusebii Pam-
phili Historiæ Eccles., lib. vi., cap. 13.

[2] Huc usque Divinæ Scripturæ Hebræorum Annales temporum continent. Ea vero quæ posthæc apud eos gesta sunt, exhibeo de Libro Mac-
cabæorum, et Josephi, et Africani scriptis.—Euseb., Chron., lib. ii., juxta
versionem S. Hieron.

[3] Ὧν οὐ καθ᾽ ἡμῖν δυνατὸν ἐξακριβάζεσθαι τὰ γένη, τῳ μηδὲ φέρεσθαι θείαν
βίβλον ἐξ ἐκείνου καὶ μέχρι τῶν τοῦ Σωτῆρος χρόνων.—Euseb., Demon. Evang.,
lib. viii.

[4] Et miror quosdam .... quum et Origines et Eusebius et Apollina-
rius aliique Ecclesiastici viri et Doctores Græciæ has visiones ut dixi non
haberi apud Hebræos fateantur, nec se debere respondere Porphyrio pro
his quæ nullam Scripturæ sacræ auctoritatem præbeant.—S. Hier. Præf.
Com. in Daniel

inspiration. He speaks of Ecclesiasticus, Wisdom, Tobit, the additions to Esther and Judith, as valuable books for beginners and those who were recently converted to Christianity, but as forming no part of the Canon of Scripture. It was the peculiar prerogative of the twenty-two books which the Jews admitted and which Protestants receive, according to him, to be the fountains of salvation, the infallible source of religious truth.[1]

Betwixt the Synod of Nice and Jerome we have a succession of distinguished writers—Epiphanius, Hilary, Basil, Gregory Nazianzen and Amphilochius, together with the Council of Laodicea—all, as we shall subsequently see, concurring not in the rejection of Judith only, but of the whole Apocrypha, from any pretensions to canonical authority. None seem to have known or ever to have heard that any such event took place at Nice as Jerome says had been somewhere read to have happened. Is it credible that if Nice had canonized Judith, all of these writers, some of whom were members of the body, should have been profoundly ignorant of the fact? How comes it that not one of them has alluded to it, but that all have spoken as if no such event had ever taken place? I cannot better express this argument than in the words of a distinguished Papist, Lindanus, the bishop of Rurmonde :[2] "If the Nicene

---

[1] Athanasius as above.

[2] Si enim Nicena Synodus librum Judith cum aliis in Canonem redegerat, cur annis 80 post eum non accenset Laodicena? Cur Nazianzenus ejus non meminit? sed *legitur* computasse (ait Hieronymus) qui mihi dubitantis suspicionem subindicare videtur. Nisi fortasse quis opinetur hunc de libris canonicis Nicenum canonem unà cum plurimis aliis, minimum (uti equidem arbitror) 47, teste Divo Julio primo Romano, hæreticorum fraude fuisse accisum, atque sublectum Ecclesiæ. Cui ne suffragemur, cogit pia de sanctissimis patribus in concilio Laodiceno congregatis existimatio. Non illos ea ætate, qua canonum scientia imprimis ornabat Episcopos, tam fuisse sui et nominis et officii oblitos, ut illos aut nescierint, aut desideratos non requisierint. Ad hæc si verè *legitur* quod ait Hieronymus legi, " *Librum Judith concilium Nicænum inter canonicas computasse:*" quid sibi vult quod idem præfatione in libris Salomonis scribit: " *Ecclesiam libros Judith, Tobiæ, Maccabeorum legere quidem, sed inter canonicas scripturas non recipere?*" Huc usque Lindanus dubitantis instar, sub-

Council held the book of Judith and the other books of that
rank to be canonical, why did the Council of Laodicea, eighty
years afterwards, omit it? And why did Nazianzen make
no mention of it? St. Hierome seems to me to speak as one
that *doubted* of it, unless a man might think that this and
many more decrees beside, which the Council of Nice made,
were afterward pared away from it by fraudulent heretics;
whereunto I cannot give my consent for the religious honour
that I bear to the Fathers of Laodicea, who in that age, when
bishops knew the canons of the Church best, and when it
was their great commendation to be skilful in them, could
not be so far negligent both of their credit and their duty
as neither to know them if they were extant nor to seek
after them if they were lost. Besides, if that were true
which St. Hierome says was read of the book of Judith,
that the Nicene Fathers took it into the Canon, how shall we
construe that which he writes in his preface before the books
of Solomon, 'that though the Church indeed reads the history of Judith and Tobit, etc., yet it doth not receive them
into the number of canonical Scripture?' But that the
Nicene Council determined nothing in this matter I am
the rather induced to believe, for the Sixth General Council
at Constantinople approved the Canon of Laodicea, which
it would never have done if the Fathers that met there had
either rejected or mutilated the Canon of Nice."

The reasoning of the bishop, coupled with the considerations which have already been adduced, seems to be conclusive. The first General Synod of the Christian Church,
whatever other follies it was permitted to perpetrate, was
kept in the merciful providence of God from corrupting those records of eternal truth from which its sublime

jungit definientis more: Verùm nihil hac de re in concilio Niceno fuisse
definitum, ut existimem invitat quòd hunc Laodicenum de scripturis
canonicis canonem, unâ cum reliquis, synodus Constantinopolitana sexta
in Trullo approbarit; quod minimè videtur fuisse factura, si designatum
à 318 illis patribus Nicenis doctissimis juxta ac sanctissimis, Laodiceni
aut non recipissent aut decurtassent Sacrarum Scripturarum Canonem.—
Rainoldus, De Libris Apocryphis, Prælectio xv., vol. i., p. 132.

and memorable creed may be most triumphantly deduced. A pure faith has nothing to apprehend from unadulterated Scriptures.

2. It is unnecessary to notice what you have said of the Provincial Synod at Alexandria, held in the year 339, or of the General Council at Constantinople, convened in 381. The principles of criticism, which have been repeatedly developed in the course of this discussion, furnish an abundant explanation of the real value of the quotations on which you have relied. In regard to Gregory Nazianzen, in particular, through whom you have represented the Council of Constantinople as endorsing the books of Ecclesiasticus and Wisdom, I shall have occasion hereafter to show that you have been grossly seduced into error. His testimony is clear and explicit for the Jewish Canon, and if he has quoted the Apocrypha as Scripture or Divine Scripture, as I am willing to admit that he has done, this fact only strengthens the position that such expressions were generic terms, comprehending the entire department of religious literature, whether inspired or not.

3. I come now to the Councils of Hippo and Carthage, which, as their testimony on this subject is one, I shall treat as one; and as my object is not to puzzle but convince, I shall take no advantage of the difficulties which press the Roman doctors in determining which of the Carthaginian Councils it was that enacted the famous decree touching the canonical books of Scripture. That decree is usually printed in the collections as the forty-seventh Canon of the third Council of Carthage, held in the year 397, and, so far as the writings of the Old Testament are concerned, is in these words: "Moreover, it is ordained that nothing beside the canonical Scriptures be read in the Church under the name of *Divine Scripture*, and the canonical Scriptures are these: Genesis, Exodus, Leviticus, Numbers, Deuteronomy, Joshua the son of Nun, Judges, Ruth, Four Books of the Kingdoms, Two Books of Chronicles, Job, David's Psalter, Five Books of Solomon, the Books of the Twelve Prophets.

Isaiah, Jeremiah, Ezekiel, Daniel, Tobit, Judith, Esther, Two Books of Esdras, Two Books of the Maccabees."

Now the question is, What are we to understand by the phrase *canonical Scriptures* as used in this decree? If it is synonymous with *inspired* Scriptures, then indeed you have produced a witness that the Apocrypha are entitled to Divine authority. If, on the other hand, it means something else, something quite distinct from *inspired* Scripture, then your cause, condemned by the voice of three centuries, is left without even the African protection which you had vainly hoped to find in the close of the fourth. Nay, if it could be proved that the Council of Carthage intended in this Canon to enumerate the books which were held to be inspired, the only protection which Rome could receive from it is the " protection which vultures give to lambs." It is as much the interest of Papists as of Protestants to find a meaning which, without doing violence to the terms that are employed, shall be consistent with itself and with the known opinions of the age, and at the same time exonerate the Fathers from the charge of ignorance, folly and wickedness, to which, if it were their purpose to draw up a list of the writings that had been given by inspiration of God, they are in some degree exposed. It cannot be denied that they were foolish, ignorant and wicked if they pronounced any book to be inspired without sufficient evidence, and it is equally indisputable that no such evidence could have been possessed in behalf of any work which the Church, in every age before and after this provincial synod, has concurred in rejecting as apocryphal. And yet a book which in the Papal editions of the Bible is placed by authority *extra seriem canonicorum librorum*, which has evidently no claims to inspiration, and which the Christian world, according to the showing of Romanists themselves, has never received as the Word of God, is inserted by Carthage in its list of canonical books. Who can believe, who can even conceive, that it was the intention of the Fathers to outrage the sentiments of the rest

of Christendom, and to incur the awful malediction of those
who add to the words of Divine Revelation? To have
perpetrated a deed of this sort, amid the light with which
they were surrounded—a light so bright that it has penetrated even to the darkened chambers of the Papacy—would
have manifested a degree of impiety and blasphemy which
we cannot attribute to a body of which Augustine was a
member. You, however, in the interpretation which you
have given of their forty-seventh canon, have charged it
upon them. It is susceptible of the clearest proof that the
two books of Esdras which they have mentioned in their
list include the *third*. What in the Latin Bellarmine himself admits[1] is denominated the *third* book of Esdras, is in
the Greek copies of the Bible entitled the first. What is
in the Latin the *first* and *second* constitute in Greek but *one*
volume, and are styled the *second* book of Esdras. So that,
according to the Greek numeration, the first and second
books of Esdras comprehend the *Apocryphal third*. Bellarmine has again informed us[2] that at the time when the
Council of Carthage was convened, the universal Church
used that translation of the Bible which Jerome was accustomed to, called the Vulgate, and which was made from
copies of the Septuagint, including the additions of the
Hellenistic Jews. Hence, the Bibles of the Fathers at Carthage, under the name of *two books* of Esdras, embraced
not only Nehemiah and Ezra, but that very *third* book of

---

[1] Nec minor est difficultas de lib. iii. Esdræ, nam in Græcis codicibus ipse
est, qui dicitur *primus Esdræ;* et qui apud nos dicuntur *primus et secundus,*
in Græco dicuntur *secundus Esdræ.* Quocirca versimile est, antiqua con-
cilia et patres, cùm ponunt in canone duos libros Esdræ, intelligere nomine
duorum librorum omnes tres. Sequebantur enim versionem septuaginta
interpretum, apud quos tres nostri duo libri Esdræ nominantur.—*Bellar.,
De Verbo Dei,* lib. i., cap. xx.

[2] Utebatur autem eo tempore universa Ecclesia libris sacris juxta eam
editionem, quam S. Hieronymus præfatione in librum Esther, et sæpe
alibi, *vulgatam* appellare solet, quæ, ut ipse ait, Græcorum lingua et literis
continetur.—*Bellar., De Verbo Dei,* lib. i., cap. vii.

Esdras which Rome declares to be Apocryphal.[1] Now, my argument is briefly this: if the Carthaginian Fathers intended to settle the Canon of inspiration, they were guilty of great folly and wickedness; but the character of the men,

[1] As the following extract so ably refutes Bellarmine's evasions, the reader, I hope, will excuse its length:

Potest autem id videri falsum, Augustinum scilicet et Carthaginiense concilium adnumerasse tertium Esdræ canonicis, cum duos tantum ejus libros in canone consignando nominent, sed si penitus introspicere volueritis, sub duorum nomine tertium quoque comprehendi intelligetis. Quod ut vobis planum fiat, principio notandum secus collocari libros Esdræ in Græca editione quam in Latina. Qui enim Latinis tertius, is est Græcis primus; qui Latinis primus et secundus, ii Græcis in unum volumen compinguntur, cui nomen *Secundus Esdræ.* Quòd verò primum et secundum Esdræ unum Græci numerent, ut Hieronymus docet, inde fieri id potuit, quia Hebræi sic numerant. Quod tertium Esdræ præfigant, inde videtur effectum, quia ille liber historiam paulò altius repetit. Fuisse autem primum Græcis, qui est Latinis tertius, manifestum est, quòd si teste opus sit, fidem faciat Athanasius, qui in enumeratione librorum duos Esdræ nominat, priorem cujus initium est, *Et obtulit Josias Pascha, etc.*, et posteriorem, cujus initium esse dicit, *In anno primo Cyri, Regis Persarum, etc.*, quæ duo cum sint initia tertii et primi libri, clarissimum inde est, tertium ab eo ut primum numeratum, secundum et primum ut secundum. Nam quod in Latinis Athanasii exemplaribus in margine adscripsit nescio quis (*Atqui hoc principium est capitis trigesimiquinti 2. Paralipomenon*) per imperitiam factum est. Non enim animadvertit ille quisquis fuit, eadem verba exordiri tertium Esdræ, sed animadvertere id debuerat, atque errorem suum corrigere ex eodem capite, ubi Athanasius agens de primo Esdræ, enumerat ea prope omnia, quæ sunt in tertio Esdræ; adscripsit autem ille idem (ut videtur) hæc haberi capite tertio et quarto libri secundi.

Id eo modo observatum est in Græcis Bibliorum editionibus; nominatim in ea quæ Venetiis ex Aldi officina exivit, ubi cum duo tantum, habeantur libri Esdræ, primus exorditur, quomodo noster tertius, secundus iisdem plane verbis, quibus Latina editio primum Esdræ inchoat. Ita manifestum est et antiquitus Athanasii tempore, et ab ejus seculo in Græcis editionibus Veteris Testamenti duobus Esdræ libris tertium comprehendi. In quo obiter notandum, doctissimos viros Franciscum Vatablum, Franciscum Junium, et Franciscum Lucam, eo parùm animadverso, existimavisse tertium Esdræ Græcè non extare. Vatablus quidem tertium Esdræ Græcè nec sibi contigisse dicit videre, nec cuiquam quod sciat alteri. Quomodo etiam Junius *Hezræ libros duos, neque Hebraicè, neque Græcè vidi* (inquit ille) *aut fuisse visos memini legere.* Franciscus Lucas, paulò asseverantiùs tertium *Esdræ nullo alio sermone extare* ait *præterquam Latino.* In quam ille opinionem inductus erat eo, quod neque in Complutensibus

particularly of Augustine, shows that they were not liable to such a charge; therefore, they *did not intend* to determine the Canon of inspired books.

This conclusion is confirmed by the fact that the decree exemplaribus, neque in Bibliis regiis habeatur tertii Esdræ Græcè; nec in Germanicis quidem Bibliis sequitur Nehemiam, sed in eam partem rejicitur, ubi Apocryphi ponuntur.   Hoc tandem Lucas vidit, et agnovit, et confessus est se deceptum, etc., sed quod ad rem præsentem facit, affirmat ibi Lucas, tertium Esdræ Latinorum, esse primum Græcis.   Atque hoc est, quod primum observatum volui.   Proximo loco animadvertere debetis Augustinum et patres Carthaginienses in Canone consignando, et alias in disputationibus suis translatione Latina è Græca 70 editione versa, uti consuevisse.   Quod ipse planum facit ubi citato illo loco, *Et formavit Deus hominem pulverem de terra:* subjungit, *Sicut Græci codices habent, unde in Latinam linguam scriptura ipsa conversa est.*   Manifestius autem id dicit, ubi rem ex professo disputat.   *Nam cum fuerint* (inquit Augustinus) *et alii interpretes, etc., hanc tamen, quæ septuaginta est, tanquam sola esset, sic recipit Ecclesia, eaque utuntur Græci populi Christiani, quorum plerique utrum alia sit aliqua ignorant.   Ex hac 70 interpretatione etiam in Latinam linguam interpretatum est, quod Ecclesiæ Latinæ tenent, quamvis non defuerit temporibus nostris presbyter Hieronymus homo doctissimus, et omnium trium linguarum peritus, qui non ex Græco, sed ex Hebræo in Latinum eloquium easdem scripturas convertit,* et quæ sequuntur.   En ut disertis verbis Augustinus non solum se usum illa Septuaginta interpretum versione significat, sed et eam perinde quasi sola esset, ab Ecclesia receptam, et Ecclesiam Latinam, quod tenet id ex illa interpretatione tenere, adeo ut quamvis, Augustini temporibus Hieronymus summa fide ex Hebraicis fontibus converteret, Ecclesia tamen præferret eam editionem, quæ ex Græca 70 Latina facta est.   Id quod et loco superiore docuit Augustinus, et præcipuè in Epistolis, ubi ad Hieronymum sic scribit, *Ego sanè te mallem Græcas potius canonicas nobis interpretari scripturas, quæ 70 interpretum authoritate perhibentur.   Perdurum erit enim, si tua interpretatio per multas Ecclesias frequentiùs ceperit lectitari, quòd à Græcis Ecclesiis-Latinæ Ecclesiæ dissonabunt, etc.,* et alibi petit à Hieronymo, ut interpretationem suam Bibliorum è 70 mittat.   *Ideò autem* (inquit) *desidero interpretationem tuam de 70, ut et tanta Latinorum, qui qualescunque hoc ausi sunt, quantum possumus imperitia careamus: et hi qui me invidere putant utilibus laboribus tuis, eandem aliquando si fieri potest, intelligant, propterea me nolle tuam ex Hebræo interpretationem in Ecclesiis legi, ne contra Septuaginta auctoritatem, tamquam novum aliquid proferentes, magno scandalo perturbemus plebes Christi, quarum aures et corda illam interpretationem audire consueverunt, qua ab apostolis approbata est.*   Denique in libris de Doctrina Christiana, vult ille Latinos codices veteris testamenti, si necesse fuerit, Græcorum auctoritate emendandos, et eorum potissimum, qui cum 70 essent, ore uno interpretati esse perhibentur, etc., locus consulatur.   Neque verò hæc Augustinus solum luculentè testatur,

itself was conditional; the Church beyond the sea, as we
gather from an ancient note, was to be consulted for its confirmation.   The Council of Carthage, then, received the
books mentioned in its list as canonical, provided the trans-
sed et reliqui scriptores, qui in eum commentarios scripserunt, vel de eo
loquuti sunt.   In quibus Ludovicus Vives in præfatione comment. ait
Augustinum versionem 70 interpretum ubique adducere.   Et in ipsis commen-
tariis *ostendit* (inquit) *olim Ecclesias Latinas usas interpretatione Latina ex
70 versa, non hac Hieronymi ut mirer esse qui tantum nefas existiment trans-
lationes attingi, modò sobriè ac prudenter fiat.*

Sixtus Senensis duas fuisse docet in Ecclesia Latina Latinas editiones
V. T. novam scilicet ac veterem. Vetus *quidem* (inquit ille) *vulgatæ et
communis nomen accepit, tùm quia nullum certum haberet auctorem, tùm quia
non de Hebræo fonte, sed de κοινη, vel de Septuaginta interpretatione sumpta
esset (quem admodum August. 18, De Civit. Dei, c. 43, et Hieronymus in
præfatione Evangeliorum testantur), cujus lectione usa est Ecclesia longè ante
tempora Hieronymi, ac etiam multo post, usque ad tempora Gregorii Papæ.
Nova verò à Hieronymo non de Græca, sed de Hebraica veritate in Latinum
eloquium versa est : qua Ecclesia usque ab ipsis Gregorii temporibus, unà cum
veteri editione usa est. Utriusque enim Gregorius in præfatione Moralium
meminit, inquiens: Novam translationem defero, sed cum probationis causa
me exigit, nunc veterem, nunc novam pro testimonio assumo: ut quia sedes
Apost. cui authore Deo præsideo utraque utitur, mei quoque labor studii ex
utroque fulciatur.* Hæc apud Sixtum, undè liquet longè ante tempora
Hieronymi, ad usque Gregorium (quasi ad 600 annos), in usu fuisse translationem Latinam è Græca 70. Adeoque rectè colligi Augustinum et
Carthaginiensis concilii patres editionem illam Græcam 70 sequutos esse.
Quid quod Bellarminus ipse hoc agnoscit, veteres sequutos esse versionem
Septuaginta? *Apud quos* (inquit) *qui nobis Esdræ tertius est, fuit primus,
siccine?* Quomodo ergo te expedies è laqueo rationis nostræ? Conatur
ille quidem expedire se, sed hæret ut mus in pisa. *Majorem revera* (ait)
esse difficultatem de tertio, Esdræ quam de quarto. Sed respondet, *Etsi duo
libri Græcorum sint nostris tertius, non tamen sequi patres antiquos cum duos
Esdræ in canone ponant, nostros tres intellexisse.* Quid ita? Quatuor
nimirum rationes adhibet è quibus pleræque non attingunt nostram sententiam, certè nullæ labefactant.

Prima ratio hæc est: *Quia Melito, Epiphanius, Hilarius, Hieronymus,
Ruffinus, apertè sequuti sunt Hebræos, qui tertium Esdræ non agnoscunt.*
Quid tum? Ergone Augustinus cum duos Esdræ accenseat, non intellexit
nostros tres? Quia scilicet, Melito, Epiphanius, Hilarius, Hieronymus,
Ruffinus, apertè sequuti sunt Hebræos, ergo Augustinus non est sequutus
editionem Græcam Septuaginta? perinde ratiocinatur ac siquis diceret,
*Socrates, Plato, veteres Academici vocarunt Deum Ideam boni, etc., ergo ac
Aristoteles et Perpateticorum schola sic vocavit.* Si nondum appareat hujus
rationis infirmitas at facillimè apparebit in ratione simili quam adjun-

marine churches would consent. Surely it could not mean
that these books are *inspired*, provided the transmarine
churches will agree that they are so. The evidence of their
inspiration was either complete to the council, or it was not.
If it was complete, they were bound as faithful ministers
of Christ to say unconditionally and absolutely that these

gam: Melito, Epiphanius, Hilarius, Hieronymus et Ruffinus rejecerunt
è canone sacrarum Scripturarum libros Sapientiæ, Ecclesiastici, Tobiæ,
Judith, etc., ergo et Augustinus hos rejecit, et concilium Carthaginiense;
hæc nisi ratio firma sit, videtis quam infirma sit altera.

Secunda Bellarmini ratio ea est *à precibus publicis et usu Ecclesiastici
officii. Quia jam diu nihil legitur ex illo libro in officio Ecclesiastico.* Quid
inde? An ergo Augustinus cum duos Esdræ libros in Canone numeraret,
non intellexit nostros tres? Aut Augustini tempore et a patribus Cartha-
giniensibus non habebatur tertius Esdræ in canonicis? Perinde hoc est ac
si quis ita ratiocinetur: *Exulat jam diu papatus ex Anglia, ergo Henrici VI.
tempore exulavit.* Imo absurdior illa ratio quam hæc, quo propriùs abfuit
ab ætate nostra Henrici VI. Regnum, quam Augustini tempora; cum ille
ab hinc non ultra 100 annos floruerit, ab Augustino ultra 1000 effluxerint,
quo temporis decursu multa mutari poterant. Bellarminus enim ipse
fatetur, Augustini tempore monachos tonderi solitos fuisse, suo radi.
Potuit tamen simili ratione uti: Jamdiu in usu fuit, ut raderentur monachi,
ergo August. tempore non solebant tonderi.

Sed fortasse tertia ratio subtilior, quæ ab auctoritate Gelasii ducitur
Is namque unum tantum Esdræ librum in canone ponit, id est (inquit Bellar.)
nostros duos. Optime. Conceditur enim, postea rem penitus introspiciemus,
et videbimus utrum unum ille tantum numeret. Interim concedant Gela-
sium, qui vixit centum annos post Aug. et Carthag. Conc. unum tantum
Esdræ lib. in canone posuisse. Quid verò hoc ad August. et Carthag.
patres? An deinde illi non numerarunt duos? an duorum nomine nostros tres non significarunt? Quidni ergo sic ratiocinent: *M. Crassus par-
tib. optimatum favit, ergo C. Marius non fuit popularis?* Hæc argumenta si
in nostris scholis supponerentur, credo riderentur à pueris. Verum cum
sufferuntur à Jesuitis, quodam ni fallor κρυψεως artificio insolubilia habe-
buntur.

Verum enim verò fortassis artificio Rhetorum firmissimam rationem
postremo loco reservavit. Ea erit palmaria. *Namque Hieronymus* (inquit
Bellarminus) *apertè docet, tertium Esdræ non modo non apud Hebræos haberi,
sed neque apud Septuaginta.* An id apertè docet Hier.? Eo certè delapsum
esse Bellarminum miror. Consulite Hieron. (Videbitis eum non modo non
apertè docere, quid ei affingit Bellar. sed nec omninò; imo contrarium sta-
tuere, quid consensu antiquorum, qui testimoniis, e tertio Esdræ persæpe
usi, postea mihi pluribus erit confirmandum.)—*Rainoldus, De Libris
Apocryphis, Prælectio* xxviii., vol. i., pp. 237-243.

books belong to the rule of faith. Under such circumstances to have enacted a conditional decree would have been treason against truth and impiety to God. Why consult the Church beyond the sea in regard to a matter which was unquestioned and notorious? If, on the other hand, the evidence was not complete or satisfactory in regard to the inspiration of the books, why make a Canon until doubts were settled and difficulties resolved? If the design of appealing to the transmarine churches was to obtain more light, why did the Fathers undertake to act until the light had been supplied? It cannot be pretended that their intention was to procure the confirmation of the Holy See. It was not the Pope alone nor a general council that they proposed to consult; it was the *Church* beyond the sea—*transmarina ecclesia*—the Bishop of Rome, or "the other bishops of those parts"; for if the end sought had been the settlement of the inspired Canon, and every bishop and doctor connected with this Church, with Boniface himself at their head, had been assembled in council, and had given their decision, their voice would have been only the voice of a *provincial synod*, and therefore not entitled to be received, according to your doctrine, as the infallible dictate of the Holy Ghost. The conduct of the Carthaginian Fathers in passing a conditional decree, if their design was to settle the Canon of inspiration, is wholly inexplicable. They virtually say, We have satisfactory evidence that these books are inspired, and yet it is not satisfactory. Such egregious trifling cannot be imputed to them, and therefore some interpretation must be evidently put upon the Canon which shall justify their appeal to a foreign Church.

No better way is left us of arriving at a just conception of this matter than by considering the testimony of Augustine, who was himself a member of the council, and who may be presumed to have known the real intentions of the body. His opinions may be taken as a true exponent of the opinions of the African Church. This illustrious advocate of the doctrines of grace has given us a list of the

canonical Scriptures which coincides precisely with the catalogue of Carthage;[1] and yet there is abundant proof that
several of the books which are mentioned in his list Augustine *did not believe* to be inspired.

In the twenty-fourth chapter of the seventeenth book of
his City of God, he remarks,[2] "that in all the time after
their return from Babylon, till the days of our Saviour, the
Jews had no prophets after Malachi, Haggai and Zechariah,
who prophesied at that time, and Ezra; except another
Zachariah, father of John, and his wife Elizabeth, just before the birth of Christ; and after his birth, old Simeon,

---

[1] Totus autem Canon Scripturarum, in quo istam considerationem ver-
sandam dicimus, his libris continetur. Quinque Moyseos, id est Genesi,
Exodo, Levitico, Numeris, Deuteronomio; ac uno libro Jesu Nave, uno
Judicum, uno libello qui appellatur Ruth, qui magis ad Regnorum prin-
cipia videtur pertinere; deinde quatuor Regnorum et duobus Paralipomenon, non consequentibus, sed quasi à latere adjunctis simulque per-
gentibus. Hæc est historia, quæ sibimet annexa tempora continet, atque
ordinem rerum: sunt aliæ tamquam ex diverso ordine, quæ neque huic
ordini, neque inter se connectuntur, sicut est Job, et Tobias, et Esther, et
Judith, et Machabæorum libri duo, et Esdræ duo, qui magis subsequi
videntur ordinatam illam historiam usque ad Regnorum vel Paralipomenon terminatam. Deinde prophetæ, in quibus David unus liber Psalmorum, et Salomonis tres, Proverbiorum, Cantica Canticorum, et Ecclesiastes. Nam illi duo libri, unus qui *Sapientia*, et alius qui *Ecclesiasticus*
inscribitur, de quadam similitudine Salomonis esse dicuntur: nam Jesus
filius Sirach eos scripsisse constantissimè perhibetur, qui tamen quoniam
in authoritatem recipi meruerunt, inter propheticos numerandi sunt.
Reliqui sunt eorum libri, qui propriè prophetæ appellati sunt, duodecim
prophetarum libri singuli, qui connexi sibimet, quoniam numquam se-
juncti sunt, pro uno habentur: quorum prophetarum nomina sunt hæc,
Osee, Joel, Amos, Abdias, Jonas, Micheas, Nahum, Habacuc, Sophonias,
Aggæus, Zacharias, Malachias: deinde quatuor prophetæ sunt majorum
voluminum, Isaias, Jeremias, Daniel, Ezechiel. His quadraginta quatuor
libris Testamenti veteris terminatur auctoritas.—*S. Augustini Episcopi de
Doctrina Christiana*, lib. ii., cap. viii.

[2] Toto autem illo tempore, ex quo redierunt de Babylonia, post Mala-
chiam, Aggæum et Zachariam, qui tum prophetaverunt et Esdram, non
habuerunt prophetas usque ad Salvatoris adventum, nisi alium Zachariam
patrem Johannis, que Elisabet ejus uxorem, Christi nativitate jam prox-
ima; et eo jam nato, Simeonem senem, et Annam viduam jàmque gran-
dævam et ipsum Johannem novissimum.—*S. Augustini, Episcopi de Civitati
Dei*, lib. xvii., cap. xxiv.

and Anna a widow of a great age; and John last of all."
Again:[1] "From Samuel the Prophet to the Babylonish
Captivity, and then to their return from it, and the rebuilding of the temple after seventy years, according to the
prophecy of Jeremiah, is the whole time of the Prophets."
To ascertain his idea of a prophet and of a prophetic composition, let us turn to the thirty-eighth chapter of the
eighteenth book of the same treatise.[2] It is there stated as
a probable explanation of the fact that some books which
were written by prophets were excluded from the Canon,
"that those to whom the Holy Spirit was accustomed to
reveal what ought to be received as authoritative in religion
wrote some things as men of historic investigation, and
others as Prophets of Divine inspiration: the two were
kept distinct, that the former might be attributed to the
men themselves, the latter to God, who spoke through the
Prophets." A Prophet, then, is a person "to whom the
Holy Spirit is accustomed to reveal what ought to be received as authoritative in religion"—he is a man who
speaks by "Divine inspiration," and does not depend upon
his diligence and industry for the truths which he communicates. He is not merely an individual who foretells the
future—he may write a history, but he must depend for his
facts, not upon historical research, but the instructions of
the Spirit. In other words, Augustine plainly treats
Prophet and *inspired man* as terms of equivalent extension.
When, therefore, he says that from Ezra to Christ no

[1] Hoc itaque tempus, ex quo sanctus Samuël prophetare cœpit, et deinceps donec populus Israël captivus in Babyloniam duceretur, atque inde
secundum sancti Jeremiæ prophetiam post septuaginta annos reversis Is-
raëlitis Dei domus instauraretur, totum tempus est Prophetarum.—*Aug.*,
De Civ. Dei, lib. xvii., c. i.

[2] Cujus rei, fateor, causa me latet; nisi quòd ego existimo, etiam ipsos,
quibus ea quæ in auctoritate religionis esse deberent Sanctus utique Spiritus revelabat, alia sicut homines historica diligentia, alia sicut Prophetas
inspiratione Divina scribere potuisse; atque hæc ita fuisse distincta, ut
illa tamquam ipsis, ista verò tamquam Deo per ipsos loquenti, judica-
rentur esse tribuenda: ac sic illa pertinerent ad ubertatem cognitionis,
hæc ad religionis auctoritatem.—*Aug.*, *De Civ. Dei*, lib. xviii., c. xxxviii.

Prophet appeared among the Jews, he unquestionably means that the gift of inspiration was withdrawn, and that, consequently, no works written during that period were entitled to be received as of authority in religion. Now, it is notorious that a large portion, if not all, of the Apocrypha was written during this very period, in which, as it is piteously lamented in the Maccabees, "a Prophet was not seen among them." Therefore, according to Augustine, a large portion of the Apocrypha is not inspired.

' In addition to this, there are several passages in his works in which he evidently treats the Hebrew Canon as complete. In his commentary on the fifty-sixth Psalm,[1] he observes, "that *all the books* in which Christ is the subject of prophecy were in the possession of the Jews. We bring our documents from the Jews, that we may put other enemies to confutation: the Jew carries the Book from which the Christian derives his faith. The Jews are our librarians." Again, he says, in another dissertation:[2] "The Jews are the escritoirs of Christians, containing the Law and the Prophets, which prove the doctrines of the Church." And in another place he expressly says that the Law, the Prophets and the Psalms comprehended " all the canonical authorities of the Sacred Books."[3] It is notorious, however, that the Jews rejected the Apocrypha—that these were documents which they refused to carry; and if Augustine received as inspired no other works but those which were

---

[1] Propterea autem adhuc Judæi sunt, ut libros nostros portent ad confu-sionem suam. Quando enim volumus ostendere prophetatum Christum, proferimus paganis istas literas. . . . . Quia omnes ipsæ literæ, quibus Christus prophetatus est, apud Judæos sunt, omnes ipsas literas habent Judæi. Proferimus codices ab inimicis, ut confundamus alios inimicos. . . . . Codicem portat Judæus, unde credat Christianus. Librarii nostri facti sunt.—*Aug. in Psa.*, lvi.

[2] Quid est aliud hodie gens ipsa [Judæorum], nisi quædam scriniaria Christianorum, bajulans legem et prophetas ad testimonium assertionis Ecclesiæ.—*Aug.*, lib. xii., *contra Faust*, cap. xxiii.

[3] Ecclesiam suam demonstrent . . . . in præscripto Legis, in Propheta-rum predictis, in Psalmorum Cantibus, ... hoc est, in omnibus canon-icis sanctorum librorum authoritatibus.—*Aug., De Unit. Eccl.*, c. xviii.

acknowledged by the Hebrew nation, it is demonstrably certain that he could not have admitted any part of the Apocrypha into the sacred Canon. We may come down, accordingly, to particular books, and show that some of them are, by him, expressly and unequivocally excluded. The book of Judith, he informs us, possessed no canonical authority among the Jews.[1] Of the Maccabees he says,[2] " The Jews do not receive the scripture of the Maccabees as they do the Law, the Prophets and the Psalms, to which our Lord bears testimony. But it is received by the Church not unprofitably, if it be read and heard soberly, especially for the sake of the history of the Maccabees, who suffered so much from the hand of persecutors for the sake of the Law of God." Whatever the reception was which the Church gave to these books, Augustine justifies it, not on account of their Divine authority, but chiefly or especially on account of the moral tendency of the history. It is plain that he could not have regarded them as inspired, since their inspiration would have been the strongest of all possible reasons for receiving them. We defer to the instructions of an inspired composition, not because its lessons are useful, but we know that its lessons must be useful because it is inspired. Speaking, in another place, of these same books, he says,[3] " The account of these times is not

[1] Per idem tempus etiam illa sunt gesta, quæ conscripta sunt in libro Judith, quem sanè in canone Scripturarum Judæi non recepisse dicuntur. —*Aug., De Civ. Dei*, lib. xviii., c. xxvi.

[2] Et hanc quidem Scripturam, quæ appellatur Macchabæorum, non habent Judæi, sicut Legem et Prophetas et Psalmos, quibus Dominus testimonium perhibet; . . . . sed recepta est ab ecclesia non inutiliter, si sobriè legatur vel audiatur, maximè propter illos Macchabæos, qui pro Dei lege, sicut veri martyres, à persecutoribus tam indigna atque horrenda perpessi sunt, etc.—*Contr. Gaudent. Donat.*, lib. i., cap. xxxi.

[3] Quorum supputatio temporum non in Scripturis Sanctis, quæ canonicæ appellantur, sed in aliis invenitur, in quibus sunt et Macchabæorum libri, quos non Judæi, sed Ecclesia pro canonicis habet, propter quorumdam Martyrum passiones vehementes atque mirabiles, qui antequam Christus venisset in carnem usque ad mortem pro Dei lege certaverunt, et mala gravissima atque horribilia pertulerunt.—*Aug., De Civ. Dei*, lib. xviii., c. xxxvi.

found in those holy Scriptures which are called *canonical*,
but in other works, among which also are the books of the
Maccabees, which the Jews do not, but which the Church
does, esteem to be canonical, on account of the violent and
extraordinary sufferings of certain martyrs, who, previously
to the advent of Christ in the flesh, contended even unto
death for the Law of God, and endured grievous and horrible calamities." Here again these books are canonical
among Christians, *not because they are inspired*, but on account of the examples of heroic martyrdom with which
they are adorned. The language of this passage is remarkable. The Maccabees are first carefully distinguished from
those Divine Scriptures which are called canonical, and then
it is immediately added that the Church receives them as
canonical. Here, then, is either a contradiction (for it is
preposterous to limit the first clause so as to make Augustine
assert that these books did not belong to the Scriptures called
canonical by the Jews,—his words are absolute and general),
or the term *canonical* is used in two distinct and separate
senses—in *one* of which it might be universally affirmed
that the Maccabees were not canonical; in the other, that
they were canonical in the Christian, though not in the
Jewish Church. I might also show—but I do not wish
to protract the argument—that Augustine rejected Ecclesiasticus and Wisdom from the list of inspired compositions.[1]

If, as we have seen, Augustine did not receive the Apocrypha as any part of the Word of God, what did he mean
by *canonical Scriptures* in the catalogue to which we have
already referred? I answer, without hesitation, *books which
might be profitably read in the churches for the public instruction of the faithful*.

That *some* of the ancient churches had a canon of reading distinct from the Canon of inspired writings, may be
gathered from the testimony of Athanasius, Jerome and
Ruffinus. The passage from Athanasius is quoted in another

[1] See Cosin's Scholastical Hist. Canon, pp. 100, 105.

part of this discussion.[1] Ruffin says,[2] "It ought, however, to be known that there are also other books which are
not canonical, but have been called by our forefathers *ecclesiastical;* as the Wisdom of Solomon, and another which
is called the Wisdom of the son of Sirach, and among the
Latins is called by the general name of *Ecclesiasticus;* by
which title is denoted, not the author of the book, but
the quality of the writing. In the same rank is the book
of Tobit and Judith and the books of the Maccabees. In
the New Testament is the book of the Shepherd, or of
Hermas, which is called the *Two Ways,* or *the Judgment
of Peter.* All which they would have to be read in the
churches, but not to be alleged by way of authority for
proving articles of faith." Jerome says,[3] "As, therefore, the
Church reads the books of Judith, Tobias and Maccabees,
but does not receive them among the canonical Scriptures,
so also it reads these two volumes [Wisdom and Ecclesias-
ticus] for the edification of the people, but not for authority
to prove the doctrines of religion."

Now, the preface to Augustine's catalogue shows conclusively that he was not answering the question, What books
were inspired? but another question, What books might be
read?[4] He first divides the Divine Scriptures into two

---

[1] Page 674.   [2] See original, quoted p. 737.

[3] Sicut ergo Judith, et Tobi, et Macchabæorum libros legit quidem Ecclesia, sed inter canonicas Scripturas non recipit, sic et hæc duo volumina [Sapientiam et Ecclesiasticum] legit ad ædificationem plebis, non ad
auctoritatem Ecclesiasticorum dogmatum confirmandam.—*Hieron., Præfat.
in Libros Salomonis.*

[4] Erit igitur Divinarum Scripturarum solertissimus indagator, qui primò
totas legerit, notasque habuerit, et si nondum intellectu, jam tamen lectione, duntaxat eas quæ appellantur *canonicæ.* Nam cæteras securius leget
fide veritatis instructus, ne præoccupent imbecillem animum, et periculosis
mendaciis atque phantasmatibus eludentes, præjudicent aliquid contra
sanam intelligentiam. In canonicis autem Scripturis Ecclesiarum Cathol-
icarum quam plurimum auctoritatem sequatur, inter quas sanè illæ sunt,
quæ Apostolicas sedes habere et Epistolas accipere meruerunt. Tenebit
igitur hunc modum in Scripturis canonicis, ut eas quæ ab omnibus accipiuntur Ecclesiis Catholicis præponat eis quas quædam non accipiunt: in
eis verò quæ non accipiuntur ab omnibus præponat eas quas plures gra-

general classes—those which were, and those which were
not, canonical—and gives the general advice that he who
would make himself skilful in the Scriptures should confine his reading to those which were canonical.   Then he
draws a distinction between the canonical books themselves,
and shows that some, even of this class, were entitled to
much more deference and respect than others.   He directs
his diligent inquirer " to prefer such as are received by all
catholic churches to those which some do not receive;" and
with regard to such as are not received by all, he advises
him "to prefer those which are received by many and
eminent churches to those which are received by few churches
and of less authority."   Now, Trent itself being witness,
all inspired Scripture is entitled to equal veneration and
respect.   No matter if every church under heaven should
agree to reject it, the obligation, supposing its inspiration to
be known, would still be perfect to receive and obey it.   Its
authority does not depend upon the numbers who submit
to it, but upon the proofs that it came from God.   These
proofs can neither be increased nor diminished by the multitude or paucity of those who are convinced by them.   If
they should be confined to a *single* church, and that church
should proclaim them to a faithless world, the world would
be as strongly bound to listen and believe as though a
thousand sees had joined in the act.   From the nature of
the case, evidence perfectly conclusive of their Divine inspiration must, in regard to some of the Epistles, have
existed, at first, only in a single congregation; and even
while other churches had not yet received them, their authority was just as perfect and complete as it afterwards
became when all Christendom confessed them to be Divine.
It is consequently preposterous to measure the authority of
inspired Scripture by the number, dignity and importance

vioresque accipiunt, eis quas pauciores minorisque auctoritatis Ecclesiæ
tenent. Si autem alias invenerit à pluribus, alias à gravioribus haberi,
quamquam hoc facilè invenire non possit, æqualis tamen auctoritatis
eas habendas puto.—*Aug.*, *De Doctrina Christ.*, lib. ii., c. viii.

of the churches that acknowledge its claims. But if the question be, What books, in the estimation of those who are competent to judge, may be safely read for practical improvement? then the rule of Augustine is just and natural, You must inquire into the experience of the Christian world if you wish to ascertain the works which God has eminently blessed to the comfort, holiness, stability and peace of his chosen children. It seems, as we gather from Augustine's Preface, that there were works in circulation, under the title of *Divine Scriptures*, abounding in falsehoods perilous to the soul, which could not, therefore, be read with safety or with profit. In contradistinction from these dangerous books those which might be read with security and advantage were pronounced to be canonical; and his whole purpose was to furnish a catalogue of safe religious works, in order to guard against the hazard and detriment to which the minds of the ignorant and unskilful would be otherwise exposed. By canonical, therefore, he means nothing more than useful or expedient as a *rule* of life. The word will evidently bear this meaning. It is a general term, and, in itself considered, expresses no more than what is fit to be a rule, without any reference to the authority which prescribes it or the end to which it is directed. In its application to the inspired Scriptures it conveys the idea of an authoritative rule or standard of faith, simply because they can be a rule of no other kind. But there is nothing in the nature of the term itself which prevents it from being used to signify a *rule* for the conduct of life, collected either from the experience of the good, the observation of the wise or the reasoning of the learned. In this sense an uninspired composition may be eminently canonical—it may supply maxims of prudence for the judicious regulation of life, which, though they are commended by no Divine authority, are yet the dictates of truth and philosophy, and will be eagerly embraced by those who are anxious to walk circumspectly, and not as fools. We do no violence, then, to the language of Augustine when we assert that by canonical books, which he opposes to those that were dangerous and deceptive, he meant books which were calculated to edify by the useful rules which they furnished, without any reference to the sources, whether supernatural or human, from which they were derived.

This interpretation is strikingly confirmed by the grounds on which, as we have already seen, Augustine admitted the Maccabees to be canonical. It also reconciles the apparent contradiction when in the same sentence he declares them to be and not to be canonical. They were not canonical in the same sense in which the Law, the Prophets and the Psalms were canonical, but they were canonical in a subordinate sense, as stimulating piety by praiseworthy examples.

Having ascertained the opinions of Augustine, we are now prepared to inquire into the meaning of the Council of Carthage. It seems from the testimony of Ruffinus that the African churches were accustomed to read other books for the public instruction of the faithful—such, for instance, as the Shepherd of Hermas—besides those which were held to be inspired. As many works were published under fallacious and deceitful titles, and were current under the name of *Divine Scriptures*, it was thought proper, in order to guard the churches against every composition of this kind, to draw up a list containing all the works which might be safely and profitably read. To furnish a catalogue of this sort was, I apprehend, the sole design of the forty-seventh canon. And for the purpose of securing uniformity in the public worship of God it was wise and judicious to consult the churches beyond the sea. This interpretation, which the language will obviously bear, saves the council from the folly, wickedness and disgrace of pronouncing the third book of Ezra to be inspired, and of contradicting the testimony of all the past ages of the Church on the subject of the sacred Canon. That this was the meaning is distinctly intimated in the very phraseology of the Council itself: " It is ordained that nothing but the canonical Scriptures be *read* in the Church under the name of *Divine Scriptures.*"

It is not said, Nothing shall be received as *inspired* by the
faithful, but, Nothing shall be *read*. Then in the close of
the Canon, as if to put the matter beyond the possibility
of doubt, it is added : " For the confirmation of this canon,
our brother and fellow-priest, Boniface, or the other bishops
of those parts, will take notice *that we have received from
our fathers these books to be read in the churches. The sufferings of the martyrs* may also *be read* when their anniver-
saries are celebrated."[1] This paragraph explains the decree.
We see from Athanasius, Jerome and Ruffinus *what* they
received from the fathers; and they expressly incorporate
uninspired legends, the sufferings of the martyrs, among the
books that may be read, showing that their object was to
regulate the public reading of the Church, and not to determine the Canon of inspiration.

This, accordingly, is the interpretation which distinguished
Romanists have themselves put upon the language of the
council. Cardinal Cajetan, at the close of his commentary
on the historical books of the Old Testament, observes:[2]

---

[1] Item placuit, ut præter Scripturas canonicas, nihil in Ecclesia legatur
sub nomine *Divinarum Scripturarum*. Sunt autem canonicæ Scripturæ,
Genesis, Exodus, Leviticus, Numeri, Deuteronomium, Jesus Nave, Judicum, Ruth, Regnorum libri quatuor, Paralipomenon libri duo, Job, Psal-
terium Davidicum, Salomonis libri quinque, libri duodecim Prophetarum,
Isaias, Jeremias, Ezechiel, Daniel, Tobias, Judith, Esther, Esdræ libri
duo, Macchabæorum libri duo. Novi autem Testamenti, Evangeliorum
libri quatuor, Actuum Apostolorum liber unus, Pauli Apostoli Epistolæ
tredecim, ejusdem ad Hebræos una, Petri Apostoli duæ, Johannis
Apostoli tres, Judæ Apostoli una, et Jacobi una, Apocalypsis Joannis
liber unus.

Hoc etiam fratri et consacerdoti nostro Bonifacio, vel aliis earum par-
tium Episcopis pro confirmando isto canone, innotescat, quia a patribus
ista accipimus in Ecclesia legenda. Liceat etiam legi passiones martyrum,
cum anniversarii dies eorum celebrantur.—*Con. Carth.*, iii., c. 47.

[2] Et hoc in loco terminamus commentaria Librorum Historialium V. T.
Nam reliqui (viz., Judith, Tobia, et Maccab. libri), a S. Hieronymo extra
canonicos libros supputantur, et inter Apocrypha locantur, cum libro Sapientiæ, Ecclesiastico, ut patet in Prologo Galeato. Nec turberis, Novitie,
si alicubi repereris libros istos inter canonicos supputari, vel in sacris conciliis, vel in sacris doctoribus. Nam ad Hieronymi limam reducenda sunt
tam verba conciliorum, quam doctorum; et juxta illius sententiam ad

"And here we close our commentaries of the historical books of the Old Testament. For the others (Judith, Tobit and Maccabees) are not reckoned by St. Jerome among the canonical books, but are placed among the Apocryphal, together with Wisdom and Ecclesiasticus, as is plain from the Prologus Galeatus. Let not the novice be disturbed if in other places he should find that these books were counted among the canonical, either by holy councils or holy doctors. For to the rule of Jerome the words as well of councils as of doctors must be reduced. And according to his opinion, these books and all similar ones in the Canon of the Bible are not canonical; that is, are not regular (or to be used as a rule) for confirming articles of faith, though they may be called *canonical*, that is, regular (or may be used as a rule), for the edification of the faithful, and are received and authorized in the Canon of the Bible only for this end;" and with this distinction, he informs us, we are to understand St. Austin and the Council of Carthage. So that, upon the showing of one of the Trent doctors—a man who was reputed to be the very prince of theologians—the Council of Carthage makes nothing in your favour. It was not treating of the Canon of inspiration, but of the canon for public reading.[1]

4. Passing over your citations from Pope Siricius and Julius Firmicus Maternus as presenting nothing worthy of a reply, I shall make a few remarks upon Ephrem the Syrian, *the Prophet of the whole world and the Lyre of the Holy Ghost.* That he has *quoted* the Apocrypha admits of no question: that he believed them to be inspired is quite

Chrom. et Heliod. Episcopos, libri isti (et si qui alii sunt in canone Bibliæ similes) non sunt canonici, hoc est, non sunt Regulares ad firmandum ea quæ sunt Fidei; possunt tamen dici *canonici*, hoc est, Regulares ad ædificationem fidelium, utpote in canone Bibliæ ad hoc recepti et authorati. Cum hoc enim distinctione discernere poteris et dicta Augustini in 2 de Doctr. Christiana, que scripta in Conc. Flor. sub Eug. 4, scripta que in provincialibus Conciliis Carthag. et Laodic. et ab Innocentio, ac Gelasio Pontificibus.—*Cajetan in lib. Esther*, sub finem.

[1] See Bingham's Origines Ecclesiast., lib. xiv., c. 3, § 16.

a different matter, and one in reference to which you have produced not a particle of proof. There are two facts, however, which you have thought proper to pass without notice, that create a very strong presumption, if they do not amount to a positive proof, against the position which you have undertaken to sustain:

(1.) Ephrem repeatedly asserts that Malachi was the *last of the Prophets*.[1] Therefore no books written subsequently to his time could have been inspired; and therefore nearly the whole of the Apocrypha must be excluded from the Canon.

(2.) Ephrem, though he commented upon all of the canonical, wrote no commentary upon any of the Apocryphal, books.[2] Why does he omit Baruch in commenting upon Jeremiah? And why omit the Song of the Three Children, the story of Susannah and the story of Bel and the Dragon, if he believed that these works were parts respectively of Jeremiah and Daniel, and entitled to equal authority with

---

[1] Judæorum sacrificia prophetæ declarant immunda fuisse. Quæ ergo Esaias hoc loco hominum canumve cadaveribus æquiparat, Malachias, Prophetarum ultimus, animalium retrimenta vocat, non offerenda Deo, sed offerentium in ora cum approbatione rejicienda. (Malach. ii. 3.)—*Comment. in Es.*, lxvi. 3, T. ii., Syr. p. 94, C. D. Malachias, omnium Prophetarum postremus, populo commendat legem, et legis coronidem Joannem, quem Eliam cognominat.—*Comm. in Malach.*, iv. 4, *ib.* p. 315, c.

[2] Hebedjesu Chaldæus, è Nestorianorum secta Episcopus Sobensis, in catalogo Scriptorum Syrorum, num. 51 Ephræmi opera enumerat, his verbis: *Ephræm magnus, qui Syrorum Propheta cognominatus est, edidit commentaria in libros Genesis, Exodi, Sacerdotum* (Levitici), *Josue filii Nun, Judicum, Samuelis* (primum et secundum Regum), *in Librum Regum* (tertium et quartum), *Davidis* (Psalmorum), *Isaiæ, Duodecim* (minorum Prophetarum), *Jeremiæ, Exechielis, et Beati Danielis. Habet etiam Libros, et Epistolas de Fide, et Ecclesia. Edidit quoque Orationes Metricas, Hymnos, et Cantica: Cantusque omnes Defunctorum: et Lucubrationes ordine Alphabetico: et Disputationem adversùs Judæos: necnon adversùs Simonem, et Bardesanem, et contra Marcionem, atque Ophitas: demùm solutionem impietatis Juliani.* Ubi Hebedjesu ea dumtaxat Ephræmi opera recenset, quæ ipse legit, vel ad manus habuit. Nam Ephræmum alia plura edidisse, quàm quæ hic numerantur, certum est ex auctoribus suprà relatis, et ex codice nostro Syriaco iii. in quo habentur commentaria ejusdem in Numeros, in Deuteronomium, etc.—*Assem., Biblioth. Orient.*, vol. i., p. 58.

the rest of the books? Asseman informs us [1] that the corrupt additions to Daniel were not contained in the vulgar
Syriac Bible, though they were subsequently added from
Greek copies, and your own citations abundantly prove that
they were known to Ephrem. He must, therefore, have
passed them over by design. His references to them show
that he held them to be historically true and practically
useful. Why, then, sever them in his commentaries from
the books to which they were generally attached, and of
which they were supposed to be a part? I know of but
one answer that can be given, and that is, that he followed
the Hebrew Canon.

5. Your appeal is just as unfortunate to the great Basil,
bishop of Cæsarea. Several of your citations are taken
from that portion of the treatise against Eunomius which
is not universally admitted to be genuine. The last two
books have been called into question. Still, upon the principles which have been repeatedly explained, the strongest
quotations which you have been able to extract from the
writings of this Father do not establish the Divine authority
of those books of the Apocrypha which he chose to accommodate. We have, however, positive evidence that he admitted as inspired only the books which were acknowledged
by the Jews. In the Philocalia, or Hard Places of Scripture, collected by him and Gregory Nazianzen out of Origen's
works, he proposes the question,[2] "Why were only twenty-

---

[1] Quæ D. Hieronymus ex Theodotione transtulit Danielis capita, nimi-
rùm Canticum trium puerorum, cap. 3, à vers. 24, ad vers. 91, Historiam
Susannæ, cap. 13, Bel idoli et Draconis, atque Danielis in locum leonum
missi, cap. 14, ea et Ephræm Hebræcum Textum sequutus, in hisce com-
mentariis tacitus præteriit. Hæc enim in vulgata Syrorum versione haud
extabant; licet postea ex Græcis exemplaribus in sermonem Syriacum à
recentioribus Interpretibus conversa fuerint.—*Assem., Biblioth. Orient.*,
vol. i., p. 72.

And yet Gregory Nyssen, as cited by Asseman, tom. i., p. 56, says that
Ephrem commented upon the *whole Bible!* Could these additions to
Daniel, then, have been a part of it?

[2] Quare xxii. Libri Divinitius inspirati? Respondeo, Quoniam in
numerorum loco, etc. Neque enim ignorandum est quòd V. T. libri (ut

two books divinely inspired?" He then goes on to tell us that, "as twenty-two letters (the number of the Hebrew alphabet) form the introduction to wisdom, so twenty-two books of Scripture are the basis and introduction of Divine wisdom and the knowledge of things."

Again, in the second book against Eunomius, having quoted the passage in the eighth chapter of Proverbs, "The Lord possessed me in the beginning of his days," Basil observes[1] that "it is *but once* found in all the Bible," as Eusebius had done before. And yet, if Ecclesiasticus is a part of the Bible, the statement is false, for substantially the very same thing is declared in the ninth verse of the twenty-fourth chapter of Ecclesiasticus. In fact, Bellarmine has represented Basil[2] as quoting it in the fourth book against Eunomius, from Ecclesiasticus, and because the Father there attributes it to Solomon, the Jesuit has inferred that he ascribed the Wisdom of Sirach to the monarch of Israel. It is plain, however, that Basil had reference to Proverbs, and Proverbs only.

6. Your next witness is Chrysostom, who, you have succeeded in proving, held the Apocrypha to be Scripture, and, if you please, Divine Scripture; but you have nowhere shown that he believed them to be inspired. On the contrary, he himself affirms in his homilies on Genesis[3] that "all the inspired books of the Old Testament were originally written in the *Hebrew tongue*." How many of those in dispute were written in this language? Again, in another

Hebræi tradunt) viginti et duo, quibus æqualis est numerus Elementorum Hebræorum. Non abs re sint. Ut enim xxii. Literæ introductio ad sapientiam, etc., ita ad sapientiam Dei, et rerum notitiam fundamentum sunt et introductio Libri Scripturæ duo et viginti.—*Philoc.*, c. 3, as quoted by Cosin. In margin p. 66.

[1] Ἅπαξ ἐν πάσαις ταῖς γραφαῖς εἴρηται· Κύριος ἔκτισε με.—*S. Bas., Adv. Eunom.*

[2] Bellar., De Ver. Dei, lib. i., c. xiv.

[3] Πᾶσαι αἱ θεῖαι βίβλοι τῆς παλαιᾶς Διαθήκης τῇ Ἑβραίων γλώττῃ ἐξ ἀρχῆς ἦσαν συντεθειμέναι, καὶ τοῦτο πάντες ἂν ἡμῖν συνομολογήσαιεν.—*Chrys. in Genes.*, Hom. 4.

place,[1] he acknowledges no other books but those which Ezra was said to have collected, and which were subsequently translated by the seventy-two Elders, acknowledged by Christ, and spread by His Apostles. But, according to your own account of the matter, Ezra collected only the books which the Jews received. Therefore Chrysostom admitted none but the Hebrew Canon. If he sometimes quoted Ecclesiasticus and Wisdom, or any other books of the Apocrypha, as the Word of God, it is evidently in the same loose way and on the same principle on which these works were ascribed to Solomon or others of the ancient Prophets. Their sentiments were approved, and their doctrine supposed to be consistent with Scripture.

7. In regard to Ambrose, bishop of Milan, all that I shall say is, that the same process of argument by which you would make him canonize the books that Rome acknowledges will also make him canonize a book which Rome rejects, which, according to Sixtus of Sienna, no Father had ever received, and which, according to Bellarmine, is disfigured with idle fables—the dreams of Rabbins and Talmudists.

His language is just as strong, pointed and precise in reference to the fourth book of Esdras as it is in reference to Tobit, Wisdom, Ecclesiasticus or Judith. In his book De Bono Mortis, having quoted the thirty-second verse of the seventh chapter of the fourth book of Esdras, Ambrose adds in the next chapter:[2] "We do not fear that end due to all, in which Esdras finds the reward of his devotion—God saying to him," etc.; and again, "Esdras *revealed* ac-

[1] Ἑτέρῳ πάλιν ἀνδρὶ θαυμαστῷ ἐνέπνευσεν, ὥστε αὐτὰς ἐκθέσθαι, τῷ Ἐσδρᾳ λέγω, καὶ ἀπὸ λειψάνων συντεθῆναι ἐποίησε. Μετὰ δὲ τοῦτο ᾠκονόμησεν ἑρμηνευθῆναι αὐτὰς ὑπὸ τῶν ἑβδομήκοντα· ἡρμήνευσαν ἐκεῖνοι. Παρεγένετο ὁ Χριστὸς, δέχεται αὐτὰς, οἱ ἀπόστολοι εἰς πάντας αὐτὰς διασπείρουσι, σημεῖα ἐποίησε καὶ θαύματα ὁ Χριστός.—*Chrys. in Hebr.*, Hom. viii.

[2] Non vereamur illum debitum omnibus finem, in quo Esdras remunerationem suæ devotionis invenit, dicente ei Domino, etc. Quis utique prior, Esdras, an Plato? nam Paulus Esdræ, non Platonis sequutus est dicta. Esdras revelavit secundum collatam in se revelationem, justos futuros cum Christo, futuros et cum sanctis.

cording to the *revelation imparted* to him;" and still again,
"Who was the elder, Esdras or Plato? For Paul followed
the sayings of Esdras, and not of Plato." Now, if Ambrose
could treat Esdras as a prophet who received a revelation
to be communicated to others, and yet not really believe
him to be inspired—if his language, in this case, must be
understood in a subordinate and modified sense—why not
understand him in the same way when he applies a similar
phraseology to the other books of the Apocrypha? Ambrose, if *strictly* interpreted, proves too much, even for the
Jesuits. They are obliged to soften his expressions, and in
doing so they completely destroy the argument by which
they would make him canonize the books which Trent has
inserted in the Sacred Library. As to his quoting Wisdom
and Ecclesiasticus under the name of Solomon, that proves
nothing, since he has distinctly informed us[1] that Solomon
was the author of only three books—Proverbs, Ecclesiastes
and Canticles.

8. It is unnecessary to dwell upon your citations from
Paulinus of Nola, as they involve only the same argument
which has been so frequently refuted; and the testimony of
Augustine, your last witness, has been abundantly considered already.

It now remains to sum up the result of this whole investigation. You undertook to prove that Rome was not
guilty of arrogance and blasphemy in adding to the Word
of God—in other words, you undertook to prove that the
Apocrypha *were inspired*. For this purpose you brought
forward *four* arguments, which I shall collect in the syllo-
gistic form.

1. The first was, Whatsoever Rome, being infallible, declares to be inspired, must be inspired.

[1] Unde et Salomonis tres libri ex plurimis videntur electi : Ecclesiastes
de naturalibus, Cantica Canticorum de mysticis, Proverbia de moralibus.—
In Ps. xxxvi., pr. t. i., p. 777. Quid etiam tres libri Salomonis, unus de
Proverbiis, alius Ecclesiastes, tertius de Canticis Canticorum, nisi trinæ
hujus ostendunt nobis Sapientiæ sanctum Salomonem fuisse solertem?—
In Lucam, pr. t. i., p. 1262, A.

Rome declares that the Apocrypha are so.

Therefore the Apocrypha must be inspired.

In a series of Essays I completely and triumphantly refuted the major; so that this argument, which was the keystone of the arch, fell to the ground.

2. Your second was, Whatsoever books Christ and His Apostles quoted must be inspired.

Christ and His Apostles quoted the Apocrypha.

Therefore the Apocrypha must be inspired.

Both premises of this syllogism were proved to be false; so that *it* is not only dead, but *twice* dead, plucked up by the roots.

3. Your third was, Whatever books were incorporated in the ancient versions of the Bible must be inspired.

The Apocrypha were so incorporated.

Therefore the Apocrypha must be inspired.

The major was shown to be without foundation, and contradicted by notorious facts.

4. Your fourth and last was, Whatever the Fathers have quoted as Scripture, Divine Scripture, etc., must be inspired.

They have so quoted the Apocrypha.

Therefore the Apocrypha must be inspired.

Here again the major was shown to be false, as these were only general expressions for religious literature, whether inspired or human. The result, then, of the whole matter is, that in three instances your conclusion is drawn from a single premiss, and in one case from no premises at all. Upon this foundation stand the claims of the Apocryphal books to a place in the Canon.

LETTER XVIII.

REAL TESTIMONY OF THE PRIMITIVE CHURCH.

HAVING now shown that Rome has utterly failed in producing a particle of proof in favour of her adulterated canon, I proceed to vindicate my original assertion, that, for four centuries, the unbroken testimony of the Christian Church is against the inspiration of the Apocryphal books. During all that period there is not only no intimation of what you have asserted to be true, that Christ and His Apostles delivered them to the faithful as a part of the Divine Rule of Faith, but there is a large amount of clear, positive and satisfactory evidence that no such event could possibly have taken place.

The testimony of the Primitive Church presents itself to us under two aspects: It is either negative, consisting in the exclusion of the disputed books from professed catalogues of Scripture; or positive, consisting in explicit declarations on the part of distinguished Fathers that they were not regarded as inspired. These two classes of proof I shall treat promiscuously, and adduce them both in the order of time.

1. Little more than half a century after the death of the last of the Apostles, flourished Melito, bishop of Sardis, one of the seven churches to which John, in the Apocalypse, was directed to write. Such was the distinguished reputation which this good man enjoyed that Polycrates, bishop of Ephesus, says of him that he was guided in all things by the Holy Ghost; and Tertullian not only praises "his elegant and oratorical genius," but adds that "he was esteemed by many as a prophet." The recorded opinions of such a man, living near enough to the times of the Apostles to have conversed with those who had listened to the Divine instructions of John, though not to be received as authority, are certainly evidence of a very high character. It so happens, in the providence of God, that we have a catalogue of the Sacred Books drawn up by him for his friend Onesimus, which he professes to have made with the utmost accuracy, after a full investigation of the subject. I shall suffer him to speak for himself: "Melito sends greeting to his brother Onesimus. Since in thy zeal for the Word thou hast often desired to have selections from the Law and the

Prophets concerning the Saviour and the whole of our faith, and hast also wished to obtain an exact statement of the ancient Books, how many they were in number and what was their arrangement, I took pains to effect this, understanding thy zeal for the faith and thy desire of knowledge in respect to the Word, and that, in thy devotion to God, thou esteemest these things above all others, striving after eternal salvation. Therefore, having come to the East and arrived at the place where these things were preached and done, and having accurately learned the books of the Old Testament, I have subjoined a list of them and sent it to thee. The names are as follows: of Moses, five books: namely, Genesis, Exodus, Leviticus, Numbers and Deuteronomy; Joshua, son of Nun, Judges, Ruth; four books of Kings, two of Chronicles, the Psalms of David, the Proverbs of Solomon, which is also called Wisdom, Ecclesiastes, Song of Songs and Job; of Prophets, the books of Isaiah and Jeremiah, writings of the twelve Prophets in one book, Daniel, Ezekiel, Ezra, from which I have made selections, distributing them into six books." [1]

This testimony, you inform us, [2] "corroborates the fact" that in the age of Melito "the practice of the Christian

---

[1] Μελίτων Ὀνησίμῳ τῷ ἀδελφῷ χαίρειν· ἐπειδή πολλάκις ἠξίωσας σπουδῇ τῇ πρὸς τὸν λόγον χρώμενος γενέσθαι σοι ἐκλογὰς, ἐκ τε τοῦ νόμου καὶ τῶν προφητῶν περὶ τοῦ σωτῆρος καὶ πάσης τῆς πίστεως ἡμῶν. ἔτι δὲ καὶ μαθεῖν τὴν τῶν παλαιῶν βιβλίων ἐβουλήθης ἀκρίβειαν, πόσα τὸν ἀριθμὸν καὶ ὁποῖα τὴν τάξιν εἶεν, ἐσπούδασα τὸ τοιοῦτο πρᾶξαι, ἐπιστάμενός σου τὸ σπουδαῖον περὶ τὴν πίστιν, καὶ φιλομαθὲς περὶ τὸν λόγον, ὅτι τε μάλιστα πάντων πόθῳ τῷ πρὸς θεὸν ταῦτα προκρίνεις, περὶ τῆς αἰωνίου σωτηρίας ἀγωνιζόμενος· ἀνελθὼν οὖν εἰς τὴν ἀνατολήν, καὶ ἕως τοῦ τόπου γενόμενος ἔνθα ἐκηρύχθη καὶ ἐπράχθη, καὶ ἀκριβῶς μαθὼν τὰ τῆς παλαιᾶς διαθήκης βιβλία ὑποτάξας ἐπέμψά σοι· ὧν ἐστὶ τὰ ὀνόματα· Μωϋσέως πέντε Γένεσις, Ἔξοδος, Λευιτικὸν, Ἀριθμοὶ, Δευτερονόμιον· Ἰησοῦς Ναυῆ, Κριταὶ, Ῥοὺθ· Βασιλειῶν τέσσαρα, Παραλειπομένων δύο. Ψαλμῶν Δαβίδ, Σολομῶνος Παροιμίαι, ἡ καὶ Σοφία, Ἐκκλησιαστής, Ἄσμα Ἀσμάτων, Ἰώβ· Προφητῶν, Ἡσαΐου, Ἱερεμίου τῶν δώδεκα ἐν μονοβίβλῳ, Δανιηλ, Ἰεζεκιηλ, Ἔσδρας. Ἐξ ὧν καὶ τὰς ἐκλογὰς ἐποιησάμην, εἰς ἓξ βιβλία διελών.—*Melito's Letter to Onesimus*, Euseb., B. iv., c. 26.

[2] "His testimony corroborates the fact, otherwise clearly proven, that at his day the practice of the Christian world was at variance with the opinion which he advanced."—*A. P. F.*, Lett. xiii.

world was at variance with the opinion which he advanced."
In other words, I understand you to assert that the Epistle
itself furnishes satisfactory proof that at the period in which
it was written a different canon of the Old Testament was
generally received from that which is presented in it.   But,
sir, in what part of the letter can this corroborating evidence
be found ?   Melitò evidently writes with the confidence of
a man who knew that he was possessed of the truth.   He
professes to give an exact statement of the names, number
and arrangement of the Sacred Books, and nowhere does he
drop the most distant hint that opposing sentiments were
held upon the subject, or that any other works had ever
been commended by any portion of Christendom as entitled
to equal veneration with those which he had enumerated.
How then does his testimony corroborate the fact that at
his day the practice of the Christian world was different
from the opinion which he advanced ?   Will the reader believe it ?[1]   Because he investigated the subject and formed
his conclusion from personal examination, it is confidently
inferred that the whole matter must previously have been
involved in uncertainty or doubt.   Sir, you have forgotten
your chronology.   That was an age of private judgment;
the Son of Perdition had not then enslaved the understandings of men.   Priestly authority was not received as a substitute for light, and the mere dicta of ghostly confessors
were not regarded as the oracles of God.   The easy art of
believing by proxy, which must always result in personal
damnation, was then wholly unknown.   Tremblingly alive
to the importance of truth, and deeply impressed with the
dangers of delusion, the faithful of that day felt the respon-

[1] " Melito, according to his own statement, came to the conclusion set
forth in his letter, after he had travelled into Palestine and had there
investigated the question. From this we are forced to infer that he had
not been taught in his youth at Sardis, and that it had not been made
known to him, even in his maturer years, while he was a priest, and perhaps the bishop of that church. It was precisely by his inquiries in Judea
that he was led to the opinion which he finally adopted."—A. P. F.,
Lett. xiii.

sibility that rested upon them to "try the spirits," "to prove all things, and hold fast that which was good." Hence, Melito determined to be guided only by evidence; and, acting in obedience to the apostolic injunction, wisely resolved to investigate the subject and to form his opinions upon accurate research. He accordingly visits the country whence the Gospel had sprung, traverses the region where Jesus had laboured, converses with the churches in which Apostles had taught, and ascertained the Books on which they were relying for the words of life.

As you are perfectly confident, however, that the testimony of Melito, commended as it is by his diligence and care, must be worthless because it is unfavourable to the interests of Rome, you invent three hypotheses,[1] by means of one of which you hope to obviate its natural result. It was either his object, according to you, to publish the Canon of the churches in Palestine, or to give that of the Jewish Synagogue, or to express his own private opinion that Christians should receive no other books of the Old Testament but those which were acknowledged by the Jews. If mere conjecture is to settle the matter, it is just as easy to make a fourth supposition—that his real design was to compare the faith of Asia and Palestine, and to give the Canon of the Christian world, so far as he was able to ascertain what it was. Let us, however, test the value of your three evasions.

(1.) If it were the object of Melito to state the books which the churches of Palestine believed to be inspired, we may regard it as settled that they received none but those which are contained in his list. Then, of course, *they* rejected the Apocrypha. Now, these churches were planted by the hands of the Apostles; they were the first fruits of

[1] "If, on the other hand, Melito, disregarding the practice of the Church, even in Palestine, and seduced by peculiar views on the authority and sanctions of the Jewish Canon, as opposed to the usage of the Church, intended in his letter to give us the Books contained in the Jewish Canon, manifestly his testimony does not touch the point before us at all."—*A. P. F.*, Lett. xiii.

the Christian ministry; and here, if anywhere, we should expect to find an accurate knowledge of the Books which the Apostles had prescribed as the rule of faith. Strange, very strange, if within sixty years after the last of the Sacred College had fallen asleep so little regard was paid to their instructions in the scene of their earliest labours that six entire works, together with divers fragments of others, had been ruthlessly torn from the inspired volume as delivered to these churches by their venerable founders! To say, as you have done,[1] that the Apostles, in tenderness to their early prejudices, permitted the Hebrew Christians to retain the Canon of the Jewish Church, to the exclusion of the Apocrypha, is to contradict what you have elsewhere said—that the Jews themselves entertained a profound respect for the disputed books, and would have admitted them into their sacred library if they had had the authority of a Prophet. These Jewish "*prejudices*," consequently, are a desperate expedient, invented solely for the purpose of reconciling the notorious faith of the churches in Judea with what Rome chooses to represent as apostolic teaching. You tell us in one breath that the Apostles delivered the Apocrypha to the primitive Christians as inspired, and then in the very next declare that they did not deliver them to the churches in Judea, because the stiff-necked children of Abraham would not receive them. But when the question was, Did the Jewish Church reject the Apocrypha from the sacred Canon? we were then informed that this was not the case—that it was a great admirer of the contested books, and would cheerfully have received them if it had been commissioned by a proper tribunal. It is certainly not a little singular that the Jews should be so warmly attached to the books as to be willing to canonize them upon suf-

[1] "The fact that a small portion of the universal Church, converts from Judaism, should cling to the observances of those ancestors whom they revered, and whom every hill and dale recalled to their minds, does not condemn other churches which, untrammelled by any such restrictions, unswayed by any such motives, walked boldly under the guidance of the Apostles."—*A. P. F.*, Lett. xiii.

ficient authority, and yet so violently prejudiced against them that the whole College of Apostles could not subdue their opposition. I have no knack at explaining riddles, and must therefore leave these high mysteries to those who can swallow transubstantiation. In the mean time I may be permitted to remark that the Apostles were not in the habit of surrendering truth to prejudice; and if the churches of Palestine knew nothing of their having endorsed the Apocrypha as inspired, the presumption is irresistible that no such thing ever took place. What they preached to the Gentiles they preached first to the Jews; and as to all the world they had proclaimed one Lord and one baptism, so they had likewise proclaimed only one faith.

(2.) Your second hypothesis, that Melito intended to state the Canon of the Jewish synagogue, and not of the Christian churches, is contradicted by his own words. How could the zeal of Onesimus in the faith be an inducement to give him only a part of its standard? And how would he be assisted in acquiring knowledge by being led into serious error? Onesimus desired an *exact statement* of the Books of the Old Testament. But, according to you, Melito furnishes him only with those books which the Jews received, and consequently omitted an important portion of the whole Old Testament. Yet Melito himself says that he had fully complied with the request of his friend. So that either your supposition must be false, or the good bishop, who, Polycrates says, was guided in all things by the Holy Ghost, was guilty of a falsehood.

(3.) Your third hypothesis, that he only intended to express his private opinion, in opposition to the prevailing practice of the Church, as to the books which *ought* to be received, hardly deserves a serious notice. That a man should travel from Sardis to Jerusalem to ascertain the documents which the apostolic churches held to be inspired, then give the result of his inquiries with the strongest expression of confidence, when his conclusions were notoriously at variance with the faith of the churches on which

he had relied—in other words, that he should entertain so
much respect for the opinion of the Hebrew and Eastern
churches as to make a long journey for the purpose of consulting them, and after all pay no attention to their opinions
at all—is a proposition too monstrous to be deliberately
maintained. I do not deny that Melito has given us
his private opinion, but I do deny that he has given an
opinion peculiar to himself. His own statement is certainly
worthy of credit; his object was to give (and he professes to
have done it) an exact account of the names, number and
arrangement of the books of the Old Testament. He fabricated no new canon for himself, but recorded the Books,
and all the Books, which the churches of the East believed
to be inspired. From Jerusalem to Sardis, consequently, in
all the churches planted by Apostles, there was but one
voice, about the middle of the second century, as to the
documents which compose the Old Testament; and that
voice, which may almost be regarded as a distant echo of the
preaching of the Twelve, condemns the Canon of Trent.

As to the objection that Melito has omitted the book of
Esther, I reply in the words of Eichhorn.[1] "It is true,"
says he, "that in this catalogue Nehemiah and Esther are
not mentioned; but whoever reads the passage and understands it will here discover both of them. Melito here arranges the books of the Old Testament manifestly according
to the time in which they were written or in which the facts
which they record occurred. Hence, he places Ruth after
the book of Judges, Daniel and Ezekiel towards the end of
his catalogue, and Ezra last of all, because he wrote after the
Babylonian captivity; and accordingly as he comprehended
the books of Samuel and Kings under the general appellation *books of Kings*, because they related to the history of
the Hebrew kingdom from Saul to Zedekiah, or until the
Babylonian captivity, in the same manner he appears to
comprise under the name of *Ezra* all historical books the
subjects of which occur in the times subsequent to the Baby-

[1] Vide Eich., Einleit., xli.

lonian captivity. As it is very common to include Ezra and Nehemiah in one book, why might not even Ezra, Nehemiah and Esther also have been regarded as a whole? If we add to this conjecture, that Nehemiah and Esther, according to Josephus, must have been parts of the Canon, and that Fathers of authority, such as Origen and Jerome, expressly enumerate both in it, no impartial inquirer can well doubt that even Melito does not reject from the Canon of the Old Testament the two books mentioned."

To this it may be added that, according to any of your three hypotheses which have just been considered, Esther must have been included. If Melito intended to state the Canon of the Hebrew Christians—and that, as you have said, coincided with the Canon of the Jewish Church—this book was confessedly a part. It was also acknowledged by the Jewish Synagogue,[1] and any private opinions in opposition to the practice of the Christian Church which Melito might have been induced to form from his intercourse with the Jews could not have led him to reject its authority. Your conjecture that he forgot to mention it is, when we consider his pretensions to accuracy, wholly incredible. As therefore it must have been included, the account which Eichhorn has given of the matter is probably the true explanation. In this opinion he is sustained by Cosin, a man as learned as himself.

2. The next writer to whom I shall appeal—and you have pronounced his eulogy—is Origen. Eusebius says of him that "in expounding the first Psalm he has given a catalogue of the sacred Books in the Old Testament, writing as follows:[2] 'Let it not be unknown that the canonical books,

[1] Vide Cosin, Scholast. Hist. Can., p. 33.

[2] Τὸν μὲν τοίγε πρῶτον ἐξηγούμενος Ψαλμὸν, ἔκθεσιν πεποίηται ['Ωριγένης] τοῦ τῶν ἱερῶν γραφῶν τῆς παλαιᾶς διαθήκης καταλόγου, ὧδέ πως γράφων κατὰ λέξιν· Οὐκ ἀγνοητέον δ᾽ εἶναι τὰς ἐνδιαθήκους βίβλους, ὡς Ἑβραῖοι παραδιδόασιν, δύο καὶ εἴκοσι· ὅσος ὁ ἀριθμὸς τῶν παρ᾽ αὐτοῖς στοιχείων ἐστίν· εἶτα μετά τινα, ἐπιφέρει λέγων· Εἰσὶ δὲ αἱ εἴκοσι δύο βίβλοι καθ᾽ Ἑβραίους αἵδε· ἡ παρ᾽ ἡμῖν Γένεσις ἐπιγεγραμμένη, παρὰ δὲ Ἑβραίοις ἀπὸ τῆς ἀρχῆς τῆς βίβλου Βρησίθ, ὅπερ ἐστιν ἐν ἀρχῇ· Ἔξοδος, Οὐαλεσμώθ, ὅπέρ ἐστι ταῦτα τὰ ὀνόματα· Λευιτικὸν

as the Hebrews transmit them, are twenty-two; for such is
the number of letters among them.'" A little farther on,
he adds, "These are the twenty-two books of the Hebrews:
the Book called Genesis with us, but among the Hebrews,
from the beginning of the Book, Bereshith, which means,
In the Beginning: Exodus, Valmoth, that is, These are the
Names: Leviticus, Vaikra, And he Called: Numbers, Am-
misphekodeum: Deuteronomy, Ellahhaddebarim, These are
the Words: Jesus, the Son of Nave, Joshua Ben Nun:
Judges, Ruth, with them united in one book called Sophetim: Kings, first and second, with them, in one called
Samuel, the Called of God: the third and fourth of Kings,
in one book, Vahammelech Dabid, that is, the Kingdom of
David: the first and second of Chronicles, in one book
called Dibre Hiamim, that is, the Records of Days: the
first and second of Esdras, in one book, called Ezra, that is,
The Assistant: the Book of Psalms, Sepher Tehillim: the
Proverbs of Solomon, Misloth: Ecclesiastes, Koheleth: the
Song of Songs, Sir Hasirim: Esaias, Jesaia: Jeremiah, with
the Lamentations and his Epistle, in one volume, Jeremiah:
Daniel, Daniel: Ezekiel, Iesekel: Job, Job: Esther, Esther:
beside these, there are also the Maccabees, which are inscribed Sarbeth Sarbaneel." In this catalogue the book of
the twelve minor Prophets is omitted through a mistake of
the transcriber. It is supplied both by Nicephorus and
Ruffinus. By the Epistle of Jeremiah we are not to understand the apocryphal letter, for the Jews never received that

ὀνϊκρὰ, καὶ ἐκάλεσεν· 'Ἀριθμὸι 'Ἀμμεσφεκοδείμ, Δευτερονόμιον ῞Ελλε ἀλδεβαρὶμ,
οὗτοι ὁι λόγοι· 'Ἰησοὺς υἱὸς Ναῦη, 'Ἰωσοῦε βὲν Νοῦν· Κριταὶ, 'Ῥοὺθ, παρ' αὑτοῖς
ἐν ἑνὶ Σωφετίμ. βασιλειῶν πρώτη, δευτέρα, παρ' αὑτοῖς ἐν Σαμουήλ, ὁ θεόκλητος·
βασιλειῶν τρίτη, τετάρτη ἐν ἑνί Οὐαμμέλεχ Δαβίδ, ὑπέρ ἐστι βασιλεία Δαβίδ.
Παραλειπομένων πρώτη, δευτέρα, ἐν ἑνὶ Διβρὴ αἱαμὶμ, ὑπέρ ἐστι λόγοι ἡμέρων·
'Ἐσδρας πρῶτος καὶ δεύτερος ἐν ἑνὶ, 'Ἐζρᾶ, ὁ ἐστι βοηθός· βίβλος Ψαλμῶν Σέφερ
θιλλίμ. Σολομῶντος Παροιμίαι Μισλώθ, 'Ἐκκλησιαστὴς, Κωέλεθ· 'Ἀσμα 'Ἀσμάτων, Σὶρ ἀσσιρίμ. 'Ἡσαίας, 'Ἰεσαιά, 'Ἰερεμίας σὺν Θρήνοις καὶ τῇ ἐπιστολῇ, ἐν
ἑνὶ 'Ἰρμία. Δανιὴλ, Δανιήλ. 'Ἰεζεκιὴλ, Ιεεζκήλ. 'Ἰὼβ 'Ἰώβ. 'Ἐσθὴρ, 'Ἐσθὴρ. ἐξω
δέ τούτων ἐστὶ τὰ Μακκαβαϊκὰ, ἅπερ ἐπιγέγραπται Σαρβὴθ Σαρβανὲ 'Ἐλ.—
Origen., Can. fr. Euseb. Eccl. Hist., vi. 25.

as canonical, but the one which occurs in the twenty-ninth chapter of the book of his Prophecy.

Such then is Origen's catalogue, in which, although he has followed the Jews, for they are the only safe guides on this subject, he has given, according to Eusebius, "the books in the Sacred Scriptures of the Old Testament." It is expressly stated that the Maccabees are *out of the Canon;* and of the other works in the Apocrypha not a syllable is mentioned.

The Epistle to Julius Africanus,[1] upon which you have relied to make Origen contradict himself, does not assert the Divine inspiration of the story of Susannah, but vindicates it simply as a historical narrative from the charge of being a fabulous imposture. Africanus had asserted the book to be a fiction, grossly spurious and utterly unworthy of credit. It was from this accusation that Origen defended it, and showed conclusively that some of the reasoning which his friend adopted, if carried out into its legitimate results, would sadly mutilate even the records which the Jews acknowledged. The Church had permitted this story *to be read,* and Origen maintains its substantial authenticity, in order that the Church might not be subject to the odious imputation of having given to her children fables for truth. Such books were recommended to the faithful as valuable helps to their personal improvement. This was evidently done upon the supposition that the facts which they contained were worthy of credit; and as this was, perhaps, the general belief, in which Africanus could not concur, Origen merely intended to prove that it was not at least without some foundation.

It is true that this Father has freely quoted the Apocryphal books under the same titles which are usually bestowed on the canonical Scriptures. So also has he quoted in the same way the spurious prophecy of Enoch, the Shepherd of Hermas, the Acts of Paul and the Gospel according to the Hebrews. He has even gone so far, in reference to the

[1] Vide Opera Origen, vol. i., p. 10, seq.

Shepherd, as to say that this Scripture was, as he supposed, *divinely inspired.*[1] I cannot believe, however, that Origen intended to convey the idea that this mystical medley should be entitled to equal veneration with the Prophets, Apostles and Evangelists. He simply meant to commend the heavenly and holy impulses under which, as he conceived, the work had been written. From incidental expressions of this sort, which are often nothing but terms of respect, we are not to gather the real position which, in the opinions of those who use them, a book is to occupy in relation to the Canon of supernatural inspiration. There is nothing, consequently, to diminish the value or obviate the force of the plain and pointed testimony which Origen has given to the books of the Old Testament in a formal catalogue in which they are professedly numbered and arranged.

3. I shall now give the Canon of Athanasius, which may be found in his Festal Epistle.[2] "For I fear," says he, "lest some few of the weaker sort should be seduced from

---

[1] Puto tamen, quod Hermas iste sit scriptor libelli illius, qui Pastor appellatur: quæ scriptura valde mihi utilis videtur, et ut puto, divinitus inspirata.—*Explan. Rom.* xvi. 14.

[2] 'Επειδήπερ τινὲς ἐπεχείρησαν ἀνατάξασθαι ἑαυτοῖς τὰ λεγόμενα 'Απόκρυφα καὶ ἐπιμίξαι ταῦτα τῇ θεοπνεύστῳ γραφῇ περὶ ἧς ἐπληροφορήθμεν, καθὼς παρέδοσαν τοῖς πατράσιν οἱ ἀπ' ἀρχῆς αὐτόπται καὶ ὑπηρέται γενόμενοι τοῦ λόγου· ἐδοξε κἀμοὶ προτραπέντι παρὰ γνησίων ἀδελφῶν καὶ μαθόντι ἄνωθεν, ἑξῆς ἐκθέσθαι τὰ Κανονιζόμενα καὶ παραδοθέντα πιστευθέντα τε θεῖα εἶναι βιβλία· ἵνα ἕκαστος, εἰ μὲν ἠπατήθη, καταγνῷ τῶν πλανησάντων· ὁ δὲ καθαρὸς διαμείνας χαίρῃ πάλιν ὑπομιμνησκόμενος. Ἐστι τοίνυν τῆς μὲν παλαιᾶς διαθήκης βιβλία τῷ ἀριθμῷ τὰ πάντα 'Εικοσιδύο. Τοσαῦτα γὰρ, ὡς ἤκουσα, καὶ τὰ στοιχεῖα τὰ παρ' Εβραίοις εἶναι παραδέδοται, τῇ δὲ τάξει καὶ τῷ ὀνόματί ἐστιν ἕκαστον οὕτω· Πρῶτον Γένεσις, εἶτα 'Εξοδος, εἶτα Λευιτικὸν, καὶ μετὰ τοῦτο 'Αριθμοὶ, καὶ λοιπὸν τὸ Δευτερονόμιον· ἑξῆς δὲ τούτοις ἐστὶν Ιησοῦς ὁ τοῦ Ναυῆ, καὶ Κριτάι. Καὶ μετὰ τοῦτο ἡ Ροὺθ. Καὶ πάλιν ἑξῆς Βασιλειῶν τέσσαρα βιβλία· καὶ τούτων τὸ μὲν πρῶτον καὶ δεύτερον εἰς ἐν βιβλίον ἀριθμεῖται· τὸ δὲ τρίτον καὶ τέταρτον ὁμοίως εἰς ἐν. Μετὰ δὲ ταῦτα Παραλειπομένων ά καὶ β' ὁμοίως εἰς ἐν βιβλίον πάλιν ἀριθμούμενα. Ἐιτα Εσδρὰς ά καὶ β' ὁμοίως εἰς ἐν. Μετὰ δὲ ταῦτα βίβλος Ψαλμῶν, καὶ ἑξῆς Παροιμίαι. Ἐιτα 'Εκκλησιαστὴς καὶ 'Ασμα 'Ασματων. Πρὸς τούτοις ἐστὶ καὶ Ιὼβ, καὶ λοιπὸν Προφῆται, οἱ μὲν δώδεκα εἰς ἐν βιβλίον ἀριθμούμενοι. Ἐιτα Ησαίας, Ιερεμίας καὶ σὺν αὐτῷ Βαροὺχ, Θρῆνοι, Επιστολὴ, καὶ μετ' αὐτὸν Εζεκιὴλ καὶ Δανιὴλ. 'Αχρι τούτων τὰ τῆς παλαιᾶς διαθήκης ἴσταται.—*Athanas. Opp.,* tom. ii. p. 38.

their simplicity and purity by the cunning of some men, and at last be led to make use of other books called *Apocryphal*, being deceived by the similarity of their names, which are like those of the true books. I therefore entreat you to forbear if I write to remind you of what you already know, because it is necessary and profitable to the Church. Now, while I am about to remind you of these things, to excuse my undertaking, I will make use of the example of Luke the Evangelist, saying also myself—'Forasmuch as some have taken in hand to set forth writings called *Apocryphal*, and to write them with the God-inspired Scripture in which we have full confidence, as they who from the first were eye-witnesses and ministers of the Word delivered them to the Fathers, it has seemed good to me, after consulting with the true brethren and inquiring from the beginning, to set forth those books which are canonical, which have been handed down to us and are believed to be Divine, so that every one who has been deceived may condemn his deceivers, and that he who remains pure may rejoice when again put in remembrance of these. All the books of the Old Testament are two and twenty in number; for, as I have heard, that is the order and number of the Hebrew letters. To name them, they are as follows: the first Genesis, the next Exodus, then Leviticus, after that the Numbers, and then Deuteronomy; next to them is Jesus the son of Nave, and Judges; after that Ruth; and again, the next in order, are the four books of the Kingdoms—of these the first and second are reckoned one book, and, in like manner, the third and fourth are one book; after them the first and second of the Remains, or Chronicles, are in like manner accounted one book; then the first and second of Esdras, also reckoned one book; after them the book of the Psalms; then the Proverbs, Ecclesiastes and the Song of Songs; besides these there is Job, and at length the Prophets; the twelve are reckoned one book; then Isaiah and Jeremiah, and with him, Baruch, the Lamentations, the Epistle; and after them Ezekiel and Daniel. Thus far the books of the Old Testament.'" Having given the

Canon of the New Testament, he proceeds : " For the sake of greater accuracy, I will add—and the addition is necessary—that there are also other books besides these, not indeed admitted into the Canon, but ordained by the Fathers to be read by such as have recently come over to us, and who wish to receive instruction in the doctrine of piety—the Wisdom of Solomon, the Wisdom of Sirach, and Esther, and Judith, and Tobit, the Doctrine of the Apostles, as it is called, and the Shepherd."

To the same purport is the account which is given in the Synopsis of Scripture, which is usually quoted under the name of Athanasius.[1] "All the Scripture of us Christians is divinely inspired. It contains not indefinite, but rather determined and canonized, books. These belong to the Old Testament." Then follows the same enumeration which has just been extracted from the Paschal Epistle. It is afterwards added : " But besides these there are other books of the same Old Testament, *not canonical*, but only read by (or to) the catechumens. Such are the Wisdom of Solomon, the Wisdom of Jesus the son of Sirach, Esther, Judith and Tobit. *These are not canonical.*"

The canonical book of Esther, though not particularly numbered in these catalogues, is included under the general name of Ezra. The additions to it, however, are expressly mentioned and repudiated ; for the Esther which is proscribed by name is not the book which the Jews received, but the one which opens with the dream of Mordecai. In this Synopsis, Athanasius not only gives a *list* of the books, but inserts the sentence with which each of them begins, in

---

[1] Πασα γραφὴ ἡμῶν χριστιανῶν θεόπνευστός ἐστιν, οὐκ ἀόριστα δὲ, ἀλλὰ μᾶλλον ὡρισμένα καὶ κεκανονισμένα ἔχει τὰ βιβλία. Καὶ ἐστι τῆς μὲν παλαιᾶς διαθήκης ταῦτα. . . . Εκτὸς δὲ τούτων εἰσὶ πάλιν ἕτερα βίβλία τῆς αὐτῆς παλαιᾶς διαθήκης. ὸν κανονιζόμενα μὲν, ἀναγινωσκόμενα δὲ μόνον τοῖς κατηχουμένοις ταῦτα· Σοφία Σολομῶντος, Σοφία Ιησοῦ υἱοῦ Σιρὰχ, Εσθὴρ· Ιουδὴθ, Τωβῖτ. Τοσᾶντα καὶ τὰ μὴ κανονιζόμενα. Τινὲς μέντοι τῶν παλαιῶν ἐιρήκασι κανονίζεσθαι παρ' Εβραίοις καὶ τὴν Εσθὴρ· καὶ τὴν μὲν Ροὺθ, μετὰ τῶν Κριτῶν ἑνουμένην, ἐις ἓν βιβλίον ἀριθμεῖσθαι, τὴν δὲ Εσθὴρ ἐις ἕτερον ἐν. καὶ οὕτω πάλιν ἐις ἔικοσι δύο συμπληροῦσθαι τὸν ἀριθμὸν τῶν κανονιζομένων παρ' αυτῖις ,βι,βλίων.—*Athan.* Opp. ii., pp. 96–98.

order that they might be easily identified, and he expressly
tells us that the Esther which he means commences in the
manner which has just been specified. We are, therefore, at
no loss to determine what he intended to condemn and repudiate under the title of *Esther*. The name of Baruch occurs
in these catalogues, as it does also in those of Cyril and the
Council of Laodicea, but it is only a fuller expression for
the book of Jeremiah. "For Baruch's name," says Bishop
Cosin,[1] "is famous in Jeremy, whose disciple and scribe he
was, suffering the same persecution and banishment that
Jeremy did, and publishing the same words and prophecies
that Jeremy had required him to write, so that in several
relations a great part of the book may be attributed to them
both. And very probable it is that for this reason the
Fathers that followed Origen did not only, after his example, join the Lamentations and the Epistle to Jeremy, but
the name of Baruch besides, whereby they intended nothing
else (as by keeping themselves precisely to the number of
twenty-two books only is clear) than what was inserted concerning Baruch in the book of Jeremy itself."

4. Hilary,[2] bishop of Poitiers in France, thus enumerates the books of the Old Testament, which, he assures us,
according to the tradition of the ancients, amounted to
twenty-two: "Five of Moses; Joshua the son of Nun, the
sixth; Judges and Ruth, the seventh; first and second

---

[1] Vide Cosin, Scholast. Hist., p. 59.

[2] Et ea causa est, ut in viginti duos libros lex Testamenti Veteris depute-
tur, ut cum literarum numero convenirent. Qui ita secundùm traditiones
veterum deputantur, ut Moysi sint libri quinque; Jesu Naue sextus;
Judicum et Ruth septimus; primus et secundus Regnorum in octavum,
tertius et quartus in nonum; Paralipomenon duo in decimum sint, ser-
mones dierum. Esdræ in undecimum; Liber Psalmorum in duodeci-
mum; Salomonis Proverbia, Ecclesiastes, Canticum Canticorum in tertium
decimum, et quartum decimum, et quintum decimum; duodecim autem
Prophetæ in sextum decimum; Esaias deinde et Jeremias cum Lamenta-
tione et Epistola; sed et Daniel, et Ezechiel, et Job, et Hester, viginti et
duum librorum numerum consumment. Quibusdam autem visum est,
additis Tobia et Judith viginti quatuor libros secundum numerum Græ-
carum literarum connumerare.—*Hilari, Prologo in Psalmos,* § xv., p. 9.

Kings, the eighth; third and fourth Kings, the ninth; two books of Chronicles, the tenth; Ezra, the eleventh; Psalms, the twelfth; Ecclesiastes and Canticles, the thirteenth, fourteenth and fifteenth; the Twelve Prophets, the sixteenth; then Isaiah and Jeremiah, together with his Lamentations and his Epistle; Daniel, and Ezekiel, and Job, and Esther make up the full number of twenty-two books."

5. Contemporary with Athanasius and Hilary was Cyril, bishop of Jerusalem, a prominent member of the second general council of Constantinople. His opinions of the Canon may be gathered from the following passage:[1] "Learn diligently from the Church what are the books of the Old Testament and what of the New, but read me none of the Apocryphal; for if you do not know the books acknowledged by all, why do you vainly trouble yourself about the disputed books? Read, then, the Divine Scriptures, the twenty-two books of the Old Testament, which have been translated by the seventy-two interpreters. Of the Law the first are the five books of Moses, then Jesus the son of Nave, and the book of Judges with Ruth, which is numbered the seventh; then follow other historical books, the first and second of the Kingdoms (one book according to the Hebrews); the third and fourth are also one book;

---

[1] Φιλομαθῶς ἐπίγνωθι παρὰ τῆς ἐκκλησίας, ποῖαι μέν εἰσιν αἱ τῆς παλαιᾶς διαθήκης βίβλοι, πῦιαι δὲ τῆς καινῆς καὶ μοι μηδὲν τῶν ἀποκρύφων ἀναγίνωσκε. Ο' γὰρ τὰ παρὰ πᾶσιν ὁμολογούμενα μὴ εἰδὼς, τὶ περὶ τὰ ἀμφιβαλλόμενα ταλαπωρεῖς μάτην; Ἀναγίνωσκε τὰς θείας γραφὰς, τὰς εἴκοσι δύο βίβλους τῆς παλαιᾶς διαθήκης, τὰς ὑπὸ τῶν ἑβδομήκοντα δύο ἑρμηνευτῶν ἑρμηνευθείσας. . . . τὸν νόμου μεν` γὰρ εἰσιν αἱ Μωσέως πρῶται πέντε βίβλοι . . . ἐξῆς δὲ, Ἰησοῦς υἱὸς Ναυῆ, καὶ τῶν Κριτῶν μετὰ τῆς Ροὶθ βιβλίον ἑβδομον ἀριθμούμενον, τῶν δὲ λοιπῶν ἱστορικῶν βιβλίων, πρώτη καὶ δευτέρα τῶν Βασιλειῶν μία παρ' Ἑβραίοις ἐστὶ βίβλος· μία δὲ καὶ ἡ τρίτη καὶ ἡ τεταρτὴ· ὁμοίως δὲ παρ' αὐτοῖς καὶ τῶν Παραλειπομένων ἡ πρώτη καὶ ἡ δευτέρα, μία τυγχάνει βίβλος, καὶ τὸν Εσδρα ἡ πρώτη καὶ ἡ δευτέρα μία λελόγισται. δωδεκάτη βίβλος ἡ Εσθήρ. Καὶ τὰ μὲν ἱστορικὰ ταῦτα. Τὰ δὲ στοιχηρὰ τυγχάνει πέντε· Ἰὼβ, καὶ βίβλος Ψαλμὼν, καὶ Παροιμίαι, καὶ Εκκλησιαστὴς, καὶ Ἀσμα Ἀσμάτων, ἑπτακαιδέκατον βιβλίον. Ἐπὶ δὲ τούτοις τὰ προφητικὰ πέντε· των δώδκα προφητῶν μία βίβλος, καὶ Ησάιου μια, καὶ Ιερεμίου μετὰ Βαροὶ'χ καὶ Θρήνων καὶ ἐπιστολῆς· εἶτα Ιεζεκὴλ· καὶ ἡ τοῦ Δανιὴλ. εἰκοστηδευτέρα βίβλος τῆς παλ'. διαθ.—Cyril., Hierosol. Cateches. iv., De Sac. Scrip.

the first and second of the Chronicles are, in like manner, reckoned as one book by them; the first and second of Ezra are counted as one book. The twelfth is Esther. These are the historical books. The books written in verse are five—Job and the book of Psalms, Proverbs, Ecclesiastes and the Song of Songs—making the seventeenth book. After these are the five prophetical books—one of the twelve Prophets, one of Isaiah, one of Jeremiah, with Baruch, Lamentations and an Epistle; then Ezekiel and the book of Daniel, the twenty-second book of the Old Testament."

6. In the writings of Epiphanius we have no less than three catalogues of the books of the Old Testament, of which, as they are all essentially the same, I shall trouble the reader with only one:[1] "Twenty-seven books acknowledged and received into the Old Testament, which, according to the letters of the Hebrew alphabet, are counted as twenty-

[1] Εἰκοσιεπτὰ βίβλοι αἱ ῥητὰι καὶ ενδιάθετοι, εἰκοσι δὲ καὶ δύο κατὰ τὴν τοῦ Ἀλφαβήτου παρ' Εβράιοις στοιχέιωσιν ἀριθμούμεναι ἡρμηνεύθησαν. Εἴκοσι γὰρ καὶ δύο ἔχουσι στοιχέιων νοήματα. πέντε δὲ εἰσιν ἐξ αὐτῶν διπλούμενα. τὸ γὰρ Κὰφ ἐστι διπλοῦν, καὶ τὸ Μεν', καὶ τὸ Νοῦν, καὶ τὸ Φὶ, καὶ τὸ ἀλέφ. Διὸ καὶ αἱ βίβλοι κατὰ τόντον τὸν τρόπον εἰκοσιδύο μὲν ἀριθμοῦνται, εἰκοσιεπτὰ δὲ εὑρίσκονται. διὰ τὸ πέντε ἐξ αὐτῶν διπλοῦσθαι. Συνάπτεται γὰρ ἡ Ροὶθ τοῖς Κριταῖς. καὶ ἀριθμεῖται παρ' Εβράιοις μία βίβλος. Συνάπτεται ἡ πρώτη τῶν Παραλειπομένων τῇ δευτέρᾳ, καὶ λέγεται μία βίβλος. Συνάπτεται ἡ πρώτη τῶν Βασιλειῶν τῇ δευτέρᾳ, καὶ λέγεται μία βίβλος. Συνάπτεται ἡ τρίτη τῇ τετάρτῃ, καὶ λέγεται μία βίβλος. Οὕτως γοῦν σύγκεινται αἱ βίβλοι ἐν Πεντατεύχοις τέταρσι. καὶ μένουσιν ἄλλαι δυο ὑστερουσαι· ὡς ἔιναι τὰς ἐνδιαθέτους βίβλους ὄντως. Πέντε μὲν νομικὰς, Γένεσιν, Εξοδον, Λευιτικὸν, Ἀριθμοὺς, Δευτερονόμιον. αὐτὴ ἡ Πεντάτευχος καὶ ἡ Νομοθεσία. Πέντε γὰρ στιχήρεις. ἡ τοῦ Ἰὼβ βίβλος. ἔιτα τὸ Ψαλτήριον, Παροιμίαι Σαλομῶντος, Εκκλησιαστὴς, Ἄσμα Ἀσμάτων. Εἶτα ἄλλη Πεντάτευχος τὰ καλούμενα Γραφεια, παρά τίσι δὲ Αγιόγραφα λεγόμενα, ἅτινά ἐστιν οὕτως· Ἰησοῦ τοῦ Ναύη βίβλος. Κριτῶν μετὰ τῆς Ροὶθ Παραλειπομένων πρώτη μετὰ τῆς δευτέρας, Βασιλειῶν πρώτη μετὰ τῆς τετάρτης. αὐτη τρίτη Πεντάτευχος. Ἄλλη Πεντάτευχος τὸ Δωδεκαπρόφητον, Ησδιας, Ιερεμίας, Ιεζεκιὴλ, Δανιήλ. Καὶ αὕτη ἡ Προφητικὴ Πεντάτευχος. Ἔμειναν δὲ ἄλλαι δύο, ἅιτινές εἰσι τὸν Εσδρα μία καὶ αὕτη λογιζομένη, καὶ ἄλλη βίβλος, ἡ τῆς Εσθήρ καλεῖται. Ἐπληρώθησαν οὖν ἁι εἰκοσιδύο βίβλοι κατὰ τόν ἀριθμὸν τῶν εἰκοσιδύο στοιχείων παρ' Εβράιοις. Αἱ γὰρ στιχήρεις δύο βίβλοι ἥ τε τοῦ Σολομῶντος ἡ Παναρέτος λεγομένη, καὶ ἡ τοῦ Ιησοῦ τοῦ υἱοῦ Σιρὰχ, ἐγγόνου δὲ τοῦ Ιησοῦ, τὸν καὶ τὴν Σοφίαν. εβραιστὶ γράψαντος ἥν ὁ ἔκγονος αὐτοῦ Ιησοῦς ἑρμηνεύσας ἑλληνιστὶ ἔγραψε, καὶ αὐται χρήσιμοι μέν εἰσι καὶ ὠφέλιμοι, ἀλλ' εἰς ἀριθμὸν ῥητῶν οὐκ ἀναφέρονται.—Epipha. De Ponderibus et Mens., iii., iv., pp. 161, 162.

two, have been interpreted. For there are twenty-two letters among the Hebrews, five of which have a double form;
for Caph is double, so also are Mem and Nun and Phi and
Zade. But since five letters among them are doubled, and
therefore there are really twenty-seven letters, which are
reduced to twenty-two, so for this reason they enumerate
their books as twenty-two, though in reality twenty-seven;
for the book of Ruth is joined to the book of Judges, and
the two together are counted as one by the Hebrews. The
first and second Kings are also counted as one book, and in like
manner the third and fourth of Kings are reckoned as one.
And in this way all the books of the Old Testament are
comprehended in five pentateuchs, with two other books
not included in these divisions. Five pertain to the Law,
Genesis, Exodus, Leviticus, Numbers, Deuteronomy. This
is the pentateuch in which the Law is contained. Five are
poetical, Job, Psalms, Proverbs of Solomon, Ecclesiastes
and Canticles. Then another pentateuch embraces the
Hagiographa, Joshua, Judges and Ruth, first and second
Chronicles, first and second Kings, and third and fourth of
Kings. This is the third pentateuch. Another pentateuch
contains the twelve Prophets, Isaiah, Jeremiah, Ezekiel and
Daniel. Besides these there remain the two books of Ezra,
which are counted as one, and the book of Esther. In this
way the twenty-two books are made out according to the
number of the Hebrew letters. As for those two books, the
Wisdom of Solomon and the Wisdom of Jesus the son of
Sirach, written by the grandfather in Hebrew and translated by the grandson into Greek, they are profitable and
useful, but not counted in the number of the received books."

7. The following is the Canon of Gregory Nazianzen:[1]

<blockquote>
[1] Ἱστορικὰι μὲν ἐασι βίβλοι δυοκαιδεκα πᾶσαι,

Τῆς αρχαιοτέρης εβραϊκῆς σοφίης.

Πρωτίστη Γένεσις, ἐιτ' Εξοδος, Λευιτικόν τε.

Επειτ' Αριθμοί· εἶτα Δεύτερος νόμος.

Επειτ' Ιησοῦς κὰι Κριταί· Ροίθ ὀγδοη.

Η δ' ἐννάτη δεκάτη τε βίβλοι πράξεις Βασιλήων,

Κὰι Παραλειπόμενα·. ἐσχατον Εσδραν ἐχεις.
</blockquote>

"There are twelve historical books of the most ancient Hebrew wisdom: the first Genesis; then Exodus, Leviticus, Numbers, Deuteronomy; the next Joshua, the Judges, Ruth, the eighth; ninth and tenth the acts of the Kings, and then the Remains, and Esdras the last. Then the five books in verse, the first Job, next David, then the three books of Solomon, Ecclesiastes, the Song and the Proverbs. The prophetic books are five; the twelve Prophets are one book, Hosea, Amos, Micah, Joel, Jonah, Obadiah, Nahum, Habakkuk, Haggai, Zachariah, Malachi, all these make one book: the second is Isaiah, then Jeremiah, Ezekiel and Daniel: which make twenty-two books, according to the number of the Hebrew letters."

8. To the same purport is the Poetical Canon of Amphilochius, the intimate friend of Gregory and Basil, given in a letter which he wrote to Zeleuchus, exhorting him to the study of piety and learning.

9. The testimony of Jerome is clear, pointed and explicit. In his famous Prologus Galeatus he says:[1] "The language

Αἱ δὲ στιχηραὶ πέντε, ὧν πρῶτος γ᾽ Ἰώβ,
Ἔπειτα Δαυίδ· εἶτα τρεῖς Σολομώντειαι,
Ἐκκλησιαστὴς, Ἀσμα, καὶ Παροιμίαι.
Καὶ πένθ᾽ ὁμοίως πνεύματος προφητικοῦ.
Μίαν μὲν εἰσιν ἐς γραφὴν᾽ οἱ δώδεκα.
Ὡσηὲ κ᾽ Ἀμὼς, καὶ Μιχαίας ὁ τρίτος.
Ἔπειτ᾽ Ἰωὴλ. ἐπ᾽ Ἰωνᾶς, Ἀβδιὰς,
Ναούμ τε, Ἀββακούμ τε, καὶ Σοφονίας,
Αγγαῖος, εἶτα Ζαχαρίας, Μαλαχίας.
Μία μὲν οἶδε. Δευτέρα δ᾽ Ἡσαίας.
Ἔπειθ᾽ ὁ κληθεὶς Ιερεμίας ἐκ βρέφους.
Εἶτ᾽ Εζεκιὴλ. καὶ Δανίηλου χάρις.
Αρχάιας μὲν ἔθηκα δύο καὶ ἔικοσι βίβλους,
Τοῖς τῶν Εβραιῶν γράμμασιν ἀντιθέτους.

Greg. Naz., Opp., tom. ii., p. 98.

[1] Viginti et duas literas [says he in the Prologus Galeatus] esse apud Hebræos, Syrorum quoque et Chaldæorum lingua testatur quæ Hebræos magna est parte confinis est. Nam et ipsi viginti duo elementa habent eodem sono sed diversis characteribus. . . Porro quinque literæ duplices apud Hebræos sunt: Caph, Mem, Nun, Pe, Sade. . . . Unde et quinque à plerisque libri duplices æstimantur, Samuel, Malachim, Dabre Hajamim, Esdras, Jeremias cum Cinoth, id est Lamentationibus suis. Quomodo igitur vi-

of the Syrians and the Chaldees is a standing proof that there are two and twenty letters among the Hebrews. But among the Hebrews five letters are double, Caph, Mem,

ginti duo elementa sunt, per quæ scribimus Hebraice omne quod loquimur, et eorum initiis vox humana comprehenditur: ita viginti duo volumina supputantur, quibus quasi literis et exordiis in Dei doctrina, tenera adhuc et lactens viri justi eruditur infantia.

Primus apud eos liber vocatur *Bresith*, quem nos Genesin dicimus. Secundus *Veelle Semoth*. Tertius *Vajicra*, id est, Leviticus. Quartus *Vajedabber*, quem Numeros vocamus. Quintus *Elle Haddebarim*, qui Deuteronomium prænotatur. Hi sunt quinque libri Mosis, quos proprie *Thora*, id est Legem, appellant.

Secundum Prophetarum ordinem faciunt, et incipiunt ab Jesu filio Nave, qui apud eos *Josue Ben Nun* dicitur. Deinde subtexunt *Sophetim*, id est Judicum librum; et in eundem compingunt Ruth, quia in diebus Judicum facta ejus narratur historia. Tertius sequitur Samuel, quem nos Regnorum primum et secundum dicimus. Quartus *Malachim*, id est Regum qui tertio et quarto Regnorum volumine continetur. Melius que multo est Malachim, id est Regum, quam Malachoth, id est Regnorum dicere. Non enim multarum gentium regna describit, sed unius Israelitici populi, qui tribibus duodecim continetur. Quintus est Esaias, sextus Jeremias, septimus Ezechiel, octavus liber duodecim Prophetarum, qui apud ilos vocatur *Thare Asra*.

Tertius ordo Hagiographa possidet. Et primus liber incipit a Job. Secundus a David, quem quinque incisionibus et uno Psalmorum volumine comprehendunt. Tertius est Salomon, tres libros habens, Proverbia, quæ illi *Parabolas*, id est *Masaloth*, appellant. Quartus Ecclesiastes, id est Coheleth. Quintus Canticum Canticorum, quem titulo *Sir Hassirim* prænotant. Sextus est Daniel, septimus *Dabre Hajamim*, id est, verba dierum, quod significantius Chronicon totius divinæ historiæ possumus appellare. Qui liber apud nos Paralipomenon primus et secundus inscribitur. Octavus Esdras, qui et ipse similiter apud Græcos et Latinos in duos libros divisus est. Nonus Esther.

Atque ita fiunt pariter veteris Legis libri viginti duo, id est, Mosis quinque, et Prophetarum octo, Hagiographorum novem.

Quanquam nonnulli Ruth et Cinoth inter Hagiographa scribent, et hos libros in suo putent numero supputandos, ac per hoc esse priscæ Legis libros viginti quatuor. . . . .

Hic Prologus Scripturarum quasi galeatum principium omnibus libris, quos de Hebræo vertimus in Latinum, convenire potest: ut scire valeamus, quicquid extra hos est, inter Apocrypha esse ponendum. Igitur Sapientia, quæ vulgo Salomonis inscribitur, et Jesu filii Sirach liber, et Judith, et Tobias, et Pastor non sunt in canone. Machabæorum primum librum Hebraicum reperi. Secundus Græcus est, quod ex ipsa quoque phrasi probari potest.

Nun, Pe, Sade. Hence, by most men, five books are considered as double; viz.: Samuel, Malachim [Kings], Dabre Hajamim [Chronicles], Ezra, Jeremiah with Kinoth, that is, the Lamentations. Therefore, as there are twenty-two letters, so twenty-two volumes are reckoned. The first book is called by them *Bresith*, by us Genesis; the second is called Exodus; the third, Leviticus; the fourth, Numbers; the fifth, Deuteronomy. These are the five books of Moses, which they call *Thora*, the Law. The second class contains the Prophets, which they begin with the book of Joshua, the son of Nun. The next is the book of the Judges, with which they join Ruth, her history happening in the time of the Judges. The third is Samuel, which we call the first and second book of the Kingdoms. The fourth is the book of the Kings, or the third and fourth book of the Kingdoms, or rather of the Kings; for they do not contain the history of many nations, but of the people of Israel only— consisting of twelve tribes. The fifth is Isaiah; the sixth, Jeremiah; the seventh, Ezekiel; the eighth, the book of the twelve Prophets. The third class is that of Hagiographa, or sacred writings: the first of which is Job; the second, David, of which they make one volume, called the Psalms, divided into five parts; the third is Solomon, of which there are three books, the Proverbs—or Parables, as they call them—the Ecclesiastes and the Song of Songs; the sixth is Daniel; the seventh is the Chronicles, consisting with us of two books, called the first and second of the Remains; the eighth is Ezra, which among the Greeks and Latins makes two books; the ninth is Esther. Thus there are in all two and twenty books of the old Law; that is, five books of Moses, eight of the Prophets and nine of the Hagiographa. But some reckon Ruth and the Lamentations among the Hagiographa; so there will be four and twenty. This prologue I write as a helmeted preface to all the books to be translated by me from the Hebrew into Latin, that we may know that all the books which are not of this number are to be reckoned Apocryphal; therefore, Wisdom,

which is commonly called Solomon's, and the book of Jesus
the son of Sirach, and Judith, and Tobit, and the Shepherd,
are not in the Canon. The first book of Maccabees I have
found in Hebrew; the second is Greek, as is evident from
the style." We have two other catalogues furnished by
Jerome—one in the Bibliotheca Divina, and the other in a
letter to Paulinus—both exactly according with this.

To these testimonies may be added a passage which occurs in the preface to his translations of the books of Solomon.[1] "I have translated," says he, "the three books of
Solomon, that is, the Proverbs, Ecclesiastes and Canticles,
from the ancient version of the Seventy. As for the book
called by many the Wisdom of Solomon, and Ecclesiasticus,
which all know to be written by Jesus the son of Sirach, I
have foreborne to translate them; for it was my intention
to send you a correct edition of the canonical Scriptures,
and not to bestow labour upon others." In the Prologue to
his translation of Jeremiah, he says [2] he "does not translate
the book of Baruch, because it was neither in the Hebrew
nor received by the Jews." He also condemns the Apocryphal additions to Daniel as not found in the Hebrew, and
as having exposed Christians to ridicule for the respect
which they paid to them.[3] Although he translated Tobit

[1] Tres libros Salomonis, id est, Proverbia, Ecclesiasten, Canticum Canticorum, veteri Septuaginta interpretum auctoritate reddidi. . . . . Porro
in eo libro, qui à plerisque Sapientia Salomonis inscribitur, et in Ecclesiastico, quem esse Jesu filii Sirach nullus ignorat, calamo temperavi;
tantummodo canonicas Scripturas vobis emendare desiderans, et studium
meum certis magis quam dubiis commendare.—*Pr. in Libr. Salom., juxta
Septuag. Interp.*, t. i., p. 1419.

[2] Librum autem Baruch, notarii ejus, qui apud Hebræos nec legitur, nec
habetur, prætermisimus.—*Prol. in Jerem.*, t. i., p. 554.

[3] Hæc idcirco, ut difficultatem vobis Danielis ostenderem; qui apud Hebræos nec Susannæ habet historiam, nec Hymnum Trium Puerorum, nec
Belis Draconisque fabulas; quas nos, quia in toto orbe dispersæ sunt, verum
† anteposito easque jugulante, subjecimus; ne videremur apud imperitos
magnam partem voluminis detruncasse. Audivi ego quemdam de præ-
ceptoribus Judæorum, quum Susannæ derideret historiam, et à Græco
nescio quo diceret esse confictam: illud opponere quod Origeni quoque
Africanus opposuit, etymologias has, ἀπὸ τὸν σχίνον σχίσαι, καὶ ἀπὸ τὸν πρι-

and Judith from Chaldee into Latin, yet he pronounces each of them to be Apocryphal. Wisdom, Ecclesiasticus and Maccabees he never translated at all.

It is perfectly plain from these testimonies that Jerome acknowledged no other books of the Old Testament to be inspired but those which were received by the Jews; and it deserves to be remarked that he characterized the Hebrew Canon as emphatically the "Canon of Hebrew verity." It alone was the infallible testimony of truth.

The testimony of Jerome is felt to be so important and conclusive that Romanists have resorted to various expedients for the purpose of obviating its force. In the first place, it has been contended that he was not treating of the Canon of the Christian Church, nor of the books which, in his own opinion, ought to be received as inspired, but only of those which the Jews acknowledged. This objection, however, is so plainly inconsistent with the language which Jerome employs, that Bellarmine, too wise to defend it, frankly confesses that it is utterly without foundation. It is amazing how Cocceius, Catharinus and Canus could gravely have proposed an explanation of this sort, when it was clearly written before them that "the *Church reads* such and such books, but does not receive them as *canonical.*"

Cardinal Perron, who admits, however, that Jerome was treating of the Christian Canon, resorts to a solution so exceedingly ridiculous that one cannot but conjecture that the cardinal himself was labouring under just the opposite infirmity. In his opinion, Jerome had not reached, when he wrote his memorable Prologue, the ripeness of his studies. It is hard to fix any precise and definite period for the development and maturity of the intellectual powers. But to

νου πρίσαι, de Græco sermone descendere. . . . . Deinde tantum fuisse otii tribus pueris cavillabatur, ut in camino æstuantis incendii metro luderent, et per ordinem et laudem Dei omnia elementa provocarent: aut quod miraculum divinæque aspirationis indicium, vel draconem interfectum offa picis, vel sacerdotum Belis machinas deprehensas? Quæ magis prudentia solertes viri quam prophetati spiritu perpetrata?—*Præf. in Dan.*, t. i., p. 989.

be an infant at fifty—and such was the age, according to the lowest calculation, which the venerable Father had then attained [1]—is an infirmity so closely approximating to absolute idiocy, that the cardinal, I apprehend, will find it much more easy to convince his readers that he himself was on the borders of dotage than that the author of such a composition as the Prologus Galeatus was either a victim of imbecility of mind or the extravagance and rashness of youth.

It has also been attempted to destroy the force of this testimony by asserting that he rejected the Epistle to the Hebrews. This, however, is so far from being true that he actually cites the Epistle under the name of Paul, and distinctly declares that he received it as authentic.[2] He says, to be sure, that *others* doubted of it, but that is very different from calling it into question himself.

It is finally contended that he subsequently changed his opinions. But of this fact no evidence can be produced. The Jesuits, indeed, tell us that in his Apology against Ruffin he retracted the censure which he had formerly pronounced upon the spurious additions to Daniel; that in his Preface to Tobit he impugns the integrity of the Hebrew Canon; in his Preface to Judith and his exposition of the Psalms he revokes what he had said of the book of Judith; and in his commentary upon Isaiah retracts his assertions in relation to the Maccabees. Such are the grounds upon which it is contended he changed his opinions. It would be very easy, by a particular examination of the passages which are cited, to show that there is no foundation whatever for any of these assumptions.

In reference to the Apocryphal additions to Daniel, Ruffinus was as far from admitting their inspiration as Jerome himself. He could not, therefore, with the least degree of

[1] Jerome wrote his Prologue about the year 392. He was born, according to Baronius, about the year 340; according to others, he was born still earlier.

[2] Hanc Epistolam . . . ab omnibus . . . quasi Pauli Apostoli suscipi . . . Apocalypsin . . . et tamen nos utramque suscipimus.—*Epist. ad Dardanum.*

propriety or consistency, censure his former friend for opinions which they held in common. But Jerome was understood to say, in his Preface to Daniel, that the stories of Susannah and of Bel and the Dragon were mere fabulous narrations. This is what he explains in his Apology against Ruffinus.[1] He asserts that he had been misunderstood, and that when he used such language in reference to these tales he was not giving his own opinion of their value, but the sentiments of the Jews. He was willing to admit that they might be usefully and profitably read, but so far was he from subscribing to their Divine inspiration that he reiterates the approbation which he had formerly given of the Reply of Origen to Porphyry, who had quoted these works —"that they were not possessed of the authority of Scripture, and therefore Christians were not bound to defend them." There is, consequently, but one principle on which Jerome can be made to endorse the claims of these wretched fictions, and that is, whatever he did not believe to be fabulous he must have believed to be inspired!

In his Preface to Tobit there is no retraction whatever. He simply states that he had yielded to the desire of the bishops who had urged him to translate it, although in so doing he was aware that he had exposed himself to the reproach of the Jews. He adds, however, that he judged it better to displease the Pharisees than to disregard the injunctions of the bishops.[2] But surely to translate a book —a book which was allowed to be read in the Church, and was commended as a fit introduction to piety (for so many of the ancients regarded it)—does not necessarily imply that it was held to be inspired. And yet Jerome's expressions of willingness to displease the Jews, and to translate Tobit at the earnest request of his friends, is all the proof upon which it is asserted that he changed his mind in regard to it. I pay no attention to the obviously-corrupted passage in which he represents the Jews as ranking this book in the class of Hagiographa. The word *Hagiographa* is an

[1] Apol. 2 advs. Ruffin.   [2] Præfat. in Tobiam.

evident mistake of the copyist for *Apocrypha;* and so the ablest doctors among the Romanists themselves have agreed.[1] The glaring falsehood of the assertion upon any other supposition is enough to show that the text is vitiated.

So, again, it is contended that he changed his opinion in reference to Judith, because he yielded to the entreaty of his friends and consented to translate it. He was the more induced to do so because the book itself presented an eminent example of chastity, and was suited to edify the people, and because the story went that the Council of Nice had inserted it in the Canon.[2] On these grounds he translated the work, but not a hint does he drop that he received it as inspired. We may therefore conclude in the words of Bishop Cosin: "And thus have we made it to appear that St. Jerome was always *constant* herein to himself. For in the year 392 he avowed his translation of the Bible, before which he placed his Prologus Galeatus, as a helmet of defence against the introduction of any other books that should pretend to be of equal authority with it. Not many years after he wrote his Preface upon Tobit and Judith, and therein he changed not his mind. About the same time he wrote his Commentary upon the Prophet Haggai and his Epistle to Turia, wherein the book of Judith remaineth uncanonized. In the year 396 he wrote his Epistle to Læta, and therein he is still constant to his Prologue. About the same year he wrote upon the Prophet Jonas, where the book of Tobit is kept out of the Canon. In the year 400 (or somewhat after) he wrote upon Daniel, and there Susannah, Bel and the Dragon have no authority of Divine Scripture. And at the same time he wrote his Apologie against Ruffin, where he referreth to his former Prologues, and expressly denieth any retraction of them. About the year 409 he wrote upon Esay, where he revoketh nothing. And in the latter end of his age he set forth his Comment-

---

[1] Comestor, Hugo the Cardinal, Tortatus, Driedo, Catharin, have all pronounced it to be a corrupt reading. See also note to Præfat. in Tobiam.

[2] Præfat. in Judith.

ary upon Ezechiel, wherein he acknowledged no more books
of the Old Testament than he had counted before, but continued his belief and judgment herein to the day of his
death, which followed not long after."

10. I shall next give the testimony of Ruffinus,[1] once the
beloved friend, and afterwards the open and avowed adver-
sary, of Jerome. In his Exposition of the Apostles' Creed he
says: "This, then, is the Holy Spirit who in the Old Testament inspired the Law and the Prophets, and in the New
the Gospels and Epistles. Wherefore the Apostle says that
'all Scripture is given by inspiration of God, and is profitable for doctrine.' It will not, therefore, be improper to

[1] Hic igitur Spiritus Sanctus est, qui in veteri Testamento Legem et
Prophetas, in novo Evangelia et Apostolos inspiravit. Unde Apostolus
dicit: omnis Scriptura divinitus inspirata utilis est ad docendum. Et
ideo quæ sunt novi ac veteris Testatamenti volumina, quæ secundum
majorum traditionem per ipsum Spiritum Sanctum inspirata creduntur,
et ecclesiis Christi tradita, competens videtur hoc in loco evidenti numero,
sicut ex patrum monumentis accepimus designare. Itaque veteris Testamenti, omnium primo Moysi quinque libri sunt traditi, Genesis, Exodus,
Leviticus, Numerus, Deuteronomium. Post hæc Jesus Nave; Judicum,
simul cum Ruth. Quatuor post hæc Regnorum libri, quos Hebræi duos
numerant. Paralipomena, qui Dierum dicitur Liber, et Esdræ duo, quia
apud illos singuli computantur, et Hester. Prophetarum vero Isaias,
Jeremias, Ezechiel, et Daniel, preterea duodecim Prophetarum, liber unus.
Job quoque, et Psalmi David singuli sunt libri. Salomon vero tres
ecclesiis tradidit, Proverbia, Ecclesiasten, Cantica Canticorum. In his
concluserunt numerum librorum veteris Testamenti. . . . Sciendum tamen
est, quod et alii libri sunt, qui non sunt canonici, sed ecclesiastici a major-
ibus appellati sunt; id est Sapientia quæ dicitur Salomonis, et alia
Sapientia, quæ dicitur filii Sirach, qui liber apud Latinos, hoc ipso gene-
rali vocabulo, *Ecclesiasticus* appellatur, quo vocabulo non autor libelli,
sed scripturæ qualitas cognominata est, ejusdem vero ordinis libellus est
Tobiæ, et Judith, et Machabæorum libri. In novo vero Testamento libellus qui dicitur Pastoris sive Hermes, qui appellatur *Duæ Viæ*, vel *Judi-
cium Petri*. Quæ omnia legi quidem in ecclesiis voluerunt, non tamen
proferi ad auctoritatem ex his fidei confirmandam. Cæteras vero scripturas apocryphas nominarunt quas in ecclesiis legi noluerunt. Hæc nobis a
patribus tradita sunt quæ ut dixi, opportunum visum est hoc in loco designare, ad instructionem eorum, qui prima sibi ecclesiæ ac fidei elementa
suscipiunt, ut sciant ex quibus sibi fontibus verbi Dei haurienda sint
pocula.—*Ruffin. in Symb. ap. Cyprian. in App.*, pp. 26, 27, et ap. *Hier.*,
tom. v., pp. 141, 142.

enumerate here the books of the New and the Old Testament, which we find by the monuments of the Fathers to have been delivered to the churches as inspired by the Holy Spirit. And of the Old Testament, in the first place, are the five books of Moses: Genesis, Exodus, Leviticus, Numbers, Deuteronomy. After these are Joshua the son of Nun, and the Judges, together with Ruth. Next, the four books of the Kingdoms (which the Hebrews reckon two), the book of the Remains, which is called the Chronicles, and two books of Ezra, which by them are reckoned one, and Esther. The Prophets are Isaiah, Jeremiah, Ezekiel and Daniel, and besides one book of the twelve Prophets. Job also and the Psalms of David. Solomon has left three books to the Church: the Proverbs, Ecclesiastes and the Song of Songs; with these they conclude the number of the books of the Old Testament. . . . However, it ought to be observed that there are also other books which are not canonical, but have been called by our forefathers ecclesiastical, as the Wisdom of Solomon, and another which is called the Wisdom of the son of Sirach, and among the Latins is called by the general name of *Ecclesiasticus*. By which title is denoted not the author of the book, but the quality of the writing. In the same rank is the book of Tobit and the books of the Maccabees. In the New Testament is the book of the Shepherd or of Hermas, which is called the *Two Ways* or the *Judgment of Peter*. All which they would have to be read in the churches, but not to be alleged by way of authority for proving articles of faith. Other Scriptures they called Apocryphal, which they would not have to be read in the churches."

11. I shall close this list of testimonies with the Canon of the Council of Laodicea, which was afterwards confirmed at Constantinople in the close of the seventh century. The closing decrees are in these words:[1] " Private Psalms should

<hr />

[1] Ὅτι οὐ δεῖ ἰδιωτικοὺς ψαλμοὺς λέγεσθαι ἐν τῇ ἐκκλησίᾳ, οὐδὲ ἀκανόνιστα βίβλια, ἀλλὰ μόνα τὰ κανονικὰ τῆς καινῆς καὶ παλαιᾶς διαθήκης.

Ὅσα δεῖ βιβλία ἀναγινώσκεσθαι τῆς παλαιᾶς διαθήκης· αʹ Γένεσις Κόσμου. βʹ

not be read in the Church, nor any books which are not canonical, but only the canonical books of the Old and New Testament. The books of the Old Testament which ought to be read are these: 1, The Genesis or generation of the World; 2, The Exodus out of Egypt; 3, Leviticus; 4, Numbers; 5, Deuteronomy; 6, Joshua the son of Nun; 7, Judges, with Ruth; 8, Esther; 9, The first and second books of Kings; 10, The third and fourth books of Kings; 11, The first and second books of Chronicles; 12, The first and second books of Esdras; 13, The book of 150 Psalms; 14, The Proverbs of Solomon; 15, The Ecclesiastes; 16, The Song of Songs; 17, Job; 18, The twelve Prophets; 19, Isaiah; 20, Jeremiah and Baruch, the Lamentations and Epistle; 21, Ezekiel; 22, Daniel."

The only serious exception which can be taken to the testimony of this council is the fact that in the Canon of the New Testament the Apocalypse of John is omitted. There are three hypotheses upon which this difficulty may be removed, each of which is fatal to the inspiration of the books in question.

In the first place, it might have been the design of the Fathers simply to prescribe the books which should be *read*, and as the Apocalypse was of an abstruse and mystical character, they might have thought it expedient to leave it out in the public services of the Church. But no such objections could have been alleged against Wisdom, Ecclesiasticus and Maccabees. These books were held to be eminently useful, and specially adapted to the instruction and improvement of recent converts. Their omission, therefore, cannot be explained upon the same principle with the omission of the Apocalypse. Why, then, were they not

Ἔξοδος ἐξ Αἰγύπτου. γ΄ Λευιτικόν. δ΄ Ἀριθμοὶ. ε΄ Δευτερονόμιον. ϛ΄ Ἰησοῦς Ναυῆ. ζ΄ Κριτάι, Ῥούθ. η΄ Ἐσθήρ. θ΄ Βασιλειῶν ά καὶ β΄. ι΄ Βασιλειῶν γ΄ δ΄. ιά Παραλειπόμενα ά, β΄. ιβ΄, Ἐσδρας ά καὶ β΄. ιγ΄ βίβλος ψαλμῶν. ιδ΄ Παροιμίαι Σολομῶντος. ιε΄ Ἐκκλησιαστῆς. ιϛ΄ Ἆσμα Ἀσματων. ιζ΄ Ἰώβ. ιη΄ δώδεκά Προφῆται. ιθ΄ Ἡσάιας. κ΄ Ἰερεμίας, καὶ Βαρούχ, Θρῆνοι καὶ Ἐπιστολὰι. κα΄ Ἰεζεκίηλ. κβ΄ Δανίηλ.—*Canon of the Council of Laodicea; Labbeus et Cossart*, tom. i., p. 1507.

admitted into the Canon? But one answer can be given, and that is, They were not canonical. Though, upon this hypothesis, the decree of Laodicea did not require *all* canonical books to be read, yet it permitted *none* to be used which were not *canonical*.

In the second place, the Fathers might not have been satisfied that the Apocalypse was really the work of John. It was the last of the sacred books, and the evidences of its inspiration might not have been fully known to the bishops at Laodicea. The primitive Christians guarded the Scriptures with diligence and care, and were willing to admit no book into the Canon of inspiration until they had thoroughly examined its credentials. This very caution gives us greater confidence in their opinions, as it is a strong security that nothing was done rashly or without adequate foundation. But if the Apocrypha had been delivered by Christ and His Apostles to the Christian Church as inspired compositions, the evidence of the fact must have been as extensive as the Gospel itself. To doubt of them, therefore, is to condemn them. If the evidence of their inspiration was unknown in the middle of the fourth century, it must for ever remain in obscurity. The authors of the books had been dead for centuries, their names and memorials had vanished from the earth; there was no possibility of directly proving that they had confirmed their commission by signs and wonders. The only evidence which the Church could enjoy was the testimony of men who were known to be inspired, and the only men to whom they could appeal were the Apostles of Christ; and if for four centuries no traces are found of any testimony borne by those chosen heralds of the truth to the Divine authority of these books, their claims must be abandoned as totally incapable of proof.

The Revelation of John and the Apocryphal books did not stand upon the same footing. There were abundant means of proving that the one was written by the disciple whom Jesus loved, while there were no means whatever of attesting the other to be the Word of God. The Fathers, therefore, might have been subsequently satisfied in reference to the one, which they never could have been in reference to the other.

Finally, the Apocalypse may have been omitted in transcribing the Canon by the negligence of copyists. This I take to be the true solution of the difficulty. In some editions, the Epistle to Philemon is left out and in others inserted. But it would have been an extraordinary blunder to have omitted through mistake such a collection of books as those which compose the Apocrypha. Whichever, therefore, of these hypotheses we may choose to adopt to explain the difficulty in reference to Revelation, the Apocrypha must be rejected.

The testimony of the Christian Church for four hundred years has now been briefly reviewed, and we find an universal concurrence in the Canon of the Jews. North and south, east and west, in Europe, Asia and Africa, the most learned and distinguished defenders of the faith, however widely they differed or warmly disputed upon other points, are cordially at one whenever they treat of the documents which constitute the Rule of Faith. In all their catalogues the Apocrypha are excluded; and in some instances it is expressly added that they were not to be received, as Trent assures us they should be, with the same piety and veneration which are due to the Law, the Prophets and the Psalms. How, if Christ and His Apostles had delivered these books to the Christian Church as inspired and authoritative records—how can we explain the amazing unanimity of the primitive Fathers in rejecting them from the sacred Canon? How comes it that in no quarter of the earth such injunctions of Apostles were respected, but that even in the churches which had been planted by their hand and bedewed by their blood, in sixty years after the last of their number had retired to his long repose, these books were excluded from a place in the list of inspired compositions? The fact is utterly inexplicable; and if with the mass of historical testimony which has already been arrayed against their pretensions to Divine authority, they are after all a veritable part of the Word of God, truth and fiction are confounded, moral reasoning is at an end, and all responsibility for conduct or opinions must for ever cease.

In the first place, they were confessedly rejected by the Jewish Church. The writers themselves were Jews; and if they had been able to attest their inspiration by signs and wonders and mighty works—the only credentials of a messenger from heaven—their own nation must have known the fact. Yet the Jews with one voice repudiate these books. In the next place, they were rejected by the Son of God, for He approved and confirmed the Hebrew Canon. And finally, they were rejected for four hundred years by the whole body of the Christian Church. And yet, with all this amount of historical evidence against them, Trent has the audacity to declare that they are entitled to equal veneration with Moses, the Prophets, Evangelists and Apostles; and when every other argument fails her, she only adds to her arrogance and blasphemy by pretending to "thunder with a voice like God"—to imitate the very style of Jehovah, and to command the nations to receive her Canon, *because she says* it is Divine!

APPENDIXES.

APPENDIX A.

[FROM THE "SPIRIT OF THE NINETEENTH CENTURY."]

THE APOCRYPHAL BOOKS.

BY PROFESSOR THORNWELL.

IN nothing is the intolerable arrogance of the Church of Rome more strikingly displayed than in the authority which, if she does not formally claim, she yet pretends to exercise, of dispensing the Holy Ghost not merely to men themselves, but also to their writings. Thus the famous Council of Trent has attempted to make that Divine which is notoriously human, and that inspired which, in the sense of the Apostle, is notoriously of "private interpretation." We allude, of course, to the conduct of Rome in placing the Apocrypha upon an equal footing with the Sacred Oracles of God. Among the books which the "holy œcumenical and general Council of Trent, lawfully assembled in the Holy Spirit," has declared should be received with equal piety and veneration with the unquestioned Word of God, and which indeed have God for their Author, are Tobit, Judith, the additions to the Book of Esther, Wisdom, Ecclesiasticus, Baruch with the Epistle of Jeremiah, the Song of the Three Children, the Story of Susannah, the Story of Bel and the Dragon, and the first and second books of Maccabees.

Having by its own authority constituted these books a part of the Word of God, the Holy Council proceeded to pronounce its usual malediction upon all who would not receive them as sacred and canonical. Now, in direct opposition to this wicked and blasphemous sentence of Rome, we assert most unhesitatingly, and shall endeavour triumphantly to prove, that these books, commonly called the *Apocrypha*, are neither "sacred nor canonical," and, of course, have no more authority in the Church of God than Seneca's Letters or Tully's Offices.

Let it be remarked, however, that the *onus probandi* rests upon the

745

Papists. The presumption is against them until they adduce satisfactory testimony in behalf of their extravagant pretensions. Nay, even defect of proof is fatal to their cause. They bring us certain documents, and declare that they were given by inspiration of God. We are bound to treat these documents as we treat all other writings, merely as human productions, until clear and cogent arguments for their Divine original are submitted to our understandings. Hence, the Protestant cause is fully made out by failure of proof on the part of the Romanists. We are not required, in justification of our position, to advance a single argument against the inspiration of these books. Our course is a righteous, a necessary one, until they are *proved* to be inspired. We think it important that this high vantage-ground of Protestantism in the argument upon this subject should be fully apprehended; not because we are unable to prove that these books are not inspired, but in order that it may be distinctly understood that all our positive arguments against them are *ex abundanti*—are over and above what is actually required of us in the case. If our position is justified by failure on the part of Rome to establish her assertion, it is more than justified—it is doubly fortified and rendered wholly impregnable—by the irresistible arguments which we are able to allege against the inspiration of the Apocryphal books. With the distinct understanding, then, that we are doing a work which justice to our own cause does not absolutely require, but which only exposes in a stronger light the arrogance and blasphemy of Rome, we proceed to show, by a few positive considerations, that these books have not the shadow of a claim to Divine inspiration.

1. Our first argument is drawn from the indisputable fact that these books were not found in the Canon of the Jews in the time of our Saviour and His Apostles. It is even doubted by learned men whether some of them existed at all until some time after the last of the Apostles had fallen asleep. But, be this as it may, they were not in the sacred Canon of the Jews or the catalogue of books which the whole nation received as coming from God. We have very clear testimony upon the subject of the Jewish Canon, in Josephus, Philo, the Talmud, and the early Christian Fathers. It is unnecessary to quote these testimonies at full length. Those who have not access to the original works may find them faithfully collated in Schmidius De Canone Sacro, and in Eichhorn's Einleitung. We would particularly commend to the reader's attention Hornemann's book, De Canone Philonis. Augustine again and again confesses that the Apocrypha formed no part of the Jewish Canon. He declares that Solomon was not the author of the books of Ecclesiasticus and Wisdom, and assures us, moreover, that these books were chiefly respected by the Western Christians. He informs us that Judith was not re-

ceived by the Jews; and his testimony in relation to Maccabees is equally decisive. We insist upon the testimony of Augustine, which may be found in his treatise De Civ. Dei, lib. i., c. 17, because he had evidently a very great respect for these books, for he frequently quotes them, and because he was a member of the bodies whose decisions in their favour have been strongly and earnestly pleaded. We take it, then, to be a fact which no scholar would think of calling into question—sustained by the concurring testimony of Jews and Christians for four hundred years after Christ—that the Jews rejected the Apocrypha from their Canon. For the purpose of our present argument it is not necessary to show what books they did receive, nor how they classed and arranged them. It is enough that they had a Canon which they believed to be inspired, and that in it the Apocrypha were not included.

Now our argument is this: Jesus Christ and His Apostles approved of the Jewish Canon, whatever it was, appealed to it as possessing Divine authority, and evidently treated it as at that time complete, or as containing the whole of God's revelation as far as it was then made. If the Apocrypha had been really a part of that revelation, and the Jews had either ignorantly or wickedly suppressed it, how comes it that Christ nowhere rebukes them for their error? We find him severely inveighing against the Pharisees for *adding to* the Word of God by their vain traditions, but not a syllable do we hear in regard to what was equally culpable—their *taking from it*, which they certainly had done if the Apocrypha were inspired. Here was confessedly a great Teacher and Prophet in Israel—their long-expected Messiah, who constituted the burden of their Scriptures, according to His own testimony—and yet while He quotes and approves the Canon of the Jews, and remands the Jews themselves to their own Scriptures, He nowhere insinuates that their sacred library was defective. If the Jews had done wrong in rejecting the Apocrypha, is it credible that He who came in the name of God, a Teacher sent from God to reveal fully the Divine will, would have passed over, without noticing it, such a flagrant fraud? We find Him reproving his countrymen for every other corruption in regard to sacred things of which they are known to have been guilty, but not a whisper escapes His lips or the lips of His Apostles touching this gross suppression of a large portion of the Word of God. The conclusion is irresistible, that neither Jesus nor His Apostles believed in the Divine authority of the Apocrypha—they knew that they were not inspired. We will grant the Romanist what he cannot prove, and what we can *disprove*—that these books are quoted in the New Testament. This will not remove the difficulty. According to his views of the Canon, the Jews were guilty of an outrageous fraud in regard to the Sacred

Oracles; and yet neither Christ nor His Apostles, whose business it was to give us the whole revelation of God, ever charged them with this fraud, or took any steps to restore the rejected books to their proper places. Christ, as the great Prophet of the Church, was unfaithful to His high and solemn trust if He stood silently by when the Word of God was trampled in the dust, or buried in obscurity, or even robbed of its full authority. To the Jews were committed the Oracles of God (Rom. iii. 2) : if they betrayed their trust we ought to have been informed of it before the lapse of sixteen centuries.

It is in vain to allege that Christ and His Apostles used the Septuagint, and that this version contained the Apocrypha. In the first place, it cannot be proved that the Septuagint at that time did contain the Apocrypha. In the second place, if it did contain them, the difficulty is rather increased than lessened. The question is, What books did the Jews, to whom were committed the Oracles of God, receive as inspired? Did Christ know that they rejected the Apocrypha from the list of inspired writings? If so, and the Septuagint version was in His hands, and really contained these rejected books, what more natural than that Christ should have told His Apostles that here are books which the Jews reject, but which you must receive—they are of equal authority with the Law, the Prophets and the Psalms? His total silence both before the Jews and His own disciples becomes more unaccountable than ever if the books were actually before Him and almost forced upon His notice by the version of the Scriptures which He used. But we do not insist upon this, because we do not believe that the Septuagint, at that time, contained the Apocrypha.[1] If it should be said that the Jews received these books as inspired, but did not insert them in the Canon because they had not the authority of a Prophet for doing so, why is it that Christ did not give the requisite authority, if not to the Jewish priests and rulers, at least to His own Apostles ?

Upon every view of the subject, then, the silence of Christ is wholly unaccountable if these writings are really inspired. It becomes simple and natural upon the supposition that they were merely human productions. The Jews had done right in rejecting them. They stood upon a footing with other literary works, and our Saviour had no more occasion to mention them than he had to mention the writings of the Greek philosophers.

2. If it should be pretended that Christ did give His Apostles authority to receive these books, though no record was made of the fact, we ask how it comes to pass—and we mention this as our second argument against them—that for four centuries the unbroken testimony of the Christian Church is against their inspiration? They are

[1] Vid. Schmidius, De Canone.

not included in the catalogues given by Melito,[1] bishop of Sardis, who flourished in the second century, of Origen,[2] Athanasius,[3] Hilary,[4] Cyril of Jerusalem,[5] Epiphanius,[6] Gregory Nazianzen,[7] Ruffinus,[8] and others; neither are they mentioned among the canonical books recognized by the Council of Laodicea. As a sample of the testimonies referred to in the margin, we will give a few passages from Jerome, the author of the authentic version commonly called the *Vulgate*. In the Preface concerning all the books of the Old Testament which he prefixed to his Latin translation of Samuel and Kings, after having given us the Jewish Canon, he says, "*Hic prologus scripturarum, quasi Galeatum principium omnibus libris quas de Hebræo vertimus in Latinum convenire potest: ut scire valeamus quicquid extra hos est inter Apocrypha esse ponendum.*" "Therefore," he adds, "Wisdom, which is vulgarly attributed to Solomon, and the book of Jesus the son of Sirach, and Judith, and Tobias, and Pastor, are not in the Canon." His testimony in relation to the Maccabees is equally decided. In the Prologue to his Commentary on Jeremiah, he declines explaining the book of Baruch, which in the edition of the LXX. is commonly joined with it, because the Jews rejected it from the Canon, and he of course knew of no authority for inserting it. In the Preface to his translation of Daniel he assures us that the Story of Susannah, the Song of the Three Children, and the fables of Bel and the Dragon, are not only not in the Jewish copies, but had exposed Christians to ridicule for the respect which they paid to them. In his Preface to Tobit and Judith he pronounces them Apocryphal!

Here, then, about the close of the fourth century, we find no remnant of any unwritten tradition from Christ and His Apostles authorizing the Church to receive these books. The early Fathers followed in the footsteps of the Jews, and unanimously concurred in receiving no other Canon of the Old Testament as inspired but that which came down to them through the Jewish Church. In this opinion learned men in every age have concurred up to the very meeting of the Council of Trent. We refer to such men as Cardinal Ximenes, Ludovicus Vives, the accomplished Erasmus and Cardinal Cajetan. How could there have been such a general concurrence in an error so deplorable if Christ and His Apostles had ever treated these books as the lively Oracles of God? Surely there would have been some record, some hint, of a fact so remarkable. We ask the Romanist to reconcile the testimonies of the Fathers with the decree of Trent. In the language of Bishop Burnet: "Here we have four centuries clear

---

[1] Euseb., lib. iv., c. 26.   [2] Expos. Psal. i., Opp. tom. ii., Euseb., vi. 25.
[3] Pasch. Epist.   [4] Prolog. in Psalmos.
[5] 4th Catech. Exer.   [6] Hæres, i. 6.
[7] Can. 23.   [8] Expos. ad. Symb. Apost.

for our Canon, in exclusion of all additions. It were easy to carry this
much farther down, and to show that these books (the Apocrypha)
were never by any express definition received into the Canon till it
was done at Trent, and that in all ages of the Church, even after they
came to be much esteemed, there were divers writers, and those generally the most learned of their time, who denied them to be a part of
the Canon.''

3. The third argument which we shall bring forward is drawn from
the books themselves. In reading them we not only are struck with
the absence of that "heavenliness of matter, efficacy of doctrine,
majesty of style, concert of all the parts and general scope of the
whole to give glory to God," by which the Sacred Scriptures abundantly evidence themselves to be the Word of God, but we are as
forcibly struck with defects utterly inconsistent with these excellences.
To say nothing of their silly and ridiculous stories, these books notoriously contain palpable lies, gross anachronisms, flat contradictions and
doctrinal statements wholly irreconcilable with what we are taught in
the unquestioned Oracles of God. Such things are totally inconsistent
with the idea of inspiration.

It would be easy to make good these charges by citations from the
books, but it is unnecessary to protract our article by quotations which
have again and again been made for the same purpose.

What, under the present head, we wish particularly to remark is,
that these books, or at least several of them, virtually disclaim all pretensions to inspiration. They do not profess to be the Word of God;
and why should Protestants be blamed for not conceding to them an
authority which they themselves do not claim? They come to us from
their authors merely as human productions: we treat them as such;
and yet we are consigned to the damnation of hell because we do not
believe that a writer was inspired when he did not believe it himself!

The author of the second book of Maccabees professes to have
abridged a work of Jason of Cyrene, and concerning his performance
he holds the following language, which can be reconciled with a belief
on his part that he was inspired when light is made to have fellowship with darkness, and God with Belial, and not till then: "Therefore, to us that have taken upon us this painful labor of abridging, it
was not easy, but a matter of sweat and watching, even as it is no ease
to him that prepareth a banquet and seeketh the benefit of others;
yet for the pleasing of many we will undertake gladly this great pains,
leaving to the author the exact handling of every particular, and labouring to follow the rules of an abridgment," etc. (2 Mac. ii. 26, seq.).
Here his motives, as assigned by himself, are such as induce ordinary
men to write, and his method is taken from the common rules of crit-

icism. In other words, it is obviously a human composition, and was intended to have no more authority than any other historical document. To the same purport is the following sentence near the close of the book : "And if I have done well, and as is fitting the story, it is that which I desired ; but if slenderly and meanly, it is that which I could attain unto." Is this the language of a man who "spake as he was moved by the Holy Ghost"? Does he seem to have drawn from the inexhaustible fountain of Divine truth, or from the shallow resources of his own mind? Verily, none but a madman could speak on this wise and yet believe that he was inspired of God. The Prologue to Ecclesiasticus—a production of Jesus the son of Sirach—is just as decisive in reference to it. As it is too long to quote, we shall content ourselves by simply referring to it. The writer asks pardon for a defective interpretation of a Hebrew document, and declares that his whole performance was the result of diligence and travail, of great watchfulness and skill. And yet, according to the Romanist, instead of being the product of human thought and labour, it was the supernatural dictation of the Holy Ghost. The pretence in this case is too absurd for argument. In the first book of Maccabees we are assured that there was not a Prophet or inspired man in Israel to direct them what to do with the altar which had been profaned. (1 Mac. iv. 46.) The same declaration is repeated in the course of the book again, and yet, contrary to his own testimony, we are required to believe that the writer himself was inspired. In fact, it was the universal opinion of the Jewish nation that inspiration ceased with Malachi, not to be revived until the dawn of the New Dispensation, and that, consequently, no books which were written after the time of Artaxerxes Longimanus were worthy of any credit as inspired records.

We might go over each of the Apocryphal books one by one, and produce such numerous instances of falsehood, error, contradiction and absurdity as to render it utterly impossible that any should attribute them to God but those whose credulity is enormous enough to swallow down the nonsense and blasphemy of transubstantiation, and to believe that God can be multiplied by the million without disturbing His unity, and made at will out of cakes and wine without detracting from His glory. Such men can believe anything, and to such men it is useless to urge the authority of Christ and His Apostles; vain to allege the concurring testimony of the leading writers of the Primitive Church ; vainer still to plead absurdity, contradiction and lies, and even implied disclaimers from the writings in question : they have an authority higher than all these. The Council of Trent has spoken—the man of sin and the son of perdition, who has given out that *he* is God, has spoken from his throne of blasphemy and abom-

inations; and the voice of a general council and the Pope is enough
to silence reason, to sanctify blasphemy and to canonize falsehood.

But to those who are not yet fastened as captives to the car of Rome
we appeal in the confident expectation of success. Can' any candid
and unprejudiced mind believe that these books proceeded from God,
when there is not a particle of evidence to establish the fact; when
the Jewish Church, to which were committed the Oracles of God, rejected them; when Christ and His Apostles rejected them; when for
four centuries united Christendom rejected them; when up to the
very time of the meeting of Trent the most enlightened members of
the Church of Rome rejected them; when, in addition to all this, the
books themselves do not profess to be inspired, and abound in absurdity,
contradiction and lies? Despising the authority of Popes and Councils, we bring the matter to the bar of sober reason and sound argument; and we challenge Rome to vindicate herself from the charge of
intolerable arrogance and blasphemy in her corrupt additions to the
Word of God. The argument which she uses with her own vassals
will not do among thinking men. Until she can adduce clear, decided,
unanswerable proof of the inspiration of the Apocrypha, all who reverence God or love their race are solemnly bound to reject these books,
and to treat them precisely as all Protestant churches always have
treated them. Rome may denounce her anathema against us, but we
know full well that the terrible malediction of God rests upon her. It
is not a light matter whether we receive or reject these writings. If
they are not inspired, those who receive them run the risk of everlasting damnation; if they are, those who reject them are exposed to
the same danger.

That Protestants reject them because they contain unpalatable doctrines is a fiction of the Roman priesthood to divert attention from
the real state of the argument. Light is death to their cause; and
therefore they resort to every trick of sophistry and of falsehood to
obscure the question at issue, and to escape unexposed in their frauds
and impostures. We reject them because *they are not inspired;* and
we shall continue to do so until the contrary is clearly proved, as well
as boldly asserted. Let the Romanists come up manfully to the point
of *inspiration.* That is the issue between us, and upon that issue we
are always ready to meet them.

APPENDIX B.

LETTERS OF A. P. F.

LETTER I.

To the Reverend JAMES H. THORNWELL, Professor of the Evidences of Christianity, etc.:

REVEREND SIR—I need offer no apology for thus publicly addressing you. The Columbia Chronicle of the 15th ult., forwarded to me a few weeks ago by a friend, contains an article under your name on what you term the *Apocryphal Books*, which at my request the Editors of the Miscellany republish together with this letter. The character of that article is such as to render it no longer an intrusion either on you or on the public thus to vindicate the Catholic Church from your attacks.

Permit me to take this occasion of expressing, once for all, my regret at finding an essay from you so plentifully interspersed with the vulgar epithets *Papist, Romanist*, and such manifestations of ill-feeling as the expressions *vassals of Rome* and *captives to the car of Rome*, the assertion that "our credulity is enormous," and your mocking language concerning the awful mystery of transubstantiation and the Church, with which, even in quotation, I am unwilling to sully my pen. Believe me, reverend sir, such invectives contain no argument. They are unbecoming the subject, and—may I presume to add?—the dignified station you occupy. Your essay would have lost none of its weight, and to Catholics would have been infinitely less revolting, had they been omitted. Catholics are neither outcasts from society nor devoid of feeling; they are neither insensible to, nor think they deserve, such words of opprobrium. It is true we have often to draw on our patience, for the rules of courtesy are frequently violated in our regard. Still it is painful to see a Professor descending from calm, gentlemanly and enlightened argument to mingle with the crowd of those whose weapons are misrepresentations and abuse. To me it is doubly painful when such language obliges me not to respect as highly as I would desire those whom I address. I will not recur to this disagreeable topic, but will endeavour to write as if your arguments were unaccompanied by what Catholics must consider as insults.

I cordially agree with you that "it is not a light matter whether we receive or reject those writings" which are contained in the Canon of the Holy Scriptures as received by the Catholic Church, and are excluded from that generally adopted by the different denominations of Protestantism. Still I am not prepared to unite unconditionally in your denunciatory clauses. Undoubtedly, all who know the truth are bound to believe and profess it; otherwise they "run the risk of eternal damnation." All too are bound according to their ability, sincerely, earnestly and perseveringly to seek the truths of revelation on this as on all other points; and those who having the means neglect to do so "are exposed to the same danger." Still there may be others to whom Divine Providence has not vouchsafed such means; and they assuredly will not be punished for not performing an impossibility.

Your essay contains some preliminary remarks on the authority of the Church to declare what books are sacred and canonical, and on the state of the question; and lays down three arguments to prove that the books in question are not inspired. I shall take up these different heads in order, and trust, by a few remarks in this and perhaps two or three other letters, to convince a "candid and unprejudiced mind by sound argument and sober reason" that the Catholic Church has not been guilty of the heinous crime you lay at her door—that of making corrupt additions to the Word of God.

You commence with the following remarks:

"In nothing is the intolerable arrogance of the Church of Rome," etc. [Here A. P. F. quotes a paragraph and more from the preceding article of Dr. Thornwell.]

I doubt not, reverend sir, you here accurately express your conception of what the Council of Trent did in regard to the Scriptures. But your terms express neither the belief of Catholics nor the action of the Council. A *Canon* I have always understood to be a list or a catalogue, *setting forth* what books *are* inspired, not giving or dispensing inspiration to uninspired books. A work to be entitled to a place in a Canon must be believed already inspired; and if believed to be inspired at any one period, it must be believed to have been always inspired. Until a Canon is formed, a catalogue of inspired works drawn up, manifestly, though many works may be *sacred* because inspired, none can be *canonical*, because none can be inserted in a catalogue which does not yet exist. He who forms a Canon must naturally first decide what books are and what are not inspired. Did the Council of Trent in making such a decision "display intolerable arrogance?" Reverend sir, your essay claims to contain a decision on that point which, according to the rules and maxims of Protestantism, proceeds from your own authority to decide for yourself, and for which you alone are responsible.   If you alone and the Fathers of Trent together are equally qualified to make that decision, then must the same terms which you apply to them be applicable to yourself.   If, on the contrary, any one should think you personally inferior to them in the qualifications of learning and research on this point, then, unless charity and courtesy forbid him, as certainly they do me, must he look for expressions, if possible, more bitter and harsh than your own.   I presume, however, that the ardour with which you engaged in the contest blinded your eyes to the fact that while you made your very first thrust at the Council, you fatally exposed yourself to the retort.

We believe that the Church of Christ will ever know and believe and teach His doctrines and precepts—that He has secured to her the possession of the truths of His revelation through the ministry of that body of pastors of which the Apostles were the first members, and whom He appointed His delegates and sent forth to "baptize all nations, teaching them to observe all things whatsoever He had taught them," guaranteeing at the same time that He would be with them in the performance of this duty ALL DAYS, even to the consummation of the world.   He promised them the Spirit of truth, who should teach them all truth.   Hence we hold that the Apostles and their successors in the ministry, in the first and second and in every succeeding century, *have* taught, and *will* continue to the end of the world to teach, all things that He taught them originally ; and when they testify that any doctrine is one of those originally taught by the Saviour, and handed down to them by their predecessors in the ministry, we feel bound to hear them, His delegated teachers, as we would hear Him from whom they received their authority, and we have the assurance that He is with them, and teaches through them.

I will not, reverend sir, enter at large on the general proofs on this point.   I might show that our doctrine is fully sustained by the words of the Saviour himself, that it has ever been recognized and acted on from the earliest days of Christianity, that the contrary is opposed to reason and the infinite wisdom of God, inasmuch as it would ever leave us in doubt and indecision, and as only through it can *all* learn, with that certainty which is required for an unhesitating assent of reason, what doctrines have been in truth revealed by the Saviour. To attempt to establish all this would be to depart too far from the subject I have undertaken to treat.   I will consider it simply in reference to the Canon of Scripture ; and hope to show that the authority claimed by the Catholic Church of determining the Canon—that is, of authoritatively declaring what books have been committed to her care

by the Apostles as inspired, and have ever been revered as such—so
far from being a "striking display of intolerable arrogance," must be
admitted if the Christian world generally is to possess any certainty
of Divine inspiration.

In the first place, it seems strange to me that you should so severely
condemn the Catholic Church for having presumed to draw up a
Canon. It is nothing more than many denominations of Protestants—
your own, reverend sir, included—have done. In the Thirty-nine Articles of the Church of England and of the Protestant Episcopal
Church in the United States, in the Articles of the Methodist Episcopal Church and in the Westminster Confession of the Presbyterians,
we find Canons of the Scriptures. Nothing is more natural than that
several ecclesiastical bodies, as these denominations are, should give
forth to its members and the world, through what each, according to its
peculiar polity, recognizes as its proper tribunal, decisions on this all-
important point. In the Catholic Church a general council is deemed
a proper tribunal, and when circumstances required it the Catholic
Church through such a tribunal gave her declaration. I am not now
speaking of the *accuracy* of the decision, but of the "authority exercised" in making it. In styling it "a striking display of intolerable
arrogance," you strike a blow which harms us not, but recoils with
tenfold force on your own denomination. Surely, if the persons assembled at Westminster could draw up a Canon or catalogue of what
they were of opinion should be received and acknowledged by all as
inspired books, the Catholic Church could through her bishops assembled in council declare too what books had ever been handed down in
her bosom as the Word of God. If it was no arrogance in the first to
put forth a decree which was valueless, because on their own principles it bound no one, and which every member of your communion has
a right to reform, and which some to my own knowledge do reform, it
was certainly none in the Catholic Church to pronounce a decree which
circumstances required, and which her children throughout the world
felt had some weight. You might contend that the Catholic Church
has no *commission* from God to make such decisions—that Catholics
err when they believe them to possess some value. That would be
attacking our doctrine. But it strikes me as strange that this particular *exercise* of authority should be singled out for condemnation by a
divine of a church which, without even claiming this commission or
this authority for its decrees, has nevertheless performed the same act.
One who rejects as uninspired the Canticle of Canticles—and, if we
may believe a recent writer in the Magnolia, there are many biblical
scholars in this country who do—must look on the declaration of the
Westminster Confession. that that book is inspired, as at least an
equally striking display of intolerable arrogance as the declaration of

the Council of Trent that the books you mention were ever preserved
in the Church, and must still be held as divinely inspired. I might
also say that it is not more arrogant to declare that a contested book is
divinely inspired than that a contested doctrine or precept is contained
in the Scripture. And yet we need not go back many months to find
your Assembly declaring this last, and enforcing its declaration under
penalty of suspension from the ministry and exclusion from your sacrament. I press this view farther than perhaps seems necessary; but
your article, like most articles written against us, breathes a spirit which
I will not qualify, but which would exclude the Catholic Church from
that right Protestants boast God has given to all men—to believe in
religious matters according to our own judgment, and to declare what
she holds true.

With these remarks on the *performance* of the act, let us pass on
to the decision itself and its truth. I have taken exception to the
idea of the decision conveyed by your words. Let the Fathers speak
for themselves:

"Sacrosancta œcumenica et generalis Tridentina Synodus, in Spiritu
Sancto legitime congregata, præsidentibus in ea iisdem tribus Apos-
tolicæ Sedis legatis, hoc sibi perpetuo ante oculos proponens, ut, sub-
latis erroribus, puritas ipsa evangelii in ecclesia conservetur; quod
promissum ante per prophetas in Scripturis sanctis, Dominus noster
Christus Dei filius proprio ore primum promulgavit; deinde per suos
Apostolos tanquam fontem omnis et salutaris veritatis et morum disci-
plinæ omni creaturæ prædicari jussit: perspiciensque hanc veritatem
et disciplinam contineri in libris scriptis, et sine scripto traditionibus,
quæ ex ipsius Christi ore ab Apostolis acceptæ, aut ab ipsis Apostolis,
Spiritu Sancto dictante, quasi per manus traditæ ad nos usque perven-
erunt: orthodoxorum Patrum exempla secuta, omnes libros tam veteris quam novi Testamenti, cum utriusque unus Deus sit auctor, nec
non traditiones ipsas, tum ad fidum tum ad mores pertinentes, tanquam vel ore tenus a Christo, vel a Spiritu Sancto dictatas, et continua
successione in Ecclesia catholica conservatas pari pietatis affectu ac
reverentia suscipit et veneratur. Sacrorum vero librorum indicem
huic decreto adscribendum censuit; ne cui dubitatio suboriri possit,
quinam sint, qui ab ipsa synodo suscipiuntur, sunt vero infra scripti.
[*Here follows the list containing the books you object to.*] Si quis autem
libros ipsos integros cum omnibus suis partibus, prout in Ecclesia catholica legi consueverunt, et in veteri vulgata Latina editione habentur,
pro sacris et canonicis non susceperit, et traditiones prædictas sciens et
prudens contempserit; anathema sit."

"The holy œcumenical and general Council of Trent, lawfully assembled in the Holy Ghost, the three aforesaid Legates of the Apostolic See presiding therein, having this always in view, that errors

being taken away, the purity of that gospel should be preserved in the
Church, which, promised by the prophets in the Holy Scriptures, our
Lord Jesus Christ, the Son of God, first promulgated with His own
mouth. and afterwards commanded should be preached by His Apostles
to every creature as the source of every saving truth and moral discipline ; and clearly seeing that this truth and discipline is contained in
the written books and in the unwritten traditions. which, received by
the Apostles from the mouth of Christ himself or from the Apostles
themselves, dictated by the Holy Ghost to them, have come down
even to us, delivered as it were from hand to hand ; following the example of the orthodox Fathers, receives with due piety and reverence,
and venerates, *all the books* as well of the Old as of the New Testament, since one God is the author of both, and also those traditions
appertaining to faith and morals which have been held in the Catholic Church in continued succession. as coming from the mouth of
Christ or dictated by the Holy Ghost. It has moreover thought
proper to annex to this decree a catalogue of the Sacred Books, lest
any doubt might arise which are the books received by this Council.
They are the following (*here follows the list, containing the books to
which entirely or in part you object*). Now, if any one does not receive as sacred and canonical those books entire, with all their parts,
as they have been usually read in the Catholic Church, and are found
in the old Latin vulgate edition, and shall knowingly and industriously
contemn the aforesaid traditions, let him be anathema.'' *Sessio
quarta celebrata die viii. Mens April, MDXLVI.*

   This decree, you perceive, reverend sir. treats of the inspired Scriptures and the unwritten traditions. Your essay takes up the first
topic : I leave the second, then, without any remark.

   From this document it appears at first glance that the Council desired to draw up for the use of the faithful a Canon or catalogue of the
inspired Books, and that they inserted therein those works which they
were convinced had ever been looked upon by the universal Church
as sacred and inspired. It is a doctrine of our Church. sustained by
the arguments at which I have hinted above, that Almighty God has
promised never to permit error under such circumstances to be taught
instead of truth. Hence the Council looked upon that decree as decisive, and as such it has been and is received by the Catholic Church
throughout the world. Were any Catholic to refuse, he would be separated from her communion. She would no longer recognize in him a
sheep of her own true fold: before the tribunal of God he would stand
or fall, according as in his own conscience he was really more or less
guilty or innocent of a violation of His supreme commands. This is
the meaning of the phrase borrowed from the Scripture, *anathema sit—*
let him be anathema—and used in every age of Christianity. You

yourself, reverend sir, have gone as far as you charge the Fathers with going when you say that if the books in question are uninspired, those who receive them "run the risk of eternal damnation." In your essay you declare that they are uninspired. The application is obvious.

Hallam, a Protestant writer, in his Introduction to the Literature of Europe, has the following passage : "No general council ever contained so many persons of eminent learning and ability as that of Trent; nor is there ground for believing that any other investigated the questions before it with so much patience, acuteness, temper and desire of truth." I might quote from Roscoe and other Protestants, who were somewhat *au fait* with the continental Catholic literature of that period, similar, if not stronger, testimonies in their favour. Considering their decree concerning the Scriptures apart from the religious value with which the doctrine of the Catholic Church invests it, I cannot think it deserves to be treated with such unceremonious disrespect as your essay exhibits. Hundreds of the most learned men in Europe, after patient examination and a thorough investigation of all the evidence they could find on the subject, decide unanimously that a certain fact took place ; for, on their own showing, the decree is based on such a decision. You, reverend sir, think they were mistaken. Still, as literary opponents, you should feel they are no despicable adversaries. If it pleases you, as a divine, to consider them as a religious body, you see the most venerable, learned and zealous pastors of a church numbering 150,000,000 in the fold, assembling together, that by mutual advice, after due consultation and earnest, persevering prayer, they may be enlightened by Him whose ministers they hold themselves to be, so as faithfully to instruct, on a most important point, the multitudes that look to them for guidance in the way of eternal salvation. If I could believe that, notwithstanding, they fell into error, while I lamented it, I would still respect, revere them. I would often turn to that assembly as a scene on which a Christian soul should love to dwell, and learn from them earnest zeal and fervent piety.

The question between us is, Did they fall into error or not?

You remark that the *onus probandi* lies on us, and that the presumption is against the inspiration of those books you combat until satisfactory evidence be brought forward to prove that point. This, reverend sir, is true, not only in reference to those books, but to all others which it may be contended are inspired. Defect of such proof would be fatal to the cause of *any* book.

Now I "assert, and shall endeavour to prove," that the only arguments which establish the inspiration of those books which you admit are inspired, in that manner, and to the extent which common sense and the nature of Christianity require that it should be proved, will also establish the inspiration of the books you repudiate; and that if these are to be rejected because of the insufficiency of those arguments in their support, the others must be at least generally rejected; the conclusive arguments, at least for the generality of Christians, being, as I shall show, identically the same in both cases.

I need not say that the question, What writings are divinely inspired? has not been debated only within this and the last two centuries. There has ever been great difference on this head among those who professed to hold a revelation from Almighty God. The Sadducees and the Samaritans rejected all the books of the Old Testament except those of Moses. The Nazarenes, on the other hand, rejected the Pentateuch. The Simonians, the Basilidians, the Marcionists with the Manichæans, the Patricians, the Severians, the Albigenses and some others, rejected the entire Old Testament. Many others have rejected various books. Nor has the New Testament escaped a similar fate. The four Gospels were rejected by the Manichæans; each book had its impugners down to the Apocalypse or book of Revelations, which you well know was rejected by many who were and are still accounted to have been orthodox. The Rationalists of Germany would smile with contempt and pity on the delusion which in the effulgence of their philosophical Christianity would believe in any supernatural aid given to the scriptural writers. The Deist among ourselves denies altogether the inspiration of the Bible, Nay, according to the principles you lay down, there is a time when *every Protestant must doubt it*. You are not, you say, at "liberty to believe" the books you attack to be inspired "until clear and decided proofs of the fact are brought forward." Neither on the same ground is any Protestant " at liberty to believe any documents to be inspired," but is solemnly bound to "treat them as he treats all other writings, merely as human productions, until clear and cogent arguments for their Divine origin are submitted to his understanding." I think it important that this high "vantage-ground," to use your own expression in the argument on this subject, "should be fully apprehended ;" for, in order to meet your preamble more directly, I will base on it the following remarks, which I offer to your serious consideration, and that of those whose sense of equity or whose curiosity may lead them to examine what a Catholic *can* say on the subject.

We cannot be called on to believe any proposition not sustained by adequate proof. When Almighty God deigned to inspire the works contained in the Holy Scriptures, He intended they should be held and believed to be inspired. Therefore there *does* exist some adequate proof of their inspiration. The nature and scheme of Christianity require that not one only in a thousand, but all those to whom Christianity is properly announced, of whatsoever age or condition they be, should believe it. Therefore, that proof of inspiration which is adapted to all those ages and conditions must be one which will strike the understanding of the wandering Indian and the unlettered negro slave as clearly and as cogently as that of the enlightened professor.

Now, reverend sir, there may be many ways of seeking to ascertain the fact of the inspiration of any writer or writers. They may, however, be all reduced to the four following methods:

1. Is every man, no matter what be his condition, to investigate by his own labour and research, and duly examine the arguments that have been or can be alleged for and against the several books which it is asserted are inspired, and on the strength of that examination to decide for himself with absolute certainty what books are and what are not inspired?

2. Is every individual to receive books as inspired, or to reject them as uninspired, according to the decision of persons he esteems duly qualified by erudition and sound judgment to determine that question accurately?

3. Must he learn the inspiration of the Scriptures from some individual whom God commissioned to announce this fact to the world?

4. Must he learn it from a body of individuals, to whom, in their collective capacity, God has given authority to make an unerring decision on this subject?

I might perhaps add a fifth method—that each one be informed what books are divinely inspired by his *private spirit*. But I omit it, as, were it true, it would be superfluous, if not a criminal intrusion on the province God would have reserved to himself, to attempt to prove or disapprove, when our duty would be simply to await in patience this revelation to every particular individual. You are not a member of the Society of Friends, and your essay is not an *exposé* of the teaching of your *private spirit*, but an effort to appeal to argument.

To some one of those four methods every plan of proving the inspiration of the Scriptures can be reduced. You for yourself use the first, appealing to the testimonies of antiquity in support of your proposition and to arguments from seeming internal imperfections. One who would rest satisfied with your dissertation, believing that your erudition and judgment must lead you to a sufficient acquaintance with those testimonies and to the proper decision thereon, and who would consequently seek nothing more, but unhesitatingly embrace your conclusion, would be using the second. The third is plain of itself. The fourth, that sustained by Catholics, "you despise."

Reverend sir, you admit that there *do* exist divinely inspired writings, and that Almighty God requires individuals of every nation,

clime and condition to receive them as inspired. Those individuals
are "solemnly bound" to reject that inspiration, to "treat those
works as they treat all other writings, merely as human productions—
of no more authority than Seneca's Letters or Tully's Offices" (if
they ever heard of them)—"until clear and cogent arguments for their
Divine origin are submitted to their understandings"—"until they
are proved to be inspired." You are forced, therefore, to allow that
God has provided such proof, suited to the capacity of all those individuals, and which when within their reach, He requires them to use.
That proof must be found in the use of some one of the four above-
mentioned methods.

Let us examine them severally, and see which is in truth suited to
the means and intelligence of men of every condition.

I. Is every man, no matter what be his condition and means, capable of investigating by his own labour and research, and duly examining the arguments that have been or can be alleged for and against
the several books which it is asserted are inspired, and on the strength
of that examination of deciding for himself, with absolute certainty
and unerring accuracy, what books are and what are not inspired?
This question, methinks, need not be asked a second time.

The arguments in this course would be of two classes, external and
internal; either or both of which would form matter for investigation.
He might seek, as you have endeavoured to do, whether there exists a
sufficient mass of testimony to establish the fact or facts that God did,
at certain times and on certain occasions, exercise over particular
writers the supernatural influence of inspiration: or, from a consideration of the perfection of the Scriptures, he might conclude that they
were above the power of unaided men, and therefore must be of Divine origin. To perform the first properly, he must be deeply versed
in the Latin, the Greek and the Hebrew, perhaps, too, in several
modern languages; must have at his command a more extensive
library than, I believe, Charleston can boast of; must spend consequently many long years of study in acquiring those languages and
obtaining authors, in searching out the thousand and one testimonies
scattered through a hundred musty tomes, and in acquiring that
thorough knowledge of times, of men, of writings which will enable
him to judge of the credibility of those witnesses; must finally possess
an unrivalled, almost supernatural, accuracy of judgment, to reconcile
this mass of conflicting statements and distinguish which are worthy
and which unworthy of credit—to conclude confidently and evidently
in favour of or against the inspiration of the books examined. The
second requires a thorough acquaintance with the Scriptures in the
original Hebrew, Greek and Chaldean, and in the ancient versions in
Samaritan, Copt, Arabic, Syriac, Greek and Latin, and with the an-

cient manuscripts; and the ability to apply to all this the subtle rules
of refined criticism, in order to determine, in the first place, as far as
can be ascertained, the exact language and meaning of the sacred
writers; a thorough knowledge of the abilities and acquirements of
each writer and the state of science and already revealed religion in
his country and age, in order to see to what extent of perfection his
own powers with such aids could naturally carry him; the faculty also
of duly appreciating the beauties of the sacred writings, and' that
knowledge of chemistry, of natural history, of geology, of the history
of nations, and of almost every science which may enable him fully
and satisfactorily to refute all the objections brought from these different sources against the intrinsic truth, and consequently internal evidence, of the Divine inspiration of the Scriptures. Need I say it is
all important he should be able to possess and peruse the books on
whose inspiration he is thus to decide?

    Whether any investigation in either or both classes, carried on even
under the most favourable circumstances, will unerringly prove the inspiration of any books of the Scripture, I leave to be mooted by those
who choose to undertake the task. The Editors of the Miscellany
have lately published several articles on the subject, under the head
Protestant Evidence of the Inspiration of Scripture. For my immediate purpose it is enough to ask you and my readers to reflect for one
moment on the past and present condition of the vast majority of those
millions who call themselves Christians, whom God *requires* to receive
the Scriptures, and who consequently have "clear and cogent arguments for their Divine origin." Is it not notorious, the great, the
overwhelming majority of Christians have ever been and must continue incapacitated by their position in the world, their want of time,
of learning, of means, from even attempting such an investigation?
Was it not, for ages before the discovery of the art of printing, morally impossible, on account of the labour and tediousness of copying
such volumes with the pen, their consequent scarcity and the enormous price at which alone they could be procured, for most individuals
to obtain even copies of the Holy Scriptures themselves, much more
of those works necessary for such an examination? Not to leave our
own State, are not more than one-half of her population debarred by
law from learning to read? Of the 550,000 souls in South Carolina,
think you there are 550 or even 50, who have the time, the means, the
ability, the opportunity of devoting themselves to this laborious task?

    If every individual is bound to reject the inspiration of a book
until it is clearly and evidently proved to his mind to be inspired, and
if such proof can only be obtained through that personal examination,
then must the negro and the Indian, and the poor and the unlettered,
and the daily labourer toiling from sunrise to sunset for his bread—

then must the OVERWHELMING MAJORITY of Christians reject the Scriptures; then were all those who, deprived of worldly learning, looked in their simplicity to God for saving wisdom, and fondly believed they possessed it in those sacred oracles of truth—I tremble to follow the awful train of thought. Reverend sir, the *first* CANNOT be the method appointed by Almighty God whereby all should learn with unerring accuracy the inspiration of the Scriptures. Let us take up the second.

II. Is every individual to receive books as inspired, or to reject them as uninspired, according to the decision of persons he esteems sufficiently qualified by erudition and sound judgment to determine that question accurately? I apprehend a candid mind can easily answer this question.

Is such a course adapted to *all* Christians? Would it lead them with unerring accuracy to the truth? If it be the means appointed by Almighty God, both questions must be answered in the affirmative. If common sense and experience show that either or both must be answered negatively, it is not.

Those who possess not learning themselves can seldom or never form a proper estimate of the learning and critical judgment of a truly erudite person whom perhaps they have scarcely looked on. Whole communities may be deceived on this point. Need I cite the case of Voltaire, once extolled by France and the *soi-disant* Philosophers of Europe as a very Briareus of erudition, and now, that in France religion and science happily go hand in hand and execrations of *l'infame* are no longer passports to celebrity, justly derided as a puny, puffed-up smatterer? The individual thus seeking the light of others (besides surrendering his Protestant privilege of judging for himself and pinning his faith to their sleeves) is in most cases unable to judge with certainty and accuracy on the sufficiency of the qualifications of those learned persons, frequently of that single individual, within his limited circle of knowledge. Of the learned in other lands and of their decisions he knows nothing. Even did he, you are aware every variety of decisions would be offered him. I cannot be brought to believe, and I am sure you will not ask me to believe, that all erudition and sound judgment is confined to Germany, Holland, Great Britain, the United States, Denmark and Sweden, and is there parceled out among those who may chance to agree with you in your list of inspired books. I cannot believe, for example, that our lamented bishop, for whom our tears yet flow, was either unsound in judgment or deficient in erudition. Not to speak of esteemed friends who, if I err not, are yet unwilling to admit *any* inspired work, I know many Catholics in the United States, whose talents and years of study render them, as they rendered him, the ornaments of the community in which they move.

I believe that "La belle France" and sunny Italy produce many champions who press forward to the van in the cause of science. I know it is the custom of some to rail against those countries as buried in ignorance and darkness, at least in matters of religion. But such language ever recalls forcibly to my mind the fable of the ant, who, till perchance she wandered forth from her hill, thought nothing could be perfect on earth but what met her limited vision within a few yards of her home. Were you, reverend sir, to devote a leisure hour or so to examining the biography of those prelates who assisted at the Council of Trent, and whose authority and decisions you so heartily "despise," you would find them eminent and worthy of respect for their sincere piety and vast erudition, albeit their decision on the books of *Tobit*, *Judith*, etc., was different from yours.

If in receiving books as inspired, or not, the ignorant and unlearned are, according to the will of God, to abide by the decisions of those learned individuals to whom they have access, or whom in their simplicity they deem qualified to act as their guides, then must we be content to say that God requires some to receive as inspired, and others to reject as uninspired, the same books. The second course seems impracticable. Were it not, it would lead to contradictory conclusions, and therefore to *error*. Such cannot be the means appointed by Divine Wisdom, whereby all the faithful shall truly learn what books of the Scripture are really inspired. Pass we on to the third.

III. Did God ordain that all Christians should learn what Scriptures were divinely inspired from some individual, whom He commissioned to announce this truth to the world? This is the next inquiry which awaits us. If He did, then will the proofs of that commission, and the declaration so made, be such as the mind of every Christian of whatsoever condition can seize.

Our Divine Saviour, taking him simply in his historical character, proved his commission from Heaven by miracles. But He left no Canon or catalogue of inspired works. The Apostles, too, proved their Divine commission. There might be some discussion respecting the works attributed to them, but neither did they leave a Canon in their writings. But did not the Saviour or the Apostles leave such a Canon, though unrecorded, to their followers, to be by them transmitted to future generations, and which all are bound to receive? This supposition, besides overturning another fundamental axiom of Protestants, that *all things* necessary to be believed are recorded in the Scriptures, turns over the question to method the first, which I have already disposed of.

After the time of the Apostles we know of no one who claimed and proved an extraordinary commission from God to establish a Canon of Scripture.

Before the coming of Christ, Esdras is said to have established a Canon for the use of the Jewish nation. It has been disputed whether he did so or not, whether he did so by his own authority or by the authority of God, whether alone or in conjunction with and as member of the Sanhedrim. It has been asserted, too, that in that catalogue were originally contained books which in the vicissitudes of that nation perished in the Hebrew, and are consequently no longer in the Jewish Canon, which consists only of books preserved in that language. I need not trouble you with my opinions on those different points. More veteran scholars than I have found some of them insoluble enigmas. I apprehend a *certain* and *accurate* answer to them all would, at least, be far beyond the capacity of the majority of Christians, and yet this much would be indispensably necessary if they are to have any Divine authority even for the Jewish Canon. At all events, that decision of Esdras would not bear on the inspiration of books then unwritten, as were all the books of the New Testament, so important to Christians, and nearly all the works the inspiration of which your essay controverts.

The third method, then, cannot be admitted, because no such clear, unequivocal testimony of the entire number of inspired books proceeding from an individual who is evidently and undoubtedly commissioned of God exists, and because in the case of Esdras the most we can say is that the substance of the declaration is tinged with doubt, while the fact that he made it and his authority for doing so cannot be ascertained by the vast majority of Christians.

IV. The fourth method alone now remains—namely, that God has ordained that each Christian shall learn what books are inspired from a body of individuals, to whom, in their collective capacity, He has given authority to make an unerring decision on that point; and we find ourselves reduced to the alternative of either admitting this, or of saying that while God *requires* all to believe the inspiration of the Scripture, and binds them to reject it unless it be clearly proved, He has left them without any such proof.

Would such a method, *if established*, be adapted to all Christians? Would it lead them to truth?

One of such a body presenting himself to instruct a Christian or an infidel would first inform him that a number of years ago a Person known by the name of Jesus Christ appeared in Judea and established a new religion. Sufficient motives of credibility can easily be brought forward to induce the novice to believe this. He proceeds to state that Christ proved His heavenly commission to do so by frequent public and manifest miracles. It will not require much to establish in those works certain striking characteristics, of themselves clearly indicative of a miraculous nature. Hence common sense is forced to conclude that the religion established by Christ was *Divine*, springing from God and binding on man. So far we find nothing above or contrary to the means and understanding even of an Indian or a negro. Our instructor then states that Christ, in order to secure the extension of His religion to every people and its perpetuation to the end of time, selected from among His followers certain persons, who, with their successors, were in His name and by the same authority He possessed to go forth and teach all nations all that He had himself taught in Judea.[1] Such a delegation is by no means unnatural or strange, and there could be found no novice, however rude and uncultivated, whose mind could not grasp it, and who would not be led to believe it on sufficiently credible testimony. The next lesson will be that the Saviour assured them that they would be opposed; that others would rise up to teach errors whom He sent not, and that some of their own number would fall away, but that God would recall to their minds all things He had taught them;[2] that He would send them the Spirit of Truth, who should abide with them for ever[3] and should teach them all truth;[4] that He himself would be with them while fulfilling that commission all days, even to the consummation of the world;[5] and that the gates of hell, the fiercest conflicts of enemies, should never prevail against that Church[6] which He sent them to found and ever to instruct. For stronger and more explicit evidence of this, he might, if necessary and convenient, recur to certain histories written by persons who lived at the same time with the Saviour, and were for years in daily and intimate intercourse with Him—who could not mistake such simple points, and the accuracy of whose reports is universally acknowledged and can easily be substantiated.

"All this," replies the novice, "my own common sense would lead me to expect. The persecutions and errors you refer to are but the natural workings of the passions of men, such as experience shows them in every-day life. It would be strange, indeed, that while men change and contradict everything else, they should not seek to change and contradict God's doctrines and precepts too. If He willed that the religion of Christ should endure always—that is, that the doctrines He revealed should be ever preached and believed, the precepts He gave ever announced and obeyed—it was necessary to make some adequate provision against this error and change-seeking tendency of man. If those doctrines and precepts are to be learned from persons He appointed to teach in His name and by His authority, as delegates whom, in virtue of the power given Him, He sent as He was sent by the Father, that provision must evidently and necessarily be directed to preserve the purity of their teaching, to preserve that body of teachers

[1] Matt. xxviii. 19, 20.   [2] John xiv. 26.   [3] John xiv. 16, 17.
[4] John xiv. 26; xvi. 13.   [5] Matt. xxviii. 20.   [6] Matt. xvi. 18.

by the power of God from error, and to make them, in fact, 'teach all things whatsoever He had taught them.' Unaided reason almost assures me this is the course the Saviour would adopt. The evidence you lay before me is satisfactory and worthy of credit. I assent."

The missionary would then inform his pupil that the body of teachers thus guaranteed to teach all truth "for ever" "to all nations" and "all days, even to the consummation of the world," and consequently ever to *exist* and to teach, does in fact exist, claiming and exercising that power—that at the present day it consists of such individuals, of whom he is a commissioned teacher. If asked, he would probably be able to point out the predecessors of those persons in the last and every preceding age, for a line of succession would have come down from the days of the Apostles claiming and exercising that authority. He might state that one hundred and seventy-five millions of every nation—from New Zealand to China, from Van Diemen's Land to the Canadian Indians, from the Cape of Good Hope to Siberia—admit and subject themselves to this authority; that this immense multitude is owing to no sudden increase, but that millions on millions in every age have done the same. The novice might inquire whether the predictions concerning persecutions and error had yet been fulfilled. In answer, the past and present persecutions might be laid before him, and the long list of those who in various ages opposed the teaching of that body by every imaginable shade of error, but with all their efforts could never overturn or suppress it.

"Truly," exclaims the pupil, "the gates of hell shall never prevail against the Church of Christ. The existence of that body, its history, its claims recognized by such multitudes, would of themselves, had I no other motive for believing, convince me of all the facts I have just admitted. Were they not true, this claim would be unfounded—this body, subject to the fate of all human bodies, would have long since perished. I see whatever Christ taught must be true. I recognize you as His commissioned teacher. I believe Him for his miracles, I believe you for His authority. What are His doctrines, that I may receive them? His precepts, that I may obey them?"

In all this there is nothing opposed to the nature or the powers of any man, or to the nature of religion. The facts to which assent is asked are as simple, and may be readily made as clear and as certain, as that there lived such a Roman as Julius Cæsar, that he warred in Gaul, afterwards turned his arms against his country, overcame Pompey, and finally met his death from assassination. An appeal is made to that principle implanted in the human mind by its Creator, and among the earliest to be developed—confiding reliance on the statements of others —while He guarantees that through His almighty providence TRUTH shall be stated. An infant would believe, by force of that nature which

God has given it, all I have proposed and the doctrines delivered in consequence, long before it would dream of asking evidence for authority to teach, and when reason is sufficiently developed to receive motives of credibility they are already at hand. We should ever bear in mind, too, that if this be the method adopted by Almighty God—if in reality, as the hypothesis requires, He speaks to that individual through this teacher—His Divine grace will influence the mind of the novice to yield a more ready and firm assent than the tendency of our nature and the unaided motives of human authority would produce. In this system there is no room for that awful but necessary, inevitable consequence of the axioms of Protestants and of your own principles, that in the life of every individual there should be a dark void of infidelity and unbelief from the time when, having attained the use of reason, he is able and most solemnly bound before his Maker to judge for himself, until the time when clear and cogent arguments for the inspiration of at least some one of the scriptural books have been laid before his mind. During that interval, be it long or short—an hour, a day, a month, a year, entire lustres or a whole life—their inspiration is *unproved* to his mind; "clear and cogent arguments for their Divine origin are not yet submitted to his understanding," and hence he is "solemnly bound" to "treat them as he treats all other writings, merely as human productions," "having no more authority than Seneca's Letters or Tully's Offices." In this interval he is without an inspired Bible, and consequently cannot believe the truths of Divine Revelation, which, on the broad ground of Protestantism, are to be learned from the Scriptures alone as the inspired Word of God; in one word, during that period he is "solemnly bound" (shall I say unless "he runs the risk of everlasting damnation?") to live a perfect INFIDEL. I know that this statement will startle many of my readers —that you will disavow it. I do not charge Protestants with holding the absurdity, for none, as far as I know, have avowed it *totidem verbis.* I see, however, a partial admission in the practice of many Protestants to let their children grow up without much religious instruction because in future years they have to examine and judge for themselves. Still, this conclusion, however absurd and awful (as you have not advanced it I may, without infringing the rules of courtesy, add), however *blasphemous,* is the necessary, unavoidable consequence of your premises. Such an inference cannot follow from TRUTH.

This fourth method is not repugnant to the nature of religion, for all true religion is based on submission of the understanding and the will to God when He speaks to us Himself—to His authorized delegates when through them He deigns to teach. Had He appointed it, that body of individuals so commissioned would evidently teach TRUTH.

The fourth method alone is therefore both practicable in the ordinary condition of the Christian world, and efficient.

Does there exist a body of men clothed with this authority guaranteed by such a Divine promise from error? Has it made a declaration setting forth, in pursuance of that authority, what works are truly inspired?

You, reverend sir, are forced to the alternative of either answering both questions in the affirmative, or of saying that the overwhelming majority of Christians are "solemnly bound" to reject the Scriptures, and if they have admitted them, it was in violation of the will of God and of their solemn duty. From this dilemma there is no escape.

Were I not unwilling to take too wide a range, I might here develop those arguments on the subject which I referred to in the beginning of this letter. Those who are desirous of investigating this question, of vital importance to every sincere Christian, I refer to Wiseman's Lectures, an English work, and one easily obtained. I trust that I have said enough to show that such a tribunal, at least for proving the inspiration of the Scriptures, does and must exist, unless we presume to tax the infinite wisdom of God with absurdity and contradiction.

Which, then, is that body? The pastors of the Catholic Church claim to compose it. No other body claims that commission. Leaving aside an appeal to the historical evidence of continued succession from the Apostles, and other arguments bearing on the subject, common sense tells us that if God has invested any body of individuals with such authority, that body cannot either be ignorant of its powers nor disclaim them. The Catholic Church, then, is that body. In the decree of the Council of Trent the Christian world has its authorized declaration.

But why delay for fifteen centuries and a half this necessary, all-important proof? Why leave the world for such a length of time without this evidence of the inspiration of the Scripture? I deny that the delay took place. In order that the sentiments of a community be known by those who move within its bosom or have intercourse with its members, it is not necessary that these should assemble in a public meeting and set forth their opinions in a preamble and resolutions. So, too, the doctrines of the Catholic Church can be known by the universal and concordant teaching of her pastors, even when her bishops have not assembled in a general council and embodied those doctrines in a list of decrees. When general councils are held, it is, on the head of doctrine, merely to declare and define what doctrines have ever been taught and believed in the Church. This is what the Council of Trent did on the Canon of Scripture.

The Apostles left to the infant Church those inspired works which

Catholics now hold. They were universally used, excepting, perhaps, in a few churches for whose variations I shall account when treating of your second argument. After a number of years circumstances arose which led some persons to doubt whether the universal Church—though she ever had and still continued to use them—did so because she looked on all as inspired, or some merely as pious and instructive works. Other works, too, were protruded as inspired, and some seemed to obtain partial circulation. An expression of the belief of the body of pastors was required. It was again and again given in the councils of Carthage and Hippo and the decisions of Innocent I. and Gelasius. In these the whole body of pastors acquiesced, and for a thousand years no objection of any importance was made. After that period arose Protestantism. Luther and his followers denounced many books—not those alone you controvert, but others also which you revere as inspired—in terms compared to which even your essay is courteous. Some Catholics, too, seemed to think the former decision had not been sufficiently explicit, and therefore the bishops at Trent, assisted by the most learned divines, canonists and scholars, after every possible research and the fullest investigation, decided again that all those books in the Catholic Bible had been handed down from the Apostles, had ever been held in the Church as inspired, and should therefore be still revered as sacred and canonical. These different assertions I shall sustain by due authority when I answer your second argument.

But many objections have been urged against the truth of that decision. I ask you, reverend sir, is there any doctrine of revelation against which many arguments have not been urged? Have not the very existence of God and His unity been assailed? Have not the mysteries of the Trinity, of the incarnation of the Son, and every doctrine of Christianity, been attacked? The fact, therefore, of opposition is no disproof. Nor is it necessary for the true believer to be able to answer every cavil or sophism. Surely the negro cannot answer, cannot even comprehend, the arguments brought against the existence of God. Is he therefore doomed to remain an Atheist? When we know positively and clearly that God requires us to believe a certain doctrine because He declares it to be true, we are bound to obey unconditionally. Common sense tells us that every objection to it must be based on error, even though we be unable to point it out. And so, too, a Catholic relies on the authorized decision of his Church concerning the inspired writings with surety, classing all the objections urged thereagainst with the numberless other objections urged in like manner against every truth of Divine revelation, against the Deity himself, which, according to his degree of knowledge, he may or may not be able to refute, but which he knows by *a priori* evidence of the strongest character *must* be false.

I trust that "a candid and unprejudiced mind" will, upon a mature consideration of the arguments I have brought forward, see that the act of the Council of Trent, so far from being a "striking display of intolerable arrogance," was a decision with the Divine authority for which, and therefore its *truth*, the inspiration of the Scriptures for the vast majority of Christians, and consequently, on Protestant principles, Christianity itself, must stand or fall.

After thus establishing the absolute necessity of admitting that authority which you impugn, and showing the frightful consequences of a contrary course—consequences from which I am certain you will shrink—I might rest satisfied that I have fully answered your essay, and proved by clear and cogent arguments the inspiration of those works against which it is directed. Whatever else I may say will be "over and above what is actually required." "With the distinct understanding, then, that I am doing a work which justice to our cause does not absolutely require," but which places the TRUTH not in a firmer position, but in a stronger light, I will proceed in my next to notice those arguments you so confidently term "irresistible." Meanwhile I remain, reverend sir,

Yours, etc.,   A. P. F.

LETTER II.

To the Reverend JAMES H. THORNWELL, Professor of the Evidences of Christianity, etc.

REVEREND SIR: In the introductory remarks to your essay you said you were not required to advance a single argument against the books of "Tobit, Judith, the additions to the book of Esther, Wisdom, Ecclesiasticus, Baruch with the Epistle of Jeremiah, the Song of the Three Children, the Story of Susannah, the Story of Bel and the Dragon, and the first and second books of Maccabees." It would at first sight appear from your article that Catholics urge only the authority of the Council of Trent in behalf of the inspiration of those books and parts of books. You have scarcely given us the credit of advancing a single argument in corroboration of the truth of that decree. "A candid and unprejudiced mind" would, methinks, have desired from you at least a full and fair statement of what reasons we do bring forward. Your position forbids my supposing you ignorant of at least some of them. Still, I cannot say I regret the course you have taken, though it is not the one I would have chosen. Every impartial, "thinking mind," even though he knew nothing of the Catholic view of the question, would see that yours is completely an *ultra* party exposition of the case, and that, before forming his decision, common

prudence requires him to hear the other side.   I trust that my letters
may fall into the hands of some such.

In my first I treated of the authority of the decree of the Council of
Trent, which declared those works "sacred and canonical," and showed
by a line of argument—which, although not conclusive to an infidel,
must be so to every Christian, because based on the very nature of
Christianity—that in the decree itself we had clear and cogent proof
of their inspiration.   I argued thus: No man can be called on to believe what is not sustained by adequate proof.   Hence, when God proposes any truth for the belief of man, He sustains it by adequate proof.
His own Divine veracity would fully constitute that proof for the individual to whom He speaks.   For others it is necessary that the additional fact that God did reveal His truth to that individual be also
sustained by adequate proof.   Nothing deserves that name which cannot be learned or understood, or which, if learned and understood,
would lead to error or leave room for reasonable doubt.

You hold that one of the truths proposed by Almighty God for the
belief of all Christians, to whom Christianity is duly announced, is, that
certain works are inspired.   Unless we betake ourselves to the tenets
of the Society of Friends, and say that He declares by a special revelation or teaching of the *Private Spirit* to every individual what books
are and what are not inspired (which neither of us is willing to do),
we must confess that this truth is one communicated to man many
ages ago, and which is now to be believed by all those Christians of
every class and condition and clime because of that communication.
Of this communication there does, therefore, there must exist, adequate
proof for all such persons.   There can be but four methods of obtaining that proof, three of which, we saw, must be rejected and the fourth
consequently admitted.

The *first*—a personal examination by each individual of the arguments, historical or intrinsic, in favour of and against the inspiration
of the Scripture, even if such an examination would ever lead to a certain result—could not be admitted, because the overwhelming majority
of Christians are prevented from instituting that examination by the
duties and the circumstances of that condition in which Divine Providence has placed them.   The *second*—that the learned should decide
for and be followed by the unlearned—would lead some to error, as
some of the learned thus to be followed have decided erroneously.
The *third*—that all Christians should learn what books are in reality
inspired from some individual commissioned by Almighty God to announce this truth to the world—was, as we saw, untenable, for the
simple reason that no such declaration from an individual thus commissioned exists.   We were forced, therefore, to admit the *fourth*,
that all Christians should learn what books compose the divinely-in-

spired Scripture from a body of individuals whom God has authorized to decide on that point, and guarantees from error in so deciding. We saw that this method was feasible, adapted to the capacity and condition of every Christian. and consonant with the essence of religion. *If* adopted, it would certainly lead to truth. In one word, it alone was feasible and effective. It *must*, therefore, be admitted. unless we say that the overwhelming majority of Christians are "solemnly bound," unless "they run the risk of everlasting damnation," to reject the inspiration of the Scriptures, and be, on Protestant principles, perfect infidels, unless we overturn Christianity itself. The pastors of the Catholic Church ALONE claim to compose that body. They, therefore, DO compose it. Their decisions on the question of inspiration are guaranteed by Almighty God from error. They have numbered the books you controvert among the inspired Scriptures Therefore those books ARE "*sacred and canonical.*"

I conceive that I have thus satisfactorily discharged the *onus probandi*. As I said above, Catholics corroborate this decree by many other arguments, improbable as this may appear to those who look on your essay as a fair and candid exposition of the state of this controversy. This might be the most proper place for introducing them; but as, in order to develop them fully, I would have to say much which I should again repeat in answering your "irresistible" arguments, I will defer doing so just now, and will proceed to test the force of those same "irresistible" arguments.

The first you state in the following words: [Here A. P. F. quotes at length Dr. Thornwell's first argument.]

Now, reverend sir, you say that a Canon is not an inspired book, but a list or catalogue of inspired works. You lay down the proposition, which I admit, that at the time of the Saviour the Jewish Synagogue had such a Canon, and that the books you controvert were not included therein. There might be some discussion as to part of what you exclude, but I will not argue the point. Even be it, if you will. that during the preaching of the Saviour not one of the books or parts of books the inspiration of which you deny was included in the Canon of the Synagogue of Jerusalem.

You then make the four following assertions:

1. That the Jews "rejected" those books from their Canon in such a manner as, were they in truth inspired, to be guilty of an outrageous fraud in regard to the "Sacred Oracles."

2. That "the Saviour and His Apostles approved of the Jewish Canon."

3. That they "appealed to it as possessing Divine authority."

4. That they "evidently treated it as complete. or as containing the whole of God's revelation as far as it was then made."

Now, reverend sir, in regard to the last three points I notice a very serious oversight in your essay. You have entirely forgotten or omitted to allege, or even by note to refer to, a single passage of the New Testament wherein the Saviour or the Apostles speaks at all of the *Canon* of the Jews. They refer to the Scriptures generally and to particular books; they quote from them; but there is not in the whole New Testament a single passage showing that Christ and His Apostles ever referred to the *canon, catalogue* or *list* of inspired books held among the Jews, much less treated that catalogue as *complete* and "containing the whole of God's revelation as far as then made."

But what you cannot sustain by an appeal to the words of the Saviour or of the Apostles you seek to establish by inference. If those works are, as the Council of Trent declared them to be, in reality divinely inspired, the Jewish nation, in not admitting them into their Canon, "betrayed their trust," were guilty of "fraud," "trampled in the dust or buried in obscurity, or even robbed of its full authority," the Word of God, were "guilty of an outrageous fraud in regard to the sacred Oracles." "It was the business of Christ and His Apostles to give us the *whole* revelation of God." Consequently, in that case they "would have charged the Jews with this fraud, or taken some steps to restore the rejected books to their proper places." He did not, neither did His Apostles. Therefore those books are not inspired, are of "no more authority than Seneca's Letters or Tully's Offices," and the Jewish Canon, which did not contain them, was then "complete," and was treated as such by the Saviour and Apostles. This, if I understand you, is the pith of your argument, in which, by the by, your third assertion is still left entirely unsupported.

Before answering this argument allow me to make a few preliminary observations:

1. That there is great difference between not inserting a work really inspired in a Canon because there is not requisite proof to establish its inspiration or sufficient authority to insert it, and rejecting it when that proof and authority both exist. The first course is proper: to insert a book under such circumstances would be criminal. The second deserves all the terms you use. The first was the case of the Jews. Without a shadow of proof therefor you charge them with the second, if those works are inspired. In your argument this distinction seems not to have struck you, or you have kept it out of sight until the end. You admit it, however, toward the close when you say, "If it should be said that the Jews received those books as inspired, but did not insert them in the Canon because they had not the authority of a Prophet for doing so," etc.

2. In case those books were in reality inspired, though not inserted in the Jewish Canon, it would have been sufficient for the Saviour or

the Apostles to place them among the divinely-inspired books of the Church. This I think evident to every Christian. You seem to admit it, also, when you ask, "Why is it that Christ did not give the requisite authority, if not to the Jewish rulers and priests, at least to His own Apostles?"

3. Christ and His Apostles might have said much in regard to the Scriptures and inspired books which is not recorded in the New Testament. I cannot quote higher and fuller authority than the New Testament itself: "But there are also many other things which Jesus did, which if they were written every one, the world itself, I think, would not be able to contain the books that should be written." John xxi. 25. "To whom (*the Apostles*) also He (*Jesus*) showed himself alive after His passion by many proofs, for forty days appearing to them and speaking of the kingdom of God." Acts i. 3. "Therefore, brethren, stand fast and hold the traditions which you have received, whether by word or by our epistle." 2 Thess. ii. 14. I might quote other texts, but my remark is evidently true. Did not the Apostles change the Jewish Sabbath for the Lord's day, making this a day of rest, consecrated to God, and abrogating the first? Where will you find that in the New Testament? This, too, you seem to allow is possible, as you begin your second argument with the following words: "If it should be pretended that Christ did give His Apostles authority to receive these books, though no record was made of the fact, we ask," etc.

4. I might also make another remark. Supposing those works inspired, as I contend they are, but not admitted at the Saviour's time into the Jewish Canon, it was not, strictly speaking, necessary that either Christ or the Apostles should testify personally to their inspiration. If the Saviour established a body of men, who, by His authority and under the guidance of His Holy Spirit of truth, were to decide that question, which, as I showed in Letter I., we are necessarily bound to admit, the decision of such a body at any subsequent period would be amply sufficient. The Christian world would have had, in the mean time, many other divinely-inspired works. If God was not pleased to give any inspired works to the children of Israel before Moses, nor to inspire the Prophets till a far later period, surely it would be the height of presumption in us now to lay down rules to Him, prescribing *when* He should inspire a work or establish its inspiration. This is more evident when we consider that the Jews had, and the Christians must still have, some method of truly and satisfactorily ascertaining the truths of Revelation other than the simple perusal of all the inspired works. In regard to the Jews this is evident, and is allowed by themselves. That Christians, too, have such a mode (a doctrine, you are aware, Catholics hold) is shown to be necessarily true by a train of argument similar to that of my preceding letter, and

equally cogent. Surely the three hundred thousand negroes in South Carolina prohibited by law from being taught to read cannot learn much from the perusal of the Scriptures. Must they, therefore, remain ignorant of the truths of Christianity? Again, has God ever declared that He will never inspire another work? And if He has not limited His omnipotence, shall we dare to place bounds to it? Now, in point of fact, as far as the Christian world is concerned there would be little if any difference between His inspiring a work five hundred, one thousand or two thousand years after Christ, and His then making known, in any way He thinks proper, that a work written any number of years before is inspired. I make this remark, not because I intend to use it in my argument, but because it is highly improper to bind down the providence of God in regard to the inspired writings to certain laws and times, as you seem to do, that have no foundation in truth. The Saviour came, if you will, to give us the whole revelation of God—that is, all the *doctrinal truths* of that revelation, but not all the inspired works, for not one of the books of the New Testament was written until years after His crucifixion. St. John wrote the last after the year 90. Many early Christians thought that the *Pastor* of Hermas, written many years still later, was inspired. They were mistaken; but even that error shows that they at that early age knew of no declaration of the Saviour or Apostles that there should be no more inspired books.

With these prefatory observations, I take up your argument as simply stated above, and meet it by answering that when the Jewish Synagogue did not admit those works into the Canon it was because of the want of proof of their inspiration, and perhaps want of authority to amend an already duly-established Canon, and that therefore they were not guilty of the heinous sin you lay at their door; and, secondly, that Christ and His Apostles *did* take some steps, not, indeed, to insert those books in the Jewish Canon, but to give them to the Christians as divinely-inspired works, and it is in consequence of those steps that the Catholic Church has ever held them as inspired and the Council of Trent enumerated them in the list of "Sacred and Canonical" works.

The distinction laid down in my first remark completely nullifies your argument. In order to convict the Jews of an "outrageous fraud in regard to the Sacred Oracles" if those works are inspired, you should show, not only that those works were not inserted in the national Canon, but also that when a work was inspired sufficient proof thereof was ever offered under the Synagogue, and that there also ever existed some individual or body of men who had authority to act on such proof and to amend accordingly that national Canon. Need I say that in your dissertation we look in vain for anything establishing

either of those points? The only remark bearing on them is that
already referred to: "If it should be said that the Jews received those
books as inspired, but did not insert them in the Canon because they
had not the authority of a Prophet for doing so, why is it that Christ
did not give the requisite authority, if not to the Jewish priests and
rulers, at least to His own Apostles?" I assert that the Saviour did
give to His Apostles and their successors every power that was necessary. This follows as a necessary consequence from the argument laid
down in my previous letter, and I will further sustain it by historical
evidence. But even had He done nothing directly or indirectly, recorded or unrecorded, in the matter, the only legitimate consequence
would be that He was not pleased ever to prove authoritatively the
inspiration of those books. I confess it would be highly probable they
were uninspired, but their want of inspiration would not be an inevitable consequence. Were not the vision of Addo, and other works I
will mention below, inspired, though now lost and known only by
name? Who can say that the other prophets of those days did not
write works, even whose names are unknown? They doubtless served
the particular end for which God designed them. But even had the
Saviour acted in such a matter as to show evidently that those works
were uninspired, this would not touch either of two points so important to the validity of your argument. These, reverend sir, you have
assumed without any show of reason or authority. Your argument
is valueless, and crumbles under its own "irresistible" weight.

I might here dismiss this part of your essay, as the *onus* was certainly on you to prove everything necessary to make your argument
conclusive. However, even though it be something "over and above"
what justice to my cause "absolutely required," I will lay before our
readers a few remarks on the national Canon of the Jews.

The earliest notice of an authoritative sanction of any work among
the Israelites is found in the command of Moses to the Levites (Deut.
xxxi. 24–26), to place in the side or by the side of the ark the volume
in which he had written the words of the law. This would appear to
designate the book of Deuteronomy alone, and certainly it does not
follow from the words used that Moses, in *writing* that volume, received the supernatural assistance of Divine Inspiration. But I am
willing to admit that the entire Pentateuch was even in that early period known to be inspired, and was used in the public services, though
this last, I think, cannot be proved. Moses died in the year 1447
before Christ, according to Calmet. Esdras returned to Jerusalem
from the Babylonian captivity, 462 B. C. During this period of
nearly one thousand years many inspired works were written. We
have a number of them in the Old Testament. Others, too, were
written which no longer exist. I might mention the book of Samuel

the Seer, that of Nathan the Prophet, and of Gad the Seer,[1] containing accounts not found in our Bible, the books of Ahias the Silonite and the vision of Addo the Seer,[2] the books of Semeias the Prophet[3] and the words of Hozai,[4] and might easily swell the catalogue. All those works, extant or lost, were in all probability known to be inspired by the contemporaries of the several writers, but we have nothing to lead us to suppose that during all this time an exact catalogue or Canon of them was formed by national or Divine authority. In the year 970 B. C., after many of them were written, the ten tribes separated from the kingdom of Judah, not a few of the Israelites retaining the true faith. After they were borne into captivity and other nations introduced into their country, these new-comers were instructed by an Israelite priest how they should worship the Lord, but for some time they joined therewith heathen profanities and idolatry. These, however, we know they afterwards abandoned. You are aware they still exist, and that they have always publicly recognized only the five books of Moses as inspired. It would appear, then, that at the time of the separation of the children of Israel under Rehoboam no Canon had been yet drawn up by due authority.

This is more evident if we advert to the fact that all the Jewish writers attribute the formation of their Canon to the *Cheneseth Ghedolah*, or great Synagogue, after the captivity of Babylon, of which Esdras was a principal member. According to the testimony of the rabbins generally, this synagogue commenced under Darius Hystaspes, and ended in Simon, surnamed the Just, high priest under Seleucus Nicanor. All agree in placing it between those two extremes, and some restrict it, at least in its flourishing condition, to a much shorter space. It seems generally to be allowed that the greater part of the duty in regard to the sacred writings devolved on Esdras himself, who expurgated the sacred works from the various faults into which copyists had fallen, and collected them all into one body, introduced the Jewish divisions of *Perishot*, *Sedarim* and *Peshuot*, and arranged the whole into books. It would seem, too, and it is generally admitted, that various additions were made, such as the conclusion of the book of Deuteronomy concerning the death of Moses. Grotius thought that the inscriptions and dates at the beginning of the prophecies originated here too. But I do not see why we need go so far, as it was natural that the original writers should place them there, and they elsewhere occur under such circumstances as show them to be evidently the work of the Prophets themselves. In speaking of this recension of the Scripture and formation of the Canon, the Jews generally attributed it

[1] 1 Paralip., or 1 Chron. xxix. 30.
[2] 2 Paralip., or 2 Chron. ix. 29; xii. 15; xiii. 22.
[3] 2 Paralip., or 2 Chron. xii. 15.   [4] 2 Paralip., or 2 Chron. xxxiii. 19.

to the *Cheneseth Ghedolah*, or great Synagogue, as, in the treatise *Meghillah*, third chapter of the Ghemara, they say this synagogue restored the pristine purity of the Scriptures, and in *Baba bathra*, chap. 1, that the men of the great Synagogue wrote the book of the twelve Prophets and the books of Daniel and Esther. Elias the Levite and other learned rabbins treat the whole work as that of the synagogue. Perhaps we would not be far from the truth in saying that Esdras, as member of the Sanhedrim, revised the copies of the sacred writings, restored the true reading, collected the scattered parts of the Psalms—as the authors of the Synopsis of Scripture, sometimes attributed to St. Athanasius and St. Hilary (Prol. in Psalm.), say—the detached Proverbs, and the other scattered parts, and arranged the whole in a body, and that the synagogue itself authoritatively sanctioned the work, thus establishing a national Canon. In this plan we must admit that some other books were superadded at a posterior date by the same synagogue. In arriving at a decision on the formation of this Canon we have to guide ourselves, not by the infallible, unvarying statements of inspired writers, but by the perplexed, sometimes contradictory, and often nearly valueless, statements of historians who wrote long afterwards. One thing is certain, the Canon was closed after the admission of the book of Nehemiah. No evidence whatever exists to prove the existence of a national Canon before the Babylonian captivity. The Jewish and the early Christian writers speak of this alone, and their testimonies, carefully weighed, would lead to the opinion I have stated.

What were the ideas of the Jews on this subject at the time of the Saviour may be learned from the following passage of Josephus Flavius, in his first book against Appion. After stating in the sixth chapter that the ancient Jews took great care about writing records of their history, and that they committed that matter to their high priests and their prophets, and that those records had been written all along down to his own times with the utmost accuracy; and in the seventh, that the best of the priests and those who attended upon the Divine worship were appointed from the beginning for that design, and that great care was taken that the race of the priests should continue unmixed and pure, he continues:

"And this is justly or rather necessarily done, because every one is not permitted of his own accord to be a writer, nor is there any disagreement in what is written, they being only prophets that have written the original and earliest account of things as they learned them of God himself by inspiration; and others have written what hath happened in their own times, and that in a very distinct manner also.

"For we have not an innumerable multitude of books among us, disagreeing from and contradicting one another [as the Greeks have], but only twenty-two books, which contain the records of all the past time, which are justly believed to be divine, and of them five belong to Moses, which contain his laws and the traditions of the origin of mankind till his death. This interval of time, from the death of Moses till the reign of Artaxerxes, king of Persia, who reigned after Xerxes, the prophets, who were after Moses, wrote down what was done in their times in thirteen books. The remaining four books contain hymns to God and precepts for the conduct of human life. It is true, our history hath been written since Artaxerxes very particularly, but hath not been esteemed of the like authority with the former by our forefathers, because there hath not been an exact succession of prophets since that time. And how firmly we have given credit to these books of our own nation is evident by what we do, for during so many ages as have already passed no one hath been so bold as either to add anything to them, to take anything from them, or to make any change in them.''

From this it appears that there were among the Jews at our Saviour's time two classes of books which were deemed worthy of respect—their canonical works and others "not esteemed of the like authority.'' In the Jewish writers we find two degrees of inspiration designated, which they term *barrahh haqqadosh* and *bath qvol*. In both they recognize an assistance of God, and say that the books of their Canon attained the first rank, while the second degree only was attained by writers after it was completed. I may refer you to the Talmud, *Baba Cama*, chap. *Hachobel*, where the work of *Ben Sirach*, as they style *Ecclesiasticus*, is declared thus inspired. St. Jerome in his preface to *Judith* expressly states that the work is classed by the Jews among the *Hagiographa*,[1] or sacred writings, not of the first class, for he elsewhere states that they were not in the Jewish Canon, but consequently in the second. The books of Tobias, Judith and the Maccabees evidently fall under the class specially mentioned by Josephus.

I do not feel it necessary, reverend sir, to dwell at length on this topic, as you have merely *assumed*, without any proof, that the Jews rejected as uninspired, mere human productions, all books not contained in their Canon.

The Jewish writers declare that their national Canon was closed and sealed by the great Synagogue, and that books written afterwards attained a lower degree of inspiration. What authority they thought necessary and sufficient to amend that Canon I have never met laid down by any one of them. They seem to presuppose that no such authority existed in fact, nor do they treat of the evidence sufficient to

---

[1] Some copies have *Apocrypha*, but Jahn, after a critical examination of the authorities, decides that Hagiographa is the true original reading, and the other a posterior change.

establish the inspiration of a work. We must conclude, then, that those
works were never brought before a competent tribunal of the Jewish
nation with sufficient evidence, if they were inspired, to prove it, and
yet were rejected. Nevertheless, all this must be proved : it must be
established that such a tribunal did exist ; that those works whose inspiration you controvert were laid before it; that if they were inspired,
sufficient evidence to prove the fact was and must have been brought
forward ; and, finally, that the tribunal rejected the evidence, condemned the books, and refused to admit them into the Canon. This
you have not endeavoured to establish. Had you endeavoured, you
would have failed, for you would have found the monuments of history
arrayed against you. And yet it should have been established before
you could reasonably assert that in regard to these books, if they are
inspired, the Jewish nation had been "guilty of an outrageous fraud
on the Sacred Oracles," and that consequently they would have merited and received a severe rebuke from the Saviour, which rebuke the
Evangelists were bound to insert in their Gospels.

But, reverend sir, even had the Jews been in reality thus heinously
guilty, was the Saviour bound to rebuke them? Did not the Sadducees and Samaritans criminally reject as uninspired, treat merely as
human productions, all the inspired works except the Pentateuch or
five books of Moses? We know that He and His Apostles conversed
with them, opposed and condemned their errors, but where did He
charge them with this heinous fraud? Or even had He rebuked the
Jews, I cannot see why the Evangelists were bound to record it more
than "all the other things that Jesus did," or all His discourses with
His Apostles for forty days after his resurrection. It surely would
have been enough to condemn and correct the outrageous fraud of the
Jews, had any been committed, to leave the books they omitted to the
Church which He founded, and for us it would be enough if we can
know this with certainty. This leads me to the second part of my
answer to your argument. Did the Saviour and His Apostles leave
those books and parts of books to the early Christians as inspired
works?

My first reply would be based on the principles of my last letter.
There must be a sure method whereby the wearied little sweep who now
cries under my window, who has trudged the streets since early dawn,
and ere another hour will bury his limbs in balmy sleep, preparing for
to-morrow's task, can answer that question as confidently and as accurately as you, reverend sir, whom years of study have made conversant
with ancient languages, and who have libraries at hand and leisure to
pore over the tomes of other days. That method is the teaching of
the Catholic Church divinely guaranteed from error. Were he to ask
me, to that Church and her testimony I would refer him, and if rea-

son and common sense prove aught. you must admit that the answer
he would receive at her hands would be unerring.

You require positive proofs from history of the fact, and I am ready
to bring them forward. We have, as I stated—and your argument is
based on the acknowledgment—no record in the New Testament of the
books the Apostles or the Saviour did leave to their followers as inspired. They refer to the Scriptures in general, and quote or allude
to particular passages, but have nowhere drawn up a list of the scriptural works. The evidence must manifestly be drawn from the history
of the Church, whence, too, you in your second argument have endeavoured to extract proofs for your cause. As I intend following the
divisions of your essay, I will reserve the testimonies of the early
Christian writers for my next letter.

Now that the difficulty you imagined so unconquerable—the fraud
of the Jews and the necessity for its recorded condemnation—has vanished, you will probably retract your concession: "We will grant"
the Catholic "what *he cannot* prove and what *we* can *disprove*, that
these books are quoted in the New Testament." It was certainly
easier and more prudent to pass by this argument in the manner you
have done than to *disprove* it, as you assert you can. I will lay before
you some of the texts of the New Testament in which the passages
of those works are quoted or referred to:

1. "See thou never do to another what thou wouldst hate to have
done to thee by another." Tob. iv. 16. "All things, therefore, whatsoever you would that men should do to you, do you also to them."
Matt. vii. 12. "And as you would that men should do to you, do you
also to them in like manner." Luke vi. 31.

2. "Happy shall I be if there shall remain of my seed to see the
glory of Jerusalem. The gates of Jerusalem shall be built of sapphire
and emerald, and all the walls thereof round about of precious stones.
All its streets shall be paved with white and clean stones, and Alleluia
shall be sung in its streets. Blessed be the Lord who hath exalted
it, and may He reign in it for ever and ever! Amen." Tobias xiii.
20, 23.

"And the building of the wall thereof was of jasper stone, but the
city itself pure gold, like to clear glass. And the foundation of the
walls of the city were adorned with all manner of precious stones.
The first foundation was jasper, the second sapphire, . . . the twelfth
an amethyst. And the twelve gates are twelve pearls, one to each,
and every several gate was of one several pearl. And the street
of the city was pure gold, as it were transparent glass." Apoc. xxi.
18-21.

3. "But they that did not receive the trials with the fear of the
Lord, but uttered their impatience and the reproach of their murmur-

ing against the Lord, were destroyed by the destroyer and perished by serpents." Jud. viii. 24, 25.

"Neither let us tempt Christ, as some of them tempted and per-ished by the serpents. Neither do you murmur, as some of them murmured and were destroyed by the destroyer." 1 Cor. x. 9, 10.

4. "The just shall shine, and shall run to and fro like sparks among the reeds." Wisdom iii. 7. "Then shall the just shine as the sun in the kingdom of their Father." Matt. xiii. 43.

5. "They [the just] shall judge nations and rule over people, and their Lord shall reign for ever." Wisdom iii. 8. "Know you not that the saints shall judge this world?" 1 Cor. vi. 2.

6. "He pleased God and was beloved, and living among sinners he was translated." Wisdom iv. 10. "By faith Henoch was translated that he should not see death, and he was not found, because God had translated him. For before his translation he had testimony that he pleased God." Heb. xi. 5.

7. "For she [Wisdom] is the brightness of eternal light and the un-spotted mirror of God's majesty, and the image of His goodness." Wisdom vii. 26. "Who [the Son of God] being the brightness of His glory and the figure of His substance," etc. Heb. i. 3. See also 2 Cor. iv. 4 and Col. i. v.

8. "For who among men is he that can know the counsel of God? or who can think what the will of God is?" Wisdom ix. 13. "For who hath known the mind of the Lord? or who hath been His coun-sellor?" Rom. xi. 34.

9. "The potter, also, tempering soft earth, with labour fashioneth every vessel for our service, and of the same clay he maketh such ves-sels as are for clean uses, and likewise such as serve to the contrary; but what is the use of these vessels the potter is the judge." Wisdom xv. 7. "Or hath not the potter power over the clay of the same lump, to make one vessel unto honour and another unto dishonour?" Rom. ix. 21.

10. "Or if they admired their power and their effects, let them un-derstand by them that He who made them is mightier than they, for by the greatness of the beauty and the creature the Creator of them may be seen so as to be known thereby." Wisdom xiii. 4, 5. "For the invisible things of Him from the creation of the world are clearly seen, being understood by the things that are made." Rom. i. 20.

11. "And His zeal will take armour, and He will arm the creature for the revenge of His enemies. He will put on justice as a breastplate, and will take true judgment instead of a helmet. He will take equity for an invincible shield, and He will sharpen His severe wrath for a spear." Wisdom v. 18, 21. "Therefore take unto you the armour of God, that you may be able to resist in the evil day and to stand in all

things perfect. Stand, therefore, having your loins girt about with truth, and having on the breastplate of justice, . . . in all things taking the shield of faith, wherewith you may be able to extinguish all the fiery darts of the most wicked one. And take unto you the helmet of salvation and the sword of the Spirit (which is the word of God).'' Eph. vi. 13, 17.

12. ''They that fear the Lord will not be incredulous to His word, and they that love Him will keep His way. They that fear the Lord will seek after the things that are well pleasing to Him, and they that love Him shall be filled with His law. . . . They that fear the Lord keep His commandments, and will have patience even until His visitation.'' Ecclesiasticus ii. 18, 21. ''If any one love me he will keep my word.'' John xiv. 23.

13. '' My son, meddle not with many matters, and if thou be rich thou shalt not be free from sin.'' Ecclus. xi. 10. ''For they that will become rich fall into temptation and into the snare of the devil, and into many unprofitable and hurtful desires which drown men into destruction and perdition.'' 1 Tim. vi. 9.

14. ''There is one that is enriched by living sparingly, and this is the portion of his reward. In that he saith, I have found me rest, and now I will eat my goods alone; and he knoweth not what time shall pass, and that death approacheth, and that he must leave all to others and shall die.'' Ecclus. xi. 18, 19, 20. ''And I [the rich man in the parable] will say to my soul, Soul, thou hast much goods laid up for many years; take thy rest, eat, drink, make good cheer. But God said to him, Thou fool, this night do they require thy soul of thee, and whose shall those things be which thou hast provided?'' Luke xii. 19, 20.

15. ''If thou wilt keep the commandments and perform acceptable fidelity for ever, they shall preserve thee.'' Ecclus. xv. 16. ''If thou wilt enter into life, keep the commandments.'' Matt. xix. 17.

16. The passage of St. Paul, ''But others were racked, not accepting deliverance, that they might find a better resurrection'' (Heb. xi. 35), has been acknowledged, even by Protestant commentators, to be, and evidently is, a reference to the account of the martyrdom of Eleazar, given in the second book of Maccabees, vi. 18–31.

I might cite many such passages, but these will be sufficient for my purpose. Any ''candid and unprejudiced mind,'' at all versed in the rules of criticism, must see that in the New Testament the passages I have brought forward are alluded to and were had in view. The identity of thought and the similarity, often striking coincidence, of expression, absolutely require this, else there is no such thing as one writer's using the thought and expression of another. You say, though you do not maintain their opinion, that some ''learned men have doubted

whether some of them existed at all until some time after the last of
the Apostles had fallen asleep." You yourself do not "believe that
the Septuagint contained them at the time of the Saviour and the
Apostles." I have not taken 'the pains to see who were those learned
men, or what books they thought were posterior to the Apostles. I
have before me—and, had your adopting their opinion rendered it
necessary, or did the space of this letter permit, might produce—testimony in abundance to prove those works anterior to the Saviour.
One of the authors you quote, Eichhorn, and Jahn, one of the most
acute of German critics, declare that Philo has drawn much from the
earlier of those works, so much so as to have been sometimes deemed
the author of the book of Wisdom. To your own "belief," and, if
you please, the authority of Schmidius, I will oppose the express declaration of Origen, the highest authority we can find or could desire on
this question of fact. In his epistle to Julius Africanus, *De Historia
Susannæ*, he says: *In nostro Græco sermone feruntur in omni ecclesia
Christi*, that these passages of Daniel "are found in our Greek tongue
throughout the entire Church;" and further on: *Apud utrumque erat
de Susanna ut tu dicis figmentum, et extremæ partes in Daniele;* "in
both (the Septuagint and the version of Theodotion) are contained
what you call the fiction of Susannah and the last parts of the book of
Daniel;" and immediately afterwards, enumerating what you term the
additions to the book of Esther, emphatically declares that though not
found in the Hebrew in his day, *Apud Septuaginta autem et Theodo-
tionem ea sunt*, "they are found, nevertheless, in the Septuagint and
Theodotion." I do not pretend to say that the Seventy translated into
Greek works written in that language, as were some of the books in
question, or not composed until they were in their graves. It is generally allowed that they translated at most only the canonical works of
the Jews shortly after that Canon was formed. Other works, however, existed in the Jewish nation, which were revered and used and
looked on as written in *Bath quol*, or the second degree of inspiration,
and were added, if you please, as an appendix to the collection of
works translated by the Seventy, the whole collection, containing both
classes of books, still retaining, at least among Christians, the name of
the *Septuagint version*. Not to multiply quotations on this point, I
will merely bring forward the testimony of Walton, the editor of the
Polyglot, whom I respect as the most learned of Protestants in such
matters, and eminently qualified, by his vast researches on the different versions, to decide authoritatively. His Protestantism effectually
prevented any *partiality* in favour of those books. In his Prol., cap.
ix., he says: " *Libri itaque Apocryphi, ut à variis auctoribus ita variis
temporibus scripti sunt, quidam Hebraicè, quidam Græcè; et licet
apud Hellenistas primum recepti fuerint, tempus tamen præcisè assig-*

nari non potest, quando cum reliquis libris sacris in unum volumen compacti fuerint. Hoc tamen clarum est, a Judœis Hellenistis cum reliqua Scriptura Ecclesiam eos recepisse." "Wherefore the Apocryphal books were written as well by different authors as at different times, some in Hebrew and some in Greek; and although they were first received by the Hellenists, yet the precise time cannot be assigned when they were united in one volume with the other sacred works. This much, however, is evident, that the Church received them from the Hellenist Jews."

Whether this transfer was made with or without the consent of the Apostles may, I think, be learned from a glance at the texts I have quoted above. What are the facts of the case? There existed a certain collection of books well known to the apostolic writers and to the faithful to whom their epistles were sent, as many, if not most, of them were converts from the number of those same Hellenist Jews. In that collection were comprised not only the canonical books of the Jews, but also those styled by the Protestants *apocryphal*. The Apostles quote frequently by name books of that collection, sometimes extract *verbatim* or with a partial change of words entire sentences, but more frequently, adopting and appealing as it were to some passage, incorporate its sentiment, and more or less of its wording, into their own train of thought. This is most frequently done by the Saviour, as may be seen by any of my readers who disdains not, in his love of the Bible *alone*, to use one with accurate marginal references. The passage from Tobias is as striking and as well defined a quotation as any other, and as such must have struck his hearers. The change of the original negative into the positive is not so striking as that of Micheas v. 2: "And thou, Bethlehem Ephrata, art a little one among the thousands of Judah," quoted thus by St. Matthew, ii. 6: "And thou Bethlehem, the land of Judah, art NOT the least among the princes of Judah." Protestants find not the least difficulty in admitting such passages of the New Testament to contain allusions to the Old as long as their canonical books alone are concerned, but when a passage of the works whose inspiration they deny is laid before them, the thought and *tournure* of expression of which an Apostle has adopted into his own Epistle so evidently as would now-a-days suffice to convict a poet of plagiary, oh! then that cannot be a quotation! Truly, reverend sir, to use your own words, "Light is death to their cause."

I have thus, reverend sir, examined your first argument. You state that at the Saviour's time the Jews had a national Canon in which the works you impugn were not contained. I am willing to admit this in regard to all the books except *Baruch with the Epistle of Jeremiah, the addition to the book of Esther,* and the parts of Daniel which you style *the Story of Susannah, the Story of Bel and the Dragon, and the Song of the Three Children.* I know that they had the books of which these were considered parts; it is allowed that those parts once existed in the original language of those books, and that at the time of Origen they no longer existed in those languages. Before I admit that they perished in those languages, not after but before the time of the Saviour, I must have proof positive, which I do not recollect having ever met, and I am of opinion does not exist. However, I waived all controversy on this point, allowing your argument all the force it could receive from the fact did it take place.

You then said that the Jews excluded them from their Canon under such circumstances as, were they in reality inspired, to render themselves "guilty of an outrageous fraud in regard to the Sacred Oracles." This was a mere assumption unsupported by any proof. It could not be the case unless there existed a tribunal in their nation capable of adding to the Canon already established, and the books were laid before this tribunal. You seem to think that the Jewish Canon was established by Divine authority. This would at once take off all responsibility from the Jewish nation and defeat your own argument. I have not taken advantage of it, however, as the Jews themselves attribute the formation of their Canon not to an immediate revelation of God, but to their *Cheneseth Ghedolah,* or Great Synagogue. I, who see therein a general Council of the Church in the old law, claiming and exercising by the authority of God the power of teaching the faithful what were their inspired works, will readily admit its Divine authority so far as the decree can be evidently shown to have gone—that is, that *those* books were inspired. It cannot be proved that it determined anything in regard to books either lost, as probably many were, or yet unwritten, or not in their possession. It would seem that it was with great difficulty they obtained even those whose inspiration they testified to. I question much whether in this view you will admit the *Divine authority* of the Jewish Canon, and yet you say the Saviour did. History informs us that this great Synagogue ended, and was not revived or succeeded by any other of equal authority to act on the Canon of Scripture. Hence, even were there noonday evidence of the inspiration of those books, the Jews could not, at least according to their own writers, place them in the Canon. It was not necessary that such full evidence should exist. We have no proof that it did exist; though that *some* evidence was in possession of the Jews may be gathered from the facts that, as Walton says, they were united in the same volume, and that the rabbins hold some of them as inferiorly inspired. At all events, it is evident the Jews were not "guilty of an outrageous fraud in regard to the Sacred Oracles" in not inserting those works, even though they be inspired, in their national Canon.

Your next assertions were, that "the Saviour and His Apostles approved of the Jewish Canon, whatever it was, and appealed to it as possessing Divine authority." Had they gone no farther, this would not have militated against us. I might, on the contrary, appeal to it as a positive Divine sanction of the fourth method of my preceding letter. Still, you have not in their words the least support for your assertions. The circumstances from which you would *infer* it exist simply in your own ardent imagination, and are not such as historical evidence sustains.

These you follow up with another statement, equally unsupported by their words or the facts of the case, that "the Saviour and His Apostles evidently treated the Jewish Canon as complete, and containing the whole of God's revelation as far as it was then made." For this, precisely, you offer no proof. You view it as the evident consequence of the other items of argument. They fall to the ground, and this must fall with them.

You think that had the Jews been guilty of the heinous crime with which, in case these books are inspired, you tax them, the Saviour and His Apostles were bound to denounce this particular offence. I think it would have been sufficient to condemn them in general and to state some of their errors, without being *bound* to go over the whole list. He proposed the truth of Christianity in general for their acceptance. If they embraced this, the acceptance of those books would have followed, as I will show it *did* follow for the early Christians. We know that as a people they "received Him not." He came not to reform the Jewish religion, but to establish another—that which it foreshadowed. He might—as He did—condemn particular errors and abuses, but the end, the grand aim, of His preaching, was to bring them to believe in Him and all those things which He taught His Apostles personally for forty days after His resurrection, or by the Spirit of truth afterward, concerning His Church, the kingdom of God. He never declared that He would, and we see no reason why He should, enumerate and condemn *every* abuse, or that He was bound to single out this particular error. We have two parallel cases: that of the Samaritans, whose schism or error He condemned in John iv. 22, and of the Sadducees, whom both He and St. Paul condemned. Both were heinously guilty of rejecting inspired writings as mere human productions, and yet we have no evidence that they charged them with this particular error or sin. Why, then, bind them to do so in regard to the Pharisees?

You finally state that Christ and His Apostles did nothing in regard to those books; and this you sustain in your first argument by saying there is not in the New Testament any record of the fact, and in your second by endeavouring to show that the Christians of the first four centuries acted in such a manner in regard to those books as they certainly would not have done if the Saviour or His Apostles had given any testimony of their inspiration.

I might answer that though the Saviour did not establish evidently the inspiration of those books then, He could have done it after four centuries with equal facility, either through such a body of individuals as I have often referred to, or by any other means He thought proper to use. The only questions for us would be, Did He adopt those means? What are the books the inspiration of which is thus declared? But I meet your assertion directly. In my next I will show that the early Christians acted in regard to these books in such a manner as they would not have done *unless* they had been received from the Saviour or the Apostles as inspired. We find nothing in the Gospels or Epistles to show that they do or must contain all that the Saviour or Apostles taught or did. St. Paul taught many things by word, as we learn from himself. The Saviour's discourse to the disciples on the road to Emmaus and a full account of all His conversations with the Apostles after His resurrection would be very valuable. Among these last you might, reverend sir, find something bearing on the number of inspired books. However, until you have *all* He said to the Jews and His Apostles, or an assurance from Him or them that this was not contained among the things omitted, venture not to assert that because He did not, as far as you can learn, say it on certain occasions to certain persons, He never said it to any one at all. That the Saviour and Apostles did do something in regard to those books, I opine, is evident from the texts I have quoted, else plagiary among authors is an imaginary crime. The identity of thought and the similarity, sometimes copied turn, of expression prove this evidently. The circumstances of the case support it. According to Walton, the collection containing these, with the canonical books of the Jews, was in the hands both of the writers and those who read their books. The subjects were the same. In their writings they avowedly quote, adopt and allude to the language and thoughts of that collection. Those instances show that such allusions were made, not only to the canonical works, but also to those you deem uninspired. I believe with Walton, that the *Septuagint*, as that collection was called, contained those books before the coming of the Saviour. You think this, if true, strengthens your argument. I think not. If those books thus united were uninspired, the Saviour and the Apostles were certainly bound positively to reject them, and not to suffer the unnatural union to pass into the Church. Now I shall show that as far back as the remnants of those early ages will carry us we find Christians uniting them both in the Septuagint, and revering both as divinely inspired. This very omission of excluding them, taken especially with the decided belief of the early Christians, is a strong proof in favour of the inspiration of those books. But you do not "believe that the Septuagint at the Saviour's time contained the Apocrypha." Reverend sir, a more disastrous avowal you could not have made. The union then took place in the Church, necessarily under the eyes and with the approbation of the Apostles and their immediate, most faithful disciples. These books are quoted and referred to as divinely-inspired Scripture. I could not desire a stronger case. Before the Apostles the contested books were not inserted. Immediately afterwards we find them already inserted. A change has taken place. It could only be effected by, it can only be attributed to, the Saviour and His Apostles. Therefore, they DID leave these works to the Christian world as INSPIRED. I remain, reverend sir, yours, etc., A. P. F.

LETTER III.

TO THE REVEREND JAMES H. THORNWELL, PROFESSOR OF THE EVIDENCES OF CHRISTIANITY, ETC.:

REVEREND SIR: We are now arrived at the most important point in the examination of the historical evidences in favour of those books, for revering which as "sacred and canonical" you charge the Catholic Church with blasphemously adding to the Word of God.

Before I enter on the task of laying before you the evidence of that character in favour of the truth of the decree passed by the Council of Trent, let me again urge on you the absolute necessity of admitting the Divine authority on which the Church based it, and its consequent truth. By denying that authority you at once overthrow the only means whereby the overwhelming majority of Christians can learn with certainty, and on which they can be *required* to believe unhesitatingly, the inspiration of the scriptural books. Even did there exist no historical testimony whatever to prove the truth set forth in that decree, as long as we have reasons for admitting, and are forced by necessity to admit, the authority of the tribunal from which it emanates, the inspiration of those books is proved to our understanding by an *a priori* argument of the strongest character.

In point of fact, millions on millions of Christians in every age have believed and must still hold the Scriptures to be Divinely inspired, simply on authority. How many are there, think you, even among Protestants in South Carolina, who believe it—not because their parents or instructors have so taught them; not because it is the general belief of persons whom they esteem, of the community of which they are members, of the denomination to which they are attached;

nor yet because they have read some dissertation like yours, wherein a few names are quoted, some books in Latin or German referred to, some extracts inserted, and then a sweeping conclusion drawn, set off with a tirade of hard names and denunciations, but scarcely warranted by the premises and wholly unsupported by facts,—how many, I ask, are there, even among Protestants, who believe the Scriptures to be inspired, not on motives like these, but because clear and cogent and *really valid* arguments have been submitted to their understandings? I have amused myself at times by asking those who assail me with texts against what they believe are our doctrines to prove the books they quote from to be inspired, and I very rarely found any one who knew even how to set about the task. They believed them to be inspired, not because any valid argument from historical or internal evidence had been laid before them, but because they had been brought up and led by education and authority to do so. Whether by acting thus, notwithstanding the want of the aforesaid arguments, they followed a course that was not "righteous and holy" and "ran the risk of everlasting damnation," I leave you, reverend sir, to decide. To me such cases are but particular examples of a general truth taught alike by common sense and experience—that not one in ten thousand Christians has the time, the means and the ability to qualify himself properly for that arduous research and to prosecute the investigation of that mass of evidence with success. Any system which would require *all* to do so must be absurd, for it supposes that possible which is morally impossible; and false, because it contradicts the infinite wisdom of God as displayed in His apportionment of men in the various conditions of life. Both among Catholics and Protestants there ever will be, there *must* be, many to whose understandings no valid arguments from reason or from historical evidence for the inspiration of Scripture will ever be submitted—whose condition in life prohibits it. Some may *think* they have them whose reasons, nevertheless, for belief are anything but valid, and would only provoke a smile from those who are qualified to estimate their value. If God requires those millions to believe that inspiration at all, He requires them to believe it on authority, for in no other manner can they learn it. And unless His works be imperfect, He has given an authority to teach them this doctrine whose teaching constitutes the necessary, clear, cogent and valid argument which is to be laid before their understandings. Now in the Protestant system there is no such authority to teach this truth, none which any one is *bound* to hear, or at least none which may not lead to error, and none, therefore, whose teaching necessarily gives truth with unerring accuracy and leaves no room for reasonable doubt and hesitation. In this system God would not have provided any means whereby those can learn certainly and unerringly the inspiration of the Scripture, who are by their circumstances unavoidably restricted to the use of authority alone on this question. In the Catholic system, on the contrary, this *hiatus* in the works of God does not exist. An authority is established by Him to teach this truth, and in fulfilling that commission is guarded by His Omnipotence from falling into error. The evidence of the commission itself and of the guarantee from error is before the world. Christians are required to believe the Scriptures to be inspired on that authority, and in believing they have an assurance from Divine Truth and Omnipotence that they err not. Historical evidence may or may not exist to corroborate the declaration of that authority. Those who believe may or may not possess it. To them it is a secondary collateral proof, placing the doctrine not in a firmer position, but, if you will, in a stronger light. A practical illustration adds nothing to the certainty of a theorem established by mathematical demonstration. If this collateral testimony were not in the possession of the person whose belief is required, or even were it not in existence, the truth of the doctrine taught would remain unchanged and the obligation of believing it equally strong.

Nay more: a person is still bound to believe even when seeming arguments which he cannot refute are urged to the contrary. Common sense tells him that what is known and *proved* to be true by one method of demonstration cannot be shown to be really false by another —that truth is never opposed to truth. Experience would tell him that there is no doctrine against which words cannot be arrayed. He may find objections, the fallacy or falsehood of which he cannot point out, brought against the inspiration of any or of all the books so declared to be inspired. But he knows that the authority which proclaims them inspired teaches TRUTH, and that whatever contradicts truth must be erroneous. He is bound still to believe. Men act thus every day in matters of life, and they are forced to carry out the principles also in doctrines of Christianity. Let me illustrate it by an example.

You hold, reverend sir, that God has declared and requires every one, even the unlettered negro, to believe unhesitatingly that there are three Divine Persons in one God. Now the negro, debarred by law from learning to read, cannot peruse his Bible; cannot (leaving aside the question of inspiration) decide whether certain texts (among them the strongest, perhaps the only decisive one, on the Trinity) be interpolations, as most Protestant critics have determined that of 1 John v. 7 to be; cannot collate all the texts on the subject, and pronounce unerringly that in them God has made such a declaration. He must learn the doctrine of the Trinity from authority. He is bound to believe it unhesitatingly, because God, who cannot declare an untruth, has declared it; and the Catholic would add, common sense requires, because the authority which communicates to him that declaration of God is prevented by Divine Omnipotence from teaching that He declared what in fact He did not. An Unitarian might say to the negro: "You are told that the Father is distinct from the Son, and the Holy Ghost from both; they are three distinct Persons. Now, if the Father is God, and the Son is God, and the Holy Ghost is God, they must, therefore, be three Gods and not one God; and to say that three distinct Persons form only one God is as absurd as to say that three men form one individual. God could not have said so, for He cannot say anything absurd, and anybody that tells you He did say so leads you into an error." Even a negro would see the force of this objection. Can he lay bare the sophism? In the Catholic system his answer would be clear and satisfactory: "My mind is feeble; I cannot by reasoning reply to what you say; but here is a tribunal which God has appointed to teach me what doctrines He has declared, and which He will not permit to mistake. That tribunal tells me that He has declared this doctrine, and when He declares it, it must be true and not absurd, and therefore I believe it, though I cannot refute your arguments." If on the Protestant principle he believed that the authority which had taught him the Trinity *could* propose doctrines which were false, and could assert that God had taught what in truth He did not teach, I confess that I do not see what answer the negro could make, or how he could *reasonably* continue in an unhesitating belief of the Trinity.

I opine, too, that even the most learned theologian would find himself in the same predicament. It would puzzle him to explain *how* three Divine Persons, each of them God, can only constitute one God, while three human persons must constitute, not one, but three beings. He can only seek to establish the fact that God did declare this to be the case. Now I certainly believe the doctrine of the Trinity as firmly as I do my own existence. But could I leave aside the authority of the Catholic Church, could I believe that it was possible for her to declare that God has revealed a doctrine which He has not, I, for one, would not admit this mystery, for the simple reason that except through her I have no positive assurance that it is one of the doctrines revealed by Almighty God. The strongest text, as I said above, is rejected by most Protestant critics as supposititious. Were it not, it is susceptible of another and very different sense. So, too, are all the other texts urged in favour of this dogma. The Unitarians strongly and earnestly urge these views. And in perusing several Protestant treatises on the subject I have not met a Trinitarian who, in my opinion at least, could, without some one-sided appeal to the authority of the Church to decide the question, overthrow their positions or make out for himself more than a plausible, perhaps a probable, case. Deprived of the authoritative teaching of the Catholic Church, I would not, on mere plausible or probable evidence, yield an unhesitating belief in so astounding a mystery as this, or expose myself to the danger of IDOL- ATRY by adoring as God one who might *perhaps* be after all a mere creature. I thank Heaven I am not left in this perplexity or unbelief. Though I cannot refute metaphysically all the metaphysical objections against the august mystery of the Trinity, though my researches of mere historical testimony or simple examination of the Scripture would not lead me to the *certain* and *evident* conclusion that God did reveal it, I have His revelation unerringly preserved by those the Saviour sent to teach all that He had taught, even as He was sent by the Father. Them I hear as I would hear Him. On His authority and their tes- timony I believe the doctrine of the Trinity firmly and unhesitatingly, despite of unsolved sophisms, and bend the knee to adore Jesus Christ as the Eternal God, no dark, horrific doubt flashing the while through my mind that *perhaps* He is but a creature and I am staining my soul with the damning sin of Idolatry.

To apply this to the subject of my letter: *If* Almighty God has been pleased to establish a tribunal with authority to declare uner- ringly, in His name, what books are sacred and canonical, we are bound to receive unhesitatingly as the Word of God the books designated as such by that tribunal, even though we possess not collateral proof from historic or intrinsic evidence to sustain it. We would be equally bound to receive them did no historical evidence whatever exist; nay, even if objections which we have not the means of solving could be urged against the inspiration of some or of all of those books.

I have shown in my first letter that every Christian at least must admit that God *did* establish such a tribunal. When that is estab- lished, collateral testimony is of secondary importance. Had the flood of time swept away every record of the early Church, as it has swept away many, the decree of the Council of Trent would still stand.

I have made these prefatory, perhaps discursive remarks, that our readers may see the nature, the bearing and the value of historical tes- timony in favour of the inspiration of the books which Catholics admit as inspired, and you reject as of no more authority than Seneca's Let- ters or Tully's Offices.

I will now proceed to redeem the promise made towards the close of my last letter, and to show that the early Christians acted in such a manner in regard to those books and parts of books as they would not have done UNLESS the Saviour and His Apostles had left them to the early Church as inspired. Here, reverend sir, we are fairly at vari- ance. I will give your second argument in your own words. [Here A. P. F. quotes Dr. Thornwell's second argument.]

This, reverend sir, might strike a reader altogether unacquainted

with those early times as very forcible, and nearly, if not quite, "irresistible." A second perusal of your essay would show him that much
as you seem to have kept the matter out of sight, even in those first four
ages there were at least two sides to the question, whereas your argument is grounded on the assertion that the unbroken testimony of the
Church during all this time was against the inspiration of those books.
St. Jerome, you state, informs us that the Christians were exposed to
ridicule from the Jews for the respect in which they held one part of
what your arguments affirm uninspired writings. Now St. Jerome
wrote before the year 400, and that respect might, for aught you say,
be some remnant of a tradition from the Apostles regarding their
inspiration. Those decisions, too, which you spoke of, made in their
favour by bodies of which St. Augustine was a member, occurred also
before the year 400. Might they not be other remnants? But, reverend sir, to one who is acquainted with those early days of the Church
it must be a matter of astonishment how, if you had read five authors
of those times (and if you had not, you should not make your second
argument so boldly), you could assert unqualifiedly and emphatically
"that for four centuries the unbroken testimony of the Christian
Church is against their inspiration."

I assert that, on the contrary, the manner in which the Christians
of the first four centuries acted in regard to those writings shows that
they were left to them by the Apostles as inspired. I presume you
will admit that while these early Christians were tried in the furnace
of persecution, and laid down their lives by thousands rather than
swerve one jot or tittle from the truth handed down to them, they
would not throughout the world unite in "blasphemously adding to
the Word of God." If they united in receiving those works as inspired, then is our cause fully sustained, for they would not have thus
united unless they had been taught by the Apostles that those books
formed part of the Word of God. You have appealed to the testimony of the Church for the first four centuries. You shall have it.
Would that you may abide by its award!

In the first place, all those books or parts of books were contained
in the Old Testament as used by the early Christians in the infancy of
the Church. That they all existed at the time of St. Jerome, and at
his day formed part of the Old Testament, cannot be denied. At the
proper place I will speak of his views on their inspiration. At present
let us investigate facts. The Latin Vulgate as used then contained
them. Now, reverend sir, if it be made evident that those works
were received universally and from the earliest day into the body of
the Old Testament, your assertion that there is no remnant of any tradition does not coincide with the fact. At what time were those works
joined to the canonical works of the synagogue? All the works, ex-

cept, perhaps, Wisdom and the second book of Maccabees, were originally written in Hebrew or Chaldaic, as their frequent Semitic idioms evidently show. St. Jerome translated Tobias and Judith from the Chaldaic, and declares that he saw Ecclesiasticus and Maccabees in the original Hebrew. Baruch with the Epistle of Jeremiah bear the indelible impress of their Hebrew origin. Origen declares emphatically that the parts of Esther and Daniel you reject were in the versions of the Septuagint and of Theodotion. We know that Theodotion, whom St. Jerome calls a *Judaizing heretic*, translated from the Hebrew into Greek, and his version of Daniel containing those parts is that anciently adopted by the Greek and Latin churches, and still followed entirely by the first, and in those parts by the latter. This clearly-ascertained origin at once shows that the works were prior to the Saviour. If the Christians had written them afterward, which this general adoption forbids, they would have done it in Greek or Latin—their languages. The book of Wisdom and the second book of Maccabees are allowed by all sane critics to be incontestably anterior to the Saviour. The translation of the Hebrew works into the Greek for the use of the Hellenist Jews is also allowed to have taken place before the Saviour's time. Without attempting now to prove this at length in regard to every book, especially as you have not denied it, I will again content myself with referring to Walton, who declares that those works were first received by the Hellenist Jews, although it cannot be ascertained at what time they were joined in one volume with the Jewish canonical works, but that this much is certain, that the Church received them with the rest of the Scripture from those Hellenist Jews. I said the transfer was made with the approbation of the Apostles, who in writing their inspired Epistles had manifestly used those works. I will now prove it by the versions of the Old Testament among the Christians. Taking the Septuagint or Greek version alone, I cannot see what valid arguments can be adduced to prove that it did not contain those works in the beginning. Not the omission of them in copies, for the oldest entire manuscripts contain them. Not any testimony of some ancient writer, for as far as they bear witness it did, and, as I will show farther on, they quote those identical works. But there is another insurmountable objection to your opinion and an irrefragable proof of my proposition. Two versions were made of the Scriptures immediately after the death of the Apostles—the Latin for the use of the Western Christians, from the Greek, and the Syriac, from the Hebrew and Greek, for those of the East. Both contain those works.

We are informed that many versions or amended versions existed among the Latins, but that there was one called the *vetus Itala vulgata*, the ancient Italian, and commonly adopted one, the first of all,

and probably the groundwork of the others. As far back as manuscripts and notices of this version in writers will carry us, we find it
containing those books. Blanchini has published part of it, but the
work is not in Charleston. The book of Psalms, both books of the
Maccabees, Wisdom and Ecclesiasticus and the parts of Esther as
now used in the Western Church are of this original version.

The Peshito, or ancient simple Syriac version, contained those works.
Walton has inserted in the fourth volume of his Polyglot the whole
of them, except the portions of Esther, and part at least of these has
been since found.

This version, made—as is allowed by all Oriental scholars, if not in
the first, at least in the beginning of the second, century—a few years
after the death of St. John, is taken from the Hebrew and Greek.
Theodotion, who translated passages of Daniel from the Hebrew, now
lost in that language, executed his versions at a later period than that
assigned by the learned to the Syriac translation. At his day those
parts existed in Hebrew. St. Jerome saw several of the other books you
contest in Hebrew or Chaldaic, and the word he uses, *reperi*, shows that
copies of them were then extremely rare; they have since perished.
Now, in looking over the Syriac version of those works, you will see that
some are taken from the Hebrew, where probably it could be found,
and others from the Greek, where the work was written originally in
that language, or the Hebrew might not probably have been at hand.
The Syriac version of Tobias and Judith apparently follows the Septuagint, or possibly both may be directly translated from the original,
which is now lost. The version of St. Jerome, also from the original,
follows avowedly the sense, not the words, of the Chaldaic or Hebrew,
and cannot guide us in determining which. The portions of Esther in
Syriac were not in the possession of Walton. They are found in the
Septuagint and the Vulgate. I said, however, that parts of them at
least have since been discovered in the Syriac. In Wisdom and Ecclesiasticus the Syriac agrees with the Septuagint, and appears to have
been translated from it. On the contrary, Baruch with the Epistle of
Jeremiah appear to have been translated into Syriac, not from the
Greek of the Septuagint, but from the Hebrew original, now no longer
extant. So, too, the Peshito Syriac version of the contested parts of
Daniel is taken, not from the Septuagint, but from the original Hebrew, whence Theodotion at a later period took them. There are
many evidences of this. For example, in the History of Susannah
the Greek says that two *ancients* were appointed judges, while the
Syriac has two *priests*. Now the original Hebrew word was undoubtedly *cohenim*, which signifies both priest and prince, or ancient. The
Syriac translator took the Hebrew word in one sense and the Greek in
another. This difference would not have happened had the Syriac

been taken simply from the Greek. On a comparison of the first and second books of Maccabees in the Greek and in the Syriac version, it will be evident that the second book in Syriac is taken from the Greek, while it seems more probable that the first is from the kindred Hebrew.

It appears, therefore, that immediately after the days of the Apostles, in the first or beginning of the second century, when, according to Walton, Wiseman and the best scholars, the Syriac and Latin versions were made, the Christians did not think that no books were contained in their Old Testament except those inserted by the Synagogue in the Jewish Canon. Whether the whole Christian world could have united in embodying the books you object to in their body of Scriptures without some testimony from the Apostles to that effect, I leave you and my readers to judge. I believe, as I said, with Walton, that those books were united to the Jewish canonical books by the Hellenist Jews before the days of Christianity, and that they came already united into the Church. The Apostles, as I showed in my last, allude to and incorporate passages and phrases from these works into their own writings. We have just seen that the early Septuagint and the two other versions made by Christians in what you will allow were the purest and palmiest days of Christianity contained them. Even were I to give that these books were not united to the others before the time of Christ, this concession would but increase your difficulty and display more strikingly the difference between the Jewish and the Christian Old Testament—a difference which could only arise from the teaching of Christ and His Apostles.

But, you may say, if this be so, the early Christian writers would quote those books. It is natural, reverend sir, that if they wrote much they should sometimes do so, and that, if their works be preserved in any quantity, we should find such quotations therein. *And we do find them.*

We have a portion of the authentic writings of four Christians before the year 100 : St. Barnabas the Apostle's catholic Epistle, St. Polycarp's Epistle to the Philippians, St. Ignatius' Epistles, and a considerable portion of St. Clement's first Epistle to the Corinthians and a fragment of his second Epistle to the same.

Now in this small collection, the earliest of the Christian writings, we have several quotations from those books.

1. St. Barnabas, in § 6 of his Epistle, has the following passage: "But what saith the Prophet against Israel? Woe be to their soul! because they have taken wicked counsel against themselves, saying, Let us lay snares for the righteous, because he is unprofitable to us." This passage is composed of the two texts, Isaias iii. 9, "Woe to their soul, for evils are rendered to them," and Wisdom ii. 12, "Let us

therefore lie in wait for the just, because he is not for our turn."
Here St. Barnabas quotes in the same sentence, and as of equal inspired authority, the book of Isaias, contained in the Canon of the
Jews, and that of Wisdom, one of those you boldly declare to be of
no more authority than Seneca's Letters or Tully's Offices.

2. Towards the end of the same Epistle the apostolical writer says:
"Thou shalt not be forward to speak, for the mouth is the snare of
death. Strive with thy soul for all thy might. Reach not out thy
hand to receive, and withhold it not when thou shouldst give." What
is this but a quotation of Ecclesiasticus (iv. 33, 34, 36), another of the
books of your heathen category? "Strive for justice for thy soul, and
even unto death fight for justice, and God will overthrow thy enemies
for thee. Be not hasty in thy tongue, and slack and remiss in thy
works. Let not thy hand be stretched out to receive and shut when
thou shouldst give."

3. St. Polycarp's Epistle to the Philippians comes next. In the
tenth section he has the following passage: "When it is in your power
to do good, defer it not, for charity delivereth from death. Be all of
you subject to one another, having your conversations honest (or irre-
proachable) among the Gentiles." St. Polycarp, like St. Barnabas,
quotes in the same breath an author whom you admit as inspired, and
one whom you reject, and condemn Catholics for revering with him.
"For alms delivereth from death." Tobias xii. 9. "Having your
conversation good among the Gentiles." 1 Pet. ii. 12.

There are one or two passages in the Epistles of St. Ignatius which
seem to me to imply quotations from the books in question, but as
they are not so clear and striking I omit them. I find, too, that several authors refer to a passage speaking of Daniel and Susannah, but
as it is not in the copy before me, I consider it most probably one of
the interpolations foisted into the saint's writings in after years. We
will leave him, then, and take up the other writer.

4. In the first Epistle to the Corinthians, § 27, St. Clement, fourth
bishop of Rome, has the following passage: "Who shall say to Him,
What dost thou? or who shall resist the power of His strength?"
These words are taken from Wisdom xi. 52 and xli. 12: "For who
shall say to thee, What hast thou done?" "And who shall resist the
strength of thy arm?"

5. In § 55 he writes thus: "And even many women, being strengthened by the grace of God, have done many glorious and manly things.
The blessed Judith, when her city was besieged, desired the elders
that they would suffer her to go to the camp of the strangers, and she
went out, exposing herself to danger for the love she bore to her country and her people that were besieged. And the *Lord delivered Holofernes into the hands of a woman.* Nor did Esther, being perfect in

faith, expose herself to any less hazard for the delivery of the twelve tribes of Israel in danger of being destroyed. For by fasting and humbling herself she entreated the great Maker of all things, the God of ages, who, beholding the humility of her soul, delivered the people for whose sake she was in peril." The passage speaks for itself. I may say that the words marked in italics are extracted from the sublime canticle of Judith (xvi. 7). In his account of Esther, too, St. Clement evidently had in his mind not only the passage in Hebrews iv. 16, v. 2, but the prayer of Esther (xiv.), one of those portions which you · reject, with which every word he uses admirably tallies.

I have been admonished not to encroach too much on the columns of the Miscellany, and must conclude here for the present.

We have seen that the Old Testament in the infancy of the Church, and from one extremity of the Christian world to the other, whether in Syriac, in Greek or in Latin, contained the books which the Catholic Canon now contains, and which you would have us exclude. We have seen three out of the four first Christian writers quoting them unequivocally, precisely as they quote the other books of the Scripture, making no distinction whatever. Add to this, if you please, the passages enumerated in my last letter, wherein the inspired writers of the New Testament have evidently used those works, and then withdraw your thoughtless assertion that "the unbroken testimony of the Christian Church is against their inspiration."

I will in my next take up some Christian writers of the second century, and shall show that they also quoted those works as parts of the Scripture. Meanwhile, I remain, reverend sir,

Yours, etc.,   A. P. F.

APPENDIX C.

COLLECTION OF THE PASSAGES IN WHICH DR. LYNCH
HAS REPRESENTED THE FATHERS AS QUOTING THE
APOCRYPHA.

N. B. The first column gives the name of the author and the book; the
second, the passages which are simply quoted or accommodated; the third,
those which are quoted with some marks of distinction, as scripture, Divine
scripture, or under the name of a prophet; the fourth gives merely allusions to the contents of the book, or assumes its history to be true.

Some few passages may have been omitted, as the syllabus has been prepared in great haste.

Names of the Fathers and of their Works.	Apocryphal passages which are simply quoted.	Those quoted as scripture or Divine scripture.	Allusions to Apocrypha.
JUSTIN MARTYR.			
1 Apol., § 44..............	Ecclus. xv. 14–18.		
IRENÆUS.			
Contra Hæres., l. iv.c.38.	Wisdom vi. 20.		
" lib. v. c. 35.	Baruch iv. 36, 37.		
" lib iv. c. 26.	Daniel xiii. 56, 52, 53.		
" lib. iv. c. 5..	" xiv. 3, 4, 24.		
CLEMENS ALEX.			
Pædag., lib. i. c. 8........	....	Ecclus. xxi. 6; i. 21, 22.	
" lib. i. c. 9.......	Ecclus. xxx. 8.		
" lib. ii. c. 5......	....	Ecclus. xxi. 20.	
" lib. ii. c. 8......	....	" xxxviii. 1.	
" lib. ii. c. 8......	....	" xxxix. 26, 27.	
" lib. iii. c. 3	....	" xxv. 6.	
Stromat., lib. iv........ ...	....	Wisdom iii. 2–8 (as Divine Wisdom).	
" lib. vi..........	....	Wisdom v. 2–5 (under name of Solomon).	
" lib. vi..........	....	Wisdom iii. 14, as Sol.	
Pædag., lib. i. c. 10.......	....	Bar. iv. 4; iii. 4, as Jer.	
" lib. ii. c. 3......	....	" iii. 16–19.	
Strom., lib. vi............	....	Tobias xii. 8.	
TERTULLIAN.			
Monog., c. 17............	....	....	Judith viii. 1.
Præscrip., c. 7............	....	Wisdom i. 1, as Sol.	
Cont. Valent., c. 2.......	....	" i. 1, as Sol.	
De Anima, c. 15...	Wisdom i. 6.		
De Virg. Vel., c. 13......	" viii. 21.		
Cont. Marc., c. 5...........	Ecclus. xv. 18.		
De Exhort. Cast., c. 2....	....	Ecclus. xv. 18.	
Scorpiauu..	....	Bar. vi. 3, 4, 5, as Jer.	

802

Names of the Fathers and of their Works	Apocryphal passages which are simply quoted.	Those quoted as scripture or Divine scripture.	Allusions to Apocrypha.
TERTULLIAN.			
De Coron Milit., c. 4......	Daniel xiii. 32.		
De Idol., c. 18...	....	....	Daniel xiv.
De Jejun., c. 9..............	....	....	" xiv. 32, 38.
Advs. Jud., c. 4.............	....	....	1 Mac. ii. 41.
De Præscrip., c. 13........	....	....	2 Mac. viii. 28.
CYPRIAN.			
Test. ad Quir., l. iii. c. 1.	Tobias ii. 2; iv. 6–12.		
" l. iii. c. 6.	" ii. 14.		
De Mortall., c. 7...........	" xii. 15.		
De Orat. Dom., c. 21......	....	Tobit. xii. 8.	
De Op. et Eleemos., c. 4.	Tobit xii. 8.		
Exhort. Mart., c. 12......	....	Wisdom iii. 4–8.	
De Mortal., c. 17...........	....	" iv. 11–14.	
Ad Demet., c. 13..........	....	" v. 1–8.	
De Habit. Virg., c. 7......	....	" v. 8.	
Ad Rogat....................	....	" iii. 4–8.	
De Mortal., c. 5............	....	Ecclus. ii. 1–4.	
De Op. et Eleemos., c. 2	....	" iii. 30.	
De Unit. Eccles., c. 19...	....	" xxviii. 28.	
Ad Rogat....................	....	" vii. 29, 31.	
De Laps., c. 19............	....	Daniel xxv. 34.	
De Unit. Eccles., c. 11...	....	....	Daniel iii. 49–50.
De Orat. Dom., c. 4.......	....	Daniel iii. 51.	
Exhort. ad Mort., c. 11.	....	" xiv. 4.	
De Orat. Dom., c. 14.....	....	....	" xiv.
De Op. et Eleemos., c. 8.	....	....	" xiv.
Epist. 40...................	....	....	" xiii.
Test. ad Quir., l. ii. c. 6.	....	Bar. iii. 35–37, as Jer.	
De Orat. Dom., c. 2.......	....	" vi. 6.	
Test. ad Quir., l. iii. c. 4.	2 Mac. ix. 12; ii. 62, 63.		
" lib. iii. c. 17.	2 Mac. vi. 30; vii. 9, 14, 16, 17, 18, 19.		
" lib. iii. c. 3...	1 Mac. ii. 60.		
Exhort. ad Mort., c. 11.	....	....	2 Mac. vi. and vii.
HIPPOLYTUS.			
Cont. Noët., c. 2..........	....	Baruch iii. 36–38.	
DIONYSIUS OF ALEXANDRIA.			
Epist. ad Germ............	....	Tobit. xii. 7.	
Cont. Paul. Samosat......	....	Wisdom i. 5, 6.	
APOS. CONSTITUTIONS.			
Lib. ii. c. 37, 49, 51.......	....	....	Daniel xiii.
Lib. viii. c. 1...............	....	....	" xiv.
Lib. v. c. 20................	Baruch iii. 36–38.		
Lib. vii. c. 23...............	" iv. 4.		
Lib. vi. c. 29...............	Wisdom iii. 1.		
Lib. iii. c. 7...............	....	....	Judith.
Lib. v. c. 19...............	....	....	"
POPE SIRICIUS.			
Epist. ad Himmer., c. 7.	Wisdom i. 4.		
JULIUS FIRMICUS MATERNUS.			
"	....	Wisdom xv. 15–17, as Solomon's.	
"	....	Baruch vi. 5–9, as Jer. " vi. 21, 25, 3, 31, 64, 50 and 57.	
EPHREM THE SYRIAN.			
De Evers. Superb.........	Daniel ix. 7.		
De Virtut., c. 3............	" iii. 40.		
De Humil., c. 9............	" iii. 39.		
Paræns., 9.................	" iii. 50.		
De Orat....................	" iii. 33.		

Names of the Fathers and of their Works.	Apocryphal passages which are simply quoted.	Those quoted as scripture or Divine scripture.	Allusions to Apocrypha.
EPHREM THE SYRIAN.			
De Pœnit., c. 23	....	....	Daniel iii.
Parœn. ad Monegit., c. 14, 11	Daniel xiii. 52.		Daniel xiii.
Epist. ad Joan	....	....	" xiii.
De Muliere	....	....	" iv. 32–36.
De Rect.Viv. Nat., c.85.	....	....	" iv. 32–38.
De Patient. etc...	....		
In D. Basylium	Tobit. xii. 7.		
Serm. Cont. Jude	Bar. ix. 4 and 20; iii.38.		
De Timore Dei	....	Wisdom iv. 12.	
De Certam., etc., c. 8...	....	Wis. iv. 7, 8, 9; v. 1–16.	
Advs. Levit	....	" iii. 1, 6, 9.	
De Humil., c. 94	....	" ii. 21, 22.	
Parœn. 39	Wisdom vi. 9.		
Exhort., 40	" i. 12.		
" 46	....	Wisdom xv. 12.	
		" v. 18–24.	
De Patient	....	Ecclus. ii. 15.	
De Virt. et Vit., c. 8...	....	" xxv. 13; iii. 7;	
De Timore Dei	Ecclus. xxxii. 1; viii. 6, 7; xxxi. 5.	xviii. 30 and 31.	
	Ecclus. vi. 18.	Eccl. xi. 5; iv. 7; vii. 40.	
De Panop., etc...		" vi. 30.	
De Cast	Ecclus. iv. 25, 26.		
Necrosima., can. 15	....		2 Mac. vi.
Testamentum	....	....	" vi.
BASIL THE GREAT.			
Cont. Eunom., lib. v., c. 15, § 2	Wisdom i. 4.		
Cont. Eunom., c. 14, § 2.	....	Wisdom i. 7.	
" c. 2	....	" ix. 1, 2, as Sol.	
"	Wisdom i. 7.		
Epist. 8, § 12 and 11	....	" i. 4, 7.	
Hom. 12	....	" i. 4, as Sol.	
" 14	....	" vi. 7.	
De Sanc. Spir., c. 23, § 54.	Wisdom i. 7.		
Hom. 12, § 13	Daniel xiii. 50.		
Hom. in 40 Mart., § 6...	" iii. 40.		
Epist. 243, § 43	" iii. 38, 39.		
Cont. Unam., lib. 2, § 19.	Esther xiv. 11.		
" " " 4, c. 3.	....	Baruch iii. 32, as Jer.	
De Sanc. Spir., c. 8, § 19.	Judith ix. 4.		
Epist. 6	....	....	2 Mac. vii.
Hom. Deut., c. 5, 9	Ecclus. ix. 20.		
Hexæm. Hom., 6, 910...	" xxvii. 12.		
Capit. Ques., 104	....	Ecclus. xxxii. 22.	
CHRYSOSTOM.			
Ad Viduam Jun	....	Ecclus. xviii. 26; xi. 5.	
Hom. de Lat	....	" xix. 16.	
Serm. 8, Cont. Jude	....	" ii. 1–5.	
Serm. de Lat	Ecclus. ii. 1, 2.		
Exhort. 2 ad. Theod	" v. 8.		
Hom. 18, ad. Pop. Anth.	" xiv. 2.		
De Fato	....	" xv. 17 and 15.	
Hom. 15, ad Pop. Anth..	....	Ec. i. 20; ix. 10, as Sol.	
Serm. 1 in Act. Apost...	....	Ecclus. xvi. 3.	
De Virginitat, c. 22	Wisdom v. 3–5.		
Serm. in Calendas	" iii. 1.		
Hom. in Gen. 11	....	Wisdom xiv. 8.	
Psalm cix	....	" xvi. 28.	
Hom. in Matt. 27	....	" vi. 7.	
Hom. in Ept. Heb. 7	....	" iv. 8, 9.	
Nous. Anom.,5	....	Baruch iii. 36, 37, 38.	
Cont. Jude et Gent	....	" iii. 36, 37, 38.	
Hom. 3, ad Pop. Anth..	Esther xiv. 13.		
Hom. 60 in Joan	....	....	Judith [mentioned.
Hom. 13 in Epis. Heb...	....	Tobit. iy. 7.	

Names of the Fathers and of their Works.	Apocryphal passages which are simply quoted.	Those quoted as scripture or Divine scripture.	Allusions to Apocrypha.
CHRYSOSTOM.			
Hom. 9 in Epis. Heb.	....	Tobit. iv. 11.	
Hom. 5, Nous. Anom....	Daniel iii. 23.		
Cont. Jude et Gent.......	" iii. 38.		
Hom. in Pentecost, 1....	" iii. 38.		
Hom. 15 in 1 Cor.........	....	Daniel xiii. 52.	
Hom. 18 "	Daniel iii. 29, 30.		
Hom. 2 in Philem........	" iii. 29, 30, 39, 32; xiv. 37.		
AMBROSE.			
Hexæm., lib. 4, c. 8....	....	Ecclus. xxvi. 12.	
In Noach., etc., c. 35.....	....	" xxxii. 13.	
In Naboth., c. 8............	....	" iv. 8.	
Tract. de 42...............	....	" ii. 5.	
Psalm cxviii...............	....	Wisdom i. 6.	
Jacob., c. 8..................	....	Wis. iv. 8, 9; xiv. 7, 8.	
Joseph......................	....	" ii. 12, as Sol.	
Psalm xliii.................	....	" vii. 7, "	
Hexæm., lib. 3, c. 14....	....	Baruch iv. 26; v. 27, as Jeremiah.	
In Tobit....................	....	Baruch iii. 24, 25.	
Cain et Abel, c. 9.........	....	" iii. 1.	
42 Mans....................	....	" iii. 29, 30.	
Hexæm., lib. ii. c. 4......	....	Dan. iii. 56, 68, 67, 74.	{ Refer to Story of Susannah
De Officiis., lib. ii. c. 9...	....	....	{ Refer to Bel and Dragon.
Joseph., c. 5...............	....	....	
Jacob., lib. i. c. 8.........	....	....	
" lib. ii. c. 9.........	....	....	
Elias, c. 9..................	Judith viii. 6.		Refer to Judith.
De Officiis, c. 13 and 14.	....	....	2 Mac. vi. & vii.
Jacob., lib. ii. c. 9.........	....	....	" iii.
De Officiis, lib. ii. c. 29.	....	....	
PAULINUS OF NOLA.			
Exhort. ad Celant........	....	Eccl. iv. 25–28; xxviii. 23, 29; iii. 20.	
Epist. ad Pamach., 37...	....	Ec. xxxviii. 16; xvii.18.	
" 30.....................	....	Ec. vii. 16; Wis. viii. 1.	
" 32.....................	....	Ec. xix. 15.	
" 39.....................	....	Ec. v. 8.	
" 37.....................	....	Wisdom iv. 7; Baruch iii. 18, 19.	

INDEX.

807

CPSIA information can be obtained
at www.ICGtesting.com
Printed in the USA
LVHW080443170622
721517LV00001B/90